D1321037

Consciousness in the Physical World

PHILOSOPHY OF MIND

Series Editor:
David J. Chalmers, Australian National University and New York University

Self Expression
Owen Flanagan

Deconstructing the Mind
Stephen Stich

The Conscious Mind
David J. Chalmers

Minds and Bodies
Colin McGinn

What's Within?
Fiona Cowie

The Human Animal
Eric T. Olson

Dreaming Souls
Owen Flanagan

Consciousness and Cognition
Michael Thau

Thinking Without Words
José Luis Bermúdez

Identifying the Mind
U.T. Place (author), George Graham,
Elizabeth R. Valentine (editors)

Purple Haze
Joseph Levine

Three Faces of Desire
Timothy Schroeder

A Place for Consciousness
Gregg Rosenberg

Ignorance and Imagination
Daniel Stoljar

Simulating Minds
Alvin I. Goldman

Gut Reactions
Jesse J. Prinz

*Phenomenal Concepts and Phenomenal
Knowledge*
Torin Alter, Sven Walter (editors)

Beyond Reduction
Steven Horst

What Are We?
Eric T. Olson

Supersizing the Mind
Andy Clark

Perception, Hallucination, and Illusion
William Fish

Cognitive Systems and the Extended Mind
Robert D. Rupert

The Character of Consciousness
David J. Chalmers

Perceiving the World
Bence Nanay (editor)

The Contents of Visual Experience
Susanna Siegel

The Senses
Fiona Macpherson (editor)

Attention is Cognitive Unison
Christopher Mole

Consciousness and the Prospects of Physicalism
Derk Pereboom

Introspection and Consciousness
Declan Smithies and Daniel Stoljar (editors)

The Conscious Brain
Jesse J. Prinz

Decomposing the Will
Andy Clark, Julian Kiverstein,
and Tillmann Vierkant (editors)

Phenomenal Intentionality
Uriah Kriegel (editor)

The Peripheral Mind
István Aranyosi

The Innocent Eye
Nico Orlandi

Does Perception Have Content?
Edited by Berit Brogaard

The Varieties of Consciousness
Uriah Kriegel

Consciousness in the Physical World
Torin Alter and Yujin Nagasawa (editors)

Consciousness in the Physical World

Perspectives on Russellian Monism

Edited by

TORIN ALTER

YUJIN NAGASAWA

OXFORD
UNIVERSITY PRESS

OXFORD
UNIVERSITY PRESS

Oxford University Press is a department of the University of
Oxford. It furthers the University's objective of excellence in research,
scholarship, and education by publishing worldwide.

Oxford   New York
Auckland   Cape Town   Dar es Salaam   Hong Kong   Karachi
Kuala Lumpur   Madrid   Melbourne   Mexico City   Nairobi
New Delhi   Shanghai   Taipei   Toronto

With offices in
Argentina   Austria   Brazil   Chile   Czech Republic   France   Greece
Guatemala   Hungary   Italy   Japan   Poland   Portugal   Singapore
South Korea   Switzerland   Thailand   Turkey   Ukraine   Vietnam

Oxford is a registered trademark of Oxford University Press
in the UK and certain other countries.

Published in the United States of America by
Oxford University Press
198 Madison Avenue, New York, NY 10016

Library of Congress Cataloging-in-Publication Data
Consciousness in the physical world : perspectives on Russellian monism / edited by Torin
Alter and Yujin Nagasawa
    pages cm
ISBN 978–0–19–992735–7 (alk. paper)
1. Consciousness.   2. Monism.   3. Russell, Bertrand, 1872–1970.   4. Materialism.
5. Dualism.   I. Alter, Torin Andrew, 1963–editor.
B808.9.C666 2015
147'.3—dc23
2014033395

9 8 7 6 5 4 3 2 1
Printed in the United States of America
on acid-free paper

Contents

Acknowledgments   vii

Contributors   ix

Editors' Introduction—TORIN ALTER AND YUJIN NAGASAWA   1

PART I: *Precursors*

1. *Monadology* 17 and Letter to De Volder
   (excerpt)—GOTTFRIED WILHELM VON LEIBNIZ   17
2. *Critique of Pure Reason,*
   A270/B326–A278/B334 (excerpt)—IMMANUEL KANT   19
3. *The Principles of Psychology* (excerpt)—WILLIAM JAMES   23

PART II: *Russell and Commentaries*

4. Excerpts from *Analysis of Matter* (1927), *Human Knowledge: Its
   Scope and Limits* (1948), *Portraits from Memory* (1956), and
   My Philosophical Development (1959)—BERTRAND RUSSELL   29
5. Russell, Russellian Monism, and
   Panpsychism—LEOPOLD STUBENBERG   58
6. Russell on Russellian Monism—DONOVAN WISHON   91

PART III: *Modern Classics and Recent Works*

7. Rigid Designators and Mind–Brain Identity
   (excerpt)—GROVER MAXWELL   121

8. The Grain Problem—MICHAEL LOCKWOOD   143

9. Real Materialism (with new
   postscript)—GALEN STRAWSON   161

10. Russellian Physicalism—BARBARA GAIL MONTERO   209

11. Causality and the Combination Problem—GREGG ROSENBERG   224

12. Panpsychism and Panprotopsychism—DAVID J. CHALMERS   246

13. The Short Slide from A Posteriori Physicalism to Russellian
    Monism—TORIN ALTER AND ROBERT J. HOWELL   277

14. Consciousness, Physicalism, and Absolutely Intrinsic
    Properties—DERK PEREBOOM   300

15. Russellian Monism or Nagelian Monism?—DANIEL STOLJAR   324

16. A Physicalist Critique of Russellian Monism—ALYSSA NEY   346

17. Against Constitutive Russellian Monism—PHILIP GOFF   370

18. Pessimism about Russellian Monism—AMY KIND   401

19. What Is Russellian Monism?—TORIN ALTER AND
    YUJIN NAGASAWA   422

Name Index   453

Subject Index   459

Acknowledgments

DAVID CHALMERS, DERK Pereboom, Howard Robinson, Seth Shabo, Galen Strawson, Leopold Stubenberg, and two anonymous reviewers gave us useful comments and suggestions. Donovan Wishon was especially helpful in recommending Russell selections. Tyler Brockett, Mitchell Dykstra, and Sarah-Louise Johnson helped us to prepare the manuscript. We thank them all. We are also grateful to the authors and publishers who let us reprint their work and especially those who wrote new papers for this volume. Finally, we thank Peter Ohlin and Lucy Randall of Oxford University Press, who both provided impeccable editorial support, and Pete Shulte, who provided the original cover art drawing.

Sources
Chapter 1

Gottfried Wilhelm von Leibniz (1714), selection from *Monadology*. Translated by Robert Merrihew Adams for this volume.

Gottfried Wilhelm von Leibniz (1699), selection from letter to De Volder, March 24/April 3, 1699. Translated by Robert Merrihew Adams for this volume.

Chapter 2

Immanuel Kant, Immanuel (1781), *Critique of Pure Reason*, A270/B326–A278/B334. Translated by John Miller Dow Mieklejohn (1855, London: Henry G. Bohn) with some alterations by Derk Pereboom.

Chapter 3

William James (1891, originally 1890), *The Principles of Psychology, Volume 1*, London: Macmillan, pp. 158–61.

Chapter 4

Bertrand Russell (1927), *Analysis of Matter*, London: Kegan Paul, pp. 382–93 and pp. 400–02. Permission by the Russell Foundation

Bertrand Russell (1948), *Human Knowledge: Its Scope and Limits*, London: Taylor and Francis, pp. 244–47. Permission by Taylor and Francis.

Bertrand Russell (1956), "Mind and Matter" in his *Portraits from Memory*, New York: Simon and Shuster, pp. 145–65. Permission by the Russell Foundation

Bertrand Russell (1959), *My Philosophical Development*, London: George Allen & Unwin Ltd. Republished by Routledge, pp. 16–27. Permission by the Russell Foundation.

Chapter 7

Grover Maxwell (1978), "Rigid Designators and Mind–Brain Identity," C. W. Savage (ed.), *Perception and Cognition*, Minneapolis: University of Minnesota Press, pp. 265–404. Permission by the publisher.

Chapter 8

Michael Lockwood (1993), "The Grain Problem," in *Objections to Physicalism*, Howard Robinson (ed.), Oxford: Clarendon Press, pp. 271–91. Permission by Gilliam Lockwood and the publisher.

Chapter 9

Galen Strawson (2008), "Real Materialism" (revised version, with postscript), Louise M. Antony and Norbert Hornstein (eds.), *Chomsky and His Critics*, Oxford: Blackwell, pp. 49–88. Permission by the author and publisher.

Chapter 12

David J. Chalmers, "Panpsychism and Panprotopsychism," first published as the 2013 Amherst Lecture in Philosophy: http://www.amherstlecture.org/index.html. Permission by the author and publisher.

Chapter 19

Alter, T., and Y. Nagasawa (2012), "What Is Russellian Monism?," *Journal of Consciousness Studies* 19 (9–10), pp. 67–95. Permission by the author and publisher.

Contributors

Torin Alter is Professor of Philosophy at the University of Alabama, USA.

David J. Chalmers is Professor of Philosophy and Director of the Centre for Consciousness at the Australian National University, Australia, and Professor of Philosophy at New York University, USA.

Philip Goff is Associate Professor of Philosophy at Central European University, Hungary.

Robert J. Howell is Professor of Philosophy at Southern Methodist University, USA.

William James was a 19th–20th–century American philosopher and psychologist. He is the founder of pragmatism and a pioneer of American psychology.

Immanuel Kant was an 18th–19th–century German philosopher. He is a central figure of late modern philosophy.

Amy Kind is Professor of Philosophy at Claremont McKenna College, USA.

Gottfried Wilhelm von Leibniz was a 17th–18th–century German philosopher. He made major contributions to a wide range of disciplines including philosophy, mathematics, physics, and technology.

Michael Lockwood is Emeritus Fellow of Green Templeton College, Oxford, UK.

Grover Maxwell was Professor of Philosophy at the University of Minnesota, USA.

Barbara Gail Montero is Associate Professor of Philosophy at the Graduate Center and the College of Staten Island, City University of New York, USA.

Yujin Nagasawa is Professor of Philosophy at the University of Birmingham, UK.

Alyssa Ney is Associate Professor of Philosophy at the University of Rochester, USA.

Derk Pereboom is Susan Linn Sage Professor of Philosophy at Cornell University, USA.

Gregg Rosenberg works as a senior executive in private business. He received his PhD in philosophy from Indiana University in 1997, with a concentration in metaphysics and logic.

Bertrand Russell was a 19th–20th–century British philosopher. He is a founding figure of Anglo-American analytic philosophy.

Daniel Stoljar is Professor of Philosophy at the Australian National University and Future Fellow of the Australian Research Council.

Galen Strawson is President's Chair in Philosophy at the University of Texas at Austin, USA.

Leopold Stubenberg is Associate Professor of Philosophy at the University of Notre Dame, USA.

Donovan Wishon is Assistant Professor of Philosophy at the University of Mississippi, USA.

Editors' Introduction

Torin Alter and Yujin Nagasawa

IN RECENT DISCUSSIONS of the mind–body problem, there has been grow-ing interest in the following view: matter has intrinsic properties that both constitute consciousness and serve as categorical bases for the dispositional properties described in physics.[1] This view, which is associated with Bertrand Russell and known as *Russellian monism*, is often advanced as an alternative to the more familiar theories in the philosophy of mind—an alternative that combines attractive components of physicalism and dualism. This volume collects various works on Russellian monism, including historical selections, recent classics, and new pieces. Most chapters are sympathetic with the view, but some are skeptical. Together, they provide an in-depth look at view itself, its relationship to other theories, its motivations, and its problems. In this introduction, we will say a bit more about the idea that Russellian monism is an alternative to more familiar versions of dualism and of physicalism, iden-tify three central Russellian monist theses, and summarize the chapters.[2]

1. Dualism, Physicalism, and Russellian Monism

Dualism is the view that the world bifurcates into two fundamentally distinct kinds of phenomena: mental and physical. In Descartes' (1641) version of

---

1. This formulation of Russellian monism is rough. We say a bit more about this later. See also chapters 12 and 14–19.

2. Limitations of space and other practical constraints prevent us from including a number of works that we would have liked to include, such as Feigl (1958/1967), Stoljar (2001), and more recent articles by Sam Coleman (2013), Emmett Holman (2008), Thomas McClelland (2013), William Seager (1995), and others.

dualism, minds are non-physical substances that can exist separately from any physical substance. Although few contemporary philosophers accept Cartesian substance dualism, many find it intuitive that phenomenal (that is, experiential) *properties*—properties that characterize phenomenal consciousness—do not reduce to objective, physical properties. But even property dualism is widely rejected on the grounds that it stands in the way of integrating mental phenomena into the natural order. In particular, if the mental and the physical are fundamentally distinct, then it is hard to see how mental events could cause physical events or vice versa.

For well over half a century, most philosophers have subscribed to physicalism (also known as materialism). This view says that the world is fundamentally physical and that mental phenomena are nothing over and above physical phenomena. Physicalism has the advantage of economy; Occam's razor seems to favor it over dualism. Also, unlike dualism, physicalism is not plagued with a seemingly intractable problem concerning mental-physical causal interaction. However, many believe that physicalism has trouble accounting for phenomenal consciousness. Consider a simple example. There is something it is like to see red. Intuitively, no amount of physical information can capture this distinctive phenomenal character. If so, then it is hard to understand how seeing red could be completely physical. Likewise for any experience—and indeed for phenomenal consciousness in general.

Russellian monism might seem to provide a happy compromise. Like dualism, it accords the properties that constitute consciousness a status that is no less fundamental than the properties physics describes, thereby accommodating the intuition that consciousness is not reducible to physical phenomena. And by taking the properties that constitute consciousness to be categorical bases of the properties physics describes, Russellian monism seems to integrate consciousness into the natural order more deeply than familiar dualist views do—and thus seems to share one of physicalism's principal virtues. To be sure, the happy-compromise argument is contentious. But it has some force. Moreover, it is but one reason among many that interest in Russellian monism is on the rise.[3]

2. Three Central Claims

How exactly Russellian monism should be formulated is controversial, and some of the chapters here address this matter. Even so, it may be useful to say

---

3. David Chalmers presents a version of the happy-compromise argument in chapter 12. For other arguments sympathetic to Russellian monism, see Chalmers (1996) and chapters 7, 9, 11, 14, 17, and 19 of this title. For less sympathetic arguments, see chapters 15, 16, and 18 of this title.

a bit more about the nature of the view. Russellian monism typically makes at least three claims, which may be stated roughly as follows:

> *Structuralism about physics*: physics describes its basic properties in only structural/dispositional terms.
>
> *Realism about the relevant intrinsic properties*: there are intrinsic properties that both constitute consciousness and serve as non-structural/categorical grounds for the structural/dispositional properties described in physics.
>
> *(Proto)phenomenal foundationalism*: at least some of those intrinsic properties are either phenomenal properties or *protophenomenal* properties—nonphenomenal properties that together (perhaps also in combination with structural/dispositional properties) constitute consciousness.[4]

Those three claims leave various issues open. For example, if the relevant intrinsic properties are phenomenal rather than protophenomenal, then the resulting view may entail panexperientialism, a version of panpsychism, on which phenomenality pervades the physical universe. And, to take another example, if the relevant intrinsic properties are construed as special sorts of physical properties, then the resulting view may come out as a version of physicalism. By contrast, construing the relevant intrinsic properties as non-physical properties would deliver a non-physicalist version of Russellian monism. Thus, Russellian monism comes in significantly different varieties. But most, if not all, varieties maintain at least the structuralist, realist, and foundationalist claims displayed above, or some variants of them.[5]

3. The Chapters

Part I: Precursors

Part I includes classical works of three philosophers who arguably anticipated Russellian monism or aspects of the view. Chapter 1 consists of two brief selections from Leibniz. In an excerpt from a letter to De Volder, Leibniz seems to anticipate the distinction between intrinsic

---

4. These claims are adapted from chapter 19 of this title, where some refinements are discussed. For criticisms of characterization of Russellian monism, see chapters 17 and 18 of this title.

5. For discussions of the varieties of Russellian monism, see chapters 12, 17, 18, and 19 of this title.

(or nonrelational) properties and extrinsic (or relational) properties on which the second thesis of Russellian monism, i.e., realism about relevant intrinsic properties, relies. He maintains that substance is not constituted by extension alone because the concept of extension is incomplete. According to him, extension is a relative notion that can be analyzed into plurality, continuity, and coexistence.

In an excerpt from *Monadology*, Leibniz suggests ideas that come close to the first and third theses of Russellian monism, i.e., structuralism about physics and (proto)phenomenal foundationalism. Here he introduces his famous thought experiment of "a machine whose structure produced thought, sensation, and perception." He imagines the machine's size increasing "while keeping the same proportions, so that we could go into it, as [we go] into a mill." He claims that, "in visiting its interior, we will find nothing but pieces that push each other, and never anything to explain a perception." This argument is often construed as an objection to physicalism, possibly anticipating the contemporary conceivability argument against physicalism. The latter tries to refute physicalism by appealing to the apparent conceivability of a situation in which the physical truths are held constant but the truths about consciousness are varied (Chalmers 2002). Yet the main point of Leibniz's argument seems to be more general: perception is not merely a matter of mechanical structure. If we replace "mechanical structure" with "physical structure," Leibniz's reasoning—especially the remark about finding "nothing but pieces that push each other"—seems to imply something in the vicinity of structuralism about physics. And by suggesting that what goes beyond mechanical structure are mental properties ("perception"), his argument can—again replacing "mechanical" with "physical"—also be construed as anticipating something akin to (proto)phenomenal foundationalism.

In chapter 2, an excerpt from *Critique of Pure Reason*, Kant argues that we cannot know the nature of things in themselves because we can know things only as they appear to our senses. In his view, we can analyze the functions and operations of matter but they are nothing but appearances. Thus, he reasons, we cannot find anything in matter that is, as he puts it, "absolutely intrinsic" (which means very roughly: being independent of extrinsic relations).[6] He does not deny that we can make progress toward understanding nature through observation and analysis of appearances. However, he does deny that we can

---

6. For a detailed discussion of absolutely intrinsic properties, see chapter 14 of this title. For further discussion, see chapter 15 of this title.

fully grasp the intrinsic aspects of nature—including the intrinsic aspects of our own minds. While he does not explicitly associate things in themselves with phenomenal properties, his reasoning could be interpreted as an argument for something close to the second thesis of Russellian monism, i.e., realism about the relevant intrinsic properties. Further, his claims about the limitations of human scientific investigation suggest something akin to the first thesis, i.e., structuralism about physics.

In chapter 3, an excerpt from *The Principles of Psychology*, William James anticipates the combination problem, which is widely recognized as one of the strongest objections to Russellian monism. He conceives of a hundred feelings being shuffled and packed as closely together as possible. Every feeling seems to remain the same and independent from the others. When they are put together appropriately, however, a consciousness that belongs to this set of feelings emerges. It is a challenge for Russellian monists to explain how the familiar smooth, homogeneous character of ordinary conscious experiences can arise from an aggregate of protophenomenal or phenomenal properties.[7]

Part II: Russell and Commentaries

How Bertrand Russell's views relate to the eponymous theory on which the present volume centers is disputed. This is the subject of Part II. It is reasonably clear that Russell accepts components of the theory. In particular, he seems to believe both structuralism about physics and the view that physical events have an intrinsic character that is not purely structural (the latter comes close to realism about the relevant intrinsic properties, minus the part about the intrinsic properties constituting consciousness). For example, he writes,

> It is not always realized how exceedingly abstract is the information that theoretical physics has to give. It lays down certain fundamental equations which enable it to deal with the logical structure of events, while leaving it completely unknown what is the intrinsic character of the events that have the structure.
>
> (Russell 1959, 17–18)

---

7. The combination problem was famously posed by William James, chapter 3 of this title. For a detailed discussion of the combination problem, see chapters 8 and 12 of this title, and Chalmers (forthcoming).

Also, he expressly advocates neutral monism, which is a related view. But it is arguable whether he should be interpreted as advocating Russellian monism in its entirety.

Chapter 4 collects selections from Russell's work that can be read as suggesting views in the vicinity of Russellian monism. The passage quoted above, from his 1959 *My Philosophical Development*, is a typical example. Similar claims may be found in the selections from his *Human Knowledge: Its Scope and Limits* (1948) and *Portraits from Memory* (1956). Relevant passages also occur in earlier works, such as *The Analysis of Matter* (1927). Chapter 4 includes the penultimate chapter of that book, in which he explains how his position differs from (traditional versions of) materialism and idealism. Along the way, he implies a commitment to structuralism about physics. And he indicates that there is more to know about perception than is revealed by "the whole of physics." Chapter 4 also includes the last three pages of *The Analysis of Matter*, where he makes further remarks along similar lines.

In chapter 5, "Russell, Russellian Monism, and Panpsychism," Leopold Stubenberg investigates the relationship between Russell's views and the panpsychist version of Russellian monism. He argues that the two differ significantly. In particular, he argues, Russell's theory of perception and his structuralism are "quite idiosyncratic and therefore difficult to accept." For example, Russell posits "unexperienced phenomenal property instances." Also, Stubenberg contends, the idea that (proto)phenomenal qualities ground fundamental properties described by physics "is entirely absent from Russell's thinking." The chapter is not only historical: Stubenberg argues that "the panpsychist version of RM [Russellian monism] could profit from borrowing many of the structural elements found in Russell's NM [neutral monism]." Doing so, Stubenberg explains, can help the panpsychist Russellian monist address the combination problem.

In chapter 6, "Russell on Russellian Monism," Donovan Wishon argues that over the roughly four decades in which Russell advocates neutral monism, "Russell holds (at least) *three* different, but related, ontological views, all of which he labels as 'neutral monism.'" One of these is a dualist theory, another is "genuine neutral monism," and the third is a physicalist version of Russellian monism. Wishon argues that Russell came to embrace physicalist Russellian monism after 1940 in (among other places) *Human Knowledge: Its Scope and Limits* and *My Philosophical Development*, relevant selections from which books are included in chapter 4 of this title. In interpreting Russell as a proponent of Russellian monism, Wishon differs from Stubenberg. Both commentaries leave little doubt but that Russell's reflections on the issues surrounding the theory that bears his name are subtle and complex.

Part III: Modern Classics and Recent Works

Part III includes modern classics and recent works on Russellian monism. Chapter 7, Grover Maxwell's "Rigid Designators and Mind-Brain Identity," is arguably the *locus classicus* of Russellian monism. In it, he defends a version of the theory that he calls "nonmaterialist physicalism." In order to establish this version, Maxwell appeals to a thesis that is now familiar: although the physical sciences provide us with the best knowledge of the structure of the neurophysiological causal networks that compose the brain, they provide us with no or little knowledge of the intrinsic properties of brain events. In relation to Saul Kripke's (1972) modal argument, Maxwell considers why it appears that we can conceive of a physical state without an associated mental state. His answer is that there can be a physical state with the same causal structure and effects without the same intrinsic nature. According to Maxwell, nonmaterialist physicalism is a genuine mind-brain identity thesis because, unlike materialism, it does not attempt to eliminate mental events. (Notice that Maxwell's claim here is based on his idiosyncratic view that materialism entails or is eliminativism.)

Michael Lockwood is another influential proponent of Russellian monism (Lockwood 1989, especially chapter 10). In chapter 8, "The Grain Problem," he argues that the so-called grain problem, which was originally introduced by Sellars (1965, 1971) and can be regarded as a version of the combination problem, resolves into three component problems: (i) The phenomenal objects of introspective awareness are far less finely structured than are any plausible physiological correlates, (ii) the structure we encounter at the phenomenal level does not match that of the underlying physiology as revealed by science, and (iii) the qualitative diversity of the phenomenal realm does not match the corresponding qualitative homogeneity of the physical ingredients out of which any corresponding brain state could realistically be composed. Lockwood explains how persistent the grain problem is and provides a few hints towards a solution. He argues that the key might be the following hypothesis: the brain is a complex, quantum-mechanical system, which can be conceptually decomposed into subsystems that can be treated as quantum-mechanical systems in their own right.

Galen Strawson is considered one of the main founders and proponents of Russellian monism, and chapter 9, "Real Materialism," is a classic articulation of the theory. He calls his distinctive version, somewhat tentatively, "real materialism." In his view, our general theoretical conception of the mental has substantial non-structural descriptive content, because we are acquainted with fundamental features of the mental nature of reality through our experiences.

However, he says, our general theoretical conception of the non-mental has substantial structure-specifying content. Apart from the possibility that the conception has non-structural content deriving from spatiotemporal concepts, we do not seem to know anything about the non-structural nature of non-mental reality. He formulates his view by appealing to these ideas and concludes that it can be appropriately construed as a form of monism. In the postscript, which he wrote for this volume, he maintains that his preferred version of Russellian monism is pure panpsychism/panexperientialism, which holds that the fundamental intrinsic nature of the basic constituents of reality treated in physics is wholly a matter of experientiality. He argues that this version of Russellian monism is the most scientifically "hard-nosed," theoretically elegant, and theoretically parsimonious.

In chapter 10, "Russellian Physicalism," Barbara Gail Montero argues, against Chalmers (2010), that there is a version of Russellian monism that avoids the conceivability argument and yet remains fully physicalistic. Russellian monists posit what she calls *inscrutables:* "properties of the fundamental world, which . . . are not revealed by physics yet ground consciousness (perhaps as well as other things)." Doing so provides Russellian monists with the resources to answer the conceivability argument. However, this need not compromise the theory's physicalist credentials. Montero argues that whether Russellian monism is fully physicalistic depends partly on the role inscrutables play in the theory. She considers the view that the inscrutables "have the sole purpose of grounding consciousness."[8] If Russellian monists accept that view, then, she argues, their theory might not be fully physicalistic. But, she continues, Russellian monists could instead hold that the inscrutables form the dependence base for the entire concrete world and that only a small portion of the base corresponds to mental phenomena. Based on that and related arguments, she presents a version of Russellian monism that, she concludes, is not anti-physicalist in spirit as "it does not bestow a place of prominence on the mental." She aptly dubs this version "Russellian physicalism."

In chapter 11, "Causality and the Combination Problem," Gregg Rosenberg summarizes and expands on the main ideas of his (2004) *A Place for Consciousness: Probing the Deep Structure of the Natural World.* Prompted by issues raised by the combination problem, he proposes "a systematic reinvention of causality from the ground up." He argues that causality should

---

8. That view appears to conflict with what we call realism about the relevant intrinsic properties. So, it is not clear that Russellian monists could accept it.

be conceived "as a *potentiality filter* . . . On one side of the filter is a set of potentialities, and on the other side is a smaller set." Although his Theory of Causal Significance makes no mention of consciousness, applying the Theory to the actual world requires positing intrinsic properties to perform certain functional roles—roles to which phenomenal properties are, he argues, well suited. For example, the requisite intrinsic properties

> would have to possess a kind of unity similar to the unity we find in consciousness, and would have to have intrinsic relations of compatibility and incompatibility similar to what we find among phenomenal properties like red and green.

The result is a panpsychist version of Russellian monism, which delivers a novel solution to the combination problem. Toward the end of the chapter, he investigates the relationship between emergence and panpsychism, a topic his book treats only briefly. In the process, he addresses two important objections due to Chalmers (forthcoming).

David J. Chalmers, more than anyone else, is responsible for the current interest in Russellian monism. Indeed, he coined the term "Russellian monism" (Chalmers 1997). In chapter 12, "Panpsychism and Panprotopsychism," he presents an argument for a version of panpsychism on which "some fundamental physical entities are conscious." On this version, "there is something it is like to be a quark or a photon or a member of some other fundamental physical type." The argument is Hegelian in form, where the conclusion (panpsychism) is a synthesis of a thesis (materialism) and an antithesis (dualism). He writes,

> we have a standoff. On the face of it, the conceivability argument refutes materialism and establishes dualism, and the causal argument refutes dualism and establishes materialism. It is time for a Hegelian synthesis.

Chalmers develops the synthesis precisely, making important points along the way, including useful taxonomic distinctions. But the argument for panpsychism takes us only through section 3 of 8. He follows with a new antithesis to panpsychism: pan*proto*psychism (a term he also coined; Chalmers 1997), on which fundamental entities "have certain special properties that are precursors to consciousness and that can collectively constitute consciousness in larger systems." And he presents Russellian monism as the subsequent synthesis—and the combination problem in turn as the antithesis to Russellian monism. He then argues that the combination problem remains unsolved, despite various attempted solutions. But he ends on an optimistic note:

> the Hegelian argument gives good reason to take both panpsychism and panprotopsychism very seriously. If we can find a reasonable solution to the combination problem for either, this view would immediately become the most promising solution to the mind–body problem.

So, Chalmers's chapter can be seen as an argument for tackling the combination problem in earnest.

In chapter 13, "The Short Slide from A Posteriori Physicalism to Russellian Monism," Torin Alter and Robert J. Howell consider the relationship between Russellian monism and a posteriori physicalism. A posteriori physicalism is the most widely accepted version of physicalism, a version that says that physicalism is true even though there is no a priori derivation from physical truths to phenomenal truths. A posteriori physicalism is normally considered an alternative to Russellian monism, but Alter and Howell argue that given certain plausible assumptions a posteriori physicalism collapses into Russellian monism. Let P be the complete microphysical truth and Q an arbitrary phenomenal truth. Alter and Howell argue that a posteriori physicalists must hold that P metaphysically necessitates Q at least partly in virtue of categorical features of properties described in P—features that are phenomenal or protophenomenal. Otherwise, they reason, the necessitation of Q by P would be implausibly inexplicable. They conclude that a posteriori physicalism requires that phenomenal or protophenomenal properties are categorical features of basic physical properties, which in turn implies Russellian monism.

In chapter 14, "Consciousness, Physicalism, and Absolutely Intrinsic Properties," Derk Pereboom explains, refines, and defends a physicalist version of Russellian monism that he presents in *Consciousness and the Prospects of Physicalism* (Oxford University Press, 2011). In this version, the categorical properties underlying the dispositional properties physics describes are *absolutely intrinsic*. An absolutely intrinsic property of an entity is both intrinsic and not necessitated by purely extrinsic properties of the entity's parts. This notion, which he derives from ideas he finds in Leibniz and Kant, allows the Russellian monist to avoid some glaring problems for the view (see Stoljar, chapter 15). For example, Russellian monism is often said to be motivated by the contention that physics describes only extrinsic properties. But that contention seems implausible. For example, physics may describe a sphere's shape, an intrinsic property. Pereboom argues that such simple counterexamples—along with other, more sophisticated ones—can be avoided by formulating the Russellian monist's claims in terms of absolutely intrinsic properties. For example, Pereboom suggests that a sphere's shape is necessitated by purely extrinsic properties such as the plurality, continuity, and coexistence of the sphere's parts.

If any absolutely intrinsic properties are instantiated, what is their nature? Pereboom argues that, "The most favorable prospect for a resolutely physicalist Russellian Monism would appear to lie in properties whose nature is currently unconceived." He notes that, "Chalmers's protophenomenalism allows for a view of this sort." The notion of absolute intrinsicality is useful for characterizing any version of Russellian monism, not just physicalist versions. The chapter also connects the contemporary theory to historical writings of Leibniz and others in intriguing ways.[9]

In chapter 15, "Russellian Monism or Nagelian Monism?," Daniel Stoljar defends what he calls Nagelian monism by contrasting it with Russellian monism. These two views share some features. For example, they both reject dualism by saying that experiential properties are not metaphysically fundamental. Also, they both reject standard forms of materialism by saying that the list of physical properties on which materialists rely is inadequate. Furthermore, they both advance an epistemic response to the conceivability argument. Stoljar notes, however, that Nagelian monism differs from Russellian monism because it does not appeal to any of the distinctions to which Russellian monism appeals, such as that between structural and non-structural properties or extrinsic and intrinsic properties. These distinctions do not play any role in Nagelian monism. Nagelian monism appeals to a more generic distinction between properties of the sort described in contemporary physics and properties of the sort described in the physics that would be formulated at the ideal limit of inquiry.

As Stoljar recognizes, Nagelian monism faces a challenge. From the perspective of the Russellian monist, even ideal scientific theory will characterize the world in terms of structure and dynamics. Thus, it seems, the current/ideal theory distinction cannot do the work done by the distinctions Russellian monists employ, such as that between structural and non-structural features. In particular, it is hard to see how the current/ideal theory distinction can help answer the conceivability argument against physicalism (op. cit.). Stoljar responds by asking what it might mean to characterize the world

---

9. Pereboom's chapter combines the main ideas of chapters 5 and 6 of *Consciousness and the Prospects of Physicalism*. But there are substantial refinements, such as a shift from a partly epistemic to a purely metaphysical characterization of absolute intrinsicality.

in terms of structure and dynamics. He distinguishes three answers to that question and argues that on all versions the threat to Nagelian monism is illusory. Further, his argument provides new challenges for Russellian monist attempts to explicate the structural/non-structural distinction in a way their theory requires.

In chapter 16, "A Physicalist Critique of Russellian Monism," Alyssa Ney argues against Russellian monism from the perspective of a committed physicalist. Her strategy is to try to undermine Russellian monism by focusing on (what we called above) structuralism about physics: the claim that physics describes its most fundamental features only relationally. Ney claims that this thesis can be interpreted in four ways: psychological/epistemological, semantic, descriptive, and normative. She devotes much of her discussion to the psychological/epistemological interpretation, which she attributes to Russell, and the semantic interpretation, which she attributes to Lewis. To defend the psychological/epistemic interpretation, Russell appeals to the causal theory of perception and the idea that we cannot know the intrinsic features of the properties that cause our experiences because they are instantiated in a distinct space from the private space of experiences. Lewis, on the other hand, appeals to his theory of theoretical terms inspired by Ramsey and Carnap and the idea that theories in physics describe only relations that objects with intrinsic properties bear to one another. Ney argues that neither of these nor the remaining two interpretations of physical structuralism succeeds and that Russellian monists fail to show that physics needs to be supplemented by additional metaphysical doctrines about intrinsic features.

Chapter 17, Philip Goff's "Against Constitutive Russellian Monism," has three main sections. In the first, Goff characterizes Russellian monism in a novel way, making use of the notion of a *transparent* concept—one that "reveals the nature" of the property denoted by the concept. The concept SPHERICITY is transparent because possessing it puts one in a position to figure out a priori what being a sphere consists in—unlike the concept WATER, for example. Goff defines Russellian monism as making this claim:

> There is no a priori entailment between the complete physicSal description of reality (i.e. the complete description of reality in the vocabulary of fundamental physics) and the phenomenal facts, but there is an a priori entailment between a transparent rendering of the complete physicSal description of reality [that is, one that uses only predicates that express transparent concepts] and the phenomenal facts.

That definition, Goff argues, has various advantages over others—including allowing him to more cleanly distinguish Russellian monism from related views, such as a posteriori (that is, type-B) physicalism.

Goff goes on to scrutinize *constitutive* Russellian monism, on which phenomenal experience is constituted by protophenomenal experience. Goff explicates the relevant notion of constitution in detail, making central use of Theodore Sider's (2012) framework for thinking about fundamentality. He then argues that constitutive Russellian monism, though favored by Chalmers, Pereboom, and others, requires a deflationary account of phenomenal facts that Russellian monists cannot accept. Goff also develops and defends a version of non-constitutive Russellian monism on which both micro- and macro-phenomenal facts are fundamental.

In chapter 18, "Pessimism about Russellian Monism," Amy Kind criticizes Russellian monism. She does not argue that the theory is false. Rather, she claims that it does not advance the debate on the problem of consciousness. She distinguishes four versions of Russellian monism: phenomenal monism, protophenomenal monism, neutral monism, and physical monism. However, she argues, on reflection only phenomenal monism and physical monism remain. This is because (i) protophenomenal monism does not carve out distinct conceptual space from the other three versions and (ii) in the context of Russellian monism, the neutral properties postulated in neutral monism are no different from physical properties of a special sort. Since phenomenal monism and physical monism correspond to dualism and physicalism in the traditional framework, Kind concludes, Russellian monism does not transcend the old dualism/physicalism divide.

In chapter 19, "What Is Russellian Monism?," Torin Alter and Yujin Nagasawa provide an analysis and defense of Russellian monism. They propose that structuralism about physics, realism about the relevant intrinsic properties (there called "realism about inscrutables"), and (proto)phenomenal foundationalism are the theory's "most central and most distinctive claims." They also distinguish several varieties of the theory and explain how those varieties relate to dualism, materialism, idealism, and neutral monism. In support of Russellian monism, they do four things. They defend it from certain misconceptions, such as the idea that it entails that phenomenal properties lack structure. They explain why it is not threatened by the conceivability argument or the knowledge argument. They argue that the arguments that do pose a threat, such as those that exploit the combination problem, are not decisive. And they present two arguments for the theory, including the happy-compromise argument mentioned in section 1 above and another, due to Chalmers (1996) and inspired by Russell, that they call "the 'solving two problems at once' argument." Alter and Nagasawa conclude that, "further development and examination of [Russellian monism] is well justified."

References

Chalmers, D. J. (1996) *The Conscious Mind: In Search of a Fundamental Theory*. New York: Oxford University Press.

Chalmers, D. J. (1997) "Moving Forward on the Problem of Consciousness," *Journal of Consciousness Studies* 4: 3–46.

Chalmers, D. J. (2002) "Does Conceivability Entail Possibility?," in T. Gendler and J. Hawthorne (eds.), *Conceivability and Possibility*. Oxford: Oxford University Press, 145–200.

Chalmers, D. J. (forthcoming) "The Combination Problem for Panpsychism," in G. Bruntrup and L. Jaskolla, (eds.), *Panpsychism*. New York: Oxford University Press.

Coleman, S. (2013) "The Real Combination Problem: Panpsychism, Micro-subjects, and Emergence," *Erkenntnis* 78: 1–26.

Descartes, R. (1641) *Meditations on First Philosophy*.

Feigl, H. (1958/1967) "The 'Mental' and the 'Physical,'" *Minnesota Studies in the Philosophy of Science* 2: 370–497. Reprinted (with a postscript) as *The 'Mental' and the 'Physical'*. Minneapolis: University of Minnesota Press.

Holman, E. (2008) "Panpsychism, Physicalism, Neutral Monism and the Russellian Theory of Mind," *Journal of Consciousness Studies* 15: 48–67.

Kripke, S. (1972) "Naming and Necessity," in G. Harman and D. Davidson, *The Semantics of Natural Language*. Dordrecht: Reidel, 253–355.

Lockwood, M. (1989) *Mind, Brain, & the Quantum: The Compound 'I.'* Oxford: Blackwell.

McClelland, T. (2013) "The Neo-Russellian Ignorance Hypothesis: A Hybrid Account of Phenomenal Consciousness," *Journal of Consciousness Studies* 20: 125–51.

Rosenberg, G. (2004) *A Place for Consciousness: Probing the Deep Structure of the Natural World*. New York: Oxford University Press.

Sellars, W. (1965) "The Identity Approach to the Mind–Body Problem," *Review of Metaphysics* 18: 430–51.

Sellars, W. (1971) "Science, Sense Impressions, and Sensa: A Reply to Cornman," *The Review of Metaphysics* 24: 391–447.

Seager, W. E. (1995) "Consciousness, Information, and Panpsychism," *Journal of Consciousness Studies* 2: 272–88.

Sider, T. (2012) *Writing the Book of the World*. Oxford: Oxford University Press.

Stoljar, D. (2001) "Two Conceptions of the Physical," *Philosophy and Phenomenological Research* 62: 253–81.

PART I

Precursors

1

Monadology 17 and Letter to De Volder (excerpt)

Gottfried Wilhelm von Leibniz

Monadology 17

Translated by Robert Merrihew Adams from the definitive text edited by André Robinet in "Monado 74": G. W. Leibniz, Discours de Métaphysique et Monadologie (Paris: Vrin, 1974), p. 49.

It must be confessed, moreover, that *perception* and what depends on it *cannot be explained by mechanical reasons*, that is to say, by shapes and motions. And imagining that there is a machine, whose structure makes it think, feel, and have perception, we could conceive of it as enlarged, while keeping the same proportions, so that we could go into it, as [we go] into a mill. And in that case, in visiting its interior, we will find nothing but pieces that push each other, and never anything to explain a perception. Hence it is in the simple substance, and not in the composite or in the machine, that we must seek it. In the simple substance also, we can't find anything but that—that is to say, the perceptions and the changes in them. It is in that alone, moreover, that all the *internal actions* of the simple substances can consist.

Letter to De Volder

Translated by Robert Merrihew Adams from Leibniz to De Volder, March 24/ April 3, 1699 (G II, 169–70).

I don't think a substance is constituted by extension alone, since the concept of extension is incomplete. Nor do I believe that extension is conceived through itself, but that it is an analyzable and relative notion. For it is analyzed into plurality, continuity, and coexistence (that is, existence of parts at one and the same time). There is plurality in number too, and continuity in time and motion too, but coexistence happens only in what is extended. But even from this it appears that something is always assumed that is continued or spread out—as whiteness is in milk; color, ductility, and weight in gold; and resistance in matter. For extension is nothing other than simultaneous continuity, and continuity as such, through itself, does not complete a substance, any more than manyness or number does, where there needs to be something that is numbered, repeated, continued. Therefore I believe that our thought is completed and finished in the notion of the dynamic, rather than in that of extension, and that no other notion of power or force is to be sought than that it is an attribute from which change follows, whose subject is a substance itself. Nor do I see what would escape [our] understanding here. The nature of the thing does not admit of anything like a clearer picture. I think there is no unity of an extended thing except in the abstract—that is, when we abstract the mind from the internal motion of parts, by which every part of matter is subdivided again into actually diverse parts, to which indeed the fullness [of things] is no obstacle. And it is not only in modes that the parts of matter differ, if they are marked off with souls and entelechies, which always subsist.

2

Critique of Pure Reason, A270/B326–A278/B334 (excerpt)

Immanuel Kant

Translated by John Miller Dow Mieklejohn, 1855
With some alterations by Derk Pereboom

DECEIVED BY THE amphiboly of the conceptions of reflection, the celebrated Leibniz constructed an intellectual system of the world, or rather, believed himself competent to cognize the intrinsic nature of things, by comparing all objects merely with the understanding and the abstract formal concepts of thought . . . [He] compared all things with each other merely by means of concepts, and naturally found no other differences than those by which the understanding distinguishes its pure concepts one from another. The conditions of sensible intuition, which contain in themselves their own means of distinction, he did not look upon as primitive, because sensibility was to him but a confused mode of representation and not any distinctive source of representations. Appearance was for him the representation of the thing in itself, though distinguished from cognition by the understanding only in respect of the logical form—the former with its usual want of analysis containing, according to him, a certain mixture of sub-representations in its conception of a thing, which it is the duty of the understanding to separate and distinguish.

In a word, Leibniz *intellectualized* appearances, just as Locke, in his system of *noogony* (if I may be allowed to make use of such expressions), *sensualized* the concepts of the understanding, that is to say, declared them to be nothing more than empirical or abstract conceptions of reflection. Instead of seeking in the understanding and sensibility two different sources of representations, which can present us with objective judgments of things only in conjunction, each of these great men recognized but one of these faculties, which, in their opinion, applied immediately to things in themselves, the other having no duty but that of confusing or arranging the representations of the former.

Accordingly, Leibniz compared the objects of sense as things in general merely in the understanding.

First. He compared them in regard to their *identity or difference*—as judged by the understanding. As, therefore, he considered merely the concepts of objects, and not their position in intuition, in which alone objects can be given, and left quite out of sight the transcendental locale of these concepts—whether, that is, their object ought to be classed among appearances, or among things in themselves, it was to be expected that he should extend the application of the principle of indiscernibles, which is valid solely for concepts of things in general, to objects of sense (*mundus phaenomenon*), and that he should believe that he had thereby contributed in no small degree to extend our knowledge of nature. In truth, if I cognize in all its intrinsic determinations a drop of water as a thing in itself, I cannot look upon one drop as different from another, if the concept of the one is completely identical with that of the other. But if it is an appearance in space, it has a place not merely in the understanding (among concepts), but also in sensible external intuition (in space), and in this case, the physical locale is a matter of indifference in regard to the intrinsic determinations of things, and one place, B, may contain a thing which is perfectly similar and the same as another in a place, A, just as well as if the two things were in every respect different from each other. Difference of place without any other conditions, makes the plurality and distinction of objects as appearances not only possible in itself, but even necessary. Consequently, the above so-called law is not a law of nature. It is merely an analytical rule for the comparison of things by means of mere concepts.

Second. The principle: "Realities (as simple affirmations) never logically contradict each other," is a proposition perfectly true respecting the relation of concepts, but, whether as regards nature, or things in themselves (of which we have not the slightest conception), is without the least meaning ...

Third. The Leibnizian monadology has really no better foundation than on this philosopher's mode of falsely representing the difference between the intrinsic and extrinsic solely in relation to the understanding. Substances, in general, must have something intrinsic, which is therefore free from extrinsic relations, consequently from that of composition also. The simple—that which can be represented by a unit—is therefore the foundation of that which is intrinsic in things in themselves. The intrinsic state of substances cannot therefore consist in place, shape, contact, or motion, determinations which are all extrinsic relations, and we can ascribe to them no other than that whereby we internally determine our faculty of sense itself, that is to say, the state of representation. This, then, resulted in the monads, which were to form the elements of the universe, the active force of which consists in representation, the effects of this force being thus entirely confined to themselves ...

Fourth. This philosopher's celebrated doctrine of space and time, in which he intellectualized these forms of sensibility, originated in the same delusion of transcendental reflection. If I attempt to represent by the mere understanding, the extrinsic relations of things, I can do so only by employing the conception of their reciprocal action, and if I wish to connect one state of the same thing with another state, I must avail myself of the notion of the order of ground and consequence. And thus Leibniz regarded space as a certain order in the community of substances, and time as the dynamical sequence of their states. That which space and time possess proper to themselves and independent of things, he ascribed to a *confusion* in our concepts of them, whereby that which is a mere form of dynamical relations is held to be a self-existent intuition, antecedent even to things themselves. Thus space and time were the intelligible form of the connection of things (substances and their states) in themselves. But things were intelligible substances (*substantiae noumena*). At the same time, he made these conceptions valid of appearances, because he did not allow to sensibility a distinctive mode of intuition, but sought all, even the empirical representation of objects, in the understanding, and left to sense nothing but the despicable task of confusing and disarranging the representation of the former.

But even if we could frame any synthetic proposition concerning things in themselves by means of the pure understanding (which is impossible), it could not apply to appearances, which do not represent things in themselves. In such a case I should be obliged in transcendental reflection to compare my conceptions only under the conditions of sensibility, and so space and time would not be determinations of things in themselves, but of appearances. What things may be in themselves, I know not and need not know, because a thing is never presented to me otherwise than as in appearance.

I must adopt the same mode of procedure with the other concepts of reflection. Matter *is substantia phaenomenon.* That in it which is intrinsic I seek to discover in all parts of space which it occupies, and in all the functions and operations it performs, and which are indeed never anything but appearances of the external sense. I cannot therefore find anything that is absolutely, but only what is comparatively intrinsic, and which itself consists of extrinsic relations. The absolutely intrinsic in matter, and as it should be according to the pure understanding, is a mere chimera, for matter is not an object for the pure understanding. But the transcendental object, which is the foundation of the appearance which we call matter, is a mere *nescio quid*, the nature of which we could not understand, even if someone were found able to tell us. This is because we can understand nothing that does not bring with it something in intuition corresponding to the expressions employed.

If, by the complaint *that we have no insight into the intrinsic nature of things*, it is meant that we do not comprehend by the pure understanding what the things which appear to us may be in themselves, it is an obtuse and unreasonable complaint; for those who talk thus really desire that we should be able to cognize, and consequently to intuit, things without senses, and therefore wish that we possessed a faculty of cognition completely different from the human faculty, not merely in degree, but even as regards intuition and the mode thereof, so that thus we should not be human beings, but belong to a class of beings the possibility of whose existence, much less their nature and constitution, we have no means of cognizing.

By observation and analysis of appearances we penetrate into the interior of nature, and no one can say what progress this knowledge may make in time. But those transcendental questions which pass beyond the limits of nature, we could never answer, even although all nature were laid open to us, because we have not the power of observing our own mind with any other intuition than that of our inner sense. For herein lies the mystery of the origin and source of our faculty of sensibility. Its application to an object, and the transcendental ground of this unity of subjective and objective, lie too deeply concealed for us, who cognize ourselves only through inner sense, consequently as appearance to be able to discover in our existence anything but appearances, the non-sensible cause of which we at the same time intently desire to comprehend.

3

The Principles of Psychology (excerpt)

William James

BUT THERE IS a still more fatal objection to the theory of mental units 'compounding with themselves' or 'integrating.' It is logically unintelligible; it leaves out the essential feature of all the 'combinations' we actually know.

All the 'combinations' which we actually know are EFFECTS, *wrought by the units said to be 'combined,'* UPON SOME ENTITY OTHER THAN THEMSELVES. Without this feature of a medium or vehicle, the notion of combination has no sense.

"A multitude of contractile units, by joint action, and by being all connected, for instance, with a single tendon, will pull at the same, and will bring about a dynamical effect which is undoubtedly the resultant of their combined individual energies ... On the whole, tendons are to muscular fibres, and bones are to tendons, combining recipients of mechanical energies. A medium of composition is indispensable to the summation of energies. To realize the complete dependence of mechanical resultants on a combining substratum, one may fancy for a moment all the individually contracting muscular elements severed from their attachments. They might then still be capable of contracting with the same energy as before, yet no co-operative result would be accomplished. The medium of dynamical combination would be wanting. The multiple energies, singly exerted on no common recipient, would lose themselves on entirely isolated and disconnected efforts."[1]

---

1. E. Montgomery, in 'Mind,' V. 18–19. See also pp. 24–25.

In other words, no possible number of entities (call them as you like, whether forces, material particles, or mental elements) can sum *themselves* together. Each remains, in the sum, what it always was; and the sum itself exists only *for a bystander* who happens to overlook the units and to apprehend the sum as such; or else it exists in the shape of some other *effect* on an entity external to the sum itself. Let it not be objected that H_2 and O combine of themselves into 'water,' and thenceforward exhibit new properties. They do not. The 'water' is just the old atoms in the new position, H-O-H; the 'new properties' are just their combined *effects*, when in this position, upon external media, such as our sense-organs and the various reagents on which water may exert its properties and be known.

"Aggregations are organized wholes only when they behave as such in the presence of other things. A statue is an aggregation of particles of marble; but as such it has no unity. For the spectator it is one; in itself it is an aggregate; just as, to the consciousness of an ant crawling over it, it may again appear a mere aggregate. No summing up of parts can make an unity of a mass of discrete constituents, unless this unity exist for some other subject, not for the mass itself."[2]

Just so, in the parallelogram of forces, the 'forces' themselves do not combine into the diagonal resultant; a *body* is needed on which they may impinge, to exhibit their resultant effect. No more do musical sounds combine *per se* into concords or discords. Concord and discord are names for their combined effects on that external medium, the *ear*.

Where the elemental units are supposed to be feelings, the case is in no wise altered. Take a hundred of them, shuffle them and pack them as close together as you can (whatever that may mean); still each remains the same feeling it always was, shut in its own skin, windowless, ignorant of what the

---

2. J. Royce, 'Mind,' VI. p. 376. Lotze has set forth the truth of this law more clearly and copiously than any other writer. Unfortunately he is too lengthy to quote. See his Microcosmus, bk. II. ch. I. § 5; Metaphysik, §§ 242, 260; Outlines of Metaphysics, part II. chap. I. §§ 3, 4, 5. Compare also Reid's Intellectual Powers, essay V, chap. III *ad fin.*; Bowne's Metaphysics, pp. 361–76; St. J. Mivart: Nature and Thought, pp. 98–101; E. Gurney: 'Monism,' in 'Mind,' VI. 153; and the article by Prof. Royce, just quoted, on 'Mind-stuff and Reality.' *In defence of the mind-stuff view*, see W. K. Clifford: 'Mind,' III. 57 (reprinted in his 'Lectures and Essays,' II. 71); G. T. Fechner, Psychophysik, Bd. II. cap. XLV; H. Taine: on Intelligence, bk. III; E. Haeckel. 'Zellseelen u. Seelenzellen,' in Gesammelte pop. Vorträge, Bd. I. p. 143; W. S. Duncan. Conscious Matter, *passim*; H. Zollner; Natur d. Cometen, pp. 320 ff.; Alfred Barratt: 'Physical Ethic' and Physical Metempiric,' *passim*' J. Soury: 'Hylozoismus,' in Kosmos,' V. Jahrg., Heft X. p. 241; A. Main: 'Mind,' I. 292, 431, 566; II. 129, 402; *Id.* Revue Philos., II. 86, 88, 419; III. 51, 502; IV. 402; F. W. Frankland: 'Mind,' VI. 116; Whittaker: 'Mind,' VI. 498 (historical); Morton Prince: The Nature of Mind and Human Automatism (1885); A. Riehl: Der philosophische Kriticismus, Bd. II. Theil 2, 2ter Abschnitt, 2tes Cap. (1887). The clearest of all these statements is, as far as it goes, that of Prince.

other feelings are and mean. There would be a hundred-and-first feeling there, if, when a group or series of such feelings were set up, a consciousness *belonging to the group as such* should emerge. And this 101st feeling would be a totally new fact; the 100 original feelings might, by a curious physical law, be a signal for its *creation*, when they came together; but they would have no substantial identity with it, nor it with them, and one could never deduce the one from the others, or (in any intelligible sense) say that they *evolved* it.

Take a sentence of a dozen words, and take twelve men and tell to each one word. Then stand the men in a row or jam them in a bunch, and let each think of his word as intently as he will; nowhere will there be a consciousness of the whole sentence.[3] We talk of the 'spirit of the age,' and the 'sentiment of the people,' and in various ways we hypostatize 'public opinion.' But we know this to be symbolic speech, and never dream that the spirit, opinion, sentiment, etc., constitute a consciousness other than, and additional to, that of the several individuals whom the words 'age,' 'people,' or 'public' denote. The private minds do not agglomerate into a higher compound mind. This has always been the invincible contention of the spiritualists against the associationists in Psychology,—a contention which we shall take up at greater length in Chapter X. The associationists say the mind is constituted by a multiplicity of distinct 'ideas' *associated* into a unity. There is, they say, an idea of *a*, and also an idea of *b*. *Therefore*, they say, there is an idea of *a* + *b*, or of *a* and *b* together. Which is like saying that the mathematical square of *a* plus that of *b* is equal to the square of *a* + *b*, a palpable untruth. Idea of *a* + idea of *b* is *not* identical with idea of (a + b). It is one, they are two; in it, what knows *a* also knows *b*; in them, what knows *a* is expressly posited as not knowing *b*; etc. In short, the two separate ideas can never by any logic be made to figure as one and the same thing as the 'associated' idea.

This is what the spiritualists keep saying; and since we do, as a matter of fact, have the 'compounded' idea, and do know *a* and *b* together, they adopt a farther hypothesis to explain that fact. The separate ideas exist, they say, but *affect* a third entity, the soul. *This* has the 'compounded' idea, if you please so to call it; and the compounded idea is an altogether new psychic fact to which the separate ideas stand in the relation, not of constituents, but of occasions of production.

---

3. "Someone might say that although it is true that neither a blind man nor a deaf man by himself can compare sounds with colors, yet since one hears and the other sees they might do so both together . . . But whether they are apart or close together makes no difference; not even if they permanently keep house together; no, not if they were Siamese twins, or more than Siamese twins, and were inseparably grown together, would it make the assumption any more possible. Only when sound and color are represented in the same reality is it thinkable that they should be compared." (Brentano; Psychologie, p. 209.)

   This argument of the spiritualists against the associationists has never been answered by the latter. It holds good against any talk about self-compounding amongst feelings, against any 'blending,' or 'complication,' or 'mental chemistry,' or 'psychic synthesis,' which supposes a resultant consciousness to float off from the constituents *per se*, in the absence of a supernumerary principle of consciousness which they may affect. The mind-stuff theory, in short, is unintelligible. Atoms of feeling cannot compose higher feelings, any more than atoms of matter can compose physical things! The 'things,' for a clear-headed atomistic evolutionist, are not. Nothing is but the everlasting atoms. When grouped in a certain way, *we* name them this 'thing' or that; but the thing we name has no existence out of our mind. So of the states of mind which are supposed to be compound because they know many different things together. Since indubitably such states do exist, they must exist as single new facts, effects, possibly, as the spiritualists say, on the Soul (we will not decide that point here), but at any rate independent and integral, and not compounded of psychic atoms.[4]

---

4. The reader must observe that we are reasoning altogether about the *logic* of the mind-stuff theory, about whether it can *explain the constitution* of higher mental states by viewing them as *identical with lower ones* summed together. We say the two sorts of fact are not identical: a higher state *is* not a lot of lower states; it is itself. When, however, a lot of lower states have come together, or when certain brain-conditions occur together which, *if they occurred separately, would produce* a lot of lower states, we have not for a moment pretended that a higher state may not emerge. In fact it does emerge under those conditions; and our Chapter IX will be mainly devoted to the proof of this fact. But such emergence is that of a new psychic entity, and is *toto coelo* different from such an 'integration' of the lower states as the mind-stuff theory affirms. It may seem strange to suppose that anyone should mistake criticism of a certain theory about a fact for doubt of the fact itself. And yet the confusion is made in high quarters enough to justify our remarks. Mr. J. Ward, in his article Psychology in the Encyclopaedia Britannica, speaking of the hypothesis that "a series of feelings can be aware of itself as a series," says (p. 39): "Paradox is too mild a word for it, even contradiction will hardly suffice." Whereupon, Professor Bain takes him thus to task: "As to 'a series of states being aware of itself, I confess I see no insurmountable difficulty. It may be a fact, or not a fact; it may be a very clumsy expression for what it is applied to; but it is neither paradox nor contradiction. A series merely contradicts an individual, or it may be two or more individuals as coexisting; but that is too general to exclude the possibility of self-knowledge. It certainly does not bring the property of self-knowledge into the foreground, which, however, is not the same as denying it. An algebraic series might know itself, without any contradiction: the only thing against it is the want of evidence of the fact." ('Mind,' XI, 459). Prof. Bain thinks, then, that all the bother is about the difficulty of seeing how a series of feelings can have the knowledge of itself *added to it!!!* As if anybody ever was troubled about that. That, notoriously enough, is a fact: our consciousness is a series of feelings to which every now and then is *added* a retrospective consciousness that they have come and gone. What Mr. Ward and I are troubled about is merely the silliness of the mind-stuffists and associationists continuing to say that the 'series of states' *is* the 'awareness of itself;' that if the states be posited severally, their collective consciousness is *eo ipso* given; and that we need no farther explanation, or 'evidence of the fact.'

PART II

Russell and Commentaries

4

Excerpts from *Analysis of Matter* (1927), *Human Knowledge: Its Scope and Limits* (1948), *Portraits from Memory* (1956), and *My Philosophical Development* (1959)

Bertrand Russell

Analysis of Matter (1927)

Physics and Neutral Monism

In this chapter, I wish to define the outcome of our analysis in regard to the old controversy between materialism and idealism, and to make it clear wherein our theory differs from both. So long as the views set forth in previous chapters are supposed to be either materialistic or idealistic, they will seem to involve inconsistencies, since some seem to tend in the one direction, some in the other. For example, when I say that my percepts are in my head, I shall be thought materialistic; when I say that my head consists of my percepts and other similar events, I shall be thought idealistic. Yet the former statement is a logical consequence of the latter.

Both materialism and idealism have been guilty, unconsciously and in spite of explicit disavowals, of a confusion in their imaginative picture of matter. They have thought of the matter in the external world as being represented by their percepts when they see and touch, whereas these percepts are really part of the matter of the percipient's brain. By examining our percepts it is possible—so I have contended—to infer certain formal mathematical properties of external matter, though the inference is not demonstrative or certain. But by examining our percepts we obtain knowledge which is not purely formal as to the matter of our brains. This knowledge, it is true, is fragmentary, but so far as it goes it has merits surpassing those of the knowledge given by physics.

The usual view would be that by psychology we acquire knowledge of our "minds," but that the only way to acquire knowledge of our brains is to have them examined by a physiologist, usually after we are dead, which seems somewhat unsatisfactory. I should say that what the physiologist sees when he looks at a brain is part of his own brain, not part of the brain he is examining. The feeling of paradox about this view comes, I should say, from wrong views of space. It is true that what we see is not located where our percept of our own brain would be located if we could see our own brain; but this is a question of perceptual space, not of the space of physics. The space of physics is connected with causation in a manner which compels us to hold that our percepts are in our brains, if we accept the causal theory of perception, as I think we are bound to do. To say that two events have no spatio-temporal separation is to say that they are compresent; to say that they have a small separation is to say that they are connected by causal chains, all of which are short. The percept must therefore be nearer to the sense-organ than to the physical object, nearer to the nerve than to the sense-organ, and nearer to the cerebral end of the nerve than to the other end. This is inevitable, unless we are going to say that the percept is not in space-time at all. It is usual to hold that "mental" events are in time but not in space; let us ask ourselves whether there is any ground for this view as regards percepts.

The question whether percepts are located in physical space is the same as the question of their causal connection with physical events. If they can be effects and causes of physical events, we are bound to give them a position in physical space-time in so far as interval is concerned, since interval was defined in causal terms. But the real question is as to "compresence" in the sense of Chapter XXVIII. Can a mental event be compresent with a physical event? If yes, then a mental event has a position in the space-time order; if no, then it has no such position. This, therefore, is the crucial question.

When I maintain that a percept and a physical event can be compresent, I am not maintaining that a percept can have to a piece of matter the sort of relation which another piece of matter would have. The relation of compresence is between a percept and a physical *event*, and physical events are not to be confounded with pieces of matter. A piece of matter is a logical structure composed of events; the causal laws of the events concerned, and the abstract logical properties of their spatio-temporal relations, are more or less known, but their intrinsic character is not known. Percepts fit into the same causal scheme as physical events, and are not known to have any intrinsic character which physical events cannot have, since we do not know of any intrinsic character which could be incompatible with the logical properties that physics assigns to physical events. There is therefore no ground for the view that percepts cannot be physical events, or for supposing that they are never compresent with other physical events.

The fact that mental events admittedly have temporal relations has much force, now that time and space are so much less distinct than they were. It has become difficult to hold that mental events, though in time, are not in space. The fact that their relations to each other can be viewed as only temporal is a fact which they share with any set of events forming the biography of one piece of matter. Relatively to axes moving with the percipient's brain, the interval between two percepts of his which are not compresent should always be temporal, if his percepts are in his head. But the interval between simultaneous percepts of different percipients is of a different kind; and their whole causal environment is such as to make us call this interval space-like. I conclude, then, that there is no good ground for excluding percepts from the physical world, but several strong reasons for including them. The difficulties that have been supposed to stand in the way seem to me to be entirely due to wrong views as to the physical world, and more particularly as to physical space. The wrong views as to physical space have been encouraged by the notion that the primary qualities are objective, which has been held imaginatively by many men who would have emphatically repudiated it so far as their explicit thought was concerned.

I hold, therefore, that two simultaneous percepts of one percipient have the relation of compresence out of which spatio-temporal order arises. It is almost irresistible to go a step further, and say that any two simultaneous perceived contents of a mind are compresent, so that all our conscious mental states are in our heads. I see as little reason against this extension as against the view that percepts can be compresent. A percept differs from another mental state, I should say, only in the nature of its causal relation to an external stimulus. Some relation of this kind no doubt always exists, but with other mental states the relation may be more indirect, or may be only to some state of the body, more particularly the brain. "Unconscious" mental states will be events compresent with certain other mental states, but not having those effects which constitute what is called awareness of a mental state. However, I have no wish to go further into psychology than is necessary, and I will pursue this topic no longer, but return to matters of more concern to physics.

The point which concerns the philosophy of matter is that the events out of which we have been constructing the physical world are very different from matter as traditionally conceived. Matter was expected to be impenetrable and indestructible. The matter that we construct is impenetrable as a result of definition: the matter in a place is all the events that are there, and consequently no other event or piece of matter can be there. This is a tautology, not a physical fact; one might as well argue that London is impenetrable because nobody can live in it except one of its inhabitants. Indestructibility, on the other hand, is an empirical property, believed to be approximately but not exactly possessed by matter. I mean by indestructibility, not conservation of mass, which is known to be only approximate, but conservation of electrons and protons. At present it is not known whether an electron and a proton sometimes enter into a suicide pact or not,[1] but there is certainly no known reason why electrons and protons should be indestructible.

Electrons and protons, however, are not the stuff of the physical world: they are elaborate logical structures composed of events, and ultimately of particulars, in the sense of Chapter XXVII. As to what the events are that compose the physical world, they are, in the first place, percepts, and then whatever can be inferred from percepts by the methods considered in Part II. But on various inferential grounds we are led to the view that a percept in which we cannot perceive a structure nevertheless often has a structure, *i.e.* that the apparently simple is often complex. We cannot therefore treat the *minimum visible* as a particular, for both physical and psychological facts may lead us to attribute a structure to it—not merely a structure in general, but such and such a structure.

Events are neither impenetrable nor indestructible. Space-time is constructed by means of co-punctuality, which is the same thing as spatio-temporal interpenetration. Perhaps it is not unnecessary to explain that spatio-temporal interpenetration is quite a different thing from logical interpenetration, though it may be suspected that some philosophers have been led to favour the latter as a result of the arguments for the former. We are accustomed to imagining that numerical diversity involves spatio-temporal separation; hence we tend to think that, if two diverse entities are in one place, they cannot be wholly diverse, but must be also in some sense one. It is this combination that is supposed to constitute logical interpenetration. For my part, I do not think that logical interpenetration can be defined without obvious self-contradiction; Bergson, who advocates it, does not define it. The

---

1 It is thought highly probable that they do. See Dr. Jeans, "Recent Developments of Cosmical Physics," *Nature*, December 4, 1926.

only author I know of who has dealt seriously with its difficulties is Bradley, in whom, quite consistently, it led to a thorough-going monism, combined with the avowal that, in the end, all truth is self-contradictory. I should myself regard this latter result as a refutation of the logic from which it follows. Therefore, while I respect Bradley more than any other advocate of inter-penetration, he seems to me, in virtue of his ability, to have done more than any other philosopher to disprove the kind of system which he advocated. However that may be, the spatio-temporal interpenetration which is used in constructing space-time order is quite different from logical interpene-tration. Philosophers have been slaves of space and time in the imagina-tive application of their logic. This is partly due to Euler's diagrams and the notion that the traditional *A, E, I, O* were elementary forms of propositions and the confounding of "*x* is a *β*" with "all *a*'s are *β*'s." All this led to a con-fusion between classes and individuals, and to the inference that individu-als can interpenetrate because classes can overlap. I do not suggest explicit confusions of this sort, but only that traditional elementary logic, taught in youth, is an almost fatal barrier to clear thinking in later years, unless much time is spent in acquiring a new technique.

On the question of the material out of which the physical world is constructed, the views advocated in this volume have, perhaps, more affinity with idealism than with materialism. What are called "mental" events, if we have been right, are part of the material of the physical world, and what is in our heads is the mind (with additions) rather than what the physiologist sees through his micro-scope. It is true that we have not suggested that all reality is mental. The positive arguments in favour of such a view, whether Berkeleyan or German, appear to me fallacious. The sceptical argument of the phenomenalists, that, whatever else there may be, we cannot know it, is much more worthy of respect. There are, in fact, if we have been right, three grades of certainty. The highest grade belongs to my own percepts; the second grade to the percepts of other peo-ple; the third to events which are not percepts of anybody. It is to be observed, however, that the second grade belongs only to the percepts of those who can communicate with me, directly or indirectly, and of those who are known to be closely analogous to people who can communicate with me. The percepts of minds, if such there be, which are not related to mine by communication—*e.g.* minds in other planets—can have, at best, only the third grade of certainty, that, namely, which belongs to the apparently lifeless physical world.

The events which are not perceived by any person who can communicate with me, supposing they have been rightly inferred, have a causal connection with percepts, and are inferred by means of this connection. Much is known about their structure, but nothing about their quality.

While, on the question of the stuff of the world, the theory of the foregoing pages has certain affinities with idealism—namely, that mental events are
part of that stuff, and that the rest of the stuff resembles them more than it
resembles traditional billiard-balls—the position advocated as regards scientific laws has more affinity with materialism than with idealism. Inference
from one event to another, where possible, seems only to acquire exactness
when it can be stated in terms of the laws of physics. There are psychological laws, physiological laws, and chemical laws, which cannot at present be
reduced to physical laws. But none of them is exact and without exceptions;
they state tendencies and averages rather than mathematical laws governing
minimum events. Take, for example, the psychological laws of memory. We
cannot say: At 12.55 G.M.T. on such and such a day, A will remember the event
e—unless, indeed, we are in a position to remind him of it at that moment.
The known laws of memory belong to an early stage of science—earlier than
Kepler's laws or Boyle's law. We can say that, if A and B have been experienced
together, the recurrence of A *tends* to cause a recollection of B, but we cannot
say that it is sure to do so, or that it will do so in one assignable class of cases
and not in another. One supposes that, to obtain an exact causal theory of
memory, it would be necessary to know more about the structure of the brain.
The ideal to be aimed at would be something like the physical explanation of
fluorescence, which is a phenomenon in many ways analogous to memory.
So far as causal laws go, therefore, physics seems to be supreme among the
sciences, not only as against other sciences of matter, but also as against the
sciences that deal with life and mind.

There is, however, one important limitation to this. We need to know in
what physical circumstances such-and-such a percept will arise, and we must
not neglect the more intimate qualitative knowledge which we possess concerning mental events. There will thus remain a certain sphere which will be
outside physics. To take a simple instance: physics might, ideally, be able to
predict that at such a time my eye would receive a stimulus of a certain sort; it
might be able to trace the physical properties of the resulting events in the eye
and the brain, one of which is, in fact, a visual percept; but it could not itself
give us the knowledge that one of them is a visual percept. It is obvious that a
man who can see knows things which a blind man cannot know; but a blind
man can know the whole of physics. Thus the knowledge which other men
have and he has not is not part of physics.

Although there is thus a sphere excluded from physics, yet physics, together
with a "dictionary," gives, apparently, all causal knowledge. One supposes that,
given the physical characteristics of the events in my head, the "dictionary"
gives the "mental" events in my head. This is by no means a matter of course.

The whole of the foregoing theory of physics might be true without entailing this consequence. So far as physics can show, it might be possible for different groups of events having the same structure to have the same part in causal series. That is to say, given the physical causal laws, and given enough knowledge of an initial group of events to determine the purely physical properties of their effects, it might nevertheless be the case that these effects could be qualitatively of different sorts. If that were so, physical determinism would not entail psychological determinism, since, given two percepts of identical structure but diverse quality, we could not tell which would result from a stimulus known only as to its physical, *i.e.* structural, properties. This is an unavoidable consequence of the abstractness of physics. If physics is concerned only with structure, it cannot, *per se*, warrant inferences to any but the structural properties of events. Now it may be a fact that (*e.g.*) the structure of visual percepts is very different from that of tactual percepts; but I do not think such differences could be established with sufficient strictness and generality to enable us to say that such-and-such a stimulus must produce a visual percept, while such another must produce a tactual percept.

On this matter, we must, I think, appeal to evidence which is partly psychological. We do know, as a matter of fact, that we can, in normal circumstances, more or less infer the percept from the stimulus. If this were not the case, speaking and writing would be useless. When the lessons are read, the congregation can follow the words in their own Bibles. The differences in their "thoughts" meanwhile can be connected causally, at least in part, with differences in their past experience, and these are supposed to make themselves effective by causing differences in the structure of brains. All this seems sufficiently probable to be worth taking seriously; but it lies outside physics, and does not follow from the causal autonomy of physics, supposing this to be established even for human bodies. It will be observed that what we are now considering is the converse of what is required for the inference from perception to physics. What is wanted there is that, given the percept, we should be able to infer, at least partially, the structure of the stimulus—or at any rate that this should be possible when a sufficient number of percepts are given. What we want now is that, given the *structure* of the stimulus (which is all that physics can give), we should be able to infer the *quality* of the percept—with the same limitations as before. Whether this is the case or not, is a question lying outside physics; but there is reason to think that it is the case.

The aim of physics, consciously or unconsciously, has always been to discover what we may call the causal skeleton of the world. It is perhaps surprising that there should be such a skeleton, but physics seems to prove that there is, particularly when taken in conjunction with the evidence that percepts are determined by the physical character of their stimuli. There is reason—though not quite conclusive reason—for regarding physics as causally dominant, in the sense that, given the physical structure of the world, the qualities of its events, in so far as we are acquainted with them, can be inferred by means of correlations. We have thus in effect a psycho-cerebral parallelism, although the interpretation to be put upon it is not the usual one. We suppose that, given sufficient knowledge, we could infer the qualities of the events in our heads from their physical properties. This is what is really meant when it is said, loosely, that the state of the mind can be inferred from the state of the brain. Although I think that this is probably true, I am less anxious to assert it than to assert, what seems to me much more certain, that its truth does not follow from the causal autonomy of physics or from physical determinism as applied to all matter, including that of living bodies. This latter result flows from the abstractness of physics, and belongs to the philosophy of physics. The other proposition, if true, cannot be established by considering physics alone, but only by a study of percepts for their own sakes, which belongs to psychology. Physics studies percepts only in their cognitive aspect; their other aspects lie outside its purview.

Even if we reject the view that the quality of events in our heads can be inferred from their structure, the view that physical determinism applies to human bodies brings us very near to what is most disliked in materialism. Physics may be unable to tell us what we shall hear or see or "think," but it can, on the view advocated in these pages, tell us what we shall say or write, where we shall go, whether we shall commit murder or theft, and so on. For all these are bodily movements, and thus come within the scope of physical laws. We are often asked to concede that the beauties of poetry or music cannot result from physical laws. I should concede that the beauty does not result from physics, since beauty depends in part upon intrinsic quality; if it were, as some writers on aesthetics contend, solely a matter of form, it would come within the scope of physics, but I think these writers do not realize what an abstract affair form really is. I should concede also that the *thoughts* of Shakespeare or Bach do not come within the scope of physics. But their thoughts are of no importance to us: their whole social efficacy depended upon certain black marks which they made on white paper. Now there seems no reason to suppose that physics does not apply to the making of these marks, which was a movement of matter just as truly as the revolution of the earth in its orbit. In any case, it is undeniable that the socially important part of their thought had a one-one relation to certain purely physical events, namely the occurrence of the black marks on the white paper. And no one can doubt that the causes of our emotions when we read Shakespeare or hear

Bach are purely physical. Thus we cannot escape from the universality of physical causation.

This, however, is perhaps not quite the last word on the subject. We have seen that, on the basis of physics itself, there may be limits to physical determinism. We know of no laws as to when a quantum transaction will take place or a radioactive atom will break down. We know fairly well what will happen *if* anything happens, and we know statistical averages, which suffice to determine macroscopic phenomena. But if mind and brain are causally interconnected, very small cerebral differences must be correlated with noticeable mental differences. Thus we are perhaps forced to descend into the region of quantum transactions, and to desert the macroscopic level where statistical averages obtain. Perhaps the electron jumps when it likes; perhaps the minute phenomena in the brain which make all the difference to mental phenomena belong to the region where physical laws no longer determine definitely what must happen. This, of course, is merely a speculative possibility; but it interposes a veto upon materialistic dogmatism. It may be that the progress of physics will decide the matter one way or other; for the present, as in so many other matters, the philosopher must be content to await the progress of science.

. . . In drawing inferences from percepts to their causes, we assume that the stimulus must possess whatever structure is possessed by the percept, though it may also have structural properties not possessed by the percept. The assumption that the structural properties of the percept must exist in the stimulus follows from the maxim "same cause, same effect" in the inverted form "different effects, different causes," from which it follows that if, *e.g.*, we see red and green side by side, there is some difference between the stimulus to the red percept and the stimulus to the green percept. The structural features possessed by the stimulus but not by the percept, when they can be inferred, are inferred by means of general laws—*e.g.* when two objects look similar to the naked eye but dissimilar under the microscope, we assume that there are differences in the stimuli to the naked-eye percepts which produce either no differences, or no perceptible differences, in the corresponding percepts.

These principles enable us to infer a great deal as to the structure of the physical world, but not as to its intrinsic character. They put percepts in their place as occurrences analogous to and connected with other events in the physical world, and they enable us to regard a dictaphone or a photographic plate as having something which, from the standpoint of physics, is not very dissimilar from perception. We no longer have to contend with what used to seem mysterious in the causal theory of perception: a series of light-waves or sound-waves or what not suddenly producing a mental event apparently totally different from themselves in character. As to intrinsic character, we do not know enough about it in the physical world to have a right to say that it is very different from that of percepts; while as to structure we have reason to hold that it is similar in the stimulus and the percept. This has become possible owing to the facts that "matter" can be regarded as a system of events, not as part of the stuff of the world, and that space-time, as it occurs in physics, has been found to be much more different from perceptual space than was formerly imagined.

This brings us to Part III, in which we endeavour to discover a possible structure of the physical world which shall at once justify physics and take account of the connection with perception demanded by the necessity for an empirical basis for physics. Here we are concerned first with the construction of points as systems of events which overlap, or are "co-punctual," in space-time, and then with the purely ordinal properties of space-time. The method employed is very general, and can be adapted to a discrete or to a continuous order; it is proved that $\aleph_0$ events are sufficient to generate a continuum of points, given certain laws as to the manner of their overlapping. The whole of this theory, however, aims only at constructing such properties of space-time as belong to *analysis situs*; everything appertaining to intervals and metrics is omitted at this stage, since causal considerations are required for the theory of intervals.

The conception of one unit of matter—say one electron—as a "substance," *i.e.* a single simple entity persisting through time, is not one which we are justified in adopting, since we have no evidence whatever as to whether it is false or true. We define a single material unit as a "causal line," *i.e.* as a series of events connected with each other by an intrinsic differential causal law which determines first-order changes, leaving second-order changes to be determined by extrinsic causal laws. (In this we are for the moment ignoring quantum phenomena.) If there are light-quanta, these will more or less fulfil this definition of matter, and we shall have returned to a corpuscular theory of light; but this is at present an open question. The whole conception of matter is less fundamental to physics than it used to be, since energy has more and more taken its place. We find that under terrestrial conditions electrons and protons persist, but there is nothing in theoretical physics to lead us to expect this, and physicists are quite prepared to find that matter can be annihilated. This view is even put forward to account for the energy of the stars.

The question of interval presents great difficulties, when we attempt to construct a picture of the world which shall make its importance seem not surprising. The same may be said of the quantum. I have endeavoured, not, I fear, with much success, to suggest hypotheses which would link these two curious facts into one whole. I suggest that the world consists of steady events accompanied by rhythms, like a long note on the violin while arpeggios are played on the piano, or of rhythms alone. Steady events are of various sorts, and many sorts have their appropriate rhythmic accompaniments. Quantum changes consist of "transactions," *i.e.* of the substitution, suddenly, of one rhythm for another. When two events have a time-like interval, if space-time is discrete, this interval is the greatest number of transitions on any causal route leading from the one event to the other. The definition of space-like intervals is derived from that of time-like intervals. The whole process of nature may, so far as present evidence goes, be conceived as discontinuous; even the periodic rhythms may consist of a finite number of events per period. The periodic rhythms are required in order to give an account of the uses of the quantum principle. A percept, at any rate when it is visual, will be a steady event, or system of steady events, following upon a transaction. Percepts are the only part of the physical world that we know otherwise than abstractly. As regards the world in general, both physical and mental, everything that we know of its intrinsic character is derived from the mental side, and almost everything that we know of its causal laws is derived from the physical side. But from the standpoint of philosophy the distinction between physical and mental is superficial and unreal.

Human Knowledge: Its Scope and Limits (1948)

When, on a common-sense basis, people talk of the gulf between mind and matter, what they really have in mind is the gulf between a visual or tactual percept and a "thought"—e.g., a memory, a pleasure, or a volition. But this, as we have seen, is a division within the mental world; the percept is as mental as the "thought." Slightly more sophisticated people may think of matter as the unknown cause of sensation, the "thing-in-itself" which certainly does not have the secondary qualities and perhaps does not have the primary qualities either. But however much they may emphasize the unknown character of the thing-in-itself, they still suppose themselves to know enough of it to be sure that it is very different from a mind. This comes, I think, of not having rid their imaginations of the conception of material things as something hard that you can bump into. You can bump into your friend's body, but not into his mind; therefore his body is different from his mind. This sort of argument persists imaginatively in many people who have rejected it intellectually.

Then, again, there is the argument about brain and mind. When a physiologist examines a brain, he does not see thoughts; therefore the brain is one thing and the mind which thinks is another. The fallacy in this argument consists in supposing that a man can see matter. Not even the ablest physiologist can perform this feat. His percept when he looks at a brain is an event in his own mind, and has only a causal connection with the brain that he fancies he is seeing. When, in a powerful telescope, he sees a tiny luminous dot, and interprets it as a vast nebula existing a million years ago, he realizes that what he sees is different from what he infers. The difference from the case of a brain looked at through a microscope is only one of degree: there is exactly the same need of inference, by means of the laws of physics, from the visual datum to its physical cause. And just as no one supposes that the nebula has any close resemblance to a luminous dot, so no one should suppose that the brain has any close resemblance to what the physiologist sees.

What, then, do we know about the physical world? Let us first define more exactly what we mean by a "physical" event. I should define it as an event which, if known to occur, is inferred, and which is not known to be mental. And I define a "mental" event (to repeat) as one with which someone is acquainted otherwise than by inference. Thus a "physical" event is one which is either totally unknown, or, if known at all, is not known to anyone except by inference–or, perhaps we should say, is not known to be known to anyone except by inference.

If physical events are to suffice as a basis for physics, and, indeed, if we are to have any reason for believing in them, they must not be *totally* unknown, like Kant's things-in-themselves. In fact, on the principle which we are assuming, they are known, though perhaps incompletely, so far as their space-time structure is concerned, for this must be similar to the space-time structure of their effects upon percipients. E.g., from the fact that the sun looks round in perceptual space we have a right to infer that it is round in physical space. We have no right to make a similar inference as regards brightness, because brightness is not a structural property.

We cannot, however, infer that the sun is *not* bright—meaning by "brightness" the quality that we know in perception. The only legitimate inferences as regards the physical sun are structural; concerning a property which is not structural, such as brightness, we must remain completely agnostic. We may perhaps say that it is unlikely that the physical sun is bright, since we have no knowledge of the qualities of things that are not percepts, and therefore there seems to be an illimitable field of choice of possible qualities. But such an argument is so speculative that perhaps we ought not to attach much weight to it.

This brings us to the question: Is there any reason, and if so what, for supposing that physical events differ in quality from mental events?

Here we must, to begin with, distinguish events in a living brain from events elsewhere. I will begin with events in a living brain.

I assume, for reasons which will be given in Part Four, that a small region of space-time is a collection of compresent events, and that space-time regions are ordered by means of causal relations. The former assumption has the consequence that there is no reason why thoughts should not be among the events of which the brain consists, and the latter assumption leads to the conclusion that, in physical space, thoughts are in the brain. Or, more exactly, each region of the brain is a class of events, and among the events constituting a region thoughts are included. It is to be observed that if we say thoughts are in the brain, we are using an ellipsis. The correct statement is that thoughts are among the events which, as a class, constitute a region in the brain. A given thought, that is to say, is a member of a class, and the class is a region in the brain. In this sense, where events in brains are concerned, we have no reason to suppose that they are not thoughts, but, on the contrary, have strong reason to suppose that at least some of them are thoughts. I am using "thoughts" as a generic term for mental events.

When we come to events in parts of physical space-time where there are no brains, we have still no positive argument to prove that they are not thoughts, except such as may be derived from observation of the differences between living and dead matter coupled with inferences based on analogy or its absence. We may contend, for instance, that habit is in the main confined to living matter, and that, since memory is a species of habit, it is unlikely that there is memory except where there is living matter. Extending this argument, we can observe that the behaviour of living matter, especially of its higher forms, is much more dependent on its past history than that of dead matter, and that, therefore, the whole of that large part of our mental life that depends upon habit is presumably only to be found where there is living matter. But such arguments are inconclusive and limited in scope. Just as we cannot be *sure* that the sun is not bright, so we cannot be *sure* that it is not intelligent.[2] We may be right in thinking both improbable, but we are certainly wrong if we say they are impossible.

I conclude that while mental events and their qualities can be known without inference, physical events are known only as regards their space-time structure. The qualities that compose such events are unknown—so completely unknown that we cannot say either that they are or that they are not different from the qualities that we know as belonging to mental events.

---

2 I do not wish the reader to take this possibility too seriously. It is of the order of "pigs might fly," dealt with by Mr. Crawshay-Williams in *The Comforts of Unreason*. London: Kegan Paul, Trench, Trubner & Co., LTD, 1947, p. 193.

Portraits from Memory (1956)

Some physiologists still imagine that they can look through a microscope and see brain tissues. This, of course, is an optimistic delusion. When you think that you look at a chair, you do not see quantum transitions. You have an experience which has a very lengthy and elaborate causal connection with the physical chair, a connection proceeding through photons, rods and cones, and optic nerve to the brain. All these stages are necessary if you are to have the visual experience which is called "seeing the chair." You may stop the photons by closing your eyes, the optic nerve may be severed, or the appropriate part of the brain may be destroyed by a bullet. If any of these things has happened you will not "see the chair." Similar considerations apply to the brain that the physiologist thinks he is examining. There is an experience in him which has a remote causal connection with the brain that he thinks he is seeing. He can only know concerning that brain such elements of structure as will be reproduced in his visual sensation. Concerning properties that are not structural, he can know nothing whatever. He has no right to say that the contents of a brain are different from those of the mind that goes with it. If it is a living brain, he has evidence through testimony and analogy that there is a mind that goes with it. If it is a dead brain, evidence is lacking either way.

I wish to suggest, as a hypothesis which is simple and unifying though not demonstrable, a theory which I prefer to that of correspondence advanced by the Cartesians. We have agreed that mind and matter alike consist of series of events. We have also agreed that we know nothing about the events that make matter, except their space-time structure. What I suggest is that the events that make a living brain are actually identical with those that make the corresponding mind. All the reasons that will naturally occur to you for rejecting this view depend upon confusing material objects with those that you experience in sight and touch. These latter are parts of your mind. I can see, at the moment, if I allow myself to talk the language of common sense, the furniture of my room, the trees waving in the wind, houses, clouds, blue sky, and sun. All these common sense imagines to be outside me. All these I believe to be causally connected with physical objects which are outside me, but as soon as I realize that the physical objects must differ in important ways from what I directly experience, and as soon as I take account of the causal trains that proceed from the physical object to my brain before my sensations occur, I see that from the point of view of physical causation the immediately experienced objects of sense are in my brain and not in the outer world. Kant was right to put the starry heavens and the moral law together, since both were figments of his brain.

If what I am saying is correct, the difference between mind and brain does not consist in the raw material of which they are composed, but in the manner of grouping. A mind and a piece of matter alike are to be considered as groups of events, or rather series of groups of events. The events that are grouped to make a given mind are, according to my theory, the very same events that are grouped to make its brain. Or perhaps it would be more correct to say that they are *some* of the events that make the brain. The important point is, that the difference between mind and brain is not a difference of quality, but a difference of arrangement. It is like the difference between arranging people in geographical order or in alphabetical order, both of which are done in the post office directory. The same people are arranged in both cases, but in quite different contexts. In like manner the context of a visual sensation for physics is physical, and outside the brain. Going backward, it takes you to the eye, and thence to a photon and thence to a quantum transition in some distant object. The context of the visual sensation for psychology is quite different. Suppose, for example, the visual sensation is that of a telegram saying that you are ruined. A number of events will take place in your mind in accordance with the laws of psychological causation, and it may be quite a long time before there is any purely physical effect, such as tearing your hair, or exclaiming "Woe is me!"

If this theory is right, certain kinds of connection between mind and brain are inescapable. Corresponding to memory, for example, there must be some physical modifying of the brain, and mental life must be connected with physical properties of the brain tissue. In fact, if we had more knowledge, the physical and psychological statements would be seen to be merely different ways of saying the same thing. The ancient question of the dependence of mind on brain, or brain on mind, is thus reduced to linguistic convenience. In cases where we know more about the brain it will be convenient to regard the mind as dependent, but in cases where we know more about the mind it will be convenient to regard the brain as dependent. In either case, the substantial facts are the same, and the difference is only as to the degree of our knowledge.

I do not think it can be laid down absolutely, if the above is right, that there can be no such thing as disembodied mind. There would be disembodied mind if there were groups of events connected according to the laws of psychology, but not according to the laws of physics. We readily believe that dead matter consists of groups of events arranged according to the laws of physics, but not according to the laws of psychology. And there seems no a priori reason why the opposite should not occur. We can say we have no empirical evidence of it, but more than this we cannot say.

Experience has shown me that the theory which I have been trying to set forth is one which people are very apt to misunderstand, and, as misunderstood, it becomes absurd. I will therefore recapitulate its main points in the hope that by means of new wording they may become less obscure.

First: the world is composed of events, not of things with changing states, or rather, everything that we have a right to say about the world can be said on the assumption that there are only events and not things. Things, as opposed to events, are an unnecessary hypothesis. This part of what I have to say is not exactly new, since it was said by Heraclitus. His view, however, annoyed Plato and has therefore ever since been considered not quite gentlemanly. In these democratic days this consideration need not frighten us. Two kinds of supposed entities are dissolved if we adopt the view of Heraclitus: on the one hand, persons, and on the other hand, material objects. Grammar suggests that you and I are more or less permanent entities with changing states, but the permanent entities are unnecessary, and the changing states suffice for saying all that we know on the matter. Exactly the same sort of thing applies to physical objects. If you go into a shop and buy a loaf of bread, you think that you have bought a "thing" which you can bring home with you. What you have in fact bought is a series of occurrences linked together by certain causal laws.

Second: sensible objects, as immediately experienced, that is to say, what we see when we see chairs and tables and the sun and the moon and so on, are parts of our minds and are not either the whole or part of the physical objects that we think we are seeing. This part of what I am saying is also not new. It comes from Berkeley, as reinforced by Hume. The arguments that I should use for it, however, are not exactly Berkeley's. I should point out that if a number of people look at a single object from different points of view, their visual impressions differ according to the laws of perspective and according to the way the light falls. Therefore no one of the visual impressions is that neutral "thing" which all think they are seeing. I should point out also that physics leads us to believe in causal chains, starting from objects and reaching our sense organs, and that it would be very odd if the last link in this causal chain were exactly like the first.

Third: I should admit that there *may* be no such thing as a physical world distinct from my experiences, but I should point out that if the inferences which lead to matter are rejected, I ought also to reject the inferences which lead me to believe in my own mental past. I should point out further that no one sincerely rejects beliefs which only such inferences can justify. I therefore take it that there are events which I do not experience, although some things about some of these can be inferred from what I do experience. Except where mental phenomena are concerned, the inferences that I can make as to the external causes of my experiences are only as to structure, not as to quality. The inferences that are warranted are those to be found in theoretical physics; they are abstract and mathematical and give no indication whatever as to the intrinsic character of physical objects.

Fourth: if the foregoing is accepted there must be two sorts of space, one the sort of space which is known through experience, especially in my visual field, the other the sort of space that occurs in physics, which is known only by inference and is bound up with causal laws. Failure to distinguish these two kinds of space is a source of much confusion. I will take again the case of a physiologist who is examining someone else's brain. Common sense supposes that he sees that brain and that what he sees is matter. Since what he sees is obviously quite different from what is being thought by the patient whom he is examining, people conclude that mind and matter are quite different things. Matter is what the physiologist sees, mind is what the patient is thinking. But this whole order of ideas, if I am right, is a mass of confusions. What the physiologist sees, if we mean by this something that he experiences, is an event in his own mind and has only an elaborate causal connection with the brain that he imagines himself to be seeing. This is obvious as soon as we think of physics. In the brain that he thinks he is seeing there are quantum transitions. These lead to emission of photons, the photons travel across the intervening space and hit the eye of the physiologist. They then cause complicated occurrences in the rods and cones, and a disturbance which travels along the optic nerve to the brain. When this disturbance reaches the brain, the physiologist has the experience which is called "seeing the other man's brain." If anything interferes with the causal chain, e.g. because the other man's brain is in darkness, because the physiologist has closed his eyes, because the physiologist is blind, or because he has a bullet in the brain at the optic center, he does not have the experience called "seeing the other man's brain." Nor does the event occur at the same time as what he thinks he sees. In the case of terrestrial objects, the difference of time is negligible, but in the case of celestial objects it may be very large, even as much as millions of years. The relation of a visual experience to the physical object that common sense thinks it is seeing is thus indirect and causal, and there is no reason to suppose that close similarity between them that common sense imagines to exist. All this is connected with the two kinds of space that I wrote of a moment ago. I horrified all the philosophers by saying that their thoughts were in their heads. With one voice they assured me that they had no thoughts in their heads whatever, but politeness forbids me to accept this assurance. Perhaps, however, it might be well to explain exactly what I mean, since the remark is elliptical. Stated accurately, what I mean is as follows: physical space, unlike the space of perception, is based upon causal contiguity. The causal contiguities of sense perceptions are with the physical stimuli immediately preceding them and with the physical reactions immediately following them. Precise location in physical space belongs not to single events but to such groups of events as physics would regard as a momentary state of a piece of matter, if it indulged in such old-fashioned language. A thought is one of a group of events, such as will count for purposes of physics as a region in the brain. To say that a thought is in the brain is an abbreviation for the following: a thought is one of a group of compresent events, which group is a region in the brain. I am not suggesting that thoughts are in psychological space, except in the case of sense impressions (if these are to be called "thoughts").

Fifth: a piece of matter is a group of events connected by causal laws, namely, the causal laws of physics. A mind is a group of events connected by causal laws, namely, the causal laws of psychology. An event is not rendered either mental or material by any intrinsic quality, but only by its causal relations. It is perfectly possible for an event to have both the causal relations characteristic of physics and those characteristic of psychology. In that case, the event is both mental and material at once. There is no more difficulty about this than there is about a man being at once a baker and a father. Since we know nothing about the intrinsic quality of physical events except when these are mental events that we directly experience, we cannot say either that the physical world outside our heads is different from the mental world or that it is not. The supposed problem of the relations of mind and matter arises only through mistakenly treating both as "things" and not as groups of events. With the theory that I have been suggesting, the whole problem vanishes.

In favour of the theory that I have been advocating, the most important thing to be said is that it removes a mystery. Mystery is always annoying, and is usually due to lack of clear analysis. The relations of mind and matter have puzzled people for a long time, but if I am right they need puzzle people no longer.

My Philosophical Development (1959)

Introductory Outline

My philosophical development may be divided into various stages according to the problems with which I have been concerned and the men whose work has influenced me. There is only one constant preoccupation: I have throughout been anxious to discover how much we can be said to know and with what degree of certainty or doubtfulness. There is one major division in my philosophical work: in the years 1899–1900 I adopted the philosophy of logical atomism and the technique of Peano in mathematical logic. This was so great a revolution as to make my previous work, except such as was purely mathematical, irrelevant to everything that I did later. The change in these years was a revolution; subsequent changes have been of the nature of an evolution.

My original interest in philosophy had two sources. On the one hand, I was anxious to discover whether philosophy would provide any defence for anything that could be called religious belief, however vague; on the other hand, I wished to persuade myself that something could be known, in pure mathematics if not elsewhere. I thought about both these problems during adolescence, in solitude and with little help from books. As regards religion, I came to disbelieve first in free will, then in immortality, and finally in God. As regards the foundations of mathematics, I got nowhere. In spite of strong bias towards empiricism, I could not believe that 'two plus two equals four' is an inductive generalization from experience, but I remained in doubt as to everything beyond this purely negative conclusion.

At Cambridge I was indoctrinated with the philosophies of Kant and Hegel, but G. E. Moore and I together came to reject both these philosophies. I think that, although we agreed in our revolt, we had important differences of emphasis. What I think at first chiefly interested Moore was the independence of fact from knowledge and the rejection of the whole Kantian apparatus of *a priori* intuitions and categories, moulding experience but not the outer world. I agreed enthusiastically with him in this respect, but I was more concerned than he was with certain purely logical matters. The most important of these, and the one which has dominated all my subsequent philosophy, was what I called 'the doctrine of external relations'. Monists had maintained that a relation between two terms is always, in reality, composed of properties of the two separate terms and of the whole which they compose, or, in ultimate strictness, only of this last. This view seemed to me to make mathematics inexplicable. I came to the conclusion that relatedness does not imply any corresponding complexity in the related terms and is, in general, not equivalent to any property of the whole which they compose. Just after developing this view in my book on *The Philosophy of Leibniz*, I became aware of Peano's work in mathematical logic, which led me to a new technique and a new philosophy of mathematics. Hegel and his disciples had been in the habit of 'proving' the impossibility of space and time and matter, and generally everything that an ordinary man would believe in. Having become convinced that the Hegelian arguments against this and that were invalid, I reacted to the opposite extreme and began to believe in the reality of whatever could not be *dis*proved—e.g. points and instants and particles and Platonic universals.

When, however, after 1910, I had done all that I intended to do as regards pure mathematics, I began to think about the physical world and, largely under Whitehead's influence, I was led to new applications of Occam's razor, to which I had become devoted by its usefulness in the philosophy of arithmetic. Whitehead persuaded me that one could do physics without supposing points and instants to be part of the stuff of the world. He considered—and in this I came to agree with him—that the stuff of the physical world could consist of events, each occupying a finite amount of space-time. As in all uses of Occam's razor, one was not obliged to deny the existence of the entities with which one dispensed, but one was enabled to abstain from ascertaining it. This had the advantage of diminishing the assumptions required for the interpretation of whatever branch of knowledge was in question. As regards the physical world, it is impossible to prove that there are not point-instants, but it is possible to prove that physics gives no reason whatever for supposing that there are such things.

At the same time, that is to say in the years from 1910 to 1914, I became interested, not only in what the physical world is, but in how we come to know it. The relation of perception to physics is a problem which has occupied me intermittently ever since that time. It is in relation to this problem that my philosophy underwent its last substantial change. I had regarded perception as a two-term relation of subject and object, as this had made it comparatively easy to understand how perception could give knowledge of something other than the subject. But under the influence of William James, I came to think this view mistaken, or at any rate an undue simplification. Sensations, at least, even those that are visual or auditory, came to seem to me not in their own nature relational occurrences. I do not, of course, mean to say that when I see something there is no relation between me and what I see; but what I do mean to say is that the relation is much more indirect than I had supposed and that everything that happens in me when I see something could, so far as its logical structure is concerned, quite well occur without there being anything outside me for me to see. This change in my opinions greatly increased the difficulty of problems involved in connecting experience with the outer world.

There was another problem which began to interest me at about the same time—that is to say, about 1917. This was the problem of the relation of language to facts. This problem has two departments: the first concerned with vocabulary; the second, with syntax. The problem had been dealt with by various people before I became interested in it. Lady Welby wrote a book about it and F. C. S. Schiller was always urging its importance. But I had thought of language as transparent—that is to say, as a medium which could be employed without paying attention to it. As regards syntax, the inadequacy of this view was forced upon me by the contradictions arising in mathematical logic. As regards vocabulary, linguistic problems arose for me in investigating the extent to which a behaviouristic account of knowledge is possible. For these two reasons, I was led to place much more emphasis than I had previously done on the linguistic aspects of epistemology. But I have never been able to feel any sympathy with those who treat language as an autonomous province. The essential thing about language is that it has meaning—i.e. that it is related to something other than itself, which is, in general, non-linguistic.

My most recent work has been connected with the problem of non-demonstrative inference. It used to be supposed by empiricists that the justification of such inference rests upon induction. Unfortunately, it can be proved that induction by simple enumeration, if conducted without regard to common sense, leads very much more often to error than to truth. And if a principle needs common sense before it can be safely used, it is not the sort of principle that can satisfy a logician. We must, therefore, look for a principle other than induction if we are to accept the broad outlines of science, and of common sense in so far as it is not refutable. This is a very large problem and I cannot pretend to have done more than indicate lines along which a solution may be sought.

Ever since I abandoned the philosophy of Kant and Hegel, I have sought solutions of philosophical problems by means of analysis; and I remain firmly persuaded, in spite of some modern tendencies to the contrary, that only by analysing is progress possible. I have found, to take an important example, that by analysing physics and perception the problem of the relation of mind and matter can be completely solved. It is true that nobody has accepted what seems to me the solution, but I believe and hope that this is only because my theory has not been understood.

My Present View of the World

The view to which I have been gradually led is one which has been almost universally misunderstood and which, for this reason, I will try to state as simply and clearly as I possibly can. I am, for the present, only endeavouring to state the view, not to give the reasons which have led me to it. I will, however, say this much by way of preface: it is a view which results from a synthesis of four different sciences—namely, physics, physiology, psychology and mathematical logic. Mathematical logic is used in creating structures having assigned properties out of elements that have much less mathematical smoothness. I reverse the process which has been common in philosophy since Kant. It has been common among philosophers to begin with how we know and proceed afterwards to what we know. I think this a mistake, because knowing how we know is one small department of knowing what we know. I think it a mistake for another reason: it tends to give to knowing a cosmic importance which it by no means deserves, and thus prepares the philosophical student for the belief that mind has some kind of supremacy over the non-mental universe, or even that the non-mental universe is nothing but a nightmare dreamt by mind in its un-philosophical moments. This point of view is completely remote from my imaginative picture of the cosmos. I accept without qualification the view that results from astronomy and geology, from which it would appear that there is no evidence of anything mental except in a tiny fragment of space-time, and that the great processes of nebular and stellar evolution proceed according to laws in which mind plays no part.

If this initial bias is accepted, it is obviously to theoretical physics that we must first look for an understanding of the major processes in the history of the universe. Unfortunately, theoretical physics no longer speaks with that splendid dogmatic clarity that it enjoyed in the seventeenth century. Newton works with four fundamental concepts: space, time, matter and force. All four have been swept into limbo by modern physicists. Space and time, for Newton, were solid, independent things. They have been replaced by space-time, which is not substantial but only a system of relations. Matter has had to be replaced by series of events. Force, which was the first of the Newtonian concepts to be abandoned, has been replaced by energy; and energy turns out to be indistinguishable from the pale ghost which is all that remains of matter. Cause, which was the philosophical form of what physicists called force, has also become decrepit. I will not admit that it is dead, but it has nothing like the vigour of its earlier days.

For all these reasons, what modern physics has to say is somewhat confused. Nevertheless, we are bound to believe it on pain of death. If there were any community which rejected the doctrines of modern physics, physicists employed by a hostile government would have no difficulty in exterminating it. The modern physicist, therefore, enjoys powers far exceeding those of the Inquisition in its palmiest days, and it certainly behooves us to treat his pronouncements with due awe. For my part, I have no doubt that, although progressive changes are to be expected in physics, the present doctrines are likely to be nearer to the truth than any rival doctrines now before the world. Science is at no moment quite right, but it is seldom quite wrong, and has, as a rule, a better chance of being right than the theories of the unscientific. It is, therefore, rational to accept it hypothetically.

It is not always realized how exceedingly abstract is the information that theoretical physics has to give. It lays down certain fundamental equations which enable it to deal with the logical structure of events, while leaving it completely unknown what is the intrinsic character of the events that have the structure. We only know the intrinsic character of events when they happen to us. Nothing whatever in theoretical physics enables us to say anything about the intrinsic character of events elsewhere. They may be just like the events that happen to us, or they may be totally different in strictly unimaginable ways. All that physics gives us is certain equations giving abstract properties of their changes. But as to what it is that changes, and what it changes from and to—as to this, physics is silent.

The next step is an approximation to perception, but without passing beyond the realm of physics. A photographic plate exposed to a portion of the night sky takes photographs of separate stars. Given similar photographic plates and atmospheric conditions, different photographs of the same portion of the sky will be closely similar. There must, therefore, be some influence (I am using the vaguest word that I can think of) proceeding from the various stars to the various photographic plates. Physicists used to think that this influence consisted of waves, but now they think that it consists of little bundles of energy called photons. They know how fast a photon travels and in what manner it will, on occasion, deviate from a rectilinear path. When it hits a photographic plate, it is transformed into energy of a different kind. Since each separate star gets itself photographed, and since it can be photographed anywhere on a clear night where there is an unimpeded view of the sky, there must be something happening, at each place where it can be photographed, that is specially connected with it. It follows that the atmosphere at night contains everywhere as many separable events as there are stars that can be photographed there, and each of these separable events must have some kind of individual history connecting it with the star from which it has come. All this follows from the consideration of different photographic plates exposed to the same night sky.

Or let us take another illustration. Let us imagine a rich cynic, disgusted by the philistinism of theatregoers, deciding to have a play performed, not before live people, but before a collection of cine-cameras. The cine-cameras—supposing them all of equal excellence—will produce closely similar records, differing according to the laws of perspective and according to their distance from the stage. This again shows, like the photographic plate, that at each cine-camera a complex of events is occurring at each moment which is closely related to the complex of events occurring on the stage. There is here the same need as before of separable influences proceeding from diverse sources. If, at a given moment, one actor shouts, 'Die, Varlet!' while another exclaims, 'Help! Murder!' both will be recorded, and therefore something connected with both must be happening at each cine-camera.

To take yet another illustration: suppose that a speech is recorded simultaneously by a number of gramophones, the gramophone records do not in any obvious way resemble the original speech, and yet, by a suitable mechanism, they can be made to reproduce something exceedingly like it. They must, therefore, have something in common with the speech. But what they have in common can only be expressed in rather abstract language concerning structure. Broadcasting affords an even better illustration of the same process. What intervenes between an orator and a man listening to him on the radio is not, on the face of it, at all similar either to what the orator says or to what the listener hears. Here, again, we have a causal chain in which the beginning resembles the end, but the intermediate terms, so far as intrinsic qualities are concerned, appear to be of quite a different kind. What is preserved throughout the causal chain, in this case as in that of the gramophone record, is a certain constancy of structure.

These various processes all belong purely to physics. We do not suppose that the cine-cameras have minds, and we should not suppose so even if, by a little ingenuity on the part of their maker, those in the stalls were made to sneer at the moments when those in the pit applauded. What these physical analogies to perception show is that in most places at most times, if not in all places at all times, a vast assemblage of overlapping events is taking place, and that many of these events, at a given place and time, are connected by causal chains with an original event which, by a sort of prolific heredity, has produced offspring more or less similar to itself in a vast number of different places.

What sort of picture of the universe do these considerations invite us to construct? I think the answer must proceed by stages differing as to the degree of analysis that has been effected. For present purposes I shall content myself by treating as fundamental the notion of 'event'. I conceive each event as occupying a finite amount of space-time and as overlapping with innumerable other events which occupy partially, but not wholly, the same region of space-time. The mathematician who wishes to operate with point-instants can construct them by means of mathematical logic out of assemblages of overlapping events, but that is only for his technical purposes, which, for the moment, we may ignore. The events occurring in any given small region of space-time are not unconnected with events occurring elsewhere. On the contrary, if a photographic plate can photograph a certain star, that is because an event is happening at the photographic plate which is connected by what we may call heredity with the star in question. The photographic plate, in turn, if it is photographed, is the origin of a fresh progeny. In mathematical physics, which is only interested in exceedingly abstract aspects of the matters with which it deals, these various processes appear as paths by which energy travels. It is because mathematical physics is so abstract that its world seems so different from that of our daily life. But the difference is more apparent than real. Suppose you study population statistics, the people who make up the items are deprived of almost all the characteristics of real people before they are recorded in the census. But in this case, because the process of abstraction has not proceeded very far, we do not find it very difficult to undo it in imagination. But in the case of mathematical physics, the journey back from the abstract to the concrete is long and arduous, and, out of sheer weariness, we are tempted to rest by the way and endow some semi-abstraction with a concrete reality which it cannot justly claim.

There is a possibility of a further stage of analysis in which events are no longer the ultimate raw material. But I will not consider this in the present discussion.

We have seen that, for purely physical reasons, events in many different places and times can often be collected into families proceeding from an original progenitor as the light from a star proceeds from it in all directions. The successive generations in a single branch of such a family have varying degrees of resemblance to each other according to circumstances. The events which constitute the journey of the light from a star to our atmosphere change slowly and little. That is why it is possible to regard them as the voyage of single entities called photons, which may be thought of as persisting. But when the light reaches our atmosphere, a series of continually odder and odder things begins to happen to it. It may be stopped or transformed by mist or cloud. It may hit a sheet of water and be reflected or refracted. It may hit a photographic plate and become a black dot of interest to an astronomer. Finally, it may happen to hit a human eye. When this occurs, the results are very complicated. There are a set of events between the eye and the brain which are studied by the physiologist and which have as little resemblance to the photons in the outer world as radio waves have to the orator's speech. At last the disturbance in the nerves, which has been traced by the physiologist, reaches the appropriate region in the brain; and then, at last, the man whose brain it is sees the star. People are puzzled because the seeing of the star seems so different from the processes that the physiologist discovered in the optic nerve, and yet it is clear that without these processes the man would not see the star. And so there is supposed to be a gulf between mind and matter, and a mystery which it is held in some degree impious to try to dissipate. I believe, for my part, that there is no greater mystery than there is in the transformation by the radio of electro-magnetic waves into sounds. I think the mystery is produced by a wrong conception of the physical world and by a Manichaean fear of degrading the mental world to the level of the supposedly inferior world of matter.

The world of which we have been speaking hitherto is entirely an inferred world. We do not perceive the sort of entities that physics talks of, and, if it is of such entities that the physical world is composed, then we do not see the eye or the optic nerve, for the eye and the optic nerve, equally, if the physicist is to be believed, consist of the odd hypothetical entities with which the theoretical physicist tries to make us familiar. These entities, however, since they owe their credibility to inference, are only defined to the degree that is necessary to make them fulfil their inferential purpose. It is not necessary to suppose that electrons, protons, neutrons, mesons, photons, and the rest have that sort of simple reality that belongs to immediate objects of experience. They have, at best, the sort of reality that belongs to 'London'. 'London' is a convenient word, but every *fact* which is stated by using this word could be stated, though more cumbrously, without using it. There is, however, a difference, and an important one, between London and the electrons: we can see the various parts of which London is composed, and, indeed, the parts are more immediately known to us than the whole. In the case of the electron, we do not perceive it and we do not perceive anything that we know to be a constituent of it. We know it only as a hypothetical entity fulfilling certain theoretical purposes. So far as theoretical physics is concerned, anything that fulfils these purposes can be taken to *be* the electron. It may be simple or complex; and, if complex, it may be built out of any components that allow the resultant structure to have the requisite properties. All this applies not only to the inanimate world but, equally, to the eyes and other sense organs, the nerves, and the brain.

But our world is not wholly a matter of inference. There are things that we know without asking the opinion of men of science. If you are too hot or too cold, you can be perfectly aware of this fact without asking the physicist what heat and cold consist of. When you see other people's faces, you have an experience which is completely indubitable, but which does not consist of seeing the things which theoretical physicists speak of. You see other people's eyes and you believe that they see yours. Your own eyes as visual objects belong to the inferred part of the world, though the inference is rendered fairly indubitable by mirrors, photographs and the testimony of your friends. The inference to your own eyes as visual objects is essentially of the same sort as the physicist's inference to electrons, etc.; and, if you are going to deny validity to

the physicist's inferences, you ought also to deny that you know you have visible eyes—which is absurd, as Euclid would say.

We may give the name 'data' to all the things of which we are aware without inference. They include all our observed sensations—visual, auditory, tactile, etc. Common sense sees reason to attribute many of our sensations to
causes outside our own bodies. It does not believe that the room in which it is
sitting ceases to exist when it shuts its eyes or goes to sleep. It does not believe
that its wife and children are mere figments of its imagination. In all this we
may agree with common sense; but where it goes wrong is in supposing that
inanimate objects resemble, in their intrinsic qualities, the perceptions which
they cause. To believe this is as groundless as it would be to suppose that a
gramophone record resembles the music that it causes. It is not, however,
the *difference* between the physical world and the world of data that I chiefly
wish to emphasize. On the contrary, it is the possibility of much closer resem-
blances than physics at first sight suggests that I consider it important to
bring to light.

I think perhaps I can best make my own views clear by comparing them
with those of Leibniz. Leibniz thought that the universe consisted of monads,
each of which was a little mind and each of which mirrored the universe. They
did this mirroring with varying degrees of inexactness. The best monads had
the least confusion in their picture of the universe. Misled by the Aristotelian
subject-predicate logic, Leibniz held that monads do not interact, and that the
fact of their continuing to mirror the same universe is to be explained by a
pre-established harmony. This part of his doctrine is totally unacceptable. It is
only through the causal action of the outer world upon us that we reflect the
world in so far as we do reflect it. But there are other aspects of his doctrine
which are more in agreement with the theory that I wish to advocate. One of
the most important of these is as to space. There are for Leibniz (though he
was never quite clear on this point) two kinds of space. There is the space in
the private world of each monad, which is the space that the monad can come
to know by analysing and arranging data without assuming anything beyond
data. But there is also another kind of space. The monads, Leibniz tells us,
reflect the world each from its own point of view, the differences of points of
view being analogous to differences of perspective. The arrangement of the
whole assemblage of points of view gives us another kind of space, different from that in the private world of each monad. In this public space, each
monad occupies a point or, at any rate, a very small region. Although in its
private world there is a private space which from its private point of view is
immense, the whole of this immensity shrinks into a tiny pin-point when the
monad is placed among other monads. We may call the space in each monad's

world of data 'private' space, and the space consisting of the diverse points of view of diverse monads 'physical' space. In so far as monads correctly mirror the world, the geometrical properties of private space will be analogous to those of physical space.

Most of this can be applied with little change to exemplify the theory that I wish to advocate. There is space in the world of my perceptions and there is space in physics. The whole of the space in my perceptions, for me as for Leibniz, occupies only a tiny region in physical space. There is, however, an important difference between my theory and that of Leibniz, which has to do with a different conception of causality and with consequences of the theory of relativity. I think that space-time order in the physical world is bound up with causation, and this, in turn, with the irreversibility of physical processes. In classical physics, everything was reversible. If you were to start every bit of matter moving backwards with the same velocity as before, the whole history of the universe would unroll itself backwards. Modern physics, starting from the Second Law of Thermodynamics, has abandoned this view not only in thermodynamics but also elsewhere. Radioactive atoms disintegrate and do not put themselves together again. Speaking generally, processes in the physical world all have a certain direction which makes a distinction between cause and effect that was absent in classical dynamics. I think that the space-time order of the physical world involves this directed causality. It is on this ground that I maintain an opinion which all other philosophers find shocking: namely, that people's thoughts are in their heads. The light from a star travels over intervening space and causes a disturbance in the optic nerve ending in an occurrence in the brain. What I maintain is that the occurrence in the brain *is* a visual sensation. I maintain, in fact, that the brain consists of thoughts—using 'thought' in its widest sense, as it is used by Descartes. To this people will reply 'Nonsense! I can see a brain through a microscope, and I can see that it does not consist of thoughts but of matter just as tables and chairs do.' This is a sheer mistake. What you see when you look at a brain through a microscope is part of your private world. It is the effect in you of a long causal process starting from the brain that you say you are looking at. The brain that you say you are looking at is, no doubt, part of the physical world; but this is not the brain which is a datum in your experience. *That* brain is a remote effect of the physical brain. And, if the location of events in physical space-time is to be effected, as I maintain, by causal relations, then your percept, which comes after events in the eye and optic nerve leading into the brain, must be located in your brain. I may illustrate how I differ from most philosophers by quoting the title of an article by Mr. H. Hudson in *Mind* of April 1956. His article is entitled, 'Why we cannot witness or observe what goes on "in our heads".' What I maintain is that we *can* witness or observe what goes on in our heads, and that we cannot witness or observe anything else at all.

We can approach the same result by another route. When we were considering the photographic plate which photographs a portion of the starry heavens, we saw that this involves a great multiplicity of occurrences at the photographic plate: namely, at the very least, one for each object that it can photograph. I infer that, in every small region of space-time, there is an immense multiplicity of overlapping events each connected by a causal line to an origin at some earlier time—though, usually, at a very slightly earlier time. A sensitive instrument, such as a photographic plate, placed anywhere, may be said in a sense to 'perceive' the various objects from which these causal lines emanate. We do not use the word 'perceive' unless the instrument in question is a living brain, but that is because those regions which are inhabited by living brains have certain peculiar relations among the events occurring there. The most important of these is memory. Wherever these peculiar relations exist, we say that there is a percipient. We may define a 'mind' as a collection of events connected with each other by memory-chains backwards and forwards. We know about one such collection of events—namely, that constituting ourself—more intimately and directly than we know about anything else in the world. In regard to what happens to ourself, we know not only abstract logical structure, but also qualities—by which I mean what characterizes sounds as opposed to colours, or red as opposed to green. This is the sort of thing that we cannot know where the physical world is concerned.

There are three key points in the above theory. The first is that the entities that occur in mathematical physics are not part of the stuff of the world, but are constructions composed of events and taken as units for the convenience of the mathematician. The second is that the whole of what we perceive without inference belongs to our private world. In this respect, I agree with Berkeley. The starry heaven that we know in visual sensation is inside us. The external starry heaven that we believe in is inferred. The third point is that the causal lines which enable us to be aware of a diversity of objects, though there are some such lines everywhere, are apt to peter out like rivers in the sand. That is why we do not at all times perceive everything.

I do not pretend that the above theory can be proved. What I contend is that, like the theories of physics, it cannot be disproved, and gives an answer to many problems which older theorists have found puzzling. I do not think that any prudent person will claim more than this for any theory.

5

Russell, Russellian Monism, and Panpsychism

Leopold Stubenberg

Introduction

One of the new "isms" to populate the philosophical landscape is Russellian monism (RM). The label is apt to mislead, for it suggests that the monism in question is the monism to which Russell himself subscribed, viz. neutral monism (NM). Instead we are dealing with a diverse family of views, united only by the fact that they all start out from two theses that Russell defended. These two theses, together with a number of other considerations, led Russell to embrace NM. But none of the Russellian monists follow Russell all the way. In the hands of some members of this group, RM turns into materialism; in the hands of others, it becomes panpsychism (or, more precisely, panexperientialism).[1] I will explore this panpsychist variety of RM. In particular, I want to investigate where and to what extent the panpsychist version of RM diverges from Russell's own views. I will try to show that the differences are numerous and significant. Once Russell's own views have come into clearer focus, I want to ask whether it is possible and desirable to bring the panpsychist version or RM into closer alignment with Russell's own views. I believe that the panpsychist version of RM could profit from borrowing many of the structural elements found in Russell's NM.

---

1. See footnote 8.

Russell's Two Theses

In their survey of the current state of RM, Alter and Nagasawa (2012) observe that contemporary versions of RM are not intended to be faithful to the letter of the monism that Russell defended, viz. NM. The Russellian element of the extant versions of RM consists in the fact that they all emerge from or are inspired by "two views Russell expressed in *The Analysis of Matter*" (Alter & Nagasawa 2012, 69). As they see it, "we are led to Russellian monism by combining Russell's structuralism about physics with a view he held about knowledge and perception" (Alter & Nagasawa 2012, 70). Let us begin by taking a brief look at Russell's structuralism and his monistic theory of perception.[2]

Russell's structuralism about physics is a claim concerning the nature of our knowledge about the physical world. It amounts to this: "the physical world is only known as regards certain abstract features of its space–time structure" (Russell 1948, 224). Neither the things that are in this spatio-temporal structure nor the spatio-temporal manifold itself are known to us directly. Such knowledge is inferential; and these inferences can only provide us with knowledge of formal features of the things and the relations that make up the physical world. Hence we get the result that "what physics says about the world is much more abstract than it seems to be, because we imagine that its space is what we know in our own experience, and that its matter is the kind of thing that feels hard when we touch it. In fact, even assuming physics true, what we know about the physical world is very little" (Russell 1948, 327).

Russell's monistic theory of perception amounts to this. Percepts—that is Russell's term for those events[3] that constitute our perceptions—are the only events whose intrinsic quality we know. "Patches of colour, noises, smells, hardnesses, etc., as well as perceived spatial relations" are examples of percepts (Russell 1927a, 257).[4] In Russell's neutral monist phase, percepts take the

---

2. I will use the expression "monistic theory of perception" to mark the fact that Russell distinguishes his (later) views about perception from dualistic views about perception—that is, any view that distinguishes between perceptual act and the perceptual object. Russell's own (earlier) sense-datum theory is an example of a dualist view of perception (see Russell 1948, 205).

3. Events—the basic particulars in Russell's philosophy from the mid 1920s onward—are "entities or structures occupying a region of space-time which is small in all four dimensions" (Russell 1927a, 286).

4. In (1927b) Russell presents a similar list of items, this time to illustrate the notion of an event: "An 'event' . . . is something having a small finite duration and a small finite extension in space . . . When I speak of an 'event' I do not mean anything out of the way. Seeing a flash of lighting is an event, so is hearing a tire burst, or smelling a rotten egg, or feeling the coldness of a frog" (Russell 1927b, 222). All these events are percepts or, as he sometimes

place of two things that Russell used to distinguish meticulously in his earlier thinking about perception: the sense-datum and the mental act directed upon the sense-datum. Since the act—the sensing—had to occur in the percipient's brain, Russell reasoned that the percept had to inherit this location. Here is one example Russell uses to illustrate this idea: "If my seeing of the sun is identical with the sun that I see, then the sun that I see is not the astronomer's sun" (Russell 1948, 205). The sun you see *is* the percept—a round, shiny yellow patch—that occurs in your brain. That is why Russell tells us that "what I maintain is that we *can* witness or observe what goes on in our heads, and that we cannot witness or observe anything else at all" (Russell 1959, 19). Inference is the only way by which we can extend our reach outside the head. And to know this percept—to know the event consisting of the instantiation of these qualities—is for it to trigger "those effects which constitute what is called awareness of the mental state" (Russell 1927a, 385). Percepts may have a structure that is hidden from you; and they can go altogether unnoticed. But some of our percepts we do know. And in knowing them, we know a part of the world in a more than merely abstract way—we get to know the intrinsic quality of the event that is our percept.

RM and the Two Theses

Brief reflection on this sketch of Russell's monistic theory of perception suggests that this view is unlikely to receive widespread support among contemporary Russellian monists. But that is a problem if Russell's views about perception are one of the two sources from which RM springs. And it appears that this problem may spread to the second Russellian source of RM. For in the literature on structuralism one can find the suggestion that Russell's structuralism derives from his views on perception.[5] Were it to turn out that RM has to reject both of Russell's views that inspire it, the claim that there is anything Russellian about RM would seem difficult to sustain.

The worry about structuralism is easily dispelled. It is true that Russell frequently argues from his views about perception (from the earlier sense-datum theory as well as from the later monistic theory) to the truth of structuralism. If our percepts are the only things whose intrinsic quality is known to us, then all of our other knowledge must be merely structural. But this is not the

---

puts it, data. It would be a mistake to conclude that all events are percepts. Russell does allow inferences to events other than your own data.

5. For a nice example of this, see Votsis (2004), chapter 2.

only way in which Russell supports his structuralism. He holds that common sense starts with a naively realistic conception of the world. But the growth of knowledge destroys this naive realism and replaces it with an increasingly abstract, scientific picture of the world. Commenting on this movement toward abstractness, Russell writes: "From this happy familiarity with the everyday world physics has been gradually driven by its own triumphs, like a monarch who has grown too grand to converse with his subjects" (Russell 1927a, 131). "Physics had to desert common sense" (Russell 1927a, 155), because "the aim of physics, consciously or unconsciously, has always been to discover the causal skeleton of the world" (Russell 1927a, 391; see also Russell 1931, 127–28). What these passages make clear is that Russell himself did not think that the structuralist picture had to await the advent of his monistic theory of perception. Inasmuch as it is the goal of science to isolate the causal skeleton of the world, science naturally tends toward an ever more abstract description of the world, leaving aside questions concerning the intrinsic qualities of the entities that obey the laws that it establishes. I believe that he took this to be an unproblematic and widely accepted view about the increasing abstractness of science—not a view in any way original to him. If this account of the sources of Russell's structuralism is correct, the Russellian monist can happily accept this thesis as one of the sources of RM.

The problem raised by the monistic theory of perception is more serious—there is no easy way of transforming it into something that might enjoy widespread acceptance among the Russellian monists. What the Russellian monist should do, in the face of this difficulty, is to make a somewhat more cautious claim about just what it is they take from Russell's theories about knowledge and perception. They are not taking on-board the whole of Russell's monistic theory; instead, it is only one feature of this theory that inspires them. It is this: in perception we get to know one part of reality intrinsically, i.e., in a way that is not merely abstract. According to Alter and Nagasawa, we should understand this as suggesting "the view that we know phenomenal properties by their intrinsic phenomenal natures" (A&N 2012, 70).

If we can agree with Alter and Nagasawa that this view is a part of Russell's monistic theory of perception (as I think we should), and if we can also agree that this view has some plausibility independently of Russell's monistic theory of perception, then it would seem that the Russellian monist is in business. She has secured Russell's structuralism (without depending on the argument that leads from the monistic theory of perception to structuralism); and it is plausible that she can secure a crucial claim contained in Russell's monistic theory of perception (without being committed to the monistic theory of perception). And with these two elements in hand, nothing seems to stand in the way of developing RM.

It remains to be seen whether the refusal to accept Russell's monistic theory of perception in its entirety has any untoward consequences. Later on I will argue that Russell's own way of combining the thesis of structuralism with the thesis about the existence of a special set of properties, revealed to us in perception, relies importantly on his locating percepts in the brain. Therefore any form of RM that tries to resist Russell's tendency to place the object of perception into the brain, will run into trouble when trying to follow his lead in the crucial task of integrating the structuralist picture of physics with the phenomenal facts as we know them in experience.[6]

The General Form of RM: Something Grounds Something

"Combining Russell's structuralism about physics with a view he held about perception and knowledge" leads to RM (Alter & Nagasawa 2012, 70). This combination is effected by identifying the percepts—the yellow patch, say—whose intrinsic qualitative nature is known to us with "the relata that stand in basic physical relations" (Alter & Nagasawa 2012, 70). This is the rough shape of the RM that emerges from the two views, found in Russell, that "have inspired most, if not all contemporary versions of Russellian monism" (Alter & Nagasawa 2012, 69).

But Alter and Nagasawa aim to formulate and discuss a generalized version of RM, one that is not limited by the specifics of Russell's views. They begin with the following definition of RM:

> Russellian monism says that there are both structural properties, which physics describes, and inscrutables [properties whose natures "are not fully characterized by structural/relational descriptions"] and that the latter ground the former.
>
> (Alter & Nagasawa 2012, 70–71)[7]

---

6. See the section "No Place for the Idea of Grounding in the Program of Logical Construction?".

7. Alter and Nagasawa borrow the term "inscrutables" from Barbara Montero. They introduce it as follows: "We will refer to properties (if such there be) that ground the physical structure/relations physics describes as *inscrutables* .... By definition, inscrutables have natures that are not fully characterized by structural/relational descriptions" (A&N, 70). Note, however, that Montero uses this term in a somewhat different way. See her (2010 and 2015).

They are quick to point out that this definition does not do full justice to the scope of their idea. While the definition is stated using the terms "structural" and "relational," the authors aim to express an idea that is more general than these words suggest. As they see it, the literature on RM has employed four different distinctions in the attempt to clarify the crucial question of how to understand the nature of the relata of the grounding relation—the relation that obtains between inscrutables and physical properties. Physical properties have been characterized as extrinsic, dispositional, relational, and structural-and-dynamic; the inscrutables, on the other hand, have been said to be intrinsic, categorical, non-relational, and non-structural-and-non-dynamic (see Alter & Nagasawa 2012, 72). The definition of RM that Alter and Nagasawa have in mind is supposed to be neutral with respect to all four of these distinctions. No matter which of these four distinctions best captures the contrast between physical and inscrutable properties, the claim of RM is that the inscrutables ground the properties that physics relies upon.

Next Alter and Nagasawa point out that their definition of RM (in its original or expanded form) is neutral with respect to another dimension along which different versions of RM can vary. We know that the inscrutables are intrinsic, or categorical, or non-relational, or not structural-dynamical properties. But what is the nature of the properties that have these interesting higher-order properties? Are they mental, physical, or neither? According to Alter and Nagasawa, the Russellian monist is free to adopt any of these options. Specifically, they enumerate the following possibilities. The inscrutables might be phenomenal properties; they might be protophenomenal properties (properties that are not themselves phenomenal but can, in combination, yield phenomenal properties); they might be neutral properties—properties that are neither physical nor mental; and, finally, they might be physical properties, albeit not the properties that figure in current physics. Barbara Montero, for example, has proposed that if the job of the inscrutables is not merely to ground consciousness, but to ground all (regular) physical properties, then, surely, these inscrutables deserve the label "physical." (See Montero 2010 and 2015.)

Based on this astonishing flexibility of the RM framework Alter and Nagasawa argue that RM can take on the appearance of most of the traditional positions in the philosophy of mind: physicalism, dualism, idealism, neutral monism, and panpsychism (see Alter & Nagasawa 2012, 77, 82).

Panpsychist Russellian Monism

There is much more to say about the various forms that RM can take, and their respective strengths and weaknesses. But from this point onward, I will focus on the panpsychist version of RM (PRM), or, more specifically, on pan-experientialist version of RM (also PRM).[8] On this picture, experience (rather than the full spread of mentality) is everywhere:

> If the inscrutables are construed as phenomenal properties and the inscrutables are assumed to be everywhere, then Russellian monism seems to entail panpsychism—the view that mind, or at any rate phenomenality, is everywhere.
>
> (Alter & Nagasawa 2012, 77)[9]

PRM is well represented in the (small) group of contemporary Russellian monists. Sam Coleman believes that "most extant forms of panpsychism have, broadly speaking, a Russellian heritage—deriving much of the structure of their ontology, if not also their philosophical motivation, from Russell's famous analysis of (micro)physics … " (Coleman 2009, 87). And Emmett L. Holman agrees that "most versions of this theory are panpsychist or panexperientialist" (Holman 2008, 49). This judgment is also borne out by the fact that Alter and Nagasawa manage to find many more philosophers who hold that the inscrutables are phenomenal properties than for any of the three other options: that they are protophenomenal, or neutral, or physical properties.[10]

While all the friends of PRM may agree that phenomenality is everywhere, they do disagree about how to answer the following questions: What are the relevant phenomenal qualities? After what manner are these properties possessed by the entities that have them? And how are these qualities related to other properties, be they the properties of physics or the properties of our conscious mental lives? Different answers to these questions yield a whole spectrum of different versions of PRM.

---

8. David Skrbina holds that panexperientialism—the view that "everything experiences, or is capable of experiencing … deserves to be considered as true panpsychism" (2007). Panpsychism makes the stronger claim that everything has a mind; there is no restriction to experience or phenomenal quality here. But in view of the fact that panexperientialism "is perhaps the most widely discussed form of panpsychism today" (Skrbina 2007), I'll use the two terms interchangeably.

9. Throughout this chapter I will only be concerned with the claim that every ultimate or fundamental constituent of the physical world has mental or experiential features. Whether such things as stones or planets have minds is a question I will not address.

10. Alter and Nagasawa (2012) and Holman (2008) provide us with lists of suspects. The following entries are found on both lists: Bolender (2001), Griffin (1998), Rosenberg (2004), Strawson (2006a). Alter and Nagasawa add Adams (2007) and Russell (1927a,b); Holman adds Coleman (2006).

Colin McGinn has argued that, for the panpsychist, "there is really no alternative but to accept that particles have minds much the same way we (and other animals) do" (McGinn 2006, 95). Barry Dainton makes the more guarded claim that "a panpsychist might conceivably hold that elementary physical particles possess conscious lives as rich and complex as our own" but immediately adds that "in practice few do" (Dainton 2011, 245). While none of the philosophers on the list of champions of the PRM (see footnote 10) makes quite as strong a claim, a few of them seem to hold that the phenomenal qualities, as we encounter them in our experience, *are* the inscrutables that ground the basic physical properties that physics describes. If we were to follow Alter and Nagasawa (2012) and Coleman (2009) in classifying Russell as a panpsychist, then he might count as a case in point.[11] And if we accept the classification of Robert Adams as a Russellian monist (a bit of a stretch, to be sure), then we find that he too comes very close identifying the inscrutables with phenomenal qualities we know from experience: "I have been making the case for these theses, first, that substances must have intrinsic non-formal qualities, and second, that qualities of consciousness, or qualities very like them, are the only intrinsic non-formal qualities of substances" (Adams 2007, 47). And then there is David Armstrong, who defended the view—a "most unfortunate" view, as he was later to maintain—that things like "colours, sounds, tastes, smells, heat and cold" might serve as "stuffing for matter" (Armstrong 1968, 282). Here is how he put it:

> So it seems that we must either fill out the physicist's account of physical objects by treating colours, etc., as real properties of objects (to pick and choose among them seems arbitrary); or else we must postulate further qualities 'I know not what' which, as it were, provide the stuffing for physical objects.
>
> (Armstrong *1961, 189*)

But, for the most part, the Russellian panpsychists have tended towards microexperientialism. This is the view that the inscrutable properties of the particles of physics, though genuinely experiential—and therefore in that respect quite unlike the so-called proto-properties frequently invoked by many fellow Russellian monists—might be profoundly different from the properties we know in experience, and possibly even completely unimaginable to us.[12] The idea that the microexperiences of the microparticles might be

---

11. See the section "Turning Neutral Monism into Panpsychism."

12. The term "microexperientiality" seems to have been introduced by Strawson in (2006a).

"wholly other" opens up many possibilities: it seems that there is no end to the different ways in which this suggestion can be filled out.

While it may seem that this path tends to dilute the panpsychist vision too much, it must also be said that the temptation of pursuing this direction of inquiry is great. Especially so, if we keep in mind that panpsychism holds that minds—not merely some free-floating mental properties—are everywhere. David Skrbina, for example, thinks that it is of the essence of panpsychism that "objects have experiences for themselves," that "this experience is singular," i.e., that this be a "unitary mental experience." And he sums this up by saying that "all objects, or systems of objects, possess a singular inner experience of the world around them" (Skrbina 2005, 16).[13] That means that the electron, for example, has a mind; that it is a subject; that it's like something to be it; that it has a point of view; that it experiences and feels. It is so much easier to regard the electron in this manner if one imagines that the phenomenal properties involved are utterly unlike those one currently experiences.

The difficulty that is felt upon attempting to conceive of the electron as an experiencing subject has led some to rethink the role of the subject in the panexperientialist theory. In this connection, it is interesting to look at Galen Strawson's reflections on experience and the self. We find that, on the one hand, Strawson is second to none in his insistence that experience without an experiencing subject is impossible (see Strawson 2006b 189–90). But, on the other hand, we discover that no one has been more unrelenting in their attempts to thin out the notion of the subject. Strawson introduces "the thin conception [of the subject] according to which a subject of experience, a true and actual subject of experience, does not and cannot exist without experience also existing, experience which it is having itself" (Strawson 2006b, 192). The thin subject of experience is short-lived (in the case of humans and,

---

13. And lest it be thought that this emphasis on the subject is an idiosyncrasy of Skrbina's understanding of panpsychism, here is the testimony of two other prominent panpsychists who share this view:

"But things do divide, in common opinion, into those such that there is and those such that there is not *something it is like to be them* (though this expression is only an idiomatic pointer to something it requires a certain sophisticated obtuseness to be unable to identify). The paradigm panpsychist maintains that each of the ultimate units of the physical world (whether particles or events or even mutually influencing fields) out of which all other physical things are made, are conscious in this sense. Of course they are not self-conscious or thoughtful, but each has some dumb feeling of its own existence and of its exchange of influence with other things" (Sprigge 1998a).

"In its more significant form, panpsychism is rather the view that all things, in all their aspects, consist exclusively of "souls," that is, of various kinds of subjects, or units of experiencing, with their qualifications, relations, and groupings or communities" (Hartshorne 1950, 442).

presumably, in the case of particles), it is not ontologically distinct from the experience or the experiencing, and it is not something that can perceive or be in intentional states (see Strawson 2006b, 192–93). And thus we get that:

> Pure panpsychism [all physical being is experiential being] has only one kind of thing in its fundamental ontology: subjects of experience in the 'thin' sense … subjects of experience each of which is at the same time an experience, an experiencing, i.e. literally identical with an experience or experiencing.
>
> (Strawson 2006b, 246–47)

It's hard to see how this differs from the "radical" position of an opponent who has decided to rid panexperientialism of the burden of the subject. That is just what Sam Coleman proposes to do: "ditch the thesis about subjects. If experience must permeate the lowest level, let us deny that mere experience suffices of subjecthood" (Coleman 2006, 49).

And, finally, the champion of PRM will have to take a stand on how these phenomenal properties—whatever their qualitative nature may be, and however they inhere in what has them—are related to the properties that they are supposed to ground. Different answers to these questions will yield versions of PRM that vary considerably.

Questions about Grounding in PRM

How can phenomenal properties accomplish the task of grounding the basic physical properties? As we have seen, Alter and Nagasawa use the term "grounding" as neutral with respect to the different ways in which the inscrutables and the basic physical properties have been construed: relational/non-relational; extrinsic/intrinsic; dispositional/categorical; and structural-dynamic/non-structural-dynamic. In their choice of the term "grounding" they seem to follow Montero, who, after flagging a number of problems with the intrinsic/extrinsic and categorical/dispositional distinctions, uses the term "grounding" to formulate RM in a manner that abstracts away from the details of these distinctions (see Montero 2010, 74). We find a similar desire to not get hung up on these details of how to characterize the nature of the inscrutables and basic physical properties in other writers as well. Coleman acknowledges that each of the following terms comes with its own difficulties: "intrinsic," "essential," "categorical," "inner," "qualitative," and "core." But rather than settle on any one of them, or introduce a new one, he prefers to "flit between those terms on the list that I feel get closest to whatever we really mean, something which

I'm hopeful may be more clearly specifiable in future" (Coleman 2009, 87). Daniel Stoljar seems to think that it matters little whether the statement of the Russellian position employs the term "categorical" or "intrinsic"—"these are labels that don't convey all that much on their own" (Stoljar 2006, 106). And perhaps Chalmers's smooth transition from talk about the intrinsic properties of fundamental particles to talk about the categorical bases of fundamental physical dispositions (see Chalmers 2002a, 265) falls in line with this tendency.

Let us then, for the time being, follow Montero and Alter and Nagasawa in adopting the term "grounding," presumably using it as a primitive, as urged by Jonathan Schaffer (2007). But we still want to be given some idea how the inscrutables manage to do their job. Take a physical particle's mass and charge. These properties "are characterized as a propensity to be accelerated in a certain way by certain forces—by relations to other entities within a spatio-temporal structure ... " (Alter & Nagasawa 2012, 69). This particle also happens to have one or more qualitative experiences—it is like something to be this particle. Does this latter fact shed any light on the question of how this particle manages to have its specific mass or charge? Or does it explain how the particle manages to have any properties like mass and charge at all? Do we really want to say that the possession of a phenomenal property (the undergoing an experience of some qualitative type or other) is a sufficient metaphysical ground for the possession of a basic physical property? Though all these questions are "merely rhetorical," it is hard to shake the suspicion that the phenomenal properties cannot play the role that has been assigned them.

According to Alter and Nagasawa, the idea of grounding is central to (all versions of) RM: to ground the properties of physics is the primary job of the inscrutables.[14] The need for such a grounding of physics is what motivates the push towards RM in the first place. This approach saddles RM with a heavy metaphysical burden, one that it may not be able to shoulder. In view of this worry it is important to note that Russell's version of RM is not motivated by the perceived need to save physics by providing a metaphysical grounding for it. Russell is moved by the epistemological worry that physics, as commonly understood, has become so remote from experience as to make it incomprehensible how the latter could afford evidence for the former: "We must therefore find an interpretation of physics which gives a due place to perceptions; if not, we have no right to appeal to the empirical

---

14. The relation between the inscrutables and the (macro)phenomenal properties of our experience will be briefly explored in the section "Turning Neutral Monism into Panpsychism."

evidence" (Russell, 1972a 7). It is this epistemic worry—not a concern about the metaphysical ungroundedness of physical properties—that leads him to undertake his neutral monist reconstruction of matter and mind. This goal "to bridge the gulf between physics ... and perception" may be more attainable than the more ambitious goal of grounding the physical in the phenomenal.

Perhaps we should be content if the Russellian framework showed us how to find a home for the phenomenal qualities in the physical world. To many it has seemed that the physical world has no room for the qualitative features of experiences. The structuralist picture has opened up a gap in the physical world into which we can slot the qualities we know from experience. That alone would be a triumph of sorts. Perhaps it is too much to ask that the phenomenal properties not merely reside in, but also metaphysically ground, the physical structures they inhabit.[15]

Russell: From Physical Sense-Data to Neutral Sensations/Percepts

While Russell is universally acknowledged as the inspirer of RM, we have seen that some panpsychist Russellian monists go so far as to count him as one of their own. The idea that Russell's NM is really some sort of mental monism is not new. On the contrary, it is perhaps the most frequently raised objection to the sort of NM we find in the works of Russell, Ernst Mach, and William James.[16] The reason for this non-neutrality suspicion is not difficult to find: initially Russell maintained that sensations were the neutral entities (see Russell 1919; 1921); later on he favored the term "percepts" (see Russell 1927a, b; 1948; 1959). And since sensations/percepts must count as paradigms of mental entities, it seems glaringly obvious that the monism in question is not neutral but mental.

This point was not lost on Russell. But no matter how hard he tried to rid the terms "sensation" and "percept" of their mentalistic flavor, this criticism would not die. In fact, Russell embarked on this (losing) battle long before embracing NM. During his dualistic sense-datum period—prior to accepting the monistic theory of perception—he staunchly insisted on the non-mentality of sense-data; and during most of this period he defended the stronger claim

---

15. David Chalmers clearly distinguishes these two issues and credits Russell with the "insight ... that we might solve both these problems at once" (Chalmers 2002, 265).

16. See Stubenberg (2005/2010).

that sense-data are physical. According to Russell, the non-mentality of sense-data is easily discerned:

> Let us ask ourselves whether the quality designated by the word 'mental' does, as a matter of observation, actually belong to objects of sense, such as colours or noises. I think any candid person must reply that, however difficult it may be to know what we mean by 'mental', it is not difficult to see that colours and noises are not mental in the sense of having that intrinsic peculiarity which belongs to beliefs and wishes and volitions, but not to the physical world.
>
> (Russell 1915, 127)

The theoretical pressure to make sense-data mental is considerable: the empiricist tradition and contemporary thought agree that sense-data "must be swept into the dustbin of the mind," as David Armstrong has so memorably put it (Armstrong & Malcolm 1984, 176). In the next section of the chapter we will see how Russell proposes to address the challenge that perceived qualities must count as mental properties that are not physical.

But there is a second problem here. If these qualities were to qualify as something physical—something in the perceiving brain, say—then it seems that we should be able to find these colorful, noisy, tasty, and so on sense-data (later on: sensations/percepts) in the brain. But we do not: the relevant noises, smells, and patches of color "are nowhere to be found in the head" (Dretske 1995, 151). In the past, this simple observation tended to push these qualities into the mind; in the present it tends to push them out of the head and onto external objects. In another passage Dretske tells us that if these qualities are in our heads, "they seem to be well camouflaged" (Dretske 1995, 36). And while he does not take this possibility seriously, Russell does. His explanation of how the "colours and noises" in our heads are hidden from plain view comes in two parts. One has to do with a peculiar feature of his theories of perception (both the earlier sense-datum theory and the later monistic theory): the grayness you see when you look at another person's brain, and the silence you hear when you put your ear up close to it, are the sense-data (sensations/percepts) in your own brain—the only sorts of things that you will ever see or hear. So, for all you know, the brain you take yourself to be seeing and hearing may be full of "colours and sounds"—but these "colours and sounds" are not things you could possibly perceive. The second part of the story explains how any "colours and sounds"—conceived of as physical (later on: neutral) items—can find a place in anybody's brain—your own brain, or the brain of the patient you are studying. This has to do with Russell's construction of matter, a construction that remained relevantly unchanged when he switched from his earlier dualism to the NM of his later period.[17]

So much for Russell's rebuttal to the objection that the sense-data of his dualist period and the sensations/percepts of his neutral monist period are obviously mental. It still remains to show that the sensations/percepts of the later period are neutral, not physical, like the sense-data of his earlier period. The physical sense-data were (among) the objects of acquaintance of the mental self/mind. When Russell convinced himself—on the grounds of introspective observation of a Humean kind—that such purely mental entities (selves, minds, mental acts) could be dispensed with, he was finally in a position to embrace NM in the style of Mach and James. Russell was very eager to adopt NM, as he himself is the first to admit. Writing about James's NM, he says: "This view is very attractive, and I have made great endeavours to believe it" (Russell 1919, 299). The "immense simplification" (Russell 1959, 103–04) in ontology is the main attraction of the view. Russell—a frequent critic of NM during his dualist period—always insisted that Occam's razor "prescribes James's theory as preferable to dualism if it can possibly be made to account for the facts" (Russell 1914a, 145–46).

It is clear, then, that Russell very much wanted to embrace NM. But how does he propose to move from the dualist framework of the sense-datum theory to the sort of monism he finds in Mach and James? His way of transitioning from physical sense-data to neutral items—the sensations of *The Analysis of Mind* and the percepts of *The Analysis of Matter*—can seem somewhat baffling. Here is a typical passage in which Russell tries to explain the transformation:

> The subject, however, appears to be a logical fiction . . . It is introduced, not because observation reveals it, but because it is linguistically convenient and apparently demanded by grammar . . . If we are to avoid a perfectly gratuitous assumption, we must dispense with the subject as one of the actual ingredients of the world. But when we do this, the possibility of distinguishing the sensation from the sense-datum vanishes; at least I see no way of preserving the distinction. Accordingly the sensation that we have when we see a patch of colour simply is that patch of colour, an actual constituent of the physical world, and part of what physics is concerned with . . . But it does not follow that

17. I will come back to this issue in the section "Russell's Construction of Matter."

the patch of colour is not also psychical, unless we assume that the
physical and the psychical cannot overlap, which I no longer consider a
valid assumption. If we admit—as I think we should—that the patch of
colour may be both physical and psychical, the reason for distinguishing the sense-datum from the sensation disappears, and we must say
that the patch of colour and our sensation in seeing it are identical.

(Russell 1921, 141–43)

Unable to discover the self or its acts—mental acts of awareness, or acquaintance, or sensing—Russell says that he can no longer distinguish the sensation (the sensing) from the sense-datum; and he goes on to say that therefore
the sense-datum (the patch of color) and the sensing of it (seeing it) are identical. This is puzzling in two ways: first, how could a physical thing (like a red
patch) be identical with a mental act (like a seeing)? Second, assuming that we
do understand this identity claim, we are faced with the fact that, according
to Russell, there are no such mental acts, no sensings; so what could it mean
that they—these nonexistent acts—are identical with patches of color, whose
existence is not in doubt?

What Russell asks us to do is to reconceptualize (visual) experience. There
are not, and there never were, two ontologically and functionally distinct parts
in visual experience: the part that we tried to capture with the concept of a
sense-datum and the part we tried to capture with the concept of the act of
sensing. This is simply a mistaken analysis of a phenomenon that has no such
inner division. The patch of color—the supposed physical object of the mental
act—the one thing that survives the critique of the sense-datum theory, now
plays both of the roles that the sense-datum theory mistakenly assigned to two
distinct entities: it can be the object that is seen, when considered in one way,
and it can be the seeing of this object, when considered in another way. The
role a given neutral element plays depends on the other elements with which
it is grouped—in the one group it is part of the perceived object, in the other
group it is part of the mental state that is aware of this object.

Does the fact that the sensation/percept plays two roles—two roles that
the sense-datum theory assigned, respectively, to a physical thing (the sense-
datum) and to a mental thing (the self with its act)—mean that sensations/
percepts are neutral: neither mental nor physical? Perhaps, but more is to be
said here.

First, it may seem that Russell himself, in the very passage quoted above,
denies the neutrality of sensations. After all, he writes that the "patch of
colour may be both physical and psychical." (Russell 1921, 143) This makes
him sound like an identity theorist, not like a neutral monist. Here, as in very

many other places, Russell speaks in an abbreviated, if somewhat misleading way. But there are just as many passages in which the basic idea of NM is stated more carefully, making it quite clear that the sensations/percepts—the neutral elements—are, indeed, neutral: neither mental nor physical, rather than being both these things. Here, for example, is how he states NM at the beginning of *The Analysis of Mind*:

> The stuff of which the world of our experience is composed is, in my belief, neither mind nor matter, but something more primitive than either. Both mind and matter seem to be composite, and the stuff of which they are compounded lies in a sense between the two, in a sense above them both, like a common ancestor.
>
> (Russell *1921, 10–11*)

A few pages later he tells us that James and the American realists are (largely) right in holding that "mind and matter are composed of neutral stuff which, in isolation, is neither mental nor material." And he adds: "I should admit this view as regards sensations: what is heard and seen belongs equally to psychology and to physics" (Russell 1921, 25). The terms "mental" and "physical" apply to groupings of neutral elements; the elements themselves are neither. There is no harm in calling a sensation/percept, when considered as a part of a mental group, mental. But it is not as if membership in this group had effected a change in the intrinsic nature of the sensation/percept in question, turning it from neutral to mental. Parallel remarks apply to the case in which this same sensation is considered as an element in a physical group. To say that the sensation/percept is now physical is just to say that it, the neutral sensation/percept, is now considered a member of a group that is governed by physical law.

Perhaps the foregoing is sufficient to show that Russell's NM can be stated in a coherent way. But what are his reasons for insisting on the neutrality of his sensations/percepts? In our discussion of sense-data we have already encountered one of the central ideas that move Russell to assert the non-mentality of sensations/percepts. Inspection of a yellow patch, a soft noise, rough texture, and so on does not reveal anything mental about the phenomenon: "it is not difficult to see that colours and noises are not mental in the sense of having that intrinsic peculiarity which belongs to beliefs and wishes and volitions, but not to the physical world" (Russell 1915, 127). This thought persuades him that there is nothing intrinsically mental about sensations/percepts. And with the exiling of the mental self as well as its mental acts—such as awareness and acquaintance—from the neutral monist universe, the idea that sensations/percepts might be mental because they "exist in the mind" can no longer persuade.

The more difficult task for Russell is to establish that sensations/percepts are non-physical. They are, after all, the direct descendants of physical things—of sense-data, as Russell understood them. To understand the recategorization of these items from physical to neutral, we must recall Russell's "supreme maxim of scientific philosophizing" (Russell 1914b, 149): "Wherever possible, substitute constructions out of known entities for inferences to unknown entities" (Russell 1924, 326). Matter, as traditionally understood by common sense and physics, is an entity not directly known but inferred. Sensations/percepts are entities that are known directly. So Russell set about constructing matter out of sensations/percepts (and other things). Reconceiving matter along these lines is, according to him, "vital for any understanding of the relations between mind and matter, between our perceptions and the world which they perceive" (Russell 1921, 306).

In the next section I will have more to say about the idea that Russell expresses here. But the relevance for our present discussion is this: matter is a construction out of things that are not themselves material. Sensations/percepts are part of the construction material for matter. So sensations/percepts are not material.

Based on these considerations, we can see how Russell was led to the astonishing view that sensations/percepts are *neither* mental *nor* physical but neutral. As he sees it, they fit into neither one of the traditional categories of mind and matter:

> The ultimate constituents of the world do not have the characteristics of either mind or matter as ordinarily understood: they are not solid persistent objects moving through space, nor are they fragments of "consciousness".
>
> (Russell 1921, 124)

This, then, is why Russell thinks that the sensations (of *The Analysis of Mind*) and the percepts (of his later neutral monist writings) are neutral—neither mental nor physical. The colored patches we see, the sounds we hear, and so on are examples of these neutral items. When you see a yellow patch, say, there is, of course, a subject involved—viz. you. But the seeing subject is not a part of the yellow patch; nor does the existence of the yellow patch depend on the existence of the seeing subject in any other way. Russell follows Hume in holding that the patches come first and that the subjects who see the patches are to be understood as constructed out of them. He is a proponent of the bundle theory of the self:

> It is supposed that thoughts cannot just come and go, but need a person to think them. Now, of course it is true that thoughts can be collected into bundles, so that one bundle is my thoughts, another is your thoughts, and a third is the thoughts of Mr. Jones. But I think the person is not an ingredient in the single thought: he is rather constituted by relations of the thoughts to each other and to the body.
>
> (Russell *1921, 18*)

Now we know why Russell would want to resist his being classified as a panpsychist. There is nothing mental about the neutral elements of his monism, not even when these elements are sensations or percepts (nor was there anything mental about the sense-data of his pre-1919 thought). He does not deny the existence of mental states and entities—beliefs, desires, selves; but these are complexes constructed out of neutral elements. Much of *The Analysis of Mind* is concerned with the difficult questions of how to construct mental states and the self from sensations and similar items. But if we are to understand the relevance of Russell's thought for panpsychism, our focus must be on his construction, not of the self, but of material objects.

Russell's Construction of Matter

In the preceding discussion the question of Russell's views about matter has arisen repeatedly; now it is time to address it. An understanding of these views will provide us with a better understanding of the relationship between Russell's views and RM. Finally I will suggest that panpsychist philosophers might profit from liberally borrowing and adapting some of Russell's ideas in this area.

Philosophy in general, and the philosophy of matter in particular, has to start with the facts that science provides—for "science has a much greater likelihood of being true in the main than any philosophy hitherto advanced" (Russell 1924, 339). Accordingly, Russell tells us that "in ontology I start by accepting the truth of physics; in epistemology I ask myself: Given the truth of physics, what can be meant by an organism having "knowledge," and what knowledge can it have?" (Russell 1946, 700). At the same time, it is the job of the philosopher to interpret science. *The Analysis of Matter* is Russell's attempt to do this for physics. What we need to do, he tells us in the preface, is to determine "the relation of "matter" to what exists"; and this takes the form of providing an "interpretation of physics in terms of what exists" (Russell 1927a, Preface). The principle guiding this process is, of course, the supreme maxim of scientific philosophizing, viz., to replace entities that are not known directly but merely inferred by constructions out of entities that are directly given to us. Russell admits that the process of constructing a point, say, out of a class of qualities may seem like a "wild and wilful paradox" (1926, 132). But the strategy recommends itself on ontological and epistemological grounds. The class of qualities can play the role of the point; the existence of the point is known only through fallible inference; but the existence of the class of qualities is known for certain. In this way we no longer need to infer the existence of points and the entities to which we are committed are better known than the ones we dispensed with (see Russell 1914/26, 132–34; Russell 1924, 326–30). Russell's most famous applications of this technique fall into the realm of logic and mathematics. But he believes that the method is equally applicable in physics: points, instants, and, most relevant for our purposes, particles of matter are among the examples he lists.

It is due to the abstractness of physics, due to the fact that it says so little about the terms or things that are related by physical law, that we are free to construct these terms in any way whatever, so long as these constructions satisfy the minimal constraints that physical theory dictates. "It is not necessary," Russell tells us, "to suppose that electrons, protons, neutrons, mesons, photons, and the rest have that sort of simple reality that belongs to immediate objects of experience." And this is so because these entities "owe their credibility to inference, [and] are only defined to the degree that is necessary to make them fulfil their inferential purpose" (Russell 1959, 16). As a consequence, we have great freedom when it comes to interpreting the true nature of, say, the electron:

> We know it only as a hypothetical entity fulfilling certain theoretical purposes. So far as theoretical physics is concerned, anything that fulfils these purposes can be taken to *be* the electron. It may be simple or complex; and, if complex, it may be built out of any components that allow the resultant structure to have the requisite properties.
>
> (Russell 1959, 16–17)

We know the electron only as a creature of theory, but "we must find some reality for the electron, or else the physical world will run though our fingers like a jelly-fish" (Russell 1927a, 319). That is, when we are dealing with the logical construction of an entity that is real (not merely logical or mathematical), the materials that go into this construction must themselves be real. What are the "known entities" that feature in the construction of merely inferred, physical entities? In the first place they are the entities we get to know in perception. And Russell holds that "we perceive events, not substances, that is to say, what we perceive occupies a volume of space-time which is small in all four dimensions" (Russell 1927a, 284). The conclusion that the building materials must be events finds strong scientific support: "the world which the theory of relativity presents to our imagination is not so much a world of 'things' in 'motion' as a world of *events* . . . It is *events* that are the stuff of relativity physics" (Russell 1925, 134). Of course, the events we know directly, our percepts, are insufficient to construct the whole world of physics. We need to infer the existence of events beyond our percepts. These inferences are non-deductive and therefore fallible. This is not ideal, but it is less bad than having to infer things—like material substances—that are completely different in kind from the events we know in experience. Hence Russell settles on events—with the pride of epistemic place given to those events that are one's percepts—as the existing real entities in terms of which matter is to be interpreted. This leaves physics untouched. But it is preferable from a philosophical point of view, in that it shrinks our ontology and gives us some measure of understanding what physics is about.

Physics, then, is concerned with "groups of "events," rather than with "things" and their "states" that change over time" (Russell 1927a, 286). We can get a sense of the sort of grouping Russell has in mind by considering our own percepts. Two temporally overlapping sounds you hear, for example, are "compresent." And if you enlarge the group of your compresent percepts—adding in further sounds, visual percepts, and so on—there will still be a place or a region of joint overlap among them. Russell builds on this idea to define a group of percepts that constitute a point in the flow of our experience: "This place will be a "point" if there is no event outside the group which is compresent with all of them" (Russell 1927a, 294). The details of the overlapping relations get considerably more complex when going beyond the "one-dimensional psychological time-series" (Russell 1927a, 294). But the basic method of construction remains the same in the construction of a point-like physical particle such as the electron. It will be a group of events, all of which overlap (or share a common region), where this overlapping is specified in a rather more complex manner.

Our grasp of the nature of matter is best for those particles that are parts of our brains, for "we do not know much about the contents of any part of the world except our own heads" (Russell 1927a, 319). Considering the brain of a living, conscious person, Russell has this to say about our knowledge of the nature of a given electron in this brain:

> While [the brain's] owner was alive, part, at least, of the contents of his brain consisted of his percepts, thoughts, and feelings. Since his brain also consisted of electrons, we are compelled to conclude that an electron is a grouping of events, and that, if the electron is in a human brain, some of the events composing it are likely to be some of the "mental states" of the man to whom the brain belongs ... Thus a percept is an event or a group of events, each of which belongs to one or more of the groups constituting the electrons in the brain. This, I think, is the most concrete statement that can be made about electrons; everything else that can be said is more or less abstract and mathematical.
>
> (Russell 1927a, 320)

If we decide to follow Russell in this matter, the next question is this: what is the relationship between a constructed physical particle and the percept that partially constitutes it? If the bright, yellow patch (that is "your seeing the sun") is among the events that constitute a given electron in your brain, that electron is not thereby made to see the sun. It does not have this experience "for itself," nor does it thereby get to be like something to be that electron. If that is so, Russell's way of putting phenomenal properties "into" physical particles does not help the (traditional) panpsychist cause. The requisite subjectivity does not arise from this construction.

As for those physical particles that do not reside in living, conscious brains, things look considerably more grim. What can we say about the events from which they are constructed? If we follow Russell, next to nothing. Here we encounter Russell's structuralist thinking again: the events inferred from your own percepts are known only as regards their structure. Nothing is known as to their intrinsic nature—"the only legitimate attitude about the physical world seems to be one of complete agnosticism as regards all but its mathematical properties" (Russell 1927a, 271). When we "see the sun," what we see is a bright patch of yellow. The yellow is the quality that composes the event that is our percept. Our ignorance about nearly everything in the universe concerns these qualities: "the qualities that compose such events are unknown—so completely unknown that we cannot say either that they are or that they are not different from the qualities that we know as belonging to mental events" (Russell 1948, 231).

This is another setback for the project of seeing Russell's metaphysics as a version of, or as an inspiration for, a panpsychist view. The first difficulty consists in the fact that those material particles that are known to "contain" percepts (phenomenal properties) do not contain them in the right way. The second difficulty is that, for the vast majority of physical particles, the Russellian framework provides no reason to think that the events that make them up are composed of the sorts of qualities we know from our percepts.[18]

The blow dealt by the second point is softened, however, by the further observation that the Russellian framework provides no reason to think that the events that make up all the particles outside of conscious brains must be entirely unlike percepts. Russell points out "the fact that physics leaves open all kinds of possibilities as to the intrinsic character of the world to which its equations apply. There is nothing in physics to prove that the physical world is radically different in character from the mental world" (Russell 1927a, 270).

No Place for the Idea of Grounding in the Program of Logical Construction?

Now that we have a somewhat fuller understanding of the nature of and the reasons for Russell's logical construction of matter, we are in a better position to assess an idea that, in one form or another, is at the heart of RM. It is this: since science deals only with dispositional, or relational, or extrinsic, or structural-dynamical properties, we *need* some categorical, or non-relational, or intrinsic, or non-structural-dynamical properties to, in some sense, provide "stuffing for matter," to anchor the scientific properties. Following Alter and Nagasawa, I call this thesis the grounding idea. Is the grounding idea, in any of its variants, part of Russell's argument as developed here? I believe that it is not.

The most detailed expression of the grounding idea has been given in terms of dispositional and categorical properties.[19] The inscrutables—be they phenomenal, or protophenomenal, or physical properties of some unusual sort—figure as the categorical bases of the dispositional properties described by physics, thereby grounding those dispositional properties of physics. But the careful reader discovers that this line of thought does not appear in Russell's writings.[20] I am not arguing that Russell holds that there can be

---

18. For more on the relationship of NM—and Russell's version of NM in particular—and panpsychism, see Stubenberg (fc).

19. Chalmers (2002), Pereboom (2011), and Stoljar (2001, 2006) like to think in these terms.

20. I am quite sure that this version of the grounding idea is not in 1927a or 1927b—the two canonical texts in this debate. I am virtually sure that it is not in (1921). I have not completely

dispositions without categorical bases. What I am saying is that, in his discussion of the question of how to "construct a theory of the physical world which makes its events continuous with perception" (Russell 1927a, 275), Russell never makes use of the idea that percepts must be "the stuffing for matter" so that they can function as the categorical base of physical, dispositional properties. The reason your bright, yellow percept ends up "in" an electron of your brain is that considerations of ontological economy and epistemological risk minimization demand that electrons be constructed out of materials that are "at hand," and that are better known than the theoretical entities of physics. As it happens, your "thoughts" turn out to be the material we are looking for. Hence your bright, yellow percept gets to be part of the group of events that is this electron in your brain. This is the only reason your "brain consists of thoughts" (Russell 1959, 18).[21]

The issue is harder to assess for other versions of the grounding idea.[22] The two claims that physics tells us nothing about the intrinsic character of the world, and that we do know the intrinsic character of our percepts, are absolutely central to Russell's project. And we also find that Russell emphasizes the importance of the terms of relations: "When we wish to describe a structure, we have to do so by means of terms and relations . . . the terms are as important as the relations, and we cannot rest content with terms which we believe to be fictitious" (Russell 1927a, 276–77). Isn't that sufficient to show that Russell uses the grounding idea in two of its forms?

Let's begin with the terms, the relata of relations. Notice that physics *does* affirm the existence of the sorts of terms (or relata) that Russell has in mind: electrons, protons, and the rest are taken to be entities in good standing. What physics says about them is abstract, of course. But these abstractly

---

reread (1940), (1948), and (1959) with this question in mind. Maybe it can be found there, or in his numerous smaller pieces on the topic. But I doubt it very much.

21. The term "thought" is here used in a broad sense to include all mental phenomena, i.e., phenomena constructed from neutral elements, such as sensations and (much more controversially) ideas and feelings (see Russell 1921). In Russell's dualist period we were said to know our thoughts through the simple relation of direct acquaintance. In the neutral monist period, knowledge, including the knowledge of our own mental states, becomes a matter of an event (or group of events) causally triggering a knowledge reaction (behavioristically conceived). This makes all knowledge fallible. But the knowledge of our own mental states is still privileged by the fact that (i) the causal distance between the thing known and the knowing of it is as short as possible; (ii) no inferences to events beyond those that trigger our knowledge reaction are involved.

22. I will discuss the case of relational/non-relational and the intrinsic/extrinsic cases. I am not sure that the structural-dynamical/non-structural-dynamical case adds anything to the previous two.

characterized terms function just fine as the relata of the complex relations that physics formulates. So it is not the case that Russell sees physics as a peculiar body of doctrine that speaks only of relations, without bothering to provide the necessary relata. He is moved by other concerns. What Russell brings to this situation is a set of philosophical beliefs and goals. Ontological and epistemological beliefs push him to prefer logical constructions to entities that have "very convenient properties," like space-time points and electrons. His views about self-knowledge and non-deductive inference push him to believe that our percepts, plus the events we can infer from them, are real and better known than entities that can only be known through inference, such as electrons. Thus he has a source of construction materials ready at hand. And the resulting metaphysics of matter solves one of the great philosophical mysteries—the mind-body problem, or, more specifically, the problem of perception. These are the reasons that move Russell to devote so much energy to the logical reconstruction of the relata of physics. It is not that physics, by some strange oversight, failed to provide the necessary relata for physical relations. It is that Russell, given his philosophical predilections, finds fault with the provided relata. Thus he takes it upon himself to logically reconstruct these relata in a, to him, more philosophically satisfying manner. As Russell makes clear, there is no guarantee that such a reconstructive project will succeed—it might turn out that no suitable construction materials can be found. This is an empirical question (see Russell 1924, 328–29). Had Russell's project of logically reconstructing physical particles failed, he would have had to take physics, with all of its basic particles, on board as is. Such an unreconstructed physics, and the world that it describes, would not vanish into thin air, for lack of solid relata of the physical relations. The failure of the constructive project would have made physics more expensive (ontologically speaking) and more dubious (epistemologically speaking). But it would still have a stronger claim on our belief "than any philosophy hitherto advanced."

What about intrinsic character—does the fact that physics speaks only of extrinsic features of matter require that there be intrinsic features of some sort? We have seen Russell's reasons for seizing upon percepts, with their known intrinsic character, when attempting his philosophically motivated reinterpretation of physics. On Russell's view of the mind, it is filled with events that are percepts—yellow patches, loud noises, sweet smells, and so on—and we are in a privileged position to know these events by their intrinsic character. This makes percepts, and the events we can infer from them, into the perfect material with which to carry out his constructions. But there is no necessity about any of this. If, for example, you were to think, as Armstrong does, that "secondary qualities are primary qualities not apprehended as such" and that you suffer "the illusion of concrete secondary quality" (Armstrong & Malcolm 1984, 180, 185) when you take yourself to know the intrinsic yellow-ness of your sun percept, then Russell's way of securing a supply of "known entities" with which to perform his logical constructions, will not impress you. You will doubt the existence of Russellian percepts and (following in Armstrong's footsteps again) you might harbor quite general reservations about the wisdom of turning to the faculty of introspection to secure knowl-edge of any kind. For reasons such as these, the details of one's logical con-structions will be determined by a variety of other philosophical views one happens to hold. The project of logically reconstructing the particles of phys-ics might be carried out from a completely different starting point, having nothing to do with percepts or their intrinsic features. All that is required is a set of real entities that is better known than the inferred theoretical entities of physics. Anything that lives up to this specification will do. The percepts with their known intrinsic properties are a prominent part of Russell's sys-tem, not because Russell thinks that a structure of purely extrinsic proper-ties could not support itself. They are there because that is the sort of thing an empiricist philosopher turns to when in search of a firm foundation for anything at all.

None of the preceding considerations so much as suggest that there is anything wrong with the different versions of the grounding idea. Nor do they show that Russell could not have used these ideas in pursuing his proj-ect. What these considerations are supposed to establish is that, as a matter of fact, Russell did not rely on the grounding idea in any of its forms. The Russellian monist may do well to adhere to the grounding strategy, in one or more of its different forms. But the Russellian monist will also do well to be aware of the fact that, in pursuing this strategy, she is not following in Russell's footsteps.

Turning Neutral Monism into Panpsychism

We have seen that some Russellian monists view Russell as a panpsychist. This is inaccurate; but perhaps we can reshape Russell's view—in small, plausible steps—to arrive at a position that is recognizably Russellian and panpsychist. If successful, this could yield an interesting new perspective on the combination problem.[23]

---

23. See Bolender (2001) for the related attempt to present an idealistic reading of Russell's position.

There is a sense in which this project of "turning Russell into a panpsychist" is perfectly in keeping with the spirit in which Russell proposed his NM. He offers it as a way of "constructing possible physical worlds which fulfill the equations of physics and yet resemble rather more closely the world of perception than does the world ordinarily presented in physics." And he explains that such constructions "are hypotheses which may hereafter prove fruitful, and which have a certain imaginative value." They are not, however, "to be regarded as necessitated by any recognized principle of scientific inference" (Russell 1927a, 271). So a panpsychist construction can be seen as simply another way of constructing a world that helps to narrow "the gulf between physics and perception" (Russell 1927a, 275).

How do we begin the transformation of NM into panpsychism? First, there is the problem of neutrality. Few seem to be persuaded by Russell's case for the neutrality of the events at the basis of NM, and there is a long tradition of classifying Russell's events as mental. One can agree with Russell that the natural place to start is with one's own perceptions. But one can hold that, pace Russell, it is *obvious* that the yellow patches, the soft sounds, the sweet smells, and so on are mental. One might follow Strawson (and many others) in holding that such items can only exist *for* a subject (however thin), and that the mentality of these items consists precisely in this subject dependence. Or one might find oneself persuaded by Coleman, who argues that *"the intrinsically qualitative* [is] *indistinguishable from the notion of the qualitatively experiential. The idea of that which has an absolutely intrinsic way of being just is the idea of the conscious-experiential"* (Coleman 2009, 94). But even if some such consideration convinces one that one's percepts are mental, one still has to face the question of how to establish the mentality of all the other events that make up the world. If Russell is right and we can only draw inferences as to the structural features of these events, the belief that they too are mental appears to be quite unsupported.

There is, however, one thought in Russell's work that may suggest a way of expanding the group of mental events beyond the small realm of our percepts:

> If there is any advantage in supposing that the light-wave, the process in the eye, and the process in the optic nerve, contain events qualitatively continuous with the final visual percept, nothing that we know of the physical world can be used to disprove the supposition ... If there is any intellectual difficulty in supposing that the physical world is intrinsically quite unlike that of precepts, this is reason for supposing that there is not this complete unlikeness.
>
> (Russell *1927a, 263–64*)

To philosophers with panpsychist inclinations, the intellectual difficulty of supposing that the events leading up to the percept are *not* similar in character to the percept itself, will be readily apparent: the failure to make this supposition saddles us with a version of David Chalmers's hard problem. We cannot comprehend how a percept, with all its intrinsic, mental quality, might arise from a chain of events devoid of such intrinsic qualities. And this consideration may be taken to provide all the support that is needed to assume that all events (not just our percepts) are mental in the appropriate panpsychist sense.

Is this all that needs to be done to arrive at a panpsychist version of Russell? Recall the emphasis on the subject that we found in Skrbina's, Sprigge's, and Hartshorne's definitions of panpsychism: the basic entities must have experiences for themselves; it must be like something to be them; they must be subjects. If we hold that the bright, yellow patch that is our seeing the sun is an experience, that all other events are relevantly similar to this event, and that Strawson is right in holding that there cannot be an experience without an experiencer, then our percepts do live up to the standard laid down by Skrbina, Sprigge, and Hartshorne: every basic entity—every event—is like something for someone, viz., the (thin) subject of the particular experience in question. But this happy result comes at a high price: "it is unintelligible how 'little' subjects of experience can sum together to form 'big' subjects of experience. Because of this, panpsychism does nothing to explain, in a way that does not appeal to brute emergence, the conscious experience of people and animals" (Goff 2006, 60). This is a well-known problem for panpsychism. Can it be avoided?

In the face of this challenge, other panpsychists have said: "let us deny that mere experience suffices for subjecthood" (Coleman 2006, 49). A similar suggestion is to be found in Thomas Nagel's seminal treatment of panpsychism: "Presumably the components out of which a point of view is constructed would not themselves have to have points of view. (How could a single self be composed of many selves?)" (Nagel 1979a, 194). The judgment on whether this idea—usually traced back to Hume—is to count as a profound insight or as an utter absurdity, is still out. If we accept it (a choice that Russell would welcome) and we also hold that the resulting world of subjectless events, composed of intrinsic phenomenal qualities, is a recognizably panpsychist one, we have arrived at a Russellian model of panpsychism. And it has one particularly interesting feature.[24]

---

24. Is there anything "recognizably panpsychist" about this picture? The following passage from Sprigge may suggest as much: "One of the main charges against idealism is that of

All the events in this system—your percepts as well as all the other events that have been inferred—are of the same basic sort: they are occurrences, small in all four dimensions, composed of phenomenal properties as we know them (in the case of our percepts), and properties that are relevantly like our phenomenal properties. That is, all events are similar in intrinsic nature and similar in size. Your bright, yellow sun percept is simply one of the many events populating your head when you "see the sun." It is *not* composed of any of these other events, be they percepts or non-percepts, in your head (or elsewhere). It is a particular, an ultimate term, as Russell puts it. Some of those other events will be part of the causal chain leading up to your sun percept; most of the other events in your head will not even have this much connection to your sun percept. Your sun percept will be a part of various sorts of groups of percepts with which physics and psychology deal—some of these groups will be physical particles, others will be beliefs, desires, and other complex mental states. And you—the only self or subject present in this construction—will be the bundle of the mental states that compose you, i.e., the bundle of mental states that the bundle theory collects together into the self you are.[25] The percepts that get bundled into you are the events you experience. The qualities that compose all the events that are not part of the bundle you are, you do not get to experience.

Nowhere in this whole account is there room for microexperientiality of any kind—no microselves, no microphenomenal properties.[26] There is only one self—the large bundle self that you are; and the only kinds of phenomenal

---

'cosmic impiety' (Santayana). Its tendency is to make the vast realm of nature simply a representation in a mind observing or thinking of it. This can hardly do justice either to its obstinacy (surely not primarily of our own making, whatever Fichte may have thought) or to its wonderfulness. Such reflections have led some of those who are persuaded of the basic idealist claim that unexperienced reality is impossible, to hold the panpsychist position that nature is composed of units which feel their own existence and relation to other things, just as truly, if less articulately, as we do" (Sprigge 1998b). Our proposal of the existence of innumerable subjectless mental events floating in the vast universe falls short of the multitude of little subjects that Sprigge envisions. But it does address the cosmic impiety worry that has been raised against idealism. On the modified Russellian picture, the universe is constituted by real, mental stuff, the existence of which does not depend on human minds. Perhaps this suffices to count this proposal as panpsychist in spirit.

25. We have seen a sketch of how Russell thinks of the construction of material particles; in *The Analysis of Mind* he tries to explain the construction of complex mental states (such as beliefs and desires) and of the self out of percepts (sensations) and other elements.

26. This is true of the original neutral monist story as well as of the panpsychist reinterpretation of it.

properties involved are those that we know from our own experience (plus the relevantly similar properties that compose all the merely inferred events). There is, therefore, no problem of composition. The events—the basic elements of the system—are full-sized instances of phenomenal properties; there is, therefore, no question about how the microphenomenal properties manage to combine into the macrophenomenal properties we know from experience. And, if we continue to adhere to our earlier decision, the events at the basis of the system do not involve selves, large or small. The only selves in the system are "macro" selves—complex bundles of self-less percepts—of the sort we know ourselves to be. So the question of the compounding of micro-selves into macroselves does not arise.

There is another problem in the vicinity that this more Russellian version of panpsychism (as well as Russell's own NM) can address elegantly. Alter and Nagasawa make the interesting suggestion that the combination problem is a version of Wilfrid Sellars's grain problem. In its original version, the grain problem concerned the question of how homogeneous colors (as we know them in experience) could be instantiated by physical bearers—by things composed of colorless microparticles. Sellars was led to the conclusion that "a whole consisting of micro-physical particles can be colored (in the naive realist sense) only if these particles are themselves colored (in the naive realist sense) which . . . "doesn't make sense"" (Sellars 1971, 412). Here I will not address Sellars's solution to this problem, nor will I pursue the question of the relationship of the grain problem and the combination problem for panpsychism. But I do want to point out how elegantly the Russellian hypothesis—in either its neutral monist or in its panpsychist interpretation—solves the original grain problem. Contrary to Sellars's assumption, the physical microparticles do not have the job of exemplifying the homogeneous colors we experience. Instead of being supports for the colors, the physical microparticles are constructions from, among other things, patches of color. The color patches are basic, the particles are derivative. The problem is not one of fitting smooth, homogeneous color into the grainy world of particles; what we need to understand is how an underlying reality of smooth homogeneous color patches can give rise to grainy particles—and that is a problem that Russell takes himself to have solved by offering methods that allow the construction of point-like particles out of extended events (where it does not matter whether the events in question are taken to be neutral or mental).

On this Russellian version of panpsychism the universe is full of events consisting of phenomenal (i.e. mental) quality instances. The vast majority of these events exists unexperienced (even by themselves). Only those events that get bound up into a bundle self are experienced. When the bright, yellow patch enters a bundle that is a self, that self changes and gets to have a yellow experience. But the bright yellow patch, which brings about this change in the experience of the bundle self, does not undergo any change in the process. On this picture the only loci of subjectivity are the bundle selves—it is like something to be them. But none of their components, large or small, share this feature. It is like nothing to be the bright, yellow patch that is your seeing the sun—nothing is like anything for it. And the same holds true of all the physical particles into whose construction the bright, yellow patch enters. This rids panpsychism of many unwanted selves; but it does so at the price of the existence of unexperienced phenomenal property instances.

Summary

In this chapter I have tried to show two things. First, RM—and panpsychist RM in particular—are considerably less Russellian than their proponents realize. Second, a panpsychism modeled closely on Russell's NM may hold considerable promise, especially as regards its ability to address certain of the standard problems encountered by more traditional versions of panpsychism. In support of the first claim I have argued that close inspection of Russell's theory of perception and of his structuralism—the two Russellian theses on which most versions of contemporary RM are based—shows them to be quite idiosyncratic and therefore difficult to accept. I went on to argue that the central idea of RM—the idea that the inscrutables ground the properties appealed to in physics—is entirely absent from Russell's thinking. His way of integrating the inscrutables and the properties of physics differs profoundly from anything that is on offer in the RM camp. In support of the second claim I have argued that it is possible to reinterpret Russell's NM in a panpsychist way and that the resulting theory has interesting things to say about the combination problem and the grain problem.[27]

27. I am very grateful to Torin Alter and Donovan Wishon for their comments on this chapter. Donovan's comments proved to be especially challenging and I have not been able to do them full justice. I urge you to read Donovan's contribution to this volume—you will find that his Russell differs considerably from mine.

Bibliography

Adams, Robert (2007), "Idealism Vindicated" in van Inwagen and Zimmerman (eds.) (2007).

Alter, Torin and Yujin Nagasawa (2012), "What Is Russellian Monism?," *Journal of Consciousness Studies* 19.9–10, 67–95.

Armstrong, D. M. (1961), *Perception and the Physical World* (London: Routledge & Kegan Paul).

Armstrong, D. M. (1968), *A Materialist Theory of the Mind* (London: Routledge & Kegan Paul).

Armstrong, D. M. and Norman Malcolm (1984), *Consciousness and Causality. A Debate on the Nature of Mind* (Oxford: Blackwell).

Bolender, John (2001), "An Argument for Idealism," *Journal of Consciousness Studies* 8.4, 37–61.

Brüntrup, Godehard and Ludwig Jaskolla (eds.) (fc.), *Panpsychism: Philosophical Essays* (Oxford: Oxford University Press).

Chalmers, David (2002a), "Consciousness and Its Place in Nature" in David Chalmers (ed.) (2002b), 247–72.

Chalmers, David (2002b), *Philosophy of Mind. Classical and Contemporary Readings* (Oxford: Oxford University Press).

Chalmers, David, David Manley and Ryan Wasserman (eds.) (2007), *Metametaphysics. New Essays in the Foundations of Ontology* (Oxford: Oxford University Press).

Coleman, Sam (2006), "Being Realistic" in Strawson et al. (2006c).

Coleman, Sam (2009), "Mind Under Matter" in Skrbina (ed.) (2009), 83–107.

Crane, Tim (2006), "Is There a Perceptual Relation?" in Gendler and Hawthorne (2006), 126–46.

Dainton, Barry (2011), "Review of Consciousness and Its Place in Nature," *Philosophy and Phenomenological Research* 83.1, 238–61.

Dretske, Fred (1995), *Naturalizing the Mind* (Cambridge: MIT Press).

Ferm, Vergilius (ed.) (1950), *A History of Philosophical Systems* (New York: The Philosophical Library).

Gendler, Tamar and John Hawthorne (2006), *Perceptual Experience* (Oxford: Oxford University Press).

Goff, Philip (2006), "Experiences Don't Sum" in Strawson et al. (2006c), 53–61.

Griffin, David Ray (1997), "Panexperientialist Physicalism and the Mind-Body Problem," *Journal of Consciousness Studies* 4.3, 248–68.

Griffin, David Ray (1998), *Unsnarling the World-Knot: Consciousness, Freedom, and the Mind-Body Problem* (Berkeley: University of California Press).

Hartshorne, Charles (1950), "Panpsychism" in Ferm (ed.) (1950).

Holman, Emmett L. (2008), "Panpsychism, Physicalism, Neutral Monism and the Russellian Theory of Mind," *Journal of Consciousness Studies* 15.5, 48–67.

McGinn, Colin (2006), "Hard Questions. Comments on Galen Strawson" in Strawson et al. (2006c), 90–99.

Montero, Barbara (2010), "A Russellian Response to the Structural Argument Against Physicalism," *Journal of Consciousness Studies* 17.3–4, 70–83.

Montero, Barbara (2015), "Russellian Physicalism" in this volume.

Nagel, Thomas (1979a), "Panpsychism" in his (1979b).

Nagel, Thomas (1979b), *Mortal Questions* (Cambridge: Cambridge University Press).

Pereboom, Derk (2011), *Consciousness and the Prospects of Physicalism* (New York: Oxford University Press).

Rosenberg, Greg (2004), *A Place for Consciousness: Probing the Deep Structure of the Natural World* (New York: Oxford University Press).

Russell, Bertrand (1914a), "On the Nature of Acquaintance," reprinted in Russell (1956), 125–74.

Russell, Bertrand (1914b), "The Relation of Sense-Data to Physics," reprinted in Russell (1917), 140–72.

Russell, Bertrand (1915), "The Ultimate Constituents of Matter," reprinted in Russell (1917), 121–39.

Russell, Bertrand (1917), *Mysticism and Logic* (London: George Allen & Unwin). (References to the London: Unwin Paperbacks 1976 edition, retitled *A Free Man's Worship and Other Essays*).

Russell, Bertrand (1919), "On Propositions. What They Are and How They Mean," reprinted Russell (1956), 283–320.

Russell, Bertrand (1921), *The Analysis of Mind* (London: George Allen & Unwin).

Russell, Bertrand (1924), "Logical Atomism," reprinted in Russell (1956), 321–43.

Russell, Bertrand (1925), *The ABC of Relativity* (London: George Allen & Unwin). (References to the London: George Allen & Unwin 1958 revised edition).

Russell, Bertrand (1926/1914), *Our Knowledge of the External World*. Revised edition. (London: George Allen & Unwin).

Russell, Bertrand (1927a), *The Analysis of Matter* (London: Kegan Paul). (References to the New York: Dover 1954 edition).

Russell, Bertrand (1927b), *An Outline of Philosophy* (London: George Allen & Unwin). (References to the London: Unwin Paperbacks 1979 edition).

Russell, Bertrand (1931), *The Scientific Outlook* (London: George Allen & Unwin). (References to the New York: The Norton Library 1962 edition).

Russell, Bertrand (1946), "Reply to My Critics" in Schilpp (1946), 679–741.

Russell, Bertrand (1948), *Human Knowledge. Its Scope and Limits* (London: George Allen & Unwin). (References to the New York: Simon and Schuster 1976 edition).

Russell, Bertrand (1956), *Logic and Knowledge. Essays 1901–1950*, edited by Robert C. Marsh (London: George Allen & Unwin).

Russell, Bertrand (1959), *My Philosophical Development* (London: George Allen & Unwin). (References to the London: Unwin Books 1975 edition).

Schaffer, Jonathan (2007), "On What Grounds What" in Chalmers et al. (eds.) (2007).

Schilpp, Paul Arthur (ed.) (1946), *The Philosophy of Bertrand Russell* (Evanston: The Library of Living Philosophers).

Sellars, Wilfrid (1971), "Science, Sense Impressions, and Sensa: A Reply to Cornman" *The Review of Metaphysics* 24, 391–447.

Skrbina, David (2005), *Panpsychism in the West* (Cambridge: MIT Press).

Skrbina, David (2007), "Panpsychism" *Internet Encyclopedia of Philosophy*, edited by James Fieser and Bradley Dowden. Retrieved from http://www.iep.utm.edu/panpsych/.

Skrbina, David (ed.) (2009), *The Mind that Abides. Panpsychism in the New Millennium* (Amsterdam: John Benjamins).

Sprigge, T.L.S. (1998a). "Panpsychism" in E. Craig (Ed.), *Routledge Encyclopedia of Philosophy* (London: Routledge). Retrieved December 21, 2012, from http://www.rep.routledge.com/article/N079.

Stoljar, Daniel (2001), "Two Conceptions of the Physical," *Philosophy and Phenomenological Research* 62, 253–81.

Stoljar, Daniel (2006), *Ignorance and Imagination. The Epistemic Origin of the Problem of Consciousness* (Oxford: Oxford University Press).

Strawson, Galen (2006a), "Realistic Monism. Why Physicalism Entails Panpsychism" in Strawson et al. (2006c).

Strawson, Galen (2006b), "Panpsychism? Reply to Commentators with a Celebration of Descartes" in Strawson et al. (2006c).

Strawson, Galen et al. (2006c), *Consciousness and Its Place in Nature. Does Physicalism Entail Panpsychism?* (Exeter: Imprint Academic).

Stubenberg, Leopold (2005/2010), "Neutral Monism" in Edward Zalta (ed.) *Stanford Encyclopedia of Philosophy*. Retrieved from http://plato.stanford.edu/entries/neutral-monism/.

Stubenberg, Leopold (fc), "Neutral Monism vs. Panpsychism" in Brüntrup and Jaskolla (eds.) (fc.).

van Inwagen, Peter and Dean Zimmerman (eds.) (2007), *Persons: Human and Devine* (Oxford: Oxford University Press).

Votsis, Ioannis (2004), *The Epistemological Status of Scientific Theories: An Investigation of the Structural Realist Account.* Doctoral dissertation submitted to the London School of Economics. Available at http://www.votsis.org/dissertation.html.

Wishon, Donovan (2015), "Russell on Russellian Monism" in this volume.

6

Russell on Russellian Monism

Donovan Wishon

1. Introduction

In recent decades, Russell's "Neutral Monism" has reemerged as a topic of great scholarly interest among philosophers of mind, philosophers of science, and historians of early analytic philosophy. One of the most controversial points of scholarly dispute regarding Russell's theory concerns how it best fits into standard classificatory schemes for understanding the relationship between mental phenomena and physical reality. The question is: Is it a genuine form of neutral monism?[1] Is it species of panpsychism (or panexperientialism)?[2] Is it a property dualism or panprotopsychism? Is it a non-standard version of physicalism or materialism?[3] On one hand, it is hoped that the answer to this question will shed light on how best to understand, on its own terms, Russell's later philosophical writings. But it is also hoped that the answer will help the growing number of contemporary proponents of "Russellian Monism" better understand how their various versions of it are continuous with, or depart from, their historical point of origin.[4]

---

1. Proponents of this interpretation include Stubenberg (2005/2010, this volume) and Tully (1988, 2003).

2. Stubenberg (this volume) makes a persuasive case against such an interpretation.

3. Proponents of this interpretation include Bostock (2012), Feigl (1975), Landini (2011), Lockwood (1981), Maxwell (1978), and perhaps Stace (1944).

4. Alter and Nagasawa (this volume) and Stubenburg (this volume) rightly note that contemporary versions of Russellian Monism are not intended to be completely faithful to Russell's Neutral Monism.

In my view, the task of classifying Russell's Neutral Monism is made all the more difficult by the fact that his conception of it evolves in significant ways over the roughly four decades that he advocates it. In fact, I would contend that during this period, Russell holds (at least) *three* different, but related, ontological views, all of which he labels as "neutral monism." And though the boundaries between these three views are somewhat nebulous, there are key changes in Russell's thought that can help us tease them apart.

To see this, we must begin by considering key aspects of his early dualism which continue to play important roles in his Neutral Monism, especially his views about acquaintance, knowledge by description, structuralism about physics, and the construction of our physical knowledge. This will be the project of §2–3. In §4, I argue that Russell revises, rather than abandons, his notion of knowledge by acquaintance in 1918 (when he gives up the act-object distinction) and contend that his resulting "neutral monism" remains a partial dualism until his 1921 *The Analysis of Mind* (hereafter *AMi*). In §5, I explain how changes in physics leads Russell to re-conceptualize his Neutral Monism in *The Analysis of Matter* (hereafter *AMa*) and *An Outline of Philosophy* (hereafter *OOP*), while challenging the relatively widespread view that his new position is a nonstandard version of physicalism. In §6, however, I argue that after 1940, Russell's mature Neutral Monism—as presented in *Human Knowledge: Its Scope and Limits* (hereafter *HK*), *My Philosophical Development* (hereafter *MPD*), and elsewhere—is very plausibly interpreted as a version of "Russellian Physicalism."[5]

2. Russellian Dualism

Many commentators rightly note that Russell's adoption of Neutral Monism is a gradual affair. In the two decades following his 1898 post-idealist "revolt into pluralism" (alongside Moore), Russell is a self-avowed mind-body dualist (*MPD*, p. 54). His interests during much of this time are dominated by problems in the philosophy of mathematics and logic, especially regarding his "Contradiction" involving the class of all classes that are not members of themselves (p. 76). Nevertheless, starting in his 1905 "On Denoting" (hereafter *OD*) and continuing through his well-known works in the 1910s, Russell develops a sophisticated theory of knowledge resting on the fundamental notion of "knowledge by acquaintance."[6]

5. See Holman (2008), Montero (2010, this volume), Pereboom (2011, this volume), Stoljar (2001, 2006, this volume), and Strawson (1999) for some recent incarnations of Russellian Physicalism.

6. For a more thorough discussion of Russell's views on acquaintance and its role in thought and talk, see my "Russellian Acquaintance and Frege's Puzzle" (forthcoming).

At the heart of Russell's theory of knowledge is the distinction, drawn from the writings of William James (1885, 1890), between two logically distinct kinds of knowledge: *knowledge of things* and *knowledge of truths* (*POP*, p. 44).[7] Knowledge of things is a matter of a subject simply being *aware of* particulars and universals such that the subject is in a position to think and talk about them. In contrast, knowledge of truths is a matter of the subject having a "take" on the objects of his or her awareness, paradigmatically in the form of *judgments* about them. Whereas the latter can be evaluated in terms of truth or falsity, there is simply no sense to be made of the truth or falsity of the former—either the subject is aware of the relevant objects, or he or she isn't.[8]

For Russell, there are two ways a subject can be aware of things.[9] A subject can be *directly* aware of things, "without the intermediary of any process of inference or any knowledge of truths," by being presented with them in experience (*POP*, p. 46). Russell calls this kind of knowledge of things "knowledge by acquaintance." A subject can also be *indirectly* aware of things by description in cases where "in virtue of some general principle, the existence of a thing answering to this description can be inferred from the existence of something with which [the subject is] acquainted" (p. 45). Russell calls this kind of knowledge of things "knowledge by description." And unlike the case of knowledge by acquaintance, the possession of knowledge by description requires the antecedent possession of knowledge of truths about things known by acquaintance, including truths about general principles.[10]

---

7. James gets this distinction from John Grote's 1865 *Exploratio Philosophica*.

8. This is the *only* sense in which knowledge of things, by acquaintance or otherwise, is infallible. In Chapter XII of *POP*, Russell says, "Our knowledge of truths, unlike our knowledge of things, has an opposite, namely error. So far as things are concerned, we may know them or not know them, but there is no positive state of mind which can be described as erroneous knowledge of things, so long, at any rate, as we confine ourselves to knowledge by acquaintance. Whatever we are acquainted with must be something; we may draw wrong inferences from our acquaintance, but acquaintance itself cannot be deceptive" (p. 119). In Wishon (2012), I further contend that acquaintance does not provide subjects with discriminating knowledge, revelatory knowledge, fully-disclosing knowledge, or transparent knowledge of its objects.

9. Russell is not entirely consistent in his uses of the terms "acquaintance" and "knowledge of things," even within the same works. Sometimes he identifies them, but other times he treats acquaintance as one kind of knowledge of things, in which case he allows for the possibility of knowledge of things by description. Given that knowledge by description puts one in a position to think and talk about things, but doesn't all by itself assert that something is thus-and-so, I prefer the latter practice.

10. On page 46 of *POP*, he says, "knowledge of things, when it is of the kind we call knowledge by acquaintance, is essentially simpler than any knowledge of truths, and *logically independent* of knowledge of truths, though it would be rash to assume that human beings ever,

Both kinds of knowledge of things play crucial roles in Russell's theory of knowledge. Knowledge by acquaintance is the ultimate enabling condition for all thought and talk. Such direct conscious awareness of things puts a subject in a position to attend to them, to introduce *genuine names* for them, and to acquire knowledge of truths about them.[11] By exploiting this knowledge of truths about the objects of acquaintance, knowledge by description then enables the subject to extend thought and talk beyond the confines of his or her personal experience. Thus, knowledge by description is the crucial material that makes scientific (and everyday) knowledge of truths about the external world possible. But it all starts from knowledge by acquaintance (*POP*, p. 48).

From 1903 until 1918, Russell thinks it important, for a number of reasons, that acquaintance is a dual (mental) relation holding between distinct relata, where one constituent of the relational fact is the mental subject and the other is the object of acquaintance. First of all, he wishes to avoid "Brentano's view that in sensation there are three elements: act, content, and object" (*MPD*, p. 134).[12] For as he expresses in his famous 1904 "Letter to Frege," Russell worries that if our awareness of objects is mediated through contents (or *senses*), we never truly acquire empirical knowledge of the world outside the mind.[13] Second, he thinks that the act-object distinction in epistemic relations is needed to resist idealisms of various sorts, including those of Berkeley and the British Monistic Idealists.[14] And third, he maintains that without viewing acquaintance as a dual relation, we cannot produce an adequate analysis of various cognitive phenomena such as consciousness, belief, memory, and selectively based indexical and demonstrative thought.[15]

But despite great continuity in Russell's view of the nature and epistemic role of acquaintance during this period, his views about the *objects* of our

---

in fact, have acquaintance with things without at the same time knowing some truth about them. Knowledge of things by description, on the contrary, always involves . . . some knowledge of truths as its source and grounds." Emphasis added.

11. The meanings of "genuine names" are just their referents. For more on these issues, see Wishon (2012, forthcoming).

12. Elsewhere, Russell associates this view with Meinong and Frege. See Russell (1904b) and (1905).

13. See Russell (1904a). Also see *MPD*, p. 134.

14. See, for instance, Chapters IV and XIV of *POP*.

15. Incidentally, Russell cites this last set of considerations as his strongest grounds for rejecting James' Neutral Monism. See Russell (1992, pp. 30–32) and (1918/1998, p. 153). For more detailed discussion, see Tully (1988, 2003).

acquaintance are in a state of flux. In the early years after his break from British Monistic Idealism, Russell (like Moore) is a naïve realist who "rejoiced in the thought that grass is really green, in spite of the adverse opinion of all philosophers from Locke onwards" (*MPD*, pp. 61–62). However, by the time of his 1910 *Philosophical Essays* (hereafter *PE*), Russell places substantial restrictions on the objects of our acquaintance.[16] A number of philosophical arguments concerning perceptual experience, including the argument from qualitative variation, the argument from hallucinations/dreams, and the argument from science, convince Russell that the objects we are directly aware of in sensation are sense-data rather than the ones of ordinary commonsense.[17] Among the candidates for other particulars with which we can be directly aware of are introspectible mental phenomena (including acquaintance itself), remembered past sense-data and mental phenomena, and (perhaps) the self (*POP*, pp. 48–51). In addition, we can be acquainted with many universals, including general principles, through conceiving them (pp. 51–52 and Chapters VII–X).

Except in the case of introspectible mental phenomena and (perhaps) the self, the objects of our acquaintance are external to the mind, even in Russell's most restrictive periods. In his view, "the faculty of being acquainted with things other than itself is the main characteristic of a mind" and "acquaintance with objects essentially consists in a relation between the mind and something other than a mind" (*POP*, p. 42). This is important because "it is this that constitutes the mind's power of knowing things" (p. 42). So it is a mistake to see sense-data as any kind of psychological entity. Rather, sense-data are sensed "qualities," such as colors, shapes, textures, hardness, and so on, which are independent of the mind, but which cannot be strictly *proved* to exist when not sensed.[18] Nevertheless, based on a number of non-deductive inferences, we have good reason to think that they are at least *caused* by the objects of physics, and are therefore *signs* of them (p. 11). And by the time of his 1914 "The Relation of Sense-Data to Physics" (hereafter *RSDP*), Russell asserts that sense-data are literally physical in nature.[19]

---

16. Most commentators believe that such restrictions are already in place in 1905 in "On Denoting." See, for example, Proops (2011, forthcoming). However, I argue against the standard interpretation in Wishon (forthcoming). It is also questioned in Soames (2003) and Kripke (2005).

17. See *PE*, pp. 181–83, *POP*, Chapters I–IV, and "The Ultimate Constituents of Matter," pp. 126–27.

18. *POP*, pp. 9–11 and *Papers*, 6, pp. 135–36 and 185–86.

19. Russell leaves open the possibility that they are also mental, noting that this would be (partially) compatible with the neutral monism of James. That is, the very same qualities

3. From Sense-Data to Knowledge of the Physical World

Two of the most pressing concerns for Russell during his dualist phase (as afterwards) are (1) how we *derive* scientific knowledge from the immediate data of experience, and (2) how such scientific knowledge can be *verified* on the basis of experience. Regarding physics in particular, he is concerned with the question of how it is that we acquire knowledge of the existence of a material world beyond the confines of personal experience, as well as what we can legitimately infer about its nature. In general outline, his answer is that we acquire knowledge about the existence and nature of the material world by means of knowledge by description and non-demonstrative inference. Like *all* knowledge of truths, such knowledge about matter "is infected with *some* degree of doubt" (*POP*, p. 135).[20] But when it comes to the material world, our epistemic situation is even more precarious than this. For all we can know about it, through science or other means, is its *structure*.

Though this acceptance of structuralism about our physical knowledge is often associated solely with Russell's neutral monist phase, it is already in place in 1912 during his dualist phase. One reason for which he embraces structuralism is that he simply sees it as part of scientific practice (*POP*, pp. 27–28). But he also sees it as a consequence of our sensory acquaintance being restricted to sense-data *caused* by physical objects, together

---

that make up the physical world could, when grouped according to psychological laws, be literally part of a subject's mind as well. He says, "I propose to assert that sense-data are physical, while yet maintaining that they probably never persist unchanged after ceasing to be data ... If there were, as some have held, a logical impossibility in sense-data persisting after ceasing to be data, that certainly would tend to show that they were mental; but if, as I contend, their non-persistence is merely a probable inference from empirically ascertained causal laws, then it carries no such implication with it, and we are quite free to treat them as part of the subject-matter of physics" (*RSDP*, p. 112). Even still, Russell's view at this time is incompatible with James' neutral monism on a different front—for he still embraces a fundamental mental subject and an act-object distinction regarding the mental relation of acquaintance. Thanks to Leopold Stubenberg for helpful discussion of these issues.

20. Contrary to widespread misinterpretation, Russell is no Cartesian when it comes to epistemology. In point of fact, he is quite explicit that "a theory which ignored this fact [i.e. that all knowledge of truths has some degree of doubt] would be plainly wrong" (*POP*, p. 135). On his view, "philosophy should show us the hierarchy of our instinctive beliefs, beginning with those we hold most strongly ... [and] it should take care to show that, in the form in which they are finally set forth, our instinctive beliefs do not clash, but form a harmonious system ... [But] it is of course *possible* that all or any of our beliefs may be mistaken, and therefore *all* ought to be held with at least some degree of doubt" (p. 25). Emphasis added. See Proops (2014, forthcoming) and Wishon (2012, forthcoming).

with considerations of perceptual variation. From this, he infers that physical objects, which we know purely by description, plausibly differ in quality from the sense-data they cause. However, we do not know what the intrinsic natures of these qualities are. Indeed, he asserts, "we find that, although the relations to physical objects have all sorts of knowable properties, derived from their correspondence with the relations of sense-data, the physical objects themselves remain unknown in their intrinsic nature, so far at least as can be discovered by means of the senses" (p. 34).[21]

What's more, all *inferences* to the intrinsic nature of physical objects are tenuous. In *POP*, Russell notes that the most natural hypothesis is that the qualities of physical objects are "more or less like" sense-data such that "physical objects will, for example, really have colours, and we might, by good luck, see an object as of the colour it really is" (p. 35). However, he maintains that the argument from science shows us that we experience the same sense-data regardless of whether the physical object causing them has color, and so "it is quite gratuitous to suppose that physical objects have colours" (p. 35). In fact, Russell thinks that "if physical objects do have an independent existence, they must differ very widely from sense-data," and so "the truth about physical objects *must* be strange . . . [and] it *may* be unattainable" (pp. 37–38).

He does not long remain content to rest our knowledge of physical reality on tenuous non-demonstrative inferences, however. Starting in his unpublished 1912 "On Matter" (hereafter *OM*), and culminating in his 1914 *Our Knowledge of the External World* (hereafter *OKEW*), Russell begins to deploy his method of logical analysis to "construct" our *knowledge* of physics from a small store of knowledge of truths about sense-data and general principles, together with assumptions which have a relatively high degree of self-evidence.[22] His goal is

---

21. And in remarks long anticipating Frank Jackson's (1982) knowledge argument, he says "we can know all [and only] those things about physical space which a man born blind might know through other people about the space of sight; but the kind of things which a man born blind could never know about the space of sight we also cannot know about physical space. We can know the properties of the relations required to preserve the correspondence with sense-data, but we cannot know the nature of the terms between which the relations hold" (*POP*, p. 32).

22. Many Russell scholars will dispute one or both of my claims that his constructions were (a) epistemic in character, but (b) not aimed at answering the skeptic once and for all. I cannot hope to settle this issue here. Instead, I will simply point to the following remarks Russell makes in his 1922 "Physics and Perception" while clarifying his aims in *OKEW*: "I have never called myself a phenomenalist, but I have no doubt sometimes expressed myself as though this were my view. In fact, however, I am not a phenomenalist. For practical purposes, I accept the truth of physics, and depart from phenomenalism so far as may be necessary for upholding the truth of physics. I do not, of course, hold that physics is certainly true, but only that it has a better chance of being true than philosophy has. Having accepted the

to provide our body of physical knowledge with as firm a foundation as possible (short of certainty), just as he attempts to do in the case of constructing our body of mathematical knowledge out of that of logic. Thus, in the first instance, this constructive project is an epistemic one, rather than an ontological one.[23] If we are to draw metaphysical conclusions about the world our constructed physical theory describes, we must still rely on non-demonstrative inferences to do so.

One of the most important parts of Russell's construction of physics is the construction of our knowledge of matter from more (epistemically) basic physical phenomena. After coming to the view in 1914 that the sense-data we are acquainted with are literally physical, he sees them as the most obvious material from which to construct this knowledge (*RSDP*, p. 111).[24] And despite having an attraction to *methodological* solipsism, Russell thinks that the construction of matter requires assuming the existence of two further sorts of inferred entities: (1) the sense-data of other people, and (2) qualities differing significantly from sense-data only in that they happen to be un-sensed, which he calls *sensibilia* (pp. 116–17). He characterizes the latter as follows:

> We have not the means of ascertaining how things appear from places not surrounded by brain and nerves and sense-organs, because we cannot leave the body; but continuity makes it not unreasonable to suppose that they present *some* appearance at such places. Any such appearance would be included among *sensibilia*. If *per impossibile*—there were a complete human body with no mind inside it, all those *sensibilia* would exist, in relation to that body, which would be sense-data if there were a mind in the body. What the mind adds to *sensibilia*, in fact, is *merely* awareness: everything else is physical or physiological (*RSDP*, p. 111).

_____

truth of physics, I try to discover the minimum of assumptions required for its truth, and to come as near to phenomenalism as I can. But I do not in the least accept the phenomenalist philosophy as necessarily right, nor do I think that its supporters always realise what a radical destruction of ordinary beliefs it involves" (p. 480).

23. Russell compares his project to Peano's in arithmetic: it does not, all by itself, have straightforward ontological implications. For an insightful discussion of Russell's method, see Hager (2003). It is also worth noting that Russell deploys his version of Ockham's Razor—"Whenever possible, substitute constructions out of known entities for inferences to unknown entities"—primarily in the epistemological project of constructing physics (1924, p. 326). In metaphysical matters, he *often* relies heavily on ontological parsimony, but his inferences are frequently guided by competing principles. His arguments against metaphysical solipsism are notable examples.

24. He puts it even clearer a year later in "The Ultimate Constituents of Matter" when he says, "I believe that the actual data of sensation, the immediate objects of sight or hearing, are extra mental, purely physical, and among the ultimate constituents of matter" (p. 96).

Thus, like sense-data, un-sensed *sensibilia* (if they exist) are qualities that are literally part of physical reality.[25]

With such assumptions in place, Russell proposes that we treat the persisting material entities of physics as collections of appropriately related sense-data and *sensibilia*, at different locations and times, grouped together into "biographies" based largely on considerations of (presumed) continuity and causal-dynamical connectedness (*RSDP*, pp. 124–26).[26] And by generalizing this strategy, he takes it to be possible, at least in principle, to construct the description of the world provided by physics by means of functions from sense-data and qualities assumed to be similar in kind to them. Of course, we have no way of knowing with any assurance the *actual* intrinsic nature of the un-sensed portions of physical reality; but we at least have a picture of it that accords well with what we know about it through acquaintance and physical theory.

4. Russellian Neutral Monism

In 1918, Russell's views about the nature of acquaintance take a radical change, resulting eventually in equally radical changes to his views about the relationship between mind and matter (*MPD*, p. 134). In particular, for a number of reasons, he "became convinced that William James had been right in denying the relational character of sensations" (p. 134). For one thing, in his 1919 "On Propositions" (hereafter *OP*), he comes to the view that in experience, we are presented neither with a mental subject (which he questioned as early as 1911 in "Knowledge by Acquaintance and Knowledge by Description" and rejected in his unpublished 1913 *Theory of Knowledge*) nor with mental acts or relations. So we have no *empirical* reason for taking them to be fundamental constituents of the world.[27] For another, he ceases to think that a relational account

---

25. Regarding the coherence and plausibility of un-sensed *sensibilia*, Russell remarks, "it may be thought monstrous to maintain that a thing can present any appearance at all in a place where no sense organs and nervous structure exist through which it could appear. I myself do not feel the monstrosity; nevertheless I should regard these supposed appearances only in the light of a hypothetical scaffolding, to be used while the edifice of physics is being raised, though possibly capable of being removed as soon as the edifice is completed" (*RSDP*, p. 117).

26. For a more detailed discussion of Russell's construction of matter, see Stubenberg (this volume).

27. In *OP*, he says, "I have to confess that the theory which analyses a presentation into act and object no longer satisfies me. The act, or subject, is schematically convenient, but not empirically discoverable. It seems to serve the same sort of purpose as is served by points and instants, by numbers and particles and the rest of the apparatus of mathematics. All

of mental occurrences is required to explain the possibility of knowledge of the external world, resist idealism, or provide an adequate analysis of consciousness, belief, memory, and selectively based indexical and demonstrative thought. Hence we have no *theoretical* grounds for holding the view, either. Consequently, we no longer have any reason to think we know of the mental subject or acts even by description.

However, Russell does not abandon acquaintance altogether, contrary to prevailing interpretation.[28] Rather, following James' "Does 'Consciousness' Exist?" (this volume), he gives up the view that sensation is a relation between numerically distinct relata: a mental subject and physical sense-data. In its place, Russell adopts James' view that the (self-presenting) qualities we are aware of in sensation are literally *part* of both our minds and physical reality (*OP*, p. 306). As he later puts it in *AMi*, "the sensation that we have when we see a patch of colour simply is that patch of colour, an actual constituent of the physical world, and part of what physics is concerned with" (p. 142). But, he continues, "it does not follow that the patch of colour is not also psychical, unless we assume that the physical and the psychical cannot overlap, which I no longer consider a valid assumption. If we admit—as I think we should—that the patch of colour may be both physical and psychical, the reason for distinguishing the sense-datum from the sensation disappears" (*AMi*, p. 143).

By giving up the act-object distinction concerning sensation, Russell took his first and most important step towards embracing a James-inspired neutral monism. On his understanding, the core of James' view is that "the mental and the physical are not distinguished by the stuff of which they are made, but only by their causal laws" (*OP*, p. 299). In other words, the qualities of which we are directly aware in sensation are *intrinsically* neither mental nor physical (and hence "neutral"); they are made mental or physical (or both) by being part of causal processes that are either psychological or physical

---

these things have to be *constructed*, not postulated: they are not stuff of the world, but assemblages which it is convenient to be able to designate as if they were single things. The same seems to be true of the subject, and I am at a loss to discover any actual phenomenon which could be called an 'act' and could be regarded as a constituent of a presentation" (p. 305).

28. In *MPD*, he simply asserts that "such words as 'awareness', 'acquaintance', and 'experience' had to be re-defined" (p. 136). And later he says, "I have maintained a principle, *which still seems to me completely valid*, to the effect that, if we can understand what a sentence means, it must be composed entirely of words denoting things with which we are acquainted or definable in terms of such words" (p. 169). Emphasis added. In §6, we'll see that he makes crucial use of acquaintance in *HK*, for instance on page 245.

(or both).[29] Comparing matters to the dual classification systems of the old British Post Office Directory, Russell remarks that on this view, "a sensation may be grouped with a number of other occurrences by a memory-chain, in which case it becomes part of a mind; or it may be grouped with its causal antecedents, in which case it appears as part of the physical world" (*MPD*, p. 139).

One of the key upshots of James' neutral monism, in Russell's estimation, is that it allows us to dispense with the mental subjects as fundamental entities. On this view, mental subjects just are constructions composed of transitory neutral qualities organized in accordance with psychological laws so as to form the right kind of "perspectives" at particular times and "biographies" across time (*AMi*, p. 296). Thus, while there *are* mental subjects, they are constructed entities rather than fundamental ones. The latter are merely "logical fictions"—it is useful for certain purposes to feign as if there are such things, but there is no reason to assume "either that they exist or that they don't exist" (*OP*, p. 306).[30]

It is important to note that at the time of *OP*, Russell's commitment to this version of neutral monism is partial and provisional. While he agrees with James that what *essentially* distinguishes psychology from physics is not a matter of the "stuff" investigated but rather a matter of the causal laws studied, he is not yet ready to conclude that there is in fact only one kind of fundamental (neutral) stuff in the world (*OP*, p. 299).[31] On the contrary, he asserts that "when we come to consider the stuff of the two sciences, it would seem that there are some particulars which obey only physical laws (namely, unperceived material things), some which obey only psychological laws (namely, images, at least), and some which obey both (namely, sensations. Thus sensations will be both physical and mental, while images will be purely mental" (p. 299).

Moreover, it is not just that images are purely mental because they *happen* to be part of causal processes that are purely psychological (when they just as well could have been part of physical causal processes, were the world arranged differently).[32] Rather, given the state of psychology and physics at

---

29. For Russell, whether qualities are mental or physical is an extrinsic matter which in no way changes their intrinsic natures, just as an individual can become an uncle or aunt due to purely extrinsic circumstances.

30. He remarks that "the practical effect of this is the same as if we assumed that [fundamental mental selves] did not exist, but the theoretical attitude is different" (*OP*, p. 306). See Stubenberg (this volume) for more on Russell's views of the mental subject as a logical construction.

31. See Bostock (2012, pp. 174–76) for a more detailed interpretation along these lines.

32. I would like to thank Russell Wahl for pressing such a reading of the passages in *OP*.

the time, Russell is led to the conclusion that "it is impossible to escape the admission of images as something *radically distinct* from sensations, particularly as being *not amenable* to the laws of physics" (*OP*, p. 296).[33] Thus it is relatively clear that Russell still accepts dualism, at least provisionally, at the time of *OP*. But at the same time, he admits, "I do not pretend to know whether the distinction between [physical and psychological laws] is ultimate and irreducible. I say only that it is to be accepted practically in the present state of science" (p. 299).

In contrast, there is little question that Russell embraces a comprehensive version of Neutral Monism by the time of his 1921 *AMi*.[34] Though he provisionally suggests his earlier *OP* view of the relation between mind and matter at its outset, he asserts in the final chapter that in the course of investigation, "we found no way of defining images except through their causation; in their intrinsic character they appeared to have no universal mark by which they could be distinguished from sensations" (p. 287). On this new version of Neutral Monism, minds are logical constructions composed of transitory sensations and images, both of which are genuinely neutral qualities, grouped together in a single process of "mnemic causation" (*AMi*, p. 306).[35] Russell characterizes mnemic causation as a process in which the "proximate cause [of an event] consists not merely of a present event, but this together with a past event" (p. 85). As illustrations of "mnemic phenomena," he includes acquired habits, images "copied" from past sensations, psychological associations, non-sensational elements in perception, memories, and thoughts.

While Russell maintains that the characteristic of an event having both present and past events as its proximate cause is not wholly confined to living organisms, he insists that "in the case of dead matter, . . . such phenomena are less frequent and important than in the case of living organisms, and it is far less difficult to invent satisfactory hypotheses as to the microscopic changes in structure which mediate between the past occurrence and the present changed response" (*AMi*, p. 78).[36] Hence, paradigmatic mnemic phenomena are "those responses of an organism which, so far as hitherto observed facts

---

33. Emphasis added.

34. Though see Bostock (2012) and Landini (2011) for the opposing view.

35. These qualities are "genuinely neutral" because they, together with similar transitory qualities lying outside any mind, literally compose "matter" (a logical construction) when grouped in accordance with physical causal laws.

36. Giving an example of a mnemic phenomenon concerning "dead matter," he remarks, "magnetized steel looks just like steel which has not been magnetized, but its behavior is in some ways different" (*AMi*, p. 78).

are concerned, can only be brought under causal laws by including past occurrences in the history of the organism as part of the causes of the present
response" (p. 78). And, he adds, they are "usually of a kind that is biologically
advantageous to the organism" (p. 78).

In fact, Russell takes very seriously the possibility "that mnemic causation may be reducible to ordinary physical causation in nervous tissue" (*AMi*,
p. 303). At first glance, this lends some credibility to those that question
whether his Neutral Monism was really neutral, rather than a nonstandard
version of materialism.[37] In fact, Russell himself notes that his view is remi-
niscent of materialism when understood as "the view that all mental phenomena are causally dependent upon physical phenomena" (p. 303). And while
he "does not profess to know" whether mnemic causation is reducible in this
way, he concedes that "the bulk of the evidence points to the materialistic
answer as the more probable" (p. 303).

However, Russell soon afterward makes clear that his ontological view is
not one of materialism. On the contrary, he maintains, "an ultimate scientific
account of what goes on in the world, if it were ascertainable, would resemble
psychology rather than physics" and "such an account would not be content to
speak, even formally, as though matter, which is a logical fiction, were the ultimate reality" (*AMi*, pp. 305–06). In fact, he continues, "it is probable that the
whole science of mental occurrences, especially where its initial definitions are
concerned, could be simplified by the development of the fundamental unifying science in which the causal laws of particulars are sought, rather than the
causal laws of those systems of particulars that constitute the material units of
physics" (pp. 306–07). As we have seen, Russell takes the relevant particulars to
be transitory qualities that are intrinsically neither mental nor material, but that
compose both when grouped in appropriate ways. And if a fundamental science
of these neutral particulars could be developed, he argues, "[it] would cause
physics to become derivative, in the sort of way in which theories of the constitution of the atom make chemistry derivative from physics; it would also cause
psychology to appear less singular and isolated among sciences" (p. 307). So
by all appearances, Russell's Neutral Monism in *AMi* is unequivocally neutral.

5. The Analysis of Matter

In recent years, a number of commentators have alleged that by the time of
Russell's 1927 *AMa*, his views about Neutral Monism shift on at least three key

---

37. See Bostock (2012), Landini (2011), and Lockwood (1981).

issues which suggest, at least to them, that it is to be counted as a non-standard version of physicalism rather than as a true neutral monism.[38] First, they argue, developments in physical science move Russell to see "events," rather than transitory particulars, as the fundamental constituents of the world.[39] Second, they rightly note, he becomes increasingly inclined to think that psychological causation is in principle reducible to physical causation. And third, they maintain, he develops a causal theory of perception that some see as at odds with a genuinely *neutral* monism.[40] In my view, however, the textual evidence suggests that despite any changes, Russell's monism at the time of *AMa* is not yet a physicalist one.

The main project of *AMa* in many respects shares the general character of *OKEW*. As with the earlier work, Russell seeks to give a logical analysis of our physical knowledge such that the propositions of physics can be deduced or constructed from "a few simple hypotheses" about "entities forming part of the empirical world" (*AMa*, pp. 2–5). By doing so, he hopes to explain how our knowledge of physics can be derived from experience, as well as how experience can provide evidence for its truth. In addition, to put physics in as secure of a position as possible (short of certainty), he aims to "construct a metaphysic of matter which shall make the gulf between physics and perception as small, and the inferences involved in the causal theory of perception as little dubious, as possible" (p. 275).

Russell mentions several times in *AMi* that physics, under the influence of relativity theory, has moved towards an event ontology. However, to my knowledge, he doesn't make *explicit* his own endorsement of this view until his 1922 "Physics and Perception" (hereafter *PP*), after having completed a series of papers on relativity and the structure of the atom. In *PP*, Russell responds to challenges leveled by C. A. Strong (1922) against his accounts of perception in both *OKEW* and *AMi*, primarily by arguing that his disagreement with Strong actually concerns the nature of matter. He says, "the main purpose of this whole outlook is, in my view, to fit our perceptions into a physical

---

38. Bostock (2012), Landini (2011), Lockwood (1981), and Feigl (1975).

39. Note that Russell *doesn't* abandon his use of the expression 'particulars' to designate "the ultimate terms of the physical structure" of the world (*AMa*, p. 277). He does, however, shift its meaning. In its new use, Russell uses it to designate "something which is concerned in the physical world merely through its qualities or its relations to other things, never through its own structure, if any" (p. 277). He is quick to add that what counts as a 'particular' (in this new sense) is relative to the current state of our knowledge; once we discover that the "ultimate terms" of our physical theories have further structure, they cease to be particulars (pp. 277–78).

40. See Bostock (2012), pp. 190–96.

context, and to show how they might, with sufficient knowledge, become part of physics" (*PP*, p. 478). And part of this project, he argues, requires giving up outdated views about what physics says regarding the nature of matter, views which Strong mistakenly continues to accept.

According to modern physics, he continues, "a piece of matter . . . has two aspects, one gravitational, the other electromagnetic . . . Both these consist of a field, extending theoretically throughout space-time. The gravitational field consists in a certain distortion of space-time, making it everywhere more or less non-Euclidean, but particularly so in a certain neighbourhood, the neigh-bourhood in which we say the matter is" (*PP*, p. 478). Thus, he says, in reality, "what we call one element of matter—say an electron—is represented by a certain selection of things that happen throughout space-time" where "these occurrences are ordered in a four-dimensional continuum [each point of which contains] many such occurrences" (p. 479). However, the orderings of these occurrences can no longer be as simple as the cross-temporal "biographies" of collections of momentary particulars which appeared in *AMi*. This is because relativity theory shows us that "the time-order of events is to a certain extent arbitrary and dependent upon the reference-body" (p. 479). Nevertheless, he argues, "each piece of matter has . . . a 'proper time,' which is indicated by clocks that share its motion; from its own point of view, this proper time may be used to define its history" (p. 479). And as a consequence of all of this, "the objects which are mathematically primitive in physics, such as electrons, pro-tons, and points in space-time, are all logically complex structures composed of entities which are epistemically more primitive, which may be conveniently called 'events' " (*AMa*, p. 9).

Strictly speaking, Russell defines *events* as "entities or structures occu-pying a region of space-time which is small in all four dimensions" (*AMa*, p. 286). Such an event might have some internal structure, but if so, it "has no space-time structure, *i.e.* it does not have parts which are external to each other in space-time" (p. 286). They may, however, be "*compresent*" with (that is, overlap with) other events at a single space-time location (p. 294).[41] Less strictly speaking, "events" ("in the broad sense") have no maximal limit with respect to their duration or, presumably, their spatial extension. Nonetheless, he insists, any event which has such a space-time structure can "be analyzed into a structure of events" which do not (pp. 286–87).

On Russell's view, the only events with which we have any acquaintance are our own *percepts*—sensible qualities such as "patches of colour, noises, smells,

41. Putting things this way can be somewhat misleading, however, since space-time points are analyzed *in terms of* the compresence of events, rather than the other way around.

hardnesses, etc., as well as perceived spatial relations"—and other events in our conscious mental lives (*AMa*, p. 257). The role they play in his causal theory of perception resembles in different respects those of the "sensations" of *AMi* and the earlier "sense-data" of *POP* and *RSDP*. As in the case of the latter, percepts are signs of the external physical objects which cause them and to which we make unreflective "physiological inferences" (*AMa*, p. 190). But, as in the case of the former, there is no act-object distinction between percepts and our awareness of them. Thus, unlike sense-data, percepts are not external to the percipient. On the contrary, Russell insists that "whoever accepts the causal theory of perception is compelled to conclude that percepts are in our heads, for they come at the end of a causal chain of physical events leading, spatially, from the object to the brain of the percipient" (p. 320).

Largely based on such causal considerations, Russell draws the notorious conclusion that "what a physiologist sees when he examines a brain is in the physiologist, not in the brain he is examining" (*AMa*, p. 320). Simply put, his proposal is that perception, properly speaking, is a complex causal process that extends from physical objects in the percipient's environment to the occurrence of events in the percipient's brain, the intrinsic qualities of which are numerically identical to the sensible qualities we naively suppose to inhere in the external objects.[42] So returning to the physiologist, if we focus on the brain that is situated at the far end of the causal process, rather than the visual percept whose intrinsic qualities the physiologist is immediately aware of, we can find brain events that are literally thoughts or percepts of the other person. Indeed, Russell asserts, "what is in the brain by the time the physiologist examines it if it is dead, I do not profess to know; but while its owner was alive, parts, at least, of the contents of this brain consisted of his percepts, thoughts, and feelings" (p. 320).[43]

---

42. According to Alter and Nagasawa (this volume), it is this view "about knowledge and perception" which, together with structuralism about physics, lead Russell to his distinctive version of Russellian Monism.

43. Russell then continues to say, "since his brain also consisted of electrons, we are compelled to conclude that an electron is a grouping of events, and that, if the electron is in the human brain, some of the events composing it are likely to be some of the 'mental states' of the man to whom the brain belongs." Stubenberg reads Russell here as endorsing the view that electrons are made up of either whole percepts or (non-physical) parts of percepts. While he certainly entertains this as a possibility, Russell immediately afterwards suggests that electrons in the brain "are likely to be *parts* of such 'mental states'—for it must not be assumed that part of a mental state must be a mental state" (*AMa*, p. 320). Thus, I read Russell as allowing for the possibility that percepts are made up of electrons and other imperceptible physical events. In my opinion, this second reading also fits better with his earlier claim that "all our percepts are composed of imperceptible parts" as well as his use of phenomenal continua cases to resist the ontological monism of the British Idealists

In claiming that percepts are literally identical to brain events, the most straightforward way to read Russell here is as endorsing some version or other of a physicalist-type identity theory. And a number of additional remarks in *AMa* lend further credibility to such a reading. For instance, he quite plainly says that "percepts are the only part of the physical world that we know otherwise than abstractly" (p. 402). Elsewhere, he contends that "there is no good ground for excluding percepts from the physical world, but several strong reasons for including them. The difficulties that have been supposed to stand in the way seem to me to be entirely due to wrong views as to the physical world, and more particularly as to physical space" (pp. 384–85). And again, he insists, "percepts fit into the same causal scheme as physical events, and are not known to have any intrinsic character which physical events cannot have, since we do not know of any intrinsic character which could be incompatible with the logical properties that physics assigns to physical events. There is therefore no ground for the view that percepts cannot be physical events, or for supposing that they are never compresent with other physical events" (p. 384).

This final point—that we are ignorant of the intrinsic nature of all but that small corner of the physical world which constitutes our own conscious experience—is what crucially opens the door to Russellian Monisms of various sorts, as all of the contributors to this volume rightly note. As for the rest of physical reality, Russell once again asserts that physical science characterizes it solely in terms of its spatiotemporal and causal structure. As he vividly puts it, "the aim of physics, consciously or unconsciously, has always been to discover what we may call the causal skeleton of the world" (*AMa*, p. 391).[44] In fact, he insists, "as regards the world in general, both physical and mental, everything that we know of its intrinsic character is derived from the mental side, and almost everything that we know of its causal laws is derived from the physical side" (p. 402).

(pp. 280–82). For more on Russell's use of phenomenal continua cases to resist British Idealism as well as Wilfrid Sellars' 1965 "grain argument" against physicalism, see Wishon (2012, forthcoming). I thank Leopold Stubenberg for helpful discussion of these issues.

44. "It is perhaps surprising that there should be such a skeleton," he continues, "but physics seems to prove that there is, particularly when taken in conjunction with the evidence that percepts are determined by the physical character of their stimuli. There is reason—though not quite conclusive reason—for regarding physics as causally dominant, in the sense that, given the physical structure of the world, the qualities of its events, in so far as we are acquainted with them, can be inferred by means of correlations" (p. 391).

The importance consequence of these facts, Russell maintains, is that they do away with any grounds for supposing there to be a deep ontological gulf between the mental and the physical. In his opinion, philosophers have struggled to solve the mind-body problem largely because they have mistaken conceptions of both the nature of physical science and the world it describes. Indeed, he says:

> Both materialism and idealism have been guilty, unconsciously and in spite of explicit disavowals, of a confusion in their imaginative picture of matter. They have thought of the matter in the external world as being represented by their percepts when they see and touch, whereas these percepts are really part of the matter of the percipient's brain. By examining our percepts it is possible—so I have contended—to infer certain formal mathematical properties of external matter, though the inference is not demonstrative or certain. But by examining our percepts we obtain knowledge which is not purely formal as to the matter of our brains (*AMa*, p. 382).

What's more, he argues, once we recognize our mistaken conception of matter for what it is, we pave the way for a far more integrated picture of where the mind fits into reality. For instance, he maintains, "we no longer have to contend with what used to seem mysterious in the causal theory of perception: a series of light-waves or sound-waves or what not suddenly producing a mental event apparently totally different from themselves in character" (*AMa*, p. 400).[45] Indeed, he similarly remarks in *OOP*:

---

45. In *Religion and Science*, Russell further argues that the difference between conscious perception and non-conscious phenomena in the natural world is a genuinely vague matter. He says, "we say that we are 'conscious,' but that sticks and stones are not; we say that we are 'conscious' when awake but not when asleep. We certainly mean *something* when we say this, and we mean something that is true . . . When we say we are 'conscious,' we mean two things: on the one hand, that we react in a certain way to our environment; on the other, that we seem to find, on looking within, some quality in our thoughts and feelings which we do not find in inanimate objects . . . So long as it could be supposed that one 'perceives' things in the outer world, one could say that, in perception, one was 'conscious' of them. Now we can only say that we react to stimuli, and so do stones, though the stimuli to which they react are fewer. So far, therefore, as external 'perception' is concerned, the difference between us and a stone is only one of degree. The more important part of the notion of 'consciousness' is concerned with what we discover by introspection. We not only react to external objects, but know that we react . . . [But] to know that we see something is not really a new piece of knowledge, over and above the seeing, unless it is in memory . . . [However] memory is a form of habit, and habit is characteristic of nervous tissue, though it may occur elsewhere, for example in a roll of paper which rolls itself up again if it is unwound" (pp. 130–32). Recently, Brogaard (2010) has also argued, in a different context, that 'consciousness' is a vague term.

Having realized the abstractness of what physics has to say, we no longer have any difficulty in fitting the visual sensation into the causal series. It used to be thought "mysterious" that purely physical phenomena should end in something mental. That was because people thought they knew a lot about physical phenomena, and were sure they differed in quality from mental phenomena (p. 154).

But, he continues:

We now realize that we know nothing of the intrinsic quality of physical phenomena except when they happen to be sensations, and therefore there is no reason to be surprised that some are sensations, or to suppose that the others are totally unlike sensations. The gap between mind and matter has been filled in, partly by new views on mind, but much more by the realization that physics tells us nothing as to the intrinsic character of matter (p. 154).

In point of fact, he asserts, given that physical causal laws are plausibly more fundamental than psychological ones, "mind is merely a cross-section in a stream of physical causation, and there is nothing odd about its being both an effect and a cause in the physical world" (p. 156).

Putting together all of the changes in Russell's views after *AMi*, it is entirely unsurprising that many commentators have interpreted him as having abandoned a genuinely *neutral* monism by the time of *AMa*. However, there is good reason to be skeptical of these claims. Most importantly, in the closing paragraph of Chapter I he says:

To show that the traditional separation between physics and psychology, mind and matter, is not metaphysically defensible will be one of the purposes of this work; but the two will be brought together, not by subordinating either to the other, but by displaying each as a logical structure composed of what, following Dr. H. M. Sheffer, we shall call "neutral stuff." (*AMa*, p. 10)

In fact, Russell further contends in *OOP*, "in a completed science, the word 'mind' and the word 'matter' would both disappear, and would be replaced by causal laws concerning 'events', the only events known to us otherwise than in their mathematical and causal properties being percepts" (pp. 292–93). As a consequence, both psychology *and* physics would cease to be independent sciences. Instead, Russell argues, they would both be reducible to what he calls "chrono-geography," an imagined future science which he suggests "begins with events having space-time relations and does not assume at the outset that certain strings of them can be treated as persistent material units or as minds" (p. 294).

Shortly thereafter, in his 1935 *Religion and Science* (hereafter *RS*), Russell makes similar pronouncements. While he claims on one hand that "physics and chemistry are supreme throughout" the world, he insists on the other that "the distinction between what is mental and what is physical is only one of convenience" (p. 203). Indeed, he continues, "the technique of physics was developed under the influence of a belief in the metaphysical reality of 'matter' which now no longer exists, and the new quantum mechanics has a different technique which dispenses with false metaphysics" (p. 204). Likewise, he says, "the technique of psychology, to some extent, was developed under a belief in the metaphysical reality of the 'mind'" (p. 204). However, he suggests, "it seems possible that, when physics and psychology have both been completely freed from these lingering errors, they will both develop into one science dealing neither with mind nor matter, but with events, which will not be labeled either 'physical' or 'mental'" (p. 204). While there remains some room for interpretation, remarks such as these strongly suggest that Russell continues to embrace a genuine neutral monism well after the writing of *AMa*.

6. Towards Russellian Physicalism?

Thus far, I have made the case that Russell's Neutral Monism encompasses two related, but distinct, views about the relation between the mind and physical reality. First, according to the Neutral Monism of Russell's 1919 *OP*, there are particulars which are purely material, images which are purely mental, and sensations which are both mental and material—and hence genuinely neutral. Plausibly, this version of Neutral Monism is an ontological dualism in all but name. Second, according to the Neutral Monism of *AMi*, both minds and matter are composed from more fundamental constituents of the world—initially labeled "transitory particulars" and later "events"—which are intrinsically neither mental nor physical, but which become mental and/or physical in virtue of playing roles in psychological and/or physical causal processes. Arguably, this version of Neutral Monism is a genuine neutral monism, one which Russell seemingly embraced well after many commentators have alleged. In what follows, I will suggest that there are strong, though far from dispositive, grounds for thinking that Russell's Neutral Monism shifts again during the 1940s—this time seemingly into a version of Russellian Physicalism.[46]

To my knowledge, the first indication of this shift occurs in his 1944 "Reply to Criticisms" (hereafter *Reply*) in the *Library of Living Philosophers* volume on his work. In the course of clarifying and addressing challenges to his Neutral Monism of *AMi*, Russell notes two points on which his views have importantly changed. Firstly, he becomes increasingly confident that mnemic causation, which he previously regarded as the causal process which renders events psychological, is fully reducible to physiological causal processes in the brain.[47] (And there is no hint here, or in later work, that Russell continues to imagine physical causation to be reducible, in turn, to chrono-geography.) Secondly, and more importantly, he revealingly remarks that "I find myself in ontology increasingly materialistic, and in theory of knowledge increasingly subjectivistic" (*Reply*, p. 700).[48] Elaborating on this shortly thereafter, Russell says, "*I wish to distinguish sharply between ontology and epistemology*. In ontology I start by accepting the truth of physics; in epistemology I ask myself: Given the truth of physics, what can be meant by an organism having 'knowledge,' and what knowledge can it have?" (p. 700, emphasis added).

In my view, these remarks suggest a significant transition in how Russell conceives of the mind-body problem, especially when considered in light of what he says elsewhere in his later work. In particular, there is compelling evidence that he no longer views the distinction between the mind and physical reality to be in any sense *ontological* in character. It is not a matter of intrinsic differences between mental and physical phenomena or even between psychological or physical causal processes. For seemingly, on his new view all

---

46. I won't here address the question of whether Russellian Physicalism genuinely counts as a version of physicalism. While I am inclined to think some versions do, making such a case is a project for another occasion.

47. He says, "As regards 'mnemic causation, I agree with Mr. [John] Laird that the hypothesis of causes acting at a distance is too violent, and I should therefore now explain habits by means of modifications of brain structure" (*Reply*, p. 700).

48. We must be careful not to conclude that Russell is here endorsing run-of-the-mill *materialism*. For he continues to repudiate it as late as 1959 in a letter to the editor originally published in *Encounter* in which he says, "I do not, in fact, think that either mind or matter is part of the stuff of the world. I think that minds and bits of matter are convenient aggregations, like cricket clubs or football clubs" (*Yours Faithfully*, p. 292). Rather, I suspect, the view to which he is increasingly attracted is what Maxwell (this volume) later calls "nonmaterialist physicalism," one according to which both matter and minds are constructed from physical events. My thanks to Russell Wahl for bringing this letter to my attention.

events and causal processes are fundamentally physical in nature.[49] Instead, the real root of the mind-body problem is *epistemic* in character; it is the result of the radical differences in the kinds of knowledge we have of the events which make up physical reality. Further evidence for this interpretation occurs a few pages later when he remarks, "beyond certain very abstract mathematical properties physics can tell us nothing about the character of the physical world. *But there is one part of the physical world which we know otherwise than through physics,* namely that part in which our thoughts and feelings are situated. These thoughts and feelings, therefore, are members of the atoms (or minimal material constituents) of our brains" (*Reply*, p. 706, emphasis added).

By the time of his 1948 *HK*, his last systematic foray into issues of epistemology and metaphysics, Russell makes his change in view even more explicit. There he reports, "my own belief is that the 'mental' and the 'physical' are not so disparate as is generally thought. I should define a 'mental' occurrence as one which some one knows otherwise than by inference; the distinction between 'mental' and 'physical' therefore belongs to theory of knowledge, not to metaphysics" (*HK*, p. 224). And not long afterwards he says,

> What, then, do we know about the physical world? Let us first define more exactly what we mean by a 'physical' event. I should define it as an event which, if known to occur, is inferred and which is not known to be mental. And I define a 'mental' event (to repeat) as one with which some one is acquainted otherwise than by inference. Thus a 'physical' event is one which is either totally unknown, or, if known at all, is not known to any one except by inference—or, perhaps we should say, is not known to be known to any one except by inference (p. 245).

On a straightforward reading of these remarks, mental phenomena are not distinguishable by any ontological feature they possess, but rather by the fact that a subject is *acquainted* with them (in the post-*OP* non-relational sense). In contrast, physical phenomena will include all of the events describable, in causal and structural terms, by physics. Hence, if it turns out that the events describable by physics include all of those with which conscious subjects are acquainted, mental events will turn out to be a subclass of the physical events that make up reality.

And there is compelling evidence that Russell thinks that mental events *are* indeed identical to events in the brain regarding which, with respect to

---

49. Consequently, there is more to physical reality than we might naively suppose.

their causal and structural features, physics can in principle provide a full *descriptive* characterization.[50] As noted earlier, by the time of *Reply*, he already sees psychological causal processes as fully reducible to physiological causal processes in the brain. And in *HK*, he goes further in maintaining that physiological causal processes are in all probability fully reducible most immediately to chemical causal processes, and ultimately to macro-level physical processes. In fact, he contends, "there is no reason to suppose living matter subject to any laws other than those to which inanimate matter is subject, and considerable reason to think that everything in the behavior of living matter is theoretically explicable in terms of physics and chemistry" (*HK*, p. 50). And concerning physiological causal processes in the brain in particular, he says, "on the evidence as it exists the most probable hypothesis is that, in the chain of events from sense-organ to muscle, everything is determined by the laws of macroscopic physics" (p. 56). Thus, it is relatively clear at this point that Russell thinks that mental events just are physical events in the brain with which a subject is acquainted. In any case, this is precisely the view that he unequivocally affirms in his 1958 review of Gilbert Ryle's *The Concept of Mind*:

> My own belief is that the distinction between what is mental and what is physical does not lie in any intrinsic character of either, but in the way in which we acquire knowledge of them. I should call an event 'mental' if it is one that somebody can notice or, as Professor Ryle would say, observe. *I should regard all events as physical*, but I should regard as only physical those which no one knows except by inference ("What is Mind?" p. 12, emphasis added).

One important consequence of the change in Russell's conception of Neutral Monism is that its neutrality becomes entirely *epistemic* character. For as he continues to emphasize, given our epistemic limitations we cannot rule out any number of competing hypotheses about the intrinsic nature of the events described by physics with which we lack acquaintance. In fact, he maintains, "the qualities that compose such events are unknown—so completely unknown that we cannot say either that they are, or that they are not, different

---

50. Of course, on Russell's view physical events have intrinsic natures which elude these descriptions. It is an open question whether he would conceive of these intrinsic natures as *additional aspects* of physical events, or whether the descriptions simply cannot capture all there is to one and the same aspects.

from the qualities that we know as belonging to mental events" (p. 247). And in *MPD*, he puts matters even more forcefully:

> It is not always realized how exceedingly abstract is the information that theoretical physics has to give. It lays down certain fundamental equations which enable it to deal with the logical structure of events, while leaving it completely unknown what is the intrinsic character of the events that have the structure. We only know the intrinsic character of events when they happen to us. Nothing whatever in theoretical physics enables us to say anything about the intrinsic character of events elsewhere. They may be just like events that happen to us, or they may be totally different in strictly unimaginable ways (*MPD*, p. 18).

But while Russell grants, and even insists, that we cannot have *conclusive* grounds for rejecting panpsychism, idealism, or even dualism for that matter, he takes there to be non-demonstrative inferences which lend greater credibility to the hypothesis that extra-mental events in physical reality differ *somewhat* in intrinsic character from those with which we are acquainted. Indeed, he contends, "when we come to events in parts of physical space-time where there are no brains, we have still no positive argument to prove that they are not thoughts, *except such as may be derived from observation of the differences between living and dead matter coupled with inferences based on analogy or its absence*" (*HK*, p. 246, emphasis added). So we needn't be forced to embrace idealism or panpsychism.

On the other hand, Russell denies that the differences in the intrinsic character of events with which we are and are not acquainted suffice to open an ontological chasm between them. Quite the contrary, he says, "there is supposed to be a gulf between mind and matter, and a mystery which it is held in some degree impious to dissipate. I believe, for my part, that there is no greater mystery than there is in the transformation by the radio of electro-magnetic waves into sounds [i.e. sound-waves]. I think the mystery is produced by a wrong conception of the physical world and by a Manichaean fear of degrading the mental world to the level of the supposedly inferior world of matter" (*MPD*, pp. 21–22).[51] Thus, by all appearances, what Russell leaves us with is a Neutral Monism with a greater affinity to Russellian Physicalism than any

---

51. Russell makes clear that instead of "sounds" he should have said "sound-waves" in his aforementioned 1959 letter to the editor in *Encounter*.

genuinely *neutral* monism, including his own previously held versions.[52] And if so, then he is not best seen as a proponent of neutral monism—he is best seen as a proponent, at different times, of *three different* Neutral Monisms: one an ontological dualism, one a genuine neutral monism, and one a Russellian Physicalism.

---

52. The strongest objection to this reading is that it is seemingly in tension with several remarks Russell makes in his "Mind and Matter," which was published in his 1956 *Portraits from Memory*. For instance, in the penultimate paragraph he says, "a piece of matter is a group of events connected by causal laws, namely the causal laws of physics. A mind is a group of events connected by causal laws, namely, the causal laws of psychology. An event is not rendered either mental or material by an intrinsic quality, but only by its causal relations" (p. 164). And elsewhere in "Mind and Matter," he remarks, "I do not think it can be laid down absolutely, if the above is right, that there can be no such thing as disembodied mind. There would be disembodied mind if there were groups of events connected according to the laws of psychology, but not according to the laws of physics. We readily believe that dead matter consists of groups of events arranged according to the laws of physics, but not according to the laws of psychology. And there seems no a priori reason why the opposite should not occur" (p. 160). Together, these passages strongly suggest that Russell is still a genuine neutral monist well into the 1950s.

However, there are a number of reasons why drawing this conclusion would be hasty. First, it is worth noting that Russell originally presented "Mind and Matter" in lectures in 1950 and it is not inconceivable that the shift in his thinking that started in 1948 hadn't yet reached full completion only two years later. Second, immediately after noting the a priori *possibility* of a disembodied mind, Russell insists that "we have no empirical evidence of it" (p. 160) and we have already seen that he thinks that the empirical evidence suggests that psychological causal processes are ultimately reducible to physical causal processes. It is perfectly consistent for Russell to think that there are only physical events and physical processes in the world while granting that we cannot a priori rule out the possibility of disembodied minds. Indeed, given his actual views about knowledge by acquaintance and knowledge by description, I think Russell is plausibly read as what we might call an "*a posteriori* Russellian Physicalist" (see Alter and Howell, this volume). (It is worth noting that some functionalists would also hold the a priori possibility of disembodied minds to be perfectly compatible with the actual world being entirely physical, though Russell obviously predated any such view.) Third, as noted in footnote 48 above, we must be careful not to conflate something's being physical with its being material. Russell clearly thinks that *matter* is constructed from more basic elements, but it doesn't follow that these events are *non-physical*. On the contrary, there are many places in his later work where he seems quite sensitive to the distinction. Thus, all things considered, I think that there is a stronger case that the later Russell is best interpreted as a Russellian Physicalist, though I grant that there might be alternative ways of interpreting him along the lines of his earlier neutral monism. But any such interpretation would have to address the passages I have noted here which strongly suggest otherwise. My thanks to Leopold Stubenberg for helpful discussion of these issues.

Acknowledgments

For helpful comments and feedback, I would like to thank Torin Alter, Heath Hamilton, Bernard Linksy, Leopold Stubenberg, Russell Wahl, and the students in my 2013 graduate seminar on Bertrand Russell at the University of Mississippi.

References

Alter, T. and R. Howell. (this volume). The Short Slide from A Posteriori Physicalism to Russellian Monism.

Alter, T. and Y. Nagasawa. (this volume). What Is Russellian Monism?

Bostock, D. (2012). *Russell's Logical Atomism*. New York: Oxford University Press.

Brogaard, B. (2010). Degrees of Consciousness. Presented at SPAWN Conference on Metaphysics, Syracuse University, July 24–28.

Feigl, H. (1975). Russell and Schlick: A Remarkable Agreement on a Monistic Solution to the Mind-Body Problem. *Erkenntniss*, 9, 11–34.

Grote, J. (1865). *Exploratio Philosophica: Rough Notes on Modern Intellectual Science*, Part 1. Cambridge: Deighton Bell.

Hager, P. (2003). Russell's Method of Analysis. (In *The Cambridge Companion to Bertrand Russell*, edited by N. Griffen, 310–31. Cambridge: Cambridge University Press.)

Holman, E. (2008). Panpsychism, Physicalism, Neutral Monism and the Russellian Theory of Mind. *Journal of Consciousness Studies*, 15, No. 5, 48–67.

Jackson, F. (1982). Epiphenomenal Qualia. *Philosophical Quarterly*, 32, 127–36.

James, W. (1885). The Function of Cognition. *Mind*, 10, No. 37, 27–44.

———. (1890/1950). *The Principles of Psychology*, Vol. 1. New York: Dover.

———. (1904). Does "Consciousness" Exist? *Journal of Philosophy, Psychology, and Scientific Methods*, 1, 477–91.

Kripke, S. (2005). Russell's Notion of Scope. *Mind*, 114, 1005–37.

Landini, G. (2011). *Russell*. New York: Routledge.

Lockwood, M. (1981). What Was Russell's Neutral Monism? *Midwest Studies in Philosophy*, 6, No. 1, 143–58.

Maxwell, G. (1978/this volume). Rigid Designators and Mind-Brain Identity.

Montero, B. (2010). A Russellian Response to the Structural Argument against Physicalism. *Journal of Consciousness Studies*, 17, No. 3–4, 70–83.

———. (this volume). Russellian Physicalism.

Pereboom, D. (2011). *Consciousness and the Prospects of Physicalism*. New York: Oxford University Press.

———. (this volume). Consciousness, Physicalism, and Absolutely Intrinsic Properties.

Proops, I. (2011). Russell on Substitutivity and the Abandonment of Propositions. *The Philosophical Review*, 120, No. 2, 151–205.

————. (2014). Russellian Acquaintance Revisited. *Journal of the History of Philosophy*, 52, No. 4, 779–811.

————. (Forthcoming). Certainty, Error, and Acquaintance in *The Problems of Philosophy*. (In *Acquaintance, Knowledge and Logic: New Essays on Bertrand Russell's The Problems of Philosophy*, edited by B. Linsky and D. Wishon. Stanford, CA: CSLI Publications.)

Russell, B. (1904a). Letter to Frege. (In G. Frege, *Philosophical and Mathematical Correspondence*, 1980, 166–70. Chicago: University of Chicago Press.)

————. (1904b). Meinong's Theory of Complexes and Assumptions. *Mind*, 13, 204–19.

————. (1905). On Denoting. *Mind*, 14, 479–93.

————. (1910). *Philosophical Essays*. New York: Longmans, Green, and Company.

————. (1912/1997). *The Problems of Philosophy*. New York: Oxford University Press.

————. (Unpublished 1912). On Matter. (In *The Collected Papers of Bertrand Russell*. Vol. 6, *Logical and Philosophical Papers, 1909–13*, edited by J. G. Slater with the assistance of B. Frohmann. London: Routledge, 1992.)

————. (1914). *Our Knowledge of the External World*. Chicago: Open Court.

————. (1914). The Relation of Sense-Data to Physics. (In *Mysticism and Logic*. 1929. New York: W. W. Norton.)

————. (1915). The Ultimate Constituents of Matter. (In *Mysticism and Logic*. 1929. New York: W. W. Norton.)

————. (1918/1985). *The Philosophy of Logical Atomism*. Chicago: Open Court.

————. (1919). On Propositions. (Reprinted in *Logic and Knowledge: Essays 1901–1950*, edited by R. Marsh, 285–320. 1956. London: George Allen and Unwin.)

————. (1921). *The Analysis of Mind*. London: George Allen and Unwin.

————. (1922). Physics and Perception. *Mind*, 31, 124, 478–85.

————. (1924). Logical Atomism. (Reprinted in *Logic and Knowledge: Essays 1901–1950*, edited by R. Marsh, 323–43. 1956. London: George Allen and Unwin.)

————. (1925) Mind and Matter. (In *Portraits from Memory and Other Essays*. 1956. New York: Simon and Schuster.)

————. (1927/1954). *The Analysis of Matter*. New York: Dover Publications.

————. (1927). *An Outline of Philosophy*. London: George Allen and Unwin.

————. (1935/1997). *Religion and Science*. New York: Oxford University Press.

————. (1944). Reply to Criticisms. (In *The Philosophy of Bertrand Russell*, edited by P. A. Schlipp, 681–741. Chicago: Northwestern University Press.)

————. (1948/1992). *Human Knowledge: Its Scope and Limits*. London: Routledge.

————. (1958). What Is Mind? *The Journal of Philosophy*, 55, 1, 5–12.

————. (1959). *My Philosophical Development*. New York: Simon and Schuster.

————. (1959). A Reply by Bertrand Russell. (Reprinted in *Yours Faithfully, Bertrand Russell: A Lifelong Fight for Peace, Justice, and Truth in Letters to the Editor*, edited by R. Perkins, Jr. 2002. Peru, IL: Open Court.)

————. (1992). *Theory of Knowledge: The 1913 Manuscript*. New York: Routledge.

Sellars, W. (1965). The Identity Approach to the Mind-Body Problem. *Review of Metaphysics*, 18, 430–51.

Soames, S. (2003). *Philosophical Analysis in the Twentieth Century*, Vol. 1. Princeton: Princeton University Press.

Stace, W. T. (1944). Russell's Neutral Monism. (In *The Philosophy of Bertrand Russell*, edited by P. A. Schlipp, 351–84. Chicago: Northwestern University Press.)

Stoljar, D. (2001). Two Conceptions of the Physical. *Philosophy and Phenomenological Research*, 62, 253–81.

———. (2006). *Ignorance and Imagination: The Epistemic Origin of the Problem of Consciousness*. New York: Oxford University Press.

———. (this volume). Russellian Monism or Nagelian Monism?

Strawson, G. (1999). Realistic Materialist Monism. (In *Towards a Science of Consciousness III*, edited by S. Hameroff, A. Kaszniak & D. Chalmers, 23–32. Cambridge, MA: MIT.)

———. (this volume). Realistic Monism: Why Physicalism Entails Panpsychism.

Strong, C. A. (1922). Mr. Russell's Theory of the External World. *Mind*, 31, 123, 307–20.

Stubenberg, L. (2005/2010). Neutral Monism. *The Stanford Encyclopedia of Philosophy*, Spring 2010 Edition. http://plato.stanford.edu/archives/spr2010/entries/neutral-monism/.

———. (this volume). Russell, Russellian Monism, and Panpsychism.

Tully, R. (1988). Russell's Neutral Monism. *Russell*, 8, 209–24.

———. (2003). Russell's Neutral Monism. (In *The Cambridge Companion to Bertrand Russell*, edited by N. Griffen, 332–70. Cambridge: Cambridge University Press.)

Wishon, D. (2012). *Russellian Acquaintance and Phenomenal Concepts*. PhD Dissertation, Stanford University.

———. (forthcoming). Russellian Acquaintance and Frege's Puzzle. *Mind*.

PART III

Modern Classics and Recent Works

7

Rigid Designators and Mind–Brain Identity (excerpt)

Grover Maxwell

A KIND OF mind–brain identity theory that is immune to recent objections by Kripke (1971 and 1972)[1] is outlined and defended in this chapter. For reasons, the details of which will be given later, I have characterized the view as a *nonmaterialist physicalism*. It is nonmaterialist in that it does not attempt to eliminate or in any way deemphasize the importance of the "truly mental." On the contrary, it accords central roles to *consciousness*, "private experience," subjectivity, "raw feels," "what it's like to be something,"[2] thoughts, pains, feelings, emotions, etc., as we live through them in all of their qualitative richness. The theory also claims, however, that all of these genuinely mental entities are also genuinely physical, from which it follows that some genuinely physical entities are genuinely mental. This should occasion no shock, for it is a consequence of any authentic mental–physical identity thesis. Of course, some call themselves identity theorists and, at the same time, deny the existence of the genuinely mental (in my sense); but the result of this is always some kind of physical–physical identity thesis rather than a genuine mental–physical identity claim. One of the main reasons that Kripke's arguments do not hold against this theory is that it incorporates a significant revision of our basic beliefs about the nature of "the physical."

This research was supported in part by the National Science Foundation and the Minnesota Center for Philosophy of Science of the University of Minnesota.

1. In subsequent references to Kripke, page numbers refer to his 1972 essay.

2. Cf. Thomas Nagel, 1974.

The revision, however, is by no means ad hoc. It is virtually forced upon us, quite independently of Kripke's argument—indeed, quite apart from the mind–brain issue—by contemporary physics, physiology, neuropsychology, and psychophysiology. It will turn out that Kripke's arguments *do* reveal, in a novel and cogent manner, the inadequacies of materialism. At the same time they provide valuable considerations that can be used to bolster the case for nonmaterialist physicalism.

All of this will become more clear later, I hope, when more detail is given. But, even at this point, perhaps I should attempt a crude and somewhat inaccurate characterization of "the physical." *The physical* is, very roughly, the subject matter of physics. By 'subject matter' I mean *not* the *theories, laws, principles,* etc., of physics, but rather what the theories and laws are about. *The physical* thus includes tables, stars, human bodies and brains, and whatever the constituents of these may be. The crucial contention is that contemporary science gives us good reason to suppose that these constituents are quite different from what common sense *and* traditional materialism believe them to be. While "the dematerialization of matter" has perhaps been overplayed in some quarters, its advocates do make an important point (see, e.g., Hanson, 1962 and Feigl, 1962); and this point is crucial for the mind–body problem. A nonmaterialist physicalism is one that rejects those erroneous prescientific beliefs about physical entities that I shall argue are endemic to common sense and are carried over, to a great extent, into traditional *and* contemporary materialism. The elimination of these beliefs clears the way for a mind–brain identity theory that avoids the antimentalist reductionism of materialism, behaviorism, and similar views. (No contempt of common sense is involved here at all. Science, at best, is modified and improved common sense. Often the improvement is minimal; but, if it is genuine, surely it ought to be preferred to the unimproved version.)

Before considering Kripke's argument against mind–brain identity, I should remark that I am assuming that his ("quasi-technical") system of "rigid designation," "reference-fixing," etc., is a viable system. This is not to assume that it provides, necessarily, an account that is in perfect accord with our customary modes of conceptualization, inference, ascription of necessity, etc. Kripke, I think, intends and believes that it does, but many disagree. This explains, no doubt, why they feel that some of his conclusions are wrong or at best highly counterintuitive or based on eccentric terminology. Be this as it may, I believe that his terminology is clear and consistent and that his system provides, if not an "analysis," at least a tenable alternative "reconstruction" of conceptualization, reasoning, etc., both in everyday and in scientific contexts. (I am *not* so sure about his *essentialism.* However, for the sake of argument—that is, for the purpose of defending the identity thesis against his objections—I shall accept his essentialism insofar as I am able to understand it.)

Let me now introduce the elements of Kripke's system that are needed for the argument in question. A *rigid designator* is a symbol the referent of which remains the same in our discourse about all possible worlds *provided two conditions obtain*. The first is the rather trivial one that the language must remain the same. Obviously if we change the meaning or the conventional (*or* stipulated) use of a term, its referent will not necessarily remain constant. The second condition is that the referent exist in the possible world in question, and this condition will, of course, fail to obtain in many possible worlds. Another way of stating the matter is to say that the referent of a rigid designator either remains constant or becomes null as our discourse ranges over different possible worlds. Proper names are, for Kripke, paradigm examples of rigid designators. As long as the term 'Richard Nixon' has its standard and established role in our language, it refers to the same entity, namely Nixon, no matter what possible world we may be talking about, *unless*, of course, we happen to be talking about a possible world in which Nixon does not exist. (Instead of using the "possible worlds" terminology, we could say that a rigid designator has the same referent in every occurrence no matter whether the statement in which it occurs is about an actual or a counterfactual state of affairs.) The most common instances of nonrigid or "accidental" designators are descriptive phrases. To use an example of Kripke, the phrase 'the inventor of bifocals' refers to Benjamin Franklin; but obviously the phrase is not a rigid designator. There are many possible worlds in which bifocals were invented by someone else—or we can easily imagine counterfactual situations such that bifocals were invented, say, by Thomas Paine. In discourse about the latter situation the referent of the phrase 'the inventor of bifocals' would be Thomas Paine instead of Benjamin Franklin.

We come now to a crucial juncture in Kripke's system. In attempting to make it as clear as possible, I shall use an example of different form and somewhat simpler than those employed by Kripke. Suppose we are convinced that one and only one man invented the incandescent electric light bulb but that we do not know who he was. Nevertheless, suppose that we stipulate that the term 'Oscar' is to be used to *rigidly designate* this so far unidentified inventor. What does this mean? It means that 'Oscar' always refers to the man who invented, as a contingent matter of fact in this the actual world, the incandescent bulb. And this referential relation holds whether or not our discourse is about the actual world or about other possible worlds—whether it is about actual or counterfactual states of affairs. There are, of course, many possible worlds in which Oscar did not invent the bulb, worlds in which someone else invented it or in which it was not invented at all. This is just to say that there are possible worlds in which the bulb was not invented by the man who actually did invent it (in this, the actual world—to be redundant). Nevertheless, in our discourse about these worlds 'Oscar' still refers to the same man—the man who invented the bulb in this, the actual world . . . .

Before proceeding to the mind–brain identity thesis, it will be helpful to continue examination of the "Oscar" example in order to understand better Kripke's views about identity in general. Suppose that, after fixing the referent of 'Oscar' as we did above, we make the (contingent) discovery that Thomas A. Edison invented the incandescent electric light bulb. It follows, obviously, that Oscar and Edison are identical—that "they" are one and the same person. It also follows, given the Kripkean system, that Edison and Oscar are *necessarily* identical. This follows simply because both 'Oscar' and 'Thomas A. Edison' are rigid designators. This means that 'Oscar' *always* refers to the same man and that, of course, the referent of 'Thomas A. Edison' *always* remains constant, whether our discourse is about the actual world (or about actual situations) or about any other possible world or any counterfactual situation. It follows that, if Edison and Oscar are identical in any possible world (including the actual world, of course), then "they" are identical in all possible worlds (in all actual and counterfactual situations). Therefore, "They" are *necessarily* identical, since something holds *necessarily* if and only if it holds in all possible worlds—in all actual and counterfactual situations. . . .

This is a good point at which to give a somewhat truncated but forceful sketch of Kripke's argument against the mind–brain identity thesis. The sketch follows:

> (1) There seems to be *no way* for a brain state (or brain event) to be *necessarily* identical with a mental state (or a mental event). So, (1′) if mind–brain identities exist, they are contingent identities. But (as we have seen above) (2) there *are no* contingent identities. Therefore, there are no mind–brain identities.

Obviously the argument is valid; if we are to reject the conclusion, we must reject at least one premise. Many—probably most—mind–brain identity theorists accept the first premise. Indeed, they emphasize and insist that mental-physical identities are contingent identities. They then proceed, either explicitly or tacitly, to reject premise (2). Needless to say, I accept (2) and shall argue that (1) and therefore (1′) are false.

Kripke emphasizes that this is just what the identity theorist *must* do if he is to retain any hope of rejecting the argument's conclusion. He then argues at some length that the first premise seems quite invulnerable. I shall argue that the first premise is false.

Kripke notes and indeed emphasizes that his apparatus provides what might seem to offer an escape route for the identity theorist, and we have already touched upon the matter earlier. If we could show that the apparent truth of premise (1) is due entirely to an *illusion of contingency*, we would have produced conclusive grounds for rejecting the premise. In order to do this we would need to indicate how there could be a *contingent associated fact* that is responsible for this "illusion of contingency." Kripke argues that the existence of such a fact seems out of the question. Before examining these arguments, it will be helpful to continue our discussion of identity and necessity. . . .

Returning now to the mind–brain identity thesis, consider a claim that, say, a certain *determinate* kind of pain, call it 'pain39,' is identical with a certain *determinate* kind of brain state $b76$.[3] Rather than speaking of *states*, it is much better, I believe, to (attempt to) identify mental *events* with physical *events*. So let us change the matter a little and take 'pain39' to refer to the *occurrence* of a certain determinate kind of pain and let '$b76$' refer to a certain determinate kind of brain event. (This is actually more in line with Kripke's main example. In it, the physical entity is C-fiber stimulation, which is a process or an event.) Let us suppose further that '$b76$' is the genuine rigid designator for the relevant physical event that Kripke suggests we use just in case 'C-fiber stimulation' is not a rigid designator.

Now, since 'pain39' and '$b76$' are both rigid designators, it follows that, if pain39 and $b76$ are identical, they are necessarily identical. So, if the identity does hold, there must be some contingent associated fact involved in fixing the reference either of 'pain39' or of '$b76$,' a fact, moreover, that would explain the all but overwhelming "illusion of contingency" about the claim of identity. Kripke argues convincingly and, in my opinion, conclusively that no such fact can exist for a designator such as 'pain39.' He says that the referent of 'pain' is picked out by a *necessary* (or "essential") property of pain, by, indeed, the property of *being pain*. This precludes the existence of a contingent reference-fixing fact for 'pain' (and for 'pain39'); for the reference of 'pain' (and 'pain39') is

---

3. Kripke directs his arguments mainly against "type-type" mental–physical identities and says that advocates of "token-token" identities are perhaps partially immune to his criticism. The reason for the immunity is not clear to me. However, I shall also consider, in the main, type-type identities. Absolving them of Kripke's charges will also absolve token-token identities, since these are entailed by the type-type ones.

fixed *ontologically without* any reference fixing fact. It is fixed *solely* by virtue of conventional linguistic practice. In contrast, fixing the reference of 'Oscar' and 'heat' involved contingent facts *in addition* to the linguistic factors. Finally, and equally importantly, language alone not only fixes ontologically the reference of 'pain,' it also *epistemically determines* what its referent *is*; in this case no contingent associated fact is involved.

So the referent of 'pain' is picked out by a necessary truth about pain, namely, the truth that pain is necessarily pain. It is *not possible* that pain (or pain39) could have been something that was not pain. This necessary truth may seem quite trivial, and in a sense it is. Note, however, that it is not a necessary truth about the inventor of the incandescent bulb that he invented the incandescent bulb. Under the appropriate arrangement of Russell's "scope operator," we can even say truthfully that it is not necessarily true that the inventor of the bulb was the inventor of the bulb; i.e., the man who *did* invent it *might* not have (cf. Kripke, p. 279). Someone other than Edison might have done it. (Or more than one person might have invented it, or it might not have been invented at all.) Or, to say it in still another manner, the man who in this, the actual, world invented the bulb did not invent it in every possible world. Or, returning to the essentialist framework, being the inventor of the bulb is not an *essential* property of the inventor of the bulb. (Or course, however, being the inventor of the bulb *is* an essential property of *being* the inventor of the bulb [as is the property of being an inventor, etc.].) Consider another example. Neither being red nor being crimson is an essential property of my sweater, which *is*, as a matter of contingent fact, crimson. But being red is of course an essential property of being crimson. Being red, therefore, is an essential property of an "accidental" property of my sweater. So we see that there are not only "illusions of contingency" but, as in the case of the inventor being the inventor, "illusions of necessity" as well. Something which, prima facie, seems necessary may turn out on closer examination to be contingent . . . .

Returning once again to Kripke's arguments, I have agreed very strongly with him that the referent of the *word* 'pain' (and the referent of the word 'pain39') is picked out by a necessary fact about (or an "essential" property of) the referent; i.e., the word 'pain39' rigidly designates the event pain39 by virtue of the necessity of pain39's *being* pain39. This precludes the possibility of fixing the reference of the term 'pain39' by means of any contingent fact. But we have seen above that this by no means precludes the existence of another, different word, say 'factor *a*' that rigidly designates the *event* pain39 and *that*, moreover, *rigidly designates it by virtue of a contingent fact*. It seems to me that such a possibility is overlooked by Kripke. However this may be, I claim that *terms referring to certain kinds of brain events*, properly construed—terms such as '*b*76'—*do rigidly refer to mental events* (events such as pain39). *Such reference is accomplished,* moreover, *by means of the (contingent) neurophysiological causal roles of the relevant events.* These "accidental" causal properties of the events *fix their reference ontologically.* However, due to our lack of neurological, psychophysiological, and neuropsychological knowledge about the details of these causal properties, the reference has *not* been, so far, *epistemically determined.* Nevertheless, the identity theorist speculates that it is mental events that are the real actors in *some* of these neurophysiological causal roles. More specifically, he speculates that there is a certain brain event, call it '*b*76,' which plays, contingently, a certain neurophysiological causal role. Moreover, the referent of '*b*76' can, in principle, be fixed by means of this (contingent) role; i.e., the relevant neurophysiological details, if only we knew them, could pick out the referent of '*b*76' ontologically. Next, he continues, the relevant (contingent) psychophysiological or neuropsychological details, if only we knew them, could epistemically determine that it is pain39 that plays the neurophysiological role in question.

Kripke stresses the disanalogies between claiming that heat (or an instance of heat) is identical with molecular motion, on the one hand, and claiming that a brain event is identical with a pain, on the other. He concludes that, although heat and molecular motion are necessarily identical, these disanalogies preclude the possibility of a brain event and a pain's being necessarily identical and therefore preclude their being identical at all. He is correct about the existence of the disanalogies but wrong, I believe, in inferring that they preclude the necessity of mind–brain identities. He summarizes his argument on this matter (p. 340) as follows:

> Thus pain, unlike heat, is not only rigidly designated by 'pain' but the reference of the designator is determined by an essential property of the referent. Thus it is not possible to say that although pain is necessarily identical with a certain physical state, a certain phenomenon can be picked out in the same way we pick out pain without being correlated with that physical state. If any phenomenon is picked out in exactly the same way we pick out pain, then that phenomenon is pain.

This is certainly correct. However, it does not preclude mind–brain identities. For what we *can* say is that, although pain39 is necessarily identical with a certain brain event (call it '*b*76'), a (different!) brain event could, in some possible worlds, be picked out in the same way that we (in the actual world) pick out *b*76 without being identical with or even correlated with pain. This is true because the referent of '*b*76' is fixed as being the event that plays such and such a neurophysiological causal role *in this world*. In some other possible worlds *that role* will be played by entities other than $b76$. The identity theorist maintains, of course, that the role in question is played by pain39 *in this world*, although it could be played by another event (which might not even be a mental event) in some other possible world. This is what is responsible for *the illusion of contingency* concerning the necessary identity of pain39 and $b76$.

It seems that Kripke assumes, tacitly at least, that designators such as 'pain39' correspond to the designator 'heat' and thus that those such as '$b76$' correspond to 'molecular motion.' I contend that the relevant analogies are rather between 'heat' and '$b76$' on the one hand and 'molecular motion' and 'pain39' on the other. For the reference of 'heat' and the reference of '$b76$' are fixed by contingent facts (by "accidental properties" of the referents). And it is the contingent associated discoveries that molecular motion causes heat sensations and that pain39 plays such and such a neurophysiological causal role that account for, respectively, the illusions of contingency about the necessary identity of heat and molecular motion and the necessary identity of pain39, and the brain event '$b76$'.

Now it may seem that Kripke has protected his flank on this score, for he does contend (p. 336) that "*being a brain state* is evidently an essential property of B (the brain state)." In other words, he would claim that every brain state of necessity *had* to be a brain state (and surely he would make the analogous claim about brain events). He goes on to say, "even being a brain state of a specific type is an essential property of [the brain state] B." If the same *is* true of brain *events* (whether Kripke so contends or not), then my counterargument *would* be unsound; for this would entail that the reference of '$b76$' is fixed by means of a necessary truth (i.e., that an "essential property" of $b76$ fixes it as the referent of '$b76$'). This would preclude fixing the reference of '$b76$' by means of one of the "accidental properties" of the referent, and therefore there could not exist any contingent associated fact to account for the apparent contingency of the correlation between $b76$ and pain39. Following Kripke (p. 336), the difficulty may also be put: "If $A = B$, then the identity of A with B is necessary, and any essential property of one must be an essential property of the other." Now suppose that being a brain event *is* an essential property of $b76$. Since being a brain event is *not* an essential property of pain39, it would follow that $b76$ and pain39 do not share all of their essential properties and thus cannot be identical.

It is time now for one of the central and, perhaps, one of the most counterintuitive contentions of this chapter: *being a brain event* is not, in general, an essential property of brain events. (Although, of course, *being a brain event* is an essential property of *being* a brain event.) Again, this is a matter of *scope* (in Russell's sense of "scope"). Just as Russell pointed out long ago how it is that we can say that a given inventor might not have been an inventor (e.g., Edison might have spent his life writing mystery novels, never inventing even a mouse trap), we are now in a position to understand how *a given brain event might not have been a brain event*. For, I claim, *to be a brain event* is to play a neurophysiological causal role of an appropriate, broadly specifiable ("*determinable*") kind; and to be a brain event of a specific ("*determinate*") kind is to play a specific, determinate kind of neurophysiological causal role (e.g., of the kind we are supposing *b*76 to play), and if we assume (in agreement with Hume) that *to say of a given event (or kind of event) that it plays a certain kind of causal role is to say something contingent*, then we see immediately that *to say of a given event (or kind of event) that it is a brain event is to say something contingent*. This follows, of course, because to say of an event that it is a brain event is merely to say that it plays a certain kind of causal role. And to say that this very brain event might not have been a brain event is merely to say that although this event, as a matter of contingent fact, plays a certain causal role, it is possible that it might not have played such a role; in some possible worlds it plays a very different role. As to the case at hand, although pain39 (alias *b*76) plays a certain specific neurophysiological causal role and is thereby (contingently) a brain event (of a certain kind), it *might not* have played such a role. It might not even have played any kind of neurological role, and thus it might not have been a brain event. Exactly the same holds for *b*76—which is, in effect, to say the same thing again, for *b*76 and pain39 are necessarily identical; '*b*76' and 'pain39' refer to one and the same event. Moreover and *obviously* by now, *being a brain event is not* an essential property of *the brain event b*76; but *being a pain is* an essential property of *the brain event b*76. And, of course, being a brain event is *not* an essential property of the *brain* (!) *event*, pain39; but being a pain *is* an essential property of the brain event[4] pain39. Pain39 and *b*76 *do* share all of "their" properties, including all of "their" essential properties; they are one and the same event. To paraphrase Russell, there is no more difficulty about a pain being both a sensation and a brain event than there is about a man being both a rational animal and a barber. . . .

What I want to do next is to argue directly that, when God made the relevant kind of brain event, say *b*76, this very act of creation was the creation

---

4. Although, as indicated earlier, being a brain event *is* an essential property of *being* a brain event; and being a brain event *is* an essential property of *being* a brain event of a specific kind. Also, being a pain is *never* an essential property of *being* a specific kind of brain event. Again, all of this is true simply because it is *necessarily* true that all neurophysiological roles are neurophysiological roles, but it is not necessarily true that pain plays any neurophysiological role at all.

of (the mental event—the sensation) pain39. After God created $b76$, there did *not* remain for Him the substantive task of creating pain39 (nor the task of then correlating it with $b76$). The creation of $b76$ *was* the creation of pain39, for "they" are one and the same event. What *was* a substantive task for the Deity was to give pain39 (alias $b76$) the kind of (contingent) neurophysiological causal role that it has. He *could* have decided to give it a different neurophysiological role or even not to give it *any neurophysiological* role at all (just as He *could* have decided not to give molecular motion the causal role of producing "heat sensations"). Our implicit recognition that the Deity had to make this contingent decision about the causal role of $b76$ is responsible for our *mistaken* feeling that the creation of $b76$ was a different act from the act of creation of pain39 and thus for the *illusion of contingency* about the *actual necessity* of the identity of (the mental event) pain39 and (the brain event) $b76$. . . .

To consider these questions we shall need to develop a small amount of "quasi technical" apparatus of our own. We need the notion of *causal structure* and the notion of a *causal network*. The accompanying greatly oversimplified sketch will serve both to explain these notions and to help answer the questions at issue [Figure 7.1]. In the diagram, the circles represent events, and the arrows connecting them represent causal connections. A lowercase letter indicates that an event is a brain event. If the letter is from the beginning portion of the alphabet, the brain event is (also) a mental event; letters toward the end of the alphabet indicate brain events (or other neurological events) that are not mental events. Capital letters indicate "input" and "output" events—input into the neurological network and output from the network. For example, the event, A, might be light striking the eyes and B sound waves entering the ears, while X and Y might be lifting an arm and uttering a word, respectively. Dots and arrows with no circles at their heads or no circles at their tails indicate that large portions of (indeed, most of) the network is not shown in the diagram.

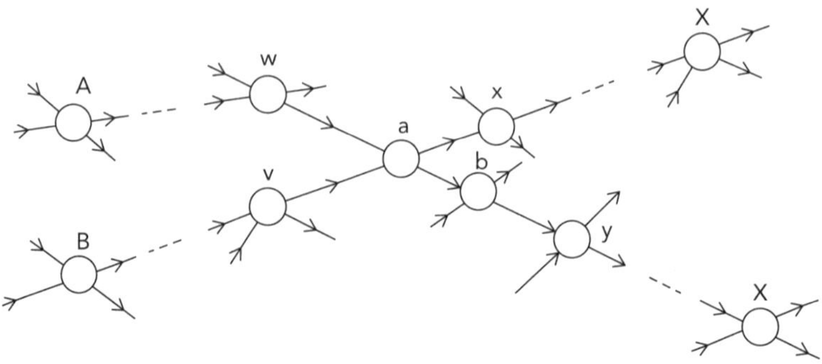

FIGURE 7.1.

The entire diagram represents a *causal network*, and every item shown is an essential part of the particular network that is illustrated. In other words, a causal network consists of a number of (causally connected) events and of the causal connections among them. The *causal structure* of the network consists entirely of the causal connections and the positions or loci of the events in the network. For example, if in the diagram event B were replaced by another event or even by an event of another *kind*, the result would be a *different* causal *network*, but the causal *structure* would remain *exactly the same*. The same holds for event a, event y, or any and all other events.

Let us now suppose that the events represented in the central part of the diagram occur in the C-fiber regions of the brain and that the event labeled 'a' is pain39 (alias *b*76). Pain39 is, thus, a part of the activity taking place in this region of the C-fibers. Its immediate causal ancestors u and v are also a part of this activity, although, unlike a (alias pain39, alias *b*76), they are not mental events. Among pain39's causal descendants are b, a brain event that is also a mental event (anger64, perhaps), and y, a brain event and perhaps a C-fiber event that is *not* a mental event. . . .

If we recognize that C-fiber activity is a complex causal network in which at least some of the events are pure events and that neurophysiology, physics, chemistry, etc., provide us *only* with knowledge of the *causal structure* of the network, the way is left entirely open for the neuropsychologist to theorize that some of the events in the network *just are pains* (in all of their qualitative, experiential, mentalistic richness).

Let us now return to Kripke's claim that, in order to create C-fiber stimulation (C-fiber activity, in our terms), "it would seem that God need only to create beings with C-fibers capable of the appropriate type of *physical* . . .[activity]; whether the beings are conscious or not is irrelevant" [my italics]. Interpreted in one way, this claim is true; but under this interpretation, it in no way counts against the identity thesis. Interpreted in another way, the claim is inconsistent with the identity thesis; however, under this second interpretation, I contend, it becomes false. Under the first interpretation, 'C-fiber activity' refers to a *causal structure*; more specifically, it refers to a certain kind of causal structure of a complex of events in the C-fiber regions of the brain. Now, quite obviously, it is (logically) possible for one and the same causal structure to be exemplified by many different complexes of events (by many different causal networks). So in order for God to create C-fiber activity *in this sense,* all He has to do is create a complex of events that has the appropriate causal structure. *The nature of the events in the complex is irrelevant;* some or all of them may be tickles, feelings of warmth, or, even, pain; or, on the other hand, every one of them could be entirely nonmental. In this sense of 'C-fiber activity,'

Kripke is entirely correct in his claim that whether or not conscious beings are involved is irrelevant. However, the identity thesis, properly formulated, does *not* attempt to identify mental activity with *C*-fiber activity *in this sense*; i.e., it does *not* identify pain with the *causal structure of the complex of events—just as Kripke does not identify heat with the causal structure of heat-sensation production.* What is identified with (a specific kind of) pain is a (specific kind of) event, or complex of events, in the causal *network*—a (kind of) event, moreover, that has the position it has in the network *in this, the actual, world.* (Analogously, what is identified with heat is a [specific kind of] event, or complex of events, that causes the heat sensations in this, the actual world.) If the term '*C*-fiber activity' is used to refer to such events (or complexes of events)—events that have the appropriate position in the causal network in this, the actual world—then, according to the identity thesis, '*C*-fiber activity' *in this* (second) *sense* refers to pain and *does so rigidly.* If Kripke's claim is interpreted according to this sense of '*C*-fiber activity,' then it must be denied; for, in this sense, '*C*-fiber activity' rigidly designates pain, and the existence of sentient beings is necessarily involved with the existence of pain and, therefore, necessarily involved with the existence of *C*-fiber activity *in this sense* (just as the existence of mobile molecules is necessarily involved with the existence of heat) . . . .

Returning to the main point, let us examine again the term '*C*-fiber activity'—or, better and less subject to ambiguity, the rigid designator that I, in response to Kripke's suggestion, have been using in its stead, '*b76*'. Once more we must emphasize that the referent of this rigid designator is *epistemically undetermined* as far as neurophysiology and other "purely physical" sciences are concerned. Physical science leaves us completely ignorant as to *what* the referent of '*C*-fiber activity' (or better, '*b76*') *is*; it provides us *only* with knowledge about the locus of the referent in the causal network. Or, stated without the quasi-technical, rigid-designator terminology, physical science leaves us entirely ignorant as to *what C*-fiber activity *is* and provides us *only* with knowledge about its causal structure (including, of course, its causal connections to the rest of the neurophysiological causal network).

We see now that when God created the *C*-fiber event, pain39 (alias a, alias *b76*), the existence of an essentially involved conscious being was *not* irrelevant; it was *necessarily* required. The creation of *this* particular bit of *C*-fiber activity *just was* the creation of pain39 (alias a, alias *b76*). Nothing *else* had to be done in order to make it be *felt* as pain; its "essence" *is* being *felt as pain.* And, of course, it would *not* be in God's powers to make pain39 (alias a and *b76*) be felt as a tickle, or as warmth, or as nothing, rather than felt as pain. Feeling a certain determinate kind of pain is one and the same event *as* pain39. (To *be* pain is to be *felt* as pain.) On the other hand, in addition to creating pain39 (alias *b76*, alias a), God did do *something* else; He made the contingent decision to give pain39 the causal role that is indicated in the diagram. He *could* have decided to give it an entirely different neurophysiological causal role or even to give it no neurophysiological role at all; for example, He might have decided to cast the world in a Cartesian mold. Analogously, God could have decided to give molecular motion (alias heat) a different causal role from the one that it has; He might, for example, have decided *not* to have it cause heat sensations. And, just as He could have decided to have events of a different kind, say low-frequency radio waves, be the principal and proximal cause of heat sensations, he also could have decided to have an event of a quite different kind play the neurophysiological causal role that, as a matter of contingent fact, is played by pain39. In particular, he could have decided to have this role played by a nonmental event.

The points illustrated by these examples follow from the more general principle: *it is* (logically) *possible for different causal networks to have the same causal structure*; or, in other words, one and the same causal structure may be realized in a number of different ways, i.e., may be exemplified by a number of different causal networks. Thus God could have created a causal network such that it differed from the one in the diagram only in that the positions occupied by a and b were occupied by different events—perhaps by events that were nonmental. This creation would have been a different causal network, but it would have been the same causal structure. Or, giving the Deity a rest, *in some possible worlds, mental events are* (some of the) *elements of C-fiber activity*, and, *in other possible worlds, none of the elements of C-fiber activity are mental events*. More generally, *in some possible worlds, mental events are brain events*, and, *in other possible worlds, no mental events are brain events*. This is true, I claim, because to be a brain event is to occupy a position in an appropriate portion of the neurophysiological causal network, and it is a contingent matter as to what kind of events occupy any such position. *With this understanding*, we may take the *identity thesis* to be *the thesis that all mental events are brain events*. *Such a thesis is contingent*, as we have just seen. But *this*, of course, *does not by any means entail that there are contingent identities*. A fortiori, it is entirely consistent with what, indeed, *must* be the case: *all the identities* that hold between mental events and brain events *hold necessarily* . . . .

Unfortunately, the strongest objection to the identity thesis is, in my opinion, yet to come. Just how it is related to Kripke's objections remains to be seen. Given what physiology and physics tell us about C-fibers and their activity, is it reasonable or even coherent to suppose that mental events comprise (a portion of) such activity? A prime—perhaps *the* prime—ingredient of this activity seems to be neuronal activity, which, let us assume, consists of chemical and (the associated) electrical activity. Chemical and electrical events, in turn, involve the transfer and transportation of electrons, ions, etc. How can one claim that (some of) the goings-on of these tiny charged particles of matter are identical with pains, joys, sorrows, thoughts that two plus two equals four, etc.? Surely, it may seem, such a claim is absurd! I once heard Benson Mates remark that it makes no more sense to identify a mental event with a brain event than it does to identify a quadratic equation with a billy goat. It is not difficult to empathize with his sentiments. Let us state the objection in a more general manner: (1) We know from common sense, from physics, from neurophysiology, etc., what brain events are like. (2) We know ("by acquaintance"—and perhaps better than we know anything else) what mental events are like. (3) This knowledge reveals that brain events differ radically from mental events; more specifically, it reveals that mental events have properties that brain events lack and that brain events have properties that mental events lack. Therefore, the objection concludes, no mental events are brain events.[5]

This, in my opinion, is *the* argument against the identity thesis, and the most important specific objections to the thesis, including Kripke's, depend upon it in one way or another. The details of the dependence need not concern us. What should be done, rather, is to acknowledge the obvious: premise (or, rather, intermediate conclusion) number (3) above must be denied if the identity thesis is to be maintained; if the thesis is to be plausible, it must be plausible to contend that some brain events share *all* of their properties, both "essential" and "accidental" ones, with mental events . . . .

The typical materialist move is to deny premise (2) above. Materialists tend to hold that knowledge of mental events, if it exists at all, is at best second- or third-rate knowledge. The belief that we are directly acquainted with the (ingredients of) mental events that comprise our very being is, according to them, at least partly and perhaps totally mistaken. Some go on to maintain that knowledge claims about our mental events (about "private experience," etc.) are so defective that they should, in principle, be abandoned entirely—that, as our knowledge from physics, physiology, etc. increases, we shall see that talk about (allegedly) mental events, private experience, etc., is on a par with talk about witches, demons, or perhaps phlogiston and epicycles. When that happy day arrives, they tell us, we shall talk only about brain events, molecules and electrons, and other "scientifically respectable" entities. This position has

---

5. The "grain" objection, attributed to Wilfrid Sellars (1965) and elaborated by Paul E. Meehl (1966), is a special case of this objection.

been called the *replacement* or the *disappearance* version of the identity thesis (see, e.g., Feyerabend, 1963, and Rorty, 1965). Quite obviously, however, it is not an identity thesis at all; it purports to eliminate mental entities altogether rather than to identify them with brain events. This is not the place to give detailed arguments against such a view. I *will* say more about it later, but now I just want to remark that this position is certainly rejected by Kripke. It is fair to say, I believe, that both he and I find it "self-evidently absurd." ...

This failure of materialism results from the fact that it must attack the objection at its strongest point, premise (2). I say this *not* because I believe that knowledge about our mental events is certain, infallible, or complete (I do not so believe), but rather because it provides us with the best (perhaps the only) knowledge that we have of the *intrinsic* properties of individual events (as opposed to *causal* and other *structural* properties). Moreover, if the objection is to retain anything at all of its great intuitive potency, premises (1) and (2) as well as intermediate conclusion (3) must be taken to refer to knowledge about *intrinsic* properties.

There is a widespread tendency to identify[6] the mind–body identity thesis with materialism. To do so, however, is to miss the point *entirely* of any genuine mind–brain identity claim. Materialism, as it is typically proposed and defended, seeks to eliminate the *genuinely mental* realm, to deny that genuinely mental events exist. But, if there *are* no mental events, then the thesis that all mental events are brain events is either nonsensical or vacuously true. A *genuine mind–brain* identity thesis must hold that there are both mental events and brain events, that all mental events are brain events, and that therefore *some brain events are mental events*—in the most full-blown "mentalistic" sense of 'mental.' Such a view I have called *nonmaterialist physicalism*[7] (see, e.g., Maxwell, 1976).

As should be apparent by now, I propose to defend the identity thesis against the prime objection by denying premise (1). More specifically: although physics, neurophysiology, etc., *do* provide us with the best knowledge we have of the *structure* of the neurophysiological causal networks that comprise the brain, they provide us with *no knowledge* (or precious little) about the *intrinsic* properties of individual brain events.[8] *Thus the possibility is entirely open that*

---

6. You should pardon the expression!

7. *Physicalism* because to be a physical event is to have a locus in the spatio-temporal causal network.

8. The claim is a general one, holding not only for the brain but for all physical systems. See, e.g., Russell, 1948, and Maxwell, 1970.

some of these brain events just are *our twinges of pain, our feelings of joy and sorrow, our thoughts that two plus two equals four, etc.* Such a brain event would, of course, "share"[9] all of its properties with the mental event which it *is*—all "essential" properties and all "accidental" properties, all intrinsic properties and all causal properties, etc., etc. By now, I hope, this is no more mysterious than the fact that the 51-year-old brother of Billy Carter "shares" all of his properties, be they accidental, essential, intrinsic, relational, etc., with the present (February 1977) president of the United States.

Well, perhaps it *is somewhat* more mysterious, for reasons to be discussed in a moment. But first it should be emphasized that the materialist has the matter entirely backwards and reversed: there is no need whatever to replace mentalistic terms with "topic-neutral" ones. For, I hold, premise (2) is correct: we *do* know (*by acquaintance*) the intrinsic nature of our mental events, i.e., we know *what* the "topic" of discourse about mental events *is*. On the other hand, we do not have this kind of knowledge about anything in the non-mental realm, i.e., we reject premise (1) insofar as it pertains to the intrinsic nature of the entities involved. Therefore, with one kind of exception, we *must* refer to physical events in a *topic-neutral* manner, unless we are willing to introduce a certain amount of confusion and unnecessary puzzlement.[10] We can refer to such physical events only with descriptions or with terms whose reference has been fixed by means of descriptions or by other *topic-neutral*, nonostensive means.[11] This is not, of course, a "disappearance" or "replacement" view of the physical. It is just that our references to physical events by means of *topic-neutral designators* is an explicit signal of our ignorance of their intrinsic nature—our ignorance as to *what* such physical entities *are*. It is a reminder that our knowledge of them is limited to their causal and other structural properties. The kind of exception to all this mentioned above is comprised by those physical events that are mental events.

---

9. The word 'share' is put in "shudder quotes" because what we are talking about, of course, is a thing "sharing" all of its properties with itself. This seems to be a somewhat atypical way of talking. The same is true of saying that if "two [!] things" are identical, "they" "share" all of "their" properties, etc. All of this results, does it not, because reflexive relations, especially identities, are somewhat atypical?

10. In most of our practical, everyday discourse, such confusion does not, of course, arise. In such contexts, there is no more need to reform our customary beliefs and modes of reference than there would be to replace, in most of its uses, the word 'salt' with the words 'sodium chloride' on the grounds that common table salt, sodium chloride, is just one out of thousands of kinds of salts, most of which are inedible and poisonous.

11. In a full-scale program, such reference-fixing can be accomplished systematically by using either Ramsey sentences or model-theoretic techniques. See Maxwell, 1970.

I have been trying to remove, layer by layer, the obstacles that stand in the way of maintaining a mind–brain identity thesis—emphasizing along the way the untenability of accomplishing this by means of antimentalist strata-gems such as materialism. So far the task has been relatively easy, if some-what tedious and repetitive due to the fact that layers tend to overlap each other. We approach now what is perhaps the last and certainly the thickest and most formidable layer. This difficulty arises from our rejection, or, rather from our *qualified* acceptance, of premise (1). We agreed that (physical[12]) sci-ence provides us with the best information that we have about the structure of the physical realm, including the structure of the brain. But, we insist, sci-ence is in the main completely silent about the intrinsic, qualitative properties exemplified by physical events.[13] The difficulty is two-fold: (a) Science does seem, sometimes, to deal explicitly with intrinsic properties. For example, we certainly seem to be dealing directly with intrinsic properties when we say that electrons are negatively charged—indeed, that each electron has a charge of 4.8×10^{-10} e.s.u. It would appear that having a negative electrical charge of 4.8×10^{-10} e.s.u. is an intrinsic property of an electron; moreover, *being an elec-tron* seems to be an intrinsic property. (b) The structures exemplified in our (private) experience, i.e., the structures we know by "acquaintance," are prima facie quite different from any known *or* hypothesized brain structures—from any structures exemplified in brain events. If these differences are actual rather than merely apparent, then the identity thesis is refuted: *unless each mental event "shares" all of its properties, both intrinsic and structural with some brain event, identity cannot hold.*

The first difficulty is not serious. *To be an electron* is to play a certain kind of *causal* (and/or otherwise *structural*) role: or more precisely, the reference of the term 'electron' is fixed (ontologically) by specifying the positions that electrons occupy in causal-structural networks. Similarly the reference of 'having a negative charge of 4.8×10^{-10} e.s.u.' is (ontologically) fixed by the causal-structural role played by such charges. However, the reference of such terms is not (to this date) *epistemically determined*. The terms *do* refer to intrinsic properties, but we do not know *what* the referents *are*, e.g., we do not know what a negative electrical charge *is*—just as we did not know what

---

12. Psychology and some social sciences, properly conducted, do deal explicitly with intrin-sic as well as structural properties.

13. This chapter cannot provide a systematic account of the distinction between intrinsic and structural properties. I *have* made preliminary efforts in this direction in Maxwell, 1970. I believe that the examples used here, however, coupled with our commonsense grasp of the distinction, will be sufficient for the purposes of this chapter.

heat *was* until we discovered that molecular motion caused heat sensation. (Actually, just as we do not know what an electron *is*, we *still* don't know what heat [alias molecular motion] *is*. We just know more about its causal roles than we used to.) Our earlier statement that physical science provides us with knowledge of structural properties but not with knowledge of intrinsic properties was an oversimplification: science *does* assert the *existence* of instances of a variety of intrinsic properties; moreover, it provides information about the various causal-structural roles that such instances play. However, it *does* leave us completely ignorant as to *what* these intrinsic properties *are*. This crucial matter calls for repeated emphasis: physics, chemistry, physiology, etc., leave us entirely ignorant about the intrinsic nature of physical entities in general and of brain events in particular; the physical sciences, properly construed, do refer to intrinsic properties, but they do so via *topic-neutral* designators—designators that leave us entirely in the dark as to *what* their referents *are*; their referents remain epistemically undetermined. This disposes of the first difficulty, (a). For it leaves entirely open the possibility that some brain events just *are* events such as the occurrence of a twinge of pain, the occurrence of a red expanse in the visual field, thinking that two plus two equals four, and exemplification of other intrinsic properties that characterize our experience (our "mental processes"). This consequence that (at least) *a portion of the physical realm may be intrinsically mental* must be entertained in complete literalness by anyone who wishes to entertain seriously a genuine mind–brain identity thesis.

What the statement of the second difficulty, (b), amounts to is a somewhat more precise statement of the "grain objection" referred to in footnote 5. The objection asks, for example, how is it that the occurrence of a smooth, continuous expanse of red in our visual experience can be identical with a brain process that must, it would seem, involve particulate, discontinuous affairs such as transfers of or interactions among large numbers of electrons, ions, or the like? Surely being smooth or continuous is a *structural* property, and being particulate or discontinuous is also a structural property, one moreover that is incompatible with being smooth and continuous. This strongly suggests, the objection continues, that at least some mental events exemplify structural properties that are not exemplified by any brain event, or, at any rate, not in any brain event that is an otherwise feasible candidate for being identical with the mental event. It follows that the mental event and the brain event do not share all of their (structural) properties, and thus, the objector concludes, they cannot be identical.

The difficulty is genuine and crucial. Unless there is good reason to hope that it can be overcome, there is no good reason to hope that mind–brain identity is possible. This difficulty is not, however, the one that has been the main concern of this chapter, which has been the difficulty posed by Kripke. Nevertheless our answer to Kripke's challenge has emphasized the indirectness, the abstractness, and the incompleteness of our knowledge of the physical realm, and reflection upon this makes the "grain objection" appear—to me, at least—somewhat less formidable. It is true that we have not, in principle, set any limits on the scope of our knowledge about the structure of the physical realm; but the indirect, highly theoretical nature of such knowledge strongly suggests that it *is* quite incomplete and imperfect. There are also strong independent grounds for the same conclusion. Surely very few historians, philosophers, and practitioners of the physical sciences believe that our knowledge of the structure of the manifold of physical events is nearing perfection or completeness. For example, what many consider to be the unsatisfactory status of the foundations of quantum theory may well be due to crucial gaps in our knowledge of structure at the micro-level; and perhaps it is not too fanciful to suspect that the failure to integrate quantum theory and general relativity is due in part to a lack of knowledge of structures of causal networks that are somewhere between the very small ones and the very large ones. Perhaps it is precisely this "middle-sized" realm that provides the relevant context for investigation of mind–brain identities. In sum, as our knowledge grows about the various manifolds of events that constitute the physical realm, perhaps we shall discover that some of the structures that are exemplified by them *are* entirely isomorphic and quite possibly identical with instances of the structures with which we are acquainted in our "private" experience.

Even within the bounds of present physical theory, we might consider a fanciful but logically coherent possibility. Fields—electrical, magnetic, or gravitational—and fluctuations in fields are, *as far as their structures are concerned*, viable candidates for identification with (some kinds of) mental states or mental events. There are, no doubt, strong objections against supposing that, say a fluctuation in an electrical field could be a mental event (such as a twinge of pain). However, such objections could not be based on a difference in structure or "grain"; as far as I can see, such a fluctuation could be entirely isomorphic in all respects with a twinge of pain. The identity theorist must hope that continued developments in physics, neurophysiology, etc., will make manifest the existence of physical entities that have such appropriate structures and that are also otherwise more feasible candidates for being identified with mental entities.

Fortunately some neurophysiologists and neuropsychologists are devoting detailed attention to these problems. For example, the holographic theories of

Pribram and others represent attempts to incorporate the structural features of mental functions (e.g., memory) and the structural features of brain processes into *one* (self-identical!) model (Pribram, Baron, & Nuwer, 1974). More accurately, they attempt to describe models in which the structural properties that characterize brain processes are ("also") structural properties of mental functions, and conversely. In other words, they are searching for a model such that, in any given case, there is only *one* process (or function), and it is both a brain process and a mental process.

Whether or not the holographic approach will survive long-range investigation is not a matter about which I would care to forecast, even if I felt competent about its details. It does seem clear that this general *kind* of approach is a necessary condition for significant future development and progress in dealing with mind–body problems. A model such as the holographic one should, obviously, warm the heart of an identity theorist. If it turned out to be "successful"—if it stood up to experimental testing, successfully predicted startling new experimental outcomes, etc.—this would provide a considerable degree of confirmation (by no means conclusive, of course) of the identity thesis.

Let us suppose the holographic model turned out to be unsuccessful. Would this refute or "falsify" the identity thesis? Would it even count very strongly against it (strongly disconfirm it)? Both questions must be answered, I believe, in the negative. This seems to me an instance of a kind of methodological situation that frequently obtains in scientific inquiry, a situation such that positive experimental results would strongly confirm the hypothesis being tested but such that negative results, far from refuting the hypothesis (pace Popper), would disconfirm it only very slightly. (For discussion of a notorious example, the experimental "detection" of the neutrino, see Maxwell, 1974.) It is true that, if there followed *repeated* failures of *other* various identity theoretic models in addition to failure of the holographic model, then the identity thesis would begin to be appreciably, perhaps strongly, disconfirmed, especially if all of this were accompanied by impressive successes of dualistic models. I mention this matter to illustrate the complexity of the relationships between experimental evidence and contingent scientific (cum philosophical) problems *such as the mind–body problem*! I have discussed this in some detail in Maxwell 1976; and I argue there that it leads to the conclusion that, in several of the traditional problem areas, the mind–body problem being a prime example, there is no sharp line or very helpful distinction between scientific inquiry and philosophical inquiry. In other words, philosophical investigation is *not* exhausted without remainder by logical, conceptual, and linguistic considerations however important, difficult, and interesting these may be. For this very general reason coupled with more specific ones such as the "grain" problem just discussed, I do not believe that philosophers are going to con-tribute a great deal more to the "solutions" of mind–brain issues until they attain something close to specialists' competence in neurophysiology, neu-ropsychology, etc. I am willing to go one step further and predict that the next important breakthrough, if it comes at all, will come from the neurosci-ences. On the other hand, the neuroscientists will probably not contribute much either unless they understand and appreciate the logical, conceptual and, *yes* (!), the contingent components of the "mind–body problem" that have concerned philosophers over the centuries. The work of Kripke that we have been considering provides valuable, fresh perspectives on these crucial components.

References

Carnap, R. Meaning postulates. *Philosophical Studies*, 1952, 3, 65–73.

Carnap, R. Beobachtungsprache und theoretische sprache. *Dialectica*, 1957, 12, 236–48.

Feigl, H. Matter still largely material. *Philosophy of Science*, 1962, 29, 39–46.

Feyerabend, P. K. Materialism and the mind-body problem. *Review of Metaphysics*, 1963, 17, 46–64.

Hanson, N. R. The dematerialization of matter. *Philosophy of Science*, 1962, 29, 27–38.

Kripke, S. Naming and necessity. In D. Davidson & G. Harman (Eds.), *Semantics of natural language*. Boston and Dordrecht: Reidel, 1972.

Kripke, S. Identity and necessity. In M. Munitz (Ed.), *Identity and individuation*. New York: New York University Press, 1971.

Maxwell, G. Meaning postulates in scientific theories. In H. Feigl & G. Maxwell (Eds.), *Current issues in the philosophy of science*. New York: Holt, Rinehart, & Winston, 1961.

Maxwell, G. Structural realism and the meaning of theoretical terms. In M. Radner & S. Winokur (Eds.), *Analyses of theories and methods of physics and psychol-ogy: Minnesota studies in the philosophy of science* (Vol. 4). Minneapolis: University of Minnesota Press, 1970.

Maxwell, G. Russell on perception: A study in philosophical method. In D. Pears (Ed.), *Bertrand Russell: A collection of critical essays*. New York: Doubleday (Anchor Paperbacks), 1972.

Maxwell, G. Corroboration with demarcation. In P. A. Schlipp (Ed.), *The philosophy of Karl Popper*. LaSalle, Ill.: Open Court, 1974.

Maxwell, G. Scientific results and the mind–brain issue: Some afterthoughts. In G. Globus, G. Maxwell, & I. Savodnik (Eds.), *Consciousness and the brain: A scien-tific and philosophical inquiry*. New York: Plenum Press, 1976.

Meehl, P. E. The compleat autocerebroscopists: A thought experiment on Professor Feigl's mind-body identity thesis. In P. K. Feyerabend & G. Maxwell (Eds.), *Mind, matter, and method: Essays in philosophy and science in honor of Herbert Feigl.* Minneapolis: University of Minnesota Press, 1966.

Nagel, T. What is it like to be a bat? *Philosophical Review*, 1974, 83, 435–50.

Pribram, K. H., Baron, R., & Nuwer, M. The holographic hypothesis of memory in brain function and perception. In R. C. Atkinson, D. H. Krantz, R. C. Luce, & P. Suppes, (Eds.), *Contemporary developments in mathematical psychology*. San Francisco: W. H. Freeman, 1974.

Rorty, R. Mind-body identity, privacy, and categories. *Review of Metaphysics*, 1965, 19, 24–54.

Russell, B. *Human knowledge: Its scope and limits*. New York: Simon & Schuster, 1948.

Russell, B. *Portraits from memory*. New York: Simon & Schuster, 1956.

Schlick, M. *General theory of knowledge* (Albert E. Blumberg, trans.). Vienna and New York: Springer-Verlag, 1974.

Sellars, W. S. The identity approach to the mind–body problem. *Review of Metaphysics*, 1965, 18, 430–51.

Shaffer, J. Could mental states be brain processes? *Journal of Philosophy*, 1961, 58, 812–22.

Smart, J. J. C. Sensations and brain processes. *Philosophical Review*, 1959, 68, 141–56.

8

The Grain Problem

Michael Lockwood

Think of what consciousness feels like, what it feels like at this moment. Does that *feel* like billions of tiny atoms wiggling in place?

(CARL SAGAN[1])

How can technicolour phenomenology arise from soggy grey matter?

(COLIN MCGINN[2])

THERE IS, TODAY, no glimmer of a consensus amongst philosophers about the mind–body problem.[3] Nevertheless, an increasing number of philosophers find themselves occupying a middle ground between physicalist reductionism, on the one hand, and dualism on the other. Physicalist reductionism I take to be the view that the physical story about what is going on in the brain and the world with which it interacts is in some sense the whole story. If there really are such things as mental states and processes—which eliminative materialists notoriously deny—then their existence must be logically implicit in facts statable in the language of physics. Space does not permit a detailed rebuttal of reductionist physicalism; nor do the arguments I have elsewhere

---

1. *Contact: A Novel* (New York, 1985), 255.

2. 'Can We Solve the Mind–Body Problem?' *Mind*, 98 (1989), 349.

3. In writing this article, I have benefited greatly from an excellent critique of my views—as set out in ch.10 of my *Mind, Brain and the Quantum: The Compound 'I'* (Oxford, 1989)—which appears in J. A. Foster's *The Immaterial Self* (London, 1991), 119–30. My statement of the grain problem, in particular, owes much to this discussion.

presented[4] admit of brief summary. But the simple intuitive argument is that a being provided with a description of you or me couched purely in the language of physics—even if it possessed unlimited powers of ratiocination—would have no way of deducing that our bodies were associated with awareness at all, much less what specifically it was *like* to be you or me.[5] There is, of course, a lot more to be said on the matter; but attempts to disarm such intuitive arguments seem to me, in the end, uniformly unsuccessful. Indeed, for those not blinded by science, the falsity of reductionist physicalism will probably seem almost too obvious to require argument: Galen Strawson aptly describes it as 'moonshine'.[6]

Dualism, on the other hand, is unattractive to most philosophers because embracing such a doctrine seems more like giving up on the mind–body problem than providing a genuine solution to it. Dualism does little or nothing to satisfy our cravings for an integrated world view. It remains obscure, on the dualist theory, just how the material is supposed to dovetail with immaterial mind. For, on the face of it, there are no mind-shaped gaps in the material fabric; the material world offers no explanatory or descriptive slots into which immaterial minds could comfortably fit. (One pictures matter saying to Cartesian mind: 'This universe ain't big enough for both of us'!)

Anyway, I shall be assuming in this chapter that, though reductionist physicalism is false, some form of materialism is nevertheless true. Conscious states and events are, on the view I favour, states of, or events within, the brain. But the very existence of consciousness shows that there is more to the matter of the brain (and hence presumably to matter in general) than is currently capable of being captured in the language of physics or physiology. How, then, is this 'more' to be conceived? Well, Bertrand Russell suggested, in the 1920s, that, in respect of the brain, awareness might be providing content, where science provides only form.[7] All that we really know of the physical world, on the basis either of sense perception or of physical theory, Russell argued, is that it possesses a certain *causal structure*. Any attribute of a physical system, whether it be shape, size, or electric charge, is really known to us only as whatever it is that occupies a certain logical niche within a causal-explanatory

---

4. Mind, Brain and the Quantum, ch. 8.

5. See T. Nagel, 'What Is It Like to Be a Bat?', *Philosophical Review*, 83 (1974), 435–50; repr. in id., *Mortal Questions* (Cambridge, 1979), 165–80.

6. G. Strawson, 'Consciousness, Free Will, and the Unimportance of Determinism', *Inquiry*, 32 (1989), 3.

7. See esp. B. Russell, *The Analysis of Matter* (London, 1927).

system. We have no way of knowing what the external world is like *in itself;* its intrinsic character is systematically hidden from the gaze of ordinary observation or experiment. But now, the brain is itself a part of the physical world, and we are assuming that conscious states are brain states. We certainly seem to know, from introspective awareness, the intrinsic character of an itch or the sound of middle C, played on the piano, or a patch of phenomenal yellow. So if conscious states *are* brain states, do we not here have a corner of the physical world whose intrinsic nature precisely *is* made manifest to us, albeit in a very limited way? This was Russell's suggestion: that in consciousness, a fragment of physical reality is, so to speak, being apprehended from within.

This idea—which seems to me the only approach to the philosophical mind–body problem, currently on offer, that holds out the slightest promise—can be thought of as a neat inversion of a celebrated theory put forward some thirty years ago by J. J. C. Smart. Smart suggested that mental state terms were, as he put it, 'topic neutral'. According to Smart, when I say that I am experiencing a yellowish-orange patch in my visual field, I am saying something like this: 'There is something going on which is like what is going on when I have my eyes open, am awake, and there is an orange illuminated in good light in front of me, that is, when I really see an orange.'[8] This then leaves it open for the physiologist to discover what, in relevant respects, actually is going on under such conditions, physiologically speaking, and identify it with the occurrence of phenomenal yellow-orange. But of course this isn't at all what I am saying when I report that I am experiencing phenomenal yellow-orange; if it were, it would follow, absurdly, that there was nothing to prevent a congenitally blind person from having as rich and complete an understanding of such introspective reports as a sighted person. Russell's view turns this unworkable theory on its head: for him it is the *physical* descriptions, rather than the mental ones, which are topic neutral.

It is at this point that we encounter the *grain problem* (a difficulty attributed to Wilfrid Sellars[9]). For if the immediate objects of introspective awareness just are states of, or events within, the brain, seen as they are in themselves, why do they *appear to be* so radically different from anything that a knowledge of the physiology of the brain would lead one to expect?

That rather vague intuitive thought may be resolved into three more specific difficulties, each of which can be regarded as an aspect of the grain

---

8. J. J. C. Smart, 'Sensations and Brain Processes', *Philosophical Review*, 68 (1959), 141–56.

9. W. Sellars, 'The Identity Approach to the Mind–Body Problem', *Review of Metaphysics*, 18 (1965), 430–51.

problem, as I conceive it. First is the fact that the phenomenal objects of introspective awareness are far less finely structured than are any plausible physiological correlates. Consider, for example, a phenomenally flawless auditory experience, of a note, say, on a violin. Its physiological substrate, presumably, is a highly structured, not to say messy, concatenation of changes in electrical potential within billions of neurons in the auditory cortex, mediated by the migration of sodium and potassium ions across cell membranes, and of molecules of transmitter substances within the chemical soup at the synapses. How do all these microstructural discontinuities and inhomogeneities come to be *glossed over,* in such a way as to generate the elegant perfection of auditory phenomenology that we associate with the playing of a Yehudi Menuhin? How are we to make philosophical sense of such phenomenological *coarse-graining?*

The second problem is that the structure we do encounter at the phenomenal level seems not to match, even in coarse-grained fashion, that of the underlying physiology, as revealed by scientific investigation. The phenomenal contents of awareness don't appear to have the *right kind* of structure; what is ostensibly lacking, here, is even the most approximate isomorphism between states of awareness and the underlying physiological goings-on that, on my view, they are supposed to be mirroring. In particular, three-dimensional spatial arrangement, and changes therein, seem central to all physical structure. Where, then, are their phenomenological counterparts? Of course, there is the visual field, and auditory and somatic-sensory space. But these are local, modality-specific *representations,* merely, of regions of the external world. We search in vain for some global, overarching mode of phenomenological organization that could plausibly be equated with introspectively encountered spatial layout. It is all very well to insist that the scientist's characterization of the brain, as of the physical world in general, is ultimately topic neutral; so that the terms of the characterization are, in the final analysis, mere placeholders for unspecified intrinsic natures. The problem is that the phenomenal pegs, as John Foster neatly puts it, seem not to be the right shape to fit these holes in the topic-neutral characterization.[10]

Someone may see in these difficulties an argument for functionalism. The functionalist would regard the relation between a phenomenological description of the contents of consciousness and a physiological description of the corresponding brain-processes as analogous to that between a description of the workings of a computer in software terms, on the one hand, and in terms,

---

10. Foster, *The Immaterial Self,* 126.

say, of the electronic configuration of the underlying circuits, on the other. Thus, brain states, for the functionalist, impinge on awareness only *qua* possessors of certain high-level causal-functional roles. Precisely what, in physiological terms, are playing those roles, and how they do so, is, at the level of phenomenology, essentially irrelevant.

Functionalism, however, has its own problems—most notably its inability to explain why functional roles should be associated with any phenomenal qualities—*qualia*—at all. And in any case, it would seem, intuitively, perfectly possible for there to be a system functionally equivalent to a human mind, in which the corresponding functional roles were associated with different *qualia* from those associated with these roles in our own case.[11] Functionalism may have some plausibility in accounting for mental structure, but, on the face of it, fails utterly to account for phenomenal *content*. Moreover, all arguments one could mount against reductionist physicalism apply *a fortiori* to functionalism; since if functionalism were true, reductionist physicalism clearly *could be* true also. If a physical system is, so to speak, running the right programs, then it follows, for the functionalist, that it has certain mental states; and this is something that a being with sufficient ratiocinative power could presumably read off from a description of the system couched in the language of physics. If, as I have been suggesting, reductionist physicalism is essentially a non-starter, then so too is functionalism—at least if put forward as a global theory of mind.

The third aspect of the grain problem that I wish to consider is raised by the profligate *qualitative diversity* of the phenomenal realm, which seems flatly at odds with the comparative qualitative homogeneity of the physical ingredients out of which any corresponding brain state could realistically be composed. There are two levels at which this might be argued. Both visual and auditory information, according to the current wisdom, are encoded—albeit in different parts of the brain—by firing rates within certain batteries of neurons. But there is (as far as I am aware) nothing qualitatively distinctive about a neuron in the auditory cortex, or the corresponding action potential, to mark it out from a neuron, or the firing of a neuron, in the visual cortex. So how, on this basis, is one to account, say, for the fundamental phenomenological difference between a sound and a flash?

The other level at which the point could be argued is that of particle physics. The most promising currently available candidate for a so-called *theory of*

---

11. See N. Block, 'Troubles with Functionalism', in *Minnesota Studies in the Philosophy of Science*, 9, ed. C. W. Savage (Minneapolis, 1978), 261–325, and also my *Mind, Brain and the Quantum*, ch. 3.

everything (TOE) is something known as *superstring theory*.[12] According to this theory, everything is ultimately composed of incredibly minute loops—the 'strings'—with length and tension, but no thickness; everything that happens is ultimately a matter of the motion and interaction of these strings; elementary particles are strings in different vibratory states. These strings are held to inhabit a ten-dimensional space–time, in which six of the spatial dimensions are curled up in such a tight radius that they are effectively undetectable *as spatial dimensions*, though their presence manifests itself in the form of forces. The details of the theory scarcely matter, for our purposes. What does matter is that, once again, it seems incomprehensible that different combinations of collective or individual string states could generate the qualitative diversity that is manifest at the phenomenal level. It seems inconceivable in much the same way, and for much the same reasons, that it is inconceivable that an artist, however skilled, should conjure the simulacrum of a Turner sunset from a palette containing only black and white paints.

What is ostensibly lacking, both at the neuronal level and at the level of particle physics, is, most obviously, the requisite qualitative potential—just as black and white paints provide the potential for an infinite number of shades of grey, but not for a yellow or a red. But there is also (as John Foster has pointed out[13]) a subtler difficulty having to do with the possibility of securing, at the fundamental level, the required qualitative *flexibility*. One might, in speculative vein, attempt some wholesale enrichment of the physical microstructure—crediting the basic ingredients of the physicist's ontology with intrinsic attributes way beyond what are called for by their explanatory roles within physical theory, but which are specifically tailored to the demands of phenomenology. The trouble then, however, is that it seems scarcely deniable that, at some level, these fundamental ontological ingredients, whatever they are, must be broadly *interchangeable*. What, one may ask, is the use of attributing, say, embryonic colour to the ultimate physical components involved in the neuronal goings-on that are supposed to be constitutive of a phenomenal patch of red, if these self-same constituents are also to be capable of figuring in auditory or olfactory experiences which are wholly devoid of visual phenomenology? Little is gained if what one does in order to account for the *presence* of phenomenal qualities in one place has the effect of making a mystery of their ostensible *absence* elsewhere.

---

12. See M. B. Green, 'Superstrings', *Scientific American*, 255 (Sept. 1986), 44–56.

13. Foster, *The Immaterial Self*, 127–28.

With regard to the first of these three difficulties, a concrete analogy may help to fix ideas. Consider a (monochrome) newspaper photograph. Seen at very close quarters, or through a magnifying glass, it stands revealed as a rectangular array of different-sized black dots on a white background. But casual inspection shows, rather, lines, edges, and patches of black, white, and varying shades of grey. Let the latter appearance correspond, in our analogy, to the phenomenal aspects of an experience, and the array of dots to the nitty-gritty of ion exchange and so forth, which is constitutive of the corresponding brain-process.

The very word 'introspection' invokes a supposed analogy with perception: the metaphor of the 'inner eye'. (Compare Kant's talk of an 'inner sense', complementary to the 'outer senses'.) Now if there really were a close parallel here, this first aspect of the grain problem would scarcely be troubling. Just as, with the photograph, the limited resolving power of the eyes ensures that, if we stand back sufficiently, we shall have the illusion of continuity, so we could envisage the mind, in introspection, as standing back from the underlying brain-processes—again, with consequent loss of resolution. Particulate and discontinuous physico-chemical activity will yield perceived continuity, just as the discrete patches of ink on paper give way to ostensibly continuous lines and patches of black, white, and grey. But of course, this picture is simply incoherent. For the mind is not supposed to exist *over and above* the relevant brain activity. And no literal sense can be attached to the notion of the conscious mind being distanced, in this fashion, *from itself*.

Coarse-graining within ordinary perception is ultimately to be explained via the concept of a *mental representation*. It is a mental representation of the external object, rather than the object itself, that is directly before the mind in ordinary perception. And this mental representation is linked to the external object by an information-conveying causal chain. Degree of resolution is largely a matter of *how much* information about the external object is conserved in transmission; though, more generally, it is also a matter of how the information is encoded and reprocessed. (Thus, 'smoothing' of the data is presumably, in part, a product of specific processing; it could hardly be accounted for on the basis merely of information degradation.)

But, as I say, there is no such story to be told in regard to introspective awareness. Introspection is not a distinct sensory modality whose objects differ from those of 'outer sense' by being internal instead of external to the conscious mind. Rather, it is distinguished by one's cognitive or intentional *focus*. Thus, any of the ordinary five senses may be exercised in introspective mode; and doing so is a matter of taking as one's cognitive focus the mental representations themselves, instead of the external objects (if any) which they represent.

(Compare the way in which, while watching the Wimbledon men's finals on television, one could switch one's mental focus from the players themselves to the corresponding images on the screen—in the context, say, of wondering whether one should adjust the contrast.) Hence, there are no distinctively introspective meta-mental representations, which stand to introspection as do ordinary visual, auditory, etc. representations to sight and hearing—and whose separation from their mental objects could help us resolve this aspect of the grain problem. And even if there were, the original problem would simply re-emerge at the level of these meta-representations themselves. Our difficulties begin at the point where the perceptual buck stops.

The force of these arguments will, I suspect, be lost on some people. Clearly, someone might protest, there are macroscopic qualities, and there is macroscopic structure: consider liquidity, for example, or temperature, or sphericity. These are perfectly genuine features of physical reality; so why shouldn't it be correspondingly macroscopic features of brain activity that manifest themselves in awareness? But macroscopic features such as those cited are not genuinely *emergent* attributes of the physical world. On the contrary, high-level descriptions like 'liquid', 'hot', or 'spherical' apply—so it would seem—entirely in virtue of what holds true at the microlevel. And if so, it appears to follow that external physical reality can, in thought and perception, present itself to the mind in such high-level terms only by courtesy of the mediating role of mental representations.

I am not, of course, suggesting that the objects of direct awareness come unconceptualized. Thus the presence, within one's visual field, of a number of black dots—even if, in contrast to the dots in our newspaper photograph, they are individually perceived as such—may inescapably carry with it the interpretation *circle*. But that does nothing to explain how what is presented to awareness can, in another instance, just *be* a phenomenally continuous circle, when the physical substrate of the experience consists of a discontinuous array of, say, discrete centres of electrical activity.

Grover Maxwell (whose statement of the grain problem is the most lucid I have come across in the published literature) suggests that, if we are looking for physical structure that is isomorphic to the phenomenal structure encountered in awareness, we might find it at what he dubs the 'middle-sized' level.[14] What he has in mind is a level of structure intermediate between, and less familiar than, quantum microstructure and quasi-classical macrostructure: a

14. G. Maxwell, 'Rigid Designators and Mind–Brain Identity', in *Minnesota Studies in the Philosophy of Science*, 9, ed. C. W. Savage (Minneapolis, 1978), 399.

level the better understanding of which might, he thinks, hold the key to the elusive goal of bringing together, into a consistent whole, quantum mechanics and general relativity. But there is a fundamental philosophical unclarity in Maxwell's proposal. For what exactly is 'middle-sized' structure supposed to consist in? Is it supposed to be structure which is, in the above sense, *high-level* with respect to electrons and the like—albeit low-level with respect to, say, blizzards, buffaloes, ball-bearings, and bacteria, hamsters, ham sandwiches, and housing estates? If so, then all he's really talking about—so it's tempting to argue—is microstructure under a (relatively) high-level description. And all the considerations invoked in the past few paragraphs still apply; it will remain a complete mystery how direct introspective contact with brain activity—unmediated by intervening mental representations—can reveal middle-sized structure to the total exclusion of the microstructure which is ultimately constitutive of it.

Perhaps, however, what Maxwell means by middle-sized structure is not merely high-level structure, with respect to the quantum microstructure, but something genuinely *emergent*, in a sense in which liquidity, temperature, and the like are not. The only sense I can attach, in the present context, to Maxwell's middle-sized structure being emergent is that it is structure which is instantiated—in part or in whole—by *emergent qualities*. By emergent qualities, I mean intrinsic attributes which are qualitatively distinct from any attributes possessed either by the low-level constituents of physical reality, considered individually, or by any configurations of them that involve relatively small numbers of these constituents, or which have a relatively low level of organization or complexity. The idea is that, at a certain number/density/ complexity (or whatever) *threshold*, new qualities emerge which are different in kind from any that are present in sub-threshold phenomena involving these same constituents; and *pari passu* with these new qualities, new behaviour also. One can imagine possessing a dynamical theory which is ostensibly equal to the task of describing the fundamental constituents, and explaining and predicting their behaviour, *up to the threshold*—at which point, however, the theory begins to prove inadequate.

Well, I daresay that something roughly along these lines may be true. Indeed, it is difficult to see how *awareness itself* could be anything other than an emergent phenomenon, in something like the above sense, assuming the truth of materialism. Nor does such emergence threaten to compromise the unity of physical science. Whatever emerged, at and above the associated threshold, would—by hypothesis—have been *latent*, all along, in the low-level constituents. Hence, a complete description of these constituents would have to include reference to dispositional properties, of which the emergent qualities and behaviour constituted a manifestation. If we assume—as is very plausible—that all dispositions must have a *categorical base* (as the disposition of a key to draw the bolt of a given lock has *shape* as its categorical base), then a description of these constituents need contain no reference to these dispositions as such. It would suffice to cite their intrinsic (non-dispositional) attributes, together with the fundamental laws; a disposition, on the part of any low-level constituent, would hold in virtue of the combination of its intrinsic, categorical attributes and laws which related these attributes to the emergent ones. And incidentally, even if awareness, say, is an emergent phenomenon in the sense just indicated (involving emergent properties and relations), it does not follow that the fundamental low-level constituents need possess any intrinsic, categorical attributes other than those which current physical theory would credit them with—at least, under the conditions prevailing in ordinary physics experiments. Their potential for generating awareness could be a matter of the application of certain currently unknown *laws* to their familiar physical attributes (in which laws, of course, there *would* be an essential reference to the emergent attributes). This fairly elementary point would appear to have escaped those authors who have argued that, if we are made out of electrons, quarks, gluons, and the like, then—given that we are conscious—electrons, quarks, and so forth must themselves be possessed of some sort of primitive proto-consciousness. As I see it, this is a complete non sequitur.

So, as I say, emergence in this sense seems to me wholly unobjectionable, philosophically speaking. But, having said that, I doubt very much whether such emergence could, realistically, be expected by itself to offer a solution to the grain problem. For we need to ask: is it really *scientifically* plausible to suppose that the distribution of these emergent qualities would possess any less microstructural complexity than that of the non-emergent ones? Let us go back to our earlier schematic example, involving a circular array of discrete centres of electrical activity in the brain. How, by appealing to emergence, might one explain how this array could present itself to consciousness as an *unbroken* circle? Well, one might suppose that, under the right conditions, such an array would give rise to an emergent field, in the immediately surrounding space, which was continuous, homogeneous, and bounded, in such a way as to match the associated phenomenal presentation, and the innate quality of which was registered in awareness (see Figure 8.1).[15]

---

15. I am here imagining that phenomenal spatial relations, say within the visual field, reflect—indeed, in some sense just *are*—actual spatial relations within the appropriate region of the cerebral cortex. But this is only for the sake of concreteness; I do not advance it as a serious hypothesis.

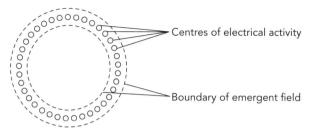

FIGURE 8.1. How a circular array of discrete centres of electrical activity in the brain might give rise to an emergent field

In short, we should have to suppose that the microstructural arrangement of the fundamental constituents was capable of giving rise to emergent distributions of qualities which were *truly* smooth and homogeneous, where their 'source' was anything but—in stark contrast to any actual field known to science, and in clear violation of the theoretical demands of quantum mechanics. Well I, for one, simply don't believe it; and I doubt if many people would. Where emergence may indeed come into its own is in accounting for the qualitative diversity that is in evidence within the phenomenal realm: McGinn's problem of how 'technicolour phenomenology [can] arise from soggy grey matter'. But as regards the problem of phenomenal coarse-graining, it seems to me that it has little or nothing to offer. A solution—if such is to be found within the confines of philosophical materialism—must be sought elsewhere.

Before we proceed further, I should make clear just what I take to be required of a solution to the grain problem. The premiss of the problem is that sensory phenomenology belongs, so to speak, to that tip of the neurophysiological iceberg which projects above the surface of awareness. We are to regard it as a part or aspect of the reality of the brain that is directly present to the conscious mind, without benefit of any intervening representation: in awareness, the intrinsic nature of some part or aspect of what is to be found within the skull stands revealed. From this it follows that the phenomenal objects of sensory awareness must be thought of as somehow *embedded* within that tract of physical reality consisting of the brain and its doings. Assuming this position to be correct, consciousness, at the phenomenal level, can only make selections from the underlying neurophysiology. There is, as we have seen, no possibility of interposing any further stage of reprocessing between awareness and the neurophysiological substrate of its phenomenal objects; for sensory phenomenology is located precisely at the point where the *output* of all processing of sensory data is delivered to the conscious mind. The challenge posed by the grain problem is, therefore, the challenge of showing how *mere selectivity*, as applied to the physical reality of the brain, can yield the form and qualitative content characteristic of sensory phenomenology.

It is often said that philosophers are better at asking questions than at answering them; and I fear that this philosopher is no exception. All that I shall try to do now (and all that space really permits) is to provide a few hints towards a solution.

Underlying the grain problem, it seems to me, are a number of tacit assumptions about the nature of reality and our relationship to it which, though intuitively natural, are philosophically far from compelling. First, I suspect that most people, when it is put to them that in awareness we are immediately aware of some part or aspect of our own brain states, will think that, on this view, the relation between what is going on in one's brain as a whole and the phenomenal contents of awareness must be something like that between a painting and a detail of that painting. But to suppose that is to make the natural but nevertheless unwarranted assumption that the *principle of selection* underlying consciousness must be purely spatial location. There is, *a priori*, no reason to assume that *any* purely *spatial* cordoning of the brain at a given time would capture all *and only* that of which the subject was directly aware. With respect to any spatially defined region, the subject could surely be aware of some but not all aspects or attributes of what lay within it. Secondly and relatedly, there is no good reason to assume that the contents of a given state of awareness correspond to *simultaneous* goings-on in the brain. Indeed, in the context of relativity, no absolute sense can be attached to the notion of spatially separated events being simultaneous. From a relativistic viewpoint, the brain corresponds to a four-dimensional *world-tube*. And it is as likely as not that what is, so to speak, *given together* in awareness is spread throughout a segment of this world-tube, rather than being confined to a time-slice. In some ways, that would square better, in any case, with the psychological phe-nomenon of the *specious present*—the fact that, subjectively speaking, states of awareness seem to possess a measure of temporal 'depth'.

These are assumptions relating to us in relation to the world. But there is, thirdly, an assumption about the nature of reality itself which one might wish to question. Kronecker once said, apropos of arithmetic, that the natural numbers were created by God and that everything else is the work of man. In a similar way, it seems to me, people are very apt to suppose that only micro-structure is, so to speak, God-given, and that any higher level of structure is, at best, ontologically or metaphysically derivative, and at worst, a mere concep-tual artefact. That assumption, in effect, was the basis of our earlier attack on Maxwell's suggestions regarding 'middle-sized structure'. But perhaps, after all, this notion of the ontological primacy of the microstructural is a dogma which should be rejected; perhaps the dilemma on whose horns we attempted to impale Maxwell is a false one. (I shall shortly advance some considerations which suggest that it is.)

None of these observations, however, penetrates to what I conceive to be the real heart of the matter, which is that the grain problem is one manifestation of a more general philosophical puzzle having to do with *subjectivity* and *objectivity*. The world of modern science, it is sometimes said, is a *centreless* world, a world which abstracts from the *point of view* of any particular observer. As Nagel neatly puts it, science is in the business of describing 'the view from nowhere'.[16] Awareness, by contrast, is inescapably centred on a point of view. What is directly present to awareness must, therefore, be conceived as a *perspective* on the brain. I wish to argue that the apparent dissonance between a physiologist's description of brain activity and the contents of our introspective judgements is to be seen, in part, as a consequence of the (relatively) perspective-transcendent character of the former.

If what is true 'subjectively' is true relative to a point of view, then the only way of reconciling subjectivity and objectivity is by incorporating *points of view* within one's objective inventory of the world. Any metaphysical theory which does not somehow include points of view in its ontology is to that extent inadequate, as a comprehensive conception of reality. One philosopher who saw this very clearly was Leibniz, who went to the extreme lengths of supposing, in effect, that the universe was entirely composed of points of view—his *monads*.

What I have just said applies as much to physics as it does to metaphysics. Indeed, it is in some sense as much a condition of the explanatory adequacy of a physical theory that one be able to locate, within it, the point of view of the observer, as it is of the practical efficacy of a map that one be able to pinpoint, on the map, one's own position.

In classical physics it was unnecessary to address this requirement explicitly, since the associated conceptual scheme was essentially continuous with that of common sense. In the theory of relativity, however, the requirement is met quite explicitly via the notion of a *frame of reference*. The currently favoured language of space–time and four-vectors would be intuitively unintelligible without the auxiliary notion of an *observer* as situated at the origin of a set of spatial co-ordinates with respect to which he is invariably at rest, with a personal flow of time which corresponds to integration of the space–time *interval* along his own *world-line*. (Einstein sometimes put this very concretely, imagining the observer as carrying around with him an apparatus consisting

---

16. T. Nagel, *The View from Nowhere* (Oxford, 1986).

of three rigid, mutually perpendicular measuring-rods, clutching it at the point where the three rods intersect—the 'origin'—to which is attached an ideal clock.)

Via this notion of a frame of reference, one comes to see how, from the observer's own point of view, space–time comes to be partitioned into the distinct space and time of common sense. Thus, the space–time interval (that is, four-dimensional separation) between two events comes to be decomposed into spatial and temporal intervals corresponding, respectively, to the *projections* of the space–time interval on to the three-dimensional space defined by the spatial co-ordinates (or the set of mutually perpendicular measuring-rods) and the one-dimensional space defined by the time co-ordinate (or the ideal clock). And, in general, a four-vector is decomposed into a three-vector and a scalar component—the four-momentum, for example, into a three-vector momentum and a scalar energy.

It is tempting to think of an observer, in the context of relativity, as the *concrete embodiment* of a frame of reference (rather than merely as 'carrying around' such a frame, à la Einstein). A description of objects and events *relative to* this frame of reference—couched, therefore, in the language of space and time, rather than of space–time—may then be thought of as corresponding to the observer's perspective: how things are from his own 'subjective' point of view.

The conception of physical science as giving us a centreless account of the world chimes well with its aim, in modern times, of finding things that remain *invariant* with respect to different ways of representing physical reality. (Einstein, it is alleged, originally wanted to call his theory the *theory of invariants.*) This notion of invariance is perhaps the single most powerful idea in modern physics and crops up everywhere—gauge invariance, in field theory, being one of its most prominent recent manifestations. But in particular, it crops up at the foundations of *quantum mechanics*. States of a physical system, in quantum mechanics, correspond to vectors in an abstract space known as *Hilbert space*. And just as the four-dimensional space of relativity can be seen through the eyes of any of an infinity of different *frames of reference*, so the Hilbert space of a quantum-mechanical system can be seen through the eyes of any of an infinity of different so-called *vector bases*. Every quantum-mechanical *observable*, that is to say, question one can ask of a quantum-mechanical system, susceptible of being answered by a suitable measurement—or more generally, every set of *compatible* observables, that is, questions capable of being simultaneously answered—corresponds to a vector basis for Hilbert space, known as the *eigenbasis* of the corresponding observable or set of observables. A set of observables, via its eigenbasis, defines a co-ordinate system for Hilbert space, just as a frame of reference defines a co-ordinate system for space–time. (The key things that remain invariant with respect to different bases are the respective probabilities of getting various outcomes, when carrying out measurements on the quantum-mechanical system in question.)

Quantum mechanics was discovered independently, in the mid-1920s, by Heisenberg and Schrödinger. But so different, in their mathematical formulation, were Heisenberg's *matrix mechanics* and Schrödinger's *wave mechanics*, that they were at first thought to be distinct, rival theories. Only subsequently were they found (by Schrödinger himself, in the first instance) to be essentially equivalent, the difference in form being due, in large part, to different choices of basis. Roughly speaking, Heisenberg chose the eigenbasis corresponding to the energy observable, and Schrödinger the eigenbasis corresponding to the position observable.

That said, I am now in a position to convey the essence of my own favoured approach to the grain problem. (Again, space does not permit more than a very approximate and compressed rendering.) First, the brain, I suggest, may legitimately be regarded as a quantum-mechanical system. (There is nothing in the formalism of quantum mechanics that prevents it from being applied to macroscopic systems.) As with most complex quantum-mechanical systems, the brain may be conceptually decomposed (doubtless, in several alternative ways) into *subsystems*, which can be treated as quantum-mechanical systems in their own right. One of these subsystems I take to coincide with the neurophysiological substrate of conscious mental functioning. (This dividing-up of the brain into subsystems need not, as remarked earlier, correspond to anything that would seem intuitively at all natural; nor need the subsystem in question correspond to what would ordinarily be thought of as a *part* of the brain. The dividing-up would not, in general, be a *spatial*, or even a *spatio-temporal* division, so much as a partitioning of the *degrees of freedom* of the larger brain system—the distinct ways in which it can change state or store energy.)

Anyway, there is, I take it, such a brain subsystem. And from the point of view of consciousness, I contend, there is (at any given time, at least) a preferred set of compatible observables on that system. The conscious observer views his or her own brain through the eyes, so to speak, of this preferred set of observables, much as the observer, in relativity, views the world through the eyes of his own frame of reference. Indeed, just as, in relativity, the observer can, in a sense, be regarded as a concrete embodiment of a particular frame of reference, so, I suggest, may a conscious subject be thought of as, in some sense, the concrete embodiment of a set of compatible observables. Every

quantum-mechanical observable has a so-called *spectrum of eigenvalues*, associated, respectively, with the eigenvectors comprising its eigenbasis; these are
numbers corresponding to the possible results of measuring the observable in
question. If we consider a *set* of observables, then their spectra can themselves
be thought of as co-ordinate axes, jointly defining a further abstract space. And
a value of each coordinate, corresponding to an eigenvalue of each observable
in the set, will define a point or vector in this abstract space. When the set of
observables is the set preferred by, or embodied in, consciousness, then this
space may be equated with phenomenal or experiential space: points or vectors in the space correspond to distinct possible states of awareness. And the
various *qualia* spaces of sense-perception—colour space, for example—are
simply subspaces of this abstract space; specific *qualia*, as they figure in awareness, represent points or regions of such spaces encountered, so to speak, in
the flesh. It is precisely here that the intrinsic character of the concrete reality
that the abstract mathematical formalism of quantum mechanics purports to
describe makes itself manifest.

But how does all this address the problem of how awareness is able to
gloss over the complex microstructure which presumably underlies the
phenomenal contents of any experience? Well, quite simply, there are, in
quantum mechanics, no observables, or sets thereof, which are *a priori* privileged. In particular, there is, in terms of quantum-mechanical observables,
no rock-bottom level of structure to be discerned in the world. In quantum
field theory, no sense can be attached, for example, to the notion of measuring the values of the field variables at a precise point—only their average values over some finite spatio-temporal region (which one can make as small
as one wishes); indeed, no sense can be attached to their *possessing* a precise
value at any precise point. (No more, in elementary quantum mechanics,
can an electron be said to have, let alone be measured as having, a precisely
defined position or momentum.) In quantum mechanics there is a sense in
which all observables, and in particular observables corresponding to every
level of structure, are to be regarded as equal in the sight of God, as are different frames of reference, relativistically conceived.[17] As I intimated earlier,

17. For the benefit of those familiar with quantum mechanics, let me say that I am, of
course, glossing over the distinction between so-called *maximal* and *non-maximal* (or *degen-
erate*) observables, or sets thereof. (A maximal observable, or set of observables, is one corresponding to a measurement, or set of simultaneous measurements, which yields a state of
maximum information about the system in question—one that cannot be improved upon by
the performance of further measurements.) In case someone thinks that maximal observables, or maximal sets of compatible observables, are privileged with respect to non-maximal
ones, in a way that vitiates my argument, it should be pointed out that one could imagine the

quantum mechanics seems to be telling us that it is a classical prejudice to suppose that the world is not *intrinsically* structured at anything but the level of elementary particles, and their actions and interactions.

According to this approach, then, the apparent dissonance between brain activity, as seen through the eyes (and concepts) of the neurophysiologist, on the one hand, and the conscious subject, on the other, is to be attributed to three distinct considerations. First, this brain activity is revealed to the awareness of the corresponding conscious subject—as it is not to the probings of the neurophysiologist—*as it is in itself* (albeit only from a certain point of view). Second, introspective awareness is focused on a *subsystem* of the brain, selected according to principles that, from the standpoint of physiology, would seem very unnatural. And finally, the contents of consciousness correspond to eigenvalues of a set of *observables* which, again, are distinct from anything that the physiologist is likely to settle on: the dissonance between the subject's view, and that of the physiologist, might be conceived as analogous to that between, say, Schrödinger's wave mechanics and Heisenberg's matrix mechanics. Thinking in terms of co-ordinate systems for the Hilbert space of the relevant brain system, it is as though the co-ordinate system of the conscious subject were, so to speak, rotated with respect to that of the external observer.[18]

The state of a physical system—on the view that I am proposing—might be compared to a block of wood, distinct cross-sections of which can reveal strikingly different sorts of patterns, depending on the angle at which it is sliced: concentric rings at one extreme, roughly parallel, gently undulating lines at the other. Though the analogy is very imperfect, one might think of the neurophysiologist, and the conscious subject in introspection, as likewise being confronted, so to speak, with different 'cross-sections' of what are in fact the same brain states. My claim is that, by appealing to the

---

space of possible states of awareness of the conscious observer being generated, so to speak, in two stages. Any non-maximal set of compatible observables can, after all, be turned into a maximal set simply by adding observables to the original set. So suppose, to begin with, that there is (from the perspective of consciousness, though not of the world) a preferred maximal set of compatible observables (having the requisite non-maximal set as a subset). The spectra of eigenvalues of the observables in the set could then be thought of as co-ordinate axes, defining a state space, with respect to which the range of possible states of awareness could then be regarded as constituting a preferred subspace.

18. Here I have been able to do no more than sketch the bare bones of the theory I favour. In *Mind, Brain and the Quantum*, I develop these ideas in far greater detail, and also, for the sake of those unversed in modern physics, provide an elementary account of quantum mechanics itself.

quantum-mechanical concept of an observable, we can render it intelligible, as with the grain of the wood, that a common underlying structure should manifest itself in superficially very different ways. On the side of introspection, moreover, such a conception removes the need to appeal to any inner representation, distinct from the state itself. For to be directly acquainted with a 'cross-section' of something is *a fortiori* to be directly acquainted with the thing itself, not merely some cognitive surrogate of it—in spite of the fact that what is thereby revealed to consciousness is revealed only under a certain aspect.

What, then, finally, is consciousness telling us about the nature of physical reality? Well, first (assuming materialism to be true), that there is more to matter than meets the physicist's eye. For there is nothing in the physicist's account of the world to explain why there should *exist* conscious points of view—why the world should contain such concrete embodiments of sets of quantum-mechanical observables. Thus we are in a position to know *a priori* that something like superstring theory, whatever its other merits, cannot literally be a theory of everything—since there is nothing in the theory that could, even in principle, explain how matter, suitably combined, is able to generate awareness. But on the positive side, it follows from what I have been saying that our states of awareness, corresponding as they do, on my account, to sequences of eigenvalues of brain observables, are providing us with the answers to specific questions concerning the intrinsic nature of a corner of the physical world—something that (as Russell rightly insisted) can never be revealed in ordinary measurement or observation. For our own awareness, so I have been urging, embodies a preferred set of observables, which in turn amounts to saying that its contents, at any given time, embody the answers to a set of questions about the state (the intrinsic state) of the underlying brain system. Sadly, however, we here find ourselves in a predicament akin to that of the characters in *The Hitch Hiker's Guide to the Galaxy*, on being told that the answer to life, the universe, and everything was 42. We know the *answers* to these questions, in a way that a scientist, merely by examining our brains from without, never could. But unfortunately, we have, as yet, no idea what the questions are!

9

Real Materialism (with new postscript)

Galen Strawson

Trinculo might have been referring to modern physics in the words, "This is the tune of our catch, played by the picture of Nobody".

EDDINGTON (*1928: 292*)

Love like Matter is much
Odder than we thought.

AUDEN (*1940, 'HEAVY DATE'*)

1 Introduction

Materialism is the view that every real, concrete[1] phenomenon[2] in the universe is physical. It's a view about the actual universe, and for the purposes of this chapter I am going to assume that it is true.

This chapter is an attempt to elaborate on 'Agnostic materialism' (Strawson 1994: 43–105), in which I argued that experiential phenomena must be among the fundamental physical phenomena, and that we must be radically ignorant of the nature of the physical in certain ways. Trailers appeared in Strawson 1998 and 1999. Daniel Stoljar and I discovered a strong and encouraging convergence in our views when I gave this chapter at the University of Boulder, Colorado, in 1998 (see Stoljar 2001). In this reprinting I've added a few more quotations and references and made a few small adjustments.

1. By 'concrete' I simply mean 'not abstract'. It's natural to think that any really existing thing is *ipso facto* concrete, non-abstract, in which case 'concrete' is redundant, but some philosophers like to say that numbers (for example) are real things—objects that really exist, but are abstract.

2. I use 'phenomenon' as a completely general word for any sort of existent, a word that carries no implication as to ontological category (the trouble with the general word 'entity' is

It has been characterized in other ways. David Lewis once defined it as 'metaphysics built to endorse the truth and descriptive completeness of physics more or less as we know it'.[3] This can't be faulted as a terminological decision, but it seems unwise to burden materialism—the view that every real concrete phenomenon in the universe is *physical*—with a commitment to the descriptive completeness of *physics* more or less as we know it. There may be physical phenomena which physics (and any non-revolutionary extension of it) cannot describe, and of which it has no inkling, either descriptive or referential.[4] Physics is one thing, the physical is another. 'Physical' is a natural-kind term—it is the ultimate natural-kind term[5]—and no sensible person thinks that physics has nailed all the essential properties of the physical. Current physics is profoundly beautiful and useful, but it is in a state of chronic internal tension.[6] It may be added, with Russell and others, that although physics appears to tell us a great deal about certain of the general structural or mathematical characteristics of the physical, it fails to give us any further insight into the nature of whatever it is that has these structural or mathematical characteristics—apart from making it plain that it is utterly bizarre relative to our ordinary conception of it.

It is unclear exactly what this last remark amounts to (is it being suggested that physics is failing to do something it could do? No.), but it already amounts to something very important when it comes to what is known as the 'mind–body problem'. For many take this to be the problem of how mental and in particular experiential phenomena can be physical phenomena *given what we already know about the nature of the physical*. But those who think this are already lost. For we have no good reason to think that we know anything

---

that it is now standardly understood to refer specifically to things or substances). Note that someone who agrees that physical phenomena are all there are, but finds no logical incoherence in the idea that physical things could be put together in such a way as to give rise to non-physical things, can define materialism as the view that every real, concrete phenomenon that there is *or could be* in the universe is physical.

3. 1986: x; when I cite a work I give the date of first publication, or occasionally the date of composition, while the page reference is to the edition listed in the bibliography.

4. Physics is trivially referentially complete, according to materialism, in so far as its object of study is the universe, i.e. the whole of concrete reality. There may nevertheless be specific, smaller-scale phenomena of which physicists have no descriptive or referential inkling.

5. Failure to recognize this simple point, long after the existence of natural-kind terms has been generally acknowledged, is one of the more disastrous legacies of positivism. (Compare the survival of the 'regularity theory of causation' after the abandonment of phenomenalism.)

6. I have in mind the old quarrel between general relativity theory and quantum mechanics, but there is also turmoil in cosmology.

about the physical that gives us any reason to find any problem in the idea that mental phenomena are physical phenomena. If we consider the nature of our knowledge of the physical, we realize with Eddington that 'no problem of irreconcilability arises' (1928: 260). Joseph Priestley saw this very clearly over two hundred years ago, and he was not the first. Noam Chomsky reached essentially the same conclusion over thirty years ago, and he was not the last (see e.g. Chomsky 1968: 6–8, 98; 1988: 142–47; 1994 passim; 1995: 1–10; 1996: 38–45; 1998: 437–41; compare Crane and Mellor 1990). Most present-day philosophers take no notice of it and waste a lot of time as a result. Much of the present debate about the 'mind–body' problem is beside the point.

2. Terminology

I'm going to use the plural-accepting, count-noun form of the word 'experience' for talking of experiences as things (events) that may (as we presume) have non-experiential being as well as experiential being. And I'm going to reserve the adjective 'experiential' and the plural-lacking form of the noun 'experience' for talking about the qualitative character that experiences have for those who have them as they have them, where this qualitative character is considered wholly independently of everything else. The phenomenon of experiential[7] qualitative character is part of what exists—it is part of reality, whatever its ontological category—and it is important to have some unequivocal way of referring to it and only to it.

One could express this terminological proposal by saying that 'experiential phenomena' and 'experience' (plural-lacking form) refer in a general way to: that part of reality which one is left with when, continuing to live and think and feel as one does, one engages in an old sceptical thought experiment and imagines that the 'external world', including one's own body, does not exist. They refer to the part or aspect of reality one has to do with when one considers experiences specifically and solely in respect of the experiential qualitative character they have for those who have them as they have them, and puts aside the fact that they may also be correctly describable in such non-experiential terms as 'a 70–20–30 Hertz coding triplet across the neurons of area V4'.[8]

---

7. 'Qualitative' has to be qualified by 'experiential' because experiences also have non-experiential qualitative character, according to materialists (every non-relational property of a thing contributes to its qualitative character). Having made the point, I will either bracket 'experiential' or follow common practice and omit it.

8. Churchland 1995: 202. Obviously 'correctly describable' doesn't entail 'fully describable'. Note that one also puts aside the fact that they can be correctly described in such non-experiential terms as 'a perception of *the Eiffel Tower*'.

3. Realistic Materialism

Realistic materialists—realistic anybodies—must grant that experiential phenomena are real, concrete phenomena, for nothing in this life is more certain.[9] They must therefore hold that they are physical phenomena, although physics contains only predicates for non-experiential being, and so cannot characterize the qualitative character of experiential being in any way. It may at first sound odd to use the word 'concrete' to characterize the qualitative character of experiences of colour, gusts of depression, thoughts about diophantine equations, and so on, but it isn't odd, because 'concrete' simply means 'not abstract'.[10] For most purposes one may take 'concrete' to be coextensive with 'possessed of spatio-temporal existence', although this will be directly question-begging in some contexts.[11]

It may also sound odd to use 'physical' to characterize mental phenomena like experiential phenomena: many materialists talk about the mental and the physical as if they were opposed categories. But this, *on their own view*, is like talking about cows and animals as if they were opposed categories. Every concrete phenomenon in the universe is physical, according to materialists, so all mental phenomena, including experiential phenomena, are physical phenomena, according to materialists: just as all cows are animals.

So what are materialists doing when they talk, as they so often do, as if the mental and the physical were entirely different? What they may mean to do is to distinguish, within the realm of the physical, which is the only realm there is, according to them, between the mental and the non-mental, or between the experiential and the non-experiential; to distinguish, that is, between mental (or experiential) features of the physical, and non-mental (or non-experiential) features of the physical.[12]

It's this difference that is in question when it comes to the 'mind-body' problem; materialists who persist in talking in terms of the difference between

---

9. Following Lewis 1994 I make no distinction between 'materialism' and 'physicalism'.

10. If 'immaterial souls' existed, they would of course be concrete phenomena.

11. Experiential phenomena would be concrete phenomena even if space and time as we currently conceive of them were not really real.

12. One needs to distinguish between mental and experiential phenomena because although all experiential phenomena are mental, not all mental phenomena are experiential, on the ordinary view of things. Certain *dispositional* states—beliefs, preferences, and so on—are generally acknowledged to be mental phenomena although they have no experiential character (there are also reasons for saying that there are *occurrent* mental phenomena that are non-experiential).

the mental and the physical perpetuate the terms of the dualism they reject in a way that is inconsistent with their own view. I use the words 'mental' and 'non-mental' ('experiential' and 'non-experiential') where many use the words 'mental' and 'physical' simply because I assume, as a (wholly conventional) materialist, that every real concrete phenomenon is physical, and find myself obliged to put things in this way (compare Chomsky 1968: 98).

There's tremendous resistance to abandoning the old mental/physical terminology in favour of the mental/non-mental, experiential/non-experiential terminology, although the latter seems to be exactly what is required. Many think the old terminology is harmless, and a few are not misled by it: they consistently use 'physical' to mean 'non-mental physical'. But it sets up the wrong frame of thought from the start, and I suspect that those who are never misled by it are members of a small minority.

When I say that the mental, and in particular the experiential, is physical, and endorse the view that 'experience is really just neurons firing', I mean something completely different from what some materialists have apparently meant by saying such things. I don't mean that all aspects of what is going on, in the case of conscious experience, can be described by current physics, or some non-revolutionary extension of it. Such a view amounts to radical 'eliminativism' with respect to consciousness,[13] and is mad. My claim is different. It is that the experiential (considered just as such)[14]—the feature of reality we have to do with when we consider experiences specifically and solely in respect of the experiential character they have for those who have them as they have them—that 'just is' physical. No one who disagrees with this is a remotely realistic materialist.

When aspiring materialists consider the living brain, in discussion of the 'mind–body problem', they often slide into supposing that the word 'brain' somehow refers only to the brain-as-revealed-by-current-physics-and -neurophysiology. But this is a mistake, for it refers just as it says, to the living brain, i.e. the living brain as a whole, the brain in its total physical existence and activity. Realistic—real—materialists must agree that the total physical existence and activity of the brain of an ordinary, living person, considered over time, is *constituted* by experiential phenomena (if only in part) in every sense in which it is (assumed to be) constituted (in part) by non-experiential phenomena characterizable by physics. Real (realistic) materialists can't think

---

13. Some doubt this, but it follows from the fact that current physics contains no predicates for experiential phenomena at all, and that no non-revolutionary extension of it could do so.

14. The parenthesis is redundant given the definition of 'experiential' in §2.

that there is something still left to say about experiential phenomena once everything that there is to say about the physical brain has been said. At the same time, they can't think that physics and neurophysiology can say everything there is to say about the brain, because physics and neurophysiology contain no predicates for experiential phenomena (considered just as such).

4. Materialism Further Defined

Materialism, then, is the view that every real concrete phenomenon is physical in every respect, but more needs to be said, for experiential phenomena— together with the subject of experience, assuming that that is something extra—are the only real, concrete phenomena that we can know with certainty to exist,[15] and as it stands this definition of materialism doesn't even rule out 'idealism'—the view that mental phenomena are the only real phenomena and have no non-mental being—from qualifying as a form of materialism! There's a sense in which this consequence of the definition is salutary (see §§14–15 below), but it may nonetheless seem silly to call an idealist view 'materialism'. Russell is right to say that 'the truth about physical objects *must* be strange' (1912: 19), but it still seems terminologically reasonable to take materialism to be committed to the existence of non-experiential being in the universe, in addition to experiential being, and I shall do so in what follows. In fact I think the most plausible version of materialism is panpsychist or panexperientialist materialism (see Strawson 1994: 62, and the quotation from Eddington on pp. 193–94 below), in which case we should override this terminological preference. But that is a subject for a different paper.

It's also reasonable to take materialism to involve the claim that *every* existing concrete phenomenon has non-mental, non-experiential being, whether or not it also has mental or experiential being. Applied to mental phenomena, then, materialism claims that each particular mental phenomenon essentially has non-mental being, in addition to mental being. This is, I think, a standard understanding of materialism (any materialism that acknowledges the existence of mental phenomena).[16]

---

15. Unless the existence of experiential phenomena of kinds that we know to exist entails the existence of non-experiential phenomena. See n. 17.

16. In the case of experiences, it amounts to saying that they are not just experiential phenomena, although experiential phenomena are of course part of what constitutes their existence. Note that to distinguish between mental being and non-mental being is not to claim to know how to draw a sharp line between them. The starting situation is simply this: we know there is mental being, and we assume, as conventional materialists, that this is not all there is.

In this chapter, then, I'll assume that all realistic materialists take it that there is both mental and experiential being and non-mental, non-experiential being. Must all realistic *monists* also take it that there is non-mental, non-experiential being? Many would say Yes, on the grounds that it is not remotely realistic to suppose either that there is, or might be, no non-mental or non-experiential being at all. But the question of what it is to be (metaphysically) realistic is far harder here than it is when it is merely the existence of experience that is in question. For the purposes of this chapter I will again *assume* that any realistic position does take it that there is non-mental or non-experiential being in addition to mental and experiential being, for this assumption accords with ordinary conceptions, and my main argument does not require me to challenge it. But it is at best an assumption, which I suspect may be false in fact. Idealists, of course, reject the assumption that realistic monism requires acknowledgement of non-mental, non-experiential phenomena, and I will enter a number of reservations along the way.[17]

It's clumsy to oscillate between 'mental' and 'experiential', or constantly double them up, and in the next few sections I'll run the discussion in terms of the mental/non-mental distinction (such as it is). This said, all my examples of mental phenomena will be experiential phenomena, for they suffice to make the relevant point and are, in the present context, what matter most. It may be added that the reference of the term 'experiential' is much clearer than that of the essentially contestable term 'mental', and that the latter may in the end deserve the treatment proposed for the term 'physical' in §15 below. Nevertheless it seems best to begin in this way.[18]

I will quote Russell—post-1926 Russell—frequently when discussing materialism, for my views converge with his in certain respects, and he has been wrongly ignored in recent discussion.[19] He was still inclined to call himself a 'neutral monist' at that time, but he is equally well read as a thoroughgoing materialist.[20] He rejects materialism in name, pointing out that

---

17. In Strawson 1994 (pp. 134–44) I argue that there couldn't be experiential or experiential-content phenomena of the sort with which we are familiar unless there were also non-experiential phenomena; I now think that that argument fails (for reasons given in Strawson 2003), and that all reality could be experiential in nature compatibly with the truth of everything that is true in physics.

18. I discuss the difference between 'experiential' and 'mental', and the vagueness of 'mental', in Strawson 1994 (see e.g. pp. 136–44 and ch. 6). Here I'm trying to avoid the issue as far as possible.

19. See, however, Lockwood 1981. (Note added in 2014: this paper was written in 1997.)

20. See e.g. Russell 1927b: 110, 119, 123, 126, 170. I don't understand everything Russell says and may misrepresent him. I aim to take what I think is right from his views without

'matter has become as ghostly as anything in a spiritualist séance'—it has, he says, disappeared 'as a "thing"' and has been 'replaced by emanations from a locality'[21]—, but he grants that 'those who would formerly have been material-ists can still adopt a philosophy which comes to much the same thing. They can say that the type of causation dealt with in physics is fundamental, and that all events are subject to physical laws' (1927b: 126–27). And this, in effect, is what he does himself.[22]

5. 'Mental' and 'Non-Mental'

It may seem odd to take 'mental' as the basic positive term when character-izing materialism, but one isn't a thoroughgoing materialist if one finds it so. For all materialists hold that every concrete phenomenon in the universe is physical, and they are neither sensible nor realistic if they have any incli-nation to deny the concrete reality of mental phenomena like experiential phenomena.[23] It follows that they have, so far, no reason to find it odd or biased to take 'mental' rather than 'non-mental' as the basic term.

  —'Surely it would be better, even so, to start with some positive term "T" for the non-mental physical, and then define a negative term, "non-T",

---

attempting exegesis, and I'll sometimes detour from the main argument in Russellian directions.

21. 1927b: 78, 84. N. R. Hanson (1962) spoke similarly of the 'dematerialization of matter' (compare Feigl, 1962), and Priestley (1777) made essentially the same point. See also Lange 1865, quoted in the next note.

22. In his introduction to Lange's *History of Materialism*, Russell notes that 'physics is not materialistic in the old sense, since it no longer assumes matter as permanent substance' (1925: xix), and he may have the following passage from Lange in mind: 'We have in our own days so accustomed ourselves to the abstract notion of forces, or rather to a notion hovering in a mystic obscurity between abstraction and concrete comprehension, that we no longer find any difficulty in making one particle of matter act upon another without immediate contact. We may, indeed, imagine that in the proposition, "No force without matter", we have uttered something very Materialistic, while all the time we calmly allow particles of matter to act upon each other through void space without any material link. From such ideas the great mathematicians and physicists of the seventeenth century were far removed. They were all in so far still genuine Materialists in the sense of ancient Materialism, that they made immediate contact a condition of influence. The collision of atoms or the attraction by hook shaped particles, a mere modification of collision, were the type of all Mechanism and the whole movement of science tended towards Mechanism' (1865: 1.308, quoted in Chomsky, 1996: 44).

23. This is so even if 'eliminativism' about other candidate mental phenomena—dispositional phenomena like preferences, beliefs, and so on—is worth serious discussion.

to cover the mental physical; or use a pair of independently positive terms?'

There are two good reasons for taking 'mental' as the basic positive term, one terminological, the other philosophical. The terminological reason is simply that we do not have a convenient positive term for the non-mental (obviously we can't use 'physical', and there is no other natural candidate). The philosophical reason is very old: it is that we have direct acquaintance with—know—fundamental features of the mental nature of (physical) reality just in having experience in the way we do, in a way that has no parallel in the case of any non-mental features of (physical)[24] reality. We do not have to stand back from experiences and take them as objects of knowledge by means of some further mental operation, in order for there to be acquaintance and knowing of this sort: the having is the knowing.[25]

This point has often been questioned, but it remains immovable. Russell may exaggerate when he says that 'we know *nothing* about the intrinsic quality of physical events except when these are mental events that we directly experience' (1956: 153; my emphasis), or that 'as regards the world in general, both physical and mental, *everything* that we know of its intrinsic character is derived from the mental side',[26] for it's arguable that the spacetime character of the world is part of its intrinsic character, and, further, that we may have some knowledge of this spacetime character. I don't think he exaggerates much, however. He's on to something important, and the epistemological asymmetry between claims to knowledge of experiential being and claims to knowledge of non-experiential being is undeniable, however unfashionable.

The asymmetry claim that concerns me is not the claim that all epistemic contact with concrete reality involves experience, and that we are inevitably a further step away from the thing with which we are in contact when it is a non-experiential phenomenon. It is, rather, the claim that we are acquainted with reality *as it is in itself*, in certain respects, in having experience as we do.

---

24. The word 'physical' is bracketed because it is redundant, here as elsewhere. See §14.

25. Compare Shoemaker's idea (rather differently applied) that many mental states and goings on are 'constitutively self-intimating' (1990). See also Maxwell 1978: 392, 396.

26. 1927a: 402; my emphasis. See Lockwood 1989: 159: 'Consciousness . . . provides us with a kind of "window" on to our brains, making possible a transparent grasp of a tiny corner of material reality that is in general opaque to us. . . . The qualities of which we are immediately aware, in consciousness, precisely *are* some at least of the intrinsic qualities of the states and processes that go to make up the material world—more specifically, states and processes within our own brains. This was Russell's suggestion'.

This second claim revolts against the tendency of much current epistemology and philosophy of mind, but there is no reason why it should trouble thoughtful materialists, and I will offer a brief defence of it in §13. Here it is worth noting that it's fully compatible with the view that there may also be fundamental things we don't know about matter considered in its experiential being.[27]

6. Aside: 'as It Is in Itself'

Does one need to defend the phrase 'as it is in itself', when one uses it in philosophy? I fear one does, for some think (incoherently) that it is somehow incoherent. Still, it is easy to defend. The supposition that reality is in fact a certain way, whatever we can manage to know or say about it, is obviously true. To be is to be somehow or other. Nothing can exist or be real without being a certain way at any given time.[28] And the way something is just is how it is in itself. This point is not threatened by the suggestion that our best models of the behaviour of things like photons credit them with properties that seem incompatible to us—wave-like properties and particle-like properties, for example. What we learn from this is just that this is how photons affect us, given their intrinsic nature—given how they are in themselves, and how we are in ourselves. We acquire no reason to think (incoherently) that photons do not have some intrinsic nature at any given time. Whatever claim anyone makes about the nature of reality—including the claim that it has apparently incompatible properties—just is a claim about the way it is. This applies as much to the Everett 'many-worlds' theory of reality as to any other.

Some think that what we learn from quantum theory is that there is, objectively, no particular way that an electron or a photon is, at a given time. They confuse an epistemological point about undecidability with a metaphysical claim about the nature of things. The problem is not just that such a claim is unverifiable. The problem is that it's incoherent. For whatever the electron's or photon's weirdness (its weirdness to us: nothing is intrinsically weird), its being thus weird just is the way it is.

So we may talk without reservation of reality as it is in itself. Such talk involves no (allegedly dubious) metaphysics of the Kantian kind. Its propriety

---

27. Not only facts about experience in sense modalities we lack, or (e.g.) about the brightness-saturation-hue complexity of seemingly simple colour-experience, but also, perhaps, murkier facts about its composition, and also, perhaps, about the 'hidden nature of consciousness' postulated by McGinn 1991: chs. 3 and 4.

28. If you are worried about the concept—or reality—of time, drop the last four words.

derives entirely and sufficiently from the thought that if a thing exists, it is a certain way. For the way it is just is how it is in itself.

7. Structure and Structured

So much, for the moment, for our theoretical conception of the mental: it has some securely anchored, positive descriptive content, and we can know that this is so; for whatever the best general account of the mental, it includes experiential phenomena in its scope; and experiential phenomena are not only indubitably real; they are also phenomena part of whose intrinsic nature just is their experiential character; and their experiential character is something with which we are directly acquainted, however hard we may find the task of describing it in words. This is so even if we can make mistakes about the nature of our experiences, and even if we can do so even when we consider them merely in respect of their (experiential) qualitative character (see e.g. Dennett 1991a: ch. 11). It is so even if we differ dramatically among ourselves in the qualitative character of our experiences, in ways we cannot know about.

Our theoretical conception of the mental, then, has clear and secure descriptive content. (Don't ask for it to be put further into words; the anchoring is sufficiently described in the last paragraph.) Our theoretical conception of the non-mental, by contrast, remains, so far, a wholly negative concept. It has, as yet, no positive descriptive content.

Can anything be done about this? On one reading, Russell thinks not: the science of physics is our fundamental way of attempting to investigate the non-mental being of physical reality, and it cannot help us. 'Physics is mathematical', he says, 'not because we know so much about the physical world, but because we know so little: it is only its mathematical properties that we can discover. For the rest, our knowledge is negative.' 'We know nothing about the intrinsic quality of physical events except when these are mental events that we directly experience.' On this view, neither physics nor ordinary experience of physical objects give us any sort of knowledge of the intrinsic nature of non-mental reality.[29]

---

29. Russell 1927b: 125, 1956: 153. Lockwood 1989: ch. 10 contains some illuminating pages on Russell and a useful historical note on versions of the idea that precede Russell's. See also Maxwell 1978, whose Russellian approach is treated sympathetically in Chalmers 1996: 153–54 (and see index), and Chalmers 1997: 405–06. Jeremy Butterfield and Bas van Fraassen have pointed out to me the link here to John Worrall's 'structural realism'; see e.g. Worrall 1989 and Ladyman 1998. Eddington explicitly endorses 'structuralism' in 1939 and also makes the point clearly in Eddington 1920 and 1928.

Is Russell right? Something needs to be said about his use of the word 'intrinsic'. It is potentially misleading, and it helps to consider other ways in which he puts the point. Thus he talks regularly of the 'abstractness' of physics. The knowledge it gives is, he says, 'purely formal'. It reveals the abstract 'structure' of physical phenomena while saying nothing about their 'quality' (1927a: 392, 382, 388).

I am not sure that the distinction between structure and quality is clear, or fundamental in such a way that it holds 'all the way down',[30] but (putting that doubt aside) it seems that the fundamental distinction that Russell has in mind can be expressed by saying that it is a distinction between *how X is structurally disposed* and *what X is apart from (over and above) its structural disposition*.[31] Physics gives the structure, but not the structure-transcendent nature, of the thing that has the structure. If we say that truths about how X is structurally disposed have purely *structure-specifying* content, while truths about what X is over and above its structural disposition also have *structure-transcendent* content, or, more simply, *non-structural* content, then we may say that 'non-structural' covers everything that Russell has in mind when he talks of the 'intrinsic' nature of things.[32]

One might dramatize Russell's idea by saying that physics can be thought of as a formal system which remains, in a peculiar sense, an *uninterpreted* formal system, even though we know that it *applies* to something = x—reality, the universe—and even though it is elaborated specifically in causal response to x. On this 'Ramseyfied' view, we may suppose that the universe has features that are *structurally homomorphic* to the structures delineated in the equations of

---

30. Structure is a matter of quality because a thing's qualitative character, exhaustively considered, is a matter of *all* aspects of how it is, and its structural character is an aspect of how it is. The converse claim—that quality (in spacetime) is in some sense a matter of structure—sounds a bit mystical, but it can on further reflection begin to seem hard to rebut, even when one maintains, as one must, a sharp distinction between epistemology and metaphysics. (The distinction between form and content may seem more robust, but may also succumb.)

31. It seems (subject to the doubt expressed in the last footnote) that this distinction must be a real one—that if there is structure, there must be something structured. Only extreme positivistic irresponsibility, or failure to 'realize what an abstract affair form [or structure] really is' (Russell 1927a: 392), can make this seem questionable.

32. At one point Russell also takes it that position in spacetime is an intrinsic property of things. Considering the relation between a perception and the object it is a perception of, he remarks that 'we cannot say whether or not it resembles the object in any intrinsic respect, except that both it and the object are brief events in space-time' (1927b: 118).

physics, but we have no account of the non-structural nature of the thing that has the structure(s) in question.[33]

So we are (to pursue the metaphor) in the peculiar position of having a known, concrete *application* (and so, in one sense, an *interpretation*) for a formal system, without that application constituting a *model* (in the sense of model-theoretic semantics) that can confer positive descriptive meaning on its terms. In being the subject matter of physics, the universe provides it with a merely referential model or object, of which it gives a merely structure-specifying description. Physics is *about* the physical, and may give a correct abstract representation of its structural disposition as far as it goes; but it does not and cannot tell us anything about what the physical actually is, over and above the fact that it exemplifies a certain formal structure.[34]

8. The Non-Mental—Space

Back now to the question whether physics can endow our general theoretical conception of the non-mental with any positive descriptive (not merely referential) content. Russell in 1927 thinks not. I disagree because correct structural description of a thing is already description of a feature of its intrinsic nature. But this disagreement is merely terminological, and the real question is this: Can one go any further than structure-specifying content, when attempting to give a satisfactory theoretical characterization of the non-mental? Again, Russell in 1927 thinks not. It seems to me, however, that we may be able to go a little further. For I think that our ordinary conception

---

33. When thinking of structural homomorphism, it is helpful to consider a version of an old example: the structural homomorphism between (1) sound waves produced by an orchestra playing Sibelius's 'Valse Triste' that are registered as (2) vibrations of a condenser plate in a microphone and sent as (3) electrical signals to a recording device that stores them as (4) pits on the surface of a compact disk that is then read as (5) digital information by a machine that transmits this information in the form of (6) radio waves to (7) a receiver that puts it through (8) an amplifier to (9) speakers that give rise to (10) sound waves that give rise to (11) electrical impulses in the auditory nerve that give rise to (12) neural occurrences in the auditory cortex and elsewhere that are conscious auditory experiences. There is a structural description that captures the respect in which all these phenomena are the same (assuming no significant loss of information even at the stage of conscious hearing). The abstract character of this description is revealed precisely by the fact that this is what it does: capture the respect in which all these substantially different phenomena are—structurally—the same. Compare Wittgenstein 1922: 4.0141.

34. In 1928, a year after the publication of *The Analysis of Matter*, Max Newman published a conclusive objection to the pure form of this view, as Russell immediately acknowledged (1967–69: 413–14). See Demopoulos and Friedman 1985.

of space may get something fundamental right about the nature of reality as it is in itself, and hence about the intrinsic nature of reality—something that survives even after the finite-but-unbounded curved gravity-constituting spacetime of relativity theory (or the ten-or eleven-or twelve-dimensional spacetime of one of the leading versions of string theory) has been granted to be closer to the truth.

I'm tempted to hold up my hands, like G. E. Moore, and to consider, not my hands, but the space—by which I mean only the spatial extension[35]—between them, and to say: 'This is space (spatial extension), and it is real, and I know its nature, in some very fundamental respect, whatever else I do not know about it or anything else (e.g. the fact that it is an aspect of spacetime).' On this view the ordinary concept of space, or indeed the concept of spacetime, in which (I claim) a fundamental feature of our ordinary conception of space survives, has correct non-structural descriptive content. It does not relate only to 'what we may call the causal skeleton of the world', (Russell 1927a: 391), if to say this is to say that it does not capture any aspect of the non-structural nature of the world. It has non-structural content, and can transmit this content to our more general conception of the non-mental.[36]

Russellians may object as follows: 'This line of thought is profoundly natural, but it depends on a fundamentally false imagining. It involves the conflation of 'objective' spatial extension, spatial extension 'as it is in itself' (where this is taken as a merely referential, structural-equivalence-class specifying term with no pretension to non-structural content) with the phenomenological space (or spaces) associated with perception. It involves an almost irresistible but entirely fatal failure to 'realize what an abstract affair form really is'.[37] All those, like yourself, who think that it is viable are 'guilty, unconsciously and in spite of explicit disavowals, of *a confusion in their imaginative picture*' of reality (Russell 1927a: 382; my emphasis).

In reply I think that some who take this line may be suffering from excessive empiricism. They take it that the notion of spatial extension—or indeed shape—that we possess is essentially informed by the character of our sensory experiences, and in this I think they are mistaken. It may well be true

---

35. I am not at all concerned with the 'substantivalist' versus 'relationalist' debate about the nature of space.

36. Cf. Hirsch 1986: 251–54. I will not here consider the 'direct realist' view that we may have some real insight into the non-mental nature of force, say, or causation, as a result of experiencing pushes and pulls and so on in the way we do.

37. Russell 1927a: 392. One could say that it is this point that Newman turns back against Russell (see n. 34).

that sensory experiences of specific kinds are necessary for the acquisition of concepts like SHAPE or SPACE, in the case of beings like ourselves.[38] Such concepts can nevertheless float free of the different possible sensory bases of their acquisition and subsequent deployment, without *ipso facto* becoming 'merely' formal or structure-specifying in character. It's easy to see that grasp of the content of SHAPE (say) does not require essential reference to any specific sensory experience. It suffices to point out that exactly the same concept of shape—that is, *the* concept of shape, for there is only one—can plausibly be supposed to be fully masterable by two different creatures A and B on the basis of sensory experiences in entirely different sensory modalities familiar to us—sight and touch.[39] One has to endorse a rather crude form of meaning-empiricism or concept-empiricism to suppose that A and B do not—cannot—have the same concept, as they do geometry together. A concept is not a faint copy or transform of a sensory experience. It is, precisely, a concept.

That's one point. Another, crucial in this context, is that the concept of shape or space that A and B have in common is not an entirely abstract or purely formal concept, as the supporters of Russell seem to suggest. There is more to A and B sharing the specific concept SHAPE or SPACE than there is to their sharing mastery of the principles of an uninterpreted formal system that is in fact suitable for the expression of shape configurations or spatial relations, although they know it only as an uninterpreted formal system. It is precisely because pure form is such a *very* 'abstract affair', as Russell says, that the concept of shape or space that A and B can have in common in spite of their different sensory experiences cannot be supposed to be a matter of pure form. To think that it is a matter of pure form is to miss out precisely their grasp of the *spatiality* of space—of that which makes their grasp of the concept of space more than grasp of (say) an abstract metric. The concept has non-structural content.

It's true that this content is abstract in one sense: it is abstract relative to all the particularities of sensation, in a way that is sufficiently indicated by reference to the fact that different creatures can acquire it (the very same concept) on the basis of experience in entirely different sensory modalities. It is indeed, and essentially, a *non-sensory* concept (see Evans 1980: 269–71;

---

38. I use small capitals for names of concepts.

39. One may contrast the case of a congenitally blind person with the hypothetical case of a fully sighted person congenitally paralysed and devoid of tactile or any other somatosensory sensation—before thinking of superintelligent echolocating bats and aliens with other sensory modalities.

McGinn 1983: 126). But it is not purely abstract in Russell's sense, because (to repeat) it involves grasp of the spatiality—rather than what one might call the mere abstract dimensionality—of space.[40] Spatiality is not abstract dimensionality: the nature of abstract dimensionality can be fully captured by a purely mathematical representation; the nature of spatiality cannot. One can give a purely mathematical representation of the dimensionality of space, but it won't distinguish three-dimensional *space* from any other possible three-dimensional 'space', e.g. the emotional state-space of a species that have just three emotions, love, anger, and despair.

Obviously questions arise about the precise nature of the non-structural content of concepts like SHAPE and SPACE, about what it is, exactly, to grasp the spatiality of space, given that SHAPE and SPACE may be fully shared by A, B, superbats, and others. But in the present context I am inclined just to hold up my hands again.[41]

Russellians may be unimpressed. Michael Lockwood, in particular, is sympathetic to the idea that knowledge of spacetime structure is not knowledge of any feature of the 'intrinsic' or non-structural nature of reality. In doing physics, Lockwood says, we may grasp the abstract structure exemplified by space while having 'no conception of its content: i.e. what it is, concretely, that fleshes out this structure. (For all we know, on this view, Henry More and Newton may be right in equating space with God's sensorium!)'[42]

But I am prepared to grant this. I am prepared to grant that we cannot rule out the possibility that space is God's sensorium,[43] or something even more unknown, and that there is therefore a sense in which we may have

---

40. Even if no finite sensory-intellectual being can possess SHAPE or SPACE without having, or without at least having grasp of the nature of, some form of sensory experience, it does not follow that specification of the content of the concept it possesses necessarily involves reference to any features of sensory experience.

41. If empiricists press me further I will offer (a) the suggestion that sensory modalities that differ qualitatively at first order (i.e. in the way that sight and touch do) may be said to be crucially similar at second order in as much as they are 'intrinsically spatial' in character, (b) the speculation that this similarity can itself be understood as a kind of similarity of (experiential) *qualitative* character, (c) the acknowledgement that it may be that one must be capable of experience in some 'intrinsically spatial' sensory modality or other (even if only in imagination) in order to possess SHAPE or SPACE, (d) the reservation that even if a *non-conceptual* experiential modality must be in play, it is not obvious that this must be a *sensory* modality. This, however, is too simple (I discuss the question further in Strawson 2002).

42. Personal communication. Eddington agrees: 'We know nothing about the intrinsic nature of space' (1928: 51–52).

43. After setting aside the problem of evil.

no idea of what it is that 'fleshes out' the abstract structure exemplified by space. For it may still be true that one grasps something fundamental about the non-structural nature of space in thinking of it as having, precisely, spatiality, rather than mere abstract dimensionality. If space is God's sensorium, so be it: God's sensorium may really have the property of spatiality. Between a fat-free, purely mathematical and thus wholly abstract representation of the structure of space and a partly structure-transcending conception of space as God's sensorium (or some such) lies a third option: an ostensibly less rich but still structure-transcending conception of space as specifically spatial (hands held up) in its dimensionality. Some may think this a fine point, but it is (I take it) a huge step away from Russell's claim that we know *nothing* about the intrinsic quality of non-mental events.[44]

I am not claiming that we do know something about the non-structural nature of space, only that we may (I hold up my hands, I move them apart—but my sense of the vulnerability of this claim has greatly increased since I wrote this in 1997). This claim allows, as it should, that there may well be more to space than we can know. SPACE, like PHYSICAL, is a natural-kind concept, and there are some atrociously good reasons for thinking that there is more to space than we know or can fully understand. In addition to the (already weighty) points that physical space is non-Euclidean, and is itself something that is literally expanding,[45] and the non-locality results,[46] and questions about the nature of the vacuum, and widespread agreement that 'there is no good a priori reason why space should be a continuum',[47] I for one still can't fully understand how space and time can be interdependent in the way that they demonstrably are. We are also told on very good authority that gravity is really

---

44. 'We know nothing about the intrinsic quality of physical events except when these are mental events that we directly experience' (1956: 153). Perhaps Russell takes this distancing step himself in his 1928 reply to Newman (see n. 34): 'It was quite clear to me, as I read your article, that I had not really intended to say what in fact I did say, that *nothing* is known about the physical world [the non-mental world as opposed to the mental world, in my terminology] except its structure. I had always assumed that there might be co-punctuality between percepts and non-percepts, and even that one could pass by a finite number of steps from one event to another compresent with it, from one end of the universe to the other ... spaciotemporal continuity of percepts and non-percepts was so axiomatic in my thought that I failed to notice that my statements appeared to deny it' (1967–69: 413).

45. In such a way that the correct answer to the question 'Where was the Big Bang taking place at the first moment in which it made sense to say that it was taking place anywhere?' is 'Right here', wherever you are.

46. Bell 1987; for an informal illustration, see Lockwood 1996: 163–64.

47. Isham and Butterfield 2000.

just a matter of the 'curvature' of space, and that string theory is an immensely promising theory of matter (especially after the 'second superstring revolution' and the growth of M-theory, and especially when it comes to understanding gravity) that entails that there are at least ten spatial dimensions... .

These points reopen the connection to the mind–body problem. For as they pile up, one can't reputably hold on to the old, powerful-seeming Cartesian intuition that there is a 'deep repugnance' or incompatibility between the nature of conscious experience and the nature of spatial extension—the intuition that 'the mental and the spatial are mutually exclusive categories' (McGinn 1995: 221). We have direct acquaintance with fundamental features of conscious experience—experiential features—just in having it; but we really have no good reason to think that we know enough about the nature of space—or rather, about the nature of matter-in-space-considered-in-so-far-as-it-has-non-mental-being—to be able to assert that there is any repugnance.[48] And if conscious experience is in time, as almost everyone agrees, then it is in spacetime, given the way in which space and time are demonstrably interdependent—in which case it is in space in every sense in which it is in time.

Note that it follows that even if our notion of space can confer some non-structural content on our best theoretical conception of the non-mental, it cannot confer any content that is guaranteed to distinguish it from any fully articulated theoretical conception of the mental, although we still intuitively feel it to fit with the former conception in a way in which we don't feel it to fit with the latter.[49]

9. The Non-Mental—Spin, Mass, and Charge

I have proposed that our theoretical conception of the non-mental may be able to acquire some non-structural content from its first lieutenant, the concept of space. Can it acquire any more? Well, I think that our more particular spatial concepts of shape, size, position, distance, and local motion (I raise my hands and bring them together) *may* also get something right about reality as it is

---

48. Foster 1982: ch. 5 and McGinn 1995 give forceful presentations of the repugnance intuition. At one point McGinn makes the funky suggestion that consciousness might be a manifestation of the non-spatial nature of pre-Big Bang reality (223–24). I think he moves in a better direction when he shifts to the very different claim that 'consciousness tests the adequacy of our spatial understanding. It marks the place of deep lack of knowledge about space' (230).

49. I'm grateful to Mark Sainsbury for encouraging me to make this point more explicit.

in itself, and so contribute to the non-structural content of our general theo-retical conception of the non-mental; I think Locke may be essentially right in his view that some of our ideas of primary qualities correctly represent how things are in themselves, although his account needs recasting.[50] It may also be that our ordinary conception of time gets something right about the nature of reality (both experiential and non-experiential)—even if we need to conceive time as part of spacetime in order to think about it properly. I just don't know.[51]

Going on from space, time, extension, shape, position, distance, and motion, in the attempt to give a positive characterization of the non-mental, one may want to mention properties like spin, mass, charge, gravitational attraction, 'colour' and 'flavour' (in the quantum-theoretic sense). But one will have to bear in mind that our grasp of these things—any grasp of them over and above that which is conveyed by their intimate relation to con-cepts of space and time—is expressed merely in equations,[52] and the truth in Russell's remark that physics is mathematical not because we know so much about the physical world, but because we know so little. So although I like to think that concepts of space and time carry non-structural content, I do not think this can be true of any of these other concepts considered independently of their relations to concepts of space and time. Here Russell is right: we know nothing of the non-mental non-structural nature of—for example—electrical phenomena apart from their spacetime structure; all we have are equations.[53]

---

50. Locke's talk of 'resemblance' between primary qualities and ideas of primary qualities is unfortunate in as much as it suggests a (mere) picturing relation, and Russell, 1927a: 385, holds that Locke is definitely wrong.

51. Perhaps it gets something right in an Augustinian sense, according to which we can be said to know what time is even though we find we don't know what to say when someone asks us what it is.

52. Unless some 'direct realist' account of our understanding of force is defensible. See n. 36. Note, though, that no sensible direct realist view can suppose that we derive understand-ing of the nature of force directly from the merely *sensory* character of experiences of pushes, pulls, and so on; that would be like thinking that we can get some real insight into the nature of electricity from the qualitative character that experiences of electric shocks have for us (compare Evans 1980: 270). Somehow, the sensory experiences would have to be the basis of an abstract, essentially cognitive, general, non-sensory concept of force.

53. The word 'non-mental' is not redundant in the last sentence, for it seems very plausible to suppose that consciousness is an electrical phenomenon, whatever else it is; in which case it may be said that we do have some knowledge of the non-structural nature of electrical phenomena just in having conscious experience.

But even if knowledge of spacetime structure is all we have, in the way of non-structural knowledge of the nature of the non-mental, it makes a huge difference to the case. Consider the difference between a characterization of the forces of electrical attraction and repulsion in which their spatial character (the way they decrease with increasing distance) is given a purely mathematical, abstract-dimensional interpretation, and one in which it is given a genuinely spatial interpretation. Consider any account of anything in which time relations have a merely mathematical abstract representation, and one in which the temporality of time is somehow represented.

10. Hens' Eggs

I want now to give a further characterization of what it is to be a genuine materialist. But I must first answer an objection that occurs to many.

—'It seems to follow, from your claim that we have no knowledge of the non-structural, intrinsic or as we may say *N-intrinsic* nature of things, that we cannot know that there are tables and chairs and hens and hens' eggs and 'that hens' eggs are generally laid by hens' (Moore 1905–06: 64). But this is a chair I'm sitting in, and it's made of wood, and this is a hen, and this is a hen's egg, and this hen laid it. These are all facts I know, and they are N-intrinsic facts—ultimate, absolute truths—about the nature of reality. They must be included in any true and full account of the history of the universe.'

My reply to this objection is similar to Moore's a hundred years ago. I agree that we know many such truths, but I take it, as a materialist, that hens are wholly made of the fundamental constituents of matter that physics discusses, and that when we consider our knowledge of these fundamental constituents we encounter the crucial and entirely general sense in which we know nothing about the fundamental N-intrinsic nature of matter. As far as I can see, this ignorance is entirely compatible with the sense in which we do have knowledge of the N-intrinsic of reality in knowing that there are hens, and what hens are, and what wood is, and so on. And this compatibility is no more surprising than the fact that I can know that this is a statue without knowing what it is made of.

—'But we know what hens are made of—carbon, hydrogen, and oxygen, mostly—and we know what carbon, hydrogen, and oxygen are made of—electrons and quarks with various characteristics. Physics gives us knowledge of the properties of these things. If you think that it fails to give us any knowledge of their ultimate, N-intrinsic nature, that's because you think that a thing is more than its properties. But that's just bad old metaphysics. A thing is not in any sense more than its properties.'

I agree that there is an irredeemably difficult but inescapable sense in which it is true to say that a thing is not more than its properties—I agree that 'in their relation to the object, the properties are not in fact subordinated to it, but are the way of existing of the object itself' (Kant 1781: A414/B441, substituting 'object' and 'property' for 'substance' and 'accident' respectively). The present claim, however, is not that a concrete phenomenon must be more than its properties, but that it must be more than its purely formal or structural properties. If you say that this is more bad metaphysics, a yearning for lumpen stuff, our disagreement will be plain. My reply will be that you have evidently forgotten 'what an abstract affair form really is'. A concrete phenomenon must be more than its purely formal or structural properties, because these, considered just as such, have a purely abstract mathematical representation, and are, concretely, nothing—nothing at all. It is true that we get out of the realm of the purely abstract when we add in spatiotemporal properties, on my account, but a thing's non-structural properties can't consist only in its spatiotemporal properties—at least so long as spacetime is conceived merely as a dimensional manifold with no physical or substantial nature.[54]

Here, then, we return to the point that—the sense in which—we have no knowledge of the N-intrinsic nature of things in spite of the sense in which it is true to say that we know what hens and hens' eggs are.

11. True Materialism

I have suggested that our general theoretical conception of the mental has substantial non-structural descriptive content, because we have acquaintance with fundamental features of the mental nature of reality just in having experience in the way we do. Our general theoretical conception of the non-mental has substantial structure-specifying content, and I have suggested, with considerable hesitation, that it may also have crucial and correct *non*-structural content deriving from spatiotemporal concepts. Apart from this, though, it is arguable (subject to note 44) that we know nothing about the intrinsic or non-structural nature of non-mental reality.

With this in place, we may ask what it is to be a genuine materialist. The first thing to do is to intone once more that realistic or real materialism entails

---

54. For the importance of this qualification, see n. 88.

full acknowledgement of the reality of experiential phenomena: they are as real as rocks, hence wholly physical, strictly on a par with anything that is correctly characterized by physics.[55] They are part of physical reality, whatever is or is not the case. It follows that current physics, considered as a general account of the general nature of the physical, is like *Othello* without Desdemona: it contains only predicates for non-experiential being, so it cannot characterize experiential being at all (recall the definition in §2). It cannot characterize a crucial feature of reality at all.

No one who doubts this is a true materialist. Partly for this reason, I think that genuine, reflective endorsement of materialism is a considerable achievement for anyone who has had a standard modern Western education. Materialism must at first provoke a feeling of deep bewilderment in anyone contemplating the question 'What is the nature of the physical?' The occurrence of such a feeling is diagnostic of real engagement with the materialist hypothesis, real engagement with the thought that experiential phenomena are physical phenomena just like spatial-extension phenomena and electrical phenomena. I think Russell is profoundly right when he says that most are 'guilty, unconsciously and in spite of explicit disavowals, of a confusion in their imaginative picture of matter'.

I suspect that some will be unable to shake off the confusion, although Locke made the crucial move long ago. Some may say that modern science has changed the situation radically since Locke's time. It has—but only in so far as it has massively reinforced Locke's point.

Perhaps I am generalizing illegitimately from my own experience, revealing my own inadequacy rather than the inadequacy of recent discussion of the 'mind–body' problem, but I don't think so. Genuine materialism requires concerted meditative effort. Russell recommends 'long reflection' (1927b: 112). If one hasn't felt a kind of vertigo of astonishment when facing the thought, obligatory for all materialists, that consciousness is a wholly physical phenomenon in every respect, including every experiential respect—a sense of having been precipitated into a completely new confrontation with the utter strangeness of the physical (the real) relative to all existing common-sense and scientific conceptions of it—, then one hasn't begun to be a thoughtful materialist. One hasn't got to the starting line.[56]

Some may find that this feeling recurs each time they concentrate on the mind-body problem. Others may increasingly think themselves—quietistically,

---

55. 'As characterized by physics' is a necessary qualification; see the remarks about 'brain' on pp. 165–6.

56. The only alternative, I think, is that one has a very rare and beautiful intellect.

apophatically, pragmatically, intuitively—into the unknownness of the (non-mental) physical in such a way that they no longer experience the fact that mental and non-mental phenomena are equally physical as involving any clash. At this point 'methodological naturalism'—the methodological attitude to scientific enquiry into the phenomena of mind recommended by Chomsky—will become truly natural for them, as well as correct.[57] I think it is creeping over me. But recidivism is to be expected: the powerfully open state of mind required by true materialism is hard to achieve as a natural attitude to the world. It involves a profound reseating of one's intuitive theoretical understanding of nature.[58]

I say 'intuitive theoretical understanding of nature', but it isn't as if there is any other kind. For (briefly) what we think of as real understanding of a natural phenomenon is always at bottom just a certain kind of *feeling*, and it is always and necessarily relative to other things one just takes for granted, finds intuitive, feels comfortable with. This is as true in science as it is in common life. I feel I fully understand why this tower casts this shadow in this sunlight, given what I take for granted about the world (I simply do not ask why light should do *that*, of all things, when it hits stone). I may also feel I understand—see—why this billiard ball does *this* when struck in this way by that billiard ball. But in this case there is already a more accessible sense in which I don't really *understand* what is going on, and it is an old point that if I were to ask for and receive an explanation, in terms of impact and energy transfer, this would inevitably invite further questions about the nature of impact and energy transfer, starting a series of questions and answers that would have to end with a reply that was not an explanation but rather had the form 'Well, that's just the way things are' (see e.g. van Fraassen 1980: ch. 5; Strawson 1994: 84–93).

The true materialist outlook may become natural for some, then, but many will find they can maintain it only for relatively short periods of time. It is not a small thing. To achieve it is to have evacuated one's natural and gripping common-sense ± science-based conception of the nature of the physical of every element that makes it seem puzzling that experiential phenomena are

---

57. See Chomsky 1994; 1995: 1–10. Chomsky is a clear example of someone who is, methodologically, a true materialist in my sense. I am not sure that he would accept the title, however; he avoids the term 'materialist' because of the point made by Lange in n. 22, which I try to counter on pp. 197–8.

58. In fact one doesn't have to be a materialist to hold that no defensible conception of the physical contains any element that gives one positive reason to doubt that experiential phenomena are physical. One can hold this even if committed to dualism.

physical. I think it is to be at ease with the idea that consciousness is a form of matter.[59]

It can help to perform special acts of concentration—focusing one's thought on one's brain and trying to hold fully in mind the idea that one's experience as one does so is part of the physical being of the brain (part of the physical being of the brain that one may be said to be acquainted with as it is in itself, at least in part, because its being as it is for one as one has it just is what it is in itself, at least in part). It is worth trying to sustain this—it is part of doing philosophy—, forcing one's thought back to the confrontation when it slips. At first one may simply encounter the curious phenomenological character of the act of concentration, but it is useful to go on—to engage, for example, in silent, understanding-engaging subvocalizations of such thoughts as 'I am now thinking about my brain, and am thinking that this experience I am now having of this very thinking—and this subvocalization—is part of the physical activity and being of my brain.' It is also useful to look at others, including young children, as they experience the world, and to think of the common-or-garden matter that is in their heads (hydrogen, oxygen, carbon, iron, potassium, sodium, and so on). It is useful to listen to music, and focus on the thought that one's auditory experience is a form of matter.[60]

12. Knowledge of Ignorance

Finding it deeply puzzling how something could be physical is not the same as finding something that one takes to be physical deeply puzzling. It is often said that quantum theory is deeply counterintuitive—in its description of the wave-like and particle-like behaviour of fundamental particles, for example—but no one seems to find it puzzling to suppose that it deals wholly with physical phenomena.[61]

---

59. I think that it requires realization that this claim is inadequately expressed by saying 'consciousness is a property of matter', or even 'consciousness is a physical property of matter', given the almost irresistible incentives to metaphysical misunderstanding that are I believe already built into the word 'property' (see Strawson 2008*b*).

60. Perhaps intuitive materialism is not always an achievement, and comes easily, and without positive error, in certain Eastern schools of thought. The requirement that there be no positive error of conception is, however, important.

61. Some may object that there is a compelling description of quantum-mechanical phenomena that completely eliminates the air of mystery attaching to wave-particle duality (see e.g. Deutsch 1997: ch. 2); but it does so at the cost of another large strangeness, because it requires one to accept Everett's many-worlds hypothesis; and although it may be that this is what one should do, I will continue to use the case of wave-particle duality as an example

The main reason for this seems to be as follows: WAVE and PARTICLE engage smoothly with standard physics concepts of shape, size, position, motion, and so on. There is, so far, a clear sense in which the two concepts are *theoretically homogeneous*, or at least non-heterogeneous; they operate on the same, single conceptual playing field of physics.[62] But when we try to integrate conscious-experience terms with the terms of physics (and common-sense physics), we find that they entirely lack any such felt theoretical homogeneity, or non-heterogeneity. To this extent, they force constantly renewed bewilderment—in a way quite different from the way in which quantum-mechanical phenomena do—on materialists who like to think they have *some* sort of coherent, theoretically unified understanding of the overall nature of the physical, however general that understanding may be, and however incomplete in its details.

But this is the central mistake: to think that one has some sort of theoretically unified understanding of the overall nature of the physical. Once one realizes that this cannot be true, if materialism is true, things change.[63] It begins to look as if there is actually *less* difficulty in the suggestion that physical phenomena have both experiential and non-experiential being than in the suggestion that photons (for example) behave both like particles and waves. For in the case of experiential terms and non-experiential terms there is no direct clash of concepts of the sort that occurs in the case of the wave-particle duality. Being a wave is incompatible with being a particle, but there is nothing in the possession of non-experiential being that we know to be intrinsically inimical to the possession of experiential being: we simply do not know enough about the nature of non-experiential being to have any good reason to suppose that this might be so. Thus the experiential terms and the non-experiential terms do not in fact *actively clash*, as the wave and particle terms do. Rather, they fail to connect or engage. One is making progress as a materialist when one has lost all sense of an active clash. It has no scientific or philosophical justification. As Russell says, 'the physical [sc non-mental] world is only known as regards certain abstract features of its space-time

---

for the purposes of discussion. (I will also put aside the view that the real intuitive difficulty resides in the phenomenon of superposition rather than in the wave-particle duality.)

62. I try to give more content to the idea of theoretical homogeneity in Strawson 1994: 88–93. Note that one can have a sense that a group of terms is theoretically homogeneous, or at least not problematically heterogeneous, without feeling that one *understands* the phenomena these terms are used to describe.

63. Although there are plenty of deep puzzles in physics even when mind is put to one side.

structure—features which, because of their abstractness, do not suffice to show whether the physical world is, or is not, different in intrinsic character from the world of mind' (1948: 240; see also 247).

Arnauld made the essential point in 1641, in his comments on Descartes's *Meditations*, and he was not the first.[64] Locke in 1689 'did not apprehend that there was any real inconsistency between the known properties of body, and those that have generally been referred to mind'.[65] Algarotti observes in 1737 that

> we are as yet but Children in this vast Universe, and are very far from having a compleat Idea of Matter; we are utterly unable to pronounce what Properties are agreeable to it, and what are not, (1737: 2.194)

and Hume in 1739 shows a very clear understanding of the point (1739–40: 246–48). Priestley in 1777 argues, with unanswerable force, and by appeal to a scientific conception of the physical that (in essence) still holds good today, 'that we have *no reason* to suppose that there are in man two substances so distinct from each other as have been represented'.[66] Kant concurs in 1781, although his special terms of debate preclude him from agreeing directly with Priestley's further materialist claim that 'mind ... is not a substance distinct from the body, but the result of corporeal organization'; that 'in man [thought]

---

64. In Descartes 1641: 2.141–43. Lange (1865) discusses many precursors.

65. Priestley 1777–82: 115. Locke doesn't fully carry through his point that our ignorance of the nature of the physical means that we lack any good reason to doubt that consciousness is wholly physical; for at one point he says that 'matter ... is evidently in its own nature void of sense and thought' (1689: 4.3.6; see also 2.10.5). But he also says that we 'possibly shall never be able to know whether any material being thinks, or no', and holds that an omnipotent being could give 'some systems of matter, fitly disposed, a power to perceive and think' (4.3.6). The force of the second quotation is less than one might suppose: it does not conclusively establish that Locke thought that God could make matter have such a power *intrinsically* or in and of itself—i.e. without any special wizardry. But Locke's correspondence with Stillingfleet very strongly suggests that his considered view is that our ignorance of the nature of the matter is in the end too great for us to have any good reason to claim that matter could not have the power of thought in and of itself (1696–99: 459–62).

66. 1777–82: 219. Priestley observes, correctly, that there is no evidence for absolute solidity: 'I ... define ... matter ... to be a substance possessed of the property of *extension*, and of *powers of attraction and repulsion*. And since it has never yet been asserted, that the powers of *sensation* and *thought* are incompatible with these (solidity, or impenetrability only, having been thought to be repugnant to them), I therefore maintain that we have no reason to suppose that there are in man two substances so distinct from each other as have been represented.'

is a property of the nervous system, or rather of the brain'; that 'sensation and thought do necessarily result from the organization of the brain'.[67] The quality of the mind-body debate is in many ways lower today than at any other time in the last three hundred years.

Substance dualism may have looked like a plausible response to the mind-body problem in Descartes's time, for classical *mechanistic* material-ism, according to which the physical world consists entirely of small, solid, intrinsically inert particles in motion, was then the dominant view, and Leibniz's famous image of the mill seemed hard to counter.[68] But the strict mechanist understanding of the physical world was fatally undermined by 1687, when Newton published his *Principia*.[69] Since then we have had no good scientific reason to think that mind is not physical. And even before Newton, in the high days of 'contact mechanics', there were no *philosophi-cally* respectable grounds for claiming that mind is not physical. The mech-anists or 'Cartesians', as Hume calls them, made a wholly unjustifiable move: they 'established it as a principle that we are *perfectly acquainted* with the essence of matter' (Hume 1739–40: 159; my emphasis). That is, they not only assumed that their fundamental theory of matter was sound as far as it went; they also assumed that it went all the way—that it was complete. It is the second of these two false assumptions that causes most trouble, for even if the Cartesians had been right that all physical change is a matter of the motion, contact, and impact of solid particles, they still would not have been justified in claiming that this fact was definitely—knowably—incompatible with some of it also being a matter of conscious goings on. Many today make exactly the same sort of mistake.

---

67. Kant 1781: A358–60; Priestley 1777–82: 220, 244, 303. John Toland in 1704 'obviously regards thought as a phenomenon which is an inherent accompaniment of the material movements in the nervous system' (Lange 1865: 1.329).

68. 'We must admit that perception, and whatever depends on it, cannot be explained on mechanical principles, i.e. by shapes and movements. If we pretend that there is a machine [e.g. a brain] whose structure makes it think, sense and have perception, then we can con-ceive it enlarged, ... so that we can go inside it as into a mill. Suppose that we do: then if we inspect the interior we shall find there nothing but parts which push one another, and never anything which could explain a perception. Thus, perception must be sought in simple sub-stances, not in what is composite or in machines' (Leibniz 1720: 150 [*Monadology* §17]).

69. Locke saw this pretty clearly after reading Newton (see e.g. Locke 1689: 2.23.24, 4.3.29; 1696–9: 467–68). Chomsky (1995: 4) quotes tellingly from Leibniz and Huygens, who con-demned Newton for abandoning sound 'mechanical principles' and reverting to mystical 'sympathies and antipathies' and 'inexplicable qualities'.

13. The Reality of Appearance

I've claimed that thoughtful materialism requires draining one's conception of the non-experiential physical of any element that, in a puzzling world, makes it seem especially puzzling that the experiential is physical. Many philosophers—all those legions who tried, for most of the twentieth century, to reduce the mental to the non-mental in some way—think this is the wrong way round. They think we have to drain our conception of the experiential of any element that produces special puzzlement, leaving our existing conception of the non-experiential physical in place. But no substantial draining can be done on the experiential side. In having experience in the way we do, we are directly acquainted with certain features of the ultimate nature of reality, as so many have remarked—whether or not we can put what we know into words in any theoretically tractable way. And this is so whatever it is best to say about any non-experiential (e.g. dispositional) aspects of the mental that there may be. We may certainly hope to *develop* our understanding of the nature of the experiential; but we can do this only by adding to what we already know of it by direct acquaintance.

> —'But in having experience we only have access to an appearance of how things are and are not cognizant, in the mere having of the experience, of how anything is in itself.'[70]

The reply is immediate. Here, how things appear or seem is how they really are: the reality that is at present in question just is the appearing or seeming. In the case of any experiential episode E there may be something X of which it is true to say that in undergoing E we only have access to an appearance of X, and not to how X is in itself. But serious materialists must hold that E itself, the event of being-appeared-to, with all the qualitative character that it has, is itself part of physical reality. They cannot say that it too is just an appearance, and not part of how things are, on pain of infinite regress. They must grant that it is itself a reality, and a reality with which we must, in plausibility, be allowed to have some sort of direct acquaintance. As Russell says, we must 'treat "seeming" with respect' (1927b: 101).

At this point some may try to adapt Ryle-type arguments for the 'systematic elusiveness of the "I" to the present case (Ryle 1949: 186–89). They may argue that anything that can count as *knowledge* of experience involves an operation

---

70. See Dennett 1991a: 365–66, and the reply in Strawson 1994: 51–52.

of taking experience as an object that necessarily precludes apprehending it in such a way that one can be said to have access to how it is in itself, rather than merely to an appearance of it. I suspect that this ancient form of argument is invalid even in its original application, where it is used to argue that the putative mental subject of experience can never directly apprehend itself as it is in the present moment of experience.[71] But even if this is not so the argument has no valid application to the present case—to things like pain and colour-experience. The way a colour-experience is experientially, for the subject of experience that has it, is part of its essential nature as a physical phenomenon. When we claim (with Russell) that to have an experience is *eo ipso* to be acquainted with certain of the intrinsic features of reality, we do not have to suppose that this acquaintance involves standing back from the experience reflectively and examining it by means of a further, distinct experience. It doesn't. This picture is too cognitivist (or perhaps too German-Idealist). The having is the knowing.

14. The Radiance of Reality

I've argued that the first thing that one needs to do, when it comes to the mind–body problem, is to reflect on one's ignorance: one's ignorance of the non-experiential. One's intuitive theoretical attitude to the nature of the non-experiential needs to evolve until any sense that there is an active clash between experiential terms and non-experiential terms has disappeared, leaving only the awareness that they fail to connect in a way that brings a sense of intuitive understanding. This awareness ought not to be merely a matter of book learning.

At this point at least two paths open up for materialists. The first goes deeper into reflection on the nature of understanding in physics. Proceeding down this path, one encounters one's sense that at least some of the terms of physics (both common-sense and scientific) connect up with one another in a way that justifies a feeling of intuitive understanding of at least some of what goes on in the world. One is then asked to examine (possibly at length) the question of what exactly one supposes this to amount to. Does it really amount to anything very solid? Is it more than a certain kind of feeling one is disposed to get (either innately or as a result of training) when considering some but not other co-occurrences of features in the world? What exactly is its significance (see, again, van Fraassen 1980: ch. 5)?

---

71. I argue for this in Strawson 2010.

Well, one probably has to go down this path at some point, as a materialist, returning to the questions raised on p. 183. But I will choose another, which has a sunnier aspect. Here one confronts the deep puzzlement one still feels when one considers experiential properties and non-experiential properties and fails to see how they coexist, and, also, one's persisting feeling that this puzzlement has, in a puzzling world, a very special if not unique status.

The question is whether one can do anything about this. I think the answer is Yes. I think physics can help us—it has already helped us a great deal—by diluting or undermining features of our natural conception of the physical that make non-experiential phenomena appear *toto coelo* different from experiential phenomena.

The basic point is simple, and can be elaborated as follows. At first, perhaps, one takes it that matter is simply solid stuff, uniform, non-particulate: Scandinavian cheese. Then, perhaps, one learns that it is composed of distinct atoms—particles that cohere more or less closely together to make up objects, but that have empty space (to put it simplistically but intelligibly) between them. Then, perhaps, one learns that these atoms are themselves made up of tiny, separate particles and full of empty space.[72] One learns that a physical object like the earth or a person is almost all empty space. One learns that matter is not at all what one thought.

Now one may accept this while holding on to the idea that matter is at root solid and dense. For this picture retains the idea that there are particles of matter: minuscule grainy bits of ultimate stuff that are in themselves perfectly solid (in Locke's phrase), 'continuum-dense'. And one may say that only these, strictly speaking, are matter: matter as such. But it is more than two hundred years since Priestley (citing Boscovich) observed that there is no positive observational or theoretical reason to suppose that the fundamental constituents of matter have any perfectly solid central part (see also Foster 1982: 67–72, Harré and Madden 1975: ch. 9).

In spite of this, a fairly robust conception of truly solid particles survived all the way into pre-1925 quantum mechanics. It suffered its most dramatic blow only in modern (1925 on) quantum mechanics, in which neither the nucleus nor the electrons of an atom are straight-up solid objects, and are more naturally thought of as fields or aspects of fields. It may be said that the basic idea

---

72. As in the old quantum-theory model of the atom, *c.*1910–24. The standard way to convey the amount of empty space inside an atom is to say that if the nucleus is imagined to be as big as a 1-mm pinhead, then the nearest electrons—themselves much smaller than the nucleus—are 100 metres away.

of the grainy particle survives even here, at least in as much as the nucleus and its components are still fairly well localized within a small central region inside the atom (albeit with small 'tails' that go out to infinity), and in as much as the probability of finding one of the (far less localized) electrons is signifi-cant only within a volume that is normally considered to be the dimensions of the atom. But this commitment to the localization of particles does not in itself amount to any sort of commitment to continuum-dense solidity, but only to fields and repulsive forces that grow stronger without any clear limit when one travels in certain directions (i.e. towards the centre of the field asso-ciated with a particle). And whatever is left of the picture of ultimate grainy bits is further etiolated in quantum field theory, in which the notion of the field more fully overrides the picture of grainy particles.[73] In this theory it becomes very hard to treat 'bound' systems like atoms at all. As for what I've been calling 'empty space'—the supposed vacuum—, it is understood to be simply the lowest energy state of fields like the electron, proton, and photon fields. It turns out to be something which 'has structure and can get squeezed, and can do work'.[74]

It may be said that quantum field theory is complicated and ill-understood, but there is a clear sense in which grainy, inert bits of matter, naively con-ceived, are already lost to us independently of quantum field theory, given only the fact that matter is a form of energy, and interconvertible with it. This fact of interconvertibility is widely known, however little it is understood, and it seems to me that it further, and utterly, confounds any understanding of matter that takes it to be in any obvious way incompatible with conscious-ness. To put it dramatically: physics thinks of matter considered in its (sup-posed) non-experiential being as a thing of spacetime-located forces, energy, fields, and it can also seem rather natural to conceive of consciousness (i.e. matter apprehended in its experiential being) as a spacetime-located form or manifestation of energy, as a kind of force, and even, perhaps, as a kind of field.[75] We may still think the two things are deeply heterogeneous, but

---

73. 'In the modern theory of elementary particles known as the Standard Model, a theory that has been well verified experimentally, the fundamental components of nature are a few dozen kinds of field' (Weinberg 1997: 20). We continue to talk in terms of particles because the quantization of the field, whereby each different (normal) mode of vibration of the field is associated with a discrete ladder of energy levels, automatically gives rise to particle-like phenomena so far as observation is concerned.

74. Harvey Brown, personal communication; see Saunders and Brown 1991. Perhaps Descartes was right, deep down, in his theory of the plenum.

75. Compare Maxwell 1978: 399; James 1890: 1.147 n. It is arguable that Schopenhauer holds something close to this view.

we have no good reason to believe this.[76] We just don't know enough about the nature of matter considered in its non-experiential being; and doubtless there are things we don't know about matter considered in its experiential being. Those who think speculations like this are enjoyable but not really serious haven't really begun on the task of being a materialist; they haven't understood the strangeness of the physical and the extent of our ignorance. It is a long time since Russell argued that 'from the standpoint of philosophy the distinction between physical and mental is superficial and unreal', and it seems that physics can back philosophy on this question (Russell 1927a: 402). In fact—and it had to come back to this—we really don't know enough to say that there is any non-mental being. All the appearances of a non-mental world may just be the way that physical phenomena—in themselves entirely mental phenomena—appear to us; the appearance being another mental phenomenon.[77]

Whatever you think of this last proposal, lumpish, inert matter, dense or corpuscled, stuff that seems essentially alien to the phenomenon of consciousness, has given way to fields of energy, essentially active diaphanous process-stuff that—intuitively—seems far less unlike the process of consciousness. When Nagel speaks of the 'squishy brain', when McGinn speaks of 'brain "gook"' and asks how 'technicolour phenomenology ... can ... arise from soggy grey matter', when the neurophysiologist Susan Greenfield describes the brain as a 'sludgy mass', they vividly and usefully express part of the 'imaginative ... confusion' in the ordinary idea of matter.[78] But physics comes to our aid: there is a clear sense in which the best description of

---

76. Kant, 1781–87: B427–28, remarks that the 'heterogeneity' of mind and body is merely assumed and not known.

77. Richard Price is consistently outclassed by Priestley in their *Free Discussion of the Doctrine of Materialism*, but he gets this point exactly right: 'if ... it comes out that [Priestley's] account of matter does not answer to the common ideas of matter, [and] is not *solid* extension, but something *not solid* that exists in space, it agrees so far with spirit', or mind (Priestley and Price 1778: 54; Price held that spirit was not only located in space but might also be extended). This is a rather good description of how things have come out, in physics. The account of matter given by current physics does not 'answer to the common ideas of matter'; it does not take matter to be 'solid extension', but rather 'something not solid that exists in space'. So far, then, it agrees with our understanding of mind or consciousness, although the agreement can only be negative, given that we have no non-mathematical grasp of the non-structural nature of the putative non-experiential being of matter—apart (perhaps) from our grasp of its spacetime structure.

78. Nagel 1998: 338; McGinn 1991: 1, 100; Greenfield BBC 21 June 1997. In spite of these quotations I think that all three of these writers are fundamentally on the right track when it comes to the mind-body problem.

the nature of the non-experiential *in non-technical, common-sense terms* comes from physics. For what, expressed in common-sense terms, does physics find in the volume of spacetime occupied by a brain? Not a sludgy mass, but an astonishingly (to us) insubstantial-seeming play of energy, an ethereally radiant vibrancy.

It finds, in other words, a physical object, which, thus far examined, is like any other. Examined further, this particular physical object turns out to have a vast further set of remarkable properties: all the sweeping sheets and scudding clouds and trains of intraneuronal and interneuronal electrochemical activity which physics (in conjunction with neurophysiology) apprehends as a further level of extraordinarily complex intensities of movement and (non-experiential) organization existing in an *n*-dimensional realm that we call spacetime although its nature is bewilderingly different from anything we ordinarily have in mind in thinking in terms of space and time. All this being so, do we have any good reason to think that we know anything about the non-mental physical (assuming it exists) that licenses surprise—even the very mildest surprise—at the thought that the experiential is physical? I do not think so. Brains are special, but they are not strange. The ghost in the machine is special, but it is certainly in the machine, and the machine, like the rest of the physical world, is already a bit of a ghost—as ghostly, in Russell's view, 'as anything in a spiritualist séance' (1927b: 78).

So when David Lewis says that 'the most formidable opposition to any form of mind-body identity comes from the friends of qualia' (1999: 5), i.e. experiential phenomena, there is no reason to agree. The main opposition to (realistic) mind–body identity comes, paradoxically, from its most passionate proponents, who are so strongly inclined to think they know more about the nature of the non-mental physical than they do. Lewis exemplifies the great mistake in his well-known summary account of his position in the philosophy of mind: 'Remember', he says, 'that the physical nature of ordinary matter under mild conditions is very well understood' (Lewis 1994: 412). But there is no reason to believe this, and every reason to disbelieve it. 'What knowledge have we of the nature of atoms that renders it at all incongruous that they should constitute a thinking [experiencing] object?', asks Eddington, who took the existence of experiential phenomena ('qualia') for granted: 'science has nothing to say as to the intrinsic nature of the atom.' The atom, so far as we know anything about it,

> is, like everything else in physics, a schedule of pointer readings [on instrument dials]. The schedule is, we agree, attached to some unknown background. Why not then attach it to something of a spiritual nature

of which a prominent characteristic is *thought* [i.e. experience or consciousness]? It seems rather *silly* to prefer to attach it to something of a so-called 'concrete' nature inconsistent with thought, and then to wonder where the thought comes from. We have dismissed all preconception as to the background of our pointer readings, and for the most part can discover nothing as to its nature. But in one case—namely, for the pointer readings of my own brain—I have an insight which is not limited to the evidence of the pointer readings. That insight shows that they are attached to a background of consciousness. (Eddington 1928: 259–60; my emphasis on 'silly')

The point is still negative. It may destroy one common source of puzzlement, but it doesn't offer any sort of positive account of the relation between the play of energy non-experientially conceived and the play of energy experientially apprehended, and some may find it no help at all. Others may say that it is a positive mistake to think that it is especially helpful, on the grounds that there is in the end no more difficulty in the thought that the existence of matter naively and grossly conceived involves the existence of consciousness than there is in the thought that matter quantum-mechanically conceived does so.[79]

We can grant them their objection for their own consumption (they are likely to be fairly sophisticated philosophers). Many others—not excluding philosophers—are likely to find the negative point rather useful, and I will conclude this section by relating it to three currently popular issues.

(1) Eliminativism

Consider any philosopher who has ever been tempted, even momentarily, by the 'eliminativist' suggestion that one has to question the reality of the experiential in some way in order to be a thoroughgoing materialist. It is an

---

79. They will find Russell's line of thought equally unnecessary as a way of reaching a conclusion they already fully accept: 'having realised the abstractness of what physics has to say, we no longer have any difficulty in fitting the visual sensation into the causal series. It used to be thought "mysterious" that purely physical [i.e. non-mental] phenomena should end in something mental. That was because people thought they knew a lot about physical phenomena, and were sure they differed in quality from mental phenomena. We now realise that we know nothing of the intrinsic quality of physical phenomena except when they happen to be sensations, and that therefore there is no reason to be surprised that some are sensations, or to suppose that the others are totally unlike sensations' (1927b: 117).

extraordinary suggestion,[80] and what is most striking about it in the present context is that it constitutes the most perfect demonstration in the history of philosophy of the grip of the very thing that it seeks to reject: dualist thinking. The eliminativists make the same initial mistake as Descartes—the mistake of assuming that they understand more about the nature of the physical than they do—but their subjugation to dualist thinking is far deeper than Descartes.[81] They are so certain that the physical excludes the experiential that they are prepared to deny the reality of the experiential in some (admittedly unclear) way—to make the most ridiculous claim ever made in philosophy—in order to retain the physical. (The mistake of thinking one may have grasped the essential nature of the physical is perhaps forgivable in the early seventeenth century, but not now.)

(2) The hard part of the mind-body problem

It can be seriously misleading to talk of 'the hard part of the mind-body problem' (Strawson 1989: 80, 1994: 93; compare McGinn 1989: 1), or 'the hard problem' (Chalmers 1995: 200). For this suggests that the problem is clearly posed. It is not, as Chomsky has observed. One might say that it is not sufficiently well defined for us to be able to say that it is hard; for although we have a clear and substantial positive fix on the non-structural nature of *experiential* reality, we have no substantial positive fix on the non-structural nature of *non-experiential* reality, apart, perhaps, from its spatiotemporal characteristics. To this extent we have no good reason to think that the mind-body problem is a harder problem than the problem posed for our understanding by the peculiarities of quantum physics. The problem is the nature of the physical, and in particular, perhaps, of the non-mental physical—if indeed it exists at all.

(3) Zombies

It is, finally, a mistake to think that we can know that 'zombies' could exist—where zombies are understood to be creatures that have no experiential properties although they are *perfect physical duplicates* (PPDs) of experiencing

---

80. It seems considerably more implausible than Xenocrates' suggestion that the soul is a self-moving number (see Aristotle *De Anima* 408b–09a).

81. In fact it is not clear that Descartes does make this mistake, although it is clear that some eliminativists do. Descartes was for a long time seen as a dangerous source of materialist views, and there are some reasons for thinking that his official dualism was motivated partly by the desire to stave off persecution by religious authorities.

human beings.[82] The argument that PPD zombies could exist proceeds from two premises: [1] it is conceivable that PPD zombies exist, [2] if something is conceivable, then it is possible. The argument is plainly valid, and (unlike many) I have no great problem with [2]. The problem is that we can't know [1] to be true, and have no reason to think it is. To be a real materialist is precisely to hold that [1] is false, and while real materialism cannot be known to be true, it cannot be refuted *a priori*, as it could be if [1] could be known to be true. PHYSICAL is a natural-kind concept, and since we know that there is much that we do not know about the nature of the physical, we cannot claim to know that an experienceless PPD—a perfect physical duplicate, no less—of a currently experiencing human being is even conceivable, and could possibly exist. One needs to be very careful how one embeds natural-kind terms in 'it is conceivable that' contexts.[83]

It is worth adding that anyone who holds that it is as a matter of *physical* fact impossible for a PPD of an actual, living normally experiencing human being to have no experience must hold that PPD zombies are *metaphysically* (if not *logically*) impossible. Physical impossibility entails metaphysical impossibility in this case, because the question is precisely what is possible given the actual nature of the physical.

15. Realistic Monism

In §1 I pointed out that the word 'physical', as used by genuine materialists, entails 'real and concrete': given that one is restricting one's attention to concrete phenomena, as we are doing here, to say something is a physical phenomenon is simply to say that it is a real phenomenon. But then why bother to use 'physical'? (compare Crane and Mellor 1990). It has become an entirely empty or vacuous term, in so far as it is supposed to mean anything more than 'real'. So why not simply use 'real'? And why bother with 'real', given that we're talking about whatever (concretely) exists, whatever it is? It is redundant. All one strictly needs, to mark the distinctions centrally at issue in the

---

82. I don't know where these zombies come from—but they may be Australian. In the 1980s and early 1990s philosophical zombies were far more plausible creatures: they were standardly defined as *outwardly* and *behaviourally* indistinguishable from human beings while having unknown—and possibly non-biological—insides (see e.g. Dennett 1991: chs. 4, 10, 11), and were, accordingly, of considerable interest to functionalists and behaviourists. (Note added in 2014: it turns out that 'PPD zombies' surfaced in Kirk 1974, and also featured, in effect, in K. Campbell 1970.)

83. It is worth noting that a perfect physical duplicate of an actual human being would have to be governed by the same physical laws.

unfortunately named 'mind–body problem', are 'mental' and 'non-mental', 'experiential' and 'non-experiential'.[84] One can simply declare oneself to be an *experiential-and-non-experiential* monist: one who registers the indubitable reality of experiential phenomena and continues to take it that there are also non-experiential phenomena.

I nominated this position for the title 'realistic monism', having explicitly assumed (p. 167) that any realistic position must take it that there is non-experiential being. This assumption can be backed by an argument that seems at first quite strong—(1) experience (experiential content) certainly exists, (2) experience (experiential content) is impossible without a subject of experience, (3) a subject of experience cannot itself be an entirely experiential (experiential-content) phenomenon, so (4) the existence of experience (experiential content) entails the existence of non-experiential phenomena. But one can have no deep confidence in the correctness of the assumption if one accepts the general principles of ignorance defended in this chapter, and this argument for it invites the reply that even if a subject of experience must have some sort of non-experiential being relative to its own experience, its non-experiential being may be the experience of some other, lower-order, subject or group of subjects, and so on down. I'm not sure this reply is cogent, in fact; but nor am I sure that premiss (3) is solid.[85] I propose in any case to leave the assumption that there is non-experiential being firmly marked as an assumption.

—'You say we can do without the word "physical". But if one can do without "physical", then "materialist", used so diligently in this paper, is just as superfluous—vacuous. You've already stated that you make no distinction between materialism and physicalism (note 9), and the word "materialist" is deeply compromised by its history.

History is two-faced, and I think that 'materialist'—an adjective formed from the natural-kind term 'matter'—can be harmlessly and even illuminatingly retained.[86] What, after all, is matter? As a materialist, I take it that it is whatever we are actually talking about when we talk about concrete reality.

---

84. According to the view presented in Strawson 1994: 162–75, the latter pair suffice on their own.

85. I argue that subjects may be wholly experiential in Strawson 2003.

86. Here I may differ from Chomsky—but only, I think, on a point of terminology. (Obviously 'physical' can also be retained in so far as it is synonymous with 'material'.)

I fix the reference of the term 'matter' in this way—giving a chair a kick, perhaps—independently of any reference to theories. I can be certain that there is such a thing as matter, as a realistic materialist monist—one who takes it that experience is wholly material in nature—because I can be certain that there is such a thing as concrete reality: experience, at the very least. What a materialist may still wish to add to this, in spite of Eddington's powerful doubt, is the insistence that nothing can count as matter unless it has some sort of non-experiential being (see §4); together with the working presumption that current physics is genuinely reality-representing in certain ways, even if any correctness of representation is only a matter of the holding of certain relations of structural correspondence between the nature of matter and the equations of physics.

In so far as I am a realistic materialist monist, then, I presume that physics' best account of the structure of reality is genuinely reality-representing in substantive ways, and that the term 'materialist' is in good order. I sail close to the wind in my use of the word 'matter', facing the charge of vacuousness and the charge (it is seen as a charge) that it may be hard to distinguish my position from idealism, because that is precisely what one has to do at this point. Kicking another chair, I grant that the term 'materialist' has travelled far from some of its past uses, but there is no good reason to think that its meaning is especially tied to its past uses rather than to the current understanding of matter.[87] And there is a sense in which its past use makes it particularly well worth retaining: it makes the claim that the present position is materialist vivid by prompting resistance that turns out to be groundless when the position is properly understood.[88]

---

87. There is, in particular, no good reason to think that it is especially tied to the seventeenth-century conception of matter as something passive and inert. The conception of matter as essentially energy-involving, or at least as something to which motion is intrinsic, is also ancient; it seems to be already present in the work of Democritus and Epicurus.

88. Let me add that I take it that spacetime itself is material (it is a disputed question). In quantum field theory, reality consists of spacetime and a collection of fields defined on spacetime; what we think of as material objects—including particles—are emergent (in the non-spooky sense) features of these fields. But spacetime is not a merely passive container, for according to general relativity the action-reaction principle applies as between spacetime and matter (this is the phenomenon Pullman, 1998: 351, usefully calls 'the vacuum-matter complementarity, or . . . the virtual-material duality of particles'). Moreover, the gravitational field, unlike the other fields, is not thought of as distinct from spacetime itself. Rather, the gravitational field, within a given region, just is the spacetime geometry of that region. The structural relations it involves are physical or material because they are spatiotemporal (they are not merely abstract-dimensional). Note also that energy can be stored and propagated within the gravitational field, and hence within the spacetime fabric itself, which again suggests that spacetime is substantial and hence—given materialism—material, in a way that

That is all I have to say about the word 'materialist'. Some will probably think that I would do better to call myself a 'neutral monist', or just a 'monist'.[89] But what about 'monist'? There is serious unclarity in this notion. Monists hold that there is, in spite of all the variety in the world, a fundamental sense in which there is only one basic kind of stuff or being. But questions about how many kinds of stuff or being there are answerable only relative to a particular point of view or interest; and what point of view is so privileged that it allows one to say that it is an absolute metaphysical fact that there is only one kind of stuff or being in reality? Materialists call themselves monists because they think that all things are of one kind—the physical kind. But most of them also hold that there is more than one kind of fundamental particle, and this claim, taken literally, entails that there isn't after all any one basic kind of being out of which everything is constituted. For it is the claim that these particles are themselves, in their diversity, the ultimate constituents of reality; in which case there is kind-plurality or stuff-plurality right at the bottom of things.

—'But these particles are nevertheless all *physical*, and in that sense of one kind.'

To say that they can be classed together as single-substanced in this way is question-begging until it's backed by a positive theoretical account of why it is correct to say that they are all ultimately (constituted) of one kind (of substance). To claim that their causal interaction sufficiently proves their same-substancehood is to beg the question in another way, on the terms of the classical debate, for classical substance-dualists simply deny that causal interaction entails same-substancehood. The claim that they are all spatio-temporally located also begs the question. For how does this prove same substancehood?

It may be replied that all the particles are just different forms of the same stuff—energy. And it may be added that the so-called fundamental particles—quarks and leptons—are not strictly speaking fundamental, and are in fact all constituted of just one kind of thing: superstrings. And these monist approaches deserve investigation—to be conducted with a properly

Newtonian space and time, say, are not. (My thanks to Michael Lockwood and Harvey Brown for discussion of this matter.)

89. For an argument that neutral monism is not an possible option, see Strawson 2015: §11.

respectful attitude to panpsychism.[90] But one can overleap them by simply rejecting the terms of the classical debate: one can take causal interaction to be a sufficient condition of same-substancehood.

I think that this is the right dialectical move in the present context, if one wants to retain any version of the terminology of substance. Dualists who postulate two distinct substances while holding that they interact causally not only face the old and seemingly insuperable problem of how to give an honest account of this interaction. They also face the (even more difficult) problem of justifying the claim that there are two substances. As far as I can see, *the only justification that has ever been attempted* has consisted in nothing more than an appeal to the *intuition* that the mental or the experiential is utterly different in nature from matter. But this intuition lacks any remotely respectable theoretical support, if the argument of this chapter is even roughly right. The truth, as Priestley saw, is that dualism has nothing in its favour—to think that it does is simply to reveal that one thinks one knows more about the nature of things than one does—and it has Occam's razor (that blunt sharp instrument) against it. This is not to rule out the theoretical possibility that substance dualism—or pluralism—is in fact the best view to take about our universe for reasons of which we know nothing.[91] The fact remains that the objection to dualism just given remains decisive when dualism is considered specifically as a theoretical response to the 'mind-body problem'.

> —'But why persist with "monist"? You might as well call yourself a "neutral pluralist", for all the difference it makes, and "monist" carries bad baggage. Why not simply call yourself a "non-committal naturalist", or a "?-ist'?"[92]

This section stirs up large questions, but I'm not too troubled. In some moods, retaining the assumption that there is non-experiential being, I'm prepared to drop the term 'monist' and call myself an 'experiential-and-non-experiential ?-ist'. At the moment, though, the physics idea (the ancient idea) that everything

---

90. See e.g. Seager 1995, Strawson 2006a. It shouldn't be necessary to say that panpsychism certainly doesn't require one to believe that tables and chairs are subjects of experience.

91. There may be phenomena in the universe that can't interact causally with other things given their nature (rather than their position in spacetime), or that do so only on the first Thursday of every seventh century, in a highly peculiar way.

92. Sebastian Gardner proposed that I am a '?-ist' in 1990. It's hard to find satisfactory names, and Grover Maxwell, who holds essentially the same position as I do, calls himself a 'nonmaterialist physicalist' (1978: 365), by which he means a physicalist who is a genuine realist about experience.

is made of the same ultimate stuff—that the deep diversity of the universe is a matter of different states or arrangements of the same fundamental *ens* or *entia*—that 'in the whole universe there is only one substance differently modified' (La Mettrie, 1747: 39)—seems to me as compelling as it is remarkable, and I choose to register my attraction to it with the word 'monism'.[93]

Postscript 2015

In *Mental Reality* (1994) I went almost all the way to panpsychist or panexperientialist materialism.[94] I argued that

> real materialists must hold at least some experiential properties to be fundamental physical properties, like electric charge ... [they must] hold that experiential properties are—that experientiality is—among the fundamental properties that must be adverted to in a completed or optimal physics (pp. 60, 61–62),

i.e.

[1] experientiality is among the fundamental properties of physical reality.

I noted (p. 77) that [1] didn't entail the fully panpsychist position

[2] experientiality is a fundamental property of all physical phenomena,

but took [2] to be the most plausible situation given [1].[95] I also noted that while it is certain that there is experiential reality, it is simply an assumption on the

---

93. I'm especially grateful to Noam Chomsky, Michael Lockwood and Undo Uus for the leads they have given me. I would also like to thank Lucy Allais, Torin Alter, Harvey Brown, Jeremy Butterfield, Arthur Collins, Tim Crane, Mark Greenberg, Isaac Levi, Barry Loewer, Brian McLaughlin, Philip Pettit, Mark Sainsbury, Simon Saunders, Stephen Schiffer, Peter Unger, Bas van Fraassen, and audiences at the University of Birmingham, CUNY Graduate Center, and Columbia University in 1997 and 1998.

94. I use 'panpsychism' and 'panexperientialism' interchangeably. The word 'materialism' marks the fact that this panpsychist position remains a thesis about *the reality which is the subject matter of physics*—the concrete reality about which we take physics to say many true things.

95. In those days reaching potentially panpsychist conclusions induced a certain bashfulness in analytic philosophers like myself. For greater forthrightness see e.g. Sprigge (1983), Griffin (1998).

part of materialist monists 'that there is more to physical reality than experiential reality' (p. 74). Most take

[3] physical reality has non-experiential being

to be essentially definitive of any materialist view, built into the meaning of the words 'physical' and 'material', but this certainly can't be taken for granted when physics and metaphysics get serious—recall the quotations from Eddington and Russell on pp. 169 and 193–4.[96]

In 'Real Materialism' I put panpsychist materialism mostly on one side while preparing a more fully panpsychist step forward.[97] It is, certainly, a large step from [2], which one might call *weak* panpsychism, to the *strong* or *pure* panpsychist claim that

[4] experientiality (experience and subjects of experience) is all there is to concrete physical reality,

and one immediately salient alternative to [4] (here I assume for purposes of argument that physical reality involves the existence of a multitude of very small fundamental entities) is *micropsychism*, according to which

[5] experientiality is a fundamental property of at least some of the fundamental physical entities

but not necessarily all. Plainly micropsychism can be true while panpsychism is false, as noted in *Mental Reality* (p. 77). One entirely speculative possibility is that only particles whose existence involves the existence of electric charge (this includes neutrons but not e.g. neutrinos) possess experientiality as a fundamental property.

There are many possibilities. With Eddington, Whitehead, and others, I think that [4], pure panpsychism/panexperientialism, is on balance the most plausible form of materialism, the most scientifically 'hard-nosed', theoretically elegant, theoretically parsimonious form of materialism, the form that appears most intuitively plausible when one has thought the matter through.

---

96. It is not in fact well supported by the dictionary definitions of 'material' and 'physical' in the *Oxford English Dictionary* (one has to go to definition 21 of 'matter' for clear support).

97. In a paper given to a one-day conference in London in 2002 with Frank Jackson and David Papineau (Strawson 2006a).

The version I favour performs a 'global replace' on physics as traditionally conceived. It proposes that the fundamental intrinsic nature of the reality treated of in physics—I like the idea that one can simply call it 'energy'—is wholly a matter of experientiality. In so doing it leaves everything that is correct in physics untouched. It doesn't have the implausible consequence that stones and tables are subjects of experience. Nor does it put in question the view that the particular qualitative character of the experience of biological subjects of experience such as ourselves is a product of evolution by natural selection.

I'm not sure there is any quick way to work a passage into a proper appreciation of the power of this position after a standard education in analytic philosophy. It's likely to be 'hard work . . . a kind of laziness pulls [one] insensibly back into one's everyday habits of thought' (Descartes 1641: 2.15), and 'we love our habits more than our income, often more than our life' (Russell 1923: 113). It took me a long time. One is making progress when one sees that 'panpsychism must be considered a species of naturalism' (Sellars 1927: 218). One is making further progress when one catches up with Eddington and Co.—noting as one goes that Russell and James, for all their talk of 'neutral monism', are also open to panpsychism (if indeed the supposed neutrality of their fundamental stuff doesn't collapse into a form of panpsychism).

Even if one can't go all the way one should, I believe, endorse the thesis of the *theoretical primacy of panpsychism*. According to this thesis, unprejudiced consideration of what we know about concrete reality obliges us to favour some version of panpsychism, or at the very least micropsychism, over all other positive substantive theories of the intrinsic non-structural nature of reality. In its strongest form, the thesis is not just that it would take extraordinarily hard work to justify preferring any substantive metaphysical position that isn't panpsychist or micropsychist—however great the difficulties panpsychism and micropsychism may also face.[98] It's rather that it can't be done. It can't be done because it requires that one assume the existence of things whose existence one has no reason to assume. It's intensely natural for us to feel certain that there is non-experiential concrete reality, in addition to the experiential reality we know to exist, so that pure panpsychism must be false. But

[6] there is no evidence—there is precisely zero evidence—for the existence of non-experiential reality.

---

98. Such as the 'combination problem'. For a classic statement see James 1890: ch. 6; but compare James 1907: ch. 5, 'The Compounding of Consciousness'. See also e.g. Clarke 1707–1718, Skrbina 2009, and papers in Blamauer 2011 and Brüntrup and Jaskolla 2015.

Nor can there ever be any. Physics is silent on the question of the intrinsic non-structural nature of concrete reality. It may be added that

[7] the assumption that non-experiential reality exists—the assumption that matter-energy has some non-experiential being—confers no theoretical advantages at all,

and finally that, given the certain existence of experience,

[8] the assumption that non-experiential reality exists creates some extremely severe—arguably unsurmountable—theoretical difficulties

in almost all existing theories that make that assumption.[99]

References

Algarotti, F. (1737/1739) *Sir Isaac Newton's Philosophy Explain'd for the Use of the Ladies,* translated by Elizabeth Carter (London: E. Cave).

Aristotle (c 340BCE/1936) *De Anima,* translated by W. S. Hett (Cambridge, MA: Harvard University Press).

Arnauld, A. (1641/1985) 'Fourth Set of Objections' in *The Philosophical Writings of Descartes,* volume 2, translated by J. Cottingham et al. (Cambridge: Cambridge University Press).

Auden, W. H. (1940) *Another Time* (New York: Random House).

Bell, J. S. (1987) *Speakable and Unspeakable in Quantum Mechanics* (Cambridge: Cambridge University Press).

Blamauer, M. (2011) *The Mental as Fundamental. New Perspectives on Panpsychism* (Frankfurt: Ontos).

Brüntrup, G. and Jaskolla, L. (2015) *Panpsychism: Philosophical Essays* (Oxford: Oxford University Press).

Chalmers, D. (1995) 'Facing up to the Problem of Consciousness' *Journal of Consciousness Studies* 2: 200–19.

Chalmers, D. (1996) *The Conscious Mind* (New York: Oxford University Press).

Chalmers, D. (1997) 'Moving Forward on the Problem of Consciousness' in *Explaining Consciousness: the Hard Problem,* edited by Jonathan Shear (Cambridge, MA: MIT Press).

Chomsky, N. (1968) *Language and Mind* (New York: Harcourt, Brace & World).

99. See again Eddington 1928. See also Griffin 1998, Seager 2012, Strawson 2006a, 2012, 2015.

Chomsky, N. (1986) *Barriers* (Cambridge, MA: MIT Press).

Chomsky, N. (1988) *Language and Problems of Knowledge* (Cambridge, MA: MIT Press).

Chomsky, N. (1993) 'Explaining Language Use' *Philosophical Topics* **20**: 205–31.

Chomsky, N. (1994) 'Naturalism and Dualism in the Study of Language' *International Journal of Philosophical Studies* **2**: 181–209.

Chomsky, N. (1995) 'Language and Nature' *Mind* **104**: 1–60.

Chomsky, N. (1996) *Powers and Prospects* (London: Pluto).

Chomsky, N. (1998) 'Comments: Galen Strawson's *Mental Reality*' *Philosophy and Phenomenological Research* **58**: 437–41.

Churchland, P. M. (1995) *The Engine of Reason, the Seat of the Soul: A Philosophical Journey into the Brain* (Cambridge, MA: MIT Press).

Clarke, S. and Collins, A. (1707–1718/2011) *The Clarke-Collins Correspondence of 1707–18*, ed. W. Uzgalis (Peterborough, ON: Broadview Press).

Crane, T. and Mellor, D. H. (1990) 'There Is No Question Of Physicalism' *Mind* **99**: 185–206.

Demopoulos, W. and Friedman, M. (1985) 'Critical Notice: Bertrand Russell's *The Analysis of Matter* and Its Historical Context and Contemporary Interest' *Philosophy of Science* **52**: 621–39.

Dennett, D. (1991) *Consciousness Explained* (Boston: Little, Brown).

Descartes, R. (1641/1985) *Meditations* and *Objections and Replies* in *The Philosophical Writings of Descartes*, volumes 1 and 2, translated by J. Cottingham et al. (Cambridge: Cambridge University Press).

Deutsch. D. (1997) *The Fabric of Reality* (Harmondsworth: Penguin).

Eddington, A. (1920) *Space Time and Gravitation* (Cambridge: Cambridge University Press).

Eddington, A. (1928) *The Nature of The Physical World* (New York: Macmillan).

Eddington, A. (1939) *The Philosophy of Physical Science* (Cambridge: Cambridge University Press).

Evans, G. (1980/1986) 'Things Without the Mind' *Collected Papers* (Oxford: Clarendon Press).

Feigl, H. (1962) 'Matter Still Largely Material (A response to N. R. Hanson's "The Dematerialization of Matter")' Philosophy of Science **29**: 39–46.

Foster, J. (1982) *The Case for Idealism* (London: Routledge).

Griffin, D. (1998) *Unsnarling the World-Knot: Consciousness, Freedom, and the Mind-Body Problem* (Berkeley, CA: University of California Press. http://ark.cdlib.org/ark:/13030/ft8c6009k3/.

Hanson, N. R. (1962) 'The Dematerialization of Matter' *Philosophy of Science* **29**: 27–38.

Harré, R. and Madden, E. H. (1975) *Causal Powers: A Theory of Natural Necessity* (Blackwell: Oxford).

Hirsch, E. (1986) 'Metaphysical Necessity and Conceptual Truth' *Midwest Studies* **11**: 243–56.

Hume, D. (1739–40/1978) *A Treatise of Human Nature*, edited by L. A. Selby-Bigge (Oxford: Clarendon Press).

Isham, C. & Butterfield, J. (2000) 'Some Possible Roles for Topos Theory in Quantum Theory and Quantum Gravity' *Foundations of Physics* **30**: 1707–35.

James, W. (1890) *The Principles of Psychology* (New York: Dover).

James, W. (1907/1987) *A Pluralistic Universe* in *William James: Writings 1902–1910* (New York: The Library of America).

Kant, I. (1781–87/1933) *Critique of Pure Reason*, translated by N. Kemp Smith (London: Macmillan).

Ladyman, J. (1998) 'What Is Structural Realism?' *Studies In History and Philosophy of Science* **29**: 409–24.

La Mettrie, J. (1747/1996) 'Machine Man' in *Machine Man and Other Writings*, edited and translated by Ann Thomson (Cambridge: Cambridge University Press).

Lange, F. A. (1865/1925) *The History of Materialism*, translated by E. C. Thomas with an introduction by Bertrand Russell (London: Routledge and Kegan Paul).

Leibniz, G. (1720/1965) *Monadology and Other Philosophical Essays*, translated by P. and A. M. Schrecker (Indianapolis: Bobbs-Merrill).

Lewis, D. (1983) 'Introduction' in D. Lewis, *Philosophical Papers*, volume 2 (Oxford: Oxford University Press).

Lewis, D. (1994) 'Reduction of Mind' in *A Companion to the Philosophy of Mind*, edited by S. Guttenplan (Oxford: Blackwell).

Lewis, D. (1999) 'Introduction' in D. Lewis, *Papers in Metaphysics and Epistemology* (Cambridge: Cambridge University Press).

Locke, J. (1690/1975) *An Essay Concerning Human Understanding*, edited by P. Nidditch (Oxford: Clarendon Press).

Locke, J. (1696–99/1964) 'The Correspondence with Stillingfleet' in *An Essay Concerning Human Understanding*, edited and abridged by A. D. Woozley (London: Collins).

Lockwood, M. (1981) 'What *Was* Russell's Neutral Monism?' *Midwest Studies in Philosophy* **6**: 143–58.

Lockwood, M. (1989) *Mind, Brain, and the Quantum*. (Oxford: Blackwell).

Lockwood, M. (1996) ' "Many Minds" Interpretation of Quantum Mechanics' *Brit. J. Phil. Sci.* **47**: 159–88.

Maxwell, G. (1978) 'Rigid Designators and Mind-Brain Identity' in *Perception and Cognition: Issues in the Foundations of Psychology*, edited by C. Wade Savage (Minneapolis: University of Minnesota Press).

McGinn, C. (1982) *The Character of Mind* (Oxford: Oxford University Press).

McGinn, C. (1991) *The Problem of Consciousness* (Oxford: Oxford University Press).

McGinn, C. (1983) *The Subjective View* (Oxford: Clarendon Press).

McGinn, C. (1989/1991) 'Can We Solve the Mind-Body Problem?' in *The Problem of Consciousness* (Oxford: Blackwell).

McGinn, C. (1995) 'Consciousness and Space' *Journal of Consciousness Studies* 2: 221–30.

Moore, G. E. (1905–06/1922) 'The Nature and Reality of Objects of Perception' in G. E. Moore, *Philosophical Studies* (London: Routledge).

Nagel, T. (1998) 'Conceiving the Impossible and the Mind-Body Problem' *Philosophy* 73: 337–52.

Priestley, J. (1777/1818) *Disquisitions Relating to Matter and Spirit*, in *The Theological and Miscellaneous Works of Joseph Priestley*, volume 3, edited by J. T. Rutt (London: Smallfield).

Priestley J. and Price, R. (1778/1819) *A Free Discussion of the Doctrines of Materialism, and Philosophical Necessity*, in *The Theological and Miscellaneous Works of Joseph Priestley*, volume 4, edited by J. T. Rutt (London: Smallfield).

Pullman, B. (1998) *The Atom in The History of Human Thought* (New York: Oxford University Press).

Russell, B. (1912/1959) *The Problems of Philosophy* (Oxford: Oxford University Press).

Russell, B. (1923/2004) 'The Need for Political Scepticism' in *Sceptical Essays* (London: Routledge).

Russell, B. (1925) 'Introduction' in F. A. Lange, *The History of Materialism*, translated by E. C. Thomas (London: Routledge and Kegan Paul).

Russell, B. (1927a/1992a) *The Analysis of Matter* (London: Routledge).

Russell, B. (1927b/1992b) *An Outline of Philosophy* (London: Routledge).

Russell, B. (1948/1992c) *Human Knowledge: Its Scope And Limits* (London: Routledge).

Russell, B. (1956/1995) 'Mind and Matter' in *Portraits from Memory* (Nottingham: Spokesman).

Russell, B. (1967–69/1978) *Autobiography* (London: Allen & Unwin).

Saunders, S. and Brown, H. (1991) *The Philosophy of Vacuum* (Oxford: Clarendon Press).

Seager, W. (1995) 'Consciousness, Information, and Panpsychism' in *Explaining Consciousness: the Hard Problem* edited by Jonathan Shear (Cambridge, MA: MIT Press).

Seager, W. (2012) *Natural Fabrications* (Dordrecht: Springer).

Shoemaker, S. (1990/1996) 'First-person access' in *The First-Person Perspective and Other Essays* (Cambridge: Cambridge University Press).

Skrbina, D. (2009) 'Panpsychism in history' in *Mind That Abides* ed. D. Skrbina (Amsterdam: John Benjamins), 1–29.

Sprigge, T. L. S. (1983) *The Vindication of Absolute Idealism* (Edinburgh: Edinburgh University Press).

Stoljar, D. (2001) 'Two Conceptions of the Physical', in *Philosophy and Phenomenological Research* 62: 253–81.

Strawson, G. (1989) *The Secret Connexion* (Oxford: Clarendon Press).

Strawson, G. (1994) *Mental Reality* (Cambridge, MA: MIT Press).

Strawson, G. (1998) Précis of *Mental Reality* and replies to Noam Chomsky, Pierre Jacob, Michael Smith, & Paul Snowdon, Symposium on *Mental Reality*, *Philosophy and Phenomenological Research* **58**: 433–35, 461–86.

Strawson, G. (1999) 'Realistic Materialist Monism' in *Towards a Science of Consciousness III*, edited by S. Hameroff, A. Kaszniak & D. Chalmers (Cambridge, MA: MIT Press), 23–32.

Strawson, G. (2002/2008a) 'Knowledge of the World' in *Philosophical Issues* **12**: 146–75. Revised as 'Can we know the nature of reality as it is in itself?' in G. Strawson 2008a.

Strawson, G. (2003/2008a) 'What is the relation between an experience, the subject of the experience, and the content of the experience?' *Philosophical Issues* **13**: 279–315, revised version in G. Strawson 2008a.

Strawson, G. (2006a) 'Why physicalism entails panpsychism' in G. Strawson *et al*, *Consciousness and its Place in Nature* (Thorverton: Imprint Academic), 3–31.

Strawson, G. (2006b) 'Reply to commentators, with a celebration of Descartes' in *Consciousness and its place in nature* edited by A. Freeman (Thorverton: Imprint Academic), 184–280.

Strawson, G. (2008a) *Real Materialism and Other Essays* (Oxford: Oxford University Press).

Strawson, G. (2008b) 'The identity of the categorical and the dispositional' *Analysis* **68/4**: 271–82.

Strawson, G. (2009) *Selves: An Essay in Revisionary Metaphysics* (Oxford: Clarendon Press).

Strawson, G. (2010) 'Radical Self-Awareness' in *Self, No Self?: Perspectives from Analytical, Phenomenological, and Indian Traditions* ed. M. Siderits, E. Thompson, and D. Zahavi (Oxford: Oxford University Press) 274–307.

Strawson, G. (2012) 'Real naturalism', Romanell Lecture, in *Proceedings of the American Philosophical Association* **86/2**: 125–54.

Strawson, G. (2015) 'Mind and being: the primacy of panpsychism'. In *Panpsychism: Philosophical Essays* edited by G. Brüntrup and L. Jaskolla (Oxford: Oxford University Press).

Toland, J. (1704) *Letters to Serena* (London: Bernard Lintot).

Van Fraassen, B. (1980) *The Scientific Image* (Oxford: Clarendon Press).

Weinberg, S. (1997) *New York Review of Books*, June 12 (New York: NYRev, Inc.).

Wittgenstein, L. (1922/1961) *Tractatus Logico-Philosophicus*, trans. B. McGuinness and D. F. Pears (London: Routledge).

Worrall, J. (1989) 'Structural Realism: The Best of Both Worlds?' *Dialectica* **43**: 99–124.

10

Russellian Physicalism

Barbara Gail Montero

ACCORDING TO DAVID Chalmers (1996, 2002, 2010) the conceivability argument against physicalism is, by and large, successful. In outline, this argument asks us to first conceive of a world that, although just like ours at the level of fundamental physics, lacks consciousness. It goes on to claim that a world matching this conception is logically possible and concludes that consciousness is not physical. Most accept that if it is possible for there to be a world that duplicates the fundamental properties of physics without duplicating consciousness, then consciousness is not physical. And many accept that we can in some sense conceive of such a world. The controversial part of the argument is the move from conceivability to possibility. Yet, according to Chalmers, when we are very careful about what is to count as conceivability, this move also is valid. Physicalism about consciousness, then, says Chalmers, must be rejected.

Or rather, it must *almost* be rejected. This qualification arises because "Russellian monism," characterized roughly by Chalmers (2002, p. 265) as the view that "consciousness is constituted by the intrinsic properties of fundamental physical entities" falls through a loophole in the antiphysicalist conceivability argument. For it may be, he thinks, that when we conceive of the fundamental physical world we fail to conceive of its intrinsic properties. Yet if Russellian monism is true, consciousness depends on these intrinsic properties, and because of this, a world that duplicates our fundamental physics without duplicating these properties may be a world without consciousness. The most, then, that even the best conceivability argument can conclude, Chalmers tells us, is either physicalism is false or Russellian monism is true (2010).

Is this good news for the physicalist? One might think so, but not Chalmers. Although he thinks that Russellian monism "may ultimately provide the best integration of the physical and the phenomenal within the natural world" and that "there appears to be no strong reasons to reject the view," he argues that it "has much in common with property dualism, and that many physicalists will want to reject [it]" (2010). He suggests that "while the view arguably fits the letter of materialism, it shares the spirit of antimaterialism" (2002, p. 265).

I aim to show that this escape clause in the conceivability argument is more significant than Chalmers indicates since there is a variation of Russellian monism, what I refer to as "Russellian physicalism," that falls through the loophole yet is fully physicalistic.[1]

Of course, physicalists who never saw conceivability arguments as bad news in the first place may have little interest in the prospects of Russellian physicalism. As they see it, not even the most careful type of conceivability can result in knowledge of (or even very good evidence for) the possibility of worlds that duplicate our physics, yet lack consciousness (e.g. Churchland 1996). But, still, these physicalists should take heed of Russellian physicalism since even if the conceivability of worlds that duplicate our physics yet lack consciousness, or what I shall refer to as "zombie worlds," is not a guide to their possibility, such worlds may be possible nonetheless.[2] Or at least, to show that they are not possible is a great deal more difficult than to show that conceivability provides neither knowledge of nor good evidence for them. Yet Russellian physicalism can be consistently maintained, even if some of these physicalists' worst zombie-riddled nightmares depict a possibility.

I shall begin with a general description of Russellian monism that, although differing from Chalmers' description in some points, remains neutral as to whether the view is antiphysicalistic in spirit. I go on to explain why this view escapes the conceivability argument (even assuming that conceivability implies possibility) and then argue that when the details of Russellian monism are filled in in a certain way, the view throws off its antiphysicalistic clothing and turns into a full-blooded form of physicalism: Russellian physicalism. In preview, I argue that since Russellian physicalism takes the fundamental grounds of everything to be neither mental nor specifically

---

1. Cf. Montero (2010).

2. My use of the phrase "zombie worlds" is atypical, as it usually means worlds that are identical to ours in every respect save for their lack of consciousness. I shall say a bit about zombie worlds in this other sense towards the end of section III.

for the purpose of generating mentality it should rightly count as a form of physicalism.

I. Russellian Monism

As Chalmers tells us, Russellian monism takes its inspiration from Bertrand Russell's view that fundamental physics tells us only about the structure of the world, about the abstract relations between things but not about the things themselves. In Chalmers' words, "current physics characterizes its underlying properties (such as mass and charge) in terms of abstract structures and relations, but it leaves open their intrinsic natures" (2002, p. 259). From physics we learn how mass behaves—we learn that a body with greater mass has more inertia, that the mass of a body does not vary with changes in gravity and so forth—but not what mass is apart from a set of behaviors. From physics we learn that opposite charges attract each other, that like charges repel, that the net charge of any isolated system never varies, but we do not learn what charge is, itself, apart from what it does. From physics we come to understand the nomological or causal role of properties, but not the nature of properties themselves. Russell (1959/1995) puts the view thus: "All that physics gives us is certain equations giving abstract properties of their changes. But as to what it is that changes, and what it changes from and to—as to this, physics is silent" (p. 18). Or as Galileo famously said, the book of nature is written in the language of mathematics.

According to the Russellian monist, however, nature itself consists of more than abstract relations; for in addition to the relations, there are the things that stand in relation to each other. Besides laws, says the Russellian monist, there is something for the laws to describe. It is difficult to say much about these first order properties, the properties of nature itself, since it is not just in physics, but in all arenas, that we explain things in terms of their relations to other things. To explain something is to describe what it does, how it affects us, and how it is related to other things. If you ask me what, say, a cantelever bridge is, I shall tell you that it is a bridge that juts out on each side from a support on that side. As opposed to a suspension bridge, or a beam bridge, it would not fall down if you were to cut it in half in the middle, and so on. But although the properties that concern the Russellian do something—according to the Russellian they form the determination base for consciousness—there is more to them than what they do. They not only do something, they also are something.

But what are they? Chalmers and others refer to them as the intrinsic properties of fundamental physical entities, but I am hesitant to use this terminology. What is an intrinsic property? Many understand the notion along Lewisian lines whereby "an intrinsic property of *a*" is a property *a* would have whether or not anything else besides *a* existed (Langton and Lewis 1998). But, arguably, physics tells us about intrinsic properties. For example, a positively charged particle existing all alone in an empty universe has the property of being such that if it were in a world with physical laws x, y, and z, (where x, y, and z describe the laws of our world) and with entities and properties u, v, w (where u, v, and w describe the other entities and properties of our world), it would be attracted to a negatively charged particle. This property counts as intrinsic on the Lewisian definition, yet, arguably, is revealed by physics.

Chalmers tells us, however, that by "intrinsic properties" he means "the categorical bases of fundamental physical dispositions." On the simple conditional interpretation of dispositions, when we learn of an object's dispositional properties we learn about what an object will do in various circumstances. For example, when we find out that a sugar cube is soluble, we learn that it has the property of being such that if it were placed in water (of a certain temperature for a certain amount of time) it would dissolve.[3] Categorical properties ground dispositional properties and, presumably, for the Russellian, the categorical properties of the fundamental dispositional properties of physics ground consciousness.

But I am also hesitant to rely on the categorical/dispositional distinction to clarify the Russellian position since, if "categorical" is supposed to imply not dispositional, it is unclear whether there are any categorical properties. For example, the purported categorical property that is supposed to ground, say, the top quark's mass, would seem to be *disposed* to give it this mass and the fundamental dispositional properties of physics, which according to the Russellian ground consciousness, would seem to be *disposed* to do so.

Though no doubt much more could be said in defense of relying on either the notion of intrinsicality or categoricity in formulating a Russellian view, these notions, as I see it, are not needed since what is significant for the Russellian monist is that there is some aspect of the fundamental world—that is, some aspect of the fundamental properties given to us by physics—that grounds consciousness, yet about which physics is silent (perhaps not permanently, but for the foreseeable future). So to highlight this, let me call the properties of the fundamental world, which, according to the Russellian, are

---

3. For an argument that this understanding of dispositions is inadequate, see Martin (1994). As I am ultimately not going to rely on the dispositional/categorical distinction, I leave the question of how to understand these notions correctly to the side.

not revealed by physics yet ground consciousness (perhaps as well as other things), "inscrutables." Chalmers seems to accept both the Russellian picture of physics and the idea that consciousness may be determined (in part) by inscrutables. But, as I shall go on to argue, once he does this, he has admitted that physicalism, both letter and spirit, might be true.

II. How Russellian Monism Slips Through the Loophole

As Chalmers (2002, 2010) points out, how a Russellian monist avoids the conceivability argument obviously depends on how we understand the argument. Recall that the conceivability argument moves from the conceivability of worlds that duplicate our physics yet lack consciousness to the possibility of such worlds and then concludes that because such worlds are possible, physicalism is false. The possibility of a world that duplicates our physics yet lacks consciousness is taken as inconsistent with physicalism since "upward determination" is thought of as a necessary condition for physicalism, where upward determination guarantees that any world that duplicates all the fundamental properties of physics of our world also duplicates all properties of our world.[4] A physicalist view that is consistent with the failure of upward determination thus would escape this argument.

Whether Russellian monism is consistent with the failure of upward determination turns on what we count as the fundamental properties of physics. On the one hand, they can be thought of as only the structural properties given to us by microphysics, while on the other hand, they can be thought of as such properties as well as that which is structured (that is, as well as the inscrutables). Only in the former sense is Russellian monism consistent with the failure of upward determination; and it is only in the latter sense, according to Chalmers, that Russellian monism "fits the letter of materialism" (2002, p. 265). This latter picture of the fundamental properties of physics results in a Russellian view that wiggles through the antiphysicalist conceivability argument by explaining away the intuition that the failure of upward determination seems possible. The Russellian monist of this stripe may argue that although a world duplicating our physics yet lacking consciousness seems conceivable, this is only because we do not imagine the full story of fundamental physics; if we did (perhaps per impossible) we would see that

---

4. See, however, Montero (2013) for an argument that physicalism does not entail upward determination.

such a world would contain consciousness as well. On the former view, the intuition need not be explained away; rather, it can be accepted as veridical.

One further clarification of the former view is needed, however, to see why this is so. All Russellian monists think that structure alone does not suffice for consciousness. And all accept that consciousness exists and its existence is determined, at least in part, by what I am calling "inscrutables." But Russellians can differ as to how they understand the relation between inscrutables and the structural properties of physics. A Russellian can think of the fundamental properties of physics as either requiring inscrutables or not requiring them. And the type of Russellian monism that is consistent with the possibility of worlds that duplicate our physics (as thought of as duplicating only the structural properties) yet lack consciousness is the type that does not require consciousness-generating inscrutables. In contrast, a Russellian who holds that the structural properties of physics require consciousness-grounding inscrutables explains away the intuition that zombie worlds are possible: the failure of upward determination of consciousness by physics is conceivable, she says, since one might conceive of a world which duplicates our physics yet lacks consciousness if one fails to imagine everything that follows from duplicating our physics. (On Chalmers' way of thinking about the issue, the failure of upward determination is conceivable for this stripe of Russellian monist because we are conceiving of only the primary intention of the world of physics, that is to say, the structure but not that which is structured.)

In each case, the Russellian has a response to the conceivability argument.

However, I would like to highlight the Russellian view that not only has a response to the conceivability argument but also is consistent with the failure of upward determination. That is, I would like to lay out a view that is compatible with the conceivability argument, even assuming that the conceivability of worlds that duplicate our physics yet lack consciousness implies the possibility of such worlds. Thus, by "the fundamental physical properties," I shall mean just the structural properties of fundamental physics, and I shall assume that these properties do not require consciousness-generating inscrutables.

III. From Monism to Physicalism

So we have a position that Chalmers admits avoids antiphysicalist conceivability arguments. Yet, why does Chalmers, one of philosophy's most eminent antiphysicalists, remain undaunted? The reason is that Russellian monism, as Chalmers sees it, isn't *really* physicalism; it can be called "physicalism," he seems to think, but it isn't the sort of physicalism most purebred physicalists would accept. The issue here, then, at least in his eyes (and in mine too) is not purely terminological: philosophers engaged in the debate over whether consciousness is physical—just like those engaged in debates over whether certain actions are morally acceptable—typically think that there is something at stake over and above our choice of words. And Chalmers, by making a distinction between the letter and spirit of materialism, is, in effect, telling us that merely applying the term "physicalism" to this view is not enough to turn it into the type of physicalism that is worthy of the name.[5]

Russellian monism, according to Chalmers, would not be to most physicalists' taste because it, "acknowledges phenomenal or protophenomenal properties as ontologically basic" (2002, p. 265). If inscrutables are themselves phenomenal, Russellian monism turns into a kind of panpsychism, imbuing the fundamental entities of physics with mentality. In this case, I agree with Chalmers that this results in a position that is at least in spirit antiphysicalist.[6]

The protophenomenal version of the view, as it does not posit that the fundamental entities are imbued with mentality, does not result in panpsychism. So why should this view be unacceptable to physicalists? Chalmers reasons that even in its protophenomenal form the view "can be seen as a sort of dualism" since it acknowledges "protophenomenal properties as ontologically fundamental, and it retains an underlying duality between structural-dispositional properties (those directly characterized in physical theory) and intrinsic protophenomenal properties (those responsible for consciousness)" (2002, p. 265). Moreover, he claims that the protophenomenal version of the view retains some of the "strangeness" of the phenomenal version of the view since "it

---

5. One way to understand the debate over physicalism is as a debate over whether mentality resides at the most fundamental level of reality. (See, for example, Montero 2009, 2001, and 1999, and Montero and Papineau 2005.)

6. Some see panpsychism as a type of physicalism (Strawson 2006). It is also sometimes said that the Russellian view must be, or at least is best thought of, as a version of panpsychism. Daniel Stoljar (2006) argues against this. He tells us that people have thought that Russellian monism entails or at least suggests panpsychism because we derive our concept of categoricity from phenomenal concepts. He then goes on to argue that even if this is so, it doesn't follow that categorical properties are phenomenal. Citing an example of Kripke's, he says that one might acquire the concept of a duck from seeing ducks in Central Park, but our concept of a duck need not be limited to ducks in Central Park. And so it could be, Stoljar claims, with categoricity. Moreover, Stoljar argues, it is unclear that we do derive our idea of categoricity from phenomenality. If a categorical property just is, as he assumes, "a nondispositional property on which dispositional properties supervene," then the notion of categoricity does not suggest phenomenality (2006, p. 119). This seems correct to me and would seem to apply to the concept of "inscrutability" just as well as categoricity. (I argue against thinking of panpsychism as a form of physicalism in Montero 2009, as well as in other papers.)

seems that any properties responsible for constituting consciousness must be strange and unusual properties, of a sort that we might not expect to find in microphysical reality" (2002, p. 266).

So as Chalmers sees it, the view should not be to a physicalist's liking since (1) it posits fundamental protophenomenal properties, (2) it is a form of dualism, and (3) protophenomenal properties are strange and unusual and not the type of thing we would expect to find in microphysical reality. I think that these last two points can be addressed rather quickly. I do not see dualism, in the sense that there are two fundamentally different sorts of substances or properties, as necessarily antiphysicalistic. If, say, dark matter turned out to be composed of something entirely different from ordinary matter, there would be two fundamentally different sorts of things, but this, I would think, should not pose a counterexample to physicalism. And I think that a physicalist should not reject a view merely because it posits strange and unusual properties of a sort that we would not expect to find in microphysical reality; each new revolution in physics itself brings with it such properties, yet these revolutions have not overturned physicalism. The first point, however, is rather more vexing.

Does the protophenomenal version of Russellian monism posit fundamental protophenomenal properties? This turns on what is to count as "protophenomenal." If the protophenomenal is just whatever it is that serves as a dependence base for the phenomenal, then certainly the view does posit such properties. But all forms of non-reductive physicalism hold that consciousness is ultimately determined by nonconscious properties, and so this alone should not make the view physicalistically suspect. On the other hand, if the protophenomenal is supposed to be tainted with the phenomenal, the view may not be to the physicalist's liking, but such a position is more in line with the panpsychist version of the view than the protophenomenal version.

If, however, Russellian monism posits that these nonconscious properties that form the dependence base for consciousness have no other role than that of determining consciousness, Chalmers' suspicions that the view is antiphysicalistic in spirit might seem better grounded. These properties would be protophenomenal because they specifically ground the phenomenal. Typical nonreductive physicalist views are not like this. For the typical nonreductivist, the fundamental physical world is the dependence base for everything including consciousness. Yet the Russellian monist, understood in this way, sees the fundamental properties of physics as the dependence base for rocks, trees, chairs, and tables, indeed, everything except for consciousness, and sees inscrutables (perhaps combined with the properties of physics) as forming the dependence base for consciousness. Is Russellian monism physicalism manqué after all?

When we understand the position as positing inscrutables that have the sole purpose of grounding consciousness, I think that the answer is not entirely clear. Perhaps if consciousness were merely the result of, say, inscrutables reaching a threshold of complexity, there would seem to be nothing to worry the physicalist. Still, Russellian monism, understood in this way, might be thought of as a borderline case of physicalism, or by some not even as a form of physicalism at all. However, Russellian monism need not be understood as positing specifically consciousness-grounding inscrutables. That is, it need not be understood as protophenomenal in the sense of grounding only the phenomenal. Rather, the Russellian can hold that inscrutables form the dependence base for the entire concrete world, only a very small portion of which is mental. The Russellian view of physics leaves us with a highly abstract picture of the world: "Our knowledge of the physical world [i.e. the world described by physics]," Russell tells us, "is only abstract and mathematical" (1946/2004, p. 274). Yet, arguably, the world is more than equations; arguably, God, with her infinite wisdom, is not only a pure mathematician but an applied one as well. And on this understanding of the Russellian view, inscrutables ground the applications.

If inscrutables are in this way the substance of the world—if they are, to use Stephen Hawking's words, what "breathes fire into the equations [of any possible grand unified theory of physics] and makes a universe for them to describe"—they are not uniquely important to the mental and so a world with them should be perfectly acceptable to a physicalist (1988, p. 174). I think that this view (the view that everything, including the mind, is determined in part by inscrutables) is no longer physicalism manqué, but the real McCoy.

This physicalistic version of Russellian monism, the view I call "Russellian physicalism," is consistent with the failure of upward determination of physics since it holds that duplicating just the fundamental physics of our world, which we are assuming is entirely structural, duplicates only more structure and not consciousness. If Russellian physicalism were true, a world that duplicates our fundamental physics yet lacks consciousness would either have inscrutables that differ from those in our world and do not ground consciousness or, perhaps, no inscrutables at all.[7] These possibilities notwithstanding, Russellian physicalism, I claim, is still a version of physicalism.

---

7. Is an entirely abstract world possible? I am not sure, but some think it is not only possible, but also actual. See, for example, Laydyman et al. (2007).

Although there is widespread disagreement about how to formulate physicalism, most more or less agree that it entails that all higher-level features of the world are, in some sense, nothing over and above the fundamental features of the world and that all fundamental features of the world are physical. Being nothing over and above is usually explained in terms of a supervenience or determination relation, though finding one such relation that is both necessary and sufficient for physicalism has proved to be no easy task.[8] However, since the reasons for thinking that the Russellian view is antiphysicalistic have nothing to do with the supervenience or determination relation it employs, but rather concerns the ontological status of inscrutables, let me merely stipulate that the Russellian who accepts Russellian physicalism, holds that all higher-level properties stand in some relation to inscrutables and structurals such that if inscrutables and structurals were physical, Russellian physicalism would be a veritable physicalism. Structurals, we are assuming, are physicalistically acceptable. But what about inscrutables?

I have said that inscrutables are neither mental nor for the sole purpose of creating mentality, and so Chalmers' worry that they are either phenomenal or protophenomenal (in any problematic sense) does not arise.[9] But perhaps there are other reasons for thinking that they pose a threat to physicalism. It may be that some would say that since inscrutables are fundamental features of the world that are not capable of being fully explained by physics, they should not count as physical. To be sure, inscrutables, as I have defined them, are inscrutable, as it were, to physics. But they are inscrutable to a physics that tells us about only the purely structural features of the world. Yet the physicalist who thinks that everything must be explainable by physics is not beholden to this notion of physics. Perhaps it is reasonable to think that all physics can and ever

---

8. For example, one particularly pressing problem is how to formulate a viable thesis of physicalism that is inconsistent with such things as a necessarily existing God and ontological emergence. For a proposed solution to this problem see Wilson (1999). Another problem is how to formulate physicalism if there are no fundamental properties. Brown and Ladyman (2009) and Montero (2006) address this issue.

9. Why should certain properties, such as fundamental properties that are mental or fundamental properties that are for the sole purpose of creating mentality, count as nonphysical? It may be that certain properties have been deemed physically unacceptable because they hint at a world that was created with us in mind. If mental phenomena were fundamental, being, for example, part of the original brew that was set in motion in the big bang or as emerging as something extra along the way, mentality would have a place of prominence in the world. And this, I think, for many suggests that the existence of a God who was looking out for us. This hint, however, is not an implication, and antiphysicalists can be atheists. However, I think that nonphysical properties have gotten their "bad" reputation because on many accounts of God, these are the sorts of properties that would exist, if She were to exist. And the reputation remains, even when its origin is forgotten.

will do is provide a structural account of the world. However, given that physics has changed in ways that would have been inconceivable to earlier generations, it seems we should leave open the possibility that physics could, someday in the unforeseeable future, explain both structural and non-structural features of the world. Inscrutables, then, as understood as features of the world that are opaque to a physics that investigates only the purely structural features of the world, may not be opaque to physics understood more broadly as investigating the fundamental aspects of the world, whatever they may be.

Apart from this, it is not even clear that being accountable for by physics, even in this broad sense, should be a necessary condition for counting as physical. Physics is a human endeavor and there seems to be little reason for why a physicalist must think that the physical world is understandable, even in principle, to humans.

Still, someone might object, inscrutables are much more important to explaining consciousness than to explaining tables and chairs, which are fairly well accounted for structurally. Because of this, the objection goes, inscrutables are protophenomenal, after all, since they exist (almost) for the sole purpose of accounting for consciousness. Related to this, perhaps one might even say that consciousness is the only phenomenon in the world that is dependent only on inscrutables, which clearly makes for a special relationship between consciousness and inscrutables. Do these objections bring dualism back into the picture?

I don't think that they do. First of all, it seems reasonable to think that a full account of consciousness is going to involve some structural claims. We want to know, for example, how consciousness is affected by various anesthetics; we want to know what types of actions consciousness facilitates; and so on. So I don't think this latter objection poses a problem for a physicalistic Russellian monist. But what about the former? Does a structural account of the world provide a good explanation of tables and so forth? On the account I have limned, it does not. It captures how things stand in relation to tables, but not tables themselves. On this account, a world without inscrutables would be a purely abstract world, a very thin world indeed. Of course, it seems to us that our structural explanations are very successful in the nonmental realm; it seems to us once the structure of the world is set, tables come along for free. But this could be simply because the concreteness of tables seems so obvious that we do not even seek an explanation for it. Nonetheless, it might be that their being concrete objects is a central feature of their tablehood that cannot be explained structurally.[10]

---

10. A purely structural explanation would leave a table, one might say, inscru-table.

Of course, it is true that most physicalists would reject the idea that pro-tophenomenal inscrutables of this stripe ground consciousness. But they would not do so based on their contention that such inscrutables are non-physical. Rather, they would reject this idea because most physicalists accept other responses to the conceivability argument (for example, they may think that a clear understanding of the properties of physics would show that con-sciousness is determined by the properties of physics or they may think that conceivability is not a guide to possibility). However, I have argued that these same physicalists should not say that physicalism is false, if it were somehow shown that Russellian physicalism were true.

If I am correct, there is a version of Russellian monism that is physicalistic through and through. But is this version of Russellian monism also consistent with the possibility of zombie worlds? If we equate zombie worlds, as I did earlier, with worlds that duplicate our physics yet lack consciousness, we have just seen that the answer is "yes." Sometimes, however, zombie worlds are thought of as not just duplicating the fundamental properties of physics, but as duplicating everything about our world save for consciousness. Russellian physicalism is not consistent with zombie worlds as such and neither is Russellian monism (of the panprotophenomenal form) since both views hold that once you've duplicated all the properties of the world at a lower level than consciousness (for example, the inscrutable properties, the structural properties, the chemical, biological and neural properties), consciousness comes along for free. However, the Russellian of either of these stripes can explain why we might think that such worlds are possible. According to the panprotophenomenal Russellian monist, when we think that there could be a world just like our world but without consciousness, we are actually imagin-ing a world just like ours yet without protopsychic-inscrutables. If Russellian monism were true, such a world would be possible. The Russellian physi-calist has a slightly different response: when we imagine the possibility of worlds that duplicate everything but consciousness, we are actually imagining a world without inscrutables (of the Russellian physicalist stripe) and mistak-enly thinking that they are not necessary for tables, chairs, bodies and brains.

So it seems that Chalmers' reasons for why we should think that Russellian monism is antiphysicalistic in spirit are either not forceful, as with the accu-sation that it is a strange view and a form of dualism, or do not apply to Russellian physicalism, as with the accusation that it posits protophenomenal properties that have the sole purpose of grounding consciousness. The ver-sion of Russellian monism I have presented does not posit protophenomenal properties in the sense of properties that have the sole, or even almost the sole, purpose of grounding consciousness, but rather posits that consciousness is grounded in the same sort of nonmental phenomena that ground rocks, tables, robots and rockets. Moreover, there seem to be no other pressing reasons for not counting this version of Russellian monism as a version of physicalism. As such, the view is not only in name, but also in spirit physicalistic.

IV. But Why Be a Russellian Physicalist?

I have tried to lay out a physicalistic view of consciousness that is consistent with the conceivability argument in its strongest form. Yet why should anyone accept the view, especially since the question of how inscrutables ground consciousness (as well as everything else) remains. Part of the motivation to accept a panpsychist Russellian view is that it is thought to solve, or at least go a long way toward solving, what Chalmers refers to as "the hard problem of consciousness," that is, the problem of explaining how it is possible for creatures like us to be conscious.[11] When it is assumed that our fundamental nature is nonconscious, this problem is especially pressing, for how can, as Colin McGinn (1989) once put it, "technicolor phenomenology arise out of soggy grey matter"?[12] Panpsychism appeals to some because it implies that this soggy gray matter is, at bottom, itself technicolor. There is still the problem of explaining how little bits of phenomenality combine to produce the rich unified type of experience that we have, but panpsychists see this problem as tractable.

Russellian physicalism does not have panpsychism's advantage of alleviating the hard problem. Rather, it claims that the world is such that we cannot, at least currently, see the solution, for according to Russellian physicalism, consciousness depends on inscrutables, yet inscrutables are just that: inscrutable. As such, Russellian physicalism leaves the explanatory gap wide open. Nonetheless, it has the advantage of not needing to posit consciousness at the ground level, for the explanatory task is only easier for the panpsychist if we can make sense of what this means for fundamental particles to have a conscious aspect.

---

11. Not everyone thinks that panpsychism has this advantage over physicalist solutions to the mind-body problem. (See for example, Block 1980 and Stoljar 2006.) I address the question of whether it does in "What Combination Problem?" (forthcoming). But whether it does or not, it still is the case that some are drawn to Russellian monism in its panpsychic clothes because they see it as alleviating the hard problem.

12. We, of course, now have an answer to this question: Technicolor phenomenology can't arise out of soggy gray matter anymore because the intensive three-strip Technicolor coloring processes that used to be popular is now deemed too expensive.

But why should we accept the view at all? My aim in this chapter has been, not to convince you that Russellian physicalism is true, but rather to show that there is a version of physicalism that is consistent with the central antiphysicalist intuition that the failure of upward determination is possible. But, in fact, if you accept that the failure of upward determination is possible yet also think that physicalism of one sort or another must be true, I have also presented an argument for the view, since Russellian physicalism is, among the current panoply of solutions to the mind-body problem, the only view that allows you to do both.

References

Block, N. (1980), "Are Absent Qualia Impossible?" *The Philosophical Review*, 89(2): 257–74.

Brown, R. and Ladyman, J. (2009), "Physicalism, Supervenience, and the Fundamental Level," *Philosophical Quarterly*, 59(234): 20–38.

Chalmers, D. (1996), *The Conscious Mind* (New York: Oxford University Press).

Chalmers, D. (2002), "Consciousness and its Place in Nature," in D. Chalmers, ed., *Philosophy of Mind: Classical and Contemporary Readings* (New York: Oxford University Press).

Churchland, P. M. (1996), "The Rediscovery of Light," *Journal of Philosophy*, 93(5): 211–28.

Hawking, S. (1988), *A Brief History of Time* (New York: Bantam).

Ladyman, J. and Ross, D. (with D. Spurrett, and J. Collier) (2007), *Every Thing Must Go: Metaphysics Naturalized* (Oxford: Oxford University Press).

Langton, R. and D. Lewis (1998), "Defining 'Intrinsic'," *Philosophy and Phenomenological Research*, 58: 333–45.

Martin, C. B. (1994), "Dispositions and Conditionals," *Philosophical Quarterly*, 44(174): 1–8.

McGinn, C. (1989), "Can We Solve the Mind-Body Problem?," *Mind*, 98: 349–66.

Montero, B. (1999), "The Body Problem," *Noûs*, 33(3): 183–200.

Montero, B. (2001), "Post-Physicalism," *Journal of Consciousness Studies*, 8(2): 61–80.

Montero, B. (2009), "What Is the Physical?," in *Oxford Handbook in the Philosophy of Mind*, B. McLaughlin and A. Beckermann, eds. (Oxford: Oxford University Press), pp. 173–88.

Montero, B. (2010), "A Russellian Response to the Structural Argument Against Physicalism," *Journal of Consciousness Studies*, 17: 3–4, 70–83.

Montero, B. (2013), "Must Physicalism Imply the Supervenience of the Mental on the Physical?" *Journal of Philosophy*, 110 (2): 93–110.

Montero, B. and Papineau, D. (2005), "The *Via Negativa* Argument for Physicalism," co-written with David Papineau, *Analysis*, 65(3): 233–37.

Montero, B. G. (forthcoming), "What Combination Problem?," in G. Bruntrup and L. Jaskolla, eds., *Panpsychism* (New York: Oxford University Press).

Russell, B. (1959/1995), *My Philosophical Development* (London: Taylor & Francis, Inc).

Russell, B. (1946/2004), *History of Western Philosophy* (London: Routledge).

Stoljar, D. (2006), *Ignorance and Imagination: The Epistemic Origin of the Problem of Consciousness* (New York: Oxford University Press).

Wilson, J. (1999), "How Superduper Does a Physicalist Supervenience Need to Be?," *Philosophical Quarterly*, 49: 33–35.

11

Causality and the Combination Problem

Gregg Rosenberg

RUSSELLIAN MONISM IS the view that intrinsic natures, which carry physical dispositions described by science, are responsible for producing the experiential quality of consciousness. Russellian Monism has a well-known problem, called the Combination Problem, focused on the question of how microphysical intrinsic qualities come to be macrophysical experiential qualities. The combination problem is a question about nature, but it is not a physics or chemistry question, so it presents issues which are different both from traditional philosophical conceptual issues and from scientific empirical issues. In *A Place for Consciousness*, I argue that the issues should prompt a re-imagination of causality itself, and I also propose a systematic reinvention of causality from the ground up. The result implies a kind of panpsychism for Russellian Monism while providing a very satisfying solution to the combination problem, by tying the presence of experience to causality-produced information without also tying it up with thorny issues of natural semantics or representation. To embrace this view, Russellian Monists and panpsychists must embrace two key re-framings of traditional problems, and also re-evaluate which questions about causality and mind are philosophically most interesting.

1. Framing the Combination Problem

Take a sentence of a dozen words, and take twelve men and tell to each one word. Then stand the men in a row or jam them in a bunch, and let each think of his word

as intently as he will; nowhere will there be a consciousness of the whole sentence ...
Where the elemental units are supposed to be feelings, the case is in no wise altered.
Take a hundred of them, shuffle them and pack them as close together as you can (whatever that might mean); still each remains the same feeling it always was, shut in its own
skin, windowless, ignorant of what the other feelings are and mean. There would be a
hundred-and-first feeling there, if, when a group or series of such feeling were set up,
a consciousness *belonging to the group as such* should emerge. And this 101st feeling
would be a totally new fact; the 100 original feelings might, by a curious physical law, be
a signal for its *creation*, when they came together; but they would have no substantial
identity with it, nor it with them, and one could never deduce the one from the others, or
(in any intelligible sense) say that they *evolved* it (1890/1950, p. 160, original emphasis).

—WILLIAM JAMES

This well-known quote from James describes a couple of difficulties which
we have come to call "the combination problem" for panpsychists. The first
is alluded to by the image of that poor twelve-word sentence which will never
exist, because its component words are trapped in the heads of twelve men.
This is a *composition of feelings* problem. What rules of composition could
blend separate feelings (or thoughts) into a single feeling or thought?

The second image of the hundred "windowless" feelings imagines success overcoming the first problem, but suggests the cost of success is a new
composition of experiencers problem. The only way to get a new feeling more
complex than the originals is to create a new substantial identity to feel it,
and this new substantial identity will be strongly emergent from the feelings
which occasioned its emergence. This is a problem because panpsychism is
supposed to be an alternative to emergentism.

James was substantially right that panpsychism leads to strong emergentism. However he and others have been wrong to frame panpsychism and
strong emergentism as competing alternatives. Both panpsychism and strong
emergentism are implied by a much deeper theory which is attractive because
of the way it makes sense of the metaphysics of causality, and many other
questions in metaphysics, as well as providing insight into important questions in the philosophy of mind. Panpsychism shouldn't be adopted simply
because it might be a solution to the mind-body problem. It is also a solution
to the carrier-causality problem, the problem of what intrinsic natures carry
the schemas of causality in our world. This makes a large difference in how
many things related to panpsychism should be viewed, particularly the motivations for adopting it, its explanatory power and its relation to emergence.

To reach this point of view, one has to switch to a new frame on certain
problems, so that oppositions and concerning questions which recur in many

contemporary discussions of panpsychism and/or the mind-body problem seem less relevant. It has been years and years since I have cared whether a view is dualist, monist or pluralist; or whether something was strongly emergent or weakly emergent; whether a view was panpsychist or merely neutral monist; whether causes have to precede effects or why there is something rather than nothing.

What follows is a discussion of a series of frame shifts which lead to an in-principle resolution of the combination problem, while changing one's point of view on whether certain ontological outcomes are "good" or "bad" and whether certain questions are interesting or not.

2. Changing the First Frame: From a Combination Problem to a Boundary Problem

James asks us to imagine twelve people thinking of twelve words. Crowd them together and we do not create a sentence. This seems like a hard problem to resolve. But is it any harder than the following problems? Imagine eight glasses of water. Crowd them together as close as you like, and they do not make a puddle. Imagine one hundred organs in a freezer. Make the freezer as small and cramped as you like, but they do not make an animal. Imagine a billion cells in a petry dish. Make the petry dish as crowded as you like, they do not form an organ.

There are related problems which are not hard: Imagine twelve waves flowing toward a beach. Have them meet, and the twelve waves combine into a single wave. Imagine two electric fields combined to create a more powerful electric field. Imagine a billion cells in a fetus, combining to make an organ.

This second set of related problems show there are good combination rules for many different kinds of things, in which these things can combine to become another unitary thing of either the same kind or a different kind. This is not a *conceptual* problem. It's a problem about understanding nature deeply enough to know when things interact and combine, and when they don't. In some cases, the combination rules are matrix or vector addition rules for things like waves and fields, in which different things can combine to make new things and the old things are lost as long as the composition holds. In other cases, the combination rules are rules of tight coupling and interaction, in which the old things combine to make qualitatively new things while still maintaining an integrity of their own.

We can imagine a panpsychist world in which phenomenal characters combine via matrix or vector-like addition rules, while experiencers combine via tight interaction rules. The difficulty is really the odd empirical fact that bounded phenomenal fields exist surprisingly at a mid-level of the physical world, at a scale corresponding to physical activity in animal brains.

In a world with a "combination problem," a panpsychist might predict primordial experiencers at the base of the world, simple fireflies of flickering experiencers at low levels of space time, without any experiencers at higher levels: feeling, feeling everywhere, but not a drop can think.

A panpsychist can avoid this surreal picture via appeal to known types of combination rules. In a world where experiences combined according to matrix or vector rules, for example, one might predict an ocean of experience constituting universal consciousness, but no experiencers below that level: a comically cosmic god-mind, experiencing itself alone forever.

The Scylla and Charybdis of these two alternatives are what I call the Boundary Problem for Phenomenal Individuals. How can one allow experiences to combine from the low level to the mid-level, but in a structured way that does not run away from us? It is a re-framing of the combination problem in terms of a different but related problem.

The hard nut of the Boundary Problem is that animal experiencers possess a kind of inherent individuality at a physical mid-level of reality, which is difficult to explain. If panpsychism is true, why do the boundaries exist *just so*? Panpsychists can easily find types of combination rules which could work to overcome the combination problem. However, once a panpsychist recognizes a known kind of combination rule might be in play, he or she can coherently hypothesize almost as many ways of determining boundaries for experiencing subjects as there are of seeing organization in the world's pattern of microphysical interaction. Constraining application of the combination rules to produce a meaningful outcome on the Boundary Problem is hard.

Moral: boundaries are harder to explain than combination. We are faced with the need to understand more deeply what it is to be an inherent individual in the natural world.

There is one relation at the borderline of physics and metaphysics which divides the world by its very nature: the relation of causal interaction. Causal interactions imply partitions: they divide the world into different, mutually influencing spaces, and do so at many levels of nature. We might discover, by looking at causality and causal interaction, that causal interactions have certain important aspects which distinguish natural individuals. For panpsychists, these individuals would be attractive candidates as the supporting ontology of experiencing subjects.

3. Changing the Second Frame: From Cause-and-Effect to Causal Significance

Mainstream discussion of causality almost always begins and ends with discussions about judgments of cause and effect or the language of cause and effect. The guiding image is that of a probability tree. Time is a tree of different outcomes, the actual world is a path through the tree, and causality is a way of influencing or setting probabilities for each branch of the tree.

A "probability tree" in which causality is a way of setting/changing probabilities is the fundamental departure point for modern discussions of causality. Significant questions within this frame include: is causality epistemic or metaphysical? Why does causality work only from the past to the future? How do we understand the relation between "cause" and "effect"? What are dispositions? This fundamental causality frame does not help a Russellian Monist or panpsychist like me, whose interest in causality is driven partly by a desire to understand causal interactions and the way causal interactions partition the world.

The probability tree is a flawed metaphor. The major problem with the probability tree is that the cause-and-effect relationship is a poor starting point for understanding the metaphysical basis of interactions and its relation to the world's structure, as our cause-and-effect concepts don't get at the essence of causal connection (the causal nexus), and contain many assumptions which could be false in a world where things interact. It is also heavily intertwined with human psychology and perception.

For example, dynamics are necessary for cause-and-effect but not necessary for interesting causality in general. If different parts of the world constrained one another so that counterfactuals about states of the world as a whole were true, one could say interesting things about laws and about causal constraints between different parts of the world, even without dynamics. Concretely, imagine a timeless world which was nothing but an unchanging Rubik's cube. Some combination of colors on its six faces is showing. Other combinations *could* show, and there is an atemporal physics describing which ones are possible and which ones are not (there is no physics of transitions). There are meaningful causal constraints in terms of constraints between components in the Rubik's cube world, even though there is no cause and effect.

Of course examples of the subjective nature of cause-and-effect are well-known. The idea of "cause" is closely related to agency and blame, and "effect" to goals and means. Negative facts such as absences can be said to cause things. Figure-ground relations, levels of granularity and so forth all impact cause-and-effect judgments so that the same facts can justifiably be viewed by different people as having different causes. And just try to get agreement about cause-and-effect in a political situation, such as the Israeli-Palestinian conflict.

Our common concept of cause-and-effect also builds in several other parameters: locality, directionality, categorical constraints on relata, the arity of the relation, all of which are baggage on a more basic notion. To think of causality in a fresh way, we need to get rid of the baggage and pare it down to its core essential truth: the world is in a constrained state, in that having one part of the world in one state places constraints on what states other parts of the world can be in. This truth captures the fundamental mystery of non-Humean causation.

It doesn't matter if the parts of the world are in different time slices, or if they are local, or if there are two of them versus three, four, or an infinite number. It doesn't matter if we think of these parts of the world as events or states or facts. It doesn't matter if one is a "cause" and the other is an "effect." If one part of the world being in one state places a meaningful physical or metaphysical constraint on the state of another part of the world, we are presented with a mystery of causality.

To express this mystery, I like to talk about the Two Canvases of Causation.

Imagine two great, blank canvases that you paint with color one drop at a time. Imagine also that the two canvases are two very different kinds of surfaces to work with. You call the first canvas the Humean Canvas. It acts like a normal canvas, as it will accept any drop of paint anywhere on its surface in any color that falls on it. If you let a drop of red paint fall onto the Humean canvas, it will stick where it lands. The same will happen if you then drop a speck of yellow paint somewhere else on the canvas. You can fill the whole canvas this way, with whatever colors you want, anywhere you want.

You call the second canvas the Canvas of Causation. It is a marvel. If your first drop of paint is a bit of green, and then you try to place a drop of red next to it, the red paint will bounce off. The canvas will not accept it. But it will accept yellow. And the more paint you put on the canvas, the pickier it seems to become. Each bit of color you put on the surface seems to place a constraint on what colors may appear elsewhere on its surface. Although the canvas will allow you to paint it in many different ways, it will accept only combinations of color that make for a beautifully covered canvas. If you try to pour many colors on it all at the same time, some will stick and some will run-off, and each time what remains after the run-off will be a beautiful pattern of color. Every color and every drop matters, jointly enforcing or excluding the colors that will finally appear on the canvas.

Although the Humean Canvas is ordinary, the Canvas of Causation seems like magic. Yet the Canvas of Causation seems to be more like the world we actually live in. It is a world in which nature includes and excludes membership based on what else has made it into the club. Making our world be like a Canvas of Causation requires some extra ingredient over and above simply having a world in which things can happen. This extra ingredient, whatever it is, should be what a theory of causality is about.

The central concept for causality, in this view, is *causal significance*, not cause-and-effect. The *causal significance* of a thing is the constraint its existence adds to the space of naturally possible ways the world can be. Though it covered other ground, *A Place for Consciousness* was chiefly about introducing and describing the metaphysics of causal significance and demonstrating its explanatory power.

An emphasis on *causal significance* is a second kind of re-framing which Russellian Monists and panpsychists need, to make progress on their world view. They need to re-frame the problem of causality from being a problem about cause-and-effect to being a problem about causal significance, because a theory of causal significance yields many unexpected and very important explanatory benefits, not only in the philosophy of mind but elsewhere.

The shift away from cause-and-effect as the core concept of causality also requires shifting away from probability trees as the core framing device for discussions of causality. If we emphasize causal significance, it seems the central job of causation is to select potentialities in ways which constrain possible states of the world. In other words, causality doesn't just make *future probabilities*. It makes the *world actual*. The proper framing device for causal significance is to think of causality as a *potentiality filter*, rather than a probability influencer. On one side of the filter is a set of potentialities, and on the other side is a smaller set.[1]

As soon as one starts thinking of causality using potentiality filters as a tool, it just becomes obvious that there is nothing inherently temporal about a potentiality filter. The potentialities fed into a potentiality filter don't need to flow from past states to future states of individuals. Efforts to restrict the formalism that way look obviously artificial and hard to justify.

The potentialities fed to the potentiality filter could come from individuals at a lower level of nature and be fed into an individual at a higher level.

---

1. In the past I've called this a *possibility filter* but I think potentiality filter is more appropriate, given that it acts on the potentialities of nomic individuals.

This scenario is mathematically, logically and metaphysically coherent. It also coheres well with known physics.

Indeed, it becomes equally obvious that a core, unargued assumption in much of classical metaphysics is that things at lower levels of nature are already, in and of themselves, in determinate states, just as we find things at higher levels in ordinary experience. It is also assumed that things at higher levels of nature *must* inherit their determinate states from the determinate states of the lower-level things which compose them. In philosophical parlance, classical metaphysics assumes that determinate macro-level states of the world *must* strongly supervene on independently determinate micro-level states of the world. This statement is a kind of *micro-determination thesis*, or *mic-d* for short.

Why do we believe mic-d? There is, in fact, no evidence for it and quite a large amount of evidence against it.

The only real reason for believing it, is it is "intuitive". But that is no reason at all. We have had no conceptual tools for thinking of anything different and so it is "intuitive" by default. Additionally, we know enough now to say with confidence that questions about fundamental nature tend to not have intuitive answers, and that things at the lowest levels of nature are not in-and-of-themselves in determinate states.

The problem is, panpsychists (and others interested) haven't had the vocabulary to raise this as an issue, or a formalism to model how an alternative could work or be resolved. The assumption has been buried so deep, there's been no good way to talk about it. There also has been no good way to model worlds in which it is true and worlds in which it is false, to examine the differences between those worlds, and the implications of those differences. To get anywhere, we need to shift from modeling probability trees extended through time, to modeling ladders of potentiality extended through levels of nature. A significant part of my project in *A Place for Consciousness* was to provide a vocabulary and formal model for asking these questions, representing differing answers, and exploring implications of those representations. What I found was that model worlds in which mic-d is false

i. tend to have physics that make the physics of our world with its randomness, backward causality, indeterminate states, non-local causality and measurement problem, look expected rather than weird;

ii. deductively require, just to make causality work, the presence of subjectivity with many of the funny properties consciousness seems to have (e.g., unified fields of intrinsic properties structured according to information-theoretic constraints);

iii. possess higher-level individuals which can easily extend to the mid-levels of the natural world.

iv. recast traditional oppositions between things like emergence and panpsychism, or dualism and monism, or mental causation and epiphenomenalism in ways which may take the bite out of them.

4. The Theory of Causal Significance

In *A Place for Consciousness*, I introduced a vocabulary and formalism for representing both the truth and falsity of mic-d within a single metaphysics for causality, and for exploring consequences of a metaphysics in which mic-d could actually be an open question. The result of this effort was the Theory of Natural Individuals (TNI), in which the Theory of Causal Significance (TCS) was its heart.

TCS describes the causal connection as a potentiality filter, of a very general nature, in which the same metaphysical device produces temporal connections of cause-and-effect, causal interactions between individuals within a time slice, and also higher-level individuals which can filter the potentialities of indeterminate lower levels and thereby be more determinate than its constituents. TCS is a unifying framework, in which these three things are all aspects of the same thing, looked at from different angles.

By achieving this unifying effect, TCS provides us a precise way to think of a world of layered individuals, in which determinate individuals can exist on top of "indeterminate" lower-level individuals and make them determinate in turn. It does this by giving us a precise way to think of what an indeterminate individual is, and how it might become determinate. From p. 209, "This kind of indefinite disjunctive state becomes easier to grasp once one realizes that a disjunctive state such as *s1 or s2* is logically equivalent to the conjunctive state: *potentially s1 and potentially s2 and not potentially anything else* . . . The indeterminate state of an individual is equivalent to a definite (note: *determinate*) state of that individual understood as a pluralistic selection from its space of potentialities."

What TCS embraces is a situation where the answer to whether an individual is in a determinate state or an indeterminate state depends on the perspective of the description. An individual may be said to be in an *indeterminate* state from the perspective that asks which of its potentials would be experienced (directly or via its influence on other individuals). TCS equates the experienced potentials of an individual with its realized or actual state and allows that the state of some individuals may be indeterminate, considered independently of their causal relations within larger individuals.

But that same individual can be said to be in a *determinate* state from the perspective that asks what subset of its potentials *could* be experienced (i.e., realized/actual). Additionally, TCS implies a realism about potentiality, in which unrealized potentialities can have causal significance. That is, the experienced/actual state of the world can depend on states of the world which could have been experienced but aren't.

This feature of TCS provides an important anticipation of the general form of quantum physics. It is a model of the causal nexus which provides a natural metaphysics for non-epistemic interpretations of the wave function in physics, in which each eigenstate is considered a real potential, with real causal power, but there is indeterminacy regarding which potential an observer would encounter. TCS provides a metaphysics in which there is an equivalency between saying an individual is in an indeterminate state (*s1 or s2*) with regard to what could be its actual observed state, and saying the individual is in a determinate state (*potentially s1 and potentially s2 and not potentially anything else*) with regard to its real causal significance.

By adopting TCS, we can ask metaphysical questions which previously were hard to ask and we can provide answers which previously were hard to even represent. Importantly for the panpsychist, TCS provides a solution to the combination problem which does not fall foul of the boundary problem.

TCS has a simple ontology, consisting of (i) two kinds of properties, (ii) one relation which holds between them, and (iii) intrinsic causal laws. Here is the furniture of TCS.

Property Types

Effective properties—Properties that intrinsically/inherently contribute to constraints on a causal nexus.

Receptive properties—Connective properties that intrinsically/inherently bind to effective properties, creating a causal nexus.

Fundamental Relation

Binding—A primitive metaphysical relation in which one property becomes part of the completed essence of another property.

Causal laws—Laws describing relationships of compatibility, incompatibility and requirement between effective properties.

The ideology of TCS is slightly more complex than the ontology, as it introduces two new concepts: receptive properties, and the concept of *completion* which occurs in the definition of the binding relationship.

Receptive properties in TCS play the role of the potentiality filter—they are the causal connection existing between effective individuals which allows them to constrain one another's potential states. It's important that there is a receptive intermediary in the causal nexus: if binding occurred directly between effective properties, the model could not simultaneously represent their interactions and establish a plurality of individuals, some at different levels of nature than others. The world would necessarily be a single-level, homogenous mesh.

In TCS, two or more effective properties can bind to the same receptive connection, which then establishes a context where the intrinsic constraints between them can be activated and structured. Think of receptivity as a kind of neutral background field, whose essence contains the possibility of interaction between effective properties, and which establishes the structure of interaction and causality in the model.

The concept of *completion* is an important ideological innovation in the theory. It is part of a cluster of concepts which also include *determination* and *concreteness*. The idea is that properties considered in isolation from their binding relation to other properties do not have *determinate* states. Lack of determinateness is interpreted to indicate a kind of essential incompleteness in a property's or individual's isolated nature. Properties *need* context (causal binding to other things) to be anything in particular.

In TCS, the state of such a context-free property gets represented as a disjunction of states (or, equivalently, a conjunction of potential states). Recall, this is the meaning of an individual being in an *indeterminate* state. When TCS says a causal relation makes an individual more determinate, it means there has been a reduction in the number of disjuncts needed to represent its state (or number of conjuncts in its list of potential states). An "indeterminate state" is defined by indeterminacy regarding the potential causal influence which would be experienced by individuals on the other side of the causal connection. One can think of this on analogy to eigenstates going flat during a process of decoherence in an object's wave function. TCS associates such indeterminate properties, considered in isolation from their contexts, with metaphysical incompleteness, and supposes they need to bind to other properties to (take on context and) become complete. This process of binding and completion is what causal interactions *are*. Importantly, it is not a temporal process. It is a vector process from an abstract space of wide multi-potentiality to a concrete space of unique potentiality.

The model example for thinking about this is to consider a property like electron spin. Inherently, electron spin can be either spin up or spin down. Considered in isolation from the context of an individual electron in the world—i.e., considered as an essence—electron spin as a property has an indeterminate state in TCS, which is represented as a disjunction of up and down values. According to TCS, spin, considered in isolation, is therefore *abstract*.

Spin is an example of an effective property. An instance of electron spin starts to become concrete when the abstract spin binds to a receptive property (the abstract may bind to many receptive properties, each of which becomes a different individual). A basic individual, such as an electron, is modeled as multiple effective properties (e.g., spin, charge, mass) bound to a common receptivity. The common receptivity gives that individual its causal unity as a particle. If the combination of properties is not further constrained, it will inherit the indeterminateness of its spin, so the particle itself may need to bind to become determinate. This process may repeat again and again, until the constraint structure is strong enough to make spin take on a determinate value and the particle be a determinate type.

The metaphysics here is one in which effective properties are determinable universals, and causal relations (in the form of receptive connections) are relations with individualized intrinsic essences which bind to universals. In binding to them, they provide context in which only some of the universal's potentials can be individualized as part of the concrete world. Causal relations are therefore the engine of creation, which take the world from abstract to concrete in a stepwise fashion, through layers of receptive binding, and the vector which represents the universal's loss of potentiality through layers of these relations was called an *ingression* in *A Place for Consciousness* (APFC). Each step in an ingression is an event, and events can be bound together into causal processes. The ontology is therefore of events, not substances, and, while variations of things may *repeat*, there are no enduring things in the concrete world.

Some people who have read APFC have reacted to this ideology as if it were strange or exotic. In a sense, it might be, compared to classical metaphysics. In the most relevant sense, I argue it is not, as it is clearly a metaphysical recasting of well-evidenced aspects of the standard model of modern physics. One might say it scores low on *intuitiveness* (it is not the first ideology one might think of) but I argue in APFC it is high on *plausibility* (it is by far the ideology most coherent with our actual evidence about causality). I believe TCS is a simple theory ontologically, a moderately complex theory ideologically, and a very plausible theory from the standpoint of what we actually have reason to believe about nature.

TCS is the heart of a theory of natural individuals because it contains at its basis a recursive combination rule, which describes how causality creates natural individuals and can do so above the base levels of reality. The combination rule is simple:

Base rule: Any primitive receptive or primitive effective property is a natural individual.

Recursive combination rule: Any receptive property which completes itself by binding to two or more other natural individuals is a natural individual.

The combination of effective properties which occurs within a binding relation is treated like a matrix or vector combination of properties, occurring within the boundary provided by the receptive connection. The receptive property itself is irreducible causality, an emergent.

The purpose of a receptive connection—its occasion for existing and what it produces—is the creation of a determinate state, or a *more* determinate state, for otherwise indeterminate individuals. Receptive connections as emergents are not otiose or indulgent. They are metaphysical ground zero. They have an essential function in causality as the engine of creation, which must somehow make a determinate world from a set of indeterminate and abstract potentials. Completion happens because a receptive context allows indeterminate individuals to place additional constraints on one another, which make them collectively more determinate than they would be without entering into the receptive context.

TCS thus describes causal significance: it gives a formalized account of how a potentiality filter—called a receptive connection—can metaphysically enable causality in the world by producing determinate states from relations between indeterminate properties. Once formalized, the theory allows us to model causality worlds which are intrinsically determinate at their lowest levels, as in classical physics (though this requires some ugly maneuvering, which speaks against the likelihood there could be a world with classical physics); but it also allows us to model worlds which are inherently *indeterminate at the lowest level but made determinate by the presence of higher-level individuals*. Additionally, it shows how the same mechanics at work between levels can produce dynamic causality across time slices.

Of the many kinds of worlds which can be modeled using TCS, the non-classical, multi-level worlds with inherently indeterminate lower-level individuals (in APFC, called "indeterminate when considered independently") are by far the most natural. Also, the intra-level structures which model interactions between individuals, and the inter-level composition relations between levels of nature, are rich and provide more insight into important metaphysical questions than does an investigation of cause-and-effect relations across time.

For example, one can clearly show a causal role for higher-level individuals (and by implication, animal consciousness) that is different than anything ever pictured in philosophical discussions of interactionism or emergent causation. The role of higher-level individuals is to act more like final causes, because the presence of the higher-level individual is a cause of determination at the lower levels, without imposing any interaction force across levels or impacting energy: it is simply a kind of selection force in a higher-level determination event. In the reverse direction, the relation between the lower-level individuals and the higher-level individuals is more like material causation rather than pure composition (because of the presence of irreducible causal connection in the form of receptive connections).

This model then provides a potential third way to think of mental causation, aside from interactionism and epiphenomenalism. Mental states are just states of certain higher-level individuals, and they are part of a universal process of causality in which there are two-way causal relations between levels of nature. Higher levels provide contexts for constraint, which make them final causes for the determination of otherwise indeterminate base levels; and the base levels, made determinate, provide material causation for the higher levels. Effective causation is limited to within-level relations.

There is a kind of strong emergentism in TCS, but it is a kind which renders the usual discussions and concerns about it uninteresting. In TCS, receptive connections bind individuals at different levels of nature, and they are not reducible. Each receptive connection is a constitutive property of its own individual, not composed from lower-level properties. But recall, the receptive connection is just *causality*. It is happening just the same everywhere—it binds fundamental properties into particles and particles into interacting systems—and is not a special thing brought in suddenly at one level of nature, or just to explain mental properties. It is in no way ad hoc or surprising.

Other traditional discussions, such as the ontological "counting" discussion, also become less interesting. One could call this a dualism of receptive and effective properties. Or a monism of the causal nexus. Or even a pluralism of intrinsic and extrinsic aspects of causality. It is a naturalism of the causal mesh or a kind of property Platonism of unrealized abstract potentials. One could make arguments to claim each of: this is a kind of Russellian neutral monism, a kind of physicalism, or a kind of non-physicalism. However, from the perspective of TCS, this sort of counting question does not advance any issue and does not grip the imagination. What matters is how much it explains—which is a lot—relative to how much it assumes, which is not so much.

5. Emergentism and The Theory of Causal Significance

The Theory of Causal Significance (TCS) described above provides a meta-physical foundation which can be combined with a Russellian view on the intrinsic character of causality, called The Carrier Theory of Causation (described in section 6), to provide a panexperientialist explanation for the existence of experience and consciousness. The combination is very fruitful, in that a great many mysteries about the properties of consciousness can be deductively explained from first principles.

The role of TCS in this total theory has caused some confusion about the relationship in APFC between emergence and panpsychism because the view can be seen as combining elements of both, even though many consider panpsychism and emergence to be rivals. This confusion has recently shown itself in the form of an objection by David Chalmers in his paper *The Combination Problem for Panpsychism*. Since the presentation in APFC is diffuse and not centrally concerned with emergence versus panpsychism as an issue, except in one short section toward the end of the book, I want to take some space here to clarify.

Chalmers describes the view in APFC as a variety of "emergent panpsychism" putting forward a "non-compositional" solution to the combination problem, including a kind of weak downward causation to resolve problems of mental causation. He finds this unattractive, as he argues the attraction of panpsychism comes from being able to avoid emergence and resolve problems of mental causation directly, without downward causation. However, I would not characterize the view in APFC in the way he does. I will first address issues of emergence and then of causation from higher to lower levels of individuals.

As far as emergence goes, it is helpful to distinguish along two dimensions: (i) what emergence views are supported as a possibility by the *model* versus what is proposed as the likely *truth*; and (ii) how to view composition as it relates to effective properties versus as it relates to receptive properties.

In section 14.2.1 of APFC, titled *Emergence*, I directly address the issues of emergence, saying clearly the model is flexible and can support a variety of truths: "The question naturally arises as to whether consciousness is *weakly emergent* or *strongly emergent* or some combination of the two . . . . Depending on the specifics of the Liberal Naturalist theory, consciousness could be weakly emergent from some nonphysical facts (e.g., from instances of protophenomenal properties) or strongly emergent given the nonphysical facts."

I do not take a stand on this issue in APFC, though I do use more space explaining how strong emergence could be true. I dwell on strong emergence because one of the novelties of TCS is that it supports a very clear model for how strongly emergent properties could exist consistently with known laws and with causality. I thought this was a new and valuable feature worth taking time to explore, but did not mean to introduce confusion about the commitments in APFC. So the model in APFC *allows* for emergent panpsychism but the view is not *committed* to it, and in the book I intentionally avoided making a commitment.

Before committing to a view here, I need to distinguish between the two kinds of properties where questions about compositional versus non-compositional behavior can arise: effective versus receptive properties. Within a TCS framework, it is possible to be compositional about one but not the other, or about both, or about neither. I believe the most fruitful view is one where effective properties are compositional but receptive connections are not. Translating to Chalmers' panpsychist taxonomy, this is a view in which experiential qualities (which carry effective properties) are compositional but in which subjects (which carry receptive connection) are emergent and exist for only a single experiential event.

But I want to be clear about what this emergence really is. The fundamental theory, TCS, is about causality, not about experience, so that experiencing is merely a carrier of the causal relation. Asserting subjects are emergent is merely to assert that *direct* causal relations between individuals are irreducible. Furthermore, the whole structure of TCS is designed to specify the difference between direct and indirect causal relationship, as it gives a precise definition early in chapter 10 in terms of influence due to a co-binding within a receptivity versus influence that travels through a chain of receptivities.

In this context, saying that subjects of experience are irreducible is trivial. Because subjects are postulated to be the carriers of irreducible causal interactions, it is only verbally different than saying irreducible causality is irreducible. That should not be objectionable, in the emergence versus non-emergence debate in metaphysics.

Hence the carriers of direct causal relationships in TCS are hypothesized to be subjects, intrinsically experiential properties which bind to the qualitative characters carrying effective properties. These receptive connections are like the 'phenomenal bonds' with intrinsic character which Chalmers elsewhere in his paper discusses under compositional theories of experience. He there offers that causality might be an appropriate kind of compositional bonding relationship, and I agree. He raises the set of questions below about this:

"One question for this view and for other phenomenal bonding views is whether the bonding relation is transitive (as co-consciousness seems to be), so that when one microphenomenal state stands in this relation to two other phenomenal states of two other subjects, all three will be jointly experienced by a single subject. If so, then given the ubiquity of spatiotemporal and causal relations, it looks as if the microphenomenal states throughout the universe may stand in this relation, yielding a single giant subject. If on the other hand the relation is not transitive and one has distinct subjects for different instances of the relation, then one will have far too many subjects and it is hard to see how we will get macrosubjects. Perhaps there are intermediate possibilities in which the relation is just nontransitive enough to yield nontrivial macrosubjects, but it is hard to see where this structure will come from."

Chalmers' objection above is describing the Boundary Problem, and the layered view of causality in TCS contains the details about what kind of causal relationships have intrinsic character and what kind do not, and it provides a metaphysical answer to his question of where to find the structure needed to resolve the Boundary Problem.

I suggest the real dispute about emergence here is not about compositionality of subjects, but about whether there are irreducible causal relationships between anything but the most fundamental microphysical entities. It's obvious the framework in APFC can succeed at explaining the existence of consciousness only if fundamental causal relationships exist between entities at multiple levels of the world.

On this point, I believe the evidence is already in and the answer is yes. We have a great deal of experimental evidence of holistic causal interaction between composite entities in quantum mechanics. We should have all agreed already to enter into the ontological transaction of admitting emergent, irreducible relations of interaction above the fundamental microphysical level, and we are just negotiating about the price. Chalmers like many others believes, if it is relevant to consciousness, the price must be brain-level quantum entanglements, but I am not convinced the answer is so cut and dried. I believe, if one superimposes the layered view of causality in APFC onto our scientific understanding of the world, it points to a kind of gradual, layered decoherence which is too complicated for current physicists to model. In APFC section 14.3.1, I quote Henry Stapp at length on why a need for this is inevitable.

Stapp argues for the opportunity (and need) to introduce irreducible causal relations, which can produce a determinate brain state in higher-level individuals with brains like ours, and he argues the need exists not because of large-scale entanglement or quantum coherence, but as an unavoidable consequence of something as fundamental as the uncertainty principle. While there is much room to argue about interpretations of quantum mechanics, the kind of decoherence view consistent with TCS falls pretty squarely into the major camps.

Chalmers' other objection to the view in APFC is that it requires "a little" downward causation to resolve problems of mental causality. In doing so, he believes, it is subject to the same objections as dualism. However, his objection here relies on an equivocation in "causation" which I believe renders it harmless. All of the discussions of downward causation in the philosophy of mind literature reference efficient causation, the kind of causation in which a force is transmitted which alters the course of events. The causality from higher-level individuals to lower levels in TCS is more like final causation, of a novel type not found in the traditional literature about either consciousness or intentionality. So it is not "a little" downward causation, as opposed to "a lot" in dualist theories, but a different kind of thing not discussed previously in the literature.

I discuss this in section 14.2.2 of APFC, where I give a mathematical treatment of it. I often say the receptive connections that potentialities pass through are like filters: they select which potentials have influence at the higher levels. Another, perhaps better, image is to say they are lenses: they focus the influences which higher-level individuals incorporate, among all the causal influences potential at the lower-levels.

What I say in APFC is that the state determination of the higher-level individual is like a *final cause* for the state-determination of the lower-level individuals. Though I was guilty in APFC of writing that lower-level individuals are "made determinate" by higher-level individuals, we do not need to think of the lower-level individuals as changed. This is what I mean in my discussion of ingressions in APFC, section 10.5, where I define the concept of "becoming actual" within the framework. It is the incorporation of a single potential to represent an individual's determinate state, from the perspective of a higher-level individual it helps to constitute. But that selection is just the tip of the lower-level individual's full ingression, and its complete nature is still there and never altered by the higher-level individual. An individual which begins its ingression with a conjunction of potential states, always has the potentials not passed along to other individuals in its context. It sheds them only *from the perspective* of the other individuals who incorporate into themselves some of those potentials but not others.

6. The Carrier Theory of Causation

The relationship between TNI and Russellian Monism comes by noticing that TCS, for all its virtues, does not avoid the kinds of critiques of physical theory put forward by Russell and Whitehead. The natural individuals in TCS need intrinsic properties to perform the functional roles laid out by the theory. These intrinsic properties are called carriers, as they carry the extrinsic descriptions for effective and receptive properties within the theory. The theory which adds this postulate to TCS is called the Carrier Theory of Causation and together the two theories make up the Theory of Natural Individuals (TNI).

The carrier theory is an additional postulate to TCS, but because TNI contains both theories as components, we are able to use TNI to deduce specific requirements about what the intrinsic carriers of effective properties must be like. One can deduce, for example, that the carriers of effective properties would have to possess a kind of unity similar to the unity we find in consciousness, and would have to have intrinsic relations of compatibility and incompatibility similar to what we find among phenomenal properties like red and green. Also, using TNI we can deduce that the intrinsic carriers of effective properties must support scalar relations also similar to what we see among phenomenal properties in their intensity dimensions (e.g., the loudness of a tone).

When we turn our attentions to receptive carriers, we can deduce the carrier of receptivity must have a kind of contentless openness, similar to what meditative practices report as characteristic of the pure experiencing self, and that the receptive carrier's relationship to effective properties would have to be much like what we see as the relationship between experiencing and phenomenal properties.

For these and other reasons, someone trying to make sense of TCS in the world will feel compelled to hypothesize that phenomenal properties are the intrinsic basis of effective properties; and that an experiential property is the intrinsic basis of receptive connection; and that the causal nexus in our world is carried by the experiencing of phenomenal properties. In more ordinary language, we would say that the experiencing of phenomenal properties *is* the causal nexus in our world. Anywhere there is direct interaction between natural individuals, there we will find experiencing occurring. So TCS endorses a panpsychist version of Russellian Monism, taking much inspiration from Whitehead in its specific form.

Furthermore, in section 10.4 of APFC, there is a proof that the effective properties existing at each level of causality are metaphysically *informational* properties, defined only by the aggregate constraint structure which integrates the information and the signaling role it plays within that structure. From p. 203, "Given the concept of an effective property in the causal significance model, only the *informationally relevant* features of [an individual's state at a level] present the true effective properties [of that individual] within a higher-level individual."

The proof of this property from 10.4 is referenced several times later in the book to resolve various paradoxes and puzzles, such as Sellar's Grain Problem. From p. 268 of APFC, "Recall that the discussion in Chapter 10, section 4 . . . explained that we can and should identify an individual's effective properties with the element of constraint it adds to the [causal nexus] in which it exists . . . In fact, the most logical structure for a carrier to have would be one matching the dimensional structure of the constraint it carried. This dimensionality would constitute its *degrees of freedom* as part in a signaling system used by a natural individual" (emphasis added).

Particularly, in section 14.3.1 the proof that effective properties are informational is used to argue that higher-level experience will exist only where there is a system of integrated information-signaling: "Additionally, we hypothesize that the bound members within [a natural individual] are encapsulated within interfaces. Their interfaces consist of their own receptivities, through which they holistically receive the constraints in their receptive fields, and their own signals, their effective properties, [through which they place constraints] . . . These interfaces create an information structure within the nexus . . . When searching for natural individuals, this characterization suggests we should view systems in the physical world as systems of information . . ."

I think now this should be considered an extremely important guideline for how the distribution of emergent experience must work, to provide guardrails on permissible versus impermissible types of 'emergence' in the theory. The law we are looking for is a law regarding *integration of information*, measured as the total degrees of freedom by which carrier qualities in a nexus can vary their qualitative character in their role as signals of effective constraint.

In TNI, for the reasons discussed above, this subjective *quantity of experience* must correspond directly to an objective *quantity of information* measured in the same way but substituting an objective measurement of variation in effective states for the experiential measurements. Information is experiencing viewed from the outside, because experiences are Russellian carriers of effective causality. TNI might metaphysically bridge the subjective and objective views of experience because it allows us to infer the total quantity of experience in the higher-level individuals is the same as the quantity of inte-grated information in that individual, like the path being pursued by Giulio Tononi and his followers, expressed by quantifying the signals leading to changes in effective states for that individual.

It should follow that it is perfectly permissible for new kinds of qualities to emerge from level to level—similar as above to new shapes of waves which come from the combining of component waves. These new qualities will be conservative of the old qualities in a way similar to how new shaped waves are conservative of their component waves, via conservation of associated quanti-ties of experience. Pulling back from the details, what is remarkable here is there is a metaphysics of causality which can tie together physics, experience, and integrated information in a way which shows they are different perspec-tives on the same thing—the causal nexus itself—and it points to ways we can move back and forth between these perspectives using a few basic first principles. I believe it can take us further—much, much further—toward an integrated understanding of many associated philosophical mysteries than competing paradigms.

Panpsychism and TNI make for an agreeable partnership. For not only can TNI benefit from panpsychism by being able to answer questions about the intrinsic basis of the world, but panpsychists can help themselves to the combination rules in TNI *for free*. This is a strong position, because these rules resolve both the traditional combination problem and the more diffi-cult boundary problem. Also, because TNI is a theory of causality, it allows for deep answers to issues about mental causation and about determinism. It can provide a framework for actually deducing explanations for a variety of traditionally mysterious aspects of consciousness, such as its unity and relationship to time as well.

Very importantly, TNI vastly strengthens the motivation for being a pan-psychist. The TNI-based panpsychist is no longer making ad hoc conjectures to resolve a specialty problem in the philosophy of mind, back-filling with more conjecture to resolve further problems which arise. Rather, he or she is making a principled conjecture to solve fundamental problems in the phi-losophy of nature, from first principles, while at the same time proposing to resolve problems in philosophy of mind and in metaphysics more broadly. The explanatory power of panpsychism when made part of TNI is vastly expanded, while nothing about it retains the whiff of ad hoc metaphysics (*speculative*, but not ad hoc).

References

Chalmers, D. J. (forthcoming). "The Combination Problem for Panpsychism." In
   G. Bruntrup and L. Jaskolla, eds., *Panpsychism*. New York: Oxford University Press.
James, W. (1890). *The Principles of Psychology*. London: Macmillan.
Rosenberg, G. (2004). A Place for Consciousness: Probing the Deep Structure of the
   Natural World. New York: Oxford University Press.
Tononi, G. (2012). *PHI: A Voyage from the Brain to the Soul*. New York: Pantheon Books.

12

Panpsychism and Panprotopsychism

David J. Chalmers

1 Introduction

Panpsychism, taken literally, is the doctrine that everything has a mind.[1] In practice, people who call themselves panpsychists are not committed to as strong a doctrine. They are not committed to the thesis that the number two has a mind, or that the Eiffel Tower has a mind, or that the city of Canberra has a mind, even if they believe in the existence of numbers, towers, and cities.

Instead, we can understand panpsychism as the thesis that some fundamental physical entities have mental states. For example, if quarks or photons have mental states, that suffices for panpsychism to be true, even if rocks and numbers do not have mental states. Perhaps it would not suffice for just one photon to have mental states. The line here is blurry, but we can read the definition as requiring that all members of some fundamental physical types (all photons, for example) have mental states.

For present purposes, the relevant sorts of mental states are conscious experiences. I will understand panpsychism as the thesis that some fundamental physical entities are conscious: that is, that there is something it

1. I first presented this material at the Munich conference on panpsychism and emergence in June 2011. I am grateful to the audience there and also to audiences at Amherst, Bogazici, Charleston, Fordham, Notre Dame, Santiago, Stanford, and Wesleyan. I owe a special debt to Daniel Stoljar, whose related work in "Two Conceptions of the Physical" greatly influenced this article. Thanks also to Torin Alter, Sam Coleman, Brian Garrett, Philip Goff, John Gregg, Bill Meacham, Daniel Stoljar, Galen Strawson, and Keith Turausky for comments on this article.

is like to be a quark or a photon or a member of some other fundamental physical type. This thesis is sometimes called *panexperientialism*, to distinguish it from other varieties of panpsychism (varieties on which the relevant entities are required to think or reason, for example), but I will simply call it panpsychism here.

Panpsychism is sometimes dismissed as a crazy view, but this reaction on its own is not a serious objection. While the view is counterintuitive to some, there is good reason to think that any view of consciousness must embrace some counterintuitive conclusions. Furthermore, intuitions about panpsychism seem to vary heavily with culture and with historical period. The view has a long history in both Eastern and Western philosophy, and many of the greatest philosophers have taken it seriously. It is true that we do not have much direct evidence for panpsychism, but we also do not have much direct evidence against it, given the difficulties of detecting the presence or absence of consciousness in other systems. And there are indirect reasons of a broadly theoretical character for taking the view seriously.

In this article I will present an argument for panpsychism. Like most philosophical arguments, this argument is not entirely conclusive, but I think it gives reason to take the view seriously. Speaking for myself, I am by no means confident that panpsychism is true, but I am also not confident that it is not true. This article presents what I take to be perhaps the best reason for believing panpsychism. A companion article, "The Combination Problem for Panpsychism," presents what I take to be the best reason for disbelieving panpsychism.

I call my argument the Hegelian argument for panpsychism. This is not because Hegel was a panpsychist. He seems to have been far from it, perhaps except insofar as he believed in a "world-soul" (which suggests a sort of cosmopsychism, the view that the world as a whole is conscious). Rather, my argument takes the dialectical form often attributed to Hegel: the form of thesis, antithesis, synthesis.[2]

In my Hegelian argument, the thesis is materialism, the antithesis is dualism, and the synthesis is panpsychism. The argument for the thesis is the causal argument for materialism (and against dualism). The argument for the antithesis is the conceivability argument for dualism (and against materialism). Synthesized, these yield the Hegelian argument for panpsychism. In effect, the argument presents the two most powerful arguments

---

2. I gather that in fact this dialectical form comes from Fichte, and that Hegel dismissed it as simplistic. Still, I will stay with the popular attribution.

for and against materialism and dualism, and motivates a certain sort of pan-psychism as a view that captures the virtues of both views and the vices of neither.

It turns out that the Hegelian argument does not support only panpsy-chism. It also supports a certain sort of *panprotopsychism*: roughly, the view that fundamental entities are *proto-conscious*, that is, that they have certain special properties that are precursors to consciousness and that can collec-tively constitute consciousness in larger systems. Later in the article, I will examine the relative merits of panpsychism and panprotopsychism, and examine problems that arise for both.

2. Thesis and Antithesis: Materialism and Dualism

Our thesis is materialism (or physicalism): roughly, the thesis that every-thing is fundamentally physical. Our antithesis is dualism: roughly, the the-sis that not everything is fundamentally physical, and the things that are not fundamentally physical are fundamentally mental. Our synthesis is panpsy-chism: very roughly, the thesis that everything is (or at least that some things are) fundamentally physical *and* fundamentally mental.

More specifically, we will be concerned with materialism and dualism about consciousness. Materialism about consciousness is the thesis that con-sciousness is fundamentally physical: that is, that truths about consciousness are grounded in the fundamental truths of a completed physics. Dualism about consciousness is the thesis that consciousness is not fundamentally physical: that is, that truths about consciousness are not grounded in the fun-damental truths of a completed physics.

Grounding is a relation of metaphysical constitution. Truths about con-sciousness are grounded in physical truths if all truths in the first set obtain wholly in virtue of truths in the second set obtaining.[3] The intuitive idea behind materialism is that physical truths somehow add up to and yield truths about consciousness. This requires at least that there is a metaphysically necessary connection between these truths, in that it is impossible for a world to be physi-cally like ours without that world being phenomenally like ours. Intuitively, once God created the entities of physics, consciousness came along for free.

---

3. For more on the notion of grounding, see Schaffer 2009 and Fine 2012. The notion of grounding at play here is what is sometimes called "full grounding," involving a "wholly in virtue of" relation, as opposed to "partial grounding," which involves a "partly in virtue of" relation. The latter is inappropriate for defining materialism, as the definition would then allow a nonmaterialist view on which truths about consciousness obtain in virtue of physical truths along with some other nonphysical truths.

We will be especially concerned with microphysical properties and with phenomenal properties. Microphysical properties are the fundamental physical properties characterized by a completed physics. Microphysical entities are the fundamental physical entities characterized by that physics. (Despite the name, it is not definitionally required that these entities be small.) Microphysical truths are positive truths about the instantiation of microphysical properties by microphysical entities. Here a positive truth is intuitively a truth about the properties that an entity has, rather than those that it lacks (for more on this, see Chalmers 2012). Macrophysical properties (entities, truths) are those that are grounded in microphysical properties (entities, truths). For ease of discussion, I will use the word "physical" to mean "microphysical" throughout what follows, sometimes using "microphysical" for explicitness.

Phenomenal (or experiential) properties are properties characterizing what it is to be a conscious subject. The most familiar phenomenal property is simply the property of phenomenal consciousness: an entity has this property when there is something it is like to be that entity. There are also many specific phenomenal properties, characterizing more specific conscious experiences. For example, phenomenal redness characterizes the distinct sort of conscious experience we have when we experience redness. An entity has the property of phenomenal redness when it has that sort of conscious experience. Phenomenal truths are positive truths about the distribution of phenomenal properties (that is, truths about what it is like to be various entities).

We can then say that materialism about consciousness is the thesis that all phenomenal truths are grounded in microphysical truths. Dualism about consciousness is the thesis that phenomenal truths are not all grounded in microphysical truths. In what follows, by "materialism" and "dualism" I mean materialism and dualism about consciousness.

We can put the conceivability argument against materialism (and for dualism) as follows. Here P is the conjunction of all microphysical truths about the universe, and Q is an arbitrary phenomenal truth (such as "I am conscious").

(1) $P\&\sim Q$ is conceivable.
(2) If $P\&\sim Q$ is conceivable, $P\&\sim Q$ is metaphysically possible.
(3) If $P\&\sim Q$ is metaphysically possible, materialism is false.

---

(4) Materialism is false.

Here we can say that a claim is conceivable when it is not ruled out a priori. So it is conceivable that there are mile-high unicycles, for example. A claim is metaphysically possible when it could have obtained: intuitively, when God could have created the world such that the claim would have been true. So it is plausibly metaphysically possible that there are mile-high unicycles.

Premise (1) here is supported by the conceivability of zombies: creatures microphysically identical to us without consciousness. Most people think that zombies do not actually exist, but there seems to be no a priori contradiction in the idea. Premise (2) is supported by general reasoning about the relationship between conceivability and possibility. The thesis needs to be refined to accommodate various counterexamples due to Kripke and others, but I will stay with the simple thesis here.[4] Premise (3) is supported by the idea that if $P\&\sim Q$ is metaphysically possible, then P does not metaphysically necessitate Q, so Q is not grounded in P, since grounding plausibly requires metaphysical necessitation. Here the intuitive idea is that if God could have created a world microphysically identical to our world but without consciousness, then the presence of consciousness involves new fundamental properties over and above those of physics, so materialism is false.

The conceivability argument is an epistemic argument against materialism, starting with an epistemological premise and proceeding to a metaphysical conclusion. There are other closely related epistemic arguments. These include the knowledge argument, which starts from the premise that Q is not deducible from P and concludes that it is not grounded in P; the explanatory argument, which starts from the premise that there is an explanatory gap between P and Q and concludes that there is an ontological gap; and the structure-dynamics argument, which starts from the premise that P can be analyzed in terms of structure and dynamics while Q cannot and concludes that Q is not grounded in P. Much of what I say will apply to all these arguments, but I will focus on the conceivability argument here.

Materialists do not just curl up and die when confronted with the conceivability argument and its cousins. Type-A materialists reject the epistemic premise, holding for example that zombies are not conceivable. Type-B materialists reject the step from an epistemic premise to an ontological conclusion, holding for example that conceivability does not entail possibility. Still, there are significant costs to both of these views. Type-A materialism seems to require something akin to an analytic functionalist view of consciousness, which most philosophers find too deflationary to be plausible. Type-B materialism seems to require a sort of brute necessity that is not found elsewhere and that is hard to justify. Of course some philosophers find these costs worth

---

4. For a much-elaborated version of the argument using two-dimensional semantics, see Chalmers 2010.

paying, or deny that these are costs. Still, I think that the argument makes at least a prima facie case against materialism.

That said, many materialists think that the conceivability argument against materialism (and for dualism) is countered by the causal argument against dualism (and for materialism). This argument runs as follows:

(1) Phenomenal properties are causally relevant to physical events.

(2) Every caused physical event has a full causal explanation in physical terms.

(3) If every caused physical event has a full causal explanation in physical terms, every property causally relevant to the physical is itself grounded in physical properties.

(4) If phenomenal properties are grounded in physical properties, materialism is true.

---

(5) Materialism is true.

Here we can say that a property is causally relevant to an event when instantiations of that property are invoked in a correct causal explanation of that event. For example, the high temperatures in Victoria were causally relevant to the Victorian bushfires. A full causal explanation of an event is one that characterizes *sufficient* causes of the event: causes that guarantee that the event will occur, at least given background laws of nature.

Premise (1) is supported by intuitive observation. My being in pain seems to cause my arm to move. If things are as they seem here, then the pain will also be causally relevant to the motion of various particles in my body. Premise (2) follows from a widely held view about the character of physics: physics is causally closed, in that there are no gaps in physical explanations of physical events. Premise (3) is a rejection of a certain sort of overdetermination. Given a full microphysical causal explanation of physical events, other causal explanations are possible only when the factors involved in the latter are grounded in the factors involved in the former (as when we explain the motion of a billiard ball both in terms of another ball and in terms of the particles that make it up).[5]

---

5. Principles such as (3) are sometimes put with "is a physical property" instead of "is grounded in a physical property." This amounts to an overly strong causal exclusion claim on which high-level events and their low-level grounds cannot both be causally relevant. Reflection on standard cases (Bennett 2003; Yablo 1992) suggests that constitutively connected events need not exclude each other as causes: these are cases of "benign overdetermination" as opposed to cases of "bad overdetermination." Premise (3) excludes only cases of the latter sort.

Any putative causal explanation that was not grounded in this way would involve causal overdetermination by independent events. Systematic overdetermination of this sort is widely rejected. Premise (4) is true by definition.

Dualists do not just curl up and die when presented with the causal argument. Epiphenomenalists reject premise (1), holding that the claim that consciousness causes behavior is just an intuition and can be rejected. Interactionists reject premise (2), holding that physics leaves room for (and perhaps is positively encouraging to) causal gaps that consciousness might fill. Still, there are costs to both of these views. Epiphenomenalism is at least inelegant and requires special coincidences between conscious experiences and macrophysical events (utterances about consciousness, for example) that seem to reflect them. Interactionism requires a view of physics that would be widely rejected by most physicists, and that involves a large bet on the future of physics. Again, some dualists (including me in some moods) deny that these are costs or hold that the costs are worth paying. Still, I think there is at least a prima facie case against dualism here.

So we have a standoff. On the face of it, the conceivability argument refutes materialism and establishes dualism, and the causal argument refutes dualism and establishes materialism. It is time for a Hegelian synthesis.

3. Synthesis: Panpsychism

Panpsychism, once again, is the thesis that some microphysical entities are conscious. For our purposes, it is useful to distinguish various more fine-grained varieties of panpsychism. To do this, we can first introduce some terminology.

Let us say that *macroexperience* is the sort of conscious experience had by human beings and other macroscopic entities (that is, entities that are not fundamental physical entities). Macroexperience involves the instantiation of *macrophenomenal properties*: properties characterizing what it is like to be humans and other macroscopic entities. Let us say that *microexperience* is the sort of conscious experience had by microphysical entities. Microexperience involves the instantiation of microphenomenal properties: properties characterizing what it is like to be microphysical entities.

If panpsychism is correct, there is microexperience and there are microphenomenal properties. We are not in a position to say much about what microexperience is like. I think we can be confident that it is very different from human experience, however. It is almost certainly much simpler than human experience. In the way that an experience of redness is much simpler than a stream of conscious thought, we can expect a quark's experience to be much simpler than an experience of redness. To get far beyond generalities like this concerning microexperience, we would need a proper panpsychist theory of consciousness, which we are currently lacking.

Constitutive panpsychism is the thesis that macroexperience is (wholly or partially) grounded in microexperience. More or less equivalently, it is the thesis that macroexperience is constituted by microexperience, or realized by microexperience. On this view, macrophenomenal truths obtain in virtue of microphenomenal truths, in roughly the same sense in which materialists hold that macrophenomenal truths obtain in virtue of microphysical truths. To put things intuitively, constitutive panpsychism holds that microexperiences somehow add up to yield macroexperience. The view can allow that macroexperience is not wholly grounded in microexperience: for example, it might be grounded in microexperience along with certain further structural or functional properties.

Panpsychists need not be constitutive panpsychists. There is also nonconstitutive panpsychism, which holds that there is microexperience and macroexperience, but the microexperience does not ground the macroexperience. Nonconstitutive panpsychists will typically be *emergent panpsychists*, holding that macroexperience is strongly emergent from microexperience and/or from microphysics. One sort of emergent panpsychist might hold that there are contingent laws of nature that specify when certain microexperiences give rise to certain macroexperiences. Another might hold that there are laws of nature connecting microphysical properties to microphenomenal properties and macrophysical properties to macrophenomenal properties, without there being any constitutive connection between microphenomenal and macrophenomenal. Still, as we will see, nonconstitutive panpsychism inherits many of the problems of dualism, while it is constitutive panpsychism that offers hope for a Hegelian synthesis. So it is this view that I will focus on.

Like materialism, constitutive panpsychism comes in type-A and type-B varieties. Type-A constitutive panpsychism holds that there is an a priori entailment from microphenomenal truths to macrophenomenal truths, while type-B constitutive panpsychism holds that there is an a posteriori necessary entailment from microphenomenal truths to macrophenomenal truths. The type-B view inherits many of the problems of type-B materialism, so it is the type-A view that offers special hope for a Hegelian synthesis. When I talk of constitutive panpsychism, it will usually be the type-A version that I have especially in mind.

Another important variety of panpsychism is *Russellian panpsychism*. This view takes its name from Russell's insight, in *The Analysis of Matter* (1927) and other works, that physics reveals the relational structure of matter but not its intrinsic nature. According to this view, classical physics tells us a lot about what mass does—it resists acceleration, attracts other masses, and so on—but it tells us nothing about what mass intrinsically is. We might say that physics tells us what the mass role is, but it does not tell us what property plays this role.

Here we can say that *quiddities* are the fundamental categorical properties that play the fundamental roles specified in physics. Alternatively, we can say that quiddities are the categorical bases of the microphysical dispositions characterized in physics. We can stipulate in addition that quiddities are distinct from the roles or the dispositions themselves. A view on which there are only role or dispositional properties, and no distinct properties playing those roles or serving as the basis for the dispositions, is a view on which there are no quiddities.

It is not obvious that there must be quiddities. There are respectable structuralist or dispositionalist views of physics on which physics involves just structure or dispositions all the way down. Still, many find these views objectionable, because they seem to yield a world devoid of substance or qualities—Russell said that on views like these "all the things in the world will merely be each others' washing" (1927, p. 325). And whether or not one accepts these objections, it is certainly not obvious that there are no quiddities. On the face of it, a worldview that postulates quiddities is perfectly coherent, and there is little clear evidence against it.

Russellian panpsychism is the view that some quiddities are microphenomenal properties. This view requires that there are quiddities—distinct properties that play the mass role, the charge role, and so on—and that at least some of these quiddities are phenomenal. For example, perhaps the property that plays the mass role is a certain phenomenal property. (Or better, as mass is really a quantity: the quantity that plays the mass role is a certain phenomenal quantity.) The Russellian panpsychist addresses two metaphysical problems—what is the place of phenomenal properties in nature, and what are the intrinsic properties underlying physical structure?—and in effect answers both of them at once. Fundamental phenomenal properties play fundamental microphysical roles and underlie fundamental microphysical structure.

Panpsychists need not be Russellian panpsychists. There is also non-Russellian panpsychism, according to which there are microphenomenal properties that do not play microphysical roles. Perhaps there are numerous microphenomenal properties quite distinct from the properties involved in the microphysical network, for example. Still, non-Russellian panpsychism faces obvious problems with mental causation, while Russellian panpsychism offers hope for a Hegelian synthesis. So it is this view that I will focus on.

In particular, I will focus on constitutive Russellian panpsychism. On this view, microphenomenal properties serve as quiddities, playing the roles associated with microphysical properties, and also serve as the grounds for macrophenomenal properties. That is, microexperience constitutes macro-experience while also playing microphysical roles. On this view, one could think of the world as fundamentally consisting in fundamental entities bearing fundamental microphenomenal properties, where these microphenomenal properties are connected to each other (and perhaps to other quiddities) by fundamental laws with the structure that the laws of physics describe. All this microphenomenal structure also serves to constitute the macrophenomenal realm, just as microphysical structure serves to constitute the macrophysical realm.

I think that constitutive Russellian panpsychism is perhaps the most important form of panpsychism, precisely because it is this form that promises to avoid the problems of physicalism and dualism and to serve as a Hegelian synthesis. In particular, one can argue that this view avoids both the conceivability argument against physicalism and the causal argument against dualism.

To assess this matter, we first need to assess a delicate question: is constitutive Russellian panpsychism a form of materialism, a form of dualism, or neither? This question turns on the answer to another delicate question: are quiddities physical properties? If quiddities are physical properties, then constitutive Russellian panpsychism entails that microphenomenal properties are physical properties, and that macrophenomenal properties are constituted by physical properties, so that materialism is true. If quiddities are not physical properties, however, then macrophenomenal properties will be constituted by nonphysical properties, and a form of dualism will be true.

To answer this question, it is useful to make a distinction. We can say that *narrowly physical* properties are microphysical role properties, such as the dispositional property associated with having a certain mass, or the second-order property of having a property that plays the mass role.[6] We can say that *broadly*

---

6. The distinction between narrowly and broadly physical properties is closely related to Stoljar's distinction between t-physical properties (properties invoked by physical theory) and o-physical properties (intrinsic properties of physical objects), but it is not the same distinction. For a start, given a view on which "mass" refers to a quiddity that plays the mass role, mass will be t-physical (assuming a property is invoked by physical theory iff it is referred to by an expression of that theory) but it will not be narrowly physical. And given a view on which physical objects have epiphenomenal intrinsic properties that are not those invoked by physical theories and that are not quiddities, these properties will be o-physical but will not be broadly physical. For related reasons (discussed later), I think the broad/narrow distinction is better suited than the t-/o- distinction to do the work that Stoljar wants the latter to do. Note that in Chalmers 2010 (p. 192) I use the broad/narrow terminology to mark a different distinction.

physical properties are physical role properties along with any properties that realize the relevant roles: categorical bases for the mass dispositions, first-order properties that play the mass role.

In effect, narrowly physical properties include structural properties of microphysical entities but exclude quiddities, while broadly physical properties include both structural properties and quiddities. Here a structural property is one that can be fully characterized using structural concepts alone, which I take to include logical, mathematical, and nomic concepts, perhaps along with spatiotemporal concepts (see Chalmers 2003 and 2012 for much more discussion). If one uses a Ramsey sentence to characterize fundamental physics, it is plausible that one can do so using structural concepts alone. At the same time, if there are quiddities, it is plausible that they (like phenomenal properties) cannot be fully characterized in structural terms.

We can then say that quiddities are not narrowly physical, but they are broadly physical. There is more to say here, particularly concerning just how we should construe the relation between quiddities and ordinary physical properties such as mass, but I will leave this for the next section.

With this distinction made, the question of whether quiddities are physical properties becomes something of a verbal question. One can use the term "physical" to cover only narrowly physical properties or to cover broadly physical properties, and the choice between these usages is a verbal matter. Some may think that there is a stronger case for one usage or the other, but little of substance turns on this.

The same applies to the question of whether constitutive Russellian panpsychism is physicalism. We can distinguish narrow physicalism, which holds that phenomenal truths are grounded in narrowly physical truths, from broad physicalism, which holds that phenomenal truths are grounded in broadly physical truths. Narrow physicalism entails broad physicalism, but broad physicalism may not entail narrow physicalism. In particular, constitutive Russellian panpsychism is incompatible with narrow physicalism, but it is a form of broad physicalism. Once again, any dispute over whether narrow or broad physicalism is really physicalism will be something of a verbal dispute. Instead, constitutive Russellian panpsychism falls into a penumbral area that might be counted either way. This is a promising area for a Hegelian synthesis.

How does constitutive Russellian panpsychism fare with respect to the conceivability argument against physicalism? Once we have the distinction between narrowly and broadly physical truths in place, we can distinguish two different versions of the argument. One version construes P as the conjunction of all positive narrowly physical truths, takes as a premise that the corresponding version of *P&~Q* is conceivable, and concludes that narrow physicalism is false. The other does the same for broadly physical truths and broad physicalism.

To assess these arguments, we can distinguish two different sorts of zombies: narrowly physical duplicates of us without consciousness, and broadly physical duplicates of us without consciousness. We can call the first group *structural zombies*, since they duplicate just our relational physical structure. We can call the second group *categorical zombies*, since they also duplicate the underlying categorical properties.[7]

It is plausible that when we typically conceive of zombies, we are really conceiving of structural zombies. We hold physical structure fixed, but we do not make any effort to hold quiddities fixed, since we have no idea what the quiddities are. This standard zombie intuition provides good reason to think that structural zombies are conceivable, but little reason to think that categorical zombies are conceivable. If this is right, adding the conceivability-possibility premise at best establishes the possibility of structural zombies but not of categorical zombies. This is a happy result for (type-A) constitutive Russellian panpsychists, who hold that categorical zombies are not conceivable and not possible.

The upshot of this is that the standard considerations about conceivability can be used at most to undermine narrow physicalism, but not broad physicalism. So these considerations have no force against constitutive Russellian panpsychism, which is a version of the latter but not the former. It follows that this view evades at least one horn of the Hegelian dilemma.

What about the other horn: the causal argument against dualism? Here it is useful to first reflect on the causal role of experience under constitutive Russellian panpsychism. According to Russellian panpsychism, microphenomenal properties certainly play a causal role in physics. They are the properties that play the most fundamental causal roles in physics: the mass role, the charge role, and so on. A microphenomenal property that plays the mass role is causally responsible for attracting other entities, and so on. This causation does not involve any violation of the laws of physics. Instead, this sort of causation underlies the laws of physics.

At the same time, constitutive panpsychism allows that macroexperience can inherit causal relevance from microexperience. This is an instance

---

7. Structural and categorical zombies are closely related to the t-zombies (t-physical duplicates without consciousness) and o-zombies (o-physical duplicates without consciousness) discussed by Stoljar (2001a). As before I think the broad/narrow distinction is more crucial than the t-/o- distinction here.

of the general claim that constituted properties can inherit causal relevance from constituting properties. For example, a billiard ball can inherit causal relevance from that of the particles that make it up. I think this is the lesson of much recent discussion of causal exclusion between the microscopic and macroscopic levels: when entities at this level are constitutively connected, there need be no causal exclusion. The moral that applies to the microphysical and the macrophysical also applies to the microphenomenal and the macrophenomenal, if they are constitutively connected.

It follows that constitutive Russellian panpsychism is compatible with a robust causal role for both microexperience and macroexperience. Given that microexperience is causally relevant (as Russellian panpsychism suggests), and that microexperience constitutes macroexperience (as constitutive panpsychism suggests), we can expect that macroexperience will be causally relevant too.

What of the causal argument? Here again we need to distinguish versions of the argument. One version of the argument invokes the causal closure of the broadly physical to argue that phenomenal properties are grounded in broadly physical properties. The premises of this version of the argument are all plausible, and the constitutive Russellian panpsychist can happily accept its conclusion. Another version invokes the causal closure of the narrowly physical to argue that phenomenal properties are grounded in narrowly physical properties. Here the constitutive Russellian panpsychist must reject the conclusion, but fortunately they can easily reject premise 2. A full causal explanation of narrowly physical events will involve broadly physical properties; a causal explanation wholly in terms of narrowly physical properties is incomplete. This is to say that on a view where there are quiddities, the broadly physical domain may be causally closed, but the narrowly physical domain will not be.[8]

The upshot is that the causal argument can be used at best to establish broad physicalism and not narrow physicalism. This is once again a happy result for the constitutive Russellian panpsychism, as it is a version of the former but not the latter. So this view evades the second horn of our Hegelian dilemma.

---

8. Alternatively, the constitutive Russellian panpsychist can accept premise (2) asserting the causal closure of the narrowly physical, while rejecting premise (3). They can hold that the narrowly physical explanation is itself grounded in a broadly physical explanation, so that these explanations are not independent and a bar on overdetermination does not render them incompatible. The case for premise (3) tacitly assumes that physical explanations do not themselves have further grounds; but on a Russellian view, narrowly physical explanations have further grounds.

We can combine our analysis of the two arguments as follows. The conceivability argument refutes narrow physicalism but is compatible with broad physicalism. The causal argument establishes broad physicalism but does not establish narrow physicalism. When these arguments are put together, they yield the Hegelian argument for the conjunction of broad physicalism with the denial of narrow physicalism. This is the ground occupied by constitutive Russellian panpsychism.[9]

It is worth noting that nonconstitutive and non-Russellian panpsychism do not evade the Hegelian dilemma. Both of these views are incompatible with broad physicalism, and so are vulnerable to the causal argument for broad physicalism. On nonconstitutive panpsychism, even if microexperience is causally relevant, macroexperience will lie outside the broad physical network, so it will lead to epiphenomenalism, interactionism, or overdetermination. On non-Russellian panpsychism, it is hard to see how even microphenomenal properties can be causally relevant, and the same trilemma ensues. Among versions of panpsychism, only constitutive Russellian panpsychism promises to serve as a Hegelian synthesis.

4. Antithesis: Panprotopsychism

It is a familiar point in the pseudo-Hegelian dialectic that every synthesis is confronted by a new antithesis and followed by a new synthesis. Our Hegelian synthesis above is panpsychism. But it turns out that another view can also escape the original Hegelian dilemma: constitutive Russellian panprotopsychism.

Recall that panprotopsychism is the view that fundamental physical entities are proto-conscious. In more detail, let us say that *protophenomenal* properties are special properties that are not phenomenal (there is nothing it is like to have a single protophenomenal property) but that can collectively constitute phenomenal properties, perhaps when arranged in the right structure. Panprotopsychism is then the view that some fundamental physical entities have protophenomenal properties.

---

9. The Hegelian argument could in principle be formalized as a six-premise argument that uses the three premises of the conceivability argument (with "physical" disambiguated to mean narrowly physical) and the three premises of the causal argument (with "physical" to mean broadly physical) to establish the conjunction of broad physicalism with the denial of narrow physicalism. An argument structure along these lines is at play in Stoljar (2001b, section 4), with the main differences being that Stoljar invokes the knowledge argument rather than the conceivability argument, uses the o-/t- distinction where I use the broad/ narrow distinction, and rejects panpsychism.

One might worry that any non-panpsychist materialism will be a form of panprotopsychism. After all, non-panpsychist materialism entails that microphysical properties are not phenomenal properties and that they collectively constitute phenomenal properties. This is an undesirable result. The thought behind panprotopsychism is that protophenomenal properties are special properties with an especially close connection to phenomenal properties. To handle this, one can unpack the appeal to specialness in the definition by requiring that (i) protophenomenal properties are distinct from structural properties and (ii) that there is an a priori entailment from truths about protophenomenal properties (perhaps along with structural properties) to truths about the phenomenal properties that they constitute. This excludes ordinary type-A materialism (which grounds phenomenal properties in structural properties) and type-B materialism (which invokes an a posteriori necessary connection). From now on I will understand protophenomenal properties this way, and will understand panprotopsychism accordingly.[10]

I have occasionally heard it said that panprotopsychism can be dismissed out of hand for the same reason as materialism. According to this objection, the epistemic arguments against materialism all turn on there being a fundamental epistemic (and therefore ontological) gap between the nonphenomenal and the phenomenal: there is no a priori entailment from nonphenomenal truths to phenomenal truths. If this were right, the gap would also refute panprotopsychism. I do not think that this is right, however. The epistemic arguments all turn on a more specific gap between the physical and the phenomenal, ultimately arising from a gap between the structural (or the structural/dynamical) and the phenomenal. We have principled reasons to think that phenomenal truths cannot be wholly grounded in structural truths. But we have no correspondingly good reason to think that phenomenal truths cannot be wholly grounded in nonphenomenal (and nonstructural) truths, as panprotopsychism suggests.

It is true that we do not have much idea of what protophenomenal properties are like. For now they are characterized schematically, in terms of their relation to phenomenal properties. A fuller account will have to wait for a full panprotopsychist theory, though I will speculate about one sort of protophenomenal property toward the end of this chapter. But our ignorance about

---

10. What about type-B views that appeal to quiddities that satisfy (i) but not (ii)? Some such views may nevertheless have a "panprotopsychist" flavor, perhaps because of the special flavor of the quiddities they appeal to, while others (say, the view advocated by Papineau 2002) seem to lack that flavor. A line between these views is hard to draw, so for present purposes I count none of them as panprotopsychism.

protophenomenal properties should not be mistaken for an objection to the truth of panprotopsychism.

Constitutive panprotopsychism is roughly the thesis that macroexperience is grounded in the protophenomenal properties of microphysical entities. That is, all phenomenal truths are grounded in protophenomenal truths concerning these entities. As before, constitutive panprotopsychism could in principle come in type-A and type-B varieties, but the definition of specialness above in effect restricts it to the type-A version (a priori entailment from protophenomenal truths to macrophenomenal truths), which is in any case the relevant version for our purposes. *Russellian* panprotopsychism is the thesis that some quiddities are protophenomenal properties. For example, perhaps protophenomenal properties play the mass role or the charge role.

Nonconstitutive and non-Russellian panprotopsychism are coherent theses as protophenomenal properties are defined above (at least if we set aside the specialness clause): perhaps protophenomenal properties only constitute some macroexperiences, and perhaps they do not serve as quiddities. As with panpsychism, however, the Hegelian motivations for panprotopsychism strongly favor (type-A) constitutive Russellian panprotopsychism, so it is this view on which I will concentrate.

Constitutive Russellian panprotopsychism, like constitutive Russellian panpsychism, is a form of broad physicalism without narrow physicalism. It therefore escapes the Hegelian dilemma in just the same way. Constitutive Russellian panpsychists will reply to the conceivability argument by saying that structural zombies are conceivable but categorical zombies are not. They will reply to the causal argument by saying that fundamental protophenomenal properties are causally relevant in virtue of playing microphysical roles, and that macrophenomenal properties inherit causal relevance from protophenomenal properties in virtue of being grounded in them. In this way it slips through the horns of the Hegelian dilemma.

5. Synthesis: Russellian Monism

Given panpsychism as thesis and panprotopsychism as antithesis, there is a natural synthesis that subsumes them both. This synthesis is Russellian monism.[11] We can understand Russellian monism as the conjunction of broad

---

11. Stoljar (2013) credits the first appearance of "Russellian monism" to Chalmers 1999. The phrase actually appears (along with "panprotopsychism") in Chalmers 1997, but in any case it is heavily inspired by Michael Lockwood's talk of the "Russellian identity theory" in *Mind, Brain, and the Quantum* (1989).

physicalism with the denial of narrow physicalism. On this view, structural properties in physics do not constitute consciousness, but quiddities (perhaps along with structure) constitute consciousness. The view is Russellian because of the appeal to quiddities and their connection to mentality. It is a sort of monism because the world on this view consists in quiddities connected by laws of nature.

It is easy to see that both constitutive Russellian panpsychism and constitutive Russellian panprotopsychism are forms of Russellian monism. In fact, Russellian monism is equivalent to the disjunction of the two. According to Russellian monism, all conscious experience is grounded in structure plus quiddities, but not in structure alone. Given the definition of protophenomenal properties above, this thesis is equivalent to the thesis that some quiddities are either phenomenal or protophenomenal, as the Russellian views hold, and that these quiddities along with structure ground all conscious experience, as the constitutive views hold.

Is Russellian monism a form of physicalism, dualism, or something else? As before, this is a largely verbal question that we need not settle. We could say that it is a form of broad physicalism but not narrow physicalism, and leave it at that. Still, it is interesting to look more closely at the question of whether, on a Russellian monist view, (proto)phenomenal properties (that is, phenomenal or protophenomenal properties) are physical properties. There are a number of different options available here, depending on what one counts as a physical property, and how one construes the semantics of physical terms such as "mass." Each of these options leads to a subtly different way of characterizing Russellian monism. The following discussion may be of most interest to aficionados of this topic; others can skip it without much loss.

An initial question is whether physical properties are restricted to the properties invoked by physical theory (space, time, mass, charge, and so on), perhaps along with those properties grounded in them. These are the properties that Stoljar calls the t-physical properties (for theory-physical) and that Strawson (2006) calls "physics-al" properties. It is most common to restrict physical properties in this sense, but one can also invoke expanded senses of the term, such as my notion of a broadly physical property, or Stoljar's notion of an o-physical property, or Strawson's notion of a physical property which appears to subsume all natural properties. Given such an expanded sense, then even if quiddities are not t-physical properties, they may count as physical in the expanded sense. The resulting position might be seen as *expansionary Russellian physicalism*, with (proto) phenomenal properties counting as physical properties in an expanded sense.[12]

In what follows, I will make the more common assumption that physical properties are restricted to t-physical properties: perhaps space, time, mass, charge, and so on. To assess the status of Russellian monism, we can then ask: what is the relationship between (proto)phenomenal properties and physical properties such as mass? This depends on just how terms such as "mass" function.

On one view, "mass" refers to the property that actually plays the mass role. So insofar as there is a quiddity that actually plays the mass role, that quiddity is identical to mass. The corresponding version of Russellian monism is the *Russellian identity theory*, because it holds that (proto)phenomenal properties are identical to physical properties such as mass. As Grover Maxwell (1978) observes, this is a sort of inversion of the more familiar identity theory due to Smart (1959) and others. The familiar identity theory offers a topic-neutral analysis of mental expressions, where "pain" refers to whatever plays the pain role, and then holds that these have physical referents, with C-fiber firing playing the pain role. The Russellian identity theory instead offers a topic-neutral analysis of physical expressions, where "mass" refers to whatever plays the mass role, and then holds that these have mental or proto-mental referents, with (proto)phenomenal quiddities playing the mass role.[13]

On another view, "mass" refers to the second-order functional property of having a property that plays the mass role. On this view, mass is not identical to the quiddity that plays the mass role, but we might say that mass is realized by that quiddity. A closely related view holds that "mass" refers to a dispositional property which is realized by the quiddity that serves as its categorical basis. The corresponding version of Russellian monism is the *Russellian realization theory*, since it holds that physical properties such as mass are realized

---

12. Stoljar and Strawson are naturally counted as expansionary Russellian physicalists. Strawson spends some time arguing with people like me (for example, questioning whether physical duplicates without consciousness are conceivable), but once it is clear that I mean by "physical" what Strawson means by "physics-al," the disagreement between us may become largely verbal.

13. Maxwell (1978) and Lockwood (1989) are certainly Russellian identity theorists: both explicitly endorse the identity theory and credit the underlying idea to Russell. Feigl (1958/1967) and Montero (2010) can easily be interpreted as holding the view. The coherence of the Russellian identity theory, on which quiddities are identical to t-physical properties and on which t-physicalism is true, suggests that Russellian monism is not best characterized (following Stoljar) as o-physicalism about consciousness without t-physicalism.

by (proto)phenomenal properties. Russellian realization theory can be seen as an inversion of the familiar functionalist realization theory, on which mental properties are second-order functional properties (pain is the property of having a property that plays the pain role) and on which these properties are realized by physical properties.

On the Russellian realization theory, quiddities are not themselves t-physical properties (at least if we assume that realizing properties are distinct from the properties they realize). So the Russellian realization theory is not a version of physicalism, assuming as above that only t-physical properties are physical properties. Instead, physical properties are themselves realized by and grounded in the (proto)phenomenal properties that serve as quiddities. The panpsychist version of this view can be seen as a form of *Russellian idealism*, with fundamental phenomenal properties serving as the grounds for physical properties. The panprotopsychist version can be seen as a form of *Russellian neutral monism*, with fundamental protophenomenal properties serving as the grounds for both physical and phenomenal properties. There may also be a mixed view, perhaps *Russellian pluralism*, if some quiddities are phenomenal and some are protophenomenal or unrelated to the phenomenal.[14]

On another view, "mass" refers to a dispositional property that is not grounded in its categorical basis: instead categorical and dispositional properties are equally fundamental, and neither is grounded in the other. Given that physical properties are restricted to t-physical properties and those grounded in them, the corresponding version of Russellian monism will be a *Russellian property dualism*, with fundamental physical properties (dispositional properties such as mass) and equally fundamental phenomenal or protophenomenal properties (the corresponding quiddities).

On a final view (the "powerful quality" view advocated by Heil 2012), dispositional properties are identical to their categorical bases. Any corresponding version of Russellian monism will be a version of the Russellian identity theory: whether "mass" functions to pick out a dispositional property or its categorical basis, it will pick out a (proto)phenomenal property. One version of this Russellian identity theory (advocated by Mørch 2014) holds that there is a sort of conceptual or a priori connection between (proto)phenomenal properties and the associated dispositions, in the same way that there is arguably such a connection between pain and certain associated dispositions (arguably, one cannot conceive of pain that does not play a certain dispositional

14. Bolender (2001) puts forward a sort of Russellian idealism, and Rosenberg (2004) may be either a Russellian idealist or pluralist.

role). Another version, which stands to the first version roughly as type-B materialism stands to type-A materialism, holds that there is an a posteriori connection between (proto)phenomenal and dispositional properties. Note that these versions of the Russellian identity theory are consistent with the version discussed a few paragraphs above, on which (for example) "mass" is equivalent to "whatever plays the mass role." They do not entail it, however, as they are also consistent with views on which "mass" picks out a disposition directly, and they are not entailed by it, as the original version is consistent with views on which dispositional and categorical properties are distinct. One could also see these views as versions of Russellian idealism or neutral monism, on which all truths are grounded in (proto)phenomenal truths.

A number of these versions of Russellian monism differ only verbally. Many of these differences turn on the correct semantics for "mass" and for "physical property," with the underlying metaphysical picture looking the same. One exception here is the difference between Russellian idealism, neutral monism, and pluralism: this turns on the (presumably substantive) issue of whether there is something it is like to have a quiddity. Another may be the differences involving Russellian property dualism and the versions of the Russellian identity theory in the previous paragraph: these turn on the (arguably substantive) issue of whether dispositional properties are grounded in, identical to, or independent of their categorical bases. For what it is worth, I am most attracted to the first version of the Russellian identity theory, with some sympathy also for the idealist, neutral monist, and property dualist versions. The only view that I am entirely unsympathetic with is the a posteriori version of the Russellian identity theory in the previous paragraph (which I think requires a sort of brute identity claim, and so stands to the first version as type-B versions of the familiar identity theory stand to type-A versions). In what follows, I will simply talk of Russellian monism, distinguishing panpsychist and panprotopsychist views as necessary.[15]

---

15. The different versions of Russellian monism will take different attitudes to the conceivability and possibility of zombies: physical duplicates without phenomenal states. Expansionary Russellian physicalism will deny that they are conceivable or possible: given the expanded sense of the physical, to conceive of a zombie requires conceiving of a categorical zombie (same structure, same quiddities, no consciousness), which cannot be done according to the view. Russellian identity theorists of the first sort discussed above may hold that zombies are conceivable but not possible, because of nontrivial two-dimensional structure in physical terms (the primary intension of "mass" picks out whatever plays the mass role, the secondary intension picks out the quiddity that actually plays the mass role). Russellian idealists, neutral monists, and property dualists may well hold that zombies are conceivable and possible, in that there are conceivable and possible situations where the structural properties are associated with different quiddities that are independent of the phenomenal, or perhaps with no quiddities at all.

6. Antithesis: The Combination Problem

Given Russellian monism as our new synthesis, a more significant antithesis now threatens. This antithesis takes the form of a major problem for both panpsychism and panprotopsychism: the combination problem.

The combination problem for panpsychism was posed by William James (1890) and named by William Seager (1995). This problem can be stated as follows: how do microexperiences combine to yield macroexperiences? It is at least very hard to see how a number of separate experiences had by separate entities could combine to yield a distinct experience had by a composite entity. It is especially hard to see how they could combine to yield the distinctive kind of macroexperience that we find in our own case.

One way to pose the combination problem is in the form of a conceivability argument. (An approach along these lines is presented by Goff (2009), to whom my presentation here is indebted.) Here PP is the conjunction of all microphysical and microphenomenal truths about the world, and Q is a macrophenomenal truth, such as "Some macroscopic entity is conscious."

(1) $PP\&{\sim}Q$ is conceivable.
(2) If $PP\&{\sim}Q$ is conceivable, it is possible.
(3) If $PP\&{\sim}Q$ is metaphysically possible, constitutive panpsychism is false.

_____

(4) Constitutive panpsychism is false.

Here premises (2) and (3) parallel the corresponding premises of the conceivability argument against materialism, and are supported by the same reasons. So the key premise here is premise (1). This premise asserts the conceivability of *panpsychist zombies*: beings that are physically and microphenomenally identical to us (and indeed whole worlds that are physically and microphenomenally identical to ours), without any macrophenomenal states.

Why believe that panpsychist zombies are conceivable? Some might find this simply intuitive: one can conceive of all the microexperiences one likes without any macroexperiences. But one can also justify it by invoking a principle in the spirit of James' objection to panpsychism in *The Principles of Psychology*. This is the principle that no set of conscious subjects necessitates the existence of a further conscious subject. Or in the key of conceivability: given any set of conscious subjects and any conscious subject not in that set, one can always conceive of all the subjects in the set without the further subject. More precisely: given any conjunction S of positive phenomenal truths about a group of conscious subjects and any positive phenomenal truth T about a conscious subject not in that group, S&~T is conceivable.

We might say that these principles invoke a subject/subject gap: an epistemic gap from the existence of subjects to the existence of distinct subjects. The principles all have intuitive appeal. Prima facie, it seems conceivable that any group of conscious subjects could exist alone, without any further subjects. But if this is right, constitutive panpsychism is in trouble. Given that all experiences are had by conscious subjects, we can say that microexperiences will be had by microsubjects and macroexperiences by macrosubjects. Then by the principle above, we can conceive of any number of microsubjects having their microexperiences without any macrosubject having macroexperiences. That is, we can conceive of the conjunction of all microphenomenal truths obtaining without any positive macrophenomenal truths obtaining.

This result (along with the conceivability-possibility premise) already rules out a version of constitutive panpsychism on which macroexperience is wholly grounded in microexperience. To rule out all versions, including those in which macroexperience is grounded in microexperience plus physical structure, we can appeal to a modified principle according to which in the case above, S&S'&~T is conceivable, where S' characterizes the physical and structural properties of the members of the original group. This principle seems just about as intuitively plausible as the original principle. Given this principle, premise (1) above follows, and if premises (2) and (3) are granted, constitutive panpsychism is ruled out.

One might think that this problem for panpsychism makes things better for panprotopsychism, as panprotopsychism does not need subjects at the bottom level. Nevertheless, there is also a combination problem for panprotopsychism. This is the problem of how protoexperiences can combine to yield experiences.

As with the combination problem for panpsychism, the combination problem for panprotopsychism can be posed in the form of a conceivability argument. Here *PPP* is the conjunction of all microphysical and protophenomenal truths (or better, purportedly protophenomenal truths, as the combination problem can be used to question whether purportedly protophenomenal properties are truly protophenomenal), and Q is a macrophenomenal truth, such as "Some macroscopic entity is conscious."

(1) *PPP*&~Q is conceivable.
(2) If *PPP*&~Q is conceivable, it is possible.

(3) If *PPP&~Q* is metaphysically possible, constitutive panprotopsychism is false.

_____

(4) Constitutive panprotopsychism is false.

Once again, the key premise is premise (1). This asserts the existence of *protophenomenal zombies*: beings that share our (purportedly) protophenomenal properties at the microphysical level, but that lack consciousness. The conceivability of protophenomenal zombies is perhaps somewhat less obvious than the conceivability of panpsychist zombies, as we have a less clear idea of what protophenomenal properties involve. Still, one might appeal to a general nonphenomenal/phenomenal gap, as on the view I discussed in chapter 4 (p. 260). One thought here is that for any nonphenomenal truths, we can conceive of all of these truths obtaining without any experience at all.

Why accept this? One possible justification is a nonsubject/subject gap. This is the claim that no set of truths about nonsubjects of consciousness can necessitate the existence of distinct subjects of consciousness. Or in the key of conceivability: for any set of nonsubjects instantiating nonphenomenal properties and any independent subject exhibiting phenomenal properties, we can conceive of the former without the latter. This principle leads naturally to premise (1) above.

Why believe this principle? One potential justification is the idea that subjects are conceptually fundamental entities. On a view where subjects are metaphysically fundamental entities, then they are not grounded in more fundamental entities, and one can make a case that they are not necessitated by the existence of other fundamental entities. Likewise, if they are conceptually fundamental entities, they are not conceptually grounded in more fundamental entities, and one can make a case that their existence is not a priori entailed by that of other entities. Certainly these principles are not obvious, but they have some intuitive appeal.

Another potential justification is a nonquality/quality gap. Here the idea is that phenomenal properties are qualitative, in that they constitutively involve qualities such as redness, greenness, and so on. And one can argue that nonqualitative truths never necessitate qualitative truths, insofar as one can always conceive of the former obtaining without the latter obtaining. Insofar as purportedly protophenomenal properties are nonqualitative, this principle yields a gap between these properties and the phenomenal that might justify premise (1).

Both panpsychism and panprotopsychism face challenging combination problems, then. As well as sharing a number of problems, each view faces one especially difficult problem that the other does not: the subject-subject gap for panpsychism, and the nonphenomenal-phenomenal gap for panprotopsychism. Reasonable people can differ on which problem is more serious. I am inclined to think the subject-subject problem is more difficult, and that panprotopsychism benefits from having fewer constraints on its building blocks, but I am far from certain about this. All of these problems have the status of challenges rather than refutations, but they are challenges that need to be addressed.

Of course physicalism is faced with its own version of the combination problem: how do microphysical entities and properties come together to yield subjects, qualities, and so on? This challenge is presumably at least as hard as the challenge to panpsychism, as the resources available to the physicalist are a subset of those available to the panpsychist. But we should be clear on the dialectic. The sympathizer with panpsychism has typically already rejected physicalism (at least in non-Russellian forms), precisely on the grounds of these gaps between the physical and the experiential. The question is then whether panpsychism can do any better. It promises to do better in at least one respect: it accommodates the very existence of experience, if only by taking it as fundamental. But it is not clear whether it does any better at explaining the complex manifest character of macroexperience. This is the challenge posed by the combination problem.

By contrast, dualism does not suffer nearly as badly from a combination problem. This is especially clear for substance dualism, which postulates fundamental entities (subjects of experience) that bear macrophenomenal properties. There is no analog of the subject combination problem for such a view. If the dualist takes macrophenomenal properties as fundamental properties, with their structure, qualities, and other features built in, then there will be no analog of the other combination problems either.

Instead of the combination problem, dualism has the familiar problem of mental causation, as well as a problem of economy (why postulate so many fundamental entities?). Panpsychism and panprotopsychism, at least in their constitutive Russellian varieties, do not suffer from these problems. They postulate only as many fundamental entities and properties as are needed to make sense of physics (at least if one thinks that physics requires quiddities), and they make a specific hypothesis about the nature of these properties. And on this picture, phenomenal properties are integrated into the causal order.

I think that substance dualism (in its epiphenomenalist and interactionist forms) and Russellian monism (in its panpsychist and panprotopsychist forms) are the two serious contenders in the metaphysics of consciousness, at least once one has given up on standard physicalism. (I divide my own credence fairly equally between them.) So in a way, our new dialectical situation confronts Russellian monism with (once again) substance dualism. In effect the problems of economy and mental causation for one are weighed against the combination problem for the other. If one of these problems can be solved or proved unsolvable, that will constitute significant progress on the mind–body problem.

7. New Synthesis: Panqualityism?

Is a new synthesis in sight? I do not have a solution to the combination problem, so I do not really have a new synthesis. But in this section I want to at least canvas options and to explore one possible new solution, before concluding that it fails. I explore options for dealing with the various aspects of the problem in much more depth in "The Combination Problem for Panpsychism."

One reaction to the combination problem is to give up on constitutive panpsychism (or panprotopsychism), and instead opt for emergent panpsychism. This view does not face nearly such a pressing form of the combination problem, as it denies that macroexperience is grounded in microexperience. Still, emergent panpsychism loses many of the key advantages of constitutive panpsychism in avoiding the Hegelian dilemma. In particular, it faces a problem of mental causation—how can macroexperience play a causal role? —that is analogous to the problems of dualism, and seems to require epiphenomenalism, interactionism, or overdetermination. So it is worth looking closely at the options for constitutive panpsychism.

A second reaction is to hold that macrosubjects are identical to certain microsubjects: that is, they are identical to certain fundamental physical entities with fundamental phenomenal properties, and they share those phenomenal properties. This view avoids the needs for subjects to combine into distinct subjects. One version of this view is akin to Leibniz's "dominant monad" view, on which human subjects are identical to single fundamental particles, perhaps in their brain. This view is subject to obvious objections, however (what happens if that particle is destroyed? how could a particle have such complex phenomenal properties, especially on a Russellian view?). Another version of the view appeals to fundamental physical entities above the level of the particle: perhaps entangled quantum systems, or perhaps the entire universe. I think that these possibilities (especially the quantum version) are worth exploring, but it is not easy to see how such entities could have fundamental phenomenal properties that yield a phenomenology like ours.

A third reaction is to *deflate the subject*, either denying that experiences must have subjects at all, or at least denying that subjects are metaphysically and conceptually simple entities. I think it is a conceptual truth that experiences have subjects: phenomenal properties must be instantiated by something, and they characterize what it is like to be that thing. But the second denial seems more tenable. Indeed, some such denial seems required to be a constitutive panpsychist, a constitutive panprotopsychist, or indeed a materialist. This view may require rejecting certain intuitions about subjects, but these intuitions are not non-negotiable.

We might define Subjects as primitive subjects of experience. I think that we have a natural conception of Subjects: these are subjects as they might have been in the Garden of Eden, as it were. Where Subjects are concerned, the subject/subject gap and the nonsubject/subject gap are both extremely plausible: the existence of a Subject is not necessitated or a priori entailed by the existence of distinct Subjects or indeed by the existence of non-Subjects. So if we are Subjects (and if we set aside the view that macrosubjects are identical to microsubjects), constitutive panpsychism and constitutive panprotopsychism are false.

Still, it is far from obvious that we are Subjects. There does not seem to be an introspective datum that we are Subjects, and it is not obvious that there are strong theoretical arguments to that effect. There are perhaps intuitions of determinacy about personal identity that tend to support the claim (see Barnett 2010 and Nida-Rümelin 2010), but these intuitions do not seem to be non-negotiable, and there are reasonably strong considerations in favor of rejecting them (see Parfit 1984). And once we deny that we are Subjects, the door is at least opened to rejecting the subject/subject gap and the nonsubject/subject gap, and to accepting constitutive panpsychism or panprotopsychism.

I think that a Russellian monist must almost certainly embrace this view (perhaps the only remotely promising alternative is the quantum version of the micro/macro identity claim above). Still, to deny that we are Subjects is not to solve the combination problem. We still need to give an account of how macroexperience can be grounded in microexperience or in protoexperience.

Here I will look briefly at a view that has been popular among sympathizers with panpsychism and panprotopsychism: panqualityism. The name of this view was introduced in an article by Herbert Feigl (1960), who credits the term to conversation with Stephen C. Pepper, but versions of the view itself were popular among the neutral monists of the early twentieth century, including William James (1904), Ernst Mach (1886), and Bertrand Russell (1921). More recently, the view has been defended by Sam Coleman (2012).

On this view, *qualities* are the properties presented in experience: Intuitively, these are properties like redness, greenness, heat, and so on. Qualities are not identical with phenomenal properties: when redness is presented to me in experience, I have a phenomenal property, but I need not be red. Instead, we would intuitively say that I am aware of redness, and that phenomenal properties involve awareness of qualitative properties. Likewise, phenomenal properties are always instantiated by conscious subjects, but qualities need not be. We can certainly make sense of the idea of a red object that is not a subject of experience.

Panqualityism typically requires rejecting a reductionist view of qualities, such as a view on which color qualities are identified with physical reflectance properties or something of the sort. Instead, it is naturally associated with what I have called an Edenic view of qualities. Here the qualities most fundamentally presented in experience are properties such as Edenic redness, a simple property that may not be instantiated by the objects that seem to have it in the external world, but which might have been instantiated in the Garden of Eden.

Panqualityism holds that fundamental physical entities instantiate qualities like these. We might imagine, for example, that fundamental particles are Edenically red. More likely, the relevant qualities involved will be more austere than this, but they will nevertheless be primitive properties that could be presented in experience. The most important kind of panqualityism, unsurprisingly, is constitutive Russellian panqualityism, on which qualities serve as quiddities and also serve to constitute human experience. Many of the panqualityists discussed above have endorsed views of this sort.

Constitutive panqualityism is a form of panprotopsychism rather than panpsychism: qualities are not phenomenal properties but serve to constitute phenomenal properties. Because qualities need not be instantiated by subjects, the view need not invoke microsubjects at all. Panqualityism is occasionally characterized as a version of panpsychism with "experiences without subjects" or "unsensed sensa," but I think the view is best regarded as a form of panprotopsychism. Still, it is a view on which the protophenomenal properties take an especially familiar form, and on which they have a close connection to phenomenal properties.

Panqualityism is not threatened by the subject/subject gap, as it does not require microsubjects to constitute macrosubjects. Likewise, it is not threatened by the nonquality/quality gap, as the purportedly protophenomenal properties here are qualitative through and through. It is threatened by the nonsubject/subject gap, but here it responds by deflating the subject. Some of the traditional panqualityists rejected subjects of experience altogether, while others have taken deflationary views of them on which they can be constituted by underlying qualities, perhaps along with structural properties.

How does panqualityism solve the combination problem? It is natural for the panqualityist to argue that simple microqualities can collectively constitute complex macroqualities, ultimately building up something as complex as the qualitative structure of a visual field, or even a full multisensory field. Then it could be suggested that the existence of these complex qualities explains the phenomenal data even without postulating an associated subject of experience; or it could be suggested that certain complex qualities entail the existence of an associated subject, perhaps in a deflated sense.

Still, I think that panqualityism is vulnerable to a version of the combination problem analogous to earlier versions. In particular, we can mount a conceivability argument against panqualityism as follows. Here QQ is a conjunction of positive qualitative truths at the microphysical level, perhaps along with any other microphysical truths, and Q is a positive macrophenomenal truth.

(1) $QQ\&{\sim}Q$ is conceivable.
(2) If $QQ\&{\sim}Q$ is conceivable, it is metaphysically possible.
(3) If $QQ\&{\sim}Q$ is metaphysically possible, constitutive panqualityism is false.

_____

(4) Constitutive panqualityism is false.

Again, all the action is in the first premise. This premise asserts the conceivability of *qualitative zombies*, beings that are qualitatively (and microphysically) identical to us without consciousness.

Why believe this premise? One could make a case that it is intuitively obvious. More deeply, it is grounded in what we might call the quality/awareness gap. Here the idea is that no instantiations of qualities ever necessitate awareness of qualities. Or in the key of conceivability: for any set of instantiated qualities and physical properties, it is conceivable that all those qualities and properties are instantiated without any awareness of the qualities. Given that all phenomenal properties involve awareness of qualities, premise (1) above follows. And even if only some phenomenal properties involve awareness of qualities, this will be enough to make the case against constitutive panqualityism.

The quality/awareness gap has much intuitive force. On the face of it, it is conceivable that Edenic redness is instantiated without anyone being aware of it. And on the face of it, this intuition scales up to arbitrarily complex qualities. Even given complex qualities corresponding to the structure of a visual field, then if it is conceivable that those qualities be instantiated at all (presumably by a situation in the world corresponding to the situation as perceived), it is conceivable that they be instantiated without any awareness of those qualities.

The panqualityist might respond in various ways. They could bring in awareness at the fundamental level, perhaps by appealing to special qualities that cannot be instantiated without awareness of those qualities (pain, maybe?); but this leads back to subjects at the fundamental level, and the associated problems. They might deny the existence of awareness, as James (1904) does, and hold that our experience involves qualities but does not involve awareness of them; but this claim runs directly counter to our phenomenology. They might combine the appeal to qualities with a functional reduction of awareness, as Coleman (2012) does; but I think that the conceivability argument above itself gives reason to reject such a reduction.

Panqualityism is also vulnerable to other aspects of the combination problem. It is vulnerable to the *structure combination problem*: the structure among qualities instantiated in the brain is very different from the structure among qualities of which we are aware, and it is hard to see how the former could constitute the latter. It is also vulnerable to the *quality combination problem*: it is hard to see how a few primitive qualities (which is all that the Russellian panqualityist can appeal to) could yield the vast array of qualities of which we are aware.

I conclude that panqualityism does not offer a solution to the combination problem. We are still in need of a new synthesis.

8. Conclusion

We started with the thesis of materialism and the antithesis of dualism, and reached the synthesis of panpsychism. This synthesis encountered the antithesis of panprotopsychism, from which we reached the new synthesis of Russellian monism. This synthesis encountered the antithesis of the combination problem, and whether there can be a new synthesis remains an open question.

Still, I think that the Hegelian argument gives good reason to take both panpsychism and panprotopsychism very seriously. If we can find a reasonable solution to the combination problem for either, this view would immediately become the most promising solution to the mind–body problem. So the combination problem deserves serious and sustained attention.

References

Barnett, D. 2010. You are simple. In (G. Bealer and R. Koons, eds.) *The Waning of Materialism*. New York: Oxford University Press.

Bennett, K. 2003. Why the exclusion problem seems intractable and how, just maybe, to tract it. *Noûs* 37:471–97.

Bolender, J. 2001. An argument for idealism. *Journal of Consciousness Studies* 8(4):37–61.

Chalmers, D. J. 1997. Moving forward on the problem of consciousness. *Journal of Consciousness Studies* 4(1): 3–46.

Chalmers, D. J. 1999. Précis of *The Conscious Mind*. *Philosophy and Phenomenological Research* 59: 435–8.

Chalmers, D. J. 2003. Consciousness and its place in nature. In (S. Stich and T. Warfield, eds.) *Blackwell Guide to the Philosophy of Mind*. Oxford: Blackwell.

Chalmers, D. J. 2010. The two-dimensional argument against materialism. In *The Character of Consciousness*. New York: Oxford University Press.

Chalmers, D. J. 2012. *Constructing the World*. New York: Oxford University Press.

Chalmers, D. J. forthcoming. The combination problem for panpsychism. In (G. Bruntrup and L. Jaskolla, eds.) *Panpsychism*. New York: Oxford University Press.

Coleman, S. 2012. Mental chemistry: Combination for panpsychists. *Dialectica* 66:137–66.

Feigl, H. 1958/1967. The 'mental' and the 'physical'. *Minnesota Studies in the Philosophy of Science* 2:370–497. Reprinted (with a postscript) as *The 'Mental' and the 'Physical'*. Minneapolis: University of Minnesota Press.

Feigl, H. 1960. Mind–body, not a pseudo-problem. In (S. Hook, ed.) *Dimensions of Mind*. New York: New York University Press.

Fine, K. 2012. The pure logic of ground. *Review of Symbolic Logic* 5:1–25.

Goff, P. 2009. Why panpsychism doesn't help to explain consciousness. *Dialectica* 63(3):289–311

Heil, J. 2012. *The Universe as We Find It*. New York: Oxford University Press.

James, W. 1890. *The Principles of Psychology*. London: Macmillan.

James, W. 1904. Does "consciousness" exist? *Journal of Philosophy, Psychology, and Scientific Methods* 1:477–91.

Lockwood, M. 1989. *Mind, Brain, and the Quantum*. New York: Oxford University Press.

Mach, E. 1886. *The Analysis of Sensations and the Relation of Physical to the Psychical*. Translated by C. M. Williams, Open Court, 1984.

Maxwell, G. 1978. Rigid designators and mind-brain identity. *Minnesota Studies in the Philosophy of Science* 9:365–403.

Montero, B. 2010. A Russellian response to the structural argument against physicalism. *Journal of Consciousness Studies* 17:70–83.

Mørch, H. H. 2014. Panpsychism and Causation: A New Argument and a Solution to the Combination Problem. Ph. D. dissertation, University of Oslo.

Nida-Rümelin, M. 2010. An argument from transtemporal identity for subject-body dualism. In (G. Bealer and R. Koons, eds.) *The Waning of Materialism*. New York: Oxford University Press.

Papineau, D. 2002. *Thinking About Consciousness.* New York: Oxford University Press.

Parfit, D. 1984. *Reasons and Persons.* New York: Oxford University Press.

Rosenberg, G. 2004. *A Place for Consciousness: Probing the Deep Structure of the Natural World.* New York: Oxford University Press.

Russell, M. 1921. *The Analysis of Mind.* London: George Allen and Unwin.

Russell, B. 1927. *The Analysis of Matter.* London: Kegan Paul.

Schaffer, J. 2009. On what grounds what. In (D. Manley, D. J. Chalmers, and R. Wasserman, eds.) *Metametaphysics: New Essays on the Foundations of Ontology.* New York: Oxford University Press.

Smart, J. J. C. 1959. Sensations and brain processes. *Philosophical Review* 68:141–56.

Seager. W. 1995. Consciousness, information, and panpsychism. *Journal of Consciousness Studies* 2:272–88.

Stoljar, D. 2001a. The conceivability argument and two conceptions of the physical. *Philosophical Perspectives* 15:393–413.

Stoljar, D. 2001b. Two conceptions of the physical. *Philosophy and Phenomenological Research* 62:253–81.

Stoljar, D. 2013. Four kinds of Russellian monism. In (U. Kriegel, ed.) *Current Controversies in the Philosophy of Mind.* New York: Routledge.

Strawson, G. 2006. Realistic monism: Why physicalism entails panpsychism. *Journal of Consciousness Studies* 13(10–11):3–31.

Yablo, S. 1992. Mental causation. *Philosophical Review* 101:245–80.

13

The Short Slide from A Posteriori Physicalism to Russellian Monism

Torin Alter and Robert J. Howell

A POSTERIORI PHYSICALISM (e.g., Block 2006, Loar 1997, Papineau 2002, 2007) seems to be the flavor of choice in today's debates about consciousness and the mind-body problem. Many philosophers, it seems, like to have their cake and eat it too. It is hard to deny the mystery of phenomenal consciousness, but few want to abandon a physicalist ontology. A posteriori, or type-B, physicalism claims that physicalism is true despite the fact that there is no way to deduce phenomenal truths from physical truths. This is why even an ideal reasoner can conceive of a zombie world (a world that lacks consciousness but is physically identical to the actual world) despite the impossibility of such worlds, and why Frank Jackson's (1982) Mary cannot know what it's like to see red from within her room, even though she knows all the physical truths.

Here we wish to put a posteriori physicalism to the test by offering a novel argument that, given plausible assumptions, a posteriori physicalism collapses into Russellian monism. The latter theory says roughly that phenomenal (or protophenomenal) properties serve as categorical grounds of the basic properties that physics describes, which are fundamentally dispositional (e.g., Russell 1927, Maxwell 1978, Chalmers 1996). The result is that a posteriori physicalism survives only by admitting that phenomenal (or protophenomenal) properties are metaphysically fundamental (or at least as fundamental as basic physical properties).[1] If this counts as a form of physicalism, it does so at best on

---

1. Some (Schaffer 2010) doubt that there is a fundamental level of reality. The debate about consciousness and physicalism is neutral on that issue; it can be framed in terms of whether the phenomenal is less (or more or equally) fundamental than the physical. But this does not

a technicality.[2] While there are ways to resist our argument, we suspect that articulating them will clarify the strong commitments of a posteriori physicalism. We also suspect that some who think of themselves as a posteriori physicalists might find themselves pushed by the argument to an a priori form of physicalism.

The Anti-Physicalist Arguments

A posteriori physicalism is best articulated as a response to anti-physicalist arguments, such as the conceivability and knowledge arguments. It will therefore be useful to have their main steps on the table. We follow David Chalmers' (2010, chapter 2) formulations. Let P be the complete microphysical truth. P specifies, in the language of microphysics, the fundamental microphysical laws and the fundamental physical features of all fundamental microphysical entities. Let Q be an arbitrary phenomenal truth, e.g., that the tallest spy is in pain. The conceivability and knowledge arguments could be stated concisely as follows.[3]

The conceivability argument
1. $P\&\sim Q$ is ideally conceivable.
2. If $P\&\sim Q$ is ideally conceivable, then $P\&\sim Q$ is metaphysically possible.
3. If $P\&\sim Q$ is metaphysically possible, then physicalism is false.
4. Therefore, physicalism is false.

The knowledge argument
1. Q is not a priori deducible from P.
2. If Q is not a priori deducible from P, then P does not metaphysically necessitate Q.
3. If P does not metaphysically necessitate Q, then physicalism is false.
4. Therefore, physicalism is false.

---

matter for present purposes, and for ease of exposition we sometimes write as though we are assuming there is a fundamental level.

2. For discussions of the relationship between physicalism and Russellian monism, see Chalmers (chapter 12 of this volume), Montero (chapter 10 of this volume), and Alter and Nagasawa 2012.

3. As Chalmers makes clear, these summaries are not fully precise. For example, P should be conjoined with T, a second-order "that's all" claim, and I, a claim that specifies indexical information. He refines his formulations to reflect those concerns (and others; see fn 6). But here those refinements are not of central importance.

On a somewhat deflationary construal of conceivability (which we will assume), to say that *P&~Q* is ideally conceivable just is to say that *Q* cannot be a priori deduced from *P*.[4] On that construal, these arguments are variants of one another. They differ principally in how the first premise, which expresses the epistemic gap, is supported. The conceivability argument's first premise is typically supported by appealing to zombie or inverted spectrum cases, whereas the knowledge argument's first premise is typically supported by appealing to the Mary case or something similar.[5]

A. Posteriori Physicalism

A posteriori physicalists reject premise 2 of both arguments, in effect denying that metaphysical necessitation requires a priori deducibility in the physical-phenomenal case. Call their central claim *necessity without deducibility*:

(NWD) *P* metaphysically necessitates *Q* even though *Q* is not a priori deducible from *P*.

NWD requires clarification. First, the operative notion of deducibility is not a strictly logico-syntactic notion. To say that *A* is deducible from *B* is to say roughly that an ideal reasoner can conclude *A* from *B* based solely on a priori reasoning.[6] Second, NWD is not the comparatively weak claim that *P* necessitates *Q* even though no one can at this point (or even ever) deduce *Q* from *P*. A posteriori physicalists, a priori physicalists, and dualists can all agree that no one will ever be able to perform that deduction. A posteriori physicalism distinguishes itself from the a priori variety by claiming that *Q* is not *deducible* from *P*, where this means roughly that *Q* cannot be a priori deduced from *P* even by an ideal reasoner. It distinguishes itself from dualism by claiming that, despite this lack of deducibility, the physical truths necessitate the phenomenal truths.

The notions of a priori knowledge and deduction by ideal reasoners are controversial. But for present purposes, we will set to one side general

---

4. This construal is deflationary in that, on it, conceiving of something does not require forming an image or other positive conception—in contrast to what Chalmers (2002) calls "positive conceivability." As he argues, however, negative ideal conceivability suffices here.

5. For example, Pereboom (1994) takes Thomas Nagel's (1974) bat case to support the knowledge argument's epistemic premise.

6. Strictly speaking, the reference to an ideal reason*er* is not needed. Instead, we could define the notion in terms of ideal reasoning. Chalmers (2002) argues that there are good reasons for doing so. But this (along with other refinements he adds) does not matter much here.

skepticism about those notions.[7] We take all parties—the anti-physicalist as well as the a posteriori and priori physicalists—to be engaged in a dispute defined against a background of agreed-upon notions. They all agree that there is such a thing as a priori knowledge and that there is a difference between failures of deduction that result from incompetence and those that result from the lack of an a priori connection between the truths. Their main difference is over (1) whether the connection between P and Q is a priori, and (2) if it isn't, whether this shows that P does not necessitate Q.

Furthermore, the necessitation involved in NWD is metaphysical. NWD cannot be established by showing that $P\&\sim Q$ is impossible in some restricted sense of possibility, such as physical possibility. Anti-physicalist proponents of the knowledge and conceivability arguments can grant that P necessitates Q given certain contingent psychophysical laws. What these philosophers usually deny, and almost all physicalists accept, is that P necessitates Q in the strict, unqualified—that is, metaphysical—sense.[8]

NWD might seem to receive support from standard Kripke (1972) cases of a posteriori necessity, such as those involving water and H_2O, lightning and electrical discharge, heat and molecular motion, and so on. If Kripke is right, then "Water is H_2O" is both a posteriori and metaphysically (not just physically) necessary. Likewise for "Heat is molecular motion," "Lightning is electrical discharge," etc. There are many cases of metaphysically necessary truths that a priori reasoning—including deductive reasoning—cannot reveal. So, one might suggest, P->Q is simply another such case. If so, the reasoning continues, perhaps NWD requires no special explanation beyond analogies to standard Kripke cases.

But that reasoning is flawed. In particular, it ignores crucial differences between standard Kripke cases and the physical-phenomenal case (Jackson 1995, 1998, Chalmers 1996, 2010). The former are usually explained along the following lines. Hydrogen-free water is metaphysically impossible. If it seems otherwise, this is likely because we confuse claims about *water* with claims about *watery stuff*, that is, stuff with superficial qualities that are associated

---

7. We might distinguish between "non–a priori physicalists" and "a posteriori physicalists" where only the latter buy into the a priori/a posteriori distinction. Our argument concerns a posteriori physicalism. We do not claim that it can be extended to non–a priori physicalism without begging the question.

8. Barbara Montero (2013) is an exception: she argues that physicalists need not accept that claim.

with water: being drinkable, being clear, filling oceans, being the typical cause of certain sorts of experiences, etc. For example, we confuse

(1) There is water without hydrogen

with

(2) There is watery stuff without hydrogen.

Claim (2) is coherent and metaphysically possible, but it does not follow that (1) is either coherent or metaphysically possible.

So, in this and the other standard cases, explaining the a posteriori necessity involves distinguishing the phenomenon in question (e.g., water) from something with the same superficial qualities (e.g., watery stuff). In particular, the explanation involves distinguishing the phenomenon itself from how we experience it. But it is doubtful that such a distinction can be coherently drawn in the case of phenomenal consciousness. To use Kripke's example, anything that feels subjectively just like pain *is* pain. Further, because P includes *all* microphysical information, it is plausible that in principle one could deduce from P that the actual watery stuff is H_2O and thus rule out (1) by a priori reasoning from P.[9] By contrast, recognizing that P includes all microphysical information does not seem to undermine either the intuition that zombies are ideally conceivable or the intuition that Mary learns something when she leaves the black-and-white room.

Such considerations have led a posteriori physicalists to devise an alternative defense of NWD, known as the phenomenal concept strategy (Stoljar 2005). The basic idea is that the epistemic gap can be explained in psychological terms and that this undermines the anti-physicalist's inference from an epistemic to a metaphysical gap. For example, some argue that while the Mary case shows that phenomenal color concepts cannot be (non-deferentially) acquired by watching black-and-white lectures, this has no tendency to show that those concepts fail to pick out wholly physical properties—and thus that the non-apriority of P->Q does not indicate that P does not metaphysically necessitate Q (e.g., Block 2006, Loar 1997, Papineau 2002, 2007).[10]

---

9. This simplifies a bit. For example, the argument here assumes that the deducer knows a priori that "water" refers (rigidly) to the actual watery stuff. For a fuller defense and elaboration, see Jackson 1995, 1998, and especially Chalmers and Jackson 2001 and Chalmers 2012.

10. We include the "non-deferentially" qualification to circumvent the concern that one can acquire a phenomenal concept by acquiring a term others use to express that concept (Ball

While most versions of a posteriori physicalism rely on the phenomenal concept strategy, some do not (e.g., see Tye 2009 and Howell 2013). Our main argument might well apply to those other versions, but here we will not attempt to settle that issue. We will focus exclusively on versions that do rely on the phenomenal concept strategy.

Russellian Monism

Russellian monism is the view that basic physical properties have categorical phenomenal or protophenomenal features, which constitute consciousness and ground the structural dispositions described by physics. This simple statement masks a good deal of complexity. The central ideas could be expressed as follows. Physics describes the spatio-temporal dispositions and implications of a property without speaking to the categorical grounds of those dispositions and implications (Armstrong 1968, p. 282).[11] What are the categorical grounds? According to Russellian monism, they are phenomenal or protophenomenal features. Thus, the (proto)phenomenal is a fundamental feature of reality, which is deeply intertwined with the world as described by physics.

Why think physics describes only dispositional properties and not categorical properties? The idea could be put roughly as follows. Physics describes the basic features of the world in terms of their spatio-temporal implications.[12] It describes properties by describing what they do—or by what entities possessing them are disposed to do in given circumstances. Any reference to categorical bases will ultimately be explicable in terms of such dispositions, e.g., mass is what grounds an object's tendency to attract other objects, etc.

Some (Ladyman and Ross 2007) argue that the dispositional properties physics describes have no categorical bases and that none are needed—that it is, in Simon Blackburn's (1990) phrase, dispositions all the way down. Russellian monists, however, insist that underlying basic physical dispositional properties are further categorical properties. What are these further

---

2009, Tye 2009, Alter 2013b). Henceforth, we will assume that the "non-deferential" qualification is understood.

11. For two ways of cashing out the notion of structure, see Chalmers 2010, 2012, and Howell 2013.

12. This is a bit quick. For a more thorough picture of how the physicalist should construe categorical bases and dispositions, see Howell 2012. See also Chalmers 2010, where he suggests that a structural truth of the sort physics describes can be fully represented in the form of a Ramsey sentence whose O-terms include only nomic and spatio-temporal expressions (in addition to logical and mathematical terms).

properties? Some Russellian monists (e.g., Rosenberg 2004) claim that those intrinsic, categorical properties are the only such properties we know: phenomenal properties. But not all do.[13] Some Russellian monists claim that the categorical properties are more properly described as protophenomenal: categorical properties that, though not themselves phenomenal, result in phenomenal properties when combined in certain ways (Chalmers 1996, pp. 126–127).[14]

The Russellian monist may respond to the anti-physicalist arguments in different ways. She might reject the arguments' first premise, which expresses a deep epistemic gap between the physical and the phenomenal. She could do this by arguing that the physical encompasses not only structural but also the associated categorical features—and that therefore Q is deducible from P, even if Q is not deducible from only the structural truths that physics describes (Stoljar 2001). She might reject the arguments' second premise, which infers a metaphysical gap from the epistemic gap (that is, she might endorse NWD). She could do that by arguing that basic physical terms such as "mass" and "charge" refer rigidly to categorical properties but not in a way that can be discovered by a priori reflection, including a priori reflection on the meanings of those terms (Chalmers 2010). And she might accept both the epistemic and metaphysical gaps, arguing that physical truths are limited to structural truths and neither a priori imply nor metaphysically necessitate phenomenal truths (Chalmers 2010). Clearly, Russellian monism faces no threat from the anti-physicalist arguments. This is not surprising, even if some versions of

---

13. Here we gloss over a number of important issues that are not central to our main argument. For example, as Derk Pereboom (chapter 14 in this volume) notes, physics describes properties that are categorical/intrinsic in some sense (e.g., shape). But as he argues, there is another, stronger sense (which he calls "absolute intrinsicality") in which those properties are not categorical/intrinsic. It is that stronger sense that Russellian monists have in mind when they appeal to a categorical/dispositional distinction (or related distinctions). Also, the categorical/dispositional distinction is contentious. For a discussion of some of the difficulties involved in making the distinction, see Heil 2003.

14. The distinction between the phenomenalist and protophenomenalist versions of Russellian monism is significant. For example, the former would seem to entail panpsychism—if the properties physics describes are ubiquitous, then so presumably are the categorical properties that ground them—but the latter would not. Also, while the phenomenalist version of the theory seems to be at odds with physicalism, the protophenomenalist version might qualify as a version of physicalism, albeit a nonstandard version. See Barbara Montero, chapter 10 of this volume. For what it's worth, at least one of us thinks protophenomenalist versions are clearly non-physicalist, and that the matter is not really just terminological. See Howell 2013.

the theory could be categorized as physicalist. The arguments were designed to refute standard versions of physicalism, not the Russellian variety.[15]

The Collapse Argument

On the face of it, Russellian monism and a posteriori physicalism have few similarities. We suspect, though, that when a posteriori physicalists are forced to give a plausible story of how the anti-physicalist arguments go awry, their view is not only similar to Russellian monism but might count as a version of it.[16]

Here is the basic argument. Whether or not one proposition is deducible from another is not really a psychological issue, as the phenomenal concept strategy seems to suggest. The issue concerns an epistemic relationship between propositions, not how they are grasped. If so, then plausibly Q is not deducible from P at least partly because of something about the propositions themselves. In particular, Q represents phenomenal properties as having, or being based on, some categorical feature F that P does not represent them as having and that P does not a priori imply.[17] This proposal is plausible for two reasons. First, as others (e.g., Stoljar 2006, Chalmers 2010, Pereboom 2011) note, phenomenal properties present themselves as categorical (or intrinsic) in an especially strong sense. Second, given the thesis that P consists in structural truths only, the proposal would seem to explain the non-deducibility of Q from P. By contrast, the non-deducibility would remain unexplained if F were a structural property. In any event, if Q represents phenomenal properties as having categorical features, then the question arises: Is that representation accurate, i.e., do phenomenal properties have such features? NWD

---

15. For this reason, in Chalmers' (2010) refined formulations, the anti-physicalist arguments conclude not that physicalism is false but that either physicalism is false or Russellian monism is true.

16. As Chalmers (2010) has noted, certain purportedly physicalist responses to the knowledge and conceivability arguments (e.g., Stoljar 2001) simply are versions of Russellian monism. And as we noted earlier, Russellian monism can accept NWD and thus take the form of a posteriori physicalism. The collapse argument makes a different claim—that the commitments of a posteriori physicalism, together with other plausible premises, entail Russellian monism.

17. Here we assume truths/propositions (such as Q) can represent states of affairs (such as phenomenal properties having categorical features). But we do not assume any particular theory of what this representation consists in or how it is achieved. Nor do we assume any particular theory of what truths/propositions are. We do, however, assume that truths/propositions are fine-grained. For example, the proposition that Superman wears a cape is distinct from the proposition that Clark Kent wears a cape.

entails that they do. Otherwise, Q would be false. But if Q were false, then there would be no truths that are non-deducible from the physical truths, contrary to the thesis of a posteriori physicalism. So, given a posteriori physicalism, P necessitates the instantiation of the categorical features of phenomenal properties mentioned in Q. Plausibly, this necessitation is not brute, that is, there is something in virtue of which that necessitation relation obtains. But in virtue of what? It can only be in virtue of the categorical features of the physical properties described in P. If this is the case, some form of Russellian monism is true—the seeds of phenomenality are present at the fundamental level as categorical grounds of structural properties described in P. Thus, if a posteriori physicalism is true, Russellian monism is true. In numbered steps:

The collapse argument

1. If a posteriori physicalism is true and P does not *brutely* metaphysically necessitate Q, then Q represents phenomenal properties as having some categorical feature F that structural physical truths do not represent phenomenal properties as having.
2. If a posteriori physicalism is true and Q represents phenomenal properties as having F, then phenomenal properties have F.
3. If a posteriori physicalism is true and phenomenal properties have F, then either (a) P brutely metaphysically necessitates Q or (b) P metaphysically necessitates Q at least partly in virtue of categorical features of properties described in P, which are phenomenal or protophenomenal.
4. (a) is false.
5. If (b), then Russellian monism is true.
6. Therefore, if a posteriori physicalism is true, then Russellian monism is true.

This argument is valid. But it involves several contentious premises. Discussing those will reveal the costs that must be borne by the a posteriori physicalist if she is to avoid Russellian monism. We take it that premise 2 is obviously true. After all, if Q is true (as a posteriori physicalism says), then phenomenal properties must have the features Q says it has. Premise 5 is also hard to deny, but it warrants discussion. The real work is done by premises 1, 3 and 4.

Premise 5

According to premise 5, if P metaphysically necessitates Q at least partly in virtue of categorical phenomenal-or-protophenomenal features of properties described in P, Russellian monism is true. This could be resisted. One could deny, for example, that the categorical phenomenal features of basic physical properties ground their structural features (even though the latter necessitate the former), or that physics describes only structural properties, thus avoiding the letter of Russellian monism as we have characterized it. But the essence of the position is there: phenomenal-or-protophenomenal properties are categorical features of basic physical properties, and this explains the presence of consciousness. It is unlikely that a posteriori physicalists will find technical differences between this view and red book Russellian monism comforting.

Premise 1: The Attribution Premise

According to premise 1 of the collapse argument, if a posteriori physicalism is true and P does not *brutely* metaphysically necessitate Q, then Q attributes some categorical feature F to phenomenal properties that structural physical truths do not attribute to phenomenal properties. This might seem unmotivated, especially if the a posteriori physicalist explains non-deducibility in terms of phenomenal concepts. This explanation does not appear to involve a commitment to brute metaphysical necessity (where what it means for T to be brutely necessary is that T is necessary but not in virtue of any other truths). Nor does the explanation appear to entail the claim that Q represents phenomenal properties as having categorical features. So, why should premise 1 be accepted?

The main reason is this. If the phenomenal concept strategy does not involve attributing some categorical feature to phenomenal properties, then the strategy will fail to do the work a posteriori physicalists demand of it. If the strategy tries to explain non-deducibility in merely psychological terms, it will not directly address the sort of non-deducibility at issue in the anti-physicalist arguments and NWD. What needs explaining is not psychological. Rather, the explanandum is a fact about the relationship between abstract propositional contents: if P metaphysically necessitates Q, then why would it be in principle impossible for an ideal reasoner to recognize the reason that is so and thereby deduce Q from P? This might not seem puzzling if the physical-phenomenal case could be straightforwardly assimilated to standard Kripkean a posteriori necessities and if the latter were correctly understood as involving both non-deducibility and metaphysical necessitation. And if the necessitation involved were brute, then there would be no reason why P necessitates Q to be recognized. But if those options are ruled out, then NWD presents a real puzzle. And again, the puzzle seems to concern abstract propositional contents, not psychology. A psychological theory might play an important role in the solution. But the solution will be incomplete until it is shown how the theory explains the puzzling facts about abstract propositions that NWD expresses.

Phenomenal concept strategists might counter by noting that the psychological theories they advance—theories of phenomenal concepts and how they relate cognitively to physical concepts—are meant to apply no less to non-human reasoners than to humans. But that response misses the mark. The concern is not that the relevant theories are about specifically human mental processes. The concern is that the theories have the wrong subject matter.

Consider an analogy. Mathematicians might wonder whether Goldbach's conjecture is deducible from the axioms of arithmetic. Would it be adequate to respond: no, there is a psychological block between those basic axioms and Goldbach's conjecture? Surely not. The mathematicians are wondering about the relationships between the axioms and the conjecture, and facts (necessary or contingent) about psychology are beside the point. Perhaps psychological facts explain why we shouldn't try to do the deduction and expect to succeed, but it says nothing directly about non-deducibility.

We will illustrate the problem by considering the version of the phenomenal concept strategy that is based on the constitutive (or quotational) theory of phenomenal concepts (e.g., Papineau 2002, Balog 1999). On the constitutive theory, phenomenal concepts involve phenomenal qualities as constituents. Phenomenal concepts might thus be construed as having a sort of demonstrative form such as, "This phenomenal quality: ____", where the relevant phenomenal quality is determined by a sort of introspective ostension. A subject fixes the reference of such a concept by attending to the phenomenal character of certain of her experiences. This account is then used to justify the claim that the reason pre-emergence Mary cannot deduce Q from P is that she fails to possess phenomenal color concepts that Q involves. Those concepts contain instances of phenomenal color qualities, and she has not yet had experiences from which such instances could be drawn.

But that cannot be the whole story. If it were, then after Mary leaves the room and comes to possess relevant phenomenal color concepts, she should be able to a priori deduce Q from P. But intuitively, she cannot do that. She now knows what it is like to see red; she knows Q. But she still cannot deduce Q from P. Rather, her new phenomenal knowledge is based on introspection (Chalmers 2004, Stoljar 2005). Her new knowledge does not render the relationship between P and Q any more transparent than it was before. If that is not clear, then consider physically alien creatures. Even after leaving the room, Mary will not be able to deduce from a complete microphysical description of Martians, who are physically different from humans, whether they have experiences with the phenomenal qualities she now enjoys (Chalmers 2004). Even if Mary knows that some human brain process B correlates with the experience of seeing red, that will not enable her to conclusively determine whether the physical states underlying Martian experiences ever give rise to red experiences—or to any experiences at all.

The problem here is not specific to the quotational theory. Any theory that aims to explain Mary's post-emergence epistemic progress in terms of her coming to acquire phenomenal concepts will run into the same difficulty. Many versions of the phenomenal concept strategy have that aim (according to Derek Ball (2009), all do). Some versions have a different emphasis. For example, Christopher Hill (1997) argues roughly that physical and phenomenal concepts play distinct functional roles in relevant cognitive systems and that the knowledge argument confuses distinct roles for distinct properties playing those roles. But views of this sort have problems that are just as serious as the other versions. Such views ultimately seem to be claiming that we are not ideal reasoners, because the functional isolation of our ways of thinking prevents us from grasping the fact that the phenomenal truths are in fact deducible from the complete physical truth.

That psychological theories fall short is not surprising if, as we have said, what demands explanation is a fact about the relationship between abstract propositional contents—the non-deducibility of Q from P—not (at least in the first instance) how those propositions are grasped. Premise 1 offers a natural explanation for that fact: Q represents consciousness as having features that P does not represent consciousness as having. And partly because P is so comprehensive—it is the *complete* physical truth—it is hard to see what else those features could be other than categorical features.

Premise 1 is perfectly compatible with the claim that Mary comes to acquire phenomenal color concepts only post-emergence. This premise is also compatible with the theories phenomenal concept strategists offer to explain why she does not acquire them while still in the room—theories such as the constitutional theory. Indeed, those theories might help explain why Q represents as it does. But on premise 1, it is not those theories but rather Q's representational content itself that explains the non-deducibility of this proposition from P.[18]

---

18. Chalmers (2007) argues that any psychological theory that phenomenal concept strategists invoke in defense of (what we call) NWD will either fail to explain our epistemic situation or fail to be physically explicable. If his argument succeeds, then this may be for a reason that we have emphasized in defense of premise 1 of the collapse argument: that what demands explanation are facts about the relationship between abstract propositional contents, not how those propositions are grasped.

Premise 3: The Necessitation of Categorical Properties

Premise 3 says that if a posteriori physicalism is true and phenomenal properties have F, then either (a) P brutely metaphysically necessitates Q or (b) P metaphysically necessitates Q at least partly in virtue of categorical features of properties described in P, which are phenomenal or protophenomenal. A lot is packed into this premise, but it all boils down to the following claims. If P necessitates Q, and the necessitation is not brute, then there is ultimately an explanation for the necessitation. This means that there must be something about the properties in P that necessitates the existence of properties with categorical phenomenal natures. Merely structural properties cannot necessitate categorical properties except partly by virtue of their categorical properties. So, P must describe properties that have categorical natures which necessitate the existence of phenomenality. That is just to say that these natures must be at least protophenomenal.

Why accept those claims? If the explanation for why P necessitated Q did not involve categorical features of properties described in P, then presumably the explanatory resources would be limited to those involved in the structural truths contained in P. But by hypothesis, those structural truths neither a priori imply truths about F nor represent phenomenal properties as having F. It is hard to see why such structural truths alone should metaphysically necessitate Q. This might be easier to see if the necessitation involved were, say, nomological. In that case, the explanation might appeal to contingent laws connecting the structural properties described in P with F. The conjunction of such laws and P might well a priori entail Q. But the necessitation in question does not depend on contingent laws. It is metaphysical necessitation. If contingent laws connecting structural properties with F are left aside, the connection between P and Q will, it seems, remain opaque. Or rather, that connection will remain opaque unless appeal is made to categorical features of structural properties described in P. Presumably, such categorical features of structural properties would bear precisely the sort of intimate connection to F that would account for P's metaphysically necessitating Q.

The foregoing reasoning suggests the following result. If P metaphysically necessitates Q in an explicable (non-brute) way, then, given that NWD is true and phenomenal properties have F, the necessitation holds at least partly in virtue of categorical features of structural properties described in P. To vindicate premise 3, it remains to be shown that those categorical features are phenomenal or protophenomenal. But it is hard to see how that conclusion could be avoided. If those features were neither phenomenal nor protophenomenal, then how else could they help explain how P necessitates Q? They need not be phenomenal, to be sure. But why wouldn't they qualify as at least protophenomenal? Remember, protophenomenal properties are not themselves phenomenal—they are defined as properties that result in phenomenal properties when appropriately combined. What exactly might be involved in the combination is left unspecified. So, the way that relevant categorical features help explain how P necessitates Q would presumably qualify as an appropriate manner of combination. If there is a problem with premise 3, it is doubtful that is resides in the final clause.

Premise 4: The Anti-Bruteness Premise

The collapse argument depends on the claim that categorical (proto)phenomenal bases of structural properties found in physics must be posited because otherwise the necessitation between P and Q would be inexplicable. If, however, that necessitation is brute, then no such explanation is needed. Premise 4 denies that this option is available.

The claim that 4 denies is not the epistemic claim that we are in no position to detect or comprehend the reason P necessitates Q, but rather that this necessitation does not obtain in virtue of any other fact—and in particular it is not explicable by some deep feature of the facts represented by P and Q. To illustrate the nature of that claim, consider a thought experiment. Suppose God stipulates that in all possible worlds where one thing obtains, so does another. So, for example, imagine that he just set everything up so that wherever there were physical systems of a certain degree of complexity there would be phenomenal states. He could stipulate that this was necessary, ensuring that this was true of every possible world. In some sense, this necessity would still not be brute—it would be in virtue of another fact, God's decision. But God here is just a heuristic. Let us take this scenario and just subtract God from the picture: the necessity that our God would set up simply obtains. This is a brute necessity.

We will argue that such brute necessitation is incoherent. But even if we are wrong about that, two things should be noted. First, if NWD is based in brute necessitation then all the talk about phenomenal concepts is unnecessary. They are introduced to explain why we cannot see the necessitation. But if the necessitation is brute such explanations aren't needed—the necessitation itself cannot be explained. Second, even if brute necessities existed, it is not clear that it would help a posteriori physicalism. Arguably, if qualitative states appear by virtue of such necessities, we have a form of dualistic emergentism, not physicalism. The qualitative features of the world do not in this case share a nature with the physical world—they are simply attached to it with modal super-glue. Physicalism should require more than just this sort of brute necessitation.

Physicalists differ on what it requires—superdupervenience (Horgan 1993), realization (Melnyk 2003), or inherited causal powers (Wilson 2005)—but a simple correlation, even if it is necessary, is not enough to secure monism of any sort, including physicalism.

It is imaginable, perhaps, that an a posteriori physicalist could endorse a brute necessitation relation that didn't hold between basic physical properties and non-physical qualia. We're not confident about what this would look like, and it might be that no one explicitly endorses it. But our purpose is in part to determine the logical space a posteriori physicalists can occupy. To do this, we need to be clear about why there is a problem with brute necessities themselves, and not just with the existence of brutely necessitated qualia in a wholly physical world.

Suppose there is a property E that gives rise necessarily to property C. Can it really be the case that this is all there is to say? Can it really be that this necessitation is not in virtue of some other fact? This is suspicious. Properties are at least in part individuated by what they necessitate. Suppose E gives rise to C in every possible world. Consider E*, which is just like E but does not give rise to C in every possible world. What distinguishes E from E*? At the very least it is the necessary fact about it that it gives rise to C. This seems to be a disposition possessed by E that is part of what makes it the property it is. If one studied properties of type E but failed to see this fact, one would not know something crucial about E's, namely, that which distinguishes them from E*'s.

One might be tempted to respond that this simply ignores the point of brute necessities and ignores the thought experiment we described earlier. God didn't have to change anything about a physical property X to make it the case that X was paired with a phenomenal property Y in every possible world. X retained its nature, and God just set the correlation across worlds. No disposition was added.

As it is told, this story does not appear to outline a coherent scenario. It seems to depend upon the confused idea that there is just a sort of modal accident in which every X world gets a Y. But there is no such thing as a modal accident in the relevant sense.[19] The space of possible worlds is necessarily what it is. It makes no sense to say it could possibly be otherwise, since talk of possibilities itself is grounded in the space of possible worlds (unless

---

19. Some (Almog 1991, Fine 1994) argue that there are properties that objects have in all possible worlds that are not part of the essential natures of those objects. In Fine's example, Socrates is a member of the set Singleton-Socrates in all possible worlds, but being a member of that set is not part of his essential nature. But these would be modal accidents in a different sense.

one equivocates on "possible"). One cannot simply posit a total distribution of worlds as a possibility—that distribution either necessarily is, or it necessarily is not. One can, perhaps, locate a possible subset of such worlds where there is an accidental match between X's and Y's, but if the match is indeed accidental, there will be other worlds where it does not occur, and there will not, therefore, be necessitation between X and Y.

This point can be put more forcefully in terms of the thought experiment in which God set Y's in every world with X's. The question is, did God have to make things this way or not? If he could have decided to have an X world without a Y, then it is possible that there is an X without a Y, and in fact X's do not necessitate Y's. If he could not have broken the pairing, why would that be? Presumably for the same reason he cannot make squares without corners—his hand was forced by the natures of the properties in question.

If this is right, the idea of brute necessitation is not fully coherent. It is on par with the notion of accidental necessities—it appears coherent only if one restricts one's focus, either equivocating on "possible" or ignoring the nature of the properties involved (Howell 2013).

Objections and Replies
Objection 1

Premise 3 says that if a posteriori physicalism is true and phenomenal properties have F, then either (a) *P* brutely metaphysically necessitates *Q* or (b) *P* metaphysically necessitates *Q* at least partly in virtue of categorical features of properties described in *P*, which are phenomenal or protophenomenal. Earlier we suggested that there is little basis for rejecting the last clause, that on (b) the relevant features are phenomenal or protophenomenal. After all, we noted, if such features are not phenomenal, then they would presumably qualify as protophenomenal simply because the way in which they help explain how *P* necessitates *Q* could qualify as an appropriate manner of combination. However, there might seem to be room for a third option here, on which the relevant features are neither phenomenal nor protophenomenal. Indeed, Pereboom (2011) provides an example of a categorical feature that might seem to fit the bill: *categorical solidity*. Categorical solidity is the categorical basis of ordinary solidity, which is dispositional (ordinary solidity can be roughly characterized as the tendency to resist penetration). He writes that Locke and Newton regarded categorical solidity as "the categorical property of matter" (p. 98).

On further reflection, however, it is not clear that categorical solidity will suffice for this purpose or that there is even room for a third option. To begin with, the notion of categorical solidity might be incoherent. The problem does not reside in the suggestion that ordinary solidity has a categorical basis but rather in the idea that this basis is a sort of solidity: a categorical sort. Is there a categorical sort of solubility too?[20] Also, Pereboom says almost nothing about the nature of categorical solidity beyond its being the categorical basis of ordinary solidity. So, why should we be confident that it is not phenomenal (Alter, 2013a)?

But leave those two concerns aside. Even if categorical solidity is coherent and non-phenomenal, why conclude that it is not protophenomenal? Presumably, the reasoning is this. Although categorical solidity helps explain how P metaphysically necessitates Q, this feature does not satisfy the descriptions usually given of protophenomenal properties. Such properties are usually described as non-phenomenal intrinsic properties that result in phenomenal properties when appropriately combined (compare Pereboom 2011, p. 4, Chalmers 2010). Categorical solidity does not fit such descriptions, the argument runs, because combining instances of categorical solidity alone (if that even makes sense) would not result in phenomenal properties. Producing phenomenality requires combining categorical solidity with other properties, such as the structural properties described in P.

But that argument is unconvincing. It is true that our description of protophenomenal properties, which is typical of those found in the literature, might seem to suggest that protophenomenal properties can combine to yield phenomenal properties without the involvement of structural properties described in P. But there is no need to accept that suggestion. Instead, it

---

20. Pereboom suggests that categorical solidity is no more obscure than other categorical properties that many philosophers would countenance. For example, he says, many maintain that our desires involve an intrinsic component that helps explain our dispositions to act in certain ways, despite their knowing that this view faces a formidable challenge from Hume's attack on the idea of causal power. He writes, "Perhaps the phenomenological feel of a desire directly acquaints us with such an explanatory component. Isolating it seems neither more nor less difficult than distinguishing the tendency-explaining or categorical component of solidity" (Pereboom 2011, p. 99). But that last claim is questionable. Desires have neural bases. Why can't this be used to help isolate the relevant explanatory component? Also, the phenomenological feel of a desire might help in this regard more than Pereboom suggests. By itself, the feel does not show that a desire explains anything. But the feel might help isolate a desire's intrinsic nature, which might do the explanatory work. By contrast, our grasp of categorical solidity seems minimal at best.

One might try to explicate the notion of categorical solidity in terms of the idea of occupying a region of spacetime. That an electron e occupies a certain spacetime region r might seem categorical. But even this is not so clear. Arguably, what it means in physics for e to occupy r is roughly that there are certain patterns of attraction and repulsion at r with respect to other entities in r and other spacetime regions; at least, something like that is all that physics seems to describe.

should be allowed that protophenomenal properties yield phenomenal properties only when appropriately combined with certain structural properties. And if this is allowed, then there is no clear reason why categorical solidity should not quality as protophenomenal. Plausibly, it is protophenomenal if it plays an essential role in P's metaphysically necessitating Q. The same point applies for other candidates. As long as it is allowed that combining protophenomenal properties results in phenomenal properties only in the presence of certain structural properties, then any candidate for the relevant categorical features of properties described in P will be protophenomenal if not phenomenal.

Objection 2

Premise 1 begs the question against a certain sort of phenomenal concept strategist. We have been insisting that there must be a difference in what properties the phenomenal concepts attribute and the properties that the scientific concepts attribute. But the best version of the phenomenal concept theory will not agree to this. Phenomenal concepts are different only in their psychological and inferential role in the subject's mind, not in their conditions of satisfaction or what they attribute/represent. It is unreasonable, therefore, to respond that these theories imply we are not ideal reasoners. Either ideal reasoners can have phenomenal concepts (as described by the psychological phenomenal concepts theorist) or they can't. If they can't, then we can easily explain why ideal reasoners can't perform the relevant deduction (despite the necessitation). If they can, then these concepts must have the features characteristic of phenomenal concepts, namely their psychological and inferential features. And the latter will explain the non-deducibility.

Reply

Although we have qualms with the objector's account of phenomenal concepts, the objector is right that insisting that phenomenal and physical concepts differ in attributive (representational/semantic) respects might beg the question in this context. Still, we contend there is significant reason to think a purely inferential difference fails to capture what is unique about phenomenal knowledge.

The phenomenal concept strategy (indeed, any strategy for defending a posteriori physicalism) should explain two things. One is the fact that Q

cannot be a priori deduced from P, even though P necessitates Q. This is not enough, however. The strategy also must explain the intuition that Mary learns something substantial when leaving her room. Inferential-role differences between phenomenal and physical concepts might explain the former but will not explain the latter. Why would Mary have an aha-moment unless the world appeared to her to be a certain way that it had not appeared before? If the two sorts of concepts were attributively the same, whence her surprise? Even if inferential-role differences would explain there being some sense in which she learns something new, this alone should not bring any surprises unless the world appears to be a different way. Perhaps we should individuate concepts according to inferential role or some other sorts of psychological difference. Nonetheless, there is a difference between concepts that differ in attributive features and those that do not. Suppose when Mary walked out of the room she suddenly lost the ability to perform certain inferences with a concept. It is not clear that she would even notice. Perhaps she would notice when she tried to perform those inferences. But whatever surprise this engenders, it is not the sort of surprise we expect Mary to experience when seeing red for the first time.[21]

Objection 3

We have overlooked a simple, obvious explanation of why P necessitates Q: phenomenal properties are identical with physical properties, and identity is necessary.

Reply

According to premise 1, Q represents phenomenal properties as having some categorical feature F that structural physical truths do not represent phenomenal properties as having. Even if F is identical with a physical property G, G is not a property attributed by the physical truths. This is just Russellian monism again—the part of the physical which explains the necessitation of the phenomenal truths is an intrinsic, categorical feature that is not described by physics.

---

21. At this point a posteriori physicalism begins to resemble the answer given to the knowledge argument by the ability hypothesis (Lewis 1988, Nemirow 1990). This hypothesis has its own problems, but to the point here is that it is usually not considered an example of a posteriori physicalism.

Conclusions

We claim that if a posteriori physicalists are to adequately account for NWD, they must ultimately accept that there are categorical phenomenal or proto-phenomenal features of basic physical properties that are not described by physics but that explain the presence of phenomenal consciousness. The reason is that if the phenomenal truths really are non-deducible from the physical truths, this must be because the phenomenal truths entail that there are categorical phenomenal-or-protophenomenal properties. Such properties cannot be necessitated by dispositional, structural properties of the sort described in physics. So, brute metaphysical necessitation notwithstanding, the necessitation must be in virtue of categorical features of base physical properties. But if a categorical base property necessitates a categorical phenomenal property in a non-brute manner, the former must be at least protophenomenal.

This argument is not obvious. And again, there are principled ways it can be resisted. Here we should emphasize *principled*. One cannot plausibly respond to the argument by, for example, merely asserting that a posteriori physicalism might be combined with a purely structuralist view on which there are no (instantiated) fundamental properties beyond the structural ones described by ideal physics. First, it is unclear that the latter structuralist view can ultimately be reconciled with NWD (more specifically, with the non-deducibility of the phenomenal from the physical). Second, even if that structuralist view can be reconciled with NWD, the challenge to *explain* NWD remains.

Further, one possible source of resistance is simply confused. We suspect that some physicalists vacillate between two views, neither of which are compatible with a posteriori physicalism:

> *Psychologically Pessimistic A Priori Physicalism*: The phenomenal truths are deducible from the physical truths in our idealized sense of deducibility, but we cannot ourselves perform the deduction because of psychological facts about us.
> *Brute Emergentism*: The phenomenal truths are not deducible from the physical truths because the necessitation involved between the two is a brute metaphysical necessity with no explanation in the nature of the physical properties.

We suggest that when these two views are taken off the table, the a posteriori physicalist will find the slide to Russellian monism hard to resist.

Perhaps some a posteriori physicalists will not mind that result. Paradigmatic a posteriori physicalist David Papineau (2002, pp. 22–23, fn.

5) indicates that he regards the version of Russellian monism Chalmers (1996) describes as "the optimal form of materialism." But Papineau's opinion is not widely shared. One indication of this is that most a posteriori physicalists feel obligated to reject arguments such as the knowledge and conceivability argument—even though those arguments pretty clearly do not threaten Russellian monism. In any event, we suspect most a posteriori physicalists will find the slide to Russellian monism contrary to their goal of saving a physicalist ontology.[22]

References

Almog, J. (1991) "The What and the How," *Journal of Philosophy* 88, pp. 225–44.

Alter, T. (2013a) "*Consciousness and the Prospects of Physicalism*, by Derk Pereboom," *Mind* 121, pp. 1115–22.

Alter, T. (2013b) "Social Externalism and the Knowledge Argument," *Mind* 122, pp. 481–96.

Alter, T. and Nagasawa, Y. (2012) "What Is Russellian Monism?," *Journal of Consciousness Studies* 19, pp. 67–95.

Armstrong, D. (1968) *A Materialist Theory of Mind*, New York: Humanities Press.

Ball, D. (2009) "There Are No Phenomenal Concepts," *Mind* 118, pp. 935–62.

Balog, K. (1999) "Conceivability, Possibility, and the Mind-Body Problem," *Philosophical Review* 108, pp. 497–528.

Blackburn, S. (1990) "Filling in Space," *Analysis* 50, pp. 62–65.

Block, N. (2006) "Max Black's Objection to Mind-Body Identity," in Zimmerman, D. (ed.) *Oxford Studies in Metaphysics* 2, New York: Oxford University Press, pp. 3–78. Also in Alter, T. and Walter, S. (eds.) *Phenomenal Concepts and Phenomenal Knowledge: New Essays on Consciousness and Physicalism*, New York: Oxford University Press, pp. 249–306.

Chalmers, D. J. (1996) *The Conscious Mind: In Search of a Fundamental Theory*, New York: Oxford University Press.

Chalmers, D. J. (2002) "Does Conceivability Entail Possibility?," in Gendler, T. and Hawthorne, J. (eds.) *Conceivability and Possibility*, New York: Oxford University Press, pp. 145–200.

Chalmers, D. J. (2004) "Phenomenal Concepts and the Knowledge Argument," in Ludlow, P., Nagasawa, Y., and Stoljar, D. (eds.) *There's Something about Mary: Essays on Phenomenal Consciousness and Frank Jackson's Knowledge Argument*, Cambridge: MIT Press, pp. 269–98.

---

22. For helpful suggestions, we thank David Chalmers, Philippe Chuard, Justin Fisher, Yujin Nagasawa, Derk Pereboom, and Brad Thompson.

Chalmers, D. J. (2007) "Phenomenal Concepts and the Explanatory Gap," in Alter, T. and Walter, S. (eds.) *Phenomenal Concepts and Phenomenal Knowledge: New Essays on Consciousness and Physicalism*, pp. 167–94.

Chalmers, D. J. (2010) *The Character of Consciousness*, New York: Oxford University Press.

Chalmers, D. J. (2012) *Constructing the World*, Oxford: Oxford University Press.

Chalmers, D. J. (chapter 12 of this volume), "Panpsychism and Panprotopsychism."

Chalmers, D. J. and Jackson, F. (2001) "Conceptual Analysis and Reductive Explanation," *Philosophical Review* 110, pp. 315–61.

Fine, K. (1994) "Essence and Modality," *Philosophical Perspectives* 8, pp. 1–16.

Heil, J. (2003) *From an Ontological Point of View*, New York: Oxford University Press.

Hill, C. (1997) "Imaginability, Conceivability, Possibility, and the Mind-Body Problem," *Philosophical Studies*, 87, pp. 61–85.

Horgan, T. (1993) "From Supervenience to Superdupervenience: Meeting the Demands of a Material World," *Mind* 102, pp. 555–86.

Howell, R. J. (2012) "Physicalism, Old School," in Alter, T. and Howell, R. J. (eds.) *Consciousness and the Mind-Body Problem: A Reader*, New York: Oxford University Press, pp. 337–48.

Howell, R. J. (2013) *Consciousness and Objectivity: The Case for Subjective Physicalism*, Oxford: Oxford University Press.

Jackson, F. (1982) "Epiphenomenal Qualia," *Philosophical Quarterly* 32, pp. 127–36.

Jackson, F. (1995) "Postscript," in Moser and Trout (eds.) *Contemporary Materialism: A Reader*, New York: Routledge, pp. 184–89.

Jackson, F. (1998) *From Metaphysics to Ethics: A Defence of Conceptual Analysis*, New York: Oxford University Press.

Kripke, S. (1972) "Naming and Necessity," in Harman, G. and Davidson, D. (eds.) *The Semantics of Natural Language*, Dordrecht: Reidel, pp. 253–355.

Ladyman, J., and Ross, D. (with D. Spurrett, and J. Collier) (2007) *Every Thing Must Go: Metaphysics Naturalized*, New York: Oxford University Press.

Lewis, D. (1988) "What Experience Teaches," *Proceedings of the Russellian Society*, Sydney: University of Sydney, reprinted in Lycan, W. 1990. (ed.) *Mind and Cognition: A Reader*, Cambridge: Basil Blackwell, pp. 499–518.

Loar, B. (1997) "Phenomenal States," in Block, Flanagan, and Güzeldere, *The Nature of Consciousness: Philosophical Debates*, Cambridge: MIT Press, pp. 597–616. Adapted from a version in *Philosophical Perspectives*, 4, 1990.

Maxwell, G. (1978) "Rigid Designators and Mind-Brain Identity," *Minnesota Studies in the Philosophy of Science* 9, pp. 365–403.

Melnyk, A. (2003) *A Physicalist Manifesto*, Cambridge: Cambridge University Press.

Montero, B. (2013) "Must Physicalism Imply the Supervenience of the Mental on the Physical?," *Journal of Philosophy* 110, pp. 95–110.

Montero, B. (chapter 10 of this volume) "Russellian Physicalism."

Nagel, T. (1974) "What Is It Like to Be a Bat?," *Philosophical Review* 83, pp. 435–50.

Nemirow, L. (1990) "Physicalism and the Cognitive Role of Acquaintance," Lycan, W. 1990. (ed.) *Mind and Cognition: A Reader*, Cambridge: Basil Blackwell, pp. 490–99.

Papineau, D. (2002) *Thinking about Consciousness*, New York: Oxford University Press.

Papineau, D. (2007) "Phenomenal and Perceptual Concepts," In Alter, T. and Walter, S. (eds.) *Phenomenal Concepts and Phenomenal Knowledge: New Essays on Consciousness and Physicalism*, pp. 111–44.

Pereboom, D. (1994) "Bats, Brain Scientists, and the Limitations of Introspection," *Philosophy and Phenomenological Research* 54, pp. 315–29.

Pereboom, D. (2011) *Consciousness and the Prospects of Physicalism*, New York: Oxford University Press.

Rosenberg, G. (2004) *A Place for Consciousness: Probing the Deep Structure of the Natural World*, New York: Oxford University Press.

Russell, B. (1927) *The Analysis of Matter*, London: Kegan Paul.

Schaffer, J. (2010) "Monism: The Priority of the Whole," *Philosophical Review* 119, pp. 31–76.

Stoljar, D. (2001) "Two Conceptions of the Physical," *Philosophy and Phenomenological Research* 62, pp. 253–81.

Stoljar, D. (2005) "Physicalism and Phenomenal Concepts," *Mind and Language* 20, pp. 469–94.

Stoljar, D. (2006) *Ignorance and Imagination: The Epistemic Origin of the Problem of Consciousness*, New York: Oxford University Press.

Tye, M. (2009) *Consciousness Revisited: Materialism without Phenomenal Concepts*, Cambridge, MA: MIT Press.

Wilson, J. (2005) "Supervenience Formulations of Physicalism," *Nous* 39, pp. 426–59.

14

Consciousness, Physicalism, and Absolutely Intrinsic Properties

Derk Pereboom

THERE'S A FAIRLY widespread consensus that it's initially reasonable to believe that consciousness is not a fundamental phenomenon, and that there are thus more fundamental features of reality that underlie and explain it. Contemporary physics encourages the hypothesis that the fundamental features of reality are physical; candidates include particles, forces, and quantum fields. But at the same time, there are serious considerations, such as the conceivability argument (explained below) that count against the view that anything physical of the sort we can now understand accounts for consciousness. This situation gives rise to the hypothesis that the account must consist at least in part in presently unknown fundamental features of reality. Add to this that the history of philosophy has witnessed a strong predilection for ontological monism, that is, for thinking that the world has fundamental features only of a single sort—materialism and idealism are cases in point. These motivations give rise to a proposal in which both consciousness and the physical features encountered in contemporary physics are grounded in presently unknown fundamental features of a single kind. This view is known as Russellian Monism, named for one of its proponents, Bertrand Russell.[1]

One specific Russellian Monist proposal involves the notions of dispositional and categorical properties. Dispositional properties are essentially tendencies to produce certain effects, and while categorical properties may have powers to produce effects, they are not essentially tendencies to produce

---

1. Russell (1927); the classic passage is on p. 384.

them. Fragility and flammability are clear examples of dispositional properties; shape and size are often cited as paradigmatic categorical properties. Many find it intuitive that categorical properties are required to account for dispositional properties. For instance, a ball's disposition to roll requires an explanation, and it is provided by its categorical properties of spherical shape and rigidity.[2] The more specific Russellian monist proposal then is this: the most basic properties contemporary physics reveals are all dispositional, and thus it leaves us ignorant of the categorical properties needed to explain them. But these unknown categorical properties account for consciousness. An electron's negative charge is one of those basic physical properties, and it is a disposition to repel other particles with negative charge and to attract particles with positive charge. This dispositional property must have a categorical basis, and it, the Russellian Monist hypothesizes, is the sort of feature that can also account for our consciousness. Russellian Monists have proposed a range of such more fundamental but yet undiscovered properties—from conscious properties of, for instance, microphysical particles, to properties similar enough to paradigmatic physical properties to qualify as physical themselves, to properties unlike any we've ever encountered, but capable of explaining consciousness.

According to the version of Russellian Monism that I set out in *Consciousness and the Prospects of Physicalism*, the yet-to-be discovered properties crucial to explaining consciousness are of the second sort, close enough in kind to our paradigmatic physical properties to count as physical.[3] What distinguishes this version is that these currently unknown properties are not only categorical but also intrinsic—that is, nonrelational—in a certain demanding sense. In what follows I explain and defend my proposal.[4]

Russellian Monism and Chalmers's Conceivability Argument

First, what reason do we have to believe that the kinds of physical properties that are revealed by current physics cannot account for consciousness? Historically, the most prominent justification for anti-physicalist views of this

---

2. Fara (2009).

3. Pereboom (2011), pp. 85–122.

4. For valuable characterizations of Russellian Monism that differ from mine in some respects, see Alter and Nagasawa (2012), and Stoljar (2012).

sort is provided by conceivability arguments against physicalism. Conceivability arguments, advanced by René Descartes and more recently by Saul Kripke and David Chalmers, propose first that certain mental truths can be conceived absent relevant physical truths or that relevant physical truths can be conceived without certain mental truths, then derive from this that such situations are metaphysically possible, and conclude that physicalism is false.[5] Such arguments assume that if physicalism is true, the complete physical truth will metaphysically necessitate all the mental truths, and this assumption is generally accepted by all parties. Thus if the conceived situations are indeed shown to be metaphysically possible, it will be generally accepted that physicalism is false.

Chalmers's influential version focuses on the phenomenal aspect of consciousness, the paradigm case of which is a subject's being in a sensory state, such as sensing red, where there is something it is like for that subject to be in that state.[6] In short, Chalmers's argument hinges on the claim that it is conceivable, in an appropriately sophisticated way, that a world that is (nothing but) an exact physical duplicate of the actual world features no phenomenal consciousness. From this premise, the argument reasons to the conclusion that the complete physical truth does not necessitate the complete phenomenal truth, or even any phenomenal truth, and that therefore physicalism is false. But a notable feature of Chalmers's version of the argument is that it allows for Russellian Monism as a potential escape from its anti-physicalist conclusion, and for this reason it is especially pertinent to our discussion.

A factor that gives rise to complexity in Chalmers's argument is that not all conceivable situations are metaphysically possible. Sometimes a subject can conceive a situation only because he is deficient in reasoning, as when someone conceives of a right triangle the square of whose hypotenuse is not equal to the sum of the squares of each of the two sides.[7] Such conceiving is less than ideal. Or else, as Kripke contends, it may be that what is really being conceived is mischaracterized, for example when someone reports that she is conceiving of water that is not H_2O but is really conceiving of something that merely appears to be water or only has the evident causal role water has in our

---

5. *Meditations on First Philosophy*, in Descartes (1984), vol. 2, p. 54 (AT VII 78); "Fourth Replies," in Descartes (1984), vol. 2, pp. 154–62 (AT VII 219–31); Kripke (1980), pp. 144–53; Bealer (2002). For an exposition of Descartes's argument, see Wilson (1978); Yablo (1991); Rozemond (1998); Almog (2002).

6. Nagel (1974).

7. This is the example Antoine Arnauld directs at Descartes's conceivability argument for dualism; "Fourth Objections," in Descartes (1984), vol. 2, p. 142 (AT VII 202).

world. Chalmers aims to ensure that none of the available ways of explaining how deficiency in conceivability fails to establish metaphysical possibility applies to the conceivability of a physical duplicate of the actual world without phenomenal consciousness, and that his argument therefore features sound reasoning to the conclusion that such a world is metaphysically possible.

Chalmers's argument involves the following elements: 'P' is a statement that details the complete microphysical truth about the actual world; 'T' is a "that's all" provision, so that 'PT' specifies all the physical truths about the actual world with the stipulation that there are no further truths (that is, other than those entailed by those physical truths); and 'Q' is an arbitrary phenomenal truth—let's suppose it's 'Mary senses red at time t'. Statement S is ideally conceivable when it is conceivable on ideal rational reflection. S is primarily possible just in case it is true in some world considered as actual, and S is secondarily possible just in case S is true in some world considered as counterfactual. Accordingly, S is primarily conceivable just in case S can be conceived as true in some world considered as actual, or alternatively, since considering-as-actual is an a priori matter, S is primarily conceivable just in case the subject can't rule out S a priori.

With these elements in place, we can now state the argument:

(1) 'PT and ~ Q' is ideally primarily conceivable.
(2) If 'PT and ~ Q' is ideally primarily conceivable, then 'PT and ~ Q' is primarily possible.
(3) If 'PT and ~ Q' is primarily possible, then 'PT and ~ Q' is secondarily possible or Russellian monism is true.
(4) If 'PT and ~ Q' is secondarily possible, materialism is false.

_____

(C) Materialism is false or Russellian monism is true.[8]

It's a crucial feature of the argument as Chalmers sees it that 'PT and ~ Q' is primarily conceivable for a subject just in case she can't rule it out a priori. Further, in his view, a subject can rule 'PT and ~ Q' out a priori just in case she can a priori derive 'Q' from 'PT.' Chalmers's Russellian Monist thought is that a subject can ideally primarily conceive 'PT and ~ Q' (that is, conceive it as true in some world considered as actual) only because she is conceiving just dispositional properties on the physical side. If 'P' were replaced with

_____

8. Chalmers (2002b).

an embellished 'P*' that includes concepts that allow for direct representation of the natures of the currently unknown categorical properties, the resulting 'P*T and ~ Q' would not be ideally primarily conceivable. For although 'Q'—'Mary senses red at time t'—is not a priori derivable from 'PT', this claim about Mary's phenomenal experience would be a priori derivable from 'P*.'[9]

Absolutely Intrinsic Properties

Let me now outline the version of Russellian Monism I develop in *Consciousness and the Prospects of Physicalism*. It's a historical story that begins with Leibniz and features the contrast between intrinsic/nonrelational and extrinsic/relational properties.[10] Leibniz contends that a conception of the physical world that does not include intrinsic properties of a certain fundamental sort is in an important sense incomplete.[11] In his view, an examination of Descartes's theory of matter, according to which the essence of matter is just extension in three spatial dimensions, reveals why this is so.[12] Leibniz contends that this theory is unsatisfactory for the reason that extension is in an important sense an extrinsic property, and that any real thing cannot feature only properties that are extrinsic in this way, but must possess intrinsic properties as well: "there is no denomination so extrinsic that it does not have an intrinsic denomination at its basis. This is itself one of my important doctrines."[13]

Leibniz's contention indicates that he assumes that properties can be more and less extrinsic. Note first that it's plausible that extrinsic properties can have intrinsic components. For example, *being wise* is an extrinsic property of Sophie because it involves a relation to a comparison class: she

9. The idea is that the a priori derivability of 'Mary senses red at time t' from 'P*T' will be on a par with the a priori derivability of 'there is water' from 'PT.' As a result, just as 'PT and there is no water' is not ideally primarily conceivable, 'P*T and Mary does not sense red at t' will not be ideally primarily conceivable. For more on this idea, see Alter and Nagasawa (2012), pp. 85–86.

10. There is considerable literature on how to characterize intrinsic and extrinsic properties more exactly. For comprehensive discussions, see Humberstone (1996), and Weatherson and Marshall (2013).

11. The material in this section is a revision of the account I set out in Pereboom (1991a, 1991b).

12. Descartes, *Principles of Philosophy*, Part II, 1–22, in Descartes (1984), pp. 223–32 (AT VIII, 40–52).

13. Leibniz to de Volder, April 1702, in Leibniz (1969) (hereafter: Loemker), pp. 526–27; Leibniz (1965) (hereafter: Gerhardt II), p. 240.

is wiser than Bill, Jane, and so on. But *being wise* also includes an intrinsic component—having a certain type and level of intelligence. Thus *being wise* is a complex property that has at least one extrinsic and one intrinsic component. It is therefore not a *purely* extrinsic property, which might be defined in this way:

> P is a *purely extrinsic property* of X just in case P is an extrinsic property of X and P has no intrinsic components.

Being one among many is a credible example of a purely extrinsic property—of a point in space, for instance.

To Leibniz's charge against Descartes, one might reply that properties like *having such-and-such an extension* and *being spherical* are paradigmatically intrinsic properties of things. But Leibniz has in mind that a sphere's extension is not intrinsic to it in a more demanding sense. He maintains that there is a respect in which the extension of a thing is extrinsic:[14]

> Nor do I think that extension can be conceived in itself, but I consider it an analyzable and relative concept, for it can be resolved into plurality, continuity, and coexistence or the existence of parts at one and the same time.[15]

The extension of the sphere can be analyzed as, or reduces to, the plurality, continuity, and coexistence of parts of the sphere. Properties of each of these three sorts are purely extrinsic properties of these parts. *Being one of several things, being spatially continuous with other things*, and *coexisting temporally with other things* are all purely extrinsic properties of their bearers. Thus it may be that P is an intrinsic property of X, while P is not in a sense fundamentally intrinsic to X, or, as James van Cleve points out, in Kant's terminology, *absolutely* intrinsic to X.[16] This is the case when X's having P can be analyzed as, or reduces to, X's parts having properties Q, R, S ... , and these properties are purely extrinsic properties of these parts. Correlatively, when P *can* be analyzed as or reduces to purely extrinsic properties of these parts, it is instead, in Kant's vocabulary, merely *comparatively* intrinsic. But it's best to avoid the

---

14. Alyssa Ney makes this point in Ney (2007), p. 50. She also suggests that the next move to make is to define a more fundamental notion of intrinsic property.

15. Leibniz to De Volder, April 1699, Loemker, p. 516 = Gerhardt II, pp. 169–70.

16. Kant (1929/1987), A277/B333; van Cleve (1988).

notions of analysis and reduction in characterizing these properties. Even if for general reasons supporting anti-reductionism, properties of a whole fail to be analyzable in terms of or to reduce to properties of its parts, an intrinsic property of the whole could still be merely comparatively intrinsic.[17] We can instead appeal to the notion of (upward) necessitation in setting out these notions:

> P is an *absolutely intrinsic* property of X just in case P is an intrinsic property of X, and P is not necessitated by purely extrinsic properties of parts of X.

By contrast,

> P is a *comparatively intrinsic* property of X just in case P is an intrinsic property of X, and P is necessitated by purely extrinsic properties of parts of X.

Leibniz then argues, in effect, that every substantial entity has at least one absolutely intrinsic property, and thus, contrary to Descartes's proposal, extension alone is implausibly constitutive of material substance. One component of Russellian Monism can be explained along the same lines: the properties that contemporary physics reveals to us are all extrinsic or only comparatively intrinsic, and thus there must be presently unknown absolutely intrinsic properties that accompany them.[18]

---

17. Chase Wrenn made this point in conversation, and as a result the definitions that follow are revised from those in Pereboom (2011), pp. 93–94. Thanks also to Ralf Bader and Nico Silins for suggestions that occasioned these revisions.

18. The notions of absolutely and comparatively intrinsic properties might also be expressed in terms of a priori derivability, although since these notions are metaphysical such epistemic characterizations will be less fundamental:

> P is an *absolutely intrinsic* property of X just in case P is an intrinsic property of X, and the proposition that X has P is not a priori derivable from R, a proposition that details all the purely extrinsic properties of X's parts.

> P is a *comparatively intrinsic* property of X just in case P is an intrinsic property of X, and the proposition that X has P is a priori derivable from R.

James van Cleve (1988) proposes alternative definitions of the notions of comparatively and absolutely intrinsic properties:

> P is a *monadic* property of X = df it is possible for something x to have P even if no individual *distinct* from x [i.e., not identical with x] exists;

and,

Thus the extension of a Cartesian sphere turns out to be a comparatively intrinsic property of it. One might object that a Cartesian sphere's extension is not necessitated by the purely extrinsic properties of the parts of the sphere, because the parts have an intrinsic property that supplements their purely extrinsic properties. But in the Cartesian theory of matter, those parts consist just in extension, and the extension of each of these parts is subject to the same metaphysical treatment of the extension of the whole: the extension of each of these parts will be necessitated by the plurality, continuity, and coexistence of their parts. The same holds for the extension of the parts of these parts, on to infinity.

As we've seen, Leibniz thinks that it is not credible that substances have only purely extrinsic properties:

> But it would appear from this that something must always be assumed which is continuous or diffused, such as the white in milk, the color, ductility, and weight in gold, and resistance in matter. For by itself, continuity (for extension is nothing but simultaneous continuity) no more constitutes substance than does multitude or number, where something is necessary to be numbered, repeated, and continued.[19]

The idea is that there must be some absolutely intrinsic property that confers substantive character on any substantial entity—one might call a property of this sort a *substantival absolutely intrinsic property*—for this substantive character cannot be accounted for by purely extrinsic and merely comparatively intrinsic properties alone. To spell out Leibniz's metaphysical intuition, a mind-independently real substantive thing can't consist just in properties such as *being next to, existing at the same time as,* and *being one of several.* Such relational properties need to be accompanied by some absolutely intrinsic property.

P is *nonrelational* = df it is possible for something x to have P even if no individual *discrete* from x [i.e., having no part in common with x] exists. (p. 235)

He then characterizes absolutely intrinsic properties as nonrelational and monadic, and comparatively intrinsic properties as nonrelational but not monadic. Absolutely intrinsic properties of X are the intrinsic properties of X that X could have if it had no parts, or if the parts it does have did not exist, while the comparatively intrinsic properties of X are the other intrinsic properties of X.

19. Leibniz to De Volder, April 1699, Loemker, p. 516 = Gerhardt II, p. 170; cf. Leibniz, *Specimen Dynamicum,* Loemker, pp. 435–52 = G. W. Leibniz, *Mathematische Schriften,* ed. C. I. Gerhardt (Berlin and Halle, 1849–56), VI, pp. 234–54.

In this last passage, Leibniz specifies the absolutely intrinsic property as that which has extension, in the sense that it is that which is continuous. What are the candidates for such an absolutely intrinsic property of a physical substance? Medieval Aristotelians proposed *prime materiality*, the fundamental subject of inherence of positive features, which is in itself just the pure potentiality for inherence of such features. This proposal is rejected by all the major modern philosophers, typically on the grounds of unintelligibility. Locke suggested *solidity*, the categorical basis of impenetrability, as the absolutely intrinsic physical property.[20] Leibniz's positive proposal is to ascribe force to matter as the property in question.[21] But is force adequate to this role? Consider gravitational force. The gravitational force exerted by a sphere on another body is a function of the gravitational force exerted by its parts, but it's not clear that the sphere's force is necessitated by purely extrinsic properties of its parts. So one possibility is that there are properties of type T intrinsic to physical thing X, and while X has property P by virtue of its parts having certain properties, X has P by virtue of its parts having properties precisely of type T itself, and these properties are intrinsic to these parts. Furthermore, these parts have these properties by virtue of *their* parts having intrinsic properties of type T, ad infinitum. If force meets this condition, then a physical thing's having force can be an absolutely intrinsic property of it.

It is important to note that, as the previous reasoning shows, force can be an absolutely intrinsic property even if there is no fundamental level, and thus no fundamental entity has force.[22] This is a welcome result because the Leibnizian principle at issue, which I will provisionally formulate as follows:

> (Intrinsicness Principle, first pass) Any substantial entity must have at least one substantival absolutely intrinsic property,

does not depend for its truth or plausibility on the existence of a fundamental level of reality—although Leibniz did maintain for unrelated reasons that there must be such a level.[23]

---

20. Locke (1975), II, iv.

21. Cf. Leibniz, *Specimen Dynamicum*, Loemker, p. 445 = G. W. Leibniz, *Mathematische Schriften*, VI, p. 246.

22. Schaffer (2003).

23. Leibniz, "On Nature Itself," Loemker, pp. 498–508 = Gerhardt IV, pp. 504–16; Schaffer (2003). For reasons to be skeptical about this principle, see McKitrick (2003); Ladyman and Ross, with Spurrett and Collier (2007).

It's important to note, however, that Leibniz denies that physical force is an absolutely intrinsic property of a physical substance. He calls physical force *derivative*, and he suggests that it is the phenomenal appearance of *primitive* force, which is an intrinsic mental property of a nonphysical soul or monad. Primitive force is a law-governed disposition of a monad to progress from one representation to another.[24] For Leibniz, the underlying ground of primitive force is to be found in the representational states of souls or monads, and it is these nonphysical representational states that yield the missing absolutely intrinsic properties. This account features no absolutely intrinsic *physical* properties. For Leibniz, this is part of the explanation for why physical things are not substantial or real in the fundamental mind-independent sense, but rather only well-founded phenomena (*phenomena bene fundata*). The fact that derivative force has an appropriate foundation in absolutely intrinsic properties of a monad nevertheless allows physical things to be substantial in the lower-grade sense in which they are real, as well-founded phenomena. This account is of particular interest given our topic, for this is the first time we see an explicit formulation of the position that the absolutely intrinsic properties of the mind-independently real world are mental.

Kant's reaction to these claims of Leibniz's is first of all to deny that we have knowledge or cognition of any absolutely intrinsic properties of material things:

> All that we cognize in matter is nothing but relations. What we call the intrinsic determinations of it are intrinsic only in a comparative sense, but among these relations some are self-subsistent and permanent, and through these we are given a determinate object.[25]

In material objects such as trees and houses we discover comparatively intrinsic properties, but never any absolutely intrinsic properties. This is not just an epistemic claim, but also a metaphysical one. For Kant contends that all properties of matter, *substantia phaenomenon*, even its apparently intrinsic properties, are ultimately purely extrinsic: "It is quite otherwise with a *substantia phaenomenon* in space; its intrinsic determinations are nothing but mere

---

24. Leibniz, Gerhardt II, p. 275.

25. Kant (1929/1987), A285/B341. In a similar vein, David Armstrong writes: "If we look at the properties of physical objects that physicists are prepared to allow them such as mass, electric charge, or momentum, these show a distressing tendency to dissolve into relations that one object has to another"; see Armstrong (1968), pp. 74–75.

relations, and it itself is entirely made up of mere relations."[26] He subsequently specifies force as a feature of matter: "We are acquainted with substance in space only through forces which are active in this and that space, either bringing objects to it (attraction), or preventing them penetrating into it (repulsion and impenetrability)." Thus for Kant force is also ultimately a purely extrinsic property of material things.[27] Specifically, in his conception forces are relations between points: attractive forces are by definition causes by which two points approach one another, and repulsive forces are causes by which two points recede from another.[28] (Kant might alternatively be interpreted here as contending that force is dispositional, and relational for that reason.)

Kant admits that it is initially unintuitive that all properties of matter are ultimately purely extrinsic: "It is certainly startling to hear that a thing is to be taken as consisting wholly of relations."[29] But the sense of implausibility can be explained away: "Such a thing is, however, mere appearance, and cannot be thought through pure categories: what it itself consists in is the mere relation of something in general to the senses."[30] Since matter is only appearance, for Kant it need not have any physical absolutely intrinsic properties. If matter were not merely appearance, but instead a thing in itself, then it would have such absolutely intrinsic properties. In making these claims, Kant indicates that he endorses a version of the Leibnizian idea that extrinsic properties require intrinsic properties. Kant's contention is that the extrinsic properties of substantial entities that are mind-independent in the sense that they are not dependent for their existence or nature on our perceiving or conceiving them—that is, things in themselves—must be grounded in absolutely intrinsic properties, although in his view we are irremediably ignorant of such properties. This suggests the following formulation of the intuition underlying the demand for absolutely intrinsic properties:

> (Intrinsicness Principle) Any mind-independently real substantial entity must have at least one substantival absolutely intrinsic property,

---

26. Kant (1929/1987), A265/B321; cf. Kant (2004), Ak IV, p. 543. See Thomas Holden's exposition of Kant's position, and also of Roger Boscovich's similar theory in Holden (2004), pp. 236–63.

27. Kant (1929/1987), A265/B321.

28. Kant (2004), Ak IV, pp. 498–91.

29. Kant (1929/1987), A285/B341; this passage conflicts with Thomas Holden's (2004, p. 261) claim that Kant was unmoved by the idea that matter must fill space by virtue of an intrinsic property.

30. Kant (1929/1987), A285/B341.

which I think best captures the intuition at play in the views of Leibniz and Kant.

Ignorance of Absolutely Intrinsic Properties

An assumption made by the various Russellian Monist proposals is that we are currently ignorant of the fundamental properties that underlie and explain consciousness. My sense is that it's implausible to account for this ignorance by our lack of acquaintance with such properties.[31] The H_2O-structural property is an intrinsic property of water, and we arguably understand the complete nature of this property and that it's the essence of water. We have this knowledge despite lacking acquaintance with this property. Our knowledge in this case is instead grounded in best explanation—we know the nature of the H_2O-structural property as the essence of water because we've conceived a model of the unobserved basis of water-dispositions that turned out to be a component of a best explanation. In principle, couldn't we do the same for absolutely intrinsic properties? We might imagine: physics provides a model for the fundamental particles in which their absolutely intrinsic property is prime materiality or categorical solidity.[32] A model of this kind turns out to be so explanatorily successful that it yields knowledge that the absolutely intrinsic property is in fact instantiated.

On this abductive model, it is credible that we presently lack knowledge of which absolutely intrinsic properties are instantiated. Several distinct candidates for such properties have been conceived that are not abductively ruled out, and it is open that we have not yet conceived all of the candidates. This will be so on David Lewis's view, according to which different fundamental properties can have the same causal role—he calls properties that satisfy this description 'quiddities.'[33] This will also be the case if, following Sydney Shoemaker, quiddities are rejected in favor of a causal structuralist view of properties, according to which the causal role of a property constitutes its individual essence, so that if P1 and P2 have the same complete causal role, they are ipso facto the same property.[34] Shoemaker's causal structuralism does not

---

31. Kant is arguably the first to claim that we lack knowledge of absolutely intrinsic properties, and he argues that for us this ignorance is irremediable. For expositions of the nature of this ignorance, see van Cleve (1988); Pereboom (1991a, 1991b, 2011: chapter 6); and Langton (1998).

32. Locke (1975), Book II, Chapter IV.

33. Lewis (2009); Locke (2009); see also Schaffer (2004).

34. Shoemaker (1980).

preclude distinct absolutely intrinsic properties with causal profiles that we are unable to distinguish, either because the distinguishing elements of these causal profiles are uninstantiated[35] or because we lack the ability to discern them. And even if we could individuate the instantiated absolutely intrinsic properties by a causal-role specification, we might yet be significantly ignorant of them because such a specification yields only limited knowledge of a property's nature.[36]

Which candidates for absolutely intrinsic properties have we already conceived? Prime materiality and categorical solidity have already been mentioned, as has Leibniz's model in which the absolute intrinsic properties are mental properties of immaterial entities. In Leibniz's conception, every entity has such mental properties, and thus his view is a variety of *panpsychism*. On Galen Strawson's view, the absolutely intrinsic properties are mental properties only of certain kinds of microphysical entities; he calls his position *micropsychism*.[37] Robert Adams defends a theistic variant on this mentalistic proposal in which the divine volitions constitute the absolutely intrinsic properties.[38] Chalmers specifies a *protophenomenal* alternative according to which the absolutely intrinsic properties are neither conscious properties nor paradigmatically physical properties, but nonetheless ground both phenomenal consciousness and the properties' current physics reveals.[39] David Armstrong has proposed primitive color as the intrinsic physical property missing from the scientific story, and this proposal might be embellished to include primitive versions of the other secondary qualities.[40] One might suspect that a number of these options can be ruled out as too wild to be in play. However, reflection on the strength of the conceivability argument against physicalism suggests that possibilities that initially seem wild remain salient

---

35. John Hawthorne makes this point in Hawthorne (2001).

36. One might think that on Shoemaker's conception all there is to a property is its causal role, but he assures me that this is not so. In his view, properties typically also feature intrinsic aptnesses for the causal roles that individuate them.

37. Strawson (2008b), pp. 54–74; cf. Strawson (2008a), pp. 19–51.

38. Adams (2007).

39. David Chalmers (2002a, 2002b).

40. Armstrong (1961); Armstrong rejects this proposal in his (1968). A primitive property is (i) one whose entire qualitative nature or essence is revealed in our sensory or introspective representation of it, and thus is not identical to a property with a qualitative nature distinct from what is revealed by the representation, and (ii) one that is metaphysically simple and thus not constituted by a plurality of other properties; Pereboom (2011), pp. 16–18; cf. Byrne and Hilbert (2007), pp. 73–105.

after all. Moreover, it seems far from certain that any proposed candidate that we understand is actually instantiated, and so it may well be that there are possibilities for such properties that we do not comprehend that are also salient alternatives.

In summary, the reason for claiming ignorance about which absolutely intrinsic properties are actually instantiated is that there is a plurality of candidates for such properties, and some of them are not currently understood. More than one of these candidates is in the running for yielding the best explanation of the relevant phenomena. But as things now stand, none of them convincingly meets this standard. The conclusion to this argument is not inevitable and permanent ignorance, but rather a sort that is potentially remediable. It is thus congenial to Chalmers's protophenomenal proposal, which leaves it open that we will come to understand the nature of the relevant intrinsic properties.

How might we assess the various proposals for currently unknown absolutely intrinsic properties as ways of filling out Russellian Monism? If we supplemented 'P' just with putative truths about prime materiality or categorical solidity, the sense that the physical is conceivable without the phenomenal is undiminished. Imagine instead, inspired by David Armstrong's suggestion, that we embellished 'P' just with putative truths about primitive colors or primitive versions of other secondary qualities. Aristotle conceived of such properties as physical, so maybe the result could be a variety of physicalism. But the idea that these are the missing absolute intrinsic properties does not seem plausible, mainly for the reason that they have been dismissed from our scientific picture of reality since the seventeenth century. At this point, we seem to have run out of candidates for the missing absolutely intrinsic physical properties that have been conceived.

What remains are the mental candidates such as panpsychism and micropsychism, proposed by Leibniz and Strawson, and, as Thomas Nagel, David Chalmers, and Colin McGinn suggest, possible candidates that we have not conceived.[41] The most favorable prospect for a resolutely physicalist Russellian Monism would appear to lie in properties whose nature is currently unconceived. Chalmers's protophenomenalism allows for a view of this sort. The kind of ignorance about the properties at issue that would be in place, together with the fact that the tradition in physics allows for properties not previously conceived as physical to come to count as physical, would seem to render protophenomenalism the physicalist Russellian Monist's best hope. If there are

---

41. Nagel (1986); David Chalmers (2002b); McGinn (2004).

currently unconceived possibilities for physical and protophenomenal absolutely intrinsic properties, they might remain unconceived. More optimistically, as physics develops, we may come to conceive them. Or as Chalmers suggests, phenomenology together with physics might arrive at such a conception.[42]

Stoljar's Challenge

In Chalmers's conception, what underwrites the conceivability argument is the following structure-and-dynamics thesis:

> (SDT) There are experiential [or phenomenal] truths that cannot be deduced from truths solely about structure and dynamics.[43]

Structural and dynamical properties contrast with intrinsic properties. As Daniel Stoljar plausibly suggests, structural properties are relational properties, and dynamical properties are changes in structural properties over time.[44] Chalmers's idea is that because the properties that contemporary physics specifies are exclusively structural and dynamical, and phenomenal properties are intrinsic properties of experiences, we can conclude that experiential truths about phenomenal properties cannot be deduced from current physics, or from any descendent that specifies only structural and dynamical properties.[45] But Stoljar argues that SDT is in error, and that these experiential truths may be derivable from exclusively structural and dynamical physical truth after all:

> The simplest way to see that the from-structure-only-structure thesis is false is to note that one can derive the instantiation of an intrinsic property from a relational one just by shifting what thing you are talking about. For example, being a husband is a relational property of Jack Spratt, and being a wife is a relational property of his wife. But being married is an intrinsic property of the pair (or the sum) of Jack Spratt and his wife. To take a different example, it seems plausible to say that I have the property of having a hand intrinsically, but my

---

42. In his presentation on structuralism in physics at the Australian National University, November 2005.

43. This formulation is from Alter (2009), at p. 760.

44. Stoljar (2013).

45. Chalmers (2002b), p. 197.

having this property obviously follows from a relation between my hand and the rest of my body, and that the truth concerning this is a relational truth.[46]

Alter agrees that Stoljar has a point: if objects x and y compose object z, then it is possible to deduce intrinsic properties of z solely from relational properties of x and y. However, this observation poses a challenge to the from-structure-only-structure thesis only if nonstructural/nondynamical properties are identified with intrinsic properties. Alter proposes that this identification is mistaken, for the reason that "the property *being married* is purely structural/dynamic despite being intrinsic to the Spratts. Any structural/dynamical duplicate of the actual world contains a corresponding married pair."[47] (A caveat: being married is plausibly extrinsic, since it builds in a relation to civic institutions. Arguably, *being a dancing pair* avoids this problem.[48]) Alter contends that such examples show not that we should reject the from-structure-only-structure thesis, but rather that it makes sense to resist identifying nonstructural/nondynamical properties with intrinsic properties.

The distinction between comparatively and absolutely intrinsic properties yields a way to vindicate Alter's claim. While the property of *being a married pair* is intrinsic to the Spratts, it is necessitated by Jack's purely extrinsic property of *being married to Jill* and Jill's purely extrinsic property of *being married to Jack*. *Being a married pair* is consequently a comparatively intrinsic property and not an absolutely intrinsic property of the Spratts. We can now propose that all nonstructural/nondynamic properties are absolutely intrinsic properties (and all nonstructural/nondynamic components of properties will be absolutely intrinsic components of properties). Stoljar's counterexample would then fail to undermine the from-structure-only-structure thesis. We can accordingly reformulate the from-structure-only-structure thesis in this way:

(2*) Truths about absolutely intrinsic properties (and absolutely intrinsic aspects of properties) are not necessitated by and cannot be deduced from truths solely about purely extrinsic properties.

---

46. Stoljar (2006), p. 152.

47. Alter (2009), p. 763.

48. Thanks to Uriah Kriegel for this point.

And the structure-and-dynamics thesis then becomes:

(SDT*) There are experiential truths that are not necessitated by and cannot be deduced from truths solely about purely extrinsic properties.

The Prospects for Russellian Monism

We've seen that Russellian Monism has versions in which the natures of the absolutely intrinsic properties are phenomenal, as in Strawson's micropsychism, or else protophenomenal, as Chalmers advocates. On a phenomenal-micropsychist option, the absolutely intrinsic properties that account for phenomenal consciousness are themselves phenomenal and irreducibly so, while on the protophenomenal alternative they are not phenomenal but are nonetheless capable of accounting for phenomenal consciousness.[49] Imagine first that 'P*' supplements 'P' by adding in the proposed micropsychist truths, statements or propositions about absolutely intrinsic phenomenal properties of fundamental physical entities that specify the natures of those properties. Suppose again that 'Q' is a phenomenal truth about Mary's visual sensory experience of red. Is 'P*T and ~ Q' ideally primarily conceivable? Philip Goff asks whether there is any less reason to believe that the resulting 'P*T and ~ Q' is ideally primarily conceivable than there is to think that 'PT and ~ Q' is.[50] Imagine that every fundamental particle has some absolutely intrinsic phenomenal property or other, and that ordinary introspectible phenomenal entities are composed of a significant number of such fundamental particles. Any such array of fundamental particles without phenomenal redness would seem as readily conceivable as any arrangement of conventionally characterized fundamental physical particles without phenomenal redness.

However, in support of the micropsychist we can invoke a misrepresentation thesis of a Leibnizian sort, according to which introspection merely fails to represent phenomenal experience as having features it in fact has.[51] While Mary's sensory experience of red is represented introspectively to feature only phenomenal redness, and this occasions the belief that phenomenal redness is a simple property, it is in fact composed of a complex

49. See Strawson (2008b). There Strawson also defends the stronger view, panpsychism; cf. Nagel (1979).

50. Goff (2009).

51. Thanks to Nico Silins for this characterization.

microphenomenal array that is normally not introspectively discerned. At this point phenomenal-micropsychism might have an advantage over a conventional physicalist proposal for the absolutely intrinsic properties, since it is arguably more plausible that phenomenal redness is composed of a complex microphenomenal array than that it is conventionally physically constituted. Micropsychism requires only that introspection mistakenly represent phenomenal redness as lacking a complex phenomenal composition. The conventional physicalist alternative would seem to demand in addition that phenomenal redness does not have any qualitative phenomenal nature of the general sort that introspection represents it as having.[52]

Note that micropsychism would specify that there are laws governing how truths about microphenomenal properties yield truths about macrophenomenal properties such as the phenomenal redness of Mary's experience. These laws would need to be derivable from 'P*T' alone (P*T adds in the micropsychist truths), for 'Q' must be derivable from 'P*T' alone. The credibility of this proposal might be enhanced by analogy with the derivability of certain macrophenomenal properties from their known components, such as phenomenal tastes from the components of sweet, sour, salty, bitter, and umami.[53] Introspectible phenomenal properties might be similarly derivable from presently unknown microphenomenal absolutely intrinsic properties together with the remainder of the base described by 'P*T.' The laws in play would then also be derivable from, and necessitated by, this base. Despite our tendency to believe that phenomenal tastes are simple properties, the discovery that phenomenal tastes are (partly) structured by sweet, sour, salty, bitter, and umami can convince us that this belief is mistaken. Note that this discovery does not challenge the claim that phenomenal tastes are absolutely intrinsic properties, for the reason that the base for derivation does not consist in purely relational properties. This lesson would apply to the micropsychist proposal more generally.

Still, there is a reason to be skeptical about the prospects of micropsychism. Building on a point developed by Karen Bennett, the worry is that the envisioned phenomenal micropsychism would need to posit brute laws linking microphenomenal absolutely intrinsic properties with the conventional microphysical properties that they underlie, without which the truths about the microphysical properties would not be derivable from the micropsychist truths.[54] This yields a reason to think that phenomenal micropsychism is

---

52. Pereboom (2011), pp. 8–28.

53. Thanks to Louis deRosset for this suggestion.

54. Karen Bennett, "Why I Am Not a Dualist," ms.

incapable of supplying illuminating explanations of the properties specified by current microphysics. At least prima facie, brute laws posit connections without explanatory illumination. It would be theoretically advantageous if the absolutely intrinsic properties did provide illuminating explanations for both phenomenal properties and the entities specified by contemporary microphysics.

Chalmers's protophenomenalist proposal appears better equipped for this twofold task. It is silent on the specific nature of the absolutely intrinsic properties, and for this reason it leaves open the possibility that they would count as physical. It is therefore also open that these protophenomenal properties yield explanations for the conventional microphysical properties they underlie without the need for brute laws linking the protophenomenal properties with the microphysical properties. The result is a potential advantage over phenomenal micropsychism. Imagine that 'P*' supplements 'P' by adding in the truths about protophenomenal absolutely intrinsic properties, employing concepts that allow for the accurate representation of the natures of these properties. Would the resulting 'P*T and ~ Q' be ideally primarily conceivable? It would seem epistemically open that there are protophenomenal properties that necessitate the phenomenal properties, and this would preclude the ideal primary conceivability of 'P*T and ~ Q.' At the same time, the resulting explanatory advantage of protophenomenalism over phenomenal micropsychism would be offset by the disadvantage that it proposes properties of which we presently have only a minimal conception.

Might we ever possess concepts that facilitate representation of the natures of protophenomenal properties? Chalmers is cautiously optimistic. Colin McGinn would be skeptical. The existence of protophenomenal properties is consistent with his position on the mind-body problem, but he would deny that concepts representing their natures are available to us. For McGinn, solving the mind-body problem would demand concepts that bridge the gap between conscious properties and conventional physical properties. But for this, we require "a perspective shift, not just a paradigm shift—a shift not merely of world view, but of ways of apprehending the world. We need to become another type of cognitive being altogether."[55] By contrast, for Nagel and Chalmers it is open that our cognitive and imaginative capacities are capable of forming this sort of concept.[56]

---

55. McGinn (2004), p. 24.

56. Nagel (1986), pp. 52–53.

What explains McGinn's reluctance to take this route is that for him any concepts available to us are closely tied to acquaintance. This limit forecloses the possibility of our acquiring concepts of the requisite bridging sort. For Nagel and Chalmers it's open that we can acquire such concepts by our imagination venturing beyond this limit. McGinn may be right to argue that these concepts cannot arise from acquaintance. What would then be needed is a creative power to form concepts not closely tied to acquaintance. Whether we have such a power is unclear, but if we do have it, what we can presently understand would not rule out our acquiring concepts of protophenomenal absolutely intrinsic properties, whereupon further investigation might also determine whether such properties are actually instantiated.

Summary and Conclusion

According to the Russellian Monist option for physicalism I've set out, presently unknown absolutely intrinsic properties account for both conventional microphysical properties and for phenomenal consciousness. Absolutely intrinsic properties of things are those that are not necessitated by purely relational properties of their parts. I've highlighted a more specific protophenomenal version Russellian Monism in which the absolutely intrinsic properties are non-mental and sufficiently similar to paradigmatic properties of current physics to count as physical. An important advantage for this position over other physicalist accounts of consciousness is that it can clearly accept an attractive accuracy claim about phenomenal representation, i.e., that introspection represents phenomenal properties as having qualitative natures that they in fact possess. This accuracy claim supplies the conceivability argument against physicalism with its characteristic force, and thus any physicalism that can unequivocally endorse it is in an advantageous dialectical position.[57] Absolutely intrinsic properties of this protophenomenal sort are currently at best only minimally conceived, and herein lies the fragility of the proposal. But for anyone with physicalist sympathies who at the same time aspires to preserve the accuracy claim, this Russellian Monism should be a live and attractive option.[58]

---

57. I set out this accuracy claim and explore a physicalist view that denies it in Pereboom (2011), pp. 9–84.

58. Thanks to Torin Alter, Ralf Bader, Karen Bennett, David Chalmers, Andrew Chignell, Louis deRosset, Tyler Doggett, Uriah Kriegel, Andrew McGonigal, Alyssa Ney, Sydney Shoemaker, Nico Silins, and Daniel Stoljar for valuable comments and discussion.

References

Adams, Robert. 2007. "Idealism Vindicated," in *Persons, Human and Divine*, ed. Peter van Inwagen and Dean Zimmerman (Oxford: Oxford University Press), pp. 35–54.

Almog, Joseph. 2002. *What Am I? Descartes and the Mind-Body Problem* (New York: Oxford University Press).

Alter, Torin. 2009. "Does the Ignorance Hypothesis Undermine the Conceivability and Knowledge Arguments?" *Philosophy and Phenomenological Research* 79, pp. 756–65.

Alter, Torin, and Yujin Nagasawa. 2012. "What Is Russellian Monism?" *Journal of Consciousness Studies* 19, n. 9–10, pp. 67–95.

Armstrong, David. 1961. *Perception and the Physical World* (London: Routledge).

Armstrong, David. 1968. *A Materialist Theory of Mind* (London: Routledge).

Arnauld, Antoine. 1984. *Fourth Set of Objections* (to René Descartes's *Meditations on First Philosophy*), in *The Philosophical Writings of Descartes*, vol. 2, tr. and ed. John Cottingham, Robert Stoothoff, and Dugald Murdoch (Cambridge: Cambridge University Press).

Bealer, George. 2002. "Modal Epistemology and the Rationalist Renaissance," in *Conceivability and Possibility*, ed. Tamar Szabó Gendler and John Hawthorne (Oxford: Oxford University Press), pp. 77–125.

Bennett, Karen. ms. "Why I Am Not a Dualist."

Byrne, Alex, and David Hilbert. 2007. "Color Primitivism," *Erkenntnis* 66, pp. 73–105.

Chalmers, David. 1996. *The Conscious Mind* (Oxford: Oxford University Press).

Chalmers, David. 1999. "Materialism and the Metaphysics of Modality," *Philosophy and Phenomenological Research* 59, pp. 473–96.

Chalmers, David. 2002a. "Consciousness and Its Place in Nature," in the *Blackwell Guide to the Philosophy of Mind* (Oxford: Blackwell); reprinted in *Philosophy of Mind: Classical and Contemporary Readings*, ed. David Chalmers (New York: Oxford University Press, 2002), pp. 247–72.

Chalmers, David. 2002b. "Does Conceivability Entail Possibility?" in *Conceivability and Possibility*, ed. Tamar Gendler and John Hawthorne (Oxford: Oxford University Press), pp. 145–200.

Chalmers, David. 2003. "The Content and Epistemology of Phenomenal Belief," in *Consciousness: New Philosophical Perspective*, ed. Q. Smith and A. Jokic (Oxford: Oxford University Press).

Chalmers, David. 2012. "The Two-Dimensional Argument against Materialism," in *The Character of Consciousness* (New York: Oxford University Press).

Chalmers, David, and Frank Jackson. 2001. "Conceptual Analysis and Reductive Explanation," *Philosophical Review* 110, pp. 315–61.

Descartes, René. 1984. *The Philosophical Writings of Descartes*, 3 vols., tr. and ed. John Cottingham, Robert Stoothoff, and Dugald Murdoch (Cambridge: Cambridge University Press).

Fara, Michael. 2009. "Dispositions," *The Stanford Encyclopedia of Philosophy* (Summer edition), ed. Edward N. Zalta, at http://plato.stanford.edu/archives/sum2009/entries/dispositions/.

Goff, Philip. 2009. "Why Panpsychism Doesn't Help Us Explain Consciousness," *Dialectica* 63, pp. 289–311.

Hawthorne, John. 2001. "Causal Structuralism," *Philosophical Perspectives* 15, pp. 361–78.

Holden, Thomas. 2004. *The Architecture of Matter* (Oxford: Oxford University Press).

Humberstone, Lloyd. 1996. "Intrinsic/Extrinsic," *Synthese* 105, pp. 205–67.

Jackson, Frank. 1998. *From Metaphysics to Ethics* (Oxford: Oxford University Press).

Kant, Immanuel. 1902–1980. *Kants* gesammelte Schriften, 29 vols., ed. Koniglichen Preussischen Akademie der Wissenschaften, Berlin: Walter de Gruyter et al. (Abbreviated as 'Ak').

Kant, Immanuel. 1929/1987. *Critique of Pure Reason*, tr. Norman Kemp Smith (London: Macmillan, 1929) and tr. Paul Guyer and Allen Wood (Cambridge: Cambridge University Press, 1987).

Kant, Immanuel. 2004. *Metaphysical Foundations of Natural Science*, tr. Michael Friedman (Cambridge: Cambridge University Press).

Kripke, Saul. 1980. *Naming and Necessity* (Cambridge: Harvard University Press).

Ladyman, James, and Don Ross, with David Spurrett and John Collier. 2007. *Every Thing Must Go* (Oxford: Oxford University Press).

Langton, Rae.1998. *Kantian Humility: Our Ignorance of Things in Themselves* (Oxford, Oxford University Press).

Leibniz, Gottfried Wilhelm. 1965. G. W. Leibniz, *Die philosophischen Schriften*, 7 vols., ed. C. I. Gerhard (Hildesheim, Germany: Olms).

Leibniz, Gottfried Wilhelm. 1969. *Philosophical Papers and Letters*, tr. and ed. L. E. Loemker (Dordrecht, The Netherlands: D. Reidel).

Lewis, David. 2009. "Ramseyan Humility," in *Conceptual Analysis and Philosophical Naturalism*, ed. David Braddon-Mitchell and Robert Nola (Cambridge: MIT Press), pp. 203–22.

Locke, Dustin. 2009. "A Partial Defense of Ramseyan Humility," *Conceptual Analysis and Philosophical Naturalism*, ed. David Braddon-Mitchell and Robert Nola (Cambridge: MIT Press), pp. 223–41.

Locke, John. 1975. *An Essay Concerning Human Understanding*, ed. P. H. Nidditch (Oxford: Oxford University Press).

McGinn, Colin. 2004. "What Constitutes the Mind-Body Problem," in his *Consciousness and Its Objects* (Oxford: Oxford University Press).

McKitrick, Jennifer. 2003. "The Bare Metaphysical Possibility of Bare Dispositions," *Philosophy and Phenomenological Research* 66, pp. 349–69.

Nagel, Thomas. 1974. "What Is It Like to Be a Bat?" *Philosophical Review* 83, pp. 435–50.

Nagel, Thomas. 1979. "Panpsychism," in his *Mortal Questions* (Oxford: Oxford University Press).

Nagel, Thomas. 1986. *The View from Nowhere* (New York: Oxford University Press).

Ney, Alyssa. 2007. "Physicalism and Our Knowledge of Intrinsic Properties," *Australasian Journal of Philosophy* 85, pp. 41–60.

Pereboom, Derk. 1991a. "Kant's Amphiboly," *Archiv für Geschichte der Philosophie* 73, pp. 50–70.

Pereboom, Derk. 1991b. "Is Kant's Transcendental Philosophy Inconsistent?" *History of Philosophy Quarterly* 8, pp. 357–71.

Pereboom, Derk. 1994. "Bats, Brain Scientists, and the Limitations of Introspection," *Philosophy and Phenomenological Research* 54, pp. 315–29.

Pereboom, Derk. 2011. *Consciousness and the Prospects of Physicalism* (New York: Oxford University Press).

Pereboom, Derk. 2012. "Russellian Monism and Absolutely Intrinsic Properties," in *Current Controversies in Philosophy of Mind*, ed. Uriah Kriegel (London: Routledge), pp. 40–69.

Russell, Bertrand. 1927. *The Analysis of Matter* (London: Kegan Paul).

Rozemond, Marleen. 1998. *Descartes's Dualism* (Cambridge: Harvard University Press).

Schaffer, Jonathan. 2003. "Is There a Fundamental Level?" *Noûs* 37, pp. 498–517.

Schaffer, Jonathan. 2004. "Quidditistic Knowledge," in *Lewisian Themes*, ed. Frank Jackson and Graham Priest (Oxford: Oxford University Press), pp. 210–30.

Shoemaker, Sydney. 1980. "Causality and Properties," in *Time and Change*, ed. P. van Inwagen (Dordrecht, The Netherlands: D. Reidel), pp. 109–35; reprinted in Sydney Shoemaker, *Identity, Cause, and Mind*, first edition (Cambridge: Cambridge University Press, 1984), pp. 206–33; and in the second, expanded, edition (Oxford: Oxford University Press, 2003), pp. 206–33.

Stoljar, Daniel. 2006. *Ignorance and Imagination: The Epistemic Origin of the Problem of Consciousness* (New York: Oxford University Press).

Stoljar, Daniel. 2013. "Four Kinds of Russellian Monism," in *Current Controversies in Philosophy of Mind*, ed. Uriah Kriegel (London: Routledge), pp. 17–39.

Strawson, Galen. 2008a. "Real Materialism," in his *Real Materialism and Other Essays* (Oxford: Oxford University Press), pp. 19–51; an earlier version appeared in *Chomsky and His Critics*, ed. L. Antony and N. Hornstein (Oxford: Blackwell, 2003).

Strawson, Galen. 2008b. "Realistic Monism," in his *Real Materialism and Other Essays* (Oxford: Oxford University Press), pp. 54–74; first published in *Consciousness and Its Place in Nature*, ed. A. Freeman, Thorverston (England: Imprint Academic, 2006), pp. 3–31.

van Cleve, James. 1988. "Inner States and Outer Relations: Kant and the Case for Monadism," in *Doing Philosophy Historically*, ed. Peter H. Hare (Buffalo, NY: Prometheus), pp. 231–47.

van Cleve, James. 2002. "Receptivity and Our Knowledge of Intrinsic Properties," *Philosophy and Phenomenological Research* 65, pp. 218–37.

Weatherson, Brian and Dan Marshall. 2013. "Intrinsic vs. Extrinsic Properties," in *The Stanford Encyclopedia of Philosophy* (Spring Edition), ed. Edward N. Zalta, <http://plato.stanford.edu/archives/spr2013/entries/intrinsic-extrinsic/>.

Wilson, Margaret. 1978. *Descartes* (London: Routledge).

Yablo, Stephen. 1991. "The Real Distinction between Mind and Body," *Canadian Journal of Philosophy* 16, pp. 149–201.

15

Russellian Monism or Nagelian Monism?

Daniel Stoljar

Introduction

A natural reaction to the usual set of options in philosophy of mind—viz., dualism and materialism—is to disagree with both. Materialism is certainly an elegant view; the world as the materialist represents it to be is a coherent system founded on a small stock of fundamental physical properties and laws. But materialism seems not to do justice to the phenomena; in particular, it seems not to adequately find a place in the world for consciousness. Dualism by contrast does justice to the phenomena—or anyway does *more* justice than materialism to at least *some* relevant phenomena. But it seems extremely inelegant, for the world as dualism represents it to be is just the material world with consciousness grafted on. But if you take something elegant and graft something onto it, the thing you end up with may well not be elegant; on the contrary, it may well be *in*elegant. And so, it turns out, unfortunately enough, with dualism.

An important task in philosophy of mind, therefore, is to develop and assess positions that are neither materialism nor dualism in the standard sense. My concern in this chapter is with two such potential positions: Russellian Monism, and a view that I will call, for the reason that it is inspired by some remarks of Thomas Nagel (cf. fn.7), Nagelian Monism. As we will see, both Russellian Monism (RM) and Nagelian Monism (NM) have a considerable

I am very much indebted to the following for their help: Torin Alter, Uziel Awret, David Chalmers, Yujin Nagasawa, Derk Pereboom, and Jon Simon.

amount in common. Both deny, as against dualism, that experiential proper-ties are metaphysically fundamental.[1] And both assert, as against standard forms of materialism, that the list of physical properties materialists usually operate with is inadequate—indeed both positions tend to be hyper critical about the usual attempts by both materialists and dualists to spell out what a physical property is. Finally, both advance an epistemic response to the conceivability argument and other arguments against materialism and for dualism—for both the apparent plausibility of these arguments is a symptom of our incomplete grasp of nature.

The difference between them is that RM relies, while NM does not, on a distinction that is in the same general class—to put it vaguely at first—as that between structural and non-structural properties, dispositional and non-dispositional properties, relational and non-relational properties, and extrinsic and intrinsic properties.[2] Nagelian Monists needn't reject dis-tinctions in this class altogether; their suggestion is rather that they play no particular role in developing the most plausible position that is neither mate-rialism nor dualism.

Even before we go into the issues in detail, there is at least the following consideration in favour of NM and against RM. Distinctions in the class I just mentioned have proved difficult to control; as Gareth Evans (1980, 102) mem-orably put it, one's views in this area seem to evince little more than a 'concep-tual prejudice'. And if that is the case, why rely on them in your philosophy of mind? For many philosophers attracted to RM, however, this line of thought is mistaken. It may be true—they will say—that other things being equal one should prefer theories that do not rely on controversial distinctions to ones that do, but that is not the situation here. For when properly understood NM is not an available position in the relevant sense; interpreted one way it is no different from RM, and interpreted another way it is no different from stan-dard materialism.

Why suppose that NM is not an available position in the relevant sense? The argument most commonly advanced to establish this has come to be called 'the structure and dynamics argument', and according to the recent literature on RM, that argument is successful; see, in particular, Alter (2009,

---

1. Some versions of Russellian Monism might allow that experiential properties of some sort are fundamental, but I will set them aside here. For some discussion of these forms, see Alter and Nagasawa 2012 and Kind, chapter 18 of this title.

2. As Alter and Nagasawa (2012) put it, a distinction like this is 'the central distinction' for RM.

2013), Alter and Nagasawa (2012), Chalmers (2010), McClelland (2013), and Pereboom (2011, 2014). By contrast, in earlier work (Stoljar 2006, 2009), I suggested it is not successful, and that NM is indeed the attractive view it seems to be. The present chapter is an elaboration and defence of that point of view; in particular, I will divide the structure and dynamics argument into various versions, and argue that none of them is successful.

Russellian Monism and Nagelian Monism

In order to put the two positions I want to discuss into sharper focus, I will begin with this simple statement of materialism:

> D1.   Materialism is true at a possible world w if and only if for every property G instantiated at w, there is some physical property (or some complex of physical properties) F instantiated at w such that F (metaphysically) necessitates G.[3]

Materialism so defined presents us with the impasse already alluded to. On the one hand, the conceivability argument—I will presume familiarity with it and similar arguments here[4]—tells us, if it is sound, that experiential properties—that is, properties constitutively connected to consciousness—are neither physical nor are necessitated by the physical. Hence materialism is false if such properties are instantiated (which I assume they are). On the other hand, the usual alternative to materialism—the sort of dualism that regards experiential properties as metaphysically fundamental—faces widely discussed problems having to do with the overall elegance of the view and, related to this, the causal and explanatory role of such properties.

The Russellian Monist offers a way out of this impasse. A good way to see the shape of this view is to start from a distinction between two kinds of physical property, which we may call 'standard' physical properties and 'non-standard' physical properties. For the Russellian, this distinction is in turn explicated in terms of a distinction in the class mentioned above, i.e.

---

3. For statements of materialism (aka physicalism) of this sort, see Stoljar 2010. The definition used in the text is a simple one; for example, it takes for granted exactly what metaphysical necessitation is. I will set aside such complications here. The definition is also incomplete in that it does not say what a physical property is; I will take up that problem below.

4. See, e.g., Stoljar 2014, Chalmers 2010, and Pereboom 2011.

between structural and non-structural, dispositional and non-dispositional, and so on. Suppose, to fix ideas, we focus on the first of these, the structural/non-structural distinction. Then the suggestion of the Russellian Monist is that standard physical properties are structural properties, and, correlatively, that non-standard physical properties are non-structural properties. The position further assumes, perhaps controversially, (a) that there is a good sense in which physics, and empirical inquiry generally, tells us only about structural properties and (b) that while this is so we nevertheless have good reason to suppose that non-structural properties are instantiated as well as structural properties.[5]

Now once we have the distinction between standard and non-standard physical properties before us, we can likewise draw a distinction between two kinds of materialism, standard materialism and non-standard materialism. Standard materialism is the view you get when you combine D1 with an assumption that the physical properties in question are standard, and so structural, properties. Non-standard materialism combines D1 with the assumption that physical properties are either standard or non-standard.

How do these distinctions show us a way out of the impasse? The suggestion of RM is that, while the conceivability argument is persuasive against standard materialism, it is not persuasive against non-standard materialism. For according to non-standard materialism there is a class of relevant instantiated physical properties (i.e. the non-structural properties) of which we are ignorant; if so, the conceivability argument loses its force since it presupposes that we know at least in outline what the relevant physical properties are.[6] On the other hand, to give up standard materialism is not to adopt dualism, and so the fundamentality of experiential properties may be denied.

So RM offers a way out of the impasse presented by materialism—what then of NM? Well, NM offers a way out too, and in fact a directly analogous way. Like RM, NM starts from a distinction between standard physical properties and non-standard physical properties, though in this case the distinction is explicated differently. For the Nagelian, standard physical properties are properties of the sort described in contemporary physics (and perhaps contemporary empirical inquiry generally). Correlatively, non-standard physical

---

5. In Stoljar 2014 I discuss four different versions of RM; the version in the text appears there as RM3. Of course any version of RM must appeal at some point to Bertrand Russell, and in particular to Russell 1927.

6. I will assume here familiarity with this epistemic style of response to the conceivability argument, which I have set out in detail elsewhere; see Stoljar 2006, 2014.

properties are properties of the sort described in the physics, whatever it is, that one will or might formulate at the ideal limit of inquiry. The position assumes, perhaps controversially, that contemporary physics is incomplete in the story it tells about nature, and so there is a difference in kind between contemporary physics and the physics that we will (or might) ideally reach.[7]

Once we have this distinction before us, NM, exactly like RM, draws a further distinction between two kinds of materialism, standard and non-standard materialism. How do these distinctions show us a way out of the impasse? The suggestion of NM—again: exactly like RM—is that while the conceivability argument is persuasive against standard materialism it is not persuasive against non-standard materialism. For according to non-standard materialism there is a class of relevant instantiated physical properties (i.e. the properties described at the ideal limit) of which we are ignorant. On the other hand, to give up standard materialism is not to adopt dualism, and so the fundamentality of experiential properties may be denied.

So we seem to have two ways out of the impasse over materialism.[8] But as we noted before, if the structure and dynamics argument is sound the only available route here *in fact* is the Russellian one. But what exactly is that argument? I now turn to that question.

The Structure and Dynamics Argument

The key text for the structure and dynamics argument is this well-known passage from David Chalmers:[9]

---

7. In *The View from Nowhere*, Nagel writes: 'The difference between the mental and the physical is far greater than the difference between the electrical and the mechanical. We need entirely new intellectual tools, and it is precisely by reflection on what appears impossible—like the generation of mind out of the recombination of matter—that we will be forced to create such tools. It may be that the eventual result of such exploration will be a new unity that is not reductionist. We and all other creatures with minds seem to be composed of the same materials as everything else in the universe. So any fundamental discoveries we make about how it is that we have minds and what they actually are, will reveal something fundamental about the constituents of the universe as a whole' (1986, 52–53). It is because of affinity with views like this that I will call the view described in the text Nagelian Monism.

8. Reader, beware: in Stoljar 2014, I classified (what I am here calling NM) as a version of RM, viz., RM4. As I say there, however, it is not clear that RM4 *is* a version of RM strictly so called, because it does not appeal to the distinction between structural and non-structural properties or any similar distinction.

9. Chalmers makes the point quoted in the course of developing an influential taxonomy of positions that includes, inter alia, a distinction between what he calls type-C materialism and

First: Physical descriptions of the world characterize the world in terms of structure and dynamics. Second: From truths about structure and dynamics, one can deduce only further truths about structure and dynamics. And third: Truths about consciousness are not truths about structure and dynamics.

(Chalmers 2002, 258)

The argument presented in this passage is, I think, fairly summarized as having the following general form:

P1. Every physical truth is a truth of a certain kind, i.e., one that 'characterizes the world in terms of structure and dynamics'.
P2. For every truth T of that kind, if T a priori entails[10] a truth T^*, then T^* is of that kind too.[11]
P3. No truth about consciousness is a truth of that kind.

On the face of it, these claims present a major problem for NM. As we have seen, the Nagelian Monist supposes that the conceivability argument is persuasive against standard materialism but is not against non-standard materialism, where in turn this distinction is founded on a distinction between the properties described in contemporary physics and the properties described in ideal physics. But if each of P1–P3 is true, this distinction makes no difference to the impasse over materialism. For according to P1, both versions of materialism described by NM entail that truths about consciousness are necessitated by truths about structure and dynamics; and, according to P2 and P3, any theory of that kind lies in the target range of the conceivability argument. Hence, while we may for other reasons find non-standard materialism more plausible than standard materialism, doing so leaves the issues surrounding the conceivability argument unaffected.[12]

---

type-F-monism (see Chalmers 2010). Since type-F monism is Russellian Monism, and type-C materialism is very close to what I am here calling Nagelian Monism, part of the message of this chapter is that the division Chalmers draws here is not as deep as he makes out.

10. I will assume here that for T to a priori entail T^* is for the material conditional 'If T then T^*' to be knowable a priori.

11. There are a number of problems with P2 as stated. For example suppose T is a truth of a certain kind, and T^* is a disjunction of T and a truth of some other kind. In that case T will a priori entail T^* and yet T^* is arguably not of the relevant kind. However, since the problems with the argument I want to raise focus on P1 and P3, I will set this aside.

12. The argument in the text is in fact a bit stronger than is dialectically necessary. One way in which it might be weakened is that the quantifier 'no truth' in P3 can be replaced with 'not

Nagelian Monists might respond by denying that both standard and non-standard materialism entail that truths about consciousness are necessitated by truths about structure and dynamics; for example, they might say that non-standard materialism permits the idea that truths about consciousness are necessitated in part by truths about structure and dynamics and in part by truths not about structure and dynamics. However, while this avoids the problem, it abandons what is distinctive about NM as opposed to RM. For RM precisely holds that truths about consciousness are necessitated in part by truths that are not structural and dynamical. Hence we arrive at the conclusion of the structure and dynamics argument: either NM is no help as far as the conceivability argument goes (and so is no better than standard versions of materialism) or else it collapses into RM.

Is this argument persuasive? In my view the crucial issue in deciding whether it is concerns what exactly 'characterizes the world in terms of structure and dynamics' means. (In what follows I will concentrate on what 'structure' means, since 'dynamics' refers to how structure changes over time.) What, then, is it for a truth to characterize the world in terms of structure; what is it (as I will say) for a truth to be a structural truth? Since there are different answers to this question, there are different versions of the structure and dynamics argument. As I have indicated, my strategy will be to distinguish three different versions of the argument, and argue that each is unpersuasive.[13]

---

every truth'; I will mention this at several points below. A different way is that a proponent of the argument may wish to weaken the premise even further and say, not that no structural and dynamical truth is a truth about consciousness, nor even that not every such truth is, but rather that the conceivability argument (however that argument turns out) concerns the relationship between truths about consciousness and structural truths, and hence the difference between standard materialism and non-standard materialism (as understood by NM) makes no difference to the argument. (I discuss this second way to weaken the argument in Stoljar 2006, 2009.)

13. In addition to the structure and dynamics argument, one might propose a second, simpler, argument for preferring NM to RM. This is that NM is clearly a kind of materialism; hence, unlike RM, it is not a view that is neither materialism nor dualism. But I think this argument is unpersuasive too. In general, whether some theory is a sort of materialism is a multi-faceted question. On what we might call a 'loose and popular' sense, a theory is a version of materialism if it rejects the view that ordinary experiential properties are fundamental. By that standard, NM certainly is a kind of materialism. But so too is RM; indeed, it was in part for that reason that I classified RM as a version of materialism in earlier work (see Stoljar 2001). So there is no reason here to prefer RM to NM. By contrast, on what we might call the 'strict and philosophical' sense, materialism is a view with a fairly definite historical meaning, a meaning that goes beyond the mere denial that ordinary experiential properties are fundamental (see Stoljar 2010). Historically, for example, materialism was a

The First Version of the Argument

According to the first and simplest suggestion, a truth is a structural truth if it concerns a relation; that is, if it concerns the instantiation of an n-place property where $n >1$. Plugging this idea into the template above we arrive at these premises:

P1.a Every physical truth is a truth of a certain kind, i.e., one that concerns relations.

P2.a For every truth T of that kind, if T a priori entails a truth T^*, then T^* is of that kind too.

P3.a No truth about consciousness is a truth of that kind.

As I have suggested elsewhere (Stoljar 2006, 2009), however, in this form the argument is not plausible. First, as against P1.a, there is no reason to suppose that physics cannot tell us about properties that are not relations. Second, as against P2.a, it is false that from truths about relations only truths about relations follow—e.g. from the truths about the relations between points in space one can derive a truth about the shape of the region these points constitute. Third, as against P3.a, some truths about consciousness are themselves relational.

Now a natural response to these points is to abandon the first version in favour of another; the bulk of the discussion to follow will be concerned with suggestions of this type. But before turning to them, it is worth mentioning a different reply prompted by a point made by Alter (2009, see also Alter and Nagasawa 2012).[14] According to this reply, 'truths about consciousness are not truths solely about structure and dynamics' (Alter 2009, 764). On the assumption that 'structure and dynamics' is here interpreted along the lines

---

positive view (though a false view, as we now think of it) about the nature of the world, the classical form of which was a kind of atomism. Contemporary materialists do not deny this; they instead suggest that their view inherits enough from the traditional doctrine to be properly called 'materialism'. In my view this is not so; there is no way to liberalize materialism and retain a view that is true to its origins and yet deserves the name. So perhaps we may put the overall point like this. In the loose and popular sense, both RM and NM are versions of materialism; in the strict and philosophical sense, neither is. Either way, we have no reason to suppose that NM is a version of materialism while RM is not.

14. Alter and Nagasawa 2012 develop this point by appealing to a notion introduced by Pereboom 2011, viz., that of a purely extrinsic property. I express some doubts about this notion below.

of the first version of the argument we are considering, the suggestion is that truths about consciousness are not truths solely about relations.

Actually, there are two ways to take this suggestion. First, in saying that truths about consciousness are not solely relational, Alter might be making the point that truths about consciousness are not *all* relational, i.e. some are relational and some are not. Now this point is indeed of some interest, for it brings out that a version of the structure and dynamics argument may go through even if P3.a—according to which *no* truth about consciousness is a relational truth—is replaced with the weaker premise that *not every* truth about consciousness is a relational truth. Combining this weaker premise with P1.a and P2.a yields the result that some truths about consciousness are not physical, and that might well be enough to generate a problem for NM. However, even if this is so, pointing it out does not help this first version of the argument. For while it may be that not every truth about consciousness is a relational truth, it is likewise the case that not every physical truth is a relational truth; indeed this is precisely one of the problems with this version of the argument.

Second, in saying that truths about consciousness are not solely relational, Alter might be making the point that such truths, even when they are relational, are not only about relations. For example, take the truth that this pain is more intense than that pain. That is a relational truth, but it is not only about a relation, i.e. because it is also about the intensity of pain. Once again, however, while this point is correct, it does not change our assessment of the first version of the structure and dynamics argument. For if P3.a is interpreted that way, then P1.a must likewise be interpreted as saying that every physical truth is solely relational. But that is not so. Take any relational physical truth—for example, that the earth is heavier than the moon. That is a truth about a relation, but it is also a truth about the physical world. (It is not about pain, for example, or about biology.) So physical truths aren't solely relational either. Thus there is no way to defend this first version of the argument by appealing to the idea that truths are not solely relational.

The Second Version of the Argument

While the first version fails, Derk Pereboom (2011, 2014) has suggested a second version, and his suggestion has become widely adopted (see, e.g. Alter 2014, Alter and Nagasawa 2012, McClelland 2013).

Pereboom's idea is to draw a distinction between two sorts of intrinsic property, a comparatively intrinsic property and an absolutely intrinsic property. To illustrate the idea of a comparative intrinsic property, consider the shape of my brain, that is, the organ currently located in my skull. That my brain has this shape is an intrinsic property of it, at least on most understandings of what an intrinsic property is. Moreover, that my brain has this shape is plausibly a function of the parts of my brain having certain properties and standing in certain relations. Now suppose something that may or may not be true, viz., that my brain has the shape that it has, not because its parts instantiate various *intrinsic* properties, but because they instantiate various *extrinsic* properties. That does not conflict with shape of my brain being an intrinsic property of it, but it would make it (in Pereboom's sense) a comparatively intrinsic property.

On the assumption that the notions of a comparatively intrinsic property and an absolutely intrinsic property may be inter-defined, we might capture the relevant notions like this:

D2. F is a comparatively intrinsic property of x if and only if (a) F is an intrinsic property of x; and (b) there are extrinsic properties G_1, $G_2 \ldots G_n$ such that (i) the (proper) parts of x exhibit a pattern of instantiation of these properties and (ii) necessarily, if the parts of x exhibit that pattern of instantiation, then x has F.

D3. F is an absolutely intrinsic property of x if and only if (a) F is an intrinsic property of x; and (b) F is not a comparatively intrinsic property of x.

This suggestion about how to understand the comparative/absolute distinction is close but not quite the same as that found in Pereboom 2014, which is in turn close but not quite the same as that found in Pereboom 2011. In his earlier discussion Pereboom did not focus squarely on necessity, and in both discussions he appeals to the idea of purely extrinsic property, which is an extrinsic property that has no intrinsic aspects or components (2014, 50). I find the latter notion obscure. For example, take the property of being one among many, which is Pereboom's main example of a purely extrinsic property. Doesn't this property have the property of being numerical, and isn't this an intrinsic aspect (i.e. an intrinsic property) of that property? Indeed, take any extrinsic property at all; does it not have the intrinsic property of *being extrinsic*? If so, it is not a purely extrinsic property, and indeed no property is a purely extrinsic property in Pereboom's sense. For these reasons, it is unclear what a purely extrinsic property is. Fortunately, however, it will not be important for our purposes here to settle this matter. In drawing our attention to the comparative/absolute distinction, Pereboom has picked out something correct and important; precisely characterizing what he has picked out may be set aside.

But how does this distinction help with the structure and dynamics argument? Well we now have a further way to understand the notion of a structural truth. On this view, a structural truth is one that concerns either extrinsic properties or comparatively intrinsic properties; equivalently, it is a truth that does not concern absolutely intrinsic properties. Plugging this into the template, we arrive at this second version of the argument:

P1.b   Every physical truth is a truth of a certain kind, i.e., one that concerns either extrinsic properties or comparatively intrinsic properties.

P2.b   For every truth T of that kind, if T a priori entails a truth T^*, then T^* is of that kind too.

P3.b   No truth about consciousness is a truth of that kind.

Once again, these premises entail that the difference between standard and non-standard materialism, as understood by NM, does not matter as far as the conceivability argument is concerned.

This second version of the argument is better than the first. For one thing, that physics can tell us about properties that are not relations does not threaten P1.b. It is consistent with P1.b that physics tells about intrinsic properties and if these are non-relational properties, then physics tells about them. For another thing, pointing out that a thing can have a non-relational property because its parts stand in various relations does not threaten P2.b. It is consistent with P2.b that this happens.

Nevertheless, a serious problem for this argument emerges when we focus on why P3.b is true.[15] On the face of it many truths about consciousness concern both relations and extrinsic properties; indeed this point was one of our criticisms of the first version of the argument above. Suppose for example I am touching a piece of velvet. This involves a relation between the velvet on the one hand and me on the other; and yet that I am touching velvet is a truth about consciousness. Or consider the idea held by many philosophers of mind, viz., that to be in a conscious state is to bear a relation to something, e.g. a relation of awareness or acquaintance either to an individual or a property or proposition. Any position of this kind entails that there are truths about consciousness that are truths about relations.

---

15. There is a second problem for Pereboom's argument as well, viz. why and in what sense physics does not tell us about absolutely intrinsic properties. I will set this problem aside here, however.

Now a proponent of the second version of the argument can revise P3.b to avoid some of these problems. One might for example draw a clear distinction between intrinsic properties and relational properties, and suggest that while truths about consciousness are truths about relations they are also truths about intrinsic properties; e.g. being acquainted with a property might be a relational feature of a person as well as an intrinsic feature.[16] One might also say that what is important here is not that *all* truths about consciousness concern absolutely intrinsic properties, but merely that *some* do (cf. Pereboom 2014); indeed we noted the possibility of this move when discussing the first version of the argument above.

But even while these manoeuvres are available, it remains unclear that P3.b is true. For suppose that I feel as if I am touching a piece of velvet; and suppose that this property—feeling as if I am touching velvet—is an intrinsic property. Is it an *absolutely* intrinsic property? Surely that is an open question; it *might* be an absolutely intrinsic property, but then again it *might* not be. Indeed, this is true for many paradigmatic intrinsic properties. Suppose my brain has some particular shape *S*; and suppose that this property is an intrinsic property of my brain. Is it an absolutely intrinsic property? Once again, that is surely an open question. But the problem with P3.b is that, according to it, it is not an open question whether feeling as if one is touching velvet is absolutely intrinsic. On the contrary, the premise says directly that it is an absolutely intrinsic property; and that that is why it should be rejected.

Pereboom has responded to an earlier and briefer (see Stoljar 2014) presentation of this point by offering two arguments that properties such as feeling as if one is touching velvet are absolutely intrinsic (see Pereboom 2014). The first argument concerns the notion of primitive property, where 'a primitive property is (i) one whose entire qualitative nature or essence is revealed in our sensory or introspective representation of it, and thus is not identical to a property with a qualitative nature distinct from what is revealed by the representation, and (ii) one that is metaphysically simple and thus not constituted by a plurality of other properties' (2014, 59). On the basis of this, Pereboom argues as follows:[17]

(1) Experiential properties are primitive.
(2) Experiential properties are intrinsic.

---

16. The literature on intrinsic properties standardly draws a distinction here; see, e.g., Weatherson and Marshall 2013.

17. While this argument is set out in Pereboom 2014, he has since indicated (p.c.) that it does not represent his considered position, in part for the reasons I go on to describe. Since it is a somewhat natural argument, however, I will consider it in the text in any case.

(3) If experiential properties are intrinsic and primitive, then they are absolutely intrinsic.

(4) Ergo, experiential properties are absolutely intrinsic.

Here, (3) is intended to be a logical truth that follows from the definitions of the relevant notions; and (1) and (2) are intended to be truths which we can come to know or at least believe on the basis of introspection.[18] Since (1–3) entail (4), we seem to have a good argument that experiential properties are absolutely intrinsic.

But this argument is unpersuasive. First, regardless of its soundness, it is not an argument that the Russellian may make against the Nagelian, and so is of limited value for the present discussion whose focus is on the contrast between these views. The reason is that (1) is inconsistent with RM, at least in the version we have been considering. For RM in that version holds as against the dualist that experiential properties are not fundamental and so are not primitive in Pereboom's sense.

Second, it is far from clear that (1) is true or is something that we are liable to believe or know on the basis of introspection, as Pereboom suggests. When I feel as if I am touching velvet, I can certainly come to know or believe certain things on the basis of introspection. For example, I can come to know or believe that I feel as if I am touching velvet. Perhaps too I can come to know (in a variety of senses) the way one feels when one feels velvet. But to say that I can come to know on the basis of introspection that feeling velvet is a primitive property seems to me extremely implausible. To adapt a phrase David Lewis used in a related context, 'making discoveries in metaphysics is not so easy'—that is, you can't tell just by introspection that some property is

---

18. In the text I use the phrase 'on the basis of introspection' with the intention of abstracting away from various controversies in the philosophy of introspection that are lying just below the surface here. For example, in Pereboom's 2011 discussion of introspection we find a distinction between non-belief-like introspective representations on the one hand and introspective beliefs (i.e. beliefs occasioned in various ways by introspective representations) on the other. From this point of view, to say that S knows or believes p on the basis of introspection might be read as entailing that S has a non-belief-like introspective representation according to which p. I don't intend the phrase that way here, for two reasons. First, while he accepts the existence of non-belief-like introspective representations, Pereboom himself does not suppose that we have introspective representations according to which (e.g.) (2) is true; his suggestion is rather that belief in (2) is occasioned by introspective representations of other sorts. Second, it is controversial whether such non-belief-like introspective representations exist in the first place, since to suppose so is to treat introspection as deeply analogous to perception in ways it may not be.

or is not determined by some other property.[19] At least, the Nagelian Monist is perfectly entitled to deny this, and so this argument is unpersuasive.

Pereboom's second argument in favour of the view that experiential properties are absolutely intrinsic is an interesting variation on the original conceivability argument against materialism.[20] Suppose T is any truth at all about extrinsic properties and comparatively intrinsic properties, and T* is any truth about consciousness—e.g., the truth that I feel as if I am touching velvet. The premise of Pereboom's second argument is that it is conceivable that T is true and T* is false, in just the sense of 'conceivable' that is at issue in the original conceivability argument. The conclusion is that T* is not a truth about extrinsic or comparatively intrinsic properties, and so is a truth about (a truth which attributes) an absolutely intrinsic property.

But this argument is unpersuasive too. As we have seen, it is an open question whether the experiential property of feeling velvet is an absolutely intrinsic property or not; hence it is an open question whether T*, the truth that I am feeling velvet, attributes an absolutely intrinsic property or not. And this means that the conjunction Pereboom has in mind is not conceivable in the sense he intends. For consider: if T* concerns an absolutely intrinsic property (which it might do), then Pereboom's conjunction will be conceivable, but if it does not (which it might not), Pereboom's conjunction is not conceivable. Either way, one cannot rely on this argument to establish that this truth about consciousness concerns an absolutely intrinsic property.

In sum, while the second version of the structure and dynamics argument offered by Pereboom is an improvement on the first, it is only successful if we have good reason to suppose that its third premise (P3.b) is true. But Pereboom has provided no reason to suppose that P3.b is true. Hence this version of the argument should be rejected.

---

19. What Lewis in fact said is 'making discoveries in neurophysiology is not so easy' (1995, 329). In effect, this is the argument from revelation against materialism as discussed in Lewis 1995 and Stoljar 2009 (see also Johnston 2002).

20. Here is Pereboom's (2014, 59) way of stating this argument: 'if we let PRP be any epistemically possible description of the world that features only purely relational properties, the intuition that 'PRP and ~Q' is ideally, primarily and positively conceivable will be very strong. If from this we can conclude that the phenomenal truths are not necessitated by or derivable from the purely relational truths, we can also conclude that the phenomenal truths are not truths exclusively about purely relational and merely comparatively intrinsic properties. And this in turn would entail that the phenomenal truths are at least partly about absolutely intrinsic properties and/or absolutely intrinsic aspects of properties'.

The Third Version of the Argument

The two versions of the structure and dynamics argument we have considered so far have in common the view that a structural truth is a truth that *concerns* or is *about* properties of a certain sort. The first version says that a structural truth is one that concerns properties that are not one-place properties; the second version says that a structural truth is one that concerns properties that are either extrinsic or comparatively intrinsic.

Now if one looks at the passage from Chalmers 2002 quoted above, it would be very natural to assume that this was in fact how the argument should be understood; that is, it would be very natural to assume that structural truths are truths with a certain metaphysical subject matter. But more recently, in *The Character of Consciousness*, Chalmers has corrected this interpretation. A structural truth, he says, is not a truth that *concerns* a property, relational or not, absolutely intrinsic or not; rather it is a truth that can be *formulated* in a certain vocabulary: 'In formal terms, a structural-dynamic description is one that is equivalent to a Ramsey sentence whose O-terms include at most spatiotemporal expressions, nomic expressions, and logical and mathematical expressions' (2010, 120n17).[21]

Plugging this into the template we arrive at this third version of the structure and dynamics argument:

P1.c   Every physical truth is a truth of a certain kind, i.e., one a priori[22] equivalent to a Ramsey sentence whose o-terms are limited to (a) spatiotemporal expressions; (b) nomic expressions; (c) mathematical and logical expressions.

P2.c   For every truth *T* of that kind, if *T* a priori entails a truth *T**, then *T** is of that kind too.

P3.c   No truth about consciousness is a truth of that kind.

Once, again, if these premises are true then the difference between standard and non-standard materialism, as understood by NM, does not matter as far as the conceivability argument goes.

---

21. In the reference to 'O-terms' and 'Ramsey-sentence', Chalmers is alluding to the Ramsey-Carnap-Lewis account of theoretical terms. For relevant presentation of these ideas see Lewis 2009, and Chalmers 2012. I also connect them to Russellian Monism in Stoljar 2014.

22. In the passage quoted, Chalmers does not specify the sense of 'equivalent'. I will assume, however, that what is intended is 'a priori equivalent', where for any sentences S and S*, S is a priori equivalent to S* just in case the bi-conditional 'S is true if and only if S* is true' is knowable a priori.

Now this version of the argument is clearly different from the previous ones, and as a consequence avoids their problems. In particular, the fact that a truth can be formulated in a certain vocabulary does not tell us anything about the metaphysical character of the properties or relations the truth is about. For suppose there is an expression in the class Chalmers describes which has as its semantic value an intrinsic property (or an absolutely intrinsic property). That would not by itself stop a sentence containing that expression from being structural in the sense he has in mind. Hence a truth can be structural in Chalmers' sense and not be structural in (e.g.) Pereboom's sense, and vice versa.

But how plausible is this version of the argument? I want to address this question by focusing on what spatiotemporal expressions are. It is clear that the argument presupposes that spatiotemporal expressions are a certain class of expression, and so to assess the argument we need to know what determines membership of that class. Now in *Constructing the World*, Chalmers offers an answer to this question which, following him, I will call 'phenomenal functionalism'. On this view, spatial expressions 'function to pick out that manifold of properties that serves as the normal causal basis of a corresponding manifold of properties in our spatial experience' (2012, 335). On the assumption that this applies to spatio*temporal* expressions and not simply to *spatial* expressions, spatiotemporal functionalism says that a spatiotemporal expression is one that functions to pick out the manifold of properties that serves as the normal causal basis of a corresponding manifold of properties in our spatiotemporal experience.

However, when we combine this suggestion with the third version of the structure and dynamics argument just outlined, we confront a major problem, viz. that if phenomenal functionalism is true, the structure and dynamics argument is unpersuasive. There are two different ways to bring out this central point.[23]

The first way starts by bringing to the surface a presupposition that is held by at least some proponents of the structure and dynamics argument, viz., that whatever physical or structural truths are exactly, no such truth a priori

---

23. Indeed the point here is of considerable interest when placed in the larger context of Chalmers' work. For the Chalmers of *The Character of Consciousness* says that the structure and dynamics argument is sound and should be interpreted in a particular way, in particular as involving the notion of a spatiotemporal expression. And the Chalmers of *Constructing the World* tells us that phenomenal functionalism is the best account of what a spatiotemporal expression is. The problem is that the first Chalmers seems to be on a collision course with the second!

entails any truth about consciousness. If we do assume this, and if we further assume that phenomenal functionalism is true, it immediately follows that P1.c is false. For P1.c says that physical truths are equivalent to various truths formulated in a certain vocabulary including spatiotemporal vocabulary; and phenomenal functionalism says that truths formulated in spatiotemporal vocabulary are a priori equivalent to (or a priori entail) truths about consciousness. Putting this together, P1.c says that physical truths are a priori equivalent to, or a priori entail, truths about consciousness. But if that is so, and if no physical truth a priori entails any truth about consciousness, P1.c is false.

The second way focuses instead on P3.c, the claim that no truth of the relevant kind is a truth about consciousness. If phenomenal functionalism is true, this claim is false too. For, given phenomenal functionalism, some truths about consciousness will indeed be structural truths on the present understanding, or at any rate will be a priori equivalent to such truths. To illustrate, take the truth 'there are spatiotemporal experiences that have causes', which is a truth about consciousness. This truth entails 'there are things which cause spatiotemporal experiences', and this is a structural truth *if* we assume phenomenal functionalism. Similarly, take the truth 'there are things which cause spatiotemporal experiences' which is a structural truth by the suggested standard. This truth entails 'there are spatiotemporal experiences that have causes', and this is a truth about consciousness.

How might one respond to the point that if phenomenal functionalism is true, the structure and dynamics argument is unpersuasive? There are four main objections to this; I will go through them one by one:[24]

Response 1: 'Phenomenal functionalism tells us *at most* that some truths about consciousness are spatiotemporal truths, viz., those about spatiotemporal experience. However, aren't there also *other* truths about consciousness, i.e., those not about spatiotemporal experience? If so, the argument will still go through for the by now familiar reason, viz., that the third premise may be weakened so that it says only that not every truth about consciousness is structural'.

Reply: This is true in principle but in practice it would require separating out experiences that are spatiotemporal from experiences that are not, and this is very difficult if not impossible to do. Any truth about consciousness will concern experiences of some sort, and almost any sort of experience arguably will be spatiotemporal at least in a sense. Take for example

---

24. I am indebted to discussion with David Chalmers in formulating these responses.

perceptual experiences; experiences of this sort seem to represent objects as having various spatial and temporal properties and so are themselves partly spatiotemporal.

Response 2: 'Phenomenal functionalism is only one sort of functionalism. In *Constructing the World*, Chalmers also describes a position called "non-phenomenal functionalism," which is the same as phenomenal functionalism except that "the roles will not involve connections to our spatial experiences, but rather will be structural roles within the physical realm" (2012, 332). If we adopt a non-phenomenal functionalism, the problem is avoided'.

Reply: The phrase 'structural roles within the physical realm' is not very clear, especially in a context in which it is contested just what 'structural' and 'physical' are supposed to mean. But as I understand him, what Chalmers intends by non-phenomenal functionalism is a position exactly like phenomenal functionalism except that spatiotemporal expressions are *themselves* defined in terms of mathematical/logical and causal/nomic expressions. So on this interpretation, P1.c says that every physical truth is one that is a priori equivalent to a truth formulable using only nomic/mathematical and causal/nomological vocabulary.

But the problem now is that this is a very implausible account of what physical truths are. To illustrate this, consider the temporal phase of the actual world from its beginning up to the point at which life (and therefore consciousness in the ordinary sense) evolved—call it *Pre-life*—and suppose I am omniscient with respect to the structural truths (in the sense at issue) that obtain there. In effect, this means that I know a huge body of truths about Pre-life of the following type:

(i)   There is an object, a, and a property F, such that a instantiates F;
(ii) There is a pair of objects a and b, and a pair of properties F and G such that a instantiates F, and b instantiates G;
(iii) There is a pair of objects a and b, and a pair of properties F and G such that a instantiates F, and b instantiates G, and F and G are lawfully correlated.

Now if physical truths are structural truths in this sense, structural omniscience with respect to Pre-life is also physical omniscience with respect to it; that is, I would know not merely all the structural truths that obtain in this part of the world but all the physical truths too. That is clearly not so, however. For consider some truth V—as it might be, the truth that the volcano at this place erupted at this time. On the face of it, no matter how many truths I know that are similar to those in (i–iii), I will not know V. The reason is that

truths of the (i–iii) type tell me only that there are certain objects that have certain properties that stand in certain lawful relations; they do not tell me what
kind of objects, properties and lawful relations these are. So, for example, even
if I know that there is some object that has some property, I will not know that
the object is a volcano and that the property is the property of erupting.[25] But
if that is true, P1.c should be rejected because it offers an implausible account
of what a physical truth is. More generally, just as phenomenal functionalism is inconsistent with the persuasiveness of the structure and dynamics
argument, so too is non-phenomenal functionalism; if either view is true, the
argument should be rejected.

Response 3: 'Functionalism in either its phenomenal or non-phenomenal
form is only one type of account of what spatiotemporal expressions are.
Another account discussed in *Constructing the World* is the primitivist account
that treats these expressions not as a priori equivalent to definite descriptions
of a certain form but instead as names for a certain class of properties and
relations. If we adopt primitivism, then the conflict between the phenomenal
functionalism and the structure and dynamics argument is avoided'.

Reply: The first point to make about primitivism is that, unlike functionalism of either sort, it does not by itself answer the question we started with,
viz., what sort of expression is a spatiotemporal expression? Hence, if one
appeals to primitivism, one would need to elaborate it to answer that question;
as I said above, spatiotemporal expressions are a type of expression and the
persuasiveness of the argument depends in part on how we understand that
type. I see two main possibilities here.

On the first—which I take to be Chalmers' own view—spatiotemporal
expressions are those that denote a certain class of property and relation,
namely, the ones that obtain in what Chalmers calls Eden, the mythical place
in which, as he puts it, 'we had unmediated contact with the world. We were
directly acquainted with objects in the world and with their properties. Objects
were simply presented to us without causal mediation, and properties were
revealed to us in their true intrinsic glory' (2010, 381). But the problem with
this is that properties instantiated in Eden, including spatiotemporal properties, are not in fact instantiated, or so Chalmers plausibly argues. And if this is
the case, introducing primitive expressions of this sort makes no difference to
the nature of the physical truths mentioned in P1.c, i.e., for no physical truth

---

25. The point in the text is closely related to a problem mentioned by Chalmers in his discussion of 'nomic structuralism', viz., that it is 'open to multiple realization, and that it will
leave certain truths about the nature of the parameter unsettled' (2013, 412).

will attribute any such property. Hence appealing to primitivism of this variety is no advance on the suggestions already considered.

On the second, a spatiotemporal expression is any expression that one might introduce in the course of explaining the scientific counterparts of Edenic properties. Since the scientific counterparts of Edenic properties are different from the Edenic properties themselves, and are presumably instanti-ated, this suggestion avoids the problem just noted. But the issue now is that, understood this way, the class of the primitive spatiotemporal expressions is extremely open ended, i.e. since it depends on what exactly those scientific counterparts are and what their explanation turns out to be. Given that it is open ended, it is in turn unclear that P3.c is true. More generally, appealing to conceptual primitivism does not alter the underlying situation.

Response 4: 'Suppose phenomenal functionalism is indeed in conflict with the structure and dynamics argument. Even so, this is merely a pyrrhic victory for the Nagelian Monist, since that position cannot appeal to phenomenal functionalism in any case. What phenomenal functionalism does in effect is treat truths about spatiotemporal experience, and experience more gener-ally, as conceptually primitive truths of the world. That does not immediately entail that experiential truths are metaphysically fundamental but it comes very close to doing so, and the path from a truth's being conceptually primi-tive to it being metaphysically fundamental is not something the Nagelian is liable to block. But Nagelian Monism is inconsistent with the truths about consciousness being fundamental'.

Reply: It is true that Nagelian Monism sits uneasily with phenomenal func-tionalism. Indeed, this is not only for the reason given but for the further reason that the program that phenomenal functionalism is central to—that is, the program of *Constructing the World*—involves a kind of rationalism accord-ing to which any truth at all follows a priori from some truth of a kind cur-rently known to us, or at least currently known to some idealized versions of us. This is something that NM rejects from the start. But none of this detracts from the points we have just made against the third version of the structure and dynamics argument, for at least three reasons. First, while, as we have seen, the argument is unpersuasive if phenomenal functionalism is true, it is likewise unpersuasive if various alternatives to phenomenal functionalism are true, e.g. non-phenomenal functionalism or primitivism. So our criticism of the argument does not depend on the truth of phenomenal functionalism. Second, it is not as if these alternatives are unavailable to NM, though admit-tedly this issue requires much more discussion than I can give it here—for example it is an open possibility that the Nagelian Monist could hold the sec-ond kind of primitivism mentioned above, the kind that treats spatiotemporal expressions as those introduced in the course of explaining the scientific counterparts of Edenic properties. Finally, recall that our interest in the structure and dynamics argument in the first place is to ascertain whether we have any reason to favour RM over NM; but if Nagelian Monism is in conflict with phenomenal functionalism, that is also true of Russellian Monism—for it too is a position that denies that experiential properties are fundamental. So, again, this third version of the argument is not successful.

Conclusion

I have considered three versions of the structure and dynamics argument, and suggested in each case that it is unpersuasive. The problem has not been—as is sometimes suggested (cf. Alter and Nagasawa 2012)—that the various notions of a structural truth we have examined are unclear or vague; by most standards they are clear enough. The problem is rather that there are lots of different notions here and no matter which one is in play the structure and dynamics argument is unpersuasive against NM.

Suppose now we agree that the structure and dynamics argument is unpersuasive; where does that leave the project we identified at the outset, the project of finding a view that is neither materialism nor dualism? In my view it leaves us much better off than we would otherwise be. For the structure and dynamics argument is one of those arguments in philosophy that is supposed to narrow the field; if successful it would suggest, in particular, that RM is the only position here that fits the bill. If what I have been saying is right, however, this is not so. RM is *one* sort of view that fits the bill but it is not the *only* sort, for NM also remains a possibility. And this makes it more, rather than less, likely that a position that is neither standard materialism nor standard dualism is the truth about nature.

References

Alter, T. 2009. 'Does the Ignorance Hypothesis Undermine the Conceivability and Knowledge Arguments?', *Philosophy and Phenomenological Research* 79: 756–65.

Alter, T. 2013. 'Review of Pereboom's *Consciousness and the Prospects of Physicalism*', *Mind*, doi: 10.1093/mind/fzt008. First published online: March 22, 2013.

Alter, T., and Y. Nagasawa. 2012. 'What Is Russellian Monism?', *Journal of Consciousness Studies* 19 (9–10): 67–95.

Chalmers, D. 2002. 'Consciousness and Its Place in Nature', in Chalmers, D. (ed.) *Philosophy of Mind: Contemporary and Classical Readings*. New York: Oxford University Press, pp. 247–72.

Chalmers, D. 2010. *The Character of Consciousness*. New York: Oxford University Press.

Chalmers, D. 2012. *Constructing the World*. Oxford: Oxford University Press.

Evans, G. 1980. 'Things without the Mind—A Commentary on Chapter 2 of Strawson's Individuals', in Zak Van Straaten (ed.) *Philosophical Subjects*. Oxford: Clarendon Press, pp. 76–116.

Johnston, M. 2002. 'How to Speak of the Colors', *Philosophical Studies* 68: 221–63.

Kind, A. 'Pessimism about Russellian Monism', chapter 18 of this volume.

Lewis, D. 1995. 'Should a Materialist Believe in Qualia?', *Australasian Journal of Philosophy* 73: 140–44.

Lewis, D. 2009. 'Ramseyan Humility', in David Braddon-Mitchell and Robert Nola (eds.) *Conceptual Analysis and Philosophical Naturalism*. Cambridge, MA: MIT Press, pp. 203–22.

McClelland, T. 2013. 'The Neo-Russellian Ignorance Hypothesis: A Hybrid Account of Phenomenal Consciousness', *Journal of Consciousness Studies* 20 (3–4): 125–51 (27).

Pereboom, D. 2011. *Consciousness and the Prospects of Physicalism*. New York: Oxford University Press.

Pereboom, D. 2014. 'Russellian Monism and Absolutely Intrinsic Properties', in U. Kriegel (ed.) *Current Controversies in Philosophy of Mind*. London: Routledge, pp. 40–69.

Russell, B. 1927. *The Analysis of Matter*. London: Kegan Paul.

Stoljar, D. 2001. 'Two Conceptions of the Physical', *Philosophy and Phenomenological Research* 62 (2): 253–81.

Stoljar, D. 2006. *Ignorance and Imagination: The Epistemic Origin of the Problem of Consciousness*. New York: Oxford University Press.

Stoljar, D. 2009. 'The Argument from Revelation', in David Braddon-Mitchell and Robert Nola (eds.) *Conceptual Analysis and Philosophical Naturalism*. Cambridge, MA: MIT Press, pp. 113–38..

Stoljar, D. 2010. *Physicalism*. London: Routledge.

Stoljar, D. 2014. 'Four Kinds of Russellian Monism', in U. Kriegel (ed.) *Current Controversies in Philosophy of Mind*. London: Routledge, pp. 17–35.

Weatherson, Brian and Dan Marshall. 2013. 'Intrinsic vs. Extrinsic Properties', in Edward N. Zalta (ed.) *The Stanford Encyclopedia of Philosophy* (Spring 2013 Edition), <http://plato.stanford.edu/archives/spr2013/entries/intrinsic-extrinsic/>.

16

A Physicalist Critique
of Russellian Monism

Alyssa Ney

ONE WAY OF understanding the view that is today called 'Russellian Monism' is as the combination of the following five interrelated theses:

(1) *Physical Structuralism*: Physics describes its most fundamental features only relationally.
(2) *The Structure-Grounding Thesis*: There must be some account of fundamental intrinsic features to supplement or support the relational description of physics (of (1)).
(3) *The Phenomenal Intrinsicality Thesis*: There exist intrinsic, phenomenal features that constitute the natures of our conscious experiences.
(4) *The Phenomenal-Grounding Thesis*: Either these intrinsic, phenomenal features (of (3)) are fundamental, or there must be more fundamental, intrinsic features on which they depend.
(5) *The Unification Thesis*: The structure-grounding intrinsic features (of (2)) are identical to the phenomenal-grounding intrinsic features (of (4)).

The present chapter will offer a critique of Russellian Monism from the perspective of a committed physicalist (i.e. one who adopts physics as an exhaustive guide to her fundamental ontological commitments). I have stated many of the above theses in a way that is purposefully vague so as to be neutral between the various statements of Russellian Monism that are found in the work of Bertrand Russell and those today whom he inspired. As will be obvious to anyone who has worked through the preceding essays in this volume, there is no one position that goes by the name 'Russellian Monism.' Rather, there are a broad variety of positions captured under this umbrella, not all of which are obviously motivated by the same considerations that moved Russell. I believe all Russellian Monists would accept something at least roughly like the five theses I have presented above. All will accept that in some sense what we learn of the fundamental features of reality from physics comes by way of a relational characterization of these features (Physical Structuralism), and that this fact motivates us to think that there is more to the world than what can be understood via this relational characterization (the Structure-Grounding Thesis). Russellian Monists also take seriously the existence of intrinsic, phenomenal features that are partly constitutive of our conscious experience of the world (the Phenomenal Intrinsicality Thesis) and believe that if these phenomenal features are not fundamental, then they must be grounded in further features of the world that are also intrinsic (the Phenomenal Grounding Thesis). And finally, Russellian Monists believe those intrinsic features that constitute or ground the nature of our conscious experience are identical to those intrinsic features that play a role in grounding the relational structure of fundamental physics. This is what makes the position a version of monism. Phenomenal and physical reality are not ultimately distinct but are each grounded in a common set of fundamental, intrinsic features. Russell himself calls the view 'Neutral Monism.'

Although all Russellian Monists would likely accept these theses as they have so far been loosely stated, there is probably no one way of making them more precise that would likely appeal to everyone.[1] Although (I believe) the third thesis, the Phenomenal Intrinsicality Thesis, is fairly precise—it is interpreted by all who discuss the position as a claim about the reality of intrinsic, phenomenal qualia that is motivated on the basis of simple (naïve) introspection—there is variation in how Russellian Monists would interpret the 'relational description' of physics. As a result of this difference, there is variation in both the reasons Russellian Monists give for thinking that physics provides only a relational characterization of the fundamental features of the world and why they think such a characterization must be incomplete. There is in addition no consensus on what it is in virtue of which the Phenomenal-Grounding thesis is true.[2] Indeed really, Russellian Monism comes in two versions: a phenomenalist version that takes the intrinsic, phenomenal features

---

1. Even as they stand, some might object to the above characterizations, for example, of (2) as a claim about grounding.

2. I will not discuss this thesis in detail here. For discussion, see Pereboom (2011), pp. 111–14.

of conscious experience to be fundamental, and a protophenomenalist version that posits a realm of more fundamental, intrinsic properties that "are not themselves phenomenal but together ... yield the phenomenal" (Chalmers 1996, p. 127). Much of what I will do here will involve distinguishing various forms of Russellian Monism and clarifying the motivations for their constituent theses. I will focus my discussion on two of the main parts of any version of Russellian Monism: Physical Structuralism and the Structure-Grounding Thesis, and show why one has good reason to be skeptical about the various versions of these claims one finds in discussion of Russellian Monism. Since I will not be focusing in later sections on either the Phenomenal Intrinsicality Thesis or the Unification Thesis, let me close the introduction by saying a bit more about each of them.

The Phenomenal Intrinsicality Thesis takes our conscious experiences to involve the instantiation of at least some intrinsic, phenomenal features, although the thesis is neutral as I have stated it as to whether these are basic, intrinsic features or intrinsic features that may be reduced in some way. To say that something is an intrinsic feature is to say that it is a feature that an entity has solely by virtue of how it is in itself, not how it is with respect to other things (Lewis 1986, p. 61). The Phenomenal Intrinsicality Thesis is rightly controversial. Over the past twenty years or more, physicalists have given compelling reasons to think that insofar as there are features that constitute the natures of our conscious experiences, these are not intrinsic features. One influential position, for example, is representationalism, the view that phenomenal character either just is or supervenes upon a particular kind of representational content (e.g. Dretske 1995, Tye 1995). On many theories of intentionality, what a system represents is a function not only of what it is like in itself, but also what it was like in the past and how it is with respect to various features of the environment in which it is embedded. Thus, if representationalism is true, this puts pressure on the Phenomenal Intrinsicality Thesis that constitutes an essential part of Russellian Monism. Now not all physicalists are sympathetic to representationalism. Some (e.g. Ned Block 2003) would argue that phenomenal features are not reducible to representational features since there are features of conscious experiences that do not represent the world as being a certain way, but characterize the experiences as they are in themselves. This is shown by presenting cases of phenomenal experiences that purportedly lack representational contents or pairs of experiences that are alike in representational content but differ in phenomenal character (e.g. inverted spectrum scenarios). Representationalists have developed responses to these purported counterexamples and the debate continues. However, the

Phenomenal Intrinsicality Thesis now faces pressure from another source, recent epistemological work which may justify skepticism about the sort of naïve introspection on which our confidence in the thesis rests. Is it so clear that our conscious experiences themselves have determinate ways they are in themselves in the first place (be they reducible to representational contents or themselves brute)? Recent work is finally bringing this claim under closer scrutiny.[3] Given all of this, no philosopher should uncritically accept the Phenomenal Intrinsicality Thesis, the claim that there exist intrinsic, phenomenal features that constitute the natures of our conscious experiences. However obvious it seems at first blush, there are good reasons to be skeptical.

Finally, I would like to briefly address the Unification Thesis. To me, it is really the prospect of the unification of phenomenal and physical reality that makes Russellian Monism such an intriguing point of view worthy of discussion. If one were to accept the other four theses that constitute the position, then the fifth, unification thesis, would be attractive. For, if one already thought there must be some intrinsic features to support the claims of physics, features of whose natures we are ignorant just on the basis of physics itself, and yet there were these other features of which we were also aware, though we were not necessarily sure about *their* respective natures either, features needed to support phenomenal reality, then it would be a very bold hypothesis, but one that would be very tempting, that what we have are not two distinct sets of fundamental intrinsic features, but just one set. This proposal strikes me, suspending disbelief about the four theses that lead up to it, at least as bold and exciting as Newton's proposed unification of terrestrial and cosmic reality. There is of course no deductive argument one may state motivating a unification like this and unlike the case of Newton's unification, there probably won't ever be evidence to confirm the hypothesis; nonetheless it is motivated on grounds of ontological parsimony and would be very interesting if true. With this concession, let's return to the first two theses, both of which are contentious and worthy of more discussion.

---

3. A pioneer here was Daniel Dennett (1991). Derk Pereboom (2011, Chapters 1–4) also suggests that introspection may mislead us as to whether our conscious experiences have any intrinsic, phenomenal features. Schwitzgebel (2011, especially Chapters 6 and 7) also tries to show us how introspection may mislead as to the characters of current conscious experiences (although of the three, Schwitzgebel is least interested in moving from this claim about the unreliability of naïve introspection to skepticism about the very existence of such determinate phenomenal characters).

1. Four Kinds of Physical Structuralism

Above, I characterized Physical Structuralism loosely as the claim that physics describes its most fundamental features only relationally. We can now be more precise and explore the specific sorts of claims that various philosophers have made along these lines. At least four distinct theses have been suggested.[4] These must be evaluated on different grounds.

> *Psychological/Epistemological*: Physics may posit fundamental intrinsic features, but the only parts of any fundamental physical theory that we may know about are that theory's relational (or extrinsic) features.
>
> *Semantic*: Physics posits fundamental, intrinsic features, but the meaning of these concepts is given only via relational descriptions.
>
> *Descriptive*: (Current and likely any future) physics posits only relational (or extrinsic) features as fundamental. It posits no fundamental, intrinsic features.
>
> *Normative*: A proper or ideal physical theory (or physics properly understood) is a theory that only posits relational (or extrinsic) features as fundamental. Ideal physics never posits fundamental, intrinsic features.

When I say 'extrinsic,' I intend a contrast with 'intrinsic.' This refers to a particular kind of feature, one that is had in virtue of an entity's relations to other things. To say that physics posits only extrinsic features is to say that it does not posit any features describing fundamental facts about what objects are like in themselves. This contrasts with my use of 'relational' which is broader and may apply to descriptions or ways of knowing about features, including intrinsic features.

It is possible to understand the structuralist thesis that forms part of Russellian Monism either as denying that our most fundamental science, physics (actual or ideal), posits any fundamental, intrinsic features (as in what I am calling the 'Descriptive' and 'Normative' versions of Physical Structuralism), or in such a way as to allow that physics posits fundamental,

---

4. In some cases, it is not clear which thesis a given Russellian Monist has in mind. I think it is especially difficult to determine which of the following four theses David Chalmers is expressing sympathy with when he discusses Physical Structuralism, e.g. in his (1996), p. 153. Here I won't primarily be so concerned to argue for historical claims about which philosophers hold (or held) which structuralist theses, but instead the philosophical issue of what may be said for or against these various positions.

intrinsic features, while claiming that for one reason or other we are in the dark as to the nature or identity of these features (as in what I am calling the 'Psychological/Epistemological' and 'Semantic' versions of Physical Structuralism). The forms of Physical Structuralism one finds in Russell and David Lewis both assume that physics posits fundamental, intrinsic features. However, for different reasons, they both come to the conclusion that we are in the dark as to the nature of these features.[5] It is something about the way physical science works that it will always leave us in the dark as to the identity of the fundamental intrinsic properties. Perhaps philosophy can help us understand what physics' story is missing.

2. Russell's Epistemological Structuralism

Let's consider Russell first. Russell comes to Physical Structuralism by considering general epistemological worries about our perceptual engagement with the world. Although the details of Russell's particular theory of perception changed over the years (e.g. Russell transitioned from having a sense datum theory to a theory where the objects of perception were physical entities, so-called 'percepts'), the elements leading to structuralism were already in place at least as early as 1912's *The Problems of Philosophy*. They start from Russell's distinction between two spaces: the physical space in which material objects (including ourselves) exist and the perceptual space in which our representation of material objects exist. Here are some key passages:

> We agreed provisionally that physical objects cannot be quite like our sense-data, but may be regarded as *causing* our sensations. These physical objects are in the space of science, which we may call 'physical' space. Now our sense-data are situated in our private spaces, either the space of sight or the space of touch or such vaguer spaces as other senses may give us. If, as science and common sense assume, there is one public all-embracing physical space in which physical objects are, the relative positions of physical objects in physical space must more or less correspond to the relative positions of sense-data in our private spaces ... (pp. 30–31)

---

5. Lewis himself was not explicitly a Russellian Monist. He considers a phenomenalist version of the hypothesis in his (2009), p. 217, but rejects it. He does not consider the protophenomenalist version.

Assuming that there is physical space, and that it does thus correspond to private spaces, what can we know about it? We can know *only* what is required in order to secure the correspondence. That is to say, we can know nothing of what it is like in itself, but we can know the sort of arrangement of physical objects which results from their spatial relations. (p. 31)

Thus, by these observations about the relationship of the mind to the world in perception, Russell gets to the conclusion that we know nothing of the intrinsic nature of physical space. He then extends this reasoning to infer that we also know nothing of the intrinsic qualities of physical objects in space.

What we have found as regards space is much the same as what we find in relation to the correspondence of the sense-data with their physical counterparts. If one object looks blue and another red, we may reasonably presume that there is some corresponding difference between the physical objects: if two objects both look blue, we may presume a corresponding similarity. But we cannot hope to be acquainted directly with the quality in the physical object which makes it look blue or red. Science tells us that this quality is a certain sort of wave-motion, and this sounds familiar, because we think of wave-motions in the space we see. But the wave-motions must really be in physical space, **with which we have no direct acquaintance**; thus the real wave-motions have not that familiarity which we might have supposed them to have. And what holds for colours is closely similar to what holds for other sense-data. Thus we find that, although the *relations* of physical objects have all sorts of knowable properties, derived from their correspondence with the relations of sense-data, the physical objects themselves remain unknown in their intrinsic nature, so far at least as can be discovered by means of the senses. (p. 34, my emphasis in bold)

I quote at length from Russell (1912) to make it clear how this form of Physical Structuralism was already endorsed by Russell at this time, and that it should be clear from this passage that it was motivated by general epistemological considerations. It is not motivated by an examination of specific physical theories as is sometimes supposed (although he uses examples from physics to illustrate the view).

By this point, Russell did not have all elements of Russellian Monism on the table. The Physical Structuralism is there, but the Unification Thesis is not. In 1927's *The Analysis of Matter*, which draws on Russell's knowledge of relativity and quantum theory, Russell thinks he has found a way to answer the question of how we could know the intrinsic natures of physical objects. This is where he proposes unification and where we find the Russellian Monist position. But the Physical Structuralism itself, this is something that is motivated by a general theory of perception, not by reflection on the specific types of features science posits. It comes from the point that although objects have intrinsic features and these cause our experiences, we don't learn through physical science what these intrinsic features are. We may only infer the extrinsic features of physical objects, the relations they bear to one another, and the relations their intrinsic features bear to each other. For example, the intrinsic physical feature responsible for our sensation of redness is different from the intrinsic physical feature responsible for our sensation of blueness. And the intrinsic physical feature responsible for our sensation of pinkness is more similar to that responsible for our sensation of redness than that responsible for our sensation of blueness. But it is impossible for us to have knowledge of these physical features that goes beyond their relational structures.

For Russell, we know our sensations much better than anything physics can tell us due to the directness of the link between ourselves and our experiences—knowledge of them is knowledge by acquaintance. There are certainly still philosophers today who find some aspects of this theory convincing (see Gertler 2011, Chapter 4), and for this reason I won't go so far as to say that such an idea is discredited. But this is by no means an obvious or uncontroversial view.[6] The knowledge physics gives us of the world is incredibly rich and informative. Consider Russell's own example of wave motions—the intrinsic features that physics takes to be responsible for our color sensations. It is not immediately clear why we should agree with Russell that we have no knowledge of these wave motions' intrinsic natures, only their similarities and dissimilarities with one another. Optics is a well-developed scientific theory. It makes very precise claims about the wave motions responsible for various sensations in us. Electromagnetic waves are assigned exact intrinsic features such as frequency, phase, and intensity. Even were we to accept a distinction between (a) the kind of knowledge we gain from physics which is indirect because it is of something outside our minds and their private spaces and (b) the knowledge we have of the intrinsic features of our sensations by acquaintance, why would this ground the claim that we can't have *any* knowledge of intrinsic features through physics? This is much stronger than what any contemporary defenders of knowledge by acquaintance want to claim. According to them, that kind of knowledge may be more reliable or perhaps immune to error in certain ways because of its directness, but that is not to say it is the only way one may have knowledge of intrinsic features.

---

6. See also the sources mentioned in footnote 3.

But perhaps Russell is presupposing a claim that goes beyond what he presented in 1912, a claim about the specific kind of knowledge we get from physics, and that physics itself doesn't even try to characterize the intrinsic features of objects in a way that goes beyond the relations these features bear to one another. (And so perhaps we should not interpret his later work as endorsing the psychological or epistemological version of Physical Structuralism.) In 1927's *Analysis of Matter*, after all, Russell did undertake an analysis of the best physical theories of his day, relativity and what then existed of quantum theory. Perhaps Russell is using his knowledge of physics rather than an *a priori* argument from the causal theory of perception to show that physics can only teach us of relational features.

But no. It is true that by 1927, as I have noted, Russell had updated his theory of perception. By this time he rejected sense-data, but he still held onto a causal theory of perception where "perception gives us no immediate knowledge of a physical object, but at best a datum for inference" (1927, p. 218) and this again is the basis for his structuralist thesis. What we get from perception are collections of percepts, which, according to Russell, are events. Using this new theory of perception, Russell again argues in a similar way to how he argued fifteen years earlier. He begins:

> The inference from perception to physics ... is one which depends upon certain postulates, the chief of which, apart from induction, is the assumption of a certain similarity of structure between cause and effect where both are complex. (p. 249)

And then, again going through first the question of our knowledge of physical space and then of physical qualities like colors, Russell argues that we only know structural features, not the natures of physical objects themselves. On space:

> My point is that the relations which physics assumes in assigning angular co-ordinates are not identical with those which we perceive in the visual field, but merely correspond with them in a manner which preserves their logical (mathematical) properties.[7] ... We need not

---

7. Here, we see confidence in the logicism of *Principia Mathematica*. One of the important developments in the attempted reduction of mathematics to logic was the ability to represent relations. Mathematical functions were analyzed in terms of relations enabling Russell to now interchange talk of mathematical features and relations.

assume that physical direction has anything in common with visual direction except the logical properties implied by the above assumption. (p. 252)

And on colors and other qualities:

The same sort of considerations apply to colours and sounds. Colours and sounds can be arranged in an order with respect to several characteristics . . . but this by itself determines only certain logical properties of the stimuli. This applies to all varieties of percepts, and accounts for the fact that our knowledge of physics is mathematical: it is mathematical because no non-mathematical properties of the physical world can be inferred from perception. (p. 253)

Again, I emphasize this conclusion derives from Russell's causal theory of perception and the assumption that our knowledge of the physical world arises from a mapping between objects in two distinct spaces: that of perception and that of the physical world. Russell's view does not entail that physics does not attempt to describe the intrinsic features of matter. Russell concedes physics describes particles as having intrinsic features like charge and mass (e.g. 1927, p. 25). It is just that when we understand the relation between our minds and the physical world, how perception works, we see that we can only know facts about the relations between these intrinsic features.

Once we see Russell's motivation for Physical Structuralism, I predict it will strike many of us today as not compelling. Our knowledge of fundamental physical features does not proceed by a mapping of them onto our experiences, yet this is an essential assumption of Russell's argument. The relationship between our fundamental physical frameworks and the world of our experience is much more complex than Russell's model reveals. The sophisticated mathematical apparatus of contemporary physics need not map 1:1 onto features of our experiences with a similar structure in order to be understood. Probably, although many Russellian Monists (and structuralists more generally) cite Russell's discussion in *Analysis of Matter* as inspiration, what they really have in mind is a different argument for a different view—that if we examine physical theories themselves, we see that physics never attempts to give intrinsic characterizations, even if it posits intrinsic features. This is more like the kind of reasoning we find in David Lewis.

3. Lewis's Semantic Structuralism

The version of Physical Structuralism found in Lewis arises out of his account of the meaning of theoretical terms from 1970. Lewis, like Russell, does not deny that physics tries to tell us about the intrinsic features of things. Physics postulates fundamental, intrinsic properties that play an important role in explanations. However, Lewis's view is that physics (like all theorizing) only characterizes features in terms of their distinctive causal or more broadly structural roles in a theory. In science, intrinsic properties like mass or charge are known and their meanings are given only in terms of relational characterizations.

Here is the rough idea. For Lewis, theoretical terms are introduced holistically in the context of an overall theory. To illustrate, let's consider the following extremely simple toy theory, T:

(T) All particles have mass and charge. All objects with mass attract one another. Those objects with the same charge repel each other. Those objects with different charge attract one another.

Here, 'mass' and 'charge' are theoretical terms introduced within T. If we want to understand the meanings of these theoretical terms, we may do so first by extracting the theory's Ramsey sentence, T_R. This is the sentence that results by replacing all of the theoretical terms with variables and introducing existential quantifiers to bind these variables:

(T_R) $\exists x \exists y$ (All particles have x and y. All objects with x attract one another. Those objects with the same y repel each other. Those objects with different y attract one another.)

According to Lewis, a theory will be true and its theoretical terms will be meaningful just in case there is a unique realization for the theory. In the case of T, since the Ramsey sentence has just two variables x and y, the theory will be uniquely realized just in case there is a unique pair of entities that realizes the theoretical roles of x and y. The definitions of the theoretical terms say that they are the unique entities that play the relevant theoretical roles. For example, in this case:

mass $=_{def}$ the unique x such that (All particles have x and charge. All objects with x attract one another. Those objects with the same charge repel each other. Those objects with different charge attract one another.)

and:

charge $=_{\text{def}}$ the unique y such that (All particles have mass and y. All objects with mass attract one another. Those objects with the same y repel each other. Those objects with different y attract one another.)

Thus, we can see that even though mass and charge may be taken to be intrinsic properties, their meanings are given by the roles they play in an overall theory. We only know these features by what the objects that possess them do, not what they are in themselves.

But, one might reasonably ask, why should we think that we are missing any knowledge of the identities of these properties when we learn a theory like T? Don't we learn which properties mass and charge are by learning their roles in the overall theory? What more could there be to know? In "Ramseyan Humility," Lewis answers this question. He notes that for theoretical terms like 'mass' and 'charge' to have meanings, there must be a unique realization for the theory's Ramsey sentence in the actual world. That is, in our example, our world must contain exactly one pair of intrinsic properties that play the mass and charge roles. However, this does not rule out that there may be other possible worlds where other intrinsic properties, distinct from the actual property mass and the actual property charge, play these theoretical roles. Let's call the pair of intrinsic properties that realize the theory in this other possible world 'schmass' and 'schmarge.' By hypothesis, schmass and schmarge are properties that are capable of playing exactly the same theoretical roles as mass and charge. So, Lewis notes, we could never acquire any means of knowing which intrinsic properties play the mass and charge roles at our world. And thus, we don't know the natures of the intrinsic properties of our physical theories:

Suppose [our theory] has multiple possible realizations, but only one of them is the actual realization. Then no possible observation can tell us which one is actual, because whichever one is actual, the Ramsey sentence will be true. There is indeed a true contingent proposition about which of the possible realizations is actual but we can never gain evidence for this proposition, and so can never know it. If there are multiple possible realizations, Humility follows. (p. 207)

Humility, as Lewis defines it, is the claim that we are ignorant of the intrinsic properties of substances. And this argument is a way into Physical Structuralism, in particular, the semantic version of that thesis. Physics posits intrinsic properties and so we know there are some, but physics can't tell us which properties these are.

Since Lewis wrote "Ramseyan Humility," many commentators have noted that this argument, what he calls 'the permutation argument,' is not a compelling argument for the conclusion that we do not know the intrinsic properties of things (Langton 2004, Schaffer 2005, Ney 2007). For this argument is a skeptical argument relying on the fact that the intrinsic properties of things could all be different without our noticing. But of course most mainstream views in epistemology today are versions of fallibilism, views that insist that just because there is a possibility (in this case a remote one) in which entities are different without our noticing, this doesn't necessarily undermine our knowledge. Yes, things would look the same to us if mass and charge were switched with schmass and schmarge. So things would look the same to us if all of the zebras at the zoo were replaced with very cleverly disguised mules. But this doesn't mean that we can't know the intrinsic properties at our world are mass and charge and the animal in the area marked with the sign 'ZEBRA' is a zebra. Indeed, as Rae Langton argues, Lewis's own contextualist epistemology (argued for in his "Elusive Knowledge") entails that he too should accept that in most contexts, 'Physics lets us know the fundamental intrinsic properties are mass and charge' expresses something true. These skeptical possibilities involving permutations are rightly ignored in most contexts and don't impact the truth of these epistemological claims. And, as has just been noted, fallibilist epistemologies will entail as well that our claims to know the natures of fundamental intrinsic properties are not undermined by remote switching possibilities.

So the argument for the particular structuralist thesis we find in Lewis relies on a controversial epistemology. But there is a more basic problem with this reasoning that arises even before we consider the possibility of switching. For it is not clear that Lewis's main point about the way theoretical terms are given meanings, that is, holistically in the context of overall theories, entails anything about their being understood merely as those features that objects have in virtue of which they bear certain relations to each other.

Lewis appears to assume as much by the time of "Ramseyan Humility." Describing the theoretical roles in terms of which the intrinsic properties of physics are understood, he describes these as nomological and locational roles.[8] A physical property's theoretical role will be a nomological role insofar as we may call the claims of the theory laws—hence 'nomological' role.[9] The locational role of a property is its pattern of instantiation at various locations in space-time. Lewis adds that the theoretical role must also include specification of locational roles because he allows that certain distinct properties of physics might exhibit enough symmetries so that there is no way to distinguish these properties in terms of their nomological roles alone. In this case, they may be individuated in our theory on the basis of their locational roles. To illustrate, Lewis notes that even if positive and negative charge are symmetric and inter-changeable according to the laws, still negative charge is what is instantiated on the "outside" of atoms and positive charge is what is instantiated on their "insides." Thus these features are individuated by their locations.

What I would like to know is how this theory of the meaning of theoretical terms is supposed to get us to Physical Structuralism. If intrinsic properties were understood in terms of their locational roles alone, then this would be clear enough. Positive charge is that which is instantiated here, here, and here. Negative charge is that which is instantiated there, there, and there. If this were our total theory, we would only understand positive and negative charge in terms of their relations to space-time. Or, if space-time is not a substance but a structure of relations, we would only understand these properties in terms of the spatiotemporal relations that obtain between the objects that instantiate them. Either way, it would make sense to say that we don't know these properties as they are in themselves, in terms of an intrinsic characterization, but only in terms of relations that things that have them bear to one another. However, the theoretical roles of the intrinsic properties of physics are not, according to Lewis, exhausted by their locational roles. The theories say more than just where properties are instantiated.

The question for us is what may be part of a physical property's nomological role. In particular, can a nomological role ever characterize what an object that instantiates a theoretical property[10] is like in itself, or must it only characterize it relationally, in terms of how it is with respect to other things?

---

8. See 2009, p. 207: "Thus the theoretical roles of positive and negative charge are not purely nomological roles; they are locational roles as well."

9. See also: "The theory T consists of all the logical consequences of a sentence we shall call the *postulate* of T. This is not a substantive assumption, since I have not said that the postulate is of finite length; but if it were not, it is hard to see how any of the theorems of T could deserve the name of laws."

10. Strictly speaking, it is terms that are theoretical, not properties. Here, for brevity, I will use 'theoretical property' as shorthand for 'property that is denoted by a theoretical term.'

There are two reasons why one might think the nomological role is a purely relational characterization, however neither is compelling in the case of the properties of our fundamental physical theories.

One reason that is unpersuasive but historically salient comes from the fact that it was Carnap's account of theoretical terms, which was in turn inspired by the theory of Ramsey, that motivated Lewis's own account. Lewis explicitly cites Carnap's *Philosophical Foundations of Physics* (1966) when he introduces his theory of theoretical terms. The main distinction between Carnap's theory of the meaning of theoretical terms and Lewis's is that for Carnap, the Ramsey sentence in terms of which we understand a theory is a sentence constituted purely by 'directly observational terms' and logical notation (1966, p. 249). Carnap motivates the view in the following way:

> Ramsey was puzzled by the fact that theoretical terms . . . are not meaningful in the same way that observational terms . . . are meaningful.. Clearly, spin is not empirically grounded in the simple, direct manner that the redness of a heated iron rod is grounded . . . How can theoretical terms, which must in some way be connected with the actual world and subject to empirical testing, be distinguished from those metaphysical terms so often encountered in traditional philosophy—terms that have no empirical meaning? (p. 248)

To solve this problem, we may understand the meaning of theoretical terms holistically in terms of their role in a theory that only makes use of observational and logical notation we already understand. How does this relate to structuralism? Because the nomological roles for Carnap described how objects having certain properties impact our observations. Saying an object has mass (say) is just to specify a complicated set of relations ultimately culminating in certain observations.

Although there is likely a route from this theory to Physical Structuralism, it is clear that this is not what Lewis intends. Lewis doesn't argue that the Ramsey sentence must be stated in a language constituted only by observational claims and logical notation. For Lewis, the language of the Ramsey sentence is just his o-language, the "old" language we had prior to the development of the theory in question. Lewis was rightly skeptical of the positivist dichotomy between observation and theory. But once we see this, we must ask what reason is there to think that the nomological role described by the Ramsey sentence will exclusively describe a system of relations?

An alternative reason would be if a property's nomological role is just a causal role, that is, when scientists introduce terms into a theory to refer to intrinsic properties, they do so just by listing the causal relationships that obtain between objects that possess those properties. This is a claim that, although it is missing from both Lewis's initial "How to Define Theoretical Terms" and "Ramseyan Humility," is found in Lewis's application of his theory to psychology, e.g. in "Psychophysical and Theoretical Identifications." It is an account of nomological role that is plausible there because functionalism is plausible in folk psychology. It is plausible to think that the meanings of terms like 'pain' and 'belief' is given by the causal relationships that obtain among mental states, sensory stimuli, and behavior. The question is whether this exhausts the description that may be given in other scientific theories, most importantly for our purposes, in fundamental physics. Must the description of causal relationships exhaust a feature's nomological role? I will argue it need not and probably does not.

To see this, let's return to the simple case of mass and charge. We've just discussed the extremely simple case of a theory that postulates two properties, mass and charge, but of course in reality physics postulates a range of quantities, the individual masses, and a range of quantities, the individual charges. Our question is: must these terms occur in our original theory T solely in descriptions of how the objects that possess these quantities interact with one another, e.g. how objects with masses attract one another as a function of their masses and the distance between them, how objects attract or repel one another based on their charges as well as the distance between them? Or, could a physical theory also use terms like 'mass' and 'charge' to specify features about how objects are in themselves as opposed to how they act with respect to other objects?

Here is one way the latter could happen. When a physicist characterizes an object as having a mass, she does not merely connect this attribution with certain causes and effects, but also with a kind of mathematical representation. She may say that the object has a property, for example, that is adequately represented as one of the numbers on the positive part of the real number line, and one that is a scalar not a vector feature. And to characterize an object as having a charge, this is to characterize it intrinsically in some other way. For example, this is to say that the object has a property that can be given a different kind of mathematical representation, say as a vector in a two-dimensional space. If this were part of our theory, and as both Carnap and Lewis agree, mathematics could be part of the old language constituting the Ramsey sentence, then this fact could be part of the nomological role assigned to these features. And yet this is not a description of what it is to have a property that amounts merely to a description of the relations objects that possess the property bear to each other. We understand what the individual masses and charges are like in themselves in terms of what are the proper sorts of mathematical objects that may be used to represent them. Mass is distinguished from charge not just as a matter of how it affects objects that have it and how they behave with respect to other things. It is also distinguished by the kind of property it is, the kind of property that permits a particular kind of mathematical representation.[11]

Now one may complain that the mathematical characterization is itself relational. For what is it to say that a value of mass is characterizable by a real number than to say that there is a complex relational structure containing that value as a part? But we must distinguish two issues here. The first is whether the mathematical objects that are being used to represent the quantities are themselves defined in terms of their relations to other mathematical objects. This is something many philosophers take to be true. Unless one is a platonist, one will very likely think all it is to be, say, the number two is just to be the successor of one and so on for the rest of the natural numbers. Reals and other species of mathematical objects will find more complicated relational characterizations. But this isn't the issue that concerns us here. Remember the question is whether we are given an intrinsic characterization of an object when we learn it is an object that is representable by a certain kind of mathematical object. I am arguing that the answer to this question is 'Yes.' A precedent is contained in the sorts of mathematical-*cum*-geometrical features that earlier physical theories ascribed: shapes. There is a way of understanding shapes that makes their attribution a way of characterizing material objects as they are in themselves. And if so, then this is a case where an object is said to be a certain way intrinsically by saying such-and-such mathematical object is capable of representing it. There is no clear reason why what is true for shape should not be the case for the more esoteric mathematical representations used in today's physical theories. Surely we may be less familiar with these types of mathematical objects. Vector spaces are less familiar than triangles. We certainly do not receive an understanding of these objects by way of perceptual experience. But this is neither here nor there when we are considering the issue of whether using them to represent an object is a way of

---

11. There is another reason to think causal/functional characterizations won't be given in our most fundamental physical theories, though it is not one to which I myself am attracted. If one holds the view found in Russell (1918) (though rejected by the time of *Analysis of Matter*) that fundamental physics does not use the concept of cause, then it is hard to see how one could be a functionalist about fundamental physical features. This "Russellianism" about causation is a position that has regained popularity in recent years. See e.g. Field (2003).

characterizing how that object is in itself as opposed to how it is with respect to other things.

Coming back to Lewis, so far as I can tell, his account of theoretical terms doesn't require that we only understand the intrinsic features postulated by our scientific theories by understanding the relations that objects that possess them bear to other objects. (Recall, this is the semantic interpretation of Physical Structuralism.) Carnap's account of theoretical terms probably entails this. Lewis's account plus functionalism probably entails this. But if scientists include more in their theories than an account of the spatiotemporal, causal, and other relations[12] that objects bear to another, then one can maintain Lewis's framework for understanding theoretical terms holistically while rejecting Physical Structuralism. And ultimately, it is plausible to reject Physical Structuralism just because our scientific theories do tell us what objects are like intrinsically when they possess properties like mass, charge, and the rest. They use what are perhaps unfamiliar, highly abstract mathematical concepts to describe what objects are intrinsically like. They don't describe objects intrinsically by using concepts with which we seem to be familiar from perceptual experience. But this doesn't mean they don't provide us with intrinsic characterizations.

We've so far discussed two ways to get to a physical structuralist thesis while assuming that physics does attempt to postulate and describe intrinsic properties: Russell's way, which relies on the causal theory of perception and the thought that we can't know the intrinsic features of the properties that cause our experiences because they are instantiated in a distinct space from the private space of experiences; and Lewis's way, which relies on his Ramsey-and-Carnap-inspired theory of theoretical terms and the thought that theories only describe relations that objects that possess intrinsic properties bear to one another. In both cases I am skeptical that we really have a good argument showing that physics fails to reveal what objects are like intrinsically. We might ask, though, what to say about the second part of Russellian Monism, the Structure-Grounding Thesis, on these interpretations of Physical Structuralism.

If Physical Structuralism is understood via either the psychological or semantic interpretations, then what the Structure-Grounding thesis says is not that there must be *additional* intrinsic properties to ground the properties of physics. Rather, it says that we need an account to supplement our scientific

---

12. Other relations might conceivably be internal relations (relations objects bear to each other that supervene on what they are like intrinsically).

understanding of what the intrinsic properties described by physics are like. My contention has been that there is no reason to think that physical theories describe objects merely relationally. The Russellian Monist might insist that the mathematical characterizations of masses, charges, and the other physical properties require supplementation by some further intrinsic characterization that allows us to distinguish these features from each other in terms we can understand, but it is not clear why this must be so. What more could we be looking for?

4. Empirical Structuralist Theses

Let's move on then to consider another way of interpreting and motivating Physical Structuralism. This is another way one might conceivably get to Russellian Monism, not by allowing that physics postulates intrinsic properties but then insisting it can't tell us anything to identify them, but instead by denying in the first place that physics is in the business of postulating intrinsic properties. The idea is that all of the properties physics talks about are really just extrinsic features, descriptions of the spatiotemporal frameworks in which objects are located and these objects' relations. Physicists use terms like 'mass' and 'charge' that may appear to denote intrinsic properties, but really they are just describing elaborate sets of relations. As we saw in Section 1, there are two ways one could go about defending this claim. On the one hand, one could present this in a normative way—maybe scientists think what they are doing is attributing intrinsic features to objects, but really, in a science that was closer to an ideal or one in which scientists understood their project better, the only postulated features would be extrinsic features.

This normative thesis is one possibility, and I won't have much to say against it here. I do wonder what the motivation could be for denying that a proper or ideal science, especially a proper or ideal version of fundamental physics, would postulate intrinsic properties. There is of course the old empiricist or positivist motivation for liking something like this. All we can understand is how objects impact our experiences and so sciences should only postulate properties that relate objects to our experiences of them. Perhaps again there might also be a preference for functionalism about scientific theories, coming from the thought that concepts are best understood when we have specified a particular causal role and seen how it may be realized. But surely this is only true for nonfundamental scientific posits, those we want to see reduced, integrated into our more fundamental, general theories. I can't see why a preference for functionalism would be motivated for a fundamental physical theory itself. But let's hang onto this normative thesis for a moment.

The last way one might interpret Physical Structuralism is in the descriptive way. It is an empirical claim about our actual physical theories that they as a matter of fact never postulate fundamental, intrinsic properties. This is a thesis that has been widely discussed in the philosophy of science of the last decade under the name 'Ontic Structural Realism,' and has been defended by Steven French, James Ladyman, and Don Ross (Ladyman and Ross 2007, French 2013). These authors appeal to specific features of quantum mechanics and relativity in order to argue that all that physics describes is relations, never intrinsic properties. Ultimately, a debate about this thesis will take us deep into the philosophy of physics. We will have to tread one by one through our physical theories and evaluate the individual features they postulate. In my (2010), I considered the situation for quantum mechanics and argued that we do not have reason to be structural realists about that theory despite interesting arguments to the contrary.

In the present chapter I don't intend to give a thorough criticism of either the descriptive or normative interpretations of Physical Structuralism. But one doesn't need to in order to criticize this way of motivating Russellian Monism. For what the Russellian Monist would need is not just the claim that physics only postulates extrinsic features, never intrinsic features, or an ideal physics would postulate only extrinsic features, never intrinsic features. The Russellian Monist would also need to move from there to what I have called the Structure-Grounding Thesis, to argue that yes, physics only posits extrinsic features, but we should in addition believe there are intrinsic features that supplement, that somehow ground, these extrinsic features. And the question is why, if the descriptive or normative structuralist thesis is true, we should believe that.

Structural realists today don't think that the extrinsic features of physics need supplementation by further intrinsic properties; they would deny the Structure-Grounding Thesis. In general, it is hard to see why if we are assuming fundamental physics can provide a satisfactory description of the world, it would need supplementation by a metaphysics of intrinsic properties (see also Ney 2007). This is almost trivial if we are assuming the normative structuralist thesis and talking about an ideal or completed fundamental theory. One might, however, still wonder about the corresponding claim for current physics, since we know it is not complete.

Even if we grant provisionally that current physics only postulates extrinsic features, it is implausible that what is required to complete physics is supplementation with a list of intrinsic properties. What is needed is a story to unify general relativity and quantum mechanics, a solution to the quantum measurement problem, a story that explains what is the nature of dark matter, if there is a story about our universe's creation beyond the Big Bang, and so on. If the physics of today makes due entirely with extrinsic features, it is dubious that to complete physics what would be needed is supplementation with a list of additional, intrinsic properties.[13]

For the kinds of explanations physics needs, it is hard to see how postulating intrinsic properties can help. However, one might argue that there are distinctly metaphysical reasons that motivate the Structure-Grounding Thesis. Frank Jackson expresses the problem with the position perhaps best. The view that objects have only extrinsic features, no intrinsic features, "makes a mystery of what it is that stands *in* the ... relations" (1998, p. 24). How can there be relations without there being something the relata are like? In his recent discussion of Russellian Monism, Derk Pereboom considers another possibility: that the instantiation of intrinsic properties is what is needed to distinguish locations that are occupied from mere empty space. He traces this thought to Leibniz and suggests what is needed is really the postulation of a class of substantial intrinsic properties (Pereboom 2011, pp. 95–96).

It is difficult to know what to make of both of these points. They are based on intuitions we have about what sorts of properties must exist in the world. One might point out that since we are talking about what fundamentally exists, it is hard to put too much weight on our intuitions, especially about matters so esoteric. Still, there are a couple of things one can say.

To Jackson's worry about relations without relata, note that to deny the existence of fundamental intrinsic properties is not necessarily to say there may be relations without relata. One might believe there are objects that serve as the relata of the relations while denying these objects have any intrinsic properties. There does not appear to be any incoherence with a description of the world of the form: $\exists x_1 \exists x_2 \exists x_3 \ldots (R_1 x_1 x_2 \& R_2 x_2 x_3 \& R_3 x_3 x_4 \& \ldots)$. This is the view one more commonly finds Ontic Structural Realists endorsing today (though by contrast, see French 2013) rather than the more extreme position suggested by Ladyman and Ross's title, *Every Thing Must Go*.

---

13. Note the issue in this section is whether current physics might need, in order to complete its own explanatory objectives, supplementation with a theory of intrinsic properties. A Russellian Monist might respond that in order for science to be completed, it would need an account of consciousness, and to do this physics needs supplementation with an account of intrinsic properties. But this is not a response to the issue considered concerning Physical Structuralism. The question is not, does *our total theory of the world* need supplementation to be complete? The question is, would *physics* need supplementation with intrinsic properties to be completed?

With respect to Pereboom's point about using the existence of intrinsic properties to mark the distinction between matter and empty space, this is historically very interesting, but it is not clear physicists use intrinsic properties with the intention of marking this distinction today nor why they should. If spatial regions are represented as possessing topological and metrical features, then as I suggested in the previous section, this may be to represent them as intrinsically one way or other. If so, the mere instantiation of intrinsic features cannot be a way of distinguishing matter-filled regions from empty space. But even if there is no way to make this distinction, this doesn't seem problematic. One way in which modern physics has challenged our previous ways of viewing the world is by challenging the distinction between empty and matter-filled space in the first place. This is most vividly demonstrated by quantum field theory where the difference between a region occupied by matter and one without amounts roughly to a difference in field amplitudes; in any case, not a dichotomous distinction between those regions that instantiate a particular type of property and those that do not. And so a motivation for the postulation of intrinsic properties that might have appeared compelling in the eighteenth century just does not carry as much weight today. I conclude that even if physicists don't postulate intrinsic properties today, it is not clear why they must. Those Russellian Monists who motivate their position using the descriptive or normative versions of Physical Structuralism combined with the Structure-Grounding Thesis need to provide us with an argument for why a purely relational physics would need the further postulation of intrinsic properties.

5. Conclusion

It is sometimes hard to tell when philosophers of mind find Russellian Monism intriguing exactly which interpretation of the Physical Structuralism thesis they have in mind and how it is supposed to be motivated. But Physical Structuralism in some form is an essential component of Russellian Monism. I have distinguished four ways this thesis may be interpreted. None of them provide convincing motivation for seeing the physical characterization of the world as in need of supplementation by further metaphysics.

The unification proposed by Russellian Monists is intriguing, but we shouldn't be tempted to favor it as a way to unify consciousness and the physical world. Philosophical reflection on our best, current physical theories lets us see that the premises that are needed to motivate the unification are under-supported and should not be accepted.

So far I have discussed Russellian Monism as a competitor to Physicalism, a view that would add fundamental properties to the catalog provided by fundamental physics, but some who discuss Russellian Monism view it not as a competitor to Physicalism, but instead as an interpretation thereof. For example, Pereboom (2011) takes Russellian Monism to be a way that Physicalism may be saved even if our experiences have intrinsic features that cannot be reduced to features found within physical science. Ultimately, I, like Russell, do not take Russellian Monism to be a way of interpreting Physicalism, but rather a position at odds with it, at least the sort of Physicalism that is most interesting: one that entails a commitment to physics and physics alone as a source of one's fundamental metaphysical commitments.[14] The Physicalist is optimistic about the ability of physics to give a complete description of the world, or at least as complete a description as we may require, and doesn't see the need for metaphysics to posit additional fundamental properties. I hope to have shown here why the arguments used to support Russellian Monism do not undermine this optimism on behalf of the Physicalist.

References

Block, Ned. 2003. Mental Paint. In *Reflections and Replies: Essays on the Philosophy of Tyler Burge*, M. Han and B. Ramberg, eds. Cambridge: MIT Press.

Carnap, Rudolf. 1966. *Philosophical Foundations of Physics*. New York: Basic Books.

Chalmers, David. 1996. *The Conscious Mind*. Oxford: Oxford University Press.

Dennett, Daniel. 1991. *Consciousness Explained*. Boston: Little, Brown.

Dretske, Fred. 1995. *Naturalizing the Mind*. Cambridge: MIT Press.

Field, Hartry. 2003. Causation in a Physical World. In *Oxford Handbook of Metaphysics*, M. Loux and D. Zimmerman, eds. Oxford: Oxford University Press, 435–60.

French, Steven. 2013. *The Structure of the World*. Oxford: Oxford University Press.

Gertler, Brie. 2011. *Self-Knowledge*. London: Routledge.

Jackson, Frank. 1998. *From Metaphysics to Ethics: A Defence of Conceptual Analysis*. Oxford: Oxford University Press.

Ladyman, James and Don Ross (with David Spurrett and John Collier). 2007. *Every Thing Must Go: Metaphysics Naturalized*. Oxford: Oxford University Press.

Langton, Rae. 2004. Elusive Knowledge of Things in Themselves. *Australasian Journal of Philosophy*, 82, 129–36.

---

14. There is another way to characterize Physicalism. This is as the position that nothing is fundamentally mental. This would be to detach Physicalism from any commitment to the ontology of physical theories. If one understands 'Physicalism' this way and then takes seriously the protophenomenalist version of Russellian Monism described in the introduction, then the two positions will be compatible. See Ney (2008) for discussion of various ways of construing Physicalism.

Lewis, David. 1970. How to Define Theoretical Terms. *Journal of Philosophy*, 67, 427–46.

Lewis, David. 1972. Psychophysical and Theoretical Identifications. *Australasian Journal of Philosophy*. 50, 249–58.

Lewis, David. 2009. Ramseyan Humility. In *Conceptual Analysis and Philosophical Naturalism*, David Braddon-Mitchell and Robert Nola, eds. Cambridge: MIT Press, 203–22.

Ney, Alyssa. 2007. Physicalism and Our Knowledge of Intrinsic Properties. *Australasian Journal of Philosophy*, 85, 41–60.

Ney, Alyssa. 2008. Defining Physicalism. *Philosophy Compass*, 3, 1033–48.

Ney, Alyssa. 2010. Are There Fundamental Intrinsic Properties? In *New Waves in Metaphysics*, A. Hazlett, ed. London: Palgrave Macmillan, 219–39.

Pereboom, Derk. 2011. *Consciousness and the Prospects for Physicalism*. Oxford: Oxford University Press.

Russell, Bertrand. 1912/1997. *The Problems of Philosophy*. Oxford: Oxford University Press.

Russell, Bertrand. 1918. On the Notion of Cause. In *Mysticism and Logic*. London: Longman, 180–208.

Russell, Bertrand. 1927/2007. *The Analysis of Matter*. Nottingham: Spokeman.

Schaffer, Jonathan. 2005. Quiddistic Knowledge. *Philosophical Studies*, 123, 1–32.

Schwitzgebel, Eric. 2011. *Perplexities of Consciousness*. Cambridge: MIT Press.

Tye, Michael. 1995. *Ten Problems of Consciousness*. Cambridge: MIT Press.

17

Against Constitutive Russellian Monism

Philip Goff

RUSSELLIAN MONISM IS a beautiful theory of matter and an attractive solution to the mind-body problem. In the first section of this chapter I give a detailed account of what I take Russellian monism to be, how it contrasts with physicalism, and what the motivation is for taking the view very seriously indeed.

In the second section, I turn to the distinction between constitutive and non-constitutive forms of Russellian monism. David Chalmers has argued that constitutive Russellian monism is the most important form of Russellian monism, avoiding disadvantages associated with dualism on the one hand, and standard forms of physicalism on the other.[1] Chalmers does not, however, explore in any detail what exactly the notion of constitution amounts to. Borrowing Theodore Sider's framework for thinking about fundamentality, I attempt to explicate the notion of constitution, and thereby to explicate constitutive forms of Russellian monism.[2] Unfortunately, when fully explicated in this way, constitutive Russellian monism turns out to be not very plausible, and perhaps incoherent.

The third and final section of the chapter brings good news: there is a form of Russellian monism Chalmers does not consider, intelligible emergentist

---

1. Chalmers, this volume.

2. Sider 2009, 2012.

Russellian monism, which remains attractive despite not possessing all the virtues Chalmers attributes to the constitutive view.

I An Elegant Theory of Matter
The Problem with Pure Physicalism

In the public imagination, physics is well on its way to giving a complete description of the fundamental nature of reality. From the scientific revolution onwards, the development of a rigorous experimental method has allowed continuous progress in understanding the nature of space, time, and matter. Of course there is a long way to go; physicists have so far been unable to unify our best theory of the very big, i.e. general relativity, with our best theory of the very small, i.e. quantum mechanics. But at some point, it is supposed, these wrinkles will be ironed out and physicists will proudly present the public with the Grand Unified Theory of everything.

Let us use the term 'pure physicalism' for the view that completed physics will reveal the complete fundamental nature of reality. The troubles with pure physicalism start from the observation that physics, from Galileo onwards, has worked with a very austere vocabulary: its predicates express only mathematical and causal concepts. Think about what physics tells us about an electron. Physics tells us that an electron has negative charge. What does physics have to tell us about negative charge? Rough and ready answer: things with negative charge repel other things with negative charge and attract other things with positive charge. Physics tells us that an electron has a certain amount of mass. What does physics have to tell us about mass? Rough and ready answer: things with mass attract other things with mass and resist acceleration. All the properties physics ascribes to fundamental particles are characterised in terms of behavioural dispositions. Physics tells us nothing about what an electron *is* beyond what it *does*.

More generally, the information physics provides us with concerning the natural world exclusively concerns its mathematico-causal structure. This is very useful information; it enables us to manipulate nature in all sorts of extraordinary ways, allowing us to build lasers and microwaves, and to fly to the moon. However, if there is more to fundamental reality than can be captured with mathematical and causal concepts, then the description of reality we get from physics must be incomplete. And many philosophers find the idea of a genuine concrete world with a purely mathematico-causal nature unintelligible. Intuitively, wherever there is mathematico-causal structure, there must be some underlying categorical nature that realises that structure; to take a specific case, there must be some categorical nature to an electron that grounds the dispositions physics tells us the electron has. If these intuitions are correct, then no possible world could be completely captured in the language of physics, and hence pure physicalism is necessarily false.

Even if there are genuine possible worlds which can be exhaustively characterised in the language of physics, there is good reason to think that the actual world is not one. For we know with certainty that our world contains phenomenal qualities, qualities such as what it's like to see red, and what it's like to feel pain. And there are powerful arguments, conceivability arguments and the knowledge argument,[3] to the conclusion that a world of pure mathematico-causal structure could not constitute a supervenience base for phenomenal qualities. If these arguments are sound then pure physicalism must be (actually even if not necessarily) false.

There is a strong case, then, that physics, for all its virtues, is unable to provide us with a complete description of fundamental reality. Physics provides us with a mathematical description of the fundamental causal workings of the natural world.[4] The formal nature of such a description entails that it necessarily abstracts not only from the reality of consciousness, but from any other real, categorical nature that material entities might happen to have. Just as a mathematical model in economics abstracts away from the concrete features of real-world consumers, for example, the nature of their labour and the specific things they buy and sell, so physics abstracts from the concrete features of space, time, and matter.

I will assume for the rest of this chapter that pure physicalist worlds are indeed incoherent, and that phenomenal qualities do not wholly supervene on mathematico-causal structure. Making these assumptions leaves us with two challenging questions:

1. What is the categorical nature of basic material entities?
2. If physics does not provide us with an adequate supervenience base for the phenomenal qualities we encounter in our experience, how do we explain their instantiation in our world?

Russellian monism provides a beautifully unified answer to both of these questions.

---

3. Chalmers 1996, 2002, Jackson 1982, 1986.

4. Perhaps we can say more cautiously that physics aims to give a complete description of the causal workings of basic entities in relatively isolated situations. There may be emergent causal powers of which physics remains silent. I discuss causal closure of the microphysical in the third section of the chapter.

The Essence of Russellian Monism

According to Russellian monism, the categorical properties of fundamental physical entities—those properties that ground the dispositions physics reveals to us—are phenomenal or protophenomenal properties. I shall say more about the definition of 'protophenomenal' presently, but let us work for now with a basic definition according to which they are properties that, although not themselves phenomenal properties, ground phenomenal properties when combined in certain ways.[5] Physics characterises mass in terms of a certain disposition (to resist acceleration and to attract other massive things), but mass itself for the Russellian monist, that is to say, the categorical property that grounds the dispositions expressed by the physical predicate 'mass', is a form of consciousness or proto-consciousness.[6] If the categorical properties of basic physical entities are taken to be phenomenal properties, the resulting view is a form of panpsychism. If the categorical properties of basic physical entities are taken to be protophenomenal properties, the resulting view is a form of panprotopsychism.[7]

This single supposition offers hope of a unified answer to both of the questions we ended the last section with. In answer to the first question, the categorical nature of basic material entities turns out to be phenomenal or protophenomenal. In answer to the second question, the presence of this phenomenal or protophenomenal nature is intended to yield a base rich enough to subvene the phenomenal qualities we encounter in our experience. Russellian monists do not in general hold that basic material entities themselves instantiate human phenomenal properties; the consciousness or proto-consciousness of electrons will be of a very basic form. But the crude experience/proto-experience of many basic material entities ground the rich experience of a working human brain.

In its most elegant form Russellian monism is a kind of unorthodox identity theory. Similarly to how physics characterises physical properties in terms of their causal roles, brain science characterises brain states in terms

---

5. Chalmers 1996: 126–27.

6. Actually, whether this is the right thing to say depends on one's view about the semantics of the expressions in physics. We may take mass to denote the disposition itself, in which case the phenomenal/protophenomenal base realises mass. For the sake of simplicity, and because it seems to me the more plausible view, I will continue to assume that the expressions of physics rigidly designate categorical properties in terms of the dispositions they ground.

7. Chalmers 1996/2002/this volume.

of (i) their causal role in relation to other brains states and behavioural or bodily effects, (ii) their chemical constituents (which are in turn characterised in chemistry in terms of (A) their causal role, (B) their physical constituents). A given brain state, say, c-fibres firing (to continue in the philosophical tradition of using this hackneyed and empirically dubious example), is described by the physical sciences 'from the outside', i.e. in terms of the dispositions it grounds and the dispositions of its constituents. But 'from the inside' we know that very state as a form of consciousness, say, the feeling of pain. So pain is identical with c-fibres firing, but the real nature of the state is understood only when it is thought of in phenomenal terms.

A popular argument for reductive physicalism is that it offers a way of reconciling platitudes about mental causation with the alleged causal closure of the physical. We want to preserve the commonsense platitude that pain 'plays the pain role', i.e. causes avoidance behaviour in response to bodily damage. But if the physical is causally closed, then there will be some physical state, c-fibres firing let us say, which plays the pain role. And hence we seem to have too many causes for my screaming and running away when you stick a knife in me. A reductive physicalist does not face the worry of avoidance behaviour being overdetermined, as pain can be identified with c-fibres firing. It is seen to be a great advantage of Russellian monism that, at least in its guise as an unorthodox identity theory, it allows us to say exactly the same thing.[8]

Distinguishing Russellian Monism from Impure Physicalism

The last section gave us an idea of what Russellian monism is, and why it is an attractive view. However, its exact definition needs refining, as the way I have characterised it thus far does not distinguish it from certain standard forms of physicalism. The problems stem from the basic definition of 'protophenomenal property' which I gave at the start of the last section, according to which protophenomenal properties are non-phenomenal properties which ground phenomenal properties when combined in certain ways. The trouble is that any physicalist who believes in phenomenal properties will take phenomenal qualities to be in some sense grounded in more basic properties, and therefore will believe in protophenomenal qualities according to that basic definition.

---

8. For some examples of Russellian monism, see Russell 1927, Eddington 1928, Feigl 1958/1967, Maxwell 1978, Lockwood, M. 1989, Strawson 1994/2003/2006a, Chalmers 1996, Griffen 1998, Stoljar 2001.

Even on this definition of 'protophenomenal' we can easily distinguish the *pure* physicalist from the Russellian monist, for the latter but not the former believes that basic physical entities have categorical properties. But not all physicalists are pure physicalists. Pure physicalists take the dispositions of fundamental particles to be *brute*, not grounded in some underlying categorical nature. But many physicalists—David Lewis and David Armstrong being two notable examples[9]—believe that the dispositions of fundamental physical entities are grounded in their categorical properties. As physics reveals to us only the dispositional properties of particles, this view entails—as Lewis and Armstrong concede—that there is more to the nature of physical entities than physics can ever reveal to us. Let us call physicalists who are not pure physicalists 'impure physicalists'.

Alter and Nagasawa have recently defined Russellian monism as the conjunction of the following three claims, in which 'protophenomenal' is understood according to the basic definition outlined above:

> *Structuralism about physics*: the basic properties physics describes are structural/relational properties.
>
> *Realism about inscrutables*: there are inscrutables [i.e. properties which ground the structures/relations physics ascribes], the natures of which are not wholly structural/relational.
>
> (Proto)*phenomenal foundationalism*: at least some inscrutables are either phenomenal or protophenomenal properties.[10]

According to the Alter/Nagasawa definition, Lewis and Armstrong count as Russellian monists. This is not a welcome result. Russellian monism is understood to be a way of incorporating the phenomenon of consciousness into nature on a *robustly realist* understanding of that phenomenon. Lewis and Armstrong, in contrast, are analytic functionalists about consciousness; the concept of a given conscious state is just the concept of a state that plays a certain causal role.[11]

Perhaps we could just stipulate that Russellian monists reject causal analyses of consciousness. However, even with this stipulation, we would be

---

9. Armstrong 1983, Lewis 2009.

10. Alter & Nagasawa 2012: 70–71.

11. Alter and Nagasawa do go on to say that they are leaving certain commitments of Russellian monism implicit. However, it is highly non-trivial what would need to be added to these three theses in order to exclude the Lewis/Armstrong view.

unable to distinguish between Russellian monism and impure versions of the most popular form of contemporary physicalism, the view David Chalmers dubbed 'type-B physicalism'.[12] Type-A physicalists, such as Armstrong and Lewis, take there to be an a priori entailment between completed physics and the phenomenal facts, and usually account for this in terms of some causal analysis of consciousness.[13] Type-B physicalists take the phenomenal to supervene on the physical, but deny that there is an a priori entailment from the latter to the former.[14] I will begin by considering the most straightforward versions of Russellian monist and type-B physicalism, according to which there is an a posteriori identity between conscious states and brain states, in order to see starkly the difficulty of distinguishing the two views.

An impure type-B physicalist who believes that the dispositions of fundamental physical entities are grounded in categorical bases will presumably also believe that the dispositions of brain states are grounded in categorical bases, categorical bases which are in turn grounded in the categorical bases of their physical constituents. Just as the categorical nature of an electron is not revealed to us by physics, so the categorical nature of c-fibres firing is not revealed to us by neurophysiology.

So we have the following situation. Both the Russellian monist and the type-B physicalist (in their most simple and elegant forms) take there to be an a posteriori identity between c-fibres firing and pain. Both the Russellian monist and the type-B physicalist take there to be a categorical nature to c-fibres firing, and to each of its fundamental physical constituents, which the physical sciences do not reveal to us. And both the type-B physicalist and the Russellian monist think that at least some of the categorical properties of fundamental physical entities are 'protophenomenal', at least if all this means is that in certain combinations they constitute conscious experience. How then do the two views differ?

I think the views can be distinguished, but we need some terminology in order to do so. Let us say that a concept C denoting a property P is 'transparent' just in case it reveals the nature of P; that is to say, it is possible for someone to come to know a priori, in virtue of possessing C, what it is for P to be instantiated. The concept *sphericity* is transparent in this sense. For something

---

12. Chalmers 2002.

13. For some examples of type-A physicalism, see Armstrong 1968, Lewis 1966/1970/1980/1994, Harman 1990, Dretske 1995, Rey 1995.

14. For some examples of type-B physicalism, see Loar 1990/2003, Papineau 1993/2002, Lycan 1996, Hill 1997, Hill & McLaughlin 1999, Block & Stalnaker 1999, Perry 2001.

to be spherical is for it to have all points on its surface equidistant from its centre; if you possess the concept *sphericity*, and you're clever enough, you can work this out a priori. In contrast we can say that a concept C denoting a property P is 'opaque' just in case it reveals nothing, or very little, of what it is for P to be instantiated. The concept *water* is an opaque concept. For something to be water is for it to be composed of H_2O molecules, but you can't work this out a priori simply in virtue of possessing the concepts *water* and H_2O.[15]

Finally, we can define a 'transparent rendering' as follows:

A transparent rendering: A transparent rendering of description D is a description which is indiscernible from D except that each predicate expressing a non-transparent concept is replaced with a predicate expressing a transparent concept of the same property.[16]

A transparent rendering leaves unchanged facts about reference and extension. It merely, as it were, opens the curtains on each concept, revealing the nature of the property denoted.

Both the Russellian monist and the type-B physicalist take there to be an a posteriori identity between pain and c-fibres firing. But, as I understood them, they disagree as to why that identity is a posteriori. For the Russellian monist, the aposteriority of psycho-physical identities is wholly due to the opacity of the *physical* concepts involved. We cannot know a priori that c-fibres firing is pain, because the concept *c-fibres firing* denotes its referent 'from the outside' rather than revealing its real nature. If brain science descriptions were transparently rendered, the real phenomenal nature of c-fibres firing would become apparent.

For the type-B physicalist, however, the a posteriority is not due, or at least not solely due, to the opacity of the physical concept. Even if we transparently rendered the concept *c-fibres firing*, revealing the real categorical nature which underlies the brain science dispositions, there would remain an a posteriori identity between that categorical nature and the phenomenal nature with which it is identical. On the most straightforward understanding of type-B physicalism, the a posteriority of psycho-physical identities is due (in part or

---

15. Jackson and Chalmers (2001) believe that, given complete physical knowledge (perhaps in conjunction with all phenomenal truths, indexical truths, and the so-called 'that's all' fact) of the actual world one could work out that water is H_2O, but even they would agree that this cannot be known without empirical information that goes beyond that required to possess the concepts.

16. I develop all these notions in more detail in Goff 2011/Forthcoming a/MS.

in whole) to the opacity of the *phenomenal* concept. It is because the phenomenal concept *pain* does not reveal the nature of its referent that we cannot
know that its referent is brain state X, even when we are conceiving of brain
state X under a transparent concept.[17]

There may be scope for a stranger form of type-B physicalism, according
to which phenomenal concepts are transparent, and yet psycho-physical identities remain a posteriori even when the relevant brain state is denoted with
a transparent concept. Such a form of type-B physicalism would be committed to what I call 'dual revelation': the thesis that, at least in some cases, the
nature of a single property can be wholly understood in two conceptually distinct ways. The view would be that I completely understand the nature of pain
when I think about it under a phenomenal concept, *and* I completely understand the nature of that same state (but in a radically different way) when
I think of it under a transparent physical concept. It is not obvious that dual
revelation is intelligible. Of course I can *refer* to a single property in numerous
conceptually distinct ways: by demonstration, by description, in virtue of a
causal connection. But it is not clear that sense can be made of my *understanding the nature* of a single property, knowing what it is, say, for something to be
spherical, in numerous conceptually distinct ways. Even if intelligible, I have
argued elsewhere that dual revelation is deeply problematic.[18]

At any rate, we can distinguish between type-B identity theory and
Russellian monist identity theory by saying that the former but not the latter
takes psycho-physical identities to be 'robustly a posteriori', in the sense that
they remain a posteriori even when the physical side of the identity is transparently rendered.

So much for the distinction between type-B physicalism and Russellian
monism in their most simple and elegant forms, i.e. when construed as
identity theories. There are forms of both type-B physicalism and Russellian
monism which do not identify conscious states with brain states. The type-B
physicalist might identify phenomenal properties with physically realised
properties, such as functional properties, rather than with specific brain
states. The Russellian monist may take c-fibres firing to be realised by, rather
than identical with, pain. To achieve a fully general distinction between the

---

17. Papineau 2006 and McLaughlin 2001 explicitly commit to this form of type-B physicalism. Whilst it is not very common for type-B physicalists to explicitly commit to phenomenal
opacity (the thesis that phenomenal concepts are opaque), they tend to defend a semantic
externalist account of phenomenal concepts, and this seems to entail phenomenal opacity.

18. Goff Forthcoming a/MS.

two views we can say that the type-B physicalist takes the supervenience of the phenomenal on the physical to be 'robustly a posteriori', in the sense that, even if the complete physical description of reality were transparently rendered, there would fail to be an a priori entailment from the (transparently rendered) physical to the phenomenal.

Russellian monists, in contrast, believe that there is an a priori entailment between a transparent rendering of the physical and the phenomenal. If you could somehow perceive the real categorical nature of my brain states, you would be able to work out the nature of my consciousness experience. If Russellian monism is true then, for a being who could see through the skulls of other people and directly perceive the categorical nature of their brain states, scepticism about other minds would be inconceivable.

This commitment distinguishes Russellian monists from type-B physicalists. However, it does not distinguish them from type-A physicalists, such as Lewis and Armstrong. For Lewis and Armstrong, a transparently rendered description of the physical facts would a priori entail the phenomenal facts in virtue of specifying the pure physical facts (the same facts that a non-transparently rendered description of the physical facts would reveal). I therefore propose to define Russellian monism as the following view:

> *Russellian Monism:* There is no a priori entailment between the complete physicSal description of reality (i.e. the complete description of reality in the vocabulary of fundamental physics) and the phenomenal facts, but there is an a priori entailment between a transparent rendering of the complete physicSal description of reality and the phenomenal facts.[19]

We now have the resources to move to a better definition of 'protophenomenal' properties, such that we avoid the implication that many type-A and type-B physicalists are committed to such properties. We can say that protophenomenal properties are properties which (i) are not phenomenal properties,

---

19. The term 'physicSal' is due to Galen Strawson (2006). In the formulation of this definition, I am assuming that physical terms like 'mass' rigidly designate categorical properties in terms of the dispositions they ground; on this understanding a transparent rendering of a 'mass' will reveal the underlying categorical nature of mass. If we take mass to be a causal role property (see footnote 6), the definition of Russellian monism would go slightly differently. In this case, we could say that the Russellian monist takes there to be an a priori entailment between a complete description of the categorical properties that underlie physicSal properties (involving transparent concepts of those properties) and the phenomenal facts.

(ii) when arranged in certain combinations form a state of affairs S such that there is an a priori entailment between a transparently rendered description of S and some positive states of affairs concerning the instantiation of phenomenal properties, (iii) there is no a priori entailment between a description of the mathematico-causal structure of S and any positive state of affairs concerning the instantiation of phenomenal properties.

One might wonder whether it is important to worry about the distinction between type-B physicalism and Russellian monism.[20] I think it is important for the following reason. There is an important debate over whether the knowledge argument and conceivability arguments are sound, in the sense that they demonstrate some metaphysically significant conclusion. Those philosophers who do not draw metaphysical conclusions from the knowledge/conceivability arguments, such as David Papineau or Michael Tye, tend to be type-B physicalists. Those who do draw metaphysical conclusions from these arguments, such as David Chalmers or Michael Lockwood, tend to be sympathetic to Russellian monism. It is important to clarify the distinction between these two positions in order to see what is at stake in the debate.

II. Against Constitutive Russellian Monism
What Is Constitution?

I turn now to the form of Russellian monism Chalmers favours: constitutive Russellian monism. Chalmers characterises the view as follows:

> *Constitutive panpsychism* is the thesis that macroexperience [i.e. the kind of experience which we pre-theoretically believe in][21] is (wholly or partially) grounded in micro[proto]experience. More or less equivalently it is the thesis that macroexperience is constituted by microexperience, or realised by microexperience.[22]

·

---

20. David Papineau and I have a long-standing debate over whether there is a significant distinction between the two views. A sample of this debate can be viewed at Goff & Papineau 2012. Our discussions have very much helped me develop the conception of Russellian monism I describe in this section of the chapter.

21. I prefer my term 'o-experience', which I introduce below, as it leaves open the (rather obscure) possibility that the kind of consciousness we pre-theoretically believe in exists at the micro-level.

22. Chalmers this volume: p. 253.

He has little to say, however, about what 'grounding' or 'constitution' or 'realisation' are, saying only that on the constitution view, 'macrophenomenal truths obtain in virtue of micro[proto]phenomenal truths, in roughly the same sense in which materialists hold that macrophenomenal truths obtain in virtue of microphysical truths'.[23]

Let us define the grounding relation as follows: fact X grounds fact Y iff Y obtains in virtue of X obtaining, where I use 'in virtue of' to express the intuitive pre-theoretical notion that something can be the case because something else is the case. Can constitution be characterised wholly in terms of the grounding relation so defined, or perhaps grounding in conjunction with a priori entailment? This would seem to be an inadequate characterisation of constitution, as a grounding relation might obtain in virtue of a relationship of intelligible causation.

Suppose X is the fact that God wills that there be light, and Y is the fact that there is light. Y obtains because X obtains, and there is an a priori entailment from X to Y: if you know that an omnipotent being has willed that there be light then you can work out a priori that there's going to be light. And yet the fact that there is light is clearly not constituted by the fact that God wills that there be light, at least if Y's being constituted by X is supposed to entail that Y is no addition in being to X: in willing that there be light God has created new being ex nihilo. To take another example, if the conjunction of dispositional essentialism and determinism is true, then knowing the fundamental nature of reality at a given time could in principle allow us to work out a priori what's going to happen at a later time. And yet this would not entail that the facts about the future are constituted by the facts about the past.

One might object that such causal connections are not instances of grounding. But one would need to move beyond the simple characterisation of grounding I have given above to show that. If grounding is just the in virtue of relation, the relation that holds when one fact obtains because another fact obtains, then causal relationships, e.g. the match lit because it was struck, would seem to constitute instances of grounding.

We might of course use the word 'constitution' in such a way that it does not imply an ontological free lunch, i.e. such that the fact that Y is 'constituted' by X does not entail that Y is nothing over and above X. However, it is clear that Chalmers does want the fact that Y is constituted by X to entail that Y is no addition in being to X, as he takes constituted properties to inherit causal relevance from their grounds. Indeed, this is the principal reason

---

23. Chalmers this volume: p. 253.

Chalmers takes constitutive forms of Russellian monism to be superior to non-constitutive forms of Russellian monism. According to Chalmers, if the fact that I feel pain, call that fact 'Q', is constituted of some micro-(proto) phenomenal fact M, then M and Q can each be individually sufficient for my pain behaviour, without my pain behaviour being problematically overdetermined. As a result, constitutive Russellian monism shares with physicalism the advantage of being able to reconcile mental causation with the causal closure of the micro-physical.

However, this use of constitution to avoid problematic overdetermination works only if constituted facts are no addition in being to their grounds. The fact that the crowd caused the disruption is not overdetermined by the fact that the members of the crowd caused the disruption, because the fact that there is a crowd is nothing over and above the fact that there are certain individuals related in certain ways. As a case of contrast, suppose that the members of the crowd are wizards, each with a powerful will akin to the powerful will of God but more limited. It could be that the angry activities bring into existence a demon, intelligibly dependent on, but ontologically additional to, the activities of the wizards. If this demon also causes disruption, we would clearly have a case of overdetermination. Only where we have an ontological free lunch do we avoid worries about causal exclusion.

Let us then define constitution as an in virtue of relation which yields an ontological free lunch: fact X constitutes fact Y iff (i) Y obtains in virtue of X, (ii) Y is nothing over and above X. What is it, though, for a certain fact to be nothing over and above another fact? Reflection on crowds, parties, or organisations makes the notion intuitive. But philosophical reflection can render it somewhat mysterious. A crowd is neither identical to its members, nor wholly distinct from them. What is this strange middle way between identity and distinctness? How can fact X involve different objects and properties to fact Y, and yet, from the perspective of serious metaphysics, add nothing beyond the objects of properties already involved in Y? Philosophers trading in 'nothing over and above' talk owe us an account of how they get their lunch for free.

The phrase 'ontological free lunch' is due to David Armstrong, who claimed that a supervenience relation is sufficient for an ontological free lunch.[24] Chalmers has in the past defended a supervenience-based account of physicalism, which suggests that he would acquiesce with Armstrong on this point.[25] However, there is a broad consensus that a mere modal notion like

---

24. Armstrong 1997: section 2.12.

25. Chalmers 1996.

supervenience is not up to the job of explicating the 'nothing over and above' relation. Consider the view Terence Horgan dubbed 'Moorean Emergentism':

> *Moorean emergentism*—(1) Both phenomenal and physical properties are equally fundamental, (2) phenomenal properties arise from physical properties in virtue of metaphysically necessary psycho-physical laws of nature.[26]

If Moorean emergentism is true, then the phenomenal facts supervene on the physical facts: any possible world W which is a minimal physical duplicate of our world will be a phenomenal duplicate of our world, given that the actual psycho-physical laws (being necessary) also obtain at W. And yet this is clearly not a world where the phenomenal facts are nothing over and above the physical facts. Hence, Moorean emergentism is a counterexample to a wholly supervenience-based account of the ontological free lunch.

Although many agree that wholly supervenience-based accounts of physicalism are problematic, there is little consensus as to what they might be replaced with. Physicalism is generally defined as 'at least' supervenience, and the details of what more is required often left hazy.[27] Fortunately, in the metaphysics literature in the last five years or so, there has been a great deal of work on the topic of *fundamentality* which can help us make sense of this notion. Perhaps most prominently, Theodore Sider has developed a detailed and systematic framework for thinking about fundamentality.[28] In the next section I outline Sider's framework; in subsequent sections I will use Sider's framework to define, and argue against, constitutive Russellian monism.

Sider on Fundamentality

In 'New work for a theory of universals', David Lewis argued for the benefits of what we might call 'predicational elitism': distinguishing an 'elite' class of metaphysically privileged predicates that 'carve nature at the joints', from the sprawling slum of metaphysically uninteresting predicates.[29] Thus we might suppose that 'is an electron' carves nature at the joints, whilst 'is grue' or 'is an

---

26. Horgan 2006.

27. There have, however, been some interesting proposals; see Horgan 1993, Wilson 1999, Melnyk 2003. I discuss these proposals in Goff MS.

28. Sider 2009/2012.

29. Lewis 1983.

elephant or an electron' does not. Lewis argues that such a distinction earns its acceptance by its theoretical utility; the distinction allows us to analyse diverse philosophical notions, such as 'intrinsic property' and 'physicalism', and to solve philosophical problems, such as the rule-following problem.

Sider develops Lewis's view in two respects. Firstly, where Lewis felt obliged to give some metaphysical account of what it is for a predicate to carve nature at the joints—perhaps all and only the elite predicates express universals—Sider takes the notion of a 'joint carving expression' as primitive. We might clarify this primitive notion in the following way: the world as it is in and of itself[30] has a certain kind of structure, and we represent better to the degree that our conceptual structure mirrors the structure of the world as it is in and of itself. To represent the world perfectly it is not enough to have representations that are true; we must have representations that employ the right concepts.

Secondly, Sider extends Lewis's elitism to linguistic expressions other than predicates. Of most importance for ontology, Sider believes in what we might call 'quantificational elitism', the view that there is a specific meaning of the quantifiers that carves nature at the joints. A candidate meaning of the quantifiers is one that preserves the distinctive inferential role of the quantifiers, for example, preserves the inference from 'Everything is physical', to 'Something is physical'. It is clear that we could invent highly artificial candidate quantifier meanings. Sider gives the following example:

> Imagine a person who is logically perfect, maximally opinionated, and totally nuts. His beliefs are logically consistent; for every proposition, he either believes it or believes its negation; and he believes that the moon is made of green cheese, that robots are stealing his luggage, and that Ludwig Wittgenstein was history's greatest philosopher. A candidate meaning on which an arbitrary sentence Φ means the same as the English sentence 'according to the (actual) beliefs of the opinionated person, Φ' is then inferentially adequate: the inference rules of quantification theory come out truth-preserving because our opinionated person, being logically perfect and maximally opinionated, believes every logical consequence of everything he believes.[31]

---

30. Sider does not in fact use the phrase 'the world as it is in and of itself' (as far as I've noticed), but I feel it helps to clarify the notion he's aiming at.

31. Sider 2009.

What is being considered above is essentially a silly meaning of the expression 'exists', according to which 'x exists' means 'according to the opinionated person x exists'. Quantifiers with this silly meaning would be inferentially adequate, but they would not carve nature at the joints. The world in and of itself is carved up into certain entities, and the silly quantifier does not range over those entities. Crucially, the quantifier of English, the meaning of which is more influenced by everyday usage than the metaphysical structure of the world, may in a more subtle way also fail to carve nature at the joints. Sider is inclined to think that the world in and of itself is carved up into and only into mereologically simple entities. But the meaning of the English quantifier may be such that when certain mereologically simple entities are arranged in certain patterns the English sentence 'There are tables' is true. In this case, the quantifier of English, although perhaps not as silly as the silly quantifier outlined above, does not range over the entities into which the reality is carved in and of itself.

Although most sentences of English will not carve nature at the joints (in the sense that they will be filled with expressions which don't carve nature at the joints), each sentence has, according to Sider, a 'metaphysical truth condition', which states what is required for its truth in a language that perfectly carves nature at the joints (in the sense of containing only expressions that carve nature at the joints). Supposing that the joint carving quantifier ranges only over particles, the metaphysical truth condition of 'There are tables' may be something like 'There are particles arranged table-wise'. I say 'something like' because presumably 'arranged table-wise' is not a predicate that carves nature at the joints. Giving the real metaphysical truth condition for 'There are tables' would require us to list all the arrangements of particles that would serve to make this sentence true using only expressions that carve nature at the joints.[32] Sider is not optimistic about our capacity to formulate complete metaphysical truth conditions for this or any very interesting sentences of English. However, he takes it to be an important part of a reductive story that we can gesture at 'toy' metaphysical truth conditions that approximate the real metaphysical truth conditions that it is beyond our ken to formulate.[33]

We can distinguish, then, between the fundamental truths—the truths of the perfectly joint carving language—and the truths of English. It may be that there are no fundamental truths about tables, but that 'There are tables' is true

---

32. In Sider 2013, he attempts to give a functionalist metaphysical truth condition for the sentence 'Moore has hands'.

33. Sider 2012: 116–18.

in English just in case something like 'There are particles arranged table-wise' is a fundamental truth. If this is so, there is then a clear sense in which the facts about tables are no addition in being to the facts about particles; table facts are not an addition in *fundamental reality*, i.e. the reality which is specified by terms which carve nature at the joints.

In summary, we can define constitution in the Siderian framework as follows:

> Truth X constitutes truth Y iff (i) X is a fundamental truth and Y is a non-fundamental truth, (ii) the fundamental reality specified by X satisfies the metaphysical truth condition of Y.

Against Constitutive Panpsychism

At this stage it would be useful to introduce some more terminology. What we really want a theory of consciousness to explain are the phenomenal properties we pre-theoretically associate with humans and other animals. Call facts about the instantiation of these phenomenal properties 'o-phenomenal facts' ('o' for 'ordinary'); call the bearers of these phenomenal properties 'o-subjects'. Call the facts about micro-level subjects/protosubjects in terms of which Russellian monists explain the facts about o-subjects 'micro-phenomenal/ protophenomenal facts'; call micro-level subjects/micro-level protosubjects 'micro-subjects'/'micro-protosubjects'.

Making sense of protophenomenal versions of constitutive Russellian monism in Sider's framework seems, on the face of it, to be quite straightforward. The constitutive panprotopsychist will say that protophenomenal predicates, but not phenomenal predicates, carve nature at the joints. Reality as it is in and of itself is carved up into particles with protophenomenal properties, but not into subjects of experience. Sentences quantifying over subjects of experience have metaphysical truth conditions that involve quantification over fundamental particles and predication over protophenomenal properties. If all this works out, there would then be a clear sense in which the o-phenomenal facts are no addition in being to the protophenomenal facts.

Interestingly, it seems that panpsychist versions of constitutive Russellian monism cannot be coherently specified using Sider's framework. The problem is that the kind term 'subject of experience' is either a joint carving expression or it is not. The fundamental truths, for the constitutive panpsychist, concern micro-level subjects of experience. All the expressions in a fundamental truth are joint carving, and hence the kind term 'subject of experience', as it appears in fundamental micro-phenomenal truths, must be joint carving. But if the kind term 'subject of experience' as it appears in certain micro-phenomenal truths is joint carving, then the kind term 'subject of experience' must also be joint carving as it appears in truths concerning o-subjects of experience, such as you and I. This follows from the sub-propositional focus of Sider's framework. Whether or not a certain expression is joint carving is not dependent on whether the truth it is contained in is a fundamental truth; rather whether or not a given truth is fundamental depends on whether or not it is formed from joint carving expressions.

We can put the argument as follows:

1. If panpsychism is true, then at least some tokens of the kind term 'subject of experience' are joint carving (i.e. those used to specify the fundamental micro-phenomenal truths).
2. If some tokens of the kind term 'subject of experience' are joint carving, then all tokens of the kind term 'subject of experience' are joint carving, including those contained in o-phenomenal truths.
3. If tokens of the kind term 'subject of experience' that are contained in o-phenomenal truths are joint carving, then o-subjects of experience are fundamental entities, i.e. entities which are quantified over in fundamental truths.
4. Therefore, if panpsychism is true, o-subjects of experience are fundamental entities.

In Sider's framework, panpsychism entails that o-subjects and micro-subjects are fundamental entities. It is, therefore, inconsistent with constitutive Russellian monism: if o-subjects are fundamental entities in their own right, then they cannot be constituted by micro-level goings on.

A bundle theorist constitutive panpsychist might respond by denying that the kind term 'subject of experience' is used in characterising the fundamental micro-phenomenal truths, claiming that the fundamental micro-phenomenal truths involve bundles of micro-phenomenal properties. However, when considering such a view, we could simply swap the property kind term 'subject of experience' in the above argument for the property kind term 'phenomenal property'. We would then reach the conclusion that o-phenomenal properties are fundamental entities, and again end up with fundamental entities involved in o-phenomenal facts. Given that such entities are fundamental, they cannot be constituted by micro-level goings on, which is inconsistent with constitutive Russellian monism.[34]

---

34. The panpsychist may be a nominalist, refusing to quantify over properties but taking phenomenal predicates to carve nature at the joints. Such a view would face essentially the same problem of ending up with fundamental o-phenomenal truths.

The constitutive panpsychist might try to claim that the joint carving expressions are not the determinables 'subject of experience' or 'phenomenal property', but terms denoting the specific determinate states of consciousness possessed by micro-subjects, states of consciousness which o-subjects do not possess. However, the panpsychist can only articulate what she takes the fundamental truths to be using phenomenal concepts that we already have, and those concepts are drawn from our understanding of o-phenomenology. To say that particles have some weird and whacky properties that we don't have a grip on is not to commit to panpsychism. The panpsychist's view of the fundamental truths is that they involve 'consciousness', that there is 'something that it is like' to be a fundamental particle. And these expressions which she takes to be involved in articulating the fundamental truths also apply to us. Once we allow that at least some of our ordinary expressions pertaining to consciousness are joint carving, it is hard to see how we could avoid there being at least some fundamental o-phenomenal truths.

I have been assuming that the panpsychist thinks truths about consciousness are amongst the fundamental truths. There could be a strange view according to which consciousness is ubiquitous at the micro-level, but there are no fundamental truths about consciousness. For example, it might be the case that the English sentence 'Particles are conscious' is true, but that this truth has a metaphysical truth condition which does not involve phenomenal predicates. I think this kind of view is best seen as an odd kind of panprotopsychism (or perhaps even type-B physicalism). In metaphysics we are ultimately interested in fundamental truth, and so a view that doesn't take fundamental truths to involve consciousness isn't appropriately classed as a form of panpsychism. In any case, the substantive point is that we have ruled out the following option: being metaphysically serious about micro-consciousness whilst being metaphysically lightweight about o-consciousness. Either 'consciousness' carves nature at the joints or it doesn't; if there are fundamental micro-phenomenal truths, then there are fundamental o-phenomenal truths.

Of course constitutive panpsychists might try to find some framework other than Sider's for making sense of their view, and so I cannot conclusively rule out panpsychist forms of constitutive Russellian monism.[35] But to my mind what this has brought out is that you're either metaphysically serious about consciousness or you're not. It doesn't really make sense to be

---

35. Fine 2001 offers a propositional rather than a sub-propositional account of metaphysically heavyweight facts. Sider argues for the superiority of his sub-propositional account in his 2012: 8.3.

metaphysically serious about some subjects (at the micro-level) and meta-physically lightweight about other subjects (o-subjects). Panpsychism entails that o-subjects are fundamental.

Against All Forms of Constitutive Russellian Monism

In the last section I argued that panpsychism is an essentially layered view of reality, and hence that we cannot make sense of panpsychist forms of constitutive Russellian monism. One might think that this gives the advantage to panprotopsychism over panpsychism. However, I will now try to show that, at least when explicated in the Siderian framework, all forms of constitutive Russellian monism are deeply implausible, and perhaps incoherent. (In what follows I will equate 'constitutive Russellian monism' with constitutive Russellian monism explicated in Sider's framework.)

If constitutive Russellian monism is true, then truths concerning o-subjects, for example, 'There is something that feels pain', have metaphysical truth conditions that quantify over particles, either non-conscious particles or particles with very different phenomenal properties to those expressed by the predicates of the original English sentence. As I said above, Sider thinks that it would be unreasonable to expect us to be able to give a precise statement of the metaphysical truth condition of any interesting ordinary language sentence, but that it is important for a reductive view of X to be able to gesture at a rough 'toy' approximation of the metaphysical truth conditions of truths about X. We can't state the complete disjunction of particle arrangements necessary for the truth of 'There are tables', but we have a (very) rough idea about what facts about particles must obtain in order for that sentence to be true.

Sider is surely right about this. In order for it to be plausible that there is a metaphysical truth condition of 'Bill is in pain' concerning a large number of particles, we must be able to gesture at it. The only way I can see that such a gesture might be given is by offering some kind of causal analysis of consciousness, i.e. analytic functionalism, analytic behaviourism, or analytic information-theoretic representationalism. Suppose we accept David Lewis's view that for something to be in pain is for it to have an inner state that plays a certain causal role mediating between bodily damage and avoidance behaviour. We would then have a rough idea of how particles must be arranged for 'Bill is in pain' to be true, akin to the rough idea we have of how particles must be arranged for 'There is a table' to be true.

However, Russellian monists reject such causal analyses of phenomenal truths. On a causal analysis of phenomenal truths, they are a priori entailed by the complete physicSal truth, whilst it is part of Russellian monism as I have defined it that o-phenomenal truths are not entailed by the complete physicSal truth. And this is not an idiosyncratic feature of my definition: Russellian monism is an attempt to find a place for the phenomenon of consciousness on a robustly realist understanding of that phenomenon.

What is required of reality as it is in and of itself for there to be something in pain? In the absence of a causal analysis, it's hard to see what metaphysical truth condition we can give for this sentence other than one that is structurally isomorphic with the original English sentence, i.e. one that employs the same predicates and quantifies over the same entities. And if the metaphysical truth condition of 'There is something that feels pain' is just 'There is something that feels pain', then 'There is something that feels pain' is a fundamental truth and subjects that feel pain are fundamental entities.

(This needs to be qualified slightly. Obviously some phenomenal predicates will not carve nature at the joints, e.g. grue-like phenomenal predicates. In what follows I will take phenomenal truths to be truths that involve only quantification and non-disjunctive/conjunctive predicates expressing direct phenomenal concepts, i.e. concepts which are formed wholly on the basis of attending to a phenomenal quality in introspection.[36])

I think the type-B physicalist would have a good response to this concern. Most type-B physicalists defend a semantic externalist account of phenomenal concepts, whereby the extension of the concept is fixed by facts outside of what is a priori accessible, such as causal or teleological facts. As a consequence, in contrast to, say, the concept *water*, phenomenal concepts lack descriptive content. Many type-B physicalists appeal to this difference to explain why there is an explanatory gap between the physical and the phenomenal facts that is lacking between the physical facts and the facts about water. It is plausible that the concept *water* connotes the description 'the colourless, odourless, stuff in oceans and lakes', and that if we know enough about the physical facts we can know that H_2O satisfies that description. In contrast, the concept *pain* lacks any such associated description, which is why we can't move a priori from knowing that someone's c-fibres are firing to knowing that they are in pain.[37]

---

36. The notion of a direct phenomenal concept comes from Chalmers 2003.

37. See Papineau 1998 for a clear expression of this kind of view.

The type-B physicalist might make a similar response to a Siderian demand to know the metaphysical truth conditions of phenomenal sentences:

> The concepts *water* and *table* refer by description, which is why the metaphysical truth conditions of truths about water and tables are a priori accessible (which is not to say the complete metaphysical truth condition is easy to access, but a toy approximation of it is easily accessible). But the extension of phenomenal concepts is determined by facts which are not a priori accessible, perhaps causal or teleological facts, and hence the metaphysical truth conditions of phenomenal truths will not be a priori accessible. The metaphysical truth condition of 'There is something that feels pain', is 'There is something with particles arranged c-fibre firing-wise', but because the metaphysical truth condition is determined by facts outside of what is a priori accessible, armchair reflection will never reveal this.

This response could be seen to constitute a kind of 'phenomenal concept strategy' response to the apparent absence of reductive metaphysical truth conditions for phenomenal truths.[38]

However, if the metaphysical truth conditions of o-phenomenal truths are not a priori accessible (because phenomenal concepts are opaque), then the necessitation of phenomenal truths by physical truths (if such a thing there be) will be robustly a posteriori. If it is not a priori what is fundamentally required for 'There is something that feels pain' to be true, then there can be no a priori connection between the fundamental facts and the truth of 'There is something that feels pain'. But constitutive Russellian monism is defined such that there is an a priori entailment between the fundamental truths and the o-phenomenal truths (at least if we assume, as I will, that the constitutive Russellian monist takes the fundamental truths to be given by a transparent rendering of a complete physicSal description of reality).

Let's bring everything together. The definition of Russellian monism has a negative component—there is no a priori entailment from the complete physicSal description of reality to the o-phenomenal facts—and a positive component—there is an a priori entailment from a transparent rendering of the complete physicSal description of reality to the o-phenomenal facts. The *negative component* of the definition supports the following premise: if the metaphysical truth conditions of phenomenal truths are a priori accessible, then

---

38. The term 'phenomenal concept strategy' comes from Stoljar 2005.

each phenomenal truth is structurally isomorphic with its metaphysical truth condition (the reason the negative component supports this premise is that only if we accept causal analyses is it plausible to suppose that a phenomenal truth has an a priori accessible metaphysical truth condition with which it is not structurally isomorphic, and the negative component rules out causal analyses). The *positive component* of the definition supports the following premise: the metaphysical truth conditions of phenomenal truths are a priori accessible.

We can present, then, the following argument against all forms of constitutive Russellian monism:

1. If constitutive Russellian monism is true, then there is no a priori entailment between the complete physicSal description of reality and the o-phenomenal truths, but there is an a priori entailment between the fundamental truths (i.e. a transparent rendering of the complete physicSal description of reality) and the o-phenomenal truths.

2. If there is no a priori entailment between the complete physicSal description of reality and the o-phenomenal truths, then either the metaphysical truth conditions of phenomenal truths are not a priori accessible, or each o-phenomenal truth is structurally isomorphic with its metaphysical truth condition and hence o-phenomenal truths are fundamental truths.

3. If there is an a priori entailment between the fundamental truths and the o-phenomenal truths, then the metaphysical truths conditions of o-phenomenal truths are a priori accessible.

4. Therefore, if constitutive Russellian monism is true, then o-phenomenal truths are fundamental truths.

5. If constitutive Russellian monism is true, then it is not the case that o-phenomenal truths are fundamental truths.

6. Therefore, constitutive Russellian monism is false.

For those who prefer symbols:

P = the complete physicSal description of reality
TP = a transparent rendering of the complete physicSal description reality
Q = an arbitrary o-phenomenal truth

1. Constitutive Russellian monism → ((P→Q) is not a priori) & ((TP→Q) is a priori).

2. ((P →Q) is not a priori) → (~(The metaphysical truth condition of Q is a priori) v (Q is a fundamental truth)).

3. ((TP →Q) is a priori) → The metaphysical truth condition of Q is a priori.
4. Therefore: constitutive Russellian monism → Q is fundamental truth.
5. Constitutive Russellian monism → ~(Q is a fundamental truth).
6. Therefore: constitutive Russellian monism is false.

Of course this argument depends on explicating constitutive Russellian monism in Sider's framework. However, the onus is on the proponent of constitutive Russellian monism to offer an account of constitution which avoids these concerns.

The Intuitive Moral of the Story

What I have offered above is a fairly complex argument, employing a fairly complex metametaphysical framework. But I take this to be an attempt to rigorously explicate a fairly intuitive thought. If you want to make sense of facts about o-consciousness being constituted of facts not involving o-consciousness, then you have to offer hope that there is some kind of *deflationary analysis* of o-consciousness: some way of understanding the o-phenomenal facts in more fundamental terms.[39] You might go the way of the type-A physicalists and give a causal analysis of phenomenal truths. Or you might go the way of the type-B physicalists and hold that we have no a priori access to the nature of consciousness, which opens us up to the possibility of discovering empirically that the real nature of consciousness can be grasped in non-experiential terms. The Russellian monist rejects both of these options, and thus is left with no alternative but to take o-phenomenal truths to be fundamental.

Couldn't the constitutive Russellian monist claim that we know *something but not everything* about the nature of phenomenal truths? This is the response one often hears from Russellian monists in conversation, and has been suggested in print by Galen Strawson[40] (in response to me[41]) and Derk Pereboom.[42] The problem is that we can now just shift the argument to focusing on *the bit of consciousness we have transparent access to*, and argue that that property must be fundamental, given that we have no way of understanding it in more fundamental terms.

---

39. I don't use the term 'deflationary analysis' such that a deflationary analysis is by definition a priori.

40. Strawson 2006b.

41. Goff 2006.

42. Pereboom 2011: 114–15. In his chapter in this volume Pereboom raises this as a response to my 2009.

In any case, constitutive Russellian monists often gesture towards the view that phenomenal concepts are *translucent*, revealing something but not everything of the states they denote, but have never as far as I'm aware worked out the details. Suppose I form a direct phenomenal concept of the phenomenal red in my experiential field right now. What is the aspect of phenomenal red which is transparently revealed in my conception? What is the aspect of phenomenal red which is opaquely denoted in my conception? (In the context of the above argument, the challenge will be to distinguish the bit of the metaphysical truth condition which is a priori accessible from the bit which is not.) This is not a matter of telling us the nature of protophenomenal properties—many Russellian monists takes these to be permanently beyond our grasp; rather, my request is for a detailed account of phenomenal *concepts* such that they turn out to be translucent.[43] If the constitutive Russellian monist wants to appeal to translucency she is obliged to fill in the details.[44]

III. Intelligible Emergentism

Chalmers contrasts constitutive Russellian monism with *emergentist* Russellian monism: the view that o-experience arises from micro-(proto)experience in virtue of causation rather than constitution. Chalmers describes a kind of brute emergentism, according to which o-experience is strongly emergent from micro-(proto)experience, i.e. o-experience arises from micro-(proto) experience but without its emergence being predicable from knowledge of the micro-(proto)phenomenal facts alone:

> One sort of emergentist panpsychist might hold that there are contingent laws of nature that specify when certain microexperiences give rise to certain macroexperiences [Chalmers' word for 'o-experience']. Another might hold that there are laws of nature connecting microphenomenal properties and macrophysical properties to macrophenomenal properties, without there being any constitutive connection between microphenomenal and macrophenomenal.[45]

---

43. See Schroer 2010 for a very good physicalist attempt to make sense of phenomenal translucency. I expect the Russellian monist who wants to appeal to phenomenal transparency to give a similarly detailed account of how phenomenal concepts work such that they are translucent.

44. I develop these objections in more detail in Goff MS.

45. Chalmers this volume: 253.

Thus, the view Chalmers uses as a contrast to constitutive Russellian monism is a kind of pan(proto)psychist version of British emergentism.[46] However, it is not clear that brute panprotopsychism is coherent, given that protophenomenal properties by definition a priori entail phenomenal properties.[47] If the relation between micro-protoexperience and o-experience is causal, then the causation must be intelligible rather than brute. Near the beginning of section II we considered divine creation and dispositional essentialism as examples of intelligible causation. Analogously, it could be that the o-phenomenal facts are intelligibly caused by the micro-protophenomenal facts. Although not conceptually obligatory, we might think of the relationship between micro-phenomenal and o-phenomenal facts in the same way.[48]

Let us call the following position 'intelligible emergentism':

(i)   o-phenomenal facts are a priori entailed by micro-(proto)phenomenal facts,

(ii) Both micro-(proto)phenomenal and o-phenomenal facts are fundamental, and hence the grounding relationship between these two kinds of fact is causal rather than constitutive.[49]

Combining intelligible emergentism and Russellian monism we get the following view:

(iii) *Intelligible emergentist Russellian Monism*: (i) There is no a priori entailment between the complete physicSal description of reality (i.e. the complete description of reality in the vocabulary of fundamental physics) and the phenomenal facts, but there is an a priori entailment between a transparent rendering of the complete physicSal description of reality and the o-phenomenal facts, (ii) both micro-(proto)phenomenal and o-phenomenal facts are fundamental, and hence the grounding relationship between these two kinds of fact is causal rather than constitutive.

---

46. See Mill 1843, Brain 1870, Lewes 1875, Alexander 1920, Morgan 1923, Broad 1925. For a very good discussion of British emergentism, see McLaughlin 1992.

47. Chalmers (this volume) also defines 'protophenomenal' such that protophenomenal properties a priori entail phenomenal properties.

48. If we define Russellian monism, as I have done, as involving a priori entailment, then it is conceptually obligatory to think of a Russellian version of emergentist panpsychism as involving intelligible rather than brute causation.

49. I think of causal relationships as non-constitutive grounding relations, i.e. grounding relations between distinct and fundamental truths.

There are strong arguments associated with the 'combination prob-lem' to the conclusion that there could be no a priori entailment from the micro-phenomenal to the o-phenomenal.[50] It seems on the face of it that we can conceive of micro-phenomenal facts obtaining in the absence of any o-phenomenal facts, which is inconsistent with there being an a priori entail-ment from the former to the latter. I have defended elsewhere a solution to this difficulty involving the notion of *phenomenal bonding*.[51] If there is a solu-tion to the combination problem, and we can make sense of an intelligible connection between micro-(proto)phenomenology and o-phenomenology, then intelligible emergentist Russellian monism provides an elegant place for o-consciousness in nature, much more elegant than standard emergentism with its reliance of brute laws.[52]

What about causal exclusion worries? Emergentist forms of Russellian monism do not seem adequately equipped to reconcile the causal efficacy of o-consciousness with *micro*-physical causal closure. However, they do have the resources to assuage exclusion concerns which come from a commitment to *macro*-physical causal closure. Suppose one thought that the event of c-fibres firing in my brain was sufficient cause for my screaming and running away after a knife had been stuck in me.[53] A non-Russellian property dualist might worry that this crowds out the possibility that my feeling pain caused me to scream and run away, and may consequently resort to epiphenomenalism. A Russellian monist, however, avoids these concerns. Either c-fibres firing just is (in its real essential nature) my feeling of pain, or my feeling of pain constitutes c-fibres firing (in the latter case c-fibres firing is a purely disposi-tional property realised by my o-experience).

In this way, the emergentist Russellian monist takes the macro-physical to be nothing over and above the macro-phenomenal, and hence there is no

---

50. Goff 2009, discussed in Chalmers this volume.

51. Goff Forthcoming b.

52. Goff Forthcoming b. The argument I present in this chapter might be seen as a way of pressing a version of the combination problem against constitutive Russellian monism. Interpreted in this way, as a challenge to constitutive pan(proto)psychism, I take the com-bination problem to be insoluble. Interpreted as a challenge to the more general view that higher-level phenomenal facts can be intelligibly grounded in more basic (proto)phenom-enal facts, I take the combination problem to be soluble. I talk about these two ways of understanding the combination problem in much more detail in Goff MS.

53. I have very much benefited from many conversations on this topic with Hedda Hassel Mørch, who provides a rich discussion of these issues in Mørch 2014.

worry about causal competition between mental and physical at the level of brains. This is a not insignificant advantage of the view. However, any emergentist takes o-experience to be something over and above micro goings on, both phenomenal and non-phenomenal. It must be conceded that if the micro-level is causally closed, this would seem to crowd out the causal efficacy of the macro-level.

How satisfactory intelligible emergentist Russellian monism is, then, may depend on the force of the arguments for micro-physical causal closure. I don't have space to pursue the matter in much detail here, but for my own part I remain unpersuaded that there is a strong argument for microphysical causal closure. Often causal closure of the physical is just assumed without argument. And where there is an argument it is often unclear whether that argument supports *microphysical* causal closure, or the causal closure of the physical more generally construed, the latter view being consistent with an indispensable role for brain-level events.[54] Until the case for micro-physical causal closure is clarified, the status of intelligible emergentist Russellian monism will also remain unclear.

Conclusion

At this stage of enquiry, intelligible emergentist Russellian monism is a view we should take seriously. For those who accept the soundness of the knowledge argument or the conceivability arguments, neither pure nor impure physicalism can be true, as they are both inconsistent with the one natural phenomenon we know with certainty to exist: consciousness. Of course, there are a range of anti-physicalist alternatives. However, even as a layered view of the world, Russellian monism looks at present to be the most elegant way of finding a home for consciousness.[55]

---

54. See the appendix of Papineau 2002 for an extended argument for the causal closure of the physical.

55. I am very grateful for fantastic comments from Torin Alter, Luke Roefls, Hedda Hassel, and David Chalmers. I gave early versions of this chapter at the 'Towards a non-physicalist solution to the mystery of consciousness' workshop organised by Yujin Nagasawa and Max Velmans, and at the 'Metaphysics and Ontology of Phenomenal Qualities' conference, which was part of the 'Phenomenal Qualities' AHRC project. I very much benefited from comments from participants at both events. I am also grateful for the precious research time afford to me by my post-doctoral position as part of the 'Phenomenal Qualities' project, and my post-doctoral position at the 'Centre for Consciousness' at the Australian National University.

References

Alter, T. & Y. Nagasawa (2012) What Is Russellian Monism? *Journal of Consciousness Studies* 19: 9–10, 67–95.

Alexander, S. (1920) *Space, Time, and Deity*, 2 Volumes, London: Macmillan.

Armstrong, D. (1968) *A Materialist Theory of Mind*, London: Routledge and Kegan Paul.

Armstrong, D. (1983) *What Is a Law of Nature?* Cambridge: Cambridge University Press.

Armstrong, D. (1997) *A World of States of Affairs*, Cambridge: Cambridge University Press.

Block, N. & R. Stalnaker (1999) Conceptual Analysis, Dualism and the Explanatory Gap, *Philosophical Review* 108/1: 1–46.

Broad, C. D. (1925) *The Mind and Its Place in Nature*, London: Routledge and Kegan Paul.

Chalmers, D. J. (1996) *The Conscious Mind: Towards a Fundamental Theory*, Oxford: Oxford University Press.

Chalmers, D. J. (2002) Consciousness and Its Place in Nature, in D. J. Chalmers (ed.), *Philosophy of Mind: Classical and Contemporary Readings*, Oxford, New York: Oxford University Press, 247–72.

Chalmers, D. J. (2003) The Content and Epistemology of Phenomenal Belief, in Q. Smith & A. Jokic (eds.) *Consciousness: New Philosophical Perspectives*, Oxford University Press.

Chalmers, D. J. (this volume) Panpsychism and Panprotopsychism.

Dretske, F. (1995) *Naturalizing the Mind*, Cambridge, MA: MIT Press.

Eddington, A. (1928) *The Nature of the Physical World*, New York: Macmillan.

Feigl, H. (1967) *The 'Mental' and the 'Physical': The Essay and a Postscript*, Minneapolis: University of Minnesota Press.

Fine, K. (2001) The Question of Realism, *Philosophers Imprint*, 1: 1–30.

Goff, P. (2006) Experiences Don't Sum, *Journal of Consciousness Studies*, 13.

Goff, P. (2009) Why Pansychism Doesn't Help Explain Consciousness, *Dialectica*, 63.

Goff, P. (2011) A Posteriori Physicalists Get Our Phenomenal Concepts Wrong, *Australasian Journal of Philosophy* 89: 2, 191–209.

Goff, P. (Forthcoming a) Real Acquaintance and the Phenomenal Concept Strategy, in S. Coates & S. Coleman (eds.), *Phenomenal Qualities*, Oxford: Oxford University Press.

Goff, P. (Forthcoming b) The Phenomenal Bonding Solution to the Combination Problem, in G. Bruntrup & L. Jaskolla (eds.), *Panpsychism*, Oxford University Press.

Goff, P. (MS) *Consciousness and Fundamental Reality*. Accessible at http://www.philipgoffphilosophy.com/.

Goff, P & D. Papineau (2012) On Physicalism, *Philosophy TV*, http://www.philostv.com/?s=papineau&submit.x=-1175&submit.y=-224&submit=Search.

Harman, G. (1990) The Intrinsic Quality of Experience, *Philosophical Perspectives* 4: 31–52.

Hill, C. & B. McLaughlin (1999) There Are Fewer Things in Reality than Are Dreamt of in Chalmers's Philosophy, *Philosophy and Phenomenological Research* 59: 2, 445–54.

Horgan, T. (1993) From Supervenience to Superdupervenience: Meeting the Demands of a Material World, *Mind* 102: 555–86.

Jackson, F. (1982) Epiphenomenal Qualia, *Philosophical Quarterly* 32.

Jackson, F. (1986) What Mary Didn't Know, *Journal of Philosophy* 83.

Lewes, G. H. (1875) *Problems of Life and Mind*, Volume 2, London: Kegan Paul, Trench, Turbner, & Co.

Lewis, D. (1966) An Argument for the Identity Theory, *Journal of Philosophy* 63/1: 17–25.

Lewis, D. (1970) How to Define Theoretical Terms, *Journal of Philosophy* 67/13: 427–46.

Lewis, D. (1980) Mad Pain and Martian Pain, in N. Block (ed.), *Readings in the Philosophy of Psychology*, Vol. I, Harvard: Harvard University Press, 216–22.

Lewis, D. (1983) New Work for a Theory of Universals, *Australasian Journal of Philosophy* 61: 343–77.

Lewis, D. (1994) Reduction of Mind, in S. Guttenplan (ed.), *Companion to the Philosophy of Mind*, Oxford: Blackwell, 412–31.

Lewis, D. (2009) Ramseyan Humility, in D. Braddon-Mitchell & R. Nolan (eds.), *Conceptual Analysis and Philosophical Naturalism*, Cambridge, MA: MIT Press.

Loar, B. (1990) Phenomenal States, *Philosophical Perspectives* 4: 81–108.

Loar, B. (2003) Qualia, Properties, Modality, *Philosophical Issues* 13/1: 113–29.

Lockwood, M. (1989) *Mind, Brain and the Quantum*, Oxford: Oxford University Press.

Lycan, W. G. (1996) *Consciousness and Experience*, Cambridge, MA: MIT Press.

Maxwell, G. (1979) Rigid Designators and Mind-Brain Identity, in C. W. Savage (ed.), *Perception and Cognition*, Minneapolis: University of Minnesota Press, 365–404.

McLaughlin, B. (1992) The Rise and Fall of British Emergentism, in A. Beckermann, H. Flohr & J. Kim (eds.), *Emergence or Reduction? Essays on the Prospects of Nonreductive Physicalism*, Berlin: Walter de Gruyter, 49–93.

McLaughlin, B. P. (2001) A Defense of New Wave Materialism: A Response to Horgan and Tienson, in Gillett and Loewer (2001).

Melnyk, A. (2003) *A Physicalist Manifesto*, Cambridge: Cambridge University Press.

Mørch, H. H. (2014) *Panpsychism and Causation: A New Argument and a Solution to the Combination Problem*, PhD Thesis, University of Oslo.

Morgan, C. L. (1923) *Emergent Evolution*, London: Williams & Norgate.

Papineau, D. (1993) Physicalism, Consciousness, and the Antipathetic Fallacy, *Australasian Journal of Philosophy* 71: 2, 169–83.

Papineau, D. (1998) Mind the Gap, in J. Tomberlin (ed.), *Philosophical Perspectives*.

Papineau, D. (2002) *Thinking about Consciousness*, Clarendon Press: Oxford.

Papineau, D. (2006) Comments on Galen Strawson, *Journal of Consciousness Studies*, 13.

Pereboom, D. (2011) *Consciousness and the Prospects for Physicalism*, Oxford: Oxford University Press.

Pereboom, D. (this volume) Consciousness, Physicalism, and Absolutely Intrinsic Properties.

Perry, J. (2001) *Knowledge, Possibility and Consciousness*, Cambridge, MA: MIT Press.

Rey, G. (1995) Towards a Projectivist Account of Conscious Experience, in T. Metzinger (ed.), *Conscious Experience*, Paderborn: Ferdinand Schoningh, 123–42.

Russell, B. (1927) *The Analysis of Matter*, London: Kegan Paul.

Sider, T. (2009) Ontological Realism, in D. Chalmers, D. Manley, & R. Wasserman (eds.), *Metametaphysics*, Oxford: Oxford University Press, 384–42.

Sider, T. (2012) *Writing the Book of the World*, Oxford: Oxford University Press.

Sider, T. (2013) 'Reply to Schaffer' in 'Symposium on *Writing the Book of the World*, *Analysis* 73: 4, 713–70.

Stoljar, D. (2001) Two Conceptions of the Physical, *Philosophy and Phenomenological Research* 62: 2, 253–81.

Stoljar, D. (2005) Physicalism and the Phenomenal Concepts Strategy, *Mind and Language* 20: 5, 469–94.

Strawson, G. (1994) *Mental Reality*. Cambridge, MA; London: MIT Press.

Strawson, G. (2003) Real Materialism, in L. Anthony & N. Hornstein (eds.), *Chomsky and His Critics*, Oxford: Blackwell, 48–88.

Strawson, G. (2006a) Realistic Monism: Why Physicalism Entails Panpsychism, in A. Freeman (ed.), *Consciousness and Its Place in Nature*, Exeter: Imprint Academic, 3–31.

Strawson, G. (2006b) Panpsychism? Reply to Commentators and a Celebration of Descartes, in A. Freeman (ed.), *Consciousness and Its Place in Nature*, Exeter: Imprint Academic.

Tye, M. (1995) *Ten Problems of Consciousness: A Representational Theory of the Phenomenal Mind*, Cambridge, MA: MIT Press.

Wilson, J. (1999) How Superduper Does a Physicalist Supervenience Need to Be?, *Philosophical Quarterly* 49: 194.

Wilson, J. (2005) Supervenience Based Formulations of Physicalism, *Nous* 39: 3, 426–59.

18

Pessimism about Russellian Monism

Amy Kind

ACCORDING TO TRADITIONAL versions of idealism, everything that exists is mental; according to traditional versions of physicalism, everything that exists is physical. In postulating the existence of only one kind of thing, both idealism and physicalism are versions of monism. However, there has recently been a resurgence of interest in a monism of a different sort, one that does not seem appropriately characterized as either idealism or physicalism, at least not as these views are usually understood. This resurgence began largely with the publication of David Chalmers' *The Conscious Mind* in 1996.[1] In arguing there for the fundamentality of consciousness, Chalmers cast himself as arguing for a version of property dualism but left open the possibility that the fundamentality of consciousness would be best captured by a version of monism: "Perhaps the physical and the phenomenal will turn out to be two different aspects of a single encompassing kind, in something like the way that matter and energy turn out to be two aspects of a single kind" (Chalmers 1996, 129).

From the perspective of many philosophers of mind in these early years of the twenty-first century, the debate between dualism and physicalism has seemed to have stalled, if not to have come to a complete standstill. There seems no way to settle the basic clash of intuitions that underlies it. But now enters—or perhaps, re-enters—Russellian monism, which promises to

---

1. Maxwell 1978, Nagel 1979, Foster 1982, and Lockwood 1989 offer contemporary explorations of issues relating to Russellian monism that pre-date *The Conscious Mind*.

show us a new way forward. As Torin Alter and Yujin Nagasawa have recently argued, this view retains the strengths of traditional versions of dualism and materialism while avoiding their weaknesses:

> Russellian monism is appealing largely because it provides an elegant way of integrating phenomenal consciousness into the natural order without disregarding or distorting the phenomenon's distinctive features. Many philosophers would agree that that result is both desirable and not delivered by traditional theories in the philosophy of mind.
> (Alter and Nagasawa 2011, 92; see also 88–89)[2]

Insofar as Russellian monism might allow us to break out of the current gridlock, it's no wonder that it's become "hot stuff."[3]

To my mind, however, the excitement about Russellian monism is misplaced. That's not to say that I'm pessimistic about the truth of the view. For all that I will say here, some version of Russellian monism might well be true. Rather, what I'm pessimistic about is the claim that Russellian monism enables us to break free of the dualism/physicalism divide. As I will argue, once we properly understand what's required to flesh out an adequate monistic story, we will see that we are in an important way right back where we started.

In the first section of the chapter, I look closely at Russellian monism in an effort to outline its basic commitments. The second section differentiates and discusses four versions of Russellian monism that have been put forward in the recent literature. Having laid this groundwork, I turn my attention in the rest of the chapter to my pessimistic argument. Section 3 argues that the four positions differentiated in section 2 are really best understood as only two different positions. This is a claim I call *the collapse thesis*. Section 4 addresses an important objection to the collapse thesis, namely, that it relies upon a faulty notion of the physical. Finally, in section 5, I use the collapse thesis to show that Russellian monism does not really transcend the traditional dualist/physicalist divide as it is usually thought. The same basic issues that arise in the

---

2. See also Holman (2008, 49): "The advertising for [Russellian monism] is that it constitutes just the insight needed to break (what many see as) the current impasse on the mind-body problem."

3. This phrase was recently used by Sam Coleman (2013) to describe panpsychism, the phenomenal version of Russellian monism. See the discussion of phenomenal monism in section 2.

debate between dualism/physicalism re-arise when we attempt to adjudicate between the two versions of Russellian monism.

1. What Is Russellian Monism?

Chalmers' own development of monism owes explicitly to Bertrand Russell, and other contemporary proponents of this sort of monism also cite Russell as a guiding inspiration for their view. In doing so, however, they typically refrain from attributing the view they espouse to Russell. In fact, as we will see in this section, there are some important respects in which many of the contemporary proponents of this sort of monism seem to depart from Russell's own version of the view—though this is hard to determine exactly, since the question of how best to understand Russell's own view is a vexed one.[4] In what follows, and in line with current terminological usage, I refer to the emerging constellation of contemporary monist views as versions of "Russellian monism," but it should be understood that, as I use this label, Russell's own view is but one of these versions of Russellian monism.

As I will understand things, there are two core claims that a view must be committed to in order for it to count as a version of Russellian monism. First, any such view must be committed to the claim that there exists only a single kind of property at the most fundamental level of reality. That's what makes the view monistic. Second, any such view must also be committed to the claim that these fundamental properties serve as the intrinsic or categorical grounds for physical properties, all of which are themselves purely structural or relational. That's what makes the view Russellian. As Russell noted in a key passage from *The Analysis of Matter*:

> Physics, in itself, is exceedingly abstract, and reveals only certain mathematical characteristics of the material with which it deals. It does not tell us anything as to the intrinsic character of this material.
>
> (Russell 1927/1954, 10)

Of course, even outside the context of discussions of Russellian monism there is considerable debate about what exactly it means for a property to be categorical in nature and, correspondingly, how the distinction between categorical and dispositional properties should be drawn. Likewise, there is

---

4. For discussion of how we should understand Russell's own version of Russellian monism, see Stubenberg 2010 and Lockwood 1981.

considerable debate about what exactly it means for property to be intrinsic in nature and, correspondingly, how the distinction between intrinsic and extrinsic properties should be drawn. A plausible articulation of at least one of these distinctions—and a defense of its coherence—will be critical for the development of Russellian monism. But that said, I will here sidestep these debates and simply assume that at least one of these distinctions can be intelligibly articulated. Moreover, however intrinsicality and categoricity are to be understood, the Russellian monist is guided by the fact that these fundamental properties, which are not themselves structural or relational, thereby seem in principle to escape the net of physical theorizing: From the perspective of physics, they are incapable of analysis or even scrutiny. Following Montero (2011), I will simply refer to the fundamental properties posited by Russellian monists as *inscrutable properties*, or more simply, as *inscrutables*.[5]

By combining these two core commitments of Russellian monism, we can now define the view as follows:

> *Russellian monism*: At the fundamental level of reality there exist inscrutable properties of a single kind.

Thus, on my way of categorizing things, someone who is committed to the existence of inscrutable properties but who denies that they are of a single kind would not count as a Russellian *monist*. Consider a view that is committed to the existence of inscrutables but divides them into many distinct kinds. By my way of categorizing things, such a view is best counted as a version of Russellian *pluralism*. A view that differentiated them into two distinct kinds would count as a version of Russellian *dualism*. Depending on how the inscrutables are characterized, such a view is not too dissimilar from traditional versions of property dualism.

Though all Russellian monists share a commitment to the existence of a unified class of inscrutable properties at the fundamental level of reality, they

---

5. Though he did not use the noun "inscrutables," John Foster had previously invoked the notion of inscrutability in this context: "Scientific analysis uncovers the internal structure of material objects, but terminates in fundamental particles whose intrinsic nature, apart from shape and size, it identifies only opaquely—as that which sustains certain causal powers and sensitivities. In short, the most that empirical investigation (whether ordinary or scientific) can reveal are the number of different fundamental forms of matter, their spatiotemporal distribution and their nomological organization. Beyond this, matter is empirically inscrutable" (1982, 66).

disagree about the nature of such properties. The current literature suggests that Russellian monism comes in four different versions:

(a) *phenomenal Russellian monism*: The inscrutables are phenomenal properties.
(b) *protophenomenal Russellian monism*: The inscrutables are protophenomenal properties.
(c) *neutral Russellian monism*: The inscrutables are neutral properties, neither phenomenal nor physical.
(d) *physical Russellian monism*: The inscrutables are physical properties of a special sort.

My discussion here is indebted to Alter and Nagasawa (2012), who helpfully distinguish these same four versions of Russellian monism. However, their understanding of Russellian monism is slightly different from mine. In attempting to specify a general formulation of the view that captures the main components "common to all versions," Alter and Nagasawa build in a claim they call *(proto)phenomenal foundationalism*: "at least some inscrutables are either phenomenal or protophenomenal properties" (71). In my view, it is a mistake to build this claim into a characterization of Russellian monism. Either the claim is empty, because anything non-phenomenal ends up counting as protophenomenal, or the claim preemptively rules out the possibility of neutral monism and physical versions of Russellian monism.[6] Thus, my own categorization of Russellian monism departs from Alter and Nagasawa's in omitting a commitment to (proto)phenomenal foundationalism as a component of the view.

My characterization also departs in an important respect from the one offered by Derk Pereboom, who defines Russellian monism as

> any view that combines (1) *categorical ignorance*, the claim that physics, or at least current physics, leaves us ignorant of certain categorical bases of physical dispositional properties, with (2) *consciousness- or*

---

6. At the very least, if we build a commitment to (proto)phenomenal foundationalism into Russellian monism, the neutral version and the physical version become significantly constrained: Neutral Russellian monists would have to identify the neutral inscrutables (which by definition are not phenomenal) with protophenomenal inscrutables, and physical Russellian monists would have to identify the physical inscrutables with either phenomenal or protophenomenal inscrutables. The four versions of Russellian monism thus immediately collapse into two. Later, in section 3, I will argue that a collapse of this sort is inevitable, but I do not want it to turn on a matter of definition.

experience-relevance, the proposal that these categorical properties have a significant role in explaining consciousness of experience.

(Pereboom 2011, 89)

Notice that Pereboom's characterization seems to omit the monistic character of such views, which I take to be central to their aim of offering a position that is importantly different from—and importantly better than—both dualism and physicalism. Pereboom's construal is consistent with there being several kinds of properties that are the categorical basis of dispositional properties. For this reason, I believe that my characterization is to be preferred.[7]

2. Four Versions of Russellian Monism

In section 1, I distinguished four versions of Russellian monism that appear to be in play in the literature. To allow us to better understand what is supposed to differentiate them from one another, this section briefly explores each of the four views. In doing so, I will drop the qualifier "Russellian" and simply refer to these views as *phenomenal monism, protophenomenal monism,* and so on.

Versions of phenomenal monism have been developed by Foster (1982), Rosenberg (2004), and Chalmers (2013a, 2002, 1996), among others. By claiming that the fundamental properties underlying all of physical reality are phenomenal properties, proponents of phenomenal monism seem to be endorsing a version of panpsychism—roughly speaking, the view that everything that exists has a mind.[8] Such a view seems, if not outright crazy, at least highly counterintuitive. We're strongly disinclined to attribute mentality even to simplistic organisms like bacteria and protozoa, let alone to non-organisms like quarks and atoms. Of course, in claiming that even quarks and atoms have mentality, phenomenal monists need not claim that these things have mentality in exactly the same way that we humans have mentality. Independent of any commitment to panpsychism, we typically accept the existence of a spectrum of simplicity when it comes to conscious experience. Compare my experience while on a crowded train, where I'm bombarded with sights and

---

7. In addition to the point made in the text, it's worth noting that Pereboom's characterization of Russellian monism has an epistemic orientation that I'd prefer to avoid. Alter and Nagasawa (2011, 71) make a similar point.

8. For a helpful discussion about how best to define the panpsychist view, see Skrbina 2005, 15–19.

sounds and smells, with my experience in an empty, quiet room staring at a white wall before me. The latter experience is considerably simpler than the former, and the phenomenal monist suggests that the experiences of a quark or an atom will be yet simpler still.[9] Importantly, such simple experiences need not be imaginable from our point of view. The fact that we cannot imagine what it is like to be a bat does not itself incline us to deny that there is something that it is like to be a bat, and likewise the fact that we cannot imagine what it is like to be an atom should not itself incline us to deny that there is something that it is like to be an atom.[10]

Ultimately, however, there's no getting around the fact that the phenomenal monist is committed to the idea that there is something it is like—perhaps not much, but *something* nonetheless—to be a quark or an atom. And even in light of the points made in the previous paragraph, this idea will still strike many as deeply counterintuitive. Much of the recent work on panpsychism has been devoted to alleviating this sense of counterintuitiveness. Relatedly, much recent work in this area has been devoted to the developing potential solutions to the infamous combination problem. Once we assume that there are little bits of consciousness everywhere, we need some explanation as to how they combine to produce the sort of unified consciousness that we experience.[11] As it is not my aim in this chapter to evaluate the plausibility of the different versions of Russellian monism, I will not here survey this literature.

In light of the perceived problems facing phenomenal monism, a Russellian monist might be tempted to endorse protophenomenal monism instead. Protophenomenal monism—at least so-called—owes almost entirely to the work of Chalmers (2013a, 2002, 1996), though he does not commit himself to the view.[12] According to Chalmers, protophenomenal properties

---

9. See, e.g., Chalmers' claim that "In the way that an experience of redness is much simpler than a stream of conscious though, we can expect a quark's experience to be much simpler than an experience of redness" (2013, 7), or Rosenberg's claim that the interactions between atoms might simply produce "flashes of extraordinary simple and brief feeling, like fireflies quietly flickering in the night" (2004, 96). I assess the plausibility of Rosenberg's view in Kind 2006.

10. See Rosenberg 2004, 95.

11. See, e.g., Coleman 2012, Chalmers 2013b.

12. In his 2013a, Chalmers develops what he takes to be the best case for views he calls *panpsychism* and *panprotopsychism*. These are the views I am here calling *phenomenal monism* and *protophenomenal monism*. Chalmers does not ultimately commit himself to the truth of either of these views. Rather, he notes that he divides his credence fairly equally between these versions of Russellian monism on the one hand and substance dualism (in either its

are not themselves phenomenal properties, though in certain cases—when, for example, a sufficiently high degree of structural complexity has been achieved—they give rise to phenomenality.[13] Assuming, as seems plausible, that atoms and quarks don't have the requisite degree of structural complexity, the protophenomenal monist need not attribute consciousness to them. Thus, the protophenomenal monist can avoid a commitment to panpsychism.

Unfortunately, however, the protophenomenal monist faces a different problem, namely, that of providing a substantive specification of what a protophenomenal property is. Obviously, it is not enough for us simply to be told that they are not phenomenal properties.[14] According to Chalmers' characterization of these protophenomenal properties, they are "special properties with an especially close connection to phenomenal properties" (2013a, 13–14). As he understands the notion of specialness, it has two components: (i) protophenomenal properties are distinct from structural properties; and (ii) there will be an *a priori* entailment between protophenomenal properties and the phenomenal properties to which they give rise.

Note that (i) applies to any inscrutable property, at least given how I am understanding the notion of inscrutability. So only (ii) can serve as a potential means for distinguishing protophenomenal properties from other candidates for the inscrutable properties. On first thought, however, there seems to be no reason that (ii) can't be true of either neutral or physical inscrutables, and we are thus left to wonder what in principle could distinguish protophenomenal monism from other versions of Russellian monism like neutral monism or physical monism. I will postpone further discussion of this question until section 3; first, we need to look more closely at both neutral monism and physical monism.

---

epiphenomenalist or interactionist forms) on the other. Moreover, he does not explicitly indicate whether he thinks one of these versions of Russellian monism is more plausible than the other—though at one point he tentatively suggests that panprotopsychism might have an advantage in "having fewer constraints on its building blocks" (2013a, 22).

13. Nagel's talk of *proto-mental* properties (Nagel 1979) and Rosenberg's talk of *protoexperiential* properties (Rosenberg 2004) should not be assimilated to Chalmers' talk of protophenomenal properties. For Nagel and Rosenberg, these "proto" properties are to some degree phenomenal or experiential. As I note in the text above, protophenomenal properties are by definition not phenomenal.

14. Strawson (2006, 22) vividly discusses the difficulty with saying something substantive about the notion of protophenomenality.

As I mentioned above, it is no easy matter to identify Russell's own version of Russellian monism. But that said, he is generally thought to have espoused some version of neutral monism. We can here look especially to the following passage from *The Analysis of Mind*:

> The stuff of which the world of our experience is composed is, in my belief, neither mind nor matter, but something more primitive than either. Both mind and matter seem to be composite, and the stuff of which they are compounded lies in a sense between the two, in a sense above them both, like a common ancestor.
>
> (Russell 1921, 10–11)

In elaborating this position, the neutral monist faces a problem parallel to the one facing the protophenomenal monist. Just as the protophenomenal monist owes us a substantive characterization of protophenomenality, the neutral monist owes us a substantive characterization of neutrality. The quoted passage from Russell suggests that we should understand the relevant sense of neutrality as simply "neither mental nor physical," or perhaps, as "neither *intrinsically* mental nor physical." Note that if we were to understand the dichotomy between the mental and the physical as exhaustive, there would be no room for neutral entities, so the neutral monist who uses this characterization of neutrality must be relying on some other understanding of the mental and the physical.[15]

There are other passages from Russell, however, that point to a way of understanding the notion of neutrality in terms of causal laws. Russell suggests that in our ultimate scientific account of the world, the causal laws will not be stated in terms of matter; rather, they will be stated in such a way as to apply equally to both psychology and physics (Russell 1921, 305–6; see also Stubenberg 2010). Insofar as we normally understand the mental as subject to distinctively psychological laws and the physical as subject to distinctively physical laws, the existence of a single set of laws governing all particulars would suggest that such particulars were not properly understood as either mental or physical but rather as neutral between the two.[16]

---

15. Papineau, for example, suggests that we can understand "physical" as simply meaning "non-mental" and thus is an example of someone who suggests that the divide between the mental and physical is exhaustive. See Papineau 2001.

16. Nagel 1979 makes a similar point, though he puts it terms of "chains of explanation" (see esp. 184–85).

The last version of Russellian monism, physical monism, has recently been advocated by Stoljar (2001), Montero (2011), and Pereboom (2011).[17] Physical monism obviously shares much in common with physicalism, but whether physical monism counts as a version of physicalism will depend on how the physicalist characterizes the nature of the physical. In positing the existence of inscrutables, the physical monist accepts the existence of properties that lie outside the domain of physics—certainly current physics, and quite possibly even ideal physics as well. But the physical monist argues that, insofar as the inscrutables are the categorical or intrinsic bases for normal physical properties, they should still be understood as physical properties in some sense. In other words, the physical monist characterizes the inscrutables as physical properties of a special sort.

Stoljar's distinction between the theory-based conception of the physical and the object-based conception of the physical helps us to clarify this point (Stoljar 2001, 256–57). According to the theory-based conception, physical properties are those that physical theory tells us about plus those that supervene on the sort of properties that physical theory tells us about. Stoljar calls these the *t-physical* properties. According to the object-based conception, physical properties are those required by a complete account of the intrinsic nature of paradigmatic physical objects and their constituents plus those that supervene on the sort of property required by such an account. Stoljar calls these the *o-physical* properties.

Traditional physicalism seems to operate with something like the theory-based conception of the physical. In contrast, physical monism operates with the object-based conception of the physical. By definition, inscrutables are not t-physical properties. But, since inscrutable properties are required by a complete account of the intrinsic nature of physical objects, they clearly count as o-physical properties. Thus, since the physical monist sees the inscrutables as o-physical properties, we might naturally redescribe physical monism as *o-physical monism*. Can this really be considered a *physical* version of monism? The question will turn on whether it's plausible

---

17. Note that the position advocated by Stoljar 2006 is importantly different from the one advocated by Stoljar 2001, and is not a version of Russellian monism as I have categorized it (see esp. 107–8; 113). Stoljar 2001 makes a commitment to inscrutables; Stoljar 2006 does not. Rather, Stoljar 2006 makes a more qualified commitment to the existence of some properties about which we are ignorant. He notes explicitly that we cannot be sure that such properties are the categorical bases of physical properties, i.e., we cannot be sure that such properties are inscrutables. Since Russellian monism is here defined partly in terms of a commitment to inscrutables, the view advocated by Stoljar 2006 does not count as a version of Russellian monism.

to consider o-physical properties as genuinely physical properties—that is, whether the object-based conception of the physical is really a conception of the physical. I return to this question in the following section. For now, however, it's worth briefly noting that some physical monists have offered specific proposals about what the o-physical inscrutables might be. Pereboom, for example, has recently explored two different possibilities: the Aristotelian notion of prime materiality and the Lockean notion of perfect solidity (Pereboom 2011, 85–101).

3. The Collapse Thesis

The previous section provided a rough overview of the four different versions of Russellian monism on offer in contemporary discussion. But as I will now argue, once we examine these views more closely we discover that there is not really room for four distinct positions here. Rather, the four versions of Russellian monism really collapse into two. Call this claim *the collapse thesis*. My argument for the collapse thesis proceeds in two steps. First, I suggest that protophenomenal monism does not carve out distinct conceptual space from the other three versions of Russellian monism, so the four versions really collapse into three versions. Second, I suggest that, in the context of Russellian monism, neutral properties are no different from physical properties of a special sort. Thus, the three remaining versions of Russellian monism really collapse into two versions.

The first step should be fairly straightforward. Above we saw that one of the standard ways of understanding the notion of neutrality is along the lines of "neither mental nor physical." On this way of understanding neutrality, whatever is not mental or physical will count as neutral by default. Thus, this understanding leaves no conceptual space for protophenomenal properties that lie outside the mental-neutral-physical trichotomy. Protophenomenal properties are by definition not phenomenal, so that means they must either be a species of neutral properties or a species of physical properties.

Granted, this is not the only way that we might understand neutrality. So what if we were instead to understand it in terms of causal laws? We saw above that if the set of laws normally thought of as psychological and the set of laws normally thought of as physical could both be recast in terms of a single kind of inscrutable property, it would seem to be plausible to treat the inscrutables as neutral. Here again, though, it seems that protophenomenal monism does not carve out a distinct position. Whatever protophenomenal properties are, it seems that both the set of laws normally thought of as psychological and the set of laws normally thought of as physical will be recast in terms of them. So on the causal law understanding of neutrality, protophenomenal inscrutables are properly understood to be neutral inscrutables.

Protophenomenal monism thus collapses into either neutral monism or physical monism, and our quartet of Russellian monist views narrows to a trio. There is no room for protophenomenal monism separate from phenomenal monism, neutral monism, and physical monism. As I am about to go on to argue that this trio of views narrows to a duo, it will not be worth worrying further here about whether it's neutral monism or physical monism into which protophenomenal monism collapses. But there is one point worth noting. In saying that protophenomenal monism collapses into one of these views, I do not mean that protophenomenal monism should be *identified* with one of these views. Rather, I mean that protophenomenal monism is best understood as a *species* of one of these views. According to Chalmers' characterization of protophenomenal properties, there will be an *a priori* entailment between protophenomenal properties and the phenomenal properties to which they give rise. Since it is open to both the neutral monist and the physical monist to deny this *a priori* entailment, we might think of protophenomenal monism as the *a priori* version of either neutral monism or physical monism.

It likely does not seem that surprising that our four initial versions of Russellian monism reduce to three, for it's likely not that surprising that protophenomenal monism is best understood as a version of either neutral or physical monism. I suspect it seems considerably more surprising, however, that the three remaining versions of Russellian monism—phenomenal monism, neutral monism, and physical monism—might themselves reduce to two versions. But this is what I will now argue. In particular, I want to suggest that there is no neutral monist position that is importantly distinct from phenomenal monism and physical monism as we have understood them.

One way to make my argument for the collapse thesis would be to push a claim that was mentioned in passing in section 2 above. Suppose that the dichotomy between the mental and the physical is exhaustive. In this case, the existence of neutral entities—entities that are neither mental nor physical—is ruled out by default. So, an argument for the claim that the mental/physical dichotomy is exhaustive would in turn show that there are no such thing as neutral inscrutables and hence that there can be no neutral version of Russellian monism. Since on this line of argumentation the alleged neutral entities are made to disappear entirely, I will call it the *disappearance strategy*.

Though my argumentative strategy has some natural affinity to the disappearance strategy, it is in other ways importantly different. In particular, I am not committed to the claim that there is no room for entities that are neutral between the mental and the physical.[18] Rather, I am committed only to the claim that there is no room for genuinely neutral *inscrutables*.

Inscrutables, recall, are the categorical or intrinsic bases for physical properties. Physical theory defines mass solely in terms of its structural role. But *what is it* that plays this role? Whatever it is, our physical theory does not have the means to tell us anything about it. This inscrutable underlies a physical property *par excellence*—and likewise for the other inscrutables. Moreover, as we saw in section 2, physical monism operates with an object-based conception of the physical. On this conception, a property is physical if it is required by (or supervenes on what is required by) a complete account of the intrinsic nature of paradigmatic physical objects and their constituents. Inscrutables clearly fit the bill. So if we accept that the object-based conception of the physical is an appropriate conception of the physical, then the kinds of inscrutables posited by the neutral monist posits are better described as physical—that is, as *o-physical*—than as neutral.[19]

This brings us back to a question about which I earlier postponed discussion: Should we accept the object-based conception of the physical? In answering this question, I am in something of a delicate position. Though I want to deny that there's room for a neutral version of Russellian monism, I do not want to deny that there's room for a phenomenal version of Russellian monism. And it looks like the object-based conception of the physical would classify even phenomenal inscrutables as physical. So if I accept that the object-based conception of the physical is really a conception of the physical, then it looks like my argument will prove too much. To show that neutral monism collapses into physical monism without also showing that phenomenal monism collapses into physical monism, I need a principled way of classifying the physical that includes neutral inscrutables without also including phenomenal inscrutables.

Fortunately, there is such a classification available. Many physicalists endorse a "no fundamental mentality" (NFM) constraint on the notion of the

---

18. Numbers, for example, might be plausibly understood as abstract objects that are neither physical nor mental. It is in part due to examples like this that I avoid the disappearance strategy and its commitment to the claim that the mental/physical dichotomy is exhaustive.

19. As Daniel Stoljar has pointed out to me, once we have the t/o distinction in play, we can then define different notions of neutrality. In particular, a t-neutral property is one which is neither t-physical nor mental. An o-physical property that is not a t-physical property will thus be t-neutral. But since physical monism is operating with an o-based conception of the physical, it seems that the notion of neutrality in play in the relevant discussion should be o-neutrality.

physical—that is, they deny that an entity that is fundamentally mental can count as a physical entity.[20] To accept such a constraint is to deny that we can fully understand the notion of the physical in terms of physics. If an ideal future physics were to incorporate entities with fundamental mentality into its theorizing, then NFM physicalists would claim that physicalism turns out to be false. NFM physicalism can accept that future physics might posit entities that are radically different from those posited by current physics, but if any such entities turn out to have fundamental mentality, then they would no longer count as physical.

Those physicalists who endorse the NFM constraint are typically working with a theory-based conception of the physical. But there is no reason that we can't incorporate an NFM constraint into an object-based conception of the physical. A property would be o*-physical if (1) it is not fundamentally mental; and (2) it is required by (or supervenes on what is required by) a complete account of the intrinsic nature of paradigmatic physical objects and their constituents. By adopting the corresponding o*-based conception of the physical, we can count the neutral inscrutables as physical without also counting the phenomenal inscrutables as physical.

4. An Objection

In the previous section, I presented my argument for the collapse thesis. If this argument is correct, then there are not really four distinct versions of Russellian monism but only two. In developing this argument, I committed myself to the claim that the o*-based conception of the physical can be properly considered to be a conception of the physical. Thus, to block my argument for the collapse thesis, someone might object to this claim. There are two ways such an objection might go. First, someone might accept that the o-based conception of the physical is really a conception of the physical, but reject the addition of the NFM constraint. Second, one might reject the o-based conception of the physical. I'll take these in reverse order.

The most obvious way of rejecting the o-based conception of the physical would be to retreat to a t-based conception of the physical.[21] But it's important

---

20. The need for such a constraint is forcefully argued by Wilson 2006. In explaining the notion of fundamental mentality she notes that an entity that lacks fundamental mentality "does not individually either possess or bestow mentality" (Wilson 2006, 72). See also Ney 2008 for discussion.

21. There might be other ways of rejecting the o-based conception of the physical without retreating to the t-based conception of the physical. Chalmers, for example, distinguishes

to note that this retreat entails rejecting altogether the possibility of a physical version of Russellian monism. Given that the inscrutables are by definition inaccessible to physical theory, they are by definition excluded from the class of t-physical properties and cannot be accommodated within the t-based conception of the physical. So an insistence that the only adequate conception of the physical is a t-physical one amounts to a denial of the coherence of physical monism.

Importantly, however, the denial of the object-based conception of the physical is consistent with the collapse thesis, i.e., with the claim that Russellian monism narrows from four options to only two options. The o-physical inscrutables are either phenomenal or not. I take it that the physical monists typically take them to be non-phenomenal.[22] Moreover, if they were phenomenal, physical monism would turn out to be a version of phenomenal monism. But if the o-physical inscrutables are not phenomenal, and they've been excluded from the class of physical properties, then that would suggest that they are best understood as neutral. In this case, the collapse thesis would still hold, though the two remaining versions would be phenomenal monism and neutral monism rather than phenomenal monism and physical monism.

In my view, at this point the dispute ends up being largely a verbal one. It is hard to see what would turn on whether we classify the non-phenomenal version of monism as neutral monism or as physical monism. But if there is a substantive issue here, there is also an easy way to avoid taking a stand on it: We could simply label the two remaining versions of Russellian monism as *phenomenal monism* and *non-phenomenal monism,* and all subsequent discussion could then be recast in terms of this way of drawing the contrast. (In what follows, I will continue to use the label *physical* monism, but a reader who is uncomfortable counting the o-physical as physical should feel free to substitute non-*phenomenal.*) As we've seen, then, a rejection of the o-physical conception of the physical does not count against the collapse thesis.

We need now to return to the first objection—that is, we need to address the concerns of someone who accepts the o-physical conception of the physical but who denies the acceptability of the NFM constraint. To my mind, there's considerable plausibility to the idea that physicalism is committed to a lack of fundamental mentality, but not everyone agrees, and to engage fully

---

between the *broadly physical* and the *narrowly physical* and argues that this distinction is not the same as Stoljar's distinction between the o-physical and the t-physical (see, e.g., his 2013a, 9–10). But the basic argument I give in the text should apply equally well, *mutatis mutandi,* were we to use Chalmers' distinction rather than Stoljar's.

22. This might suggest commitment to the NFM constraint.

with this debate here would take us too far afield.[23] Recall the role played by the NFM constraint: It enables us to argue that neutral monism collapses into physical monism without having to claim that phenomenal monism collapses into physical monism. In the absence of this constraint, even phenomenal inscrutables could be classified as physical inscrutables. Our initial quartet of versions of Russellian monism would then be reduced to but a single version.

Importantly, however, even if we are left with only physical monism, the distinction in which I am primarily interested—and which underlies the overall pessimistic argument of this chapter—would not disappear. That distinction is between the phenomenal and the non-phenomenal. If someone wants to treat phenomenal monism as a version of physical monism, so be it—but notice that there will still be two importantly different kinds of positions here: one we might call *phenomenal physical monism* and the other what we might call *non-phenomenal physical monism*. Ultimately, it does not matter for my purposes whether we say that there are two versions of Russellian monism, or whether we say that there are two sub-types of physical monism. In both cases, we are forced to confront the basic dichotomy between the phenomenal and the non-phenomenal. As I will argue in the following section, the re-appearance of this basic dichotomy means that, contrary to its advance billing, Russellian monism is unable to meaningfully transcend the dualism/ physicalism divide.

5. The Case for Pessimism

I begin this final section with two tales.

First, the tale of the disenchanted dualist. Once upon a recent time there was a philosopher with deeply entrenched dualist inclinations, but who had grown disenchanted with the traditional forms of dualism on offer. She was deeply convinced that no reductive theory of consciousness will succeed, that consciousness is a fundamental part of reality. But she was also deeply frustrated by the inability of existing versions of dualism to account adequately for the reality of mental causes. Then one day she was visited by the ghost of Russell past, who showed her that Russellian monism could provide her with almost exactly what she's looking for. Sure there was a cost: She had to give up on her intuition that the mental and the physical are as radically different as she had thought, since Russellian monism claims that both the mental and the physical would arise from the inscrutables of a single sort. But there

---

23. See Dowell 2006 and Ney 2008 for useful discussions.

was also a benefit: She now had a potential answer to the problem of mental causation, since it would be plausible for mental causes to inherit causal efficacy from the inscrutables that underlie them. The details would have to be worked out, of course. But she had good reason for hope, and she lived happily ever after.

Next, the tale of the disenchanted physicalist. Once upon a recent time there was a philosopher with deeply entrenched physicalist inclinations, but who had grown disenchanted with the traditional forms of physicalism on offer. She was deeply convinced that some reductive theory of consciousness will succeed, that consciousness is not a fundamental part of reality. But she was also deeply frustrated by the inability of existing versions of physicalism adequately to address the array of conceivability arguments (e.g., zombie arguments) leveled against them. Then one day she was visited by the ghost of Russell past, who showed her that Russellian monism could provide her with almost exactly what she's looking for. Sure there was a cost: She had to give up on her intuition that physicalism can be explained in terms of physics, since inscrutables are by definition out of the reach of physics. But there was also a benefit: She now had a potential answer to the conceivability arguments, since it would be plausible to deny that we can conceive of a zombie who is identical to a conscious being even with respect to inscrutables but yet who lacked consciousness. The details would have to be worked out, of course. But she had good reason for hope, and she lived happily ever after.

Hearing these two tales, it might appear that the disenchanted dualist and the disenchanted physicalist have both happened upon the same bag of magic beans, as it were. The tales suggest that they have converged on a single position—that they have transcended the dualist/physicalist divide. But this is simply an illusion. There are no magic beans. Or, perhaps better: The disenchanted dualist is planting a completely different sort of magic beans from those being planted by the disenchanted physicalist. While it is true that they have both adopted versions of Russellian monism, the distance between them seems to me as great as ever. In particular, they still disagree on the basic question of whether consciousness is part of the fundamental nature of reality. The disenchanted dualist will insist that the inscrutables are phenomenal, while the disenchanted physicalist will insist that the inscrutables are non-phenomenal. And the clash of intuitions between them will be just as great as it has always been.

To my mind, this simple point has been obfuscated by the proliferation of different views in the recent philosophical literature that have been classified as versions of Russellian monism. I don't mean to suggest that this classification is incorrect. Insofar as each of the views is committed to a single class of inscrutables, they seem appropriately considered as views of this type. But by focusing on the respects in which these views depart from traditional versions of dualism and traditional versions of physicalism, and by focusing on what they have in common, we appear to have a made a certain kind of progress that, in my view, we have not made.

Consider, for example, the following claims made about Russellian monism (or particular versions of Russellian monism):

> [Phenomenal monism] offers resolutions to mind-body problems that dualism and materialism find intractable. Present philosophy of mind is dominated by materialist theories that cannot adequately address issues of consciousness, qualia, or the role of mind in the universe. Dualism is the traditional alternative, but it too suffers from long-standing weaknesses and unanswered questions. [Phenomenal monism] offers a third way.
>
> (Skrbina 2005, 4)

> But even where there is substantial overlap with traditional theories, Russellian monism provides a distinctive perspective on conscious-ness, the world as revealed by physical science, and the relationship between the two.
>
> (Alter and Nagasawa 2011, 83)

The discussion of this chapter helps us to see how these claims can be mislead-ing. Once we clear away the clutter, so to speak, we see that there are really only two possibilities for the nature of inscrutables: they must be either phenom-enal or physical. That means that a Russellian monist must endorse either phe-nomenal monism and physical monism. To my mind, these two views are as different from one another as traditional dualism and traditional physicalism are. Any attempt to adjudicate between them will have to settle the question as to whether consciousness is a fundamental part of nature—the same question that needs to be adjudicated in the debate between dualism and physicalism.

Granted, we often describe the basic issue that divides dualism and physi-calism in a slightly different way. As defined by the *Stanford Encyclopedia of Philosophy*, dualism "is the theory that the mental and the physical—or mind and body or mind and brain—are, in some sense, radically different kinds of thing" (Robinson 2012). This claim is denied by both physicalists and ide-alists; physicalists conjoin their denial that the mental and the physical are radically different kinds of things with the further claim that the physical kind of thing is more basic. So the issue between dualism and physicalism might seem to be an issue about how many kinds of things there are—two or one. Notice, however, that the reason that the dualist thinks that there are two kinds of things is that she thinks that consciousness is an irreducible part of nature. And it's this that the physicalist denies. Thus, the common description of what separates dualism from physicalism cannot be invoked to dispel my pessimistic conclusion.

Does this mean that phenomenal monism is just a version of dualism, while physical monism is a version of physicalism? In collapsing into these two versions, does Russellian monism simply collapse back into dualism and physicalism? To properly answer these questions, we would first have to undertake a careful look at the commitments of both traditional dualism and traditional physicalism. We would then have to evaluate whether the respect in which phenomenal monism departs from the commitments of traditional dualism outweighs the respect in which it shares such commitments. We would have to do likewise for physical monism/traditional physicalism. But how exactly should these things be weighed? At this point, we might worry that things have devolved into merely a verbal dispute. Chalmers, for example, claims exactly this. In considering the question of whether Russellian monism is "a form of physicalism, dualism, or something else," he notes that it "is a largely verbal question that we need not settle" (2013a, 16).

I myself do not feel the temptation to dismiss the debate here as merely verbal. Moreover, I'm myself inclined to give affirmative answers to the questions above, i.e., I'm inclined to see Russellian monism as dividing into a version of dualism and a version of physicalism, both of which would be non-traditional in important respects. Insofar as this non-traditionality might be thought to count against the classification, or to make it seem as if it's only a verbal question, it might be helpful to consider, for example, two views that are both uncontroversially counted as versions of dualism: Cartesian dualism and epiphenomenalism. Cartesian dualism is a view about substances. It is also interactionist in nature. Epiphenomenalism is a view about properties, and it rejects interactionism. It seems clear that it differs in pretty crucial ways from the Cartesian picture. Yet we count epiphenomenal dualism as a version of dualism, and we're not at all inclined to consider the question of whether this classification is correct as merely a verbal one.

Fortunately, however, the overall argument of this chapter does not require me to take a stance on these issues. My pessimism about Russellian monism will still be warranted even if one is not inclined to accept that Russellian monism collapses into either dualism or physicalism, and it will likewise be warranted even if one is inclined to dismiss the issue itself as one that is not substantive. For whatever one's stance on these issues, it remains the case that the Russellian monist owes us an account of the nature of the inscrutables. As I have argued in this chapter, the development of this account will involve a choice between two options: phenomenal monism and physical monism. This choice hinges on the issue of whether the inscrutables are phenomenal. If this choice is not flatly the choice between dualism and physicalism, it is at the very least not too far removed from that choice. And so we are thus essentially back where we started. Of course, that's not to deny that *some* progress has been made along the way. There might be reasons to think that phenomenal monism improves upon traditional dualism. There might likewise be reasons to think that physical monism improves upon traditional physicalism. But the central divide in philosophy of mind remains unbridged.

In conclusion, nothing that I've said in this chapter is meant to show that Russellian monism is false. Though my argument here has been a pessimistic one, my pessimism concerns not the truth of the view but rather its ability to transcend the dualist/physicalist divide. I started this section with two tales, but in my view, philosophy of mind can be largely seen as a tale of two philosophies. It's been hoped that Russellian monism would close the chapter on that story, and begin a new one—one that provides us with the best of times without the worst of times. As I've suggested in this chapter, however, that hope is misguided.[24]

References

Alter, Torin and Yujin Nagasawa. 2012. "What Is Russellian Monism?" *Journal of Consciousness Studies* 19: 67–95.

Chalmers, David. 2013a. "Panpsychism and Panprotopsychism." Draft available at http://consc.net/papers/panpsychism.pdf.

Chalmers, David. 2013b. "The Combination Problem for Panpsychism." Draft available at http://consc.net/papers/combination.pdf.

Chalmers, David. 2002. "Consciousness and Its Place in Nature." In *Philosophy of Mind: Classic and Contemporary Readings*, ed. David Chalmers, 247–72. Oxford: Oxford University Press.

Chalmers, David. 1996. *The Conscious Mind*. Oxford: Oxford University Press.

Coleman, Sam. 2013. Review of Michael Blamauer, ed., *The Mental as Fundamental: New Perspectives on Panpsychism. Notre Dame Philosophical Reviews.* http://ndpr.nd.edu/news/28297-the-mental-as-fundamental-new-perspectives-on-panpsychism/.

Coleman, Sam. 2012. "Mental Chemistry: Combination for Panpsychists." *Dialectica* 66: 137–66.

---

24. I'm grateful to Peter Ross and Peter Thielke for helpful discussion of issues related to Russellian monism. Thanks also to Torin Alter, Dustin Locke, Frank Menetrez, Yujin Nagasawa, and Daniel Stoljar for helpful comments on a previous draft of this chapter.

Dowell, Janice. 2006. "Formulating the Thesis of Physicalism: An Introduction." *Philosophical Studies* 131: 1–23.

Foster, John. 1982. *The Case for Idealism*. London: Routledge & Kegan Paul.

Holman, Emmett L. 2008. "Panpsychism, Physicalism, Neutral Monism and the Russellian Theory of Mind." *Journal of Consciousness Studies* 15: 28–67.

Kind, Amy. 2006. "Panexperientialism, Cognition, and the Nature of Experience." *Psyche* 12, http://www.theassc.org/files/assc/2657.pdf.

Lockwood, Michael. 1989. *Mind, Brain, and the Quantum*. Oxford: Blackwell Publishers.

Lockwood, Michael. 1981. "What *Was* Russell's Neutral Monism?" *Midwest Studies in Philosophy* 6: 143–58.

Maxwell, Grover. 1978. "Rigid Designators and Mind-Brain Identity." In *Minnesota Studies in the Philosophy of Science*, Vol. 9, ed. C. Wade Savage, 365–403. Minneapolis: University of Minnesota Press.

Montero, Barbara. 2011. "A Russellian Response to the Structural Argument Against Physicalism." *Journal of Consciousness Studies* 17: 70–83.

Nagel, Thomas. 1979. *Mortal Questions*. Cambridge: Cambridge University Press.

Ney, Alyssa. 2008. "Defining Physicalism." *Philosophy Compass* 3: 1033–48.

Pereboom, Derk. 2011. *Consciousness and the Prospects of Physicalism*. Oxford: Oxford University Press.

Robinson, Howard. 2012. "Dualism." In *The Stanford Encyclopedia of Philosophy* (Winter 2012 Edition), ed. Edward N. Zalta, http://plato.stanford.edu/archives/win2012/entries/dualism/.

Rosenberg, Gregg. 2004. *A Place for Consciousness*. Oxford: Oxford University Press.

Russell, Bertrand. 1927/1954. *The Analysis of Matter*. New York: Dover Publications.

Russell, Bertrand. 1921. *The Analysis of Mind*. New York: The Macmillan Company.

Skrbina, David. 2005. *Panpsychism in the West*. Cambridge, Mass.: The MIT Press.

Stoljar, Daniel. 2006. *Ignorance and Imagination*. Oxford: Oxford University Press.

Stoljar, Daniel. 2001. "Two Conceptions on the Physical." *Philosophy and Phenomenological Research* 62: 253–2181.

Strawson, Galen. 2006. "Realistic Monism: Why Physicalism Entails Panpsychism." *Journal of Consciousness Studies* 13: 3–31.

Stubenberg, Leopold. 2010. "Neutral Monism." In *The Stanford Encyclopedia of Philosophy* (Spring 2010 Edition), ed. Edward N. Zalta. Available at http://plato.stanford.edu/archives/spr2010/entries/neutral-monism/.

Wilson, Jessica. 2006. "On Characterizing the Physical." *Philosophical Studies* 131: 61–99.

What Is Russellian Monism?

Torin Alter and Yujin Nagasawa

Introduction

Russellian monism is a view about phenomenal consciousness, the physical world, and the relationship between them.[1] On this view, the phenomenal and the physical are deeply intertwined—more so, at least, than traditional inter-actionist dualism allows. But there is no attempt to reduce the phenomenal to the physical, at least not in the manner of traditional versions of physicalism (or materialism). Instead, on Russellian monism phenomenal consciousness fills a gap in the picture of nature painted by physics. For example, on one well-known version of the view, phenomenal properties are the categorical bases of fundamental physical properties, such as mass and charge, which are dispositional.[2]

In this chapter, we provide some background on Russellian monism (sections 1–2); specify what we take to be the core of the view (section 3); distinguish its main variations and examine the central concepts it employs (sections 4–6); explain how it relates to traditional theories (section 7) and to the conceivability and knowledge arguments against physicalism (section 8); and discuss the main arguments for and against Russellian monism (sections 9 and 10).

To the extent that this chapter is an overview, it is a decidedly opinionated one. We are neutral on certain issues, such as which version of Russellian

---

1. A mental state is *phenomenally conscious* if there is something it is like to be in that state. See T. Nagel 1974.

2. For examples of traditional dualism and traditional physicalism, see R. Descartes 1641 and D. M. Armstrong 1968, respectively.

monism is the most plausible. But on other issues we take stands. For example, the general formulation of Russellian monism that we propose in section 3 differs from others in the literature. We explain our reasons for doing so, but not all will find those reasons sufficient.

1. Monism

Ontological monism comes in at least two varieties: token and type.[3] Token monism says roughly that there is (ultimately) only one object. Historically, this view is associated with Spinoza and Parmenides, among others. There are also contemporary versions. Terence Horgan and Matjaž Potrč (2009) defend existence monism, according to which there is only one concrete object, which they call "the blobject."[4] And Jonathan Schaffer (2010) defends priority monism, according to which there is only one *basic* object, the whole cosmos.

Where token monism tends to concern objects specifically, type monism tends to concern entities more generally construed—objects, properties, tropes, etc. Type monism says that there is (ultimately) only one type of entity. Examples of type monism include physicalism, which says that all entities are ultimately of the physical type, and idealism, which says that all entities are ultimately of the mental type. Russellian monism is a version of type monism, not token monism. More precisely, Russellian monism is a version of type monism insofar as it is a version of monism. As we will explain (section 7), some versions of Russellian monism posit more than one type of entity and thus are monistic in name only.[5]

2. Russell

Bertrand Russell's writings have inspired most, if not all, contemporary versions of Russellian monism. David J. Chalmers (1996), Michael Lockwood

---

3. We qualify "monism" with "ontological" because the former is sometimes used to name views that apply outside ontology. For example, value monism says that there is only one value, such as hedonic pleasure.

4. One might think that existence monism is clearly false because, for example, you have two distinct hands. In response, Horgan and Potrč would argue that, although the blobject has spatiotemporal and structural complexity, hands are neither concrete particulars nor genuine parts of the blobject.

5. In contemporary philosophy of mind, it is common to apply the type/token distinction to mental and physical states (or events). That application should not be confused with our application to kinds of monism.

(1992), Grover Maxwell (1978), and others trace the view specifically to *The Analysis of Matter* (Russell 1927a). There Russell describes his position as neutral monism, a version of type monism on which the one type of entity that ultimately exists is intrinsically neither of the mental nor physical type (Stubenberg 2005/10). However, neutral monism is but one version of Russellian monism (see section 5). We do not intend "Russellian monism" to abbreviate "the version of monism Russell held."[6]

Even so, it will be instructive to see how Russellian monism emerges from two views Russell expressed in *The Analysis of Matter*. One is structuralism about physics. According to structuralism, physics describes its basic entities in highly abstract, purely structural/relational terms. For example, a particle's mass and charge are characterized as a propensity to be accelerated in a certain way by certain forces—by relations to other entities within a spatiotemporal structure. Those other entities are characterized by further such relations, which in turn are characterized by yet further such relations, and so on. So, for Russell, physics describes the structure of the universe in great detail but is silent on what, if anything, has the structure in itself. That is, physics does not characterize the intrinsic nature of basic physical entities—the relata that stand in basic physical relations.[7]

What are these relata, if such there be? According to Russell (1927a, p. 402), "Percepts are the only part of the physical world that we know otherwise than abstractly." That claim can be taken to suggest the view that we know phenomenal properties by their intrinsic phenomenal natures. And the idea that phenomenal properties have intrinsic natures with which we are familiar—natures not exhausted by extrinsic, structural features—makes them natural candidates for the relata that stand in basic physical relations.

---

6. The definite description would be improper in any case. Russell adopted different versions of the view over the years (Stubenberg 2005/10). Given that Russellian monism does not necessarily represent Russell's view and that Russellian monism can be seen as a form of dualism, one might think that Russellian monism is analogous to the Holy Roman Empire, which is neither holy, Roman, nor an empire. Thanks to an anonymous referee for this observation.

7. Pure structuralism, on which every term in physical theory is defined structurally, faces a well-known difficulty, first raised by Newman (1928): the theory can be satisfied by any set of the appropriate cardinality and thus seems vacuous (or nearly so). However, the problem can be avoided by allowing certain primitives that are not defined structurally. For example, "cause" and "law" might refer to causation and lawhood independently of any structural roles played by causation and lawhood. Russell (1951, p. 271) responded to Newman in roughly this way, where the primitive he assumed was "spacio-temporal continuity with the world of percepts." Note that even on such impure versions of structuralism, the question of what, if anything, has the structure physics describes still arises.

This identification results in a version of Russellian monism.[8] Thus, we are led to Russellian monism by combining Russell's structuralism about physics with a view he held about knowledge and perception.

3. General Formulation

There are many distinct versions of Russellian monism but it would be useful to have a general formulation of the view: one that expresses its main components, which are common to all versions. In this section, we will attempt to provide such a general formulation, inspired by the Russellian reasoning traced in the preceding section.

First, however, it will be convenient to introduce some terminology. We will refer to properties (if such there be) that ground the physical structure/relations physics describes as *inscrutables* (Montero 2014). By definition, inscrutables have natures that are not fully characterized by structural/relational descriptions.[9] We will also refer to *protophenomenal properties*—properties that, though not themselves phenomenal, result in phenomenal properties when combined in certain ways (Chalmers 1996, pp. 126–27).

We are now in a position to specify the main components of Russellian monism. We propose that Russellian monism be understood as a conjunction of three claims:

> *Structuralism about physics*: the basic properties physics describes are structural/relational properties.
>
> *Realism about inscrutables*: there are inscrutables, the natures of which are not wholly structural/relational.
>
> (Proto)*phenomenal foundationalism*: at least some inscrutables are either phenomenal or protophenomenal properties.

Russellian monism implies additional claims that we leave implicit, e.g., that there are physical properties; and that these properties are indeed structural, as descriptions in physics imply. We isolate structuralism about physics,

---

8. This version of Russellian monism does not, however, imply neutral monism, which Russell favored. But it is consistent with neutral monism given the further assumption that phenomenal properties are or reduce to neutral properties.

9. We use "inscrutables" simply as a name for the properties we have described. The term is not ideal, because it has epistemic connotations we do not intend, e.g., that knowledge about such properties is difficult or impossible to acquire. We hope this does not mislead.

realism about inscrutables, and (proto)phenomenal foundationalism because we believe they are the most central and most distinctive claims that Russellian monism makes.

So, on our formulation Russellian monism says that there are both structural properties, which physics describes, and inscrutables—and that the latter ground the former. Our formulation differs from some others in the literature. Derk Pereboom writes:

> . . . Russellian monism is any view that combines (1) *categorical igno-rance*, the claim that physics, or at least current physics, leaves us igno-rant of certain categorical bases of physical dispositional properties, with (2) *consciousness- or experience-relevance*, the proposal that these categorical properties have a significant role in explaining conscious-ness or experience.[10]
>
> (Pereboom *2011, p. 89*)

Pereboom's formulation is in many ways consonant with ours. However, his has an epistemic orientation that ours lacks. In particular, ours does not mention categorical ignorance.[11] It is understandable that Pereboom's does; proponents of Russellian monism often emphasize categorical ignorance. However, categorical ignorance is an *epistemic* claim. But as we understand Russellian monism, it is supposed to be a theory in the same category as dualism and physicalism, namely, *metaphysical*. Such theories primarily concern the nature of the mental and its (metaphysical) relationship to the physical world. Of course, such theories tend to have epistemic commitments. But today those are usually regarded as consequences rather than basic tenets of these theories.[12] We believe that the same attitude should be taken toward Russellian monism.[13]

---

10. Compare Chalmers 2003, Stoljar 2001a, 2001b, 2006, Montero 2014. Pereboom (2011) advances this characterization of Russellian monism only provisionally, and refines some of its key concepts in useful ways. However, he does not expressly reject the epistemic orienta-tion of his provisional characterization.

11. Clause (2) in Pereboom's formulation also has an epistemic orientation, if the intended notion of explanation is epistemic. But this may not be his intention.

12. This was not always the case. For example, in chapter 1 of his influential work, *The Concept of Mind*, Gilbert Ryle (1949) characterizes Cartesian dualism partly in epistemic terms.

13. The nature of Russellian monism's epistemic commitments is a topic for another essay. But a few points can be made concisely. First, Pereboom's view that Russellian monism implies categorical ignorance is plausible, whether or not it should be included in a definition

Our formulation is schematic in certain respects. In particular, much is left open about: the relationship between physical properties and the inscrutables; what the inscrutables are; and the relationship between the inscrutables and phenomenal properties. We will address these matters in turn.

4. Physical Properties and the Inscrutables

Central to Russellian monism is the idea that there is a substantial distinction between the properties found in physics and inscrutables. Call this *the central distinction*. In this section, we will discuss the main ways the central distinction has been explicated.

Explications typically involve the following contrasts:

(i)   extrinsic vs. intrinsic properties
(ii) dispositional vs. categorical properties
(iii) relational vs. non-relational properties
(iv) structural-and-dynamic vs. non-structural-and-non-dynamic properties.[14]

Differences between these contrasts are not much emphasized in the literature on Russellian monism, and some of the terms are often used interchangeably (especially "relational/non-relational" and "extrinsic/intrinsic").

However, distinctive controversies surround each of the four contrasts. For example, consider the dispositional/categorical contrast. Sydney

---

of Russellian monism. Second, some versions of Russellian monism may imply that we know phenomenal properties in a distinctive way, a way in which we know nothing else. Witness Russell's claim, quoted in section 2, about percepts being the only aspects of the physical world that we know otherwise than abstractly. Third, Russellian monism may have implications concerning Ramseyan Humility, the doctrine that "we are irremediably ignorant about the identities of the fundamental properties that figure in the actual realization of the true final theory [of reality]" (Lewis 2009, p. 214). Ramseyan Humility assumes a metaphysical framework in which there are what we call inscrutables. So, Russellian monism involves a Humility-friendly metaphysical framework. Moreover, according to some versions of Russellian monism—namely, all versions except those that identify the inscrutables with phenomenal properties (see section 5)—we do not know much about inscrutables, and our ignorance will not be removed by acquiring more of the sort of information physics provides. The latter sort of ignorance falls short of Ramseyan Humility, which says that our ignorance is incurable. But the subject matter of both ignorance claims is the same.

14. Sometimes explications of the central distinction also invoke epistemic contrasts, e.g., that between properties we know and properties about which we are ignorant (Stoljar 2006). See section 7.

Shoemaker (1980) argues that all properties are dispositional, and David Armstrong (1996) argues that dispositional properties should be identified with their categorical bases. Either conclusion would complicate the use of the dispositional/categorical contrast in explicating the central distinction. Shoemaker's and Armstrong's arguments are disputed (see Fara 2006). But it is not clear that one should have to take a stand on those particular disputes in order to endorse at least some versions of Russellian monism (cf. Stoljar 2006, chapter 6). Similar considerations apply to the other three contrasts.

Let us therefore stipulate that the general formulation of Russellian monism proposed in the preceding section is neutral on how the central distinction is explicated. References to structural/relational properties should be regarded as mere examples. Thus, structuralism about physics need not strictly involve claims about structure *per se*. A more precise statement of structuralism would be the following: the basic properties physics describes are structural (or structural-and-dynamic) or relational or extrinsic or dispositional. Realism about inscrutables and (proto)phenomenal foundationalism should likewise be regarded as neutral in this respect.

At least three problems arise in connection to how the central distinction is explicated. We will refer to them as *impurity, relativity*, and *vagueness*, and address them in turn.

Impurity

Proponents of Russellian monism sometimes describe inscrutables as intrinsic and properties found in physics as extrinsic. But as Pereboom observes, extrinsic properties can have intrinsic aspects:

> ... *being wise* is an extrinsic property of Sophie since it involves a relation to a comparison class. But *being wise* also includes an intrinsic aspect—having a certain type and level of intelligence. *Being wise* is therefore a complex property that has at least one extrinsic and one intrinsic aspect ...
>
> (Pereboom 2011, pp. 92–93)

This leads Pereboom to define a *purely* extrinsic property of a thing X as an extrinsic property of X that has no intrinsic aspects. *Being one of many* is a clear example of a purely extrinsic property. When proponents of Russellian monism characterize properties found in physics as extrinsic, they likely mean not that those properties are purely extrinsic but rather that physics describes only their extrinsic aspects.[15] And when these philosophers characterize inscrutables as intrinsic, they likely mean not that inscrutables lack extrinsic aspects altogether but only that such properties have intrinsic aspects. Likewise for the other three contrasts in play.[16]

Failing to recognize this point can cause confusion. For example, it is sometimes noted that phenomenal properties have structure and dynamics. The series of auditory phenomenal properties typically caused by hearing a musical scale plausibly has a structure corresponding to the scale. And your headache might become more intense over time. At first glance, such simple observations might seem to create problems for Russellian monism (Stoljar 2006, pp. 144–49). But the point made in the previous paragraph shows that this concern is unfounded. The relevant claim is not that phenomenal properties lack structure or dynamics, but only that phenomenal properties are not merely structural/dynamic (Alter 2009).

Relativity

Proponents of Russellian monism sometimes describe inscrutables as categorical and properties found in physics as dispositional. The implication is that categorical properties are not found in physics. But this seems wrong. A typical example of a categorical property is an object's shape, e.g., the roundness of a ball. Yet shapes are described in physics.

However, proponents of Russellian monism need not deny that shape is categorical in a sense. The ball's round shape helps explain its tendency to roll. Proponents of Russellian monism will thus agree that its shape is categorical *relative to* its tendency to roll. But they will argue that its shape is not *absolutely* categorical, in the sense that this property can be analyzed in purely

---

15. The latter claim should not be confused with the stronger claim, to which Russellian monists are not committed, that the properties found in physics have no intrinsic aspects.

16. On this line of reasoning, it might be the case that *both* the inscrutables and the properties found in physics have intrinsic and extrinsic aspects. But there is an important difference. Inscrutables are intrinsic properties that might or might not have extrinsic aspects. By contrast, the properties found in physics are extrinsic properties that might or might not have intrinsic aspects. In other words, the inscrutables are purely or impurely intrinsic, whereas the properties found in physics are purely or impurely extrinsic.

dispositional terms. Simon Blackburn (1990, 60–62) expresses this idea in a frequently cited passage:

> When we think of categorical grounds, we are apt to think of spatial configurations of things—hard, massy, shaped things, resisting penetration and displacement by others of their kind. But the categorical credentials of any item on this list are poor. Resistance is *par excellence* dispositional; extension is only of use, as Leibniz insisted, if there is some other property whose instancing defines the boundaries; hardness goes with resistance, and mass is knowable only by its dynamical effects. Turn up the magnification and we find things like an electrical charge at a point, or rather varying over a region, but the magnitude of a field at a region is known only through its effects on other things in spatial relations to that region. A region with charge is very different from a region without: perhaps different enough to explain all we could ever know about nature. It differs precisely in its dispositions or powers. But science finds only dispositions all the way down.[17]

Similar points apply to the other three contrasts. For example, the ball's roundness can be said to be intrinsic to the ball because it may seem that the ball is round independently of its relation to other objects. But proponents of Russellian monism will argue that its roundness is not *absolutely* intrinsic, in the sense that this property can be analyzed in purely extrinsic terms—more specifically, in terms of the extrinsic properties of its parts, such as their spatial arrangement (van Cleve 1988; Pereboom 2011, p. 93).

Vagueness

At least some of the concepts used to explicate the central distinction are vague in potentially objectionable ways (Stoljar 2006, pp. 144–53, 2009). Perhaps the clearest example is the concept of *structure*. Consider the Russellian monist claim that basic physical properties are structural and dynamic. What is implied by "structural"? One might suggest that a structural property is one that can be defined using only relational terms, indexicals, and logical and mathematical vocabulary. But this will not do. At least, there would have

---

17. For a similar view, see Holden 2004, p. 272. Blackburn's argument, though influential, does not settle the matter. For one thing, consider his statement, "mass is knowable only by its dynamical effects." That claim is epistemic: it concerns how mass can be known, not what mass is. Even if true, it does not follow that mass is dispositional. For critical discussion of Blackburn's argument, see Pereboom 2011, pp. 90–91.

to be constraints on which relational terms are allowed. The term "standing next to someone who is in pain" is relational, and proponents of Russellian monism will reject the idea that the property expressed by that term is merely structural (Alter 2009).

In response, one might suggest stipulating that the terms used to define structural properties do not refer to phenomenal properties. But that would be dialectically unacceptable. Proponents of Russellian monism wish to *argue* that the structural/dynamic truths physics discovers are incomplete—that there are truths involving phenomenal properties that are not entailed by any structural/dynamic truths (see section 8). That is supposed to be a substantial claim, not a trivial consequence of a stipulation.[18] Further, the proposed stipulation would do little to clarify the relevant notion of structure.

There is a more promising suggestion. For the purposes of Russellian monism, we propose that "structure" be understood to refer specifically to nomic (or causal) spatiotemporal structure.[19] This seems to be what at least some leading proponents of Russellian monism (e.g., Maxwell (1978), Chalmers (1996, 2003)) have in mind.

Daniel Stoljar, who raises (what we call) the vagueness concern, considers and rejects that suggestion (which he attributes to Chalmers). But his basis for rejecting it seems to us inadequate. He writes, "some possible physical truths are clearly not about causal and spatiotemporal structure" (Stoljar 2009, p. 778). However, this is not really so clear. Familiar physical truths, at least those found in physics, would appear to concern precisely (and only) nomic spatiotemporal structure. If there are exceptions, this would need to be shown. In any event, Stoljar does not elaborate, and so his objection is hard to assess.

Stoljar gives a second objection to treating structure as nomic spatiotemporal structure for the purposes of Russellian monism:

> . . . there are phenomenal truths that are causal or spatiotemporal—e.g. the sense of agency is presumably causal in one good sense but

---

18. Strictly, the stipulation alone does not establish the conclusion, if only because the conclusion rests on the additional claim that there are truths involving phenomenal properties. But this is plainly beside the point.

19. It might be possible to define structural-and-dynamic truths as those that can be fully represented in the form of a Ramsey sentence whose O-terms include only nomic and spatiotemporal expressions (in addition to indexicals and logical and mathematical terms). For the notions of a Ramsey sentence and O-terms, see Lewis 2009. Thanks to David Chalmers for this suggestion (in correspondence).

contributes according to many philosophers to the overall phenomenal state of the subject.

(Stoljar *2009, p. 778*)

But this is beside the point. Proponents of Russellian monism do not deny that there are phenomenal truths that are—in part—about causal spatiotemporal structure. Their claim (on the current suggestion) is rather that there are phenomenal truths that are not exhausted by truths about nomic spatiotemporal structure.

5. What Are the Inscrutables?

Proponents of Russellian monism differ on what the inscrutables are. In this section, we discuss the four main candidates.

Proposal One: The Inscrutables Are Phenomenal Properties

Proponents of proposal one include Adams (2007), Bolender (2001), Foster (1982), Griffin (1998), Rosenberg (2004), Russell (1927a), Strawson (2006a), and various others. This proposal is a natural one for Russellian monists to consider. Phenomenal properties appear to have natures that are not fully captured by the sorts of truths found in physics.[20] Additionally, identifying the inscrutables as phenomenal properties allows for precisely the sort of integration between phenomenal and physical properties that Russellian monism is designed to achieve.

If the inscrutables are construed as phenomenal properties and the inscrutables are assumed to be everywhere, then Russellian monism seems to entail panpsychism—the view that mind, or at any rate phenomenality, is everywhere.[21] The argument here is straightforward. Basic physical properties are ubiquitous: they are instantiated throughout the universe. By definition, the inscrutables ground basic physical properties. So, if the inscrutables are

---

20. This point is vividly illustrated by various thought experiments used in standard anti-physicalist arguments, such as Frank Jackson's (1982) Mary case. See section 8.

21. Rosenberg (2004, p. 91) prefers the term "panexperientialism" introduced by Griffin (1998) partly on the grounds that "panpsychism" suggests the ubiquity of mind, whereas the view in question implies only the ubiquity of phenomenality. Chalmers (1996, pp. 298–99) raises the same concern (plus two others) about "panpsychism."

phenomenal properties, then phenomenal properties too must be instantiated everywhere.

Few contemporary philosophers accept panpsychism, and some find it repugnant. This is understandable. Panpsychism seems to imply that there is something it is like to be a thermometer, a rock, and even an electron. Such claims are at least highly surprising, and some (Searle 1997) regard them as obviously false. But they do not appear to be incoherent, and they have been defended (Chalmers 1996, chapter 8, Rosenberg 2004, Strawson 2006a, 2006b). Some attribute resistance to panpsychism to assumptions that panpsychists need not make. One of these is the assumption that the phenomenality associated with rocks and thermometers would have to strongly resemble the phenomenality with which we are familiar—strongly enough so that we could *imagine* what it is like to be a rock or a thermometer. Additionally, defenders of panpsychism note that the alternative also has a counterintuitive consequence: that phenomenal consciousness would either have to "wink in" at a certain level of complexity, or that it is sometimes indeterminate whether a system is conscious. Even so, panpsychism is a consequence many philosophers otherwise sympathetic to Russellian monism would prefer to avoid.[22] That result is achieved by a second proposal:

Proposal Two: The Inscrutables Are Protophenomenal Properties

Again, protophenomenal properties are nonphenomenal properties the combination of which results in phenomenality (Chalmers 1996, 2003). On this proposal, Russellian monism seems to entail not panpsychism but pan*proto*psychism, the weaker claim that the components of phenomenality pervade the physical world. On panprotopsychism, if there is nothing it is like to be a rock, then this is only because the protophenomenal properties underlying the basic physical properties instantiated in the rock are not combined in the right way. Chalmers writes:

> [P]erhaps there is some *other* class of novel fundamental properties from which phenomenal properties are derived . . . [T]hese cannot be physical properties, but perhaps they are nonphysical properties of a new variety, on which phenomenal properties are logically supervenient.

---

22. For further discussion of the costs and benefits of panpsychism, see Chalmers 1996; Rosenberg 2004; Alter 2004; and Freeman 2006.

Such properties would be related to experience in the same way that basic physical properties are related to nonbasic properties such as [the] temperature [of a gas]. We could call these properties *protophenomenal* properties, as they are not themselves phenomenal but together they can yield the phenomenal.

(Chalmers 1996, pp. 126–27)

The crucial question here is what exactly protophenomenal properties are if they are not themselves phenomenal.

Proposal Three: The Inscrutables Are Neutral Properties, Properties That Are Neither Physical Nor Mental

This proposal is associated with neutral monism. It entails neutral monism if combined with three other assumptions: the assumption that neutral properties ground not only basic physical properties (as all inscrutables do, by definition) but also phenomenal properties; the assumption that physical and phenomenal properties are nothing over and above neutral properties; and the assumption that there are no further properties that are over and above neutral, physical, and mental properties.[23] Thomas Nagel (1986, 1998) suggests a view roughly along these lines (see also Feigl 1958/1967).[24]

Proposal Four: The Inscrutables Are Physical Properties of a Special Sort

Such physical properties would be special in that they would have natures that are not exhausted by the sorts of properties found in physics. At first glance, that condition might seem relatively weak. Biological properties such as *being a cell* might seem to satisfy it: this property has no place in fundamental physics, and yet it seems to be a physical property *par excellence*. However, it does not follow that it has a nature that is not exhausted by the sorts of properties found in physics. On the contrary, it seems plausible that biological properties have no such natures. This is reflected by a claim that is defended by Chalmers

---

23. The conjunction of the first assumption and the third proposal seems to entail the second proposal, that the inscrutables are protophenomenal properties.

24. This version of Russellian monism could be conceived roughly as a type analogue of Spinoza's dual-aspect theory about tokens. On Spinoza's theory there is only one token entity with two (physical and mental) aspects, and on this version of Russellian monism there is only one type of entity with two aspects.

and Jackson (2001): that (roughly put) there are no truths about such proper-ties that fail to be a priori deducible from the complete microphysical truth (the latter includes all and only truths found in fundamental microphysics).[25] So, by having natures that are not similarly exhausted by the sorts of proper-ties found in physics, physical inscrutables would indeed be special.

Proposal four is suggested by Papineau (2002, pp. 22–23), Stoljar (2001a, 2001b), Montero (2014), and Pereboom (2011). Pereboom considers two can-didates for what specific sorts of physical properties the inscrutables might be: Aristotelian prime materiality; and absolute (or perfect) solidity, the notion of which he attributes to Locke and Newton. The former is notoriously obscure, but Pereboom implies that the latter should be regarded as a serious option. If absolute solidity is to qualify as an inscrutable, then it would have to differ from ordinary solidity, which seems manifestly dispositional. Whether we can make sense of this idea is not entirely clear. Also, absolute solidity would have to do what Russellian monism requires of inscrutables, namely, it would have to ground basic physical properties and account for phenomenal consciousness. Whether it (or any other physical property) can satisfy those conditions is an open question.

The four proposals do not all exclude each other. Proposal one (the inscru-tables are phenomenal) is incompatible with proposal two (the inscrutables are protophenomenal) and proposal three (the inscrutables are neutral). Proposal three is incompatible with proposal one and proposal four (the inscrutables are physical). But depending on how the notion of the physical is explicated, proposals one and four may be compatible, and proposal two may be compat-ible with proposals three and four. [26] It is also possible to devise hybrid views,

---

25. This simplifies a bit. For example, the deduction base should include the complete indexical truth (Chalmers and Jackson 2001, section 2.2). Such complications do not affect the point we are making here, concerning the way in which the relevant physical properties would have to be special.

26. In his 1996 book Chalmers rejects the claim that protophenomenal properties are physi-cal properties. He writes:

> Some people will think that the view [Russellian monism] should count as a ver-sion of materialism rather than dualism, because it posits such a strong lawful dependence of the phenomenal facts on the physical facts, and because the physi-cal domain remains autonomous. Of course there is little point arguing over a name, but it seems to me that the existence of further contingent facts over and above the physical facts is a significant enough modification to the received mate-rialist world view to deserve a different label. (p. 126)

However, in his 2003 paper Chalmers seems to affirm that protophenomenal proper-ties can be regarded as physical properties. He writes, "From one perspective, [Russellian monism] can be seen as a sort of materialism. If one holds that physical terms refer not

by allowing that there is variation among the inscrutables. For example, one might propose that the inscrutables include both nonphenomenal (protophenomenal, neutral, or physical) and phenomenal properties (Holman 2008).

6. The Inscrutables and Phenomenal Properties

What relations obtain between the inscrutables and phenomenal properties? Once again, there are multiple options. Here are three:

a. Identity: the inscrutables are identical to phenomenal properties.
b. Constitution: the inscrutables constitute phenomenal properties.
c. Necessitation/supervenience: phenomenal properties are necessitated by/supervene on the inscrutables; more precisely, all phenomenal truths (truths involving phenomenal properties) are necessitated by/supervene on inscrutable truths (truths involving the inscrutables).[27]

(b) and (c) are compatible with any of the four proposals discussed in the previous section, concerning the nature of the inscrutables. But (a) seems compatible only with proposal one, that the inscrutables are phenomenal properties.[28]

A fourth option may be

d. Causation: the inscrutables cause phenomenal properties, or more precisely, the instantiation of inscrutables causes the instantiation of phenomenal properties.

---

to dispositional properties but the underlying intrinsic properties, then the protophenomenal properties can be seen as physical properties, thus preserving a sort of materialism" (p. 134).

27. The necessitation/supervenience relation to which we here refer is metaphysical, as opposed to epistemic or nomological. We do not mean to deny that the latter relations obtain between inscrutable and phenomenal truths. They well might. Chalmers describes (1996, pp. 126–27) protophenomenal properties as properties on which phenomenal properties would logically supervene—by which he means that phenomenal truths would be a priori deducible from protophenomenal truths (truths involving protophenomenal properties).

28. (a) entails proposal one, but the reverse entailment does not strictly hold. One might maintain that the inscrutables *are* phenomenal properties in the sense that the latter *constitute* the former. But so construing proposal one would make it hard to distinguish from proposal two, that the inscrutables are protophenomenal properties. So, we set this construal aside.

(d) is compatible with proposals two, three, and four. Whether (d) is compatible with proposal one (that the inscrutables are identical with phenomenal properties) depends on whether, in property causation, causes and effects must be distinct.

However, it is unclear whether proponents of Russellian monism should consider (d) an option. (d) is compatible with the three main components of Russellian monism: structuralism about physics, realism about inscrutables, and (proto)phenomenal foundationalism. However, many consider Russellian monism's implication that phenomenality is deeply integrated into the natural order as one of the theory's principal virtues. Construing the inscrutable/phenomenal relation as merely causal threatens to undermine that virtue. Those with this concern might therefore insist that, if Russellian monism is true, then the inscrutables must relate to phenomenal properties in a more intimate way, such as by identity, constitution, or necessitation/supervenience.[29]

7. Traditional Theories

How does Russellian monism relate to other theories concerning consciousness and the physical world? This depends on how the details are filled in. In section 5, we noted that Russellian monism becomes a version of neutral monism if the inscrutables are construed as neutral properties (given a few further assumptions, such as the assumption that the inscrutables ground phenomenal properties). In this section, we will explain how filling in the details in other ways yields versions of the three main traditional theories: physicalism, dualism, and idealism.

Turning Russellian monism into a version of physicalism may seem simple: we need merely construe the inscrutables as physical properties of a special sort (Montero 2014; Strawson 2006a; Papineau 2002, pp. 22–23; Pereboom 2011). In that case, it seems, everything would be physical. But this is misleading. On traditional versions of physicalism, physics (or perhaps objective science more generally conceived) catalogues all the fundamental properties there are. Traditional theories leave no room for any further properties (or perhaps more precisely: any further property instantiations). Yet

---

29. In theory, proponents of Russellian monism might reject options (a) through (d) and instead hold that the relevant relations—identity, constitution, supervenience, or causation—obtain between the inscrutables and *combinations* of phenomenal properties and properties found in physics. But we are not aware of proponents of Russellian monism who endorse, or even consider, this option.

so-called physicalist versions of Russellian monism do posit further properties, namely, the inscrutables. As we explained earlier (section 5), even if these are construed as physical properties, they would be unlike physical properties as traditionally conceived, such as prime materiality or absolute solidity. So, if there are physicalist versions of Russellian monism, they are nontraditional physicalist theories.

Russellian monism can become a version of dualism if two assumptions are made. The first is that the inscrutables are phenomenal properties. The second is that the properties found in physics (or at least the basic ones) are not constituted by (and do not supervene on) relations among the inscrutables. Given these assumptions, Russellian monism seems to posit a dualism of the phenomenal and the physical (Rosenberg 2004). But this version of dualism encourages a tighter connection between the phenomenal and the physical than traditional versions of dualism, such as interactionism, posit. Traditional versions tend to construe that connection as merely causal. On Russellian monism, the connection is conceived as being closer than that. For example, on some versions phenomenal properties are categorical bases of physical, dispositional properties. That is a significant departure from traditional versions of dualism.

Russellian monism can become a version of idealism too. Here we again assume that the inscrutables are phenomenal properties. But this time we assume that the properties found in physics (and all properties other than the inscrutables) *are* constituted by relations among the inscrutables. The result is a view that posits only the inscrutables and what they constitute. So, we have a Russellian monist version of idealism (Adams 2007; Bolender 2001; Chalmers 2012; Foster 1982).

So, Russellian monism would seem to be compatible with neutral monism, physicalism, dualism, and idealism. Russellian monism can also be construed such that it does not fit neatly into any of those four categories. Suppose, for example, that we assume that the inscrutables are neutral but also that phenomenal properties are over and above neutral properties. The resulting version of Russellian monism posits two basic sorts of properties, which seems to imply that it is not a version of neutral monism, physicalism, or idealism. But it is also not a version of mental-physical dualism, because the physical is accorded a derivative status. The view could be described as a hybrid view: neutral-phenomenal dualism. But even where there is substantial overlap with traditional theories, Russellian monism provides a distinctive perspective on consciousness, the world as revealed by physical science, and the relationship between the two.

8. The Conceivability Argument and the Knowledge Argument

Recent philosophical treatment of consciousness tends to center on two powerful arguments against physicalism: the conceivability argument and the knowledge argument. In this section we consider how Russellian monism fits into this discussion. Following Chalmers (2003), we will argue that neither argument threatens Russellian monism.

The conceivability argument usually begins with a thought experiment, such as the case of zombies—creatures that lack (phenomenal) consciousness but are physically identical to ordinary human beings.[30] The argument runs roughly as follows. Intuitively, zombies would seem to be conceivable. Moreover, the apparent conceivability of zombies does not seem to disappear upon further reflection. As Chalmers (2002, 2010) suggests, this is so even on ideal reflection. No a priori reasoning whatsoever would reveal any inconsistency (or incoherence of any sort) in the zombie hypothesis. Not even a thinker with limitless reasoning abilities would detect any such inconsistency. But if zombies are, as Chalmers puts it, *ideally conceivable*, then they are metaphysically possible, i.e., then zombies could have existed. This indicates that the complete physical truth about the world is incomplete. For example, consider the visual experience you are now having. The complete physical truth—including all the physical truth about your brain and body—does not distinguish between you and your zombie twin, who experiences nothing whatsoever. In other words, there are truths about consciousness that are not necessitated by the complete physical truth. If so, then it seems to follow that physicalism is false.

To summarize:

1. It is ideally conceivable that there be zombies.
2. If it is ideally conceivable that there be zombies, then it is metaphysically possible that there be zombies.
3. If it is metaphysically possible that there be zombies, then physicalism is false.
4. Therefore, physicalism is false.[31]

---

30. The conceivability argument can also begin with other thought experiments, such as inverted spectrum cases (Chalmers 1996).

31. Both premises 1 and 2 are disputed. See Gendler and Hawthorne (2002). The link between conceivability and possibility is especially controversial, and even defenders of premise 2 such as Chalmers (2002) reject the unqualified thesis that if p is ideally conceivable then p is metaphysically possible.

The knowledge argument was introduced by Frank Jackson (1982, 1986), who reasons as follows. Imagine Mary, who was raised in an entirely black-and-white environment. She has never seen colors. Nevertheless, she learns everything physics can teach—not just the physics of today, but *completed* physics. She acquires all such information by watching lectures on black-and-white television. If physicalism were true, her complete scientific knowledge would amount to complete knowledge *simpliciter*. But there are truths that she does not know. To see this, suppose she leaves her room and looks at, say, a ripe tomato for the first time. When this happens, she will learn something new, namely, what it is like to see red. Therefore, physicalism is false.[32]

The knowledge argument's general form can be represented in a way that parallels the above summary of the conceivability argument, as follows:

1. There are truths about consciousness that cannot be deduced from the complete physical truth (that is why Mary learns something when she leaves the room).
2. If there are truths about consciousness that cannot be deduced from the complete physical truth, then there are truths about consciousness that are not necessitated by the complete physical truth.
3. If there are truths about consciousness that are not necessitated by the complete physical truth, then physicalism is false.
4. So, physicalism is false.[33]

Like the conceivability argument, the knowledge argument uses a thought experiment to establish an epistemic gap between the physical and the phenomenal—though here the gap is expressed in terms of non-deducibility rather than conceivability (Chalmers 2003). Also like the conceivability argument, the knowledge argument then proceeds to infer a corresponding metaphysical gap, from which the falsity of physicalism is in turn inferred.

Russellian monists have at least three options for responding to the conceivability and knowledge arguments. Russellian monists who reject physicalism can, of course, accept the anti-physicalist conclusion. But those more sympathetic to physicalism have at least two other options.

---

32. Jackson (1998, 2003, 2007) now rejects the knowledge argument. For criticisms of his rejection, see Alter 2007; Robinson 2002; and Robinson 2008.

33. Both arguments involve some simplification. For example, references to the complete physical truth in the knowledge argument should instead refer to a conjunction of the complete physical truth, a second-order "that's all" claim, and the complete indexical truth. See Chalmers 2010. But these details do not matter much here.

Jackson assumes that the truths discovered by ideal physics exhaust the complete physical truth. Russellian monists might reject that assumption on the grounds that the truths discovered by physics do not include one class of physical truths, namely, the truths about the inscrutables. On this view, the black-and-white lectures Mary watches while still in the room would leave out part of the complete physical truth (Stoljar 2001a). Her pre-release physical knowledge would therefore be incomplete. And if her physical knowledge *were* complete, then she presumably would be able to deduce what it is like to see red—because, on this view, the truths about inscrutables are or ground phenomenal truths, including the truths about what it is like to see red. For these reasons, Russellian monists could reject premise 1 of the knowledge argument (which says that there are truths about consciousness that cannot be deduced from the complete physical truth).

Alternatively, Russellian monists might reject premise 2 of the knowledge argument (which says that if there are truths about consciousness that cannot be deduced from the complete physical truth, then there are truths about consciousness that are not necessitated by the complete physical truth). Here is the reasoning. The reason some phenomenal truths cannot be deduced from the complete physical truth is that the former are or are grounded in truths that physics does not describe, namely, truths about inscrutables. Nevertheless, the truths that physics does describe completely determine the truth about inscrutables—just not in a way that can be discerned by a priori reflection. Thus, the physical necessitates the phenomenal despite the impossibility of deducing phenomenal truths from physical truths.[34]

Parallel points apply to the conceivability argument. Russellian monists could accept its anti-physicalist conclusion. Alternatively, they could reject that argument's first premise, arguing that zombies seem conceivable only because we ignore the parts of the physical world that concern the inscrutables. Duplicating the complete physical world, Russellian monists could argue, would require duplicating all the truths about inscrutables which, on their view, includes (or a priori implies) the truths about consciousness (Stoljar 2001b). Also, Russellian monists could dispute the conceivability argument's second premise, arguing that although the complete physical truth necessitates all truths about consciousness, this cannot be discerned by a priori reflection alone.

---

34. This move could be based on the semantic view that basic physical terms such as "mass" and "charge" rigidly refer to the inscrutables but not in a way that can be discovered by a priori reflection on the meanings of those terms. See Chalmers (2003, 2010).

Thus, the conceivability and knowledge arguments do not threaten Russellian monism. This is not surprising, for at least two reasons. First, those arguments are directed against traditional versions of physicalism, which do not emphasize the central distinction between the properties found by physics and inscrutables. Second, the relevant thought experiments, such as the zombie and Mary cases, can all be seen as simply vivid illustrations of a general principle that arguably constitutes the foundation of both arguments. This is *the structure-and-dynamics thesis*: the claim that there are truths about consciousness that are not a priori deducible from truths solely about structure and dynamics (Chalmers 2003). For example, the reason pre-release Mary cannot figure out what it is like to see red while still in the room is that what this experience is like includes more than just structural and dynamic information, and yet the latter sort of information is all that the science lectures convey. But the structure-and-dynamics thesis fits well with Russellian monism. Indeed, Russellian monism would appear to assume the thesis. Such considerations suggest that the target of the conceivability and knowledge arguments is not physicalism *per se* but rather physicalist views that are not also versions of Russellian monism.[35]

9. Arguments for Russellian Monism

That Russellian monism comports well with the conceivability and knowledge arguments will for some constitute an argument for Russellian monism, or at least a reason to take the view seriously. In this section, we will present two further arguments for Russellian monism.

A. A Comparative Argument

It can be argued that Russellian monism retains strengths of traditional versions of physicalism and dualism, while overcoming their weaknesses. Consider traditional physicalism first. As we noted earlier in section 1, physicalism is a version of monism, and as such it has the advantage of ontological parsimony. However, traditional physicalism has trouble accommodating a claim that many take to be obvious, namely, the claim that consciousness is fundamentally distinct from any property found in physics. This is, for those

---

35. Chalmers (2010) expresses this idea by saying that the arguments' conclusion should be presented not as "physicalism is false" but instead as "physicalism is false or Russellian monism is true."

philosophers, a substantial drawback. To be sure, there are versions of traditional physicalism that go to considerable lengths to try to accommodate the uniqueness of consciousness. These are the views that Chalmers (2003) classifies as type-B physicalism: views that accept a deep epistemic gap between the physical and the phenomenal but deny a corresponding metaphysical gap (e.g., Papineau 2007; Block 2007). However, many think that these views face serious objections (which we do not have space to explain); see Chalmers 2007, 2010.

Consider now traditional dualism. Some philosophers are attracted to this view because it affirms the uniqueness of consciousness. However, traditional dualism is not parsimonious, in comparison to monist views. Moreover, it has trouble accommodating a claim that many take to be obvious, namely, the claim that consciousness is a fundamentally natural phenomenon—a phenomenon that is fully integrated into the physical world. Traditional dualist views tend to make the physical-phenomenal connection appear accidental and arbitrary, and many naturalistically inclined philosophers find that consequence implausible. For example, traditional interactionist dualism says that the physical and the phenomenal affect each other. But it can seem mysterious as to how they could affect each other if, as this view maintains, the two are fundamentally different (Kim 2005, chapter 3). Traditional interactionist dualism also threatens to violate the widely held view that the physical domain is causally closed (Papineau 2002). Epiphenomenalist versions of dualism avoid the latter problem by maintaining that consciousness has no physical effects. But epiphenomenalism retains the problem of making it mysterious how the physical can affect the phenomenal. And by denying that the phenomenal affects the physical, epiphenomenalism arguably does even worse than interactionist dualism with respect to integrating consciousness into nature.

It can be argued that Russellian monism retains the strengths of these traditional theories while avoiding their weaknesses. Monist versions of Russellian monism share the ontological elegance of physicalism. And like traditional dualism, all versions of Russellian monism succeed in affirming the uniqueness of consciousness. Yet Russellian monism allows consciousness to be integrated into nature in a much more substantial way than does traditional dualism. The causal roles phenomenal properties play on Russellian monism are not necessarily those that folk wisdom ascribes to consciousness. For example, folk wisdom has it that a sharp pain can cause you to flinch. Although Russellian monism does not exclude the possibility that pain causes flinching, the causal roles some versions of Russellian monism ascribe to phenomenal properties do not necessarily support such claims. Instead, Russellian monism says (on some versions) that phenomenal or protophenomenal properties constitute categorical bases for fundamental physical dispositions. Nevertheless, Russellian monism does support a naturalistic perspective on consciousness, according to which consciousness (or its components) fits crucially into the causal nexus. Further, unlike traditional versions of dualism, an intimate physical-phenomenal connection is built into Russellian monism from the start.

B. The 'Solving Two Problems at Once' Argument

Another argument for Russellian monism is that it provides a unified solution to two basic philosophical problems that may be closely related. Chalmers (1996) presents this argument and attributes it to Russell.[36]

In the philosophy of science, there is a problem of a lack of metaphysical grounding. All fundamental physics gives us is nomic spatiotemporal structure. That is, it gives us little more than structure without any underlying non-structural properties. Some believe that what we should conclude from this is that nature consists in nothing but structure (Ladyman and Ross 2007). But Russell and others think that we must look outside of physics for properties that ground the network of causes and effects that physics describes.[37]

In the philosophy of mind, there is a problem about integrating consciousness into nature. There are powerful arguments—principally the knowledge argument and the conceivability argument—that indicate that the truth about consciousness is not exhausted by the sorts of truths we find in physics. But many who are sympathetic to that conclusion are concerned that accepting it creates a serious integration problem. As we noted above, many find traditional versions of dualism, to which proponents of the knowledge argument and the conceivability argument often subscribe, unattractive precisely because these views fail to adequately integrate consciousness into nature.

At first glance, these problems may seem to have nothing to do with each other. But on reflection, they might be related. The philosophy of science problem could be described as a help-wanted problem. Physics wants to hire help: it wants to employ something outside its purview to ground the structure it so elegantly describes. The philosophy of mind problem could likewise

---

36. Russell does not present the argument explicitly, but comes close. See Russell 1927a and 1927b, p. 116.

37. Jennifer McKitrick (2003) argues that there *could* be pure dispositions, dispositions without categorical bases. Russellian monists can agree but argue that in fact basic physical properties have categorical bases. Cf. Chalmers 2003, p. 131.

be described as a job-seeking problem. Consciousness wants a job: it wants to be integrated into nature by playing a role in the causal nexus known as the cosmos. Seen in this way, a unified solution suggests itself: consciousness can be employed to ground fundamental physical relations—which is what Russellian monism says, with the one qualification that on some versions of Russellian monism it is not consciousness itself but its components (pro-tophenomenal properties) that ground the properties found in physics. So, Russellian monism provides what seems on reflection to be a natural solution to two significant philosophical problems. This speaks in favor of the view.[38]

10. Arguments Against Russellian Monism

We have seen two arguments for Russellian monism in the previous section. In this section we will consider two arguments that have been advanced *against* Russellian monism. We will argue that neither is decisive but that the second identifies a serious challenge for Russellian monism.

A. *The Argument from Weirdness*

Perhaps the most common reaction to Russellian monism is that it is weird or highly counterintuitive. This reaction tends to be particularly strong when Russellian monism is formulated as a version of panpsychism, which says that phenomenal consciousness is ubiquitous. For example, John Searle (1997) attributes panpsychism to Chalmers and describes the view as "absurd." Searle criticizes (what he takes to be) Chalmers' acceptance of panpsychism as follows: "when faced with a *reductio ad absurdum* argument [Chalmers] just accepts the absurdity ... It is as if someone got the result that 2 + 2 = 7 and said, 'Well, maybe 2 plus 2 does equal 7'" (Searle 1997, p. 156).[39]

But Searle's arithmetic analogy is questionable. We know that 2 + 2 does not equal 7. There is no serious disagreement about the falsity of that equation. By contrast, it is an open question which theory best describes the relationship between consciousness and the physical world. Moreover, on reflection it is

---

38. We hope it is not too pedantic to mention that our talk of what physics and conscious-ness "want" is metaphorical. We risk pedantry here only because we have discussed panpsy-chism, which is sometimes taken to imply that inanimate entities literally have such things as desires. Russellian monist versions of panpsychism have no such implication.

39. In fact, as he notes in his response to Searle, Chalmers (1996, 1997, p. 166) does not endorse panpsychism but rather claims only that it is "not as unreasonable as is often supposed."

not surprising that we end up with a weird theory of the physical-phenomenal relationship. From the perspective of objective science, consciousness seems fundamentally different from every other natural phenomenal; from that perspective, its very existence can seem bizarre.[40] In any event, if Russellian monism's weirdness provides a reason to reject Russellian monism, the reason is hardly compelling. If weirdness were a compelling reason to reject a theory about the fundamental nature of the world, then we would be rationally compelled to reject counterintuitive theories in physics, such as string theory and, on some interpretations (such as the many-worlds interpretation), quantum mechanics. But we are not so compelled.

B. The Combination Problem

Despite the shortcomings of the argument from weirdness, there is a serious problem in the vicinity. Familiar experiences present themselves as smooth, continuous, and unified. And they seem to belong to a single subject. To be sure, they have various aspects. But these aspects have an underlying homogeneity. In summary, our experience seems to have a specific, homogeneous character. Now, according to Russellian monism, familiar phenomenal properties result from combinations of inscrutables. But how is this supposed to work? It is hard to see how phenomenal or protophenomenal properties of microphysical systems could somehow add up to the phenomenal properties with which we are familiar—properties with the specific, homogeneous character with which we are all acquainted.

This is a version of *the combination problem* for panpsychism (James 1890, chapter 6, Chalmers 2003), which is also known as *the grain problem* (Sellars 1965). The problem is substantial. Chalmers writes, 'It is certainly the hardest problem for any sort of Russellian view' (Chalmers 1996, p. 307). ('Any' might be too strong; the problem might not arise for versions of the view that identify the inscrutables with familiar phenomenal properties.) Some disagree. For example, Stoljar suggests that the grain problem rests on a mistaken assumption. He considers Maxwell's claim that a visual experience of red is smooth and continuous and writes,

> ... the answer [to the combination problem] emerges when we focus on what precisely it is in Maxwell's example that is supposed to be smooth and continuous. It seems plausible to say that it is the expanse

---

40. See Campbell (1970) and Jackson (1982).

that is smooth and continuous, and also that the expanse is something that we represent in visual experience, i.e., Maxwell's example is an example in which we are having an experience which represents an expanse as being smooth and continuous. But of course, it does not follow from this that the experience *itself* is smooth and continuous. Consider: an experience of red represents something as being red, but it itself is not red. So the answer to the grain problem is that it gets the phenomenology wrong and mislocates the absence of grain: absence of grain is not a feature of experiences, but a feature of something that experiences represent.

(Stoljar 2001a, p. 276)

However, many will find this response to the problem unconvincing, at least as an answer to the combination problem. Experience itself seems at least much more smooth and continuous than what one would expect based on panprotopsychism. There is a striking discrepancy between how experience presents itself and how it is construed by panprotopsychism. It is not clear that this discrepancy can be explained adequately in terms of misattributing a property of what is represented (such as an expanse in physical space) to that which does the representing (an experience).[41]

Even so, similar problems arise for at least some competing theories. Wilfrid Sellars (1965) develops a version for traditional physicalism. More importantly, the problem should properly be seen not as a refutation of Russellian monism but instead as a challenge to develop a concept that is central to the theory: the concept of (proto)phenomenal composition (cf. Chalmers 2003). We understand how physical composition works, but this notion does not readily apply to the phenomenal realm. Russellian monism will not become a mature, complete account until a theory of (proto)phenomenal composition that yields a plausible solution to the combination problem is devised.[42]

---

41. In response to this sort of objection, Stoljar appeals to the doctrine, popular among representationalists (e.g., Tye 2000), that experience is diaphanousness—the doctrine that, as Stoljar puts it, "introspection reveals the intentional objects of experiences to us, but not the experiences themselves" (Stoljar 2001a, p. 276). However, the diaphanousness doctrine is controversial (see Kind 2003). Russellian monists tend to accept that experience itself is at least dissimilar enough from protophenomenal properties to give rise to a serious combination problem.

42. For discussions of the combination problem, see Chalmers 1996, pp. 306–8; Chalmers 2003, pp. 136–37; Lockwood 1992; Maxwell 1978; Goff 2006; and Strawson 2006b, pp. 246–56.

11. Conclusion

Russellian monism is at once strange and appealing. It is strange because it requires reconceiving of the relationship between the physical and the phenomenal in surprising ways. For example, on some versions of the view phenomenal properties are instantiated in inanimate, microphysical systems such as photons and quarks. That consequence can be avoided by construing the inscrutables posited by the view as protophenomenal properties. But there would still be implications, such as panprotopsychism, that are foreign to mainstream conceptions of the phenomenal-physical relationship. Russellian monism is appealing largely because it provides an elegant way of integrating phenomenal consciousness into the natural order without disregarding or distorting the phenomenon's distinctive features. Many philosophers would agree that that result is both desirable and not delivered by traditional theories in the philosophy of mind. Further, there appear to be no decisive arguments against the view. We believe further development and examination of it is well justified.[43]

References

Adams, R. (2007) 'Idealism Vindicated', in P. van Inwagen and D. Zimmerman (eds.), *Persons: Human and Divine*, Oxford: Oxford University Press, pp. 35–54.

Alter, T. (ed.) (2004) Book Symposium on Gregg Rosenberg's *A Place for Consciousness*, *Psyche* 12:5. http://journalpsyche.org/archive/volume-12-2006/.

Alter, T. (2007) 'Does Representationalism Undermine the Knowledge Argument?', in Alter, T. & Walter, S. (eds.) *Phenomenal Concepts and Phenomenal Knowledge: New Essays on Consciousness and Physicalism*, New York: Oxford University Press, pp. 65–76.

Alter, T. (2009) 'Does the Ignorance Hypothesis Undermine the Conceivability and Knowledge Arguments?', *Philosophy and Phenomenological Research* 79, pp. 756–65.

Armstrong, D. (1968) *A Materialist Theory of Mind*, New York: Humanities Press.

Armstrong, D., Martin, C. & Place, U. (1996) *Dispositions: A Debate*, London: Routledge.

Blackburn, S. (1990) 'Filling in Space', *Analysis* 50, pp. 62–65.

Block, N. (2007) *Consciousness, Function, and Representation: Collected Papers, Volume 1*, Cambridge, MA: MIT Press.

---

43. For constructive comments and helpful suggestions, we would like to thank David Chalmers, Alyssa Ney, Derk Pereboom, Leopold Stubenberg, and two anonymous referees for the *Journal of Consciousness Studies*.

Bolender, J. (2001) 'An Argument for Idealism', *Journal of Consciousness Studies* 8, pp. 37–61.

Campbell, K. (1970) *Body and Mind*, Garden City, New York: Doubleday Anchor books. Second edition published in 1984 from University of Notre Dame Press.

Chalmers, D. (1996) *The Conscious Mind: In Search of a Fundamental Theory*. New York: Oxford University Press.

Chalmers, D. (1997) Reply to Searle's review of *The Conscious Mind* in *The New York Review of Books*, reprinted in Searle 1997, pp. 164–67.

Chalmers, D. (2002) 'Does Conceivability Entail Possibility?', in T. Gendler and J. Hawthorne (eds.) *Conceivability and Possibility*, New York: Oxford University Press, pp. 145–200.

Chalmers, D. (2003) 'Consciousness and Its Place in Nature', in Stephen P. Stich and Ted A. Warfield (eds.), *Blackwell Guide to the Philosophy of Mind*, Oxford: Blackwell, pp. 247–72. Revised version in Chalmers 2010, pp. 103–40.

Chalmers, D. (2007) Phenomenal concepts and the explanatory gap, in Alter, T. & Walter, S. (eds.) *Phenomenal Concepts and Phenomenal Knowledge: New Essays on Consciousness and Physicalism*, New York: Oxford University Press, pp. 167–94.

Chalmers, D. (2010) *The Character of Consciousness*, New York: Oxford University Press.

Chalmers, D. (2012) *Constructing the World*, New York: Oxford University Press.

Chalmers, D. & Jackson, F. (2001) 'Conceptual Analysis and Reductive Explanation', *Philosophical Review* 110, pp. 315–61.

Descartes, R. (1641) *Meditations on First Philosophy*.

Fara, M. (2006) 'Dispositions' in *The Stanford Encyclopedia of Philosophy*, http://plato.stanford.edu/entries/dispositions/.

Feigl, H. (1958/1967) 'The 'Mental' and the 'Physical'', *Minnesota Studies in the Philosophy of Science* 2, pp. 370–497. Reprinted (with a postscript) as *The 'Mental' and the 'Physical'*, Minneapolis: University of Minnesota Press.

Foster, J. (1982) *The Case for Idealism*. London: Routledge & Kegan Paul.

Freeman, A. (ed.) (2006) *Consciousness and Its Place in Nature: Does Physicalism Entail Panpsychism?*, Exeter: Imprint Academic.

Gendler, T. & Hawthorne, J. (eds.) (2002) *Conceivability and Possibility*, New York: Oxford University Press.

Goff, P. (2006) 'Experiences Don't Sum', in Freeman, A. (ed.) *Consciousness and Its Place in Nature: Does Physicalism Entail Panpsychism?*, Exeter: Imprint Academic, pp. 53–61.

Griffin, D. (1998) *Unsnarling the World-Knot: Consciousness, Freedom, and the Mind-Body Problem*, Berkeley: University of California Press.

Holden, T. (2004) *The Architecture of Matter*, Oxford: Oxford University Press.

Holman, E. (2008) 'Panpsychism, Physicalism, Neutral Monism and the Russellian Theory of Mind', *Journal of Consciousness Studies* 15: 48–67.

Horgan, T. & Potrč, M. (2000)''Blobjectivism and Indirect Correspondence', *Facta Philosophica* 2, 249–70.

Jackson, F. (1982) 'Epiphenomenal Qualia', *Philosophical Quarterly* 32, pp. 127–36.

Jackson, F. (1986) 'What Mary Didn't Know', *Journal of Philosophy* 83, pp. 291–95.

Jackson, F. (1998) 'Postscript on Qualia', in *Mind, Method and Conditionals*, London: Routledge, pp. 76–79.

James, W. (1890) *The Principles of Psychology*, New York: Henry Holt and Co.

Kim, J. (2005) *Physicalism, or Something Near Enough*, Princeton: Princeton University Press.

Kind, A. (2003) 'What's so Transparent About Transparency?' *Philosophical Studies* 115 (3), pp. 225–44.

Ladyman, J., & Ross, D. (with D. Spurrett, and J. Collier) (2007) *Every Thing Must Go: Metaphysics Naturalized*, New York: Oxford University Press.

Lewis, D. (2009) 'Ramseyan Humility', in David Braddon-Mitchell & Robert Nola (eds.), *Conceptual Analysis and Philosophical Naturalism*, Cambridge, MA: MIT Press, pp. 203–22.

Lockwood, M. (1992) 'The Grain Problem', in Howard Robinson (ed.), *Objections to Physicalism*, Oxford: Oxford University Press, pp. 271–92.

Maxwell, G. (1978) 'Rigid Designators and Mind-Brain Identity', *Minnesota Studies in the Philosophy of Science* 9, pp. 365–403.

McKitrick, J. (2003) 'The Bare Metaphysical Possibility of Bare Dispositions', *Philosophy and Phenomenological Research* 66, pp. 349–69.

Montero, B. G. (2014) 'Russellian Physicalism', this volume, chapter 10.

Nagel, T. (1974) 'What Is It Like to Be a Bat', *Philosophical Review* 83, pp. 435–50.

Nagel, T. (1986) *The View from Nowhere*, Oxford: Oxford University Press.

Nagel, T. (1998) 'Conceiving the Impossible and the Mind-Body Problem', *Philosophy* 73, pp. 337–52.

Newman, M. (1928) 'Mr. Russell's Causal Theory of Perception', *Mind* 5, pp. 26–43.

Papineau, D. (2002) *Thinking about Consciousness*, New York: Oxford University Press.

Papineau, D. (2007) 'Phenomenal and Perceptual Concepts', in Alter, T. & Walter, S. (eds.) *Phenomenal Concepts and Phenomenal Knowledge: New Essays on Consciousness and Physicalism*, New York: Oxford University Press, pp. 145–67.

Pereboom, D. (2011) *Consciousness and the Prospects of Physicalism*, New York: Oxford University Press.

Robinson, H. (2008) 'Why Frank Should Not Have Jilted Mary', in E. Wright (ed.) *The Case for Qualia*, Cambridge: MIT Press, pp. 223–46.

Robinson, W. (2002) 'Jackson's Apostasy', *Philosophical Studies* 111 (3), pp. 277–93.

Rosenberg, G. (2004) *A Place for Consciousness: Probing the Deep Structure of the Natural World*, New York: Oxford University Press.

Russell, B. (1927a) *The Analysis of Matter*, London: Kegan Paul.

Russell, B. (1927b) *An Outline of Philosophy*, London: Unman Hyman Ltd.

Russell, B. (1951) *The Autobiography of Bertrand Russell 1914–1944*, Boston: Little, Brown and Company.

Ryle, G. (1949) *The Concept of Mind*, Chicago: University of Chicago Press.

Schaffer, J. (2010) 'Monism: The Priority of the Whole', *Philosophical Review* 119, pp. 31–76.

Searle, J. (1997) *The Mystery of Consciousness*, New York: New York Review of Books.

Sellars, W. (1965) 'The Identity Approach to the Mind-Body Problem', *Review of Metaphysics* 18, pp. 430–51.

Shoemaker, S. (1980) 'Causality and Properties', in *Time and Change*, ed. P. van Inwagen, Dodrecht, The Netherlands: D. Reidel, pp. 109–35.

Stoljar, D. (2001a) 'Two Conceptions of the Physical', *Philosophy and Phenomenological Research* 62, pp. 253–81.

Stoljar, D. (2001b) 'The Conceivability Argument and Two Conceptions of the Physical', *Philosophical Perspectives* 15, pp. 393–413.

Stoljar, D. (2006) *Ignorance and Imagination: The Epistemic Origin of the Problem of Consciousness*, New York: Oxford University Press.

Stoljar, D. (2009) 'Response to Alter and Bennett', *Philosophy and Phenomenological Research* 79, pp. 775–84.

Strawson, G. (2006a) 'Realistic Monism: Why Physicalism Entails Panpsychism' *Journal of Consciousness Studies* 13, pp. 3–31.

Strawson, G. (2006b) 'Panpsychism? Reply to Commentators with a Celebration of Descartes', in Freeman, A. (ed.) *Consciousness and Its Place in Nature: Does Physicalism Entail Panpsychism?*, Exeter: Imprint Academic, pp. 184–280.

Stubenberg, L. (2005/2010) 'Neutral Monism', *The Stanford Encyclopedia of Philosophy* (Spring 2010 Edition). http://plato.stanford.edu/archives/spr2010/entries/neutral-monism/.

Tye, M. (2000) *Consciousness, Color, and Content*, Cambridge, MA: MIT Press.

Van Cleve, J. (1988) 'Inner States and Outer Relations: Kant and the Case for Monadism', in Hare, P. H. (ed.) *Doing Philosophy Historically*, Buffalo, NY: Prometheus Books, pp. 231–47.

Name Index

Adams, Robert, 17, 64–65, 312, 432, 438
Alexander, Samuel, 395
Algarotti, Francesco, 186
Allais, Lucy, 201
Almog, Joseph, 291, 302
Alter, Torin, 10, 13–14, 59, 61–68, 79, 86–87, 91, 106, 116, 201, 246, 278, 282, 293, 301, 304, 314–315, 319, 324–326, 331–332, 344, 375, 397, 402, 405–406, 418, 420, 429, 431, 433, 440
Aristotle, 195, 313
Armstrong, David, 65, 70, 81–82, 282, 309, 312–313, 375–376, 379, 382, 422, 428
Arnauld, Antoine, 186, 302

Bader, Ralf, 306, 319
Bain, Alexander, 26
Ball, Derek, 281–282, 288
Balog, Katalin, 287
Barnett, David, 271
Baron, Robert, 140
Barratt, Alfred, 24
Bealer, George, 302
Bell, John Stuart, 177
Bennett, Karen, 251, 317, 319
Berkeley, George, 33, 44, 57, 94

Blackburn, Simon, 282, 430
Blamauer, Michael, 203
Block, Ned, 147, 221, 277, 281, 348, 376, 443
Bolender, John, 64, 82, 264, 432, 438
Boscovich, Roger, 190, 310
Bostock, David, 91, 101–104
Bowne, Borden Parker, 24
Brentano, Franz, 25, 94
Broad, C.D., 395
Brogaard, Berit, 108
Brown, Harvey, 191, 199, 201, 218
Brütrup, Godehard, 203
Butterfield, Jeremy, 171, 177, 201
Byrne, Alex, 312

Campbell, Keith, 196, 446
Carnap, Rudolf, 12, 338, 360–361, 363
Chalmers, David J., 2, 4–5, 8–11, 13–14, 68–69, 79, 84, 171, 195, 209–222, 238–241, 249–250, 255–256, 261, 277–284, 287–288, 293, 297, 301–303, 312–314, 316–319, 324, 326, 328–329, 338–342, 348, 350, 370–374, 376–377, 380–382, 390, 394–397, 401, 403, 406–408, 412, 414–415, 419, 423, 425–426, 431–436, 438–448

Chignell, Andrew, 319
Chomsky, Noam, 163, 165, 168, 183, 187,
    195, 197, 201
Chuard, Phillipe, 297
Churchland, Paul M., 163, 210
Clarke, Samuel, 203
Clifford, W. K., 24
Coleman, Sam, 1, 64–65, 67–68, 83–84,
    246, 271, 274, 402, 407
Collier, John, 308
Collins, Arthur, 201
Crane, Tim, 163, 196, 201
Crawshay-Williams, Rupert, 41

Dainton, Barry, 65
De Volder, Burchard, 3, 17, 304–305, 307
Democritus, 198
Demopoulos, William, 173
Dennett, Daniel C., 171, 188, 196, 349
deRosset, Louis, 317, 319
Descartes, René, 1, 56, 186–187, 191, 195,
    203, 302–306, 422
Deutsch, David, 184
Doggett, Tyler, 319
Dowell, Janice, 416
Dretske, Fred, 70, 348, 376
Duncan, W. C., 24

Eddington, Arthur, 161, 163, 166, 171,
    176, 193–194, 198, 202–204, 374
Einstein, Albert, 155–156
Epicurus, 198
Evans, Gareth, 175, 179, 325

Fara, Michael, 301, 428
Fechner, Gustav Theodore, 24
Feigl, Herbert, 1, 91, 104, 122, 168, 263,
    271, 374, 434
Feyerabend, Paul, 135
Fichte, Johann Gottlieb 85, 247
Field, Hartry, 362
Fine, Kit, 248, 291, 388

Fisher, Justin, 297
Foster, John, 143, 146, 148, 178, 190,
    401–402, 404, 406, 432, 438
Frankland, F. W., 24
Freeman, Anthony, 433
Frege, Gottlob, 92, 94
French, Steven, 365–366
Friedman, Michael, 173

Galileo (Galilei), 211, 371
Gardner, Sebastian, 200
Garrett, Brian, 246
Gendler, Tamar, 439
Gerhardt, C. I., 307
Goff, Philip, 12–13, 84, 246, 266,
    316, 377–378, 380, 383, 393–394,
    396, 447
Green, M. B., 148
Greenberg, Mark, 201
Greenfield, Susan, 192
Greg, John, 246
Griffin, David, 64, 201, 204, 374, 432
Grote, John, 93
Gurney, Edmund, 24

Haeckel, Ernst, 24
Hager, Peter J., 98
Hanson, N. R., 122, 141, 168
Harman, Gilbert, 376
Harré, Rom, 190
Hartshorne, Charles, 66, 84
Hawking, Stephen, 217
Hawthorne, John, 312, 439
Hegel, G. W. F, 9, 10, 47, 49, 247–248,
    252–259, 261, 270, 274
Heil, John, 264, 283
Heisenberg, Werner, 157–159
Heraclitus, 44
Hilbert, David, 156–157, 312
Hill, Christopher S., 288, 376
Hirsch, Eli, 174
Holden, Thomas, 310, 430

Holman, Emmett, 1, 64, 92, 402, 436

Horgan, Terence, 291, 383, 423

Howell, Robert J., 10, 115, 282–283, 292

Humberstone, Lloyd, 304

Hume, David, 44, 71, 74, 84, 129, 186–187, 229–230, 293

Huygens, Christiaan, 187

Isham, Christopher, 177

Jackson, Frank, 97, 202, 277, 280–281, 366, 372, 377, 432, 435, 440–441, 446

James, William, 5, 48, 69, 71, 73, 93–96, 99–101, 191, 203, 225–226, 266, 271, 274

Jaskolla, Ludwig, 203

Jeans, J. H., 32

Johnston, Mark, 337

Kant, Immanuel, 4, 10, 40, 42, 47, 49–50, 149, 170, 181, 186–187, 192, 305, 309–311

Kim, Jaegwon, 443

Kind, Amy, 13, 325, 407, 447

Kirk, Robert, 196

Kriegel, Uriah, 315, 319

Kripke, Saul, 7, 95, 121–141, 215, 250, 280–281, 286, 302

Kronecker, Leopold, 154

Ladyman, James, 171, 218, 282, 308, 365–366, 444

Laird, John, 111

La Mettrie, Julian, 201

Landini, Gregory, 91, 102–104

Lange, F. A., 168, 183, 186–187

Langton, Rae, 212, 311, 358

Leibniz, Gottfried Wilhelm von, 3–4, 10–11, 17, 19–21, 47, 55–56, 155, 187, 270, 304–316, 366, 430

Levi, Isaac, 201

Lewes, George H., 395

Lewis, David, 12, 162, 164, 193, 212, 295, 311, 336–338, 348, 351, 355–363, 375–376, 379, 383–384, 389, 427, 431

Loar, Brian, 277, 281, 376

Locke, Dustin, 420

Locke, John, 19, 95, 179, 182, 186–187, 190, 292, 308, 311, 411, 420, 435

Lockwood, Michael, 7, 91, 103–104, 167, 169, 171, 176–177, 199, 201, 261, 263, 374, 380, 401, 403, 423, 447

Loewer, Barry, 201

Lotze, Rudolph Hermann, 24

Lycan, William G., 376

Mach, Ernest, 69, 71, 271

Madden, E. H., 190

Main, Alexander, 24

Malcolm, Norman, 70, 82

Marshall, Dan, 304, 335

Martin, C. B., 212

Maxwell, Grover, 7, 91, 111, 135–137, 140, 150–155, 169, 171, 191, 200, 263, 277, 374, 401, 424, 434, 446–447

McClelland, Thomas, 1, 326, 332

McGinn, Colin, 65, 153, 170, 176, 178, 192, 195, 221, 313, 318–319

McGonigal, Andrew, 319

McKitrick, Jennifer, 308, 444

McLaughlin, Brian, 201, 376, 378, 395

Meacham, Bill, 246

Meehl, Paul E., 134

Meinong, Alexius, 94

Mellor, D. H., 163, 196

Melnyk, Andrew, 291, 383

Menetrez, Frank, 420

Mill, John Stuart, 395

Mivart, St. George Jackson, 24

Montero, Barbara Gail, 8, 62–63, 67–68, 92, 210, 213, 215, 218, 263, 278, 280, 283, 404, 410, 425–426, 435, 437

Montgomery, Edmund, 23

Moore, G. E., 47, 92, 95, 174, 180, 383, 385

Mørch, Hedda Hassel, 264, 396–397

Morgan, C. Lloyd, 395

Nagasawa, Yujin, 13–14, 59, 61–65, 67–68, 79, 86, 91, 106, 278, 297, 301, 304, 324–326, 331–332, 344, 375, 397, 402, 405–406, 418, 420

Nagel, Thomas, 84, 121, 144, 155, 192, 279, 302, 313, 316, 318–319, 324, 328, 401, 408–409, 422, 434

Nemirow, Laurence, 295

Newman, Max, 173–174, 177, 424

Newton, Issac, 50, 176, 187, 199, 292, 349, 435

Ney, Alyssa, 12, 305, 319, 358, 365, 368, 414, 416, 448

Nida-Rümelin, Martine, 271

Nuwer, Marc, 140

Papineau, David, 202, 215, 260, 277, 281, 287, 296–297, 376, 378, 380, 390, 397, 409, 435, 437, 443

Parfit, Derek, 271

Peano, Giuseppe, 47, 98

Pepper, Stephen, 271

Pereboom, Derk, 10–11, 13, 79, 92, 279, 283–284, 292–293, 297, 301, 304, 306, 311–312, 317, 319, 324, 326, 331–339, 347, 349, 366–368, 393, 405–406, 410–411, 426, 428, 430, 435, 437, 448

Perry, John, 376

Pettit, Phillip, 201

Potrč, Matjaž, 423

Pribram, Karl, 140

Price, Richard, 192

Priestley, Joseph, 163, 168, 186–187, 190, 192, 200

Prince, Morton, 24

Proops, Ian N., 95–96

Pullam, Geoffrey K., 198

Reid, Thomas, 24

Rey, Georges, 376

Robinson, Howard, 418, 440

Robinson, William S., 440

Roefls, Luke, 397

Rorty, Richard, 135

Rosenberg, Gregg, 8, 64, 264, 283, 406–408, 432–433, 438

Ross, Don, 282, 308, 365–366, 444

Ross, Peter, 420

Royce, Josiah, 24

Rozemond, Marleen, 302

Russell, Bertrand, 1, 5–6, 12, 14, 58–87, 91–115, 126, 135, 144–145, 160, 162, 166–169, 171–177, 179, 182, 185, 188–189, 192–194, 202–203, 211, 217, 242, 253–254, 263, 271, 277, 300, 327, 346–347, 351–356, 362–363, 368, 374, 403, 409, 416–417, 423–425, 427, 432, 444

Ryle, Gilbert, 113, 188, 426

Sainsbury, Mark, 178, 201

Santayana, George, 85

Saunders, Simon, 191, 201

Savage, C. W., 147, 150

Schaffer, Jonathan, 68, 248, 277, 308, 311, 358, 423

Schiffer, Stephen, 201

Schiller, F. C. S., 48

Schrödinger, Erwin, 157–159

Schroer, Robert, 394

Schwitzgebel, Eric, 349

Seager, William, 1, 200, 204, 266
Searle, John, 433, 445
Sellars, Wilfrid, 7, 86, 107, 134, 145, 203, 446–447
Shoemaker, Sydney, 169, 311–312, 319, 428
Sider, Theodore, 13, 370, 383–393
Silins, Nico, 306, 316, 319
Skrbina, David, 64, 66, 84, 203, 406, 418
Smart, J. J. C., 145, 263
Soames, Scott, 95
Soury, Jules, 24
Spinoza, Baruch, 423, 434
Sprigge, Timothy, 66, 84–85, 201
Spurrett, David, 308
Stalnaker, Robert, 376
Stapp, Henry, 240
Stillingfleet, Edward, 186
Stoljar, Daniel, 1, 10–11, 68, 79, 92, 161, 215, 221, 246, 255, 257, 259, 261–263, 281, 283–284, 287, 301, 314–315, 319, 326–328, 330–331, 335, 337–338, 374, 391, 410, 413, 415, 420, 426–432, 435, 441, 446–447
Strawson, Galen, 7, 64–67, 83–84, 92, 144, 161, 166–167, 176, 183–185, 188–189, 195, 197, 200, 202, 204, 215, 246, 262–263, 312–313, 316, 374, 379, 393, 408, 432–433, 437, 447
Stubenberg, Leopold, 6, 69, 79, 91, 96, 99, 101, 106–107, 115–116, 403, 409, 424, 448

Taine, Hippolyte, 24
Thielke, Peter, 420
Thompson, Brad, 297
Toland, John, 187
Tully, Robert, 91, 94
Turausky, Keith, 246
Tye, Michael, 282, 348, 380, 447

Unger, Peter, 201
Uus, Undo, 201

van Cleve, James, 305–306, 311, 430
van Fraassen, Bas, 171, 183, 189, 201
Velmans, Max, 397
Votsis, Ioannis, 60

Wahl, Russell, 101, 111, 116
Ward, James, 26
Weatherson, Brian, 304, 335
Whittaker, T. 24
Wilson, Jessica, 218, 291, 302, 383, 414
Wilson, Margaret, 302
Wishon, Donovan, 6, 87, 93–96, 107
Wittgenstein, Ludwig, 173, 384
Worrall, John, 171
Wrenn, Chase, 306

Xenocrates, 195

Yablo, Stephen, 251, 302

Zollner, Johan Karl Friedrich, 24

Subject Index

acquaintance, 7, 36, 40, 71–73, 80, 92–100, 105–107, 112–115, 134–139, 160, 169–171, 178–189, 293, 310–311, 319, 334–335, 342, 352–353, 446

a posteriori, 10–13, 115, 253, 260, 265, 277–297, 376–379, 391; physicalism, *see* materialism, type-B

a priori, 10–12, 43, 47, 115, 154, 158–160, 177, 196, 249–253, 260–264, 268–271, 278–289, 295–296, 303–306, 329–334, 338–343, 354, 376–381, 390–396, 408, 412, 435–436, 439–442; physicalism, *see* materialism, type-A

Cartesian dualism, 2, 42, 96, 133, 144, 178, 419, 426.

categorical property, 1–2, 10, 63, 67–68, 79–80, 152, 212–215, 229, 254–257, 261–265, 277, 282–296, 300–304, 308–313, 371–379, 403–413, 422, 426–430, 438, 444. *See also* dispositional property, quiddity

causal network, *see* causal structure

causal skeleton, 35, 61, 107, 174. *See also* causal structure

causal structure, 7, 107, 130–139, 144–145, 311, 371–372, 380, 444. *See also* structure

combination problem, 5–13, 23–26, 82, 86–87, 143–160, 203, 221, 224–244, 266–274, 396, 407, 446–447. *See also* grain problem

conceivability argument, 4, 8–13, 196, 209–222, 246–274, 277–297, 300–319, 325–330, 334–338, 372, 380, 396–397, 417, 422, 439–444

concept, phenomenal, 215, 281–295, 377–380, 388–394; physical, 287, 295, 377–378; spatiotemporal, 8, 181, 256, 338–344; structural, 112, 256, 430–432

content, 7–8, 31, 42, 78, 94, 106, 144–147, 154–160, 167, 171–181, 197, 286–288, 348–349, 390. *See also* proposition

contingency, 123–133, 140–141, 253, 280, 287–289, 357, 435. *See also* necessity

dispositional property, 1–3, 10, 63, 67–68, 79–80, 151–152, 164, 168, 172–173, 188, 212–215, 224, 254–256, 264–265, 277, 282–283, 291–296, 300–303, 309–311, 325–327, 371–381, 395, 403–406, 422, 426–430, 435–438, 444. *See also* categorical property

eliminativism, 7, 121, 135, 143, 165–168,
     194–195
emergence, 9, 26, 84, 150–153, 198,
     218, 225–226, 232, 236–246, 253,
     270, 290, 296, 370–372, 383,
     394–397
epiphenomenalism, 232, 237,
     252–255, 259, 269–270, 396,
     408, 419, 443
extrinsic property, 4, 10–11, 20–22,
     38, 63, 67, 79–82, 101, 237, 242,
     304–310, 315–316, 325, 331–338,
     350–353, 364–366, 404, 424–430

foundationalism, 3–4, 13, 375, 405,
     425–428, 437
functionalism, 115, 146–147, 196, 250,
     263–264, 274, 339–344, 361–364,
     375–378, 385, 389

grain problem, 7, 86–87, 107, 134,
     138–160, 243, 446–447. *See also*
     combination problem

idealism, 6, 13, 29, 33–34, 63, 82–85,
     92, 94–95, 100, 106–108, 114,
     166–167, 189, 198, 264–265, 300,
     401, 423, 437–438
identity theory, 7, 20, 25–26, 42, 72,
     106–107, 112–113, 121–141, 145,
     150, 193, 261–265, 271–277, 295,
     373–378, 382
introspection, 7, 71, 82, 95, 108, 145–151,
     155, 159–160, 271, 287, 312, 316–317,
     335–336, 347–349, 390, 447

knowledge argument, 13, 97, 250,
     259, 278–280, 288, 297, 372,
     380, 397, 422, 439–444. *See also*
     Mary case

macrophenomenal property, *see*
     microphenomenal property
Mary case, 277–281, 287–288,
     295, 303–304, 316–317, 432,
     440–442. *See also* knowledge
     argument
materialism, type-A, 250–253, 257–261,
     265, 376–379, 393, *see also* a priori;
     type-B, 13, 250–253, 260–261, 265,
     277, 376–380, 388–393, 443, *see*
     also a posteriori.
microphenomenal property, 85–86,
     240, 252–261, 266–269,
     273, 317, 381, 394. *See also*
     micropsychism
micropsychism, 202–203, 312–318.
     See also panpsychism,
     microphenomenal property

natural kind, 162, 177, 196–197
necessity, 10–11, 20, 38, 81–83, 122–130,
     213, 248–253, 260, 268–296,
     302, 306–308, 315–319, 326–333,
     337, 383, 436–441. *See also*
     contingency, rigid designators,
     supervenience
neutral monism, 6, 13, 29, 58–104,
     109–116, 167, 199–203, 226, 237,
     264–265, 271, 347, 405–416,
     424–425, 434–438
nonphenomenal property, 3, 260,
     268–269, 293, 341–343, 374, 397,
     405, 415–417, 433, 436
nonphysical property, 2–3, 74, 106, 115,
     162, 218–220, 237–238, 248, 255,
     291, 309, 433. *See also* physical
     property
nonrelational property, 4, 63, 67, 79–80,
     112, 163, 301–307, 325, 334, 427. *See*
     also quiddity, relational property

nonstructural property, 3, 7–12, 42, 63, 67, 79–80, 172–181, 192–195, 203–204, 219, 260, 315, 325–328, 427, 444. *See also* quiddity, structural property

Occam's razor, 2, 48, 71, 200

pain, 121–139, 188–189, 251, 263–264, 274, 278–281, 332, 361, 372–378, 382, 389–391, 396, 431, 443
panexperientialism, 3, 8, 58, 64–67, 91, 166, 201–202, 238, 247, 432. *See also* panpsychism
panprotopsychism, 9–10, 91, 220, 246–274, 373, 386–389, 395, 407–408, 433, 447–448. *See also* protophenomenal, protophenomenalism
panpsychism, 3–10, 58–87, 91, 114, 166, 200–203, 215–216, 221–233, 238–274, 283, 312–316, 373, 380, 386–389, 394–395, 402, 406–408, 432–433, 445–446. *See also* panexperientialism, micropsychism
phenomenology, 143–148, 153–154, 174, 184, 192, 221, 270, 274, 293, 314, 388, 396, 447
physical property, 1–3, 10–13, 34–36, 43, 63–69, 79, 184, 201, 214, 249–265, 273, 277, 281–286, 291, 295–296, 301, 308–313, 317–319, 324–328, 359, 364, 373, 383, 394, 403–405, 410–415, 422–438, 444. *See also* nonphysical property
proposition, 20–21, 33–36, 99, 104, 168, 284–288, 306, 316, 334, 357, 384–388. *See also* content

protophenomenal property, 3–5, 10–13, 63–64, 79, 215–220, 238, 259–268, 272, 277, 282–296, 312–319, 348, 373–379, 386, 394–395, 405–412, 425, 433–436, 444–448. *See also* panprotopsychism, protophenomenalism
protophenomenalism, 11, 283, 313, 318, 348, 368. *See also* protophenomenal property

qualia, 147, 158, 193, 291, 347, 418
quiddity, 254–265, 269–272, 311. *See also* categorical property, nonrelational property, nonstructural property

Ramsey sentence, 136, 256, 282, 338, 356–363, 431
realism, 3–8, 13, 61, 73, 86, 95, 164–174, 179–181, 193–200, 233, 347, 365–366, 375, 425–428, 437
relational property, 4, 12, 48, 62–63, 67, 79–80, 94, 99, 136, 253, 257, 307–310, 314–319, 325, 331–338, 346–368, 375, 404, 424–431. *See also* nonrelational property
representation, 19–21, 85, 146–153, 160, 173–181, 198, 224, 231, 284, 288, 294, 304, 309–312, 316–319, 335–336, 348–351, 361–362, 384
representationalism, 348, 389, 447
rigid designators, 7, 121–141, 150, 281–283, 373, 379, 441

spatiotemporality, 8, 30–33, 59, 68, 107, 135, 157–158, 164, 181, 195–199, 240, 256, 282, 338–343, 359, 363–364, 404, 423–424, 431–432, 444

structural property, 3–12, 35–40,
58, 62–63, 83, 113, 135–140,
146, 152–154, 162, 172–181, 198,
213–220, 253–267, 272, 282–296,
403–404, 408, 413, 426–427.
See also nonstructural property,
structuralism, structure
structuralism, 3–6, 12–13, 59–62, 78, 87,
92, 96, 106, 171, 254, 296, 311–314,
342, 346–368, 375, 424–425,
428, 437
structure, *and* dynamics, 11–12, 63, 67,
79–80, 250, 260, 314–316, 325–344,
427–431, 442; logical, 5, 30–32,

48–51, 57, 114, 243, 351; structural
concept: *see* concept, structural.
See also structural property,
structuralism
supervenience, 215–218, 231, 348,
363, 372, 376–383, 410–414,
433–438

topic neutral, 136–138, 145–146, 263

zombie, 195–196, 210, 214, 220,
250, 257, 261, 265–268, 273,
277–281, 417, 439–442. *See also*
conceivability argument